LONDON

AND ITS

ENVIRONS
1900

A HANDBOOK FOR TRAVELLERS
BY
KARL BAEDEKER

WITH A FOLDOUT MAP, 27 BUILDING PLANS
AND 31 PAGES OF STREET MAPS

OLD HOUSE BOOKS
MORETONHAMPSTEAD DEVON
www.OldHouseBooks.co.uk

'Go, little book, God send thee good passage
And specially let this be thy prayere
Unto them all that thee will read or hear,
Where thou art wrong, after their help to call
Thee to correct in any part or all.

PREFACE.

The chief object of the Handbook for London, like that of the Editor's other guide-books, is to enable the traveller so to employ his time, his money, and his energy, that he may derive the greatest possible amount of pleasure and instruction from his visit to the greatest city in the modern world.

As several excellent English guide-books to London already existed, the Editor in 1878 published the first English edition of the present Handbook with some hesitation, notwithstanding the encouragement he received from numerous English and American correspondents, who were already familiar with the distinctive characteristics of 'Baedeker's Handbooks'. So favourable a reception, however, was accorded to the first edition that the issue of a second became necessary in little more than a year, while ten other editions have since been called for. The present volume embodies the most recent information, down to the month of July, 1900, obtained in the course of personal visits to the places described, and from the most trustworthy sources.

In the preparation of the Handbook the Editor has received most material assistance from several English and American friends who are intimately acquainted with the great Metropolis.

Particular attention has been devoted to the description of the great public collections, such as the National Gallery, the British Museum, the Wallace Collections, the National Portrait Gallery, the Tate Gallery, and the South Kensington Museum, to all of which the utmost possible space has been allotted.

The Introduction, which has purposely been made as comprehensive as possible, is intended to convey all the information, preliminary, historical, and practical, which is best calculated to make a stranger feel at home in London, and to familiarise him with its manners and customs. While the descriptive part of the work is topographically arranged, so that the reader may see at a glance which of the sights of London may be visited together, the introductory portion classifies the principal sights according to their subjects, in order to present the reader with a convenient index to their character, and to facilitate his selection of those most congenial to his taste. As, however, it has not been the Editor's purpose to write an exhaustive account of so stupendous a city, but merely to describe the most important objects of general interest contained in it, he need hardly observe that the information required by specialists of any kind can be given only to a very limited extent in the present work. The most noteworthy sights are indicated by asterisks.

The list of Hotels and Restaurants enumerated in the Handbook comprises the most important establishments and many of humbler pretension. Those which the Editor has reason to believe especially worthy of commendation in proportion to their charges are denoted by asterisks; but doubtless there are many of equal excellence among those not so distinguished. The hotels at the West End and at the principal railway-stations are the most expensive, while the inns in the less fashionable quarters of the Metropolis generally afford comfortable accommodation at moderate charges.

The Maps and Plans, upon which the utmost care has been bestowed, will also, it is hoped, be found serviceable. Those relating to London itself (one large plan, four special plans of the most important quarters of the city and a railway map) are situated at the end of the volume. The subdivision of the Plan of the city into three west to east sections of a different colour (Northern section brown, Central section red and the Southern section grey) will be found greatly to facilitate reference as it obviates the necessity of unfolding a large sheet of paper at each consultation. Each of the three coloured sections is presented within seven consecutive pages with ample overlap, both north to south as well as west to east.

The Routes to places of interest in the Environs of London, although very brief, will probably suffice for the purposes of an ordinary visit. Some of the longer excursions that appeared in earlier editions have now been transferred to *Baedeker's Handbook to Great Britain*.

To hotel-owners, tradesmen, and others the Editor begs to intimate that a character for fair dealing and courtesy towards travellers forms the sole passport to his commendation, and that advertisements of every kind are strictly excluded from his Handbooks.

Abbreviations

M. = Engl. mile; hr. = hour; min. = minute; r. = right; l = left; N.= north, northwards, northern; S. = south, etc.; E. = east, etc.; W. = west, etc.; R. = Route or room; B. = breakfast; D. = dinner; A. = attendance; L. = luncheon; pens = pension (*i.e.* board, lodging, and attendance); rfmts = refreshments; carr = carriage; c., ca. = circa. about. The letter *d*, with a date, after a name indicates the year of the person's death.

Asterisks are used as marks of commendation

CONTENTS.

Introduction.

Sights of London.
I. The City.

CONTENTS.

Excursions from London.   Page

List of Maps and Plans

St. Paul's Cathedral, p.113; Tower, p.156; National Gallery, p 190; National Portrait Gallery, between pp.220 and 221; Houses of Parliament, between pp 238 and 239; Westminster Abbey, p 248; National Gallery of British Art, p. 275; Zoological Gardens, between pp. 294 and 295; British Museum, between pp. 300 and 301; Natural History Museum, between pp. 346 and 347; South Kensington Museum, survey-plan, p.350; special plans, pp. 351 and 360; Crystal Palace, p. 397; Environs of Hampton Court Palace, p. 406; Windsor Castle, p.423.

INTRODUCTION.

1. Money. Expenses. Season. Passports. Custom House. Time.

Money. In Great Britain alone of the more important states of Europe the currency is arranged without much reference to the decimal system. The ordinary British *Gold* coins are the sovereign or pound (*l.* = libra) equal to 20 shillings, and the half-sovereign. The *Silver* coins are the crown (5 shillings), the half-crown, the double florin (4 shillings; seldom seen), the florin (2 shillings), the shilling (*s.* = solidus), and the six-penny and three-penny pieces. The *Bronze* coinage consists of the penny (*d.* = denarius), of which 12 make a shilling, the halfpenny ($^1/_2 d$.), and the farthing ($^1/_4 d$.). The *Guinea*, a sum of 21*s.*, though still used in reckoning, is no longer in circulation as a coin. A sovereign is approximately equal to 5 American dollars, 25 francs, 20 German marks, or 10 Austrian florins (gold). The *Bank of England* issues notes for 5, 10, 20, 50, and 100 pounds, and upwards. These are useful in paying large sums; but for ordinary use, as change is not always readily procured, gold is preferable. The number of each note should be taken down in a pocket-book, as there is a bare possibility of its being in this way traced and recovered, if lost or stolen. *Foreign Money* does not circulate in England, and should always be exchanged on arrival (see p. 76). A convenient and safe mode of carrying money from America or the Continent is in the shape of letters of credit, or circular notes, which are readily procurable at the principal banks. A larger sum than will suffice for the day's expenses should never be carried on the person, and gold and silver coins of a similar size (*e.g.* sovereigns and shillings) should not be kept in the same pocket.

Expenses. The cost of a visit to London depends, of course, on the habits and tastes of the traveller. If he lives in a first-class hotel, dines at the table-d'hôte, drinks wine, frequents the theatre and other places of amusement, and drives about in cabs or flys instead of using the economical train or omnibus, he must be prepared to spend 30-40*s.* a day or upwards. Persons of moderate requirements, however, will have little difficulty, with the aid of the information in the Handbook, in living comfortably and seeing the principal sights of London for 15-20*s.* a day or even less.

Season. The 'London Season' is chiefly comprised within the months of May, June, and July, when Parliament is sitting, the aristocracy are at their town-residences, the greatest artistes in the world are performing at the Opera, and the Picture Exhibitions are open. Families who desire to obtain comfortable accommodation had better be in London to secure it by the end of April; single travellers can, of course, more easily find lodgings at any time.

Passports. These documents are not necessary in England, though occasionally useful in procuring delivery of registered and *poste restante* letters (comp. p. 79). A *visa* is quite needless. American travellers, who intend to proceed from London to the Continent, should provide themselves with passports before leaving home. Passports, however, may also be obtained by personal application at the American Embassy in London (p. 75). The *visa* of the American consul, and that of the minister in London of the country to which the traveller is about to proceed, are sometimes necessary.

Passport Agents. *C. Smith & Son*, 63 Charing Cross; *E. Stanford*, 26 Cockspur Street, Charing Cross; *Buss*, 440 West Strand; *W. J. Adams*, 59 Fleet Street; *Thos. Cook & Son* (see p. 76); *Gaze* (see p. 76). Charge 2*s.*, agent's fee 1*s.* 6*d.*

Custom House. Almost the only articles likely to be in the possession of ordinary travellers on which duty is charged are spirits and tobacco, but half-a-pint of the former and 1/2lb. of the latter (including cigars) are usually passed free of duty, if duly declared and not found concealed. Passengers from the Channel Islands are allowed only half these quantities. On larger quantities duty must be paid at the rate of 10*s.* 10*d.* to 17*s.* 3*d.* per gallon of spirits and 2*s.* 8*d.* to 5*s.* per pound of tobacco. A small fine is also leviable on packets of tobacco or cigars weighing less than 80lbs.; but a quantity of 7lbs. from non-European ports or 3lbs. from European ports beyond the Straits of Gibraltar are passed without fine. Foreign reprints of copyright English books are confiscated. The custom house examination is generally lenient. — Dogs are not at present allowed to land in Great Britain without a licence previously obtained from the Board of Agriculture (4 Whitehall Place, London, S.W.).

Time. Uniformity of time throughout Great Britain is maintained by telegraphic communication with Greenwich Observatory (p. 381).

2. Routes to and from London. Arrival.

The following lists include the principal routes between America and Great Britain and between London and the Continent, which may prove useful to travellers in either direction. The times and fares are liable to alteration. On the more popular routes and at the most frequented seasons it is desirable to secure berths and staterooms in advance. On the Atlantic steamers fares are reduced during the winter season (Nov. 1st to March 31st), and children between 1 and 8 years of age are generally charged half-fare (between 1 and 12 in the second cabin). There is no reduction on first cabin return-tickets by some of the largest lines, but as a rule a reduction of 5-10 per cent on the combined out and home fares is granted. The largest and finest steamers on the Atlantic Ocean at present are the *Lucania* and *Campania* of the Cunard Line, the *Oceanic* (17,200 tons), *Teutonic*, and *Majestic* of the White Star Line, the *St. Louis*, *St. Paul*, *Philadelphia* (late *Paris*), and *New York* of the American Line, the *Winefredian* of the Leyland Line, the *Bavarian* of the Allan Line, the *Commonwealth* of the Dominion Line, the *City of Rome* of the Anchor Line, the *Kaiser Wilhelm der Grosse* of the North German Lloyd, and the *Deutschland* (16,000 tons) of the Hamburg-American Line. — The records for the quickest passages between Queenstown and New York are held by the *Lucania* (westward, 5 days, 7 hrs., 23 min.; eastward, 5 days, 8 hrs., 38 min.; average speed 22 knots; highest day's run 562 knots or about 650 statute miles). The *Kaiser Wilhelm* has accomplished the voyage from Southampton to New York in 5 days, 20 hrs., and that from New York to Southampton in 5 days, 17 hrs., 8 min.; highest day's run 580 knots (670 M.).

Routes to England from the United States of America and Canada. The steamers of any of the following companies afford comfortable accommodation and speedy transit.

Cunard Line. A steamer of this company starts every Sat. and every second Tues. from New York and every Wed. from Boston for Queenstown and Liverpool. Cabin fare 75-175 dollars; second cabin 42¹/₂-57 dollars. Steamers from Liverpool for New York every Sat. and every second Tues., for Boston every Tuesday. Fare 15-35*l.*; second cabin 8-12*l.* London offices, 93 Bishopsgate Street and 13 Pall Mall.

White Star Line. Steamer every Wed. from New York to Queenstown and Liverpool. Cabin 75-175 dollars; second cabin 40 50 dollars. From Liverpool to New York every Wednesday. Cabin 15-35*l*; second cabin 7*l* 5*s.* to 9*l.* 10*s.* London offices, 34 Leadenhall Street, E.C., and 41 Maddox Street, W.

American Line. Every Wed. from New York to Southampton. Cabin 75-175 dollars; second cabin from 45 dollars. From Southampton to New York every Saturday. Fare from 15*l.*; second cabin from 8*l.* 10*s.* Also from Philadelphia to Liverpool, and *vice versâ*, every Wed. (no first cabin; second cabin from 7*l.* 5*s.* or 36 dollars). London offices, 116 Leadenhall Street, E.C., and 3 Cockspur Street, S.W.

North German Lloyd Line. From New York to Southampton or Plymouth every Tues. and every Thurs. in summer. Cabin from 100 dollars; second cabin from 45 dollars. From Southampton to New York every Wed. and every Sun. in summer. Cabin from 15*l.*; second saloon from 10*l.* London offices, 2 King William Street, E.C., and 32 Cockspur Street, W.C

Hamburg-American Line. From New York to Plymouth every Thursday. Saloon 75-375 dollars; second cabin 60-75 dollars. From Southampton to New York on Friday, and from Plymouth to New York on Tuesday. Saloon from 15*l*; second cabin from 10*l.* 10*s.* London offices, 9 Fenchurch Street, E.C., and 22 Cockspur Street, S W.

Anchor Line. From New York to Glasgow every Sat.; from Glasgow to New York every Thursday. Saloon from 9*gs.*, return-tickets from 19*l.* 19*s.*, second cabin from 6*l.* 10*s.* London address, 18 Leadenhall Street, E.C.

Allan Line. From Montreal (in summer) or Portland (in winter) to Liverpool every Sat., returning every Sat. or Thursday. Cabin from 10*l.* 10*s.* (52¹/₂ dollars); second cabin from 7*l.* 5*s.* (36 dollars). London address, 103 Leadenhall Street.

Dominion Line. From Quebec and Montreal weekly in summer, and

from Halifax and Portland fortnightly in winter, to Liverpool. Saloon
10-20gs. Also from Boston to Liverpool weekly. Saloon fare 15-30l.; second
cabin 8l. London offices, 14 Waterloo Place, S.W., and Billiter Buildings, E.C.

Leyland Line. Weekly, between Liverpool and Boston. Saloon passengers only; fare from 10l. London agency, 3½ Leadenhall Street, E.C.

Atlantic Transport Line. From New York to London every Thursday. Saloon passengers only; fares 10-18gs.; return, double
fare, less 5 per cent.

Wilsons & Furness-Leyland Line. From New York to London every
Sat.; returning every Thursday. Saloon passengers only; fares from 10l.
10s.; return-ticket from 19l. 19s. London office, 38 Leadenhall St., E.C.

The average duration of the passage across the Atlantic is 6-9 days.
The best time for crossing is in summer. Passengers should pack clothing and other necessaries for the voyage in small flat boxes (*not* portmanteaus),
such as can lie easily in the cabin, as all bulky luggage is stowed away
in the hold. Stateroom trunks should not exceed 3 ft. in length, 1½-2 ft.
in breadth, and 15 inches in height. Trunks not required on board should
be m rked 'Hold' or 'Not Wanted', the others 'Cabin' or 'Wanted'. The
steamship companies generally provide labels for this purpose. Dress for
the voyage should be of a plain and serviceable description, and it is advisable, even in midsummer, to be provided with warm clothing. Ladies
should not forget a thick veil. A deck-chair, which may be purchased
(from 6-7s. upwards) or hired (2-4s.) at the dock or on the steamer before
sailing, is a luxury that may almost be called a necessary. Bought chairs
should be distinctly marked with the owner's name or initials, and may
be left in charge of the Steamship Co.'s agents until the return-journey.
Seats at table, retained thr.ughout the voyage, are usually assigned by the
Saloon Steward immediately after starting; and those who wish to sit at
a particular table or beside a particular person should apply to him. It is
usual to give a fee of 10s. (2½ dollars) to the table-steward and to the
stateroom steward, and small gratuities are also expected by the boot-
cleaner, the bath-steward, etc. The stateroom steward should not be 'tipped'
until he has brought all the passenger's small baggage safely on to the
landing-stage or tender.

On landing, passengers remain in a large waiting-room until all the
baggage has been placed in the custom-house shed. Here the owner will
find his property expeditiously by looking for the initial of his surname
on the wall. The examination is generally soon over (comp. p. 2). Porters
then convey the luggage to a cab (3d. for small articles, 6d. for a large
trunk). — Baggage may now be 'expressed' from New York to any
city in Eur'pe. Agents of the English railway-companies, etc., also meet
the steamers on arrival at Liverpool and undertake to 'express' baggage
on the American system to any address given by the traveller.

FROM LIVERPOOL TO LONDON there are five different railway
routes (202-240 M., in 4½-8 hrs.; fares by all trains 29s., 20s. 8d.,
16s. 6d.; no second class by Midland or Great Northern Railways).

The *Midland Railway* (to St. Pancras Station) runs by Matlock, Derby,
and Bedford. The route of the *London and North Western Railway* (to
Euston Square Station) goes viâ Crewe and Rugby. A special service,
for Atlantic passengers only, runs from the Riverside Station on the landing-stage to Euston Square in 4 hrs. The *Great Central Railway* (to Marylebone Station) runs viâ Sheffield, Nottingham, Leicester, and Rugby. By
the *Great Western Railway* (to Paddington Station) we may travel either
viâ Chester, Birmingham. Warwick, and Oxford; or viâ Hereford and
Gloucester; or viâ Worcester. Or, lastly. we may take a train of the *Great
Northern Railway* (to King's Cross Station), passing Grantham and Peterborough. — The following are comfortable hotels at Liverpool: *North
Western Hotel*, Lime Street Station; *Adelphi*, near Central Station; *Lancashire & Yorkshire*, at the Exchange Station; *Grand*, Lime Street; *Alexandra*,
Dale Street; *Shaftesbury Temperance Hotel*, Mount Pleasant.

From Southampton to London, by *South Western Railway* to Waterloo Station (79 M., in $2^1/_4$-$3^1/_4$ hrs. ; fares 13s., 8s. 2d., 6s. 6d.). Hotels at Southampton: *South Western; Radley's; Royal; Dolphin; Polygon House; Flower's Temperance*.

From Plymouth to London, by *Great Western Railway* to Paddington Station, or by *South Western Railway* to Waterloo Station (247 or 231 M., in $5^1/_2$-8 hrs.; fares 37s. 4d., 23s. 4d., 18s. 8d.). Hotels at Plymouth: *Grand; Duke of Cornwall; Royal; Chubb's; Globe; Westminster Temperance*.

For details of these routes, see *Baedeker's Great Britain*.

Routes from England to the Continent.

From *Dover* to *Calais* thrice a day, in $1^1/_4$-$1^3/_4$ hr.; cabin 10s. 5d., fore-cabin 8s. 5d. (Railway from London to Dover, or *vice versâ*, in $1^3/_4$-$2^3/_4$ hrs.; express fares 19s. 9d., 12s. 8d.; ordinary fares 13s., 8s. 2d., 6s. $5^1/_2$d.)

From *Dover* to *Ostend*, thrice a day, in 3-$3^1/_2$ hrs.; 8s. 6d. or 6s. 8d.

From *Folkestone* to *Boulogne*, twice a day, in $1^1/_2$-2 hrs.; cabin 9s. 5d., fore-cabin 7s. 5d. (Railway from London to Folkestone *Harbour* in 2-4 hrs.; express fares 17s. 9d., 11s.; ordinary fares 12s., 7s. 6d, 6s.)

From *Queenborough* to *Flushing*, twice daily, in 6 hrs. (3 hrs. at sea); train from London to Queenborough in $1^1/_4$ hr., from Flushing to Amsterdam in 6-9 hrs.; through-fare 37s. 1d. or 25s. 6d.

From *Newhaven* to *Dieppe*, twice daily, in 5-7 hrs.; 15s. 3d. or 11s. 7d. (Railway from London to Newhaven, or *vice versâ*, in $1^1/_2$-3 hrs.; fares 9s. 4d., 5s. 8d., and 4s. 8d.)

From *Harwich* to *Hoek van Holland* and *Rotterdam*, daily, in 7-8 and 9-10 hrs. Great Eastern Railway from London to Harwich in $1^1/_2$-$2^1/_2$ hrs. (fares 13s. 3d., 5s. $11^1/_2$d.); fare from London to Rotterdam, 29s. or 18s. (second-class passengers pay 7s. extra for the first cabin).

From *Harwich* to *Antwerp*, daily (Sun. in summer only), in 12-13 hrs. (train from London to Harwich in $1^1/_2$-$2^1/_2$ hrs.); 2.3s. or 15s. (from London).

From *London* to *Ostend*, twice a week, in 12 hrs. (6 hrs. at sea); 7s. 6d. or 6s.

From *Tilbury* to *Ostend* and to *Boulogne*, see p. 64.

From *London* to *Rotterdam*, daily, in 16-18 hrs. (12 hrs. at sea); 17s. or 11s.

From *London* to *Amsterdam*, four times weekly; fares 23s., 15s.

From *London* to *Antwerp*, twice or thrice a week, in 17-20 hrs. (8-9 hrs. of which are on the open sea); 16s. or 11s.

From *Harwich* to *Hamburg*, twice weekly (Wed. & Sat.; train from London in $1^1/_2$-$2^1/_2$ hrs.); 1l. 7s. 6d . 1l. (from London 1l. 17s. 6d., 1l. 5s. 9d.).

From *Harwich* to *Esbjerg* (Denmark), thrice weekly, in 30 hrs. (from London to Harwich, see above); fares from London 1l. 17s. 6d., 1l. 5s.

From *London* to *Gothenburg*, every Frid., in 42-45 hrs.; 3l. 3s., 2l. 2s.

From *London* to *Christiansand* and *Christiania*, weekly, in two days; 3l. 13s., 2l. 18s.

From *London* to *Bremen*, thrice a week, in 40 hrs.; 1l. 15s., 1l. 5s.

From *London* to *Hamburg*, five times a week, in 36-40 hrs.; 1l. 10s. or 1l.

From *Southampton* to *Bremen*, by North German Lloyd Transatlantic steamer (p. 3) in 25 hrs., twice weekly; fares 3l., 2l.

From *Plymouth* to *Cuxhaven* by Hamburg-American steamer (p. 3), in 23 hrs.; fares 3l. 10s. or 2l. 10s.

From *Southampton* to *Cherbourg*, thrice a week, in 8-9 hrs.; fares 20s., 14s.

From *Southampton* to *Havre*, nightly, in 7-8 hrs.; fares (from London) 1l. 7s. 6d., 1l.

From *London* to *Bordeaux*, every Sat., in 55-65 hrs.; 50s., 35s.

From *Newhaven* to *Caen*, thrice weekly, in 10-12 hrs.; fares 15s., 9s.

From *Southampton* to *Caen*, daily; fares from London 30s., 21s.

From *Newhaven* to *Trouville*, thrice weekly.

From *Southampton* to *Trouville*, daily.

From *Southampton* to *St. Malo*, four times a week, in 16-18 hrs.; fares 23*s.* 10*d.*, 17*s.* 10*d.*

Steamers also sail regularly from *Hull* to *Norway*, *Sweden*, *Denmark*, etc.; from *Grimsby* to *Hamburg*, *Antwerp*, *Rotterdam*, *Denmark*, etc.; from *Leith* to *Norway*, *Hamburg*, etc.; from *London* and from *Liverpool* to *Spain*, *Portugal*, *Egypt*, etc. See the advertisements in *Bradshaw's Railway Guide*.

On the longer voyages (10 hrs. and upwards), or when special attention has been required, the steward expects a gratuity of 1*s.* or more. Food and liquors are supplied on board all the steamboats at fixed charges, but the viands are sometimes not very inviting. An official *Interpreter* accompanies the chief trains on the more important routes.

Arrival. Those who arrive in London by water have sometimes to land in small boats. The tariff is 6*d.* for each person, and 3*d.* for each trunk. The traveller should take care to select one of the watermen who wear a badge, as they alone are bound by the tariff.

Cabs (see p. 33) are in waiting at most of the railway-stations, and also at the landing-stages. The stranger had better let the porter at his hotel pay the fare in order to prevent an overcharge. At the more important stations *Private Omnibuses*, holding 6-10 persons, may be procured on previous application to the Railway Co. (fare 1*s.* per mile, with two horses 1*s.* 6*d.*-2*s.*, minimum charge 3-4*s.*)

3. Hotels. Boarding Houses. Private Lodgings.

Hotels. The attempt made in the following pages to arrange the hotels of London in geographical groups is necessarily based on somewhat arbitrary distinctions, but will, it is hoped, nevertheless prove useful to the visitor. Within each group the arrangement is made as far as possible according to tariff. The most expensive houses are naturally those in the fashionable quarters of the West End, while those in such districts as Bloomsbury and the City are considerably cheaper. Charges for rooms vary according to the floor; and it is advisable to make enquiry as to prices on or soon after arrival. When a prolonged stay is contemplated, the bill should be called for every two or three days, in order that errors, whether accidental or designed, may be detected. In some hotels the day of departure is charged for, unless the rooms are given up by noon. Many hotels receive visitors *en pension*, at rates depending on whether it is or is not the Season. Numerous as the London hotels are, it is often difficult to procure rooms in the height of the Season, and it is therefore advisable to apply in advance by letter or telegram.

Several of the West End hotels are equipped in the most luxurious manner, and even in the smaller houses most of the rooms are fairly well furnished, while the beds are clean and comfortable. Breakfast is generally taken in the hotel, the Continental habit of breakfasting at a café being almost unknown in England. The meal consists of tea or coffee with meat, fish, and eggs, and is charged for by tariff. A fixed charge per day (almost invariably 1s. 6d.) is made for attendance, beyond which no gratuity need be given. It is, however, usual to give the 'boots' (*i.e.* boot-cleaner and errand man) a small fee on leaving, and the waiter who has specially attended to the traveller also expects a shilling or two. The excellent American custom of paying one's bill at the office instead of through a waiter has not yet become usual in London. Lights (*i.e.* candles, electricity, or gas) are seldom or never charged for, but travellers accustomed to the American system of heating must remember that fires in bedrooms or private sitting-rooms are an extra. — In most hotels smoking is prohibited except in the *Smoking Rooms* provided for the purpose. — In the more old-fashioned houses the dining-room is called the Coffee Room. — Wine is generally expensive at London hotels; but the expectation that guests should order it 'for the good of the house' has fallen largely into abeyance, and there are many *Temperance Hotels*, where no intoxicating drinks are served. — Attendance at table-d'hôte is not obligatory. — English newspapers are provided at every hotel, but foreign journals are rarely met with.

The ordinary charges at London hotels vary from about 8s. a day in the least pretentious houses up to 20s. and upwards in the most expensive. The prices given below will enable the traveller to form an approximate idea of the expense at the hotel he selects. The charge for room is that for an ordinary room occupied by a single person. The charge for two persons occupying the same room is often proportionately much less, while that for the best bedrooms may be much higher. Private sitting-rooms are usually expensive. The ordinary charge for a hot bath is 1s., for a cold sponge-bath in bedroom 6d. The prices here given for breakfast, luncheon, and dinner generally refer to table-d'hôte meals. The average *à la carte* charges for breakfast are 2s.-3s. 6d., for luncheon 2s. 6d.-5s., for dinner from 3s. upwards. 'Pension' as used in this Handbook includes board, lodging, and attendance.

Almost all the great terminal railway-stations of London are provided with large hotels, often belonging to the railway-companies and offering accommodation at varied rates. These hotels, which are specially convenient for passing travellers, are noted in their proper places in the following lists.

a. Hotels in or near Charing Cross and the Strand.

The objects of interest in this district include the National Gallery, the National Portrait Gallery, and most of the theatres.

Hôtel Cecil (Pl. R, 30; *II*), an enormous house on the Victoria Embankment, near Waterloo Bridge, overlooking the Thames and extending back to the Strand; 700 bedrooms, 200 private sitting rooms, large ball and concert rooms, restaurant (p. 15), lifts, terrace, etc.; R. & A. from 6s., B. from 2s., L. 3s. 6d., D. 6s.

Savoy Hotel, another large hotel on the Embankment, adjoining the Cecil, with an entrance in Beaufort Buildings, Strand; R. & A. (including bath) from 7s. 6d., B. from 2s., L. 5s., D. 7s. 6d.; restaurant, see p. 15.

Hôtel Métropole (550 bedrooms), *Hôtel Victoria* (500 beds; orchestra during meals), and *Grand Hôtel* (400 beds; facing Trafalgar Square; restaurant, p. 15), three large and handsomely furnished hotels in Northumberland Avenue, belonging to the same company; R. & A. from 5s., B. 3s. 6d., L. 3s. 6d., D. 5-6s.

Charing Cross Hotel, at Charing Cross Railway Station, with 350 rooms, restaurant (p. 15), and lifts; R. & A. from 4s., D. from 3s. 6d. — *Morley's Hotel*, Trafalgar Square, a comfortable family hotel with 100 beds; R. & A. from 4s. 6d., D. from 3s. 6d., pension from 13s. — *Golden Cross Hotel*, 352 Strand, opposite the Charing Cross Hotel, R. & A. 5s., B. 3s. 6d., L. 3s., D. 5s.

The streets leading from the Strand to the Thames (Pl. R, 31; *II*) contain a number of quiet and comfortable hotels with reasonable charges. Among these are the following: — In Arundel Street: *Arundel Hotel* (No. 8), on the Embankment, R., A., & B. from 6s., D. 3s., pens. from 9s. 6d.; *Temple* (No. 11), R., A., & B. from 6s., pens. from 9s. 6d. — In Norfolk Street: *Howard* (100 beds), R., A., & B. from 6s., D. 3s., pens. from 9s. 6d., well spoken of. — In Surrey Street: *Loudoun* (No. 24; 90 beds), R., A., & B. from 6s., D. 3s. 6d., pens. from 9s. 6d.; *Lay's* (Nos. 5, 6, 8, & 9); *Norfolk* (No. 30). R., A., & B. from 6s. — *Adelphi* (50 beds), John Street, R. & A. from 3s. 6d., pens. from 3l. 3s. per week; *Caledonian*, 10 Adelphi Terrace.

In Covent Garden, to the N. of the Strand: — *Tavistock* (200 beds), Piazza, Covent Garden, for gentlemen only, R., A., & B. 7s. 6d., D. from 3s., good wines; *Hummums, Bedford*, also in the Piazza; *Covent Garden*, at the corner of Southampton Street, pens. from 10s.

Philp's New Cockburn Hotel (temperance), 13 Henrietta St.; *Buckingham Temperance Hotel*, 28 Buckingham Street, R. & A. from 4s. 6d.; *Temperance Hotel*, 12 Catherine Street, for gentlemen only, R. from 2s., these three in streets leading N. from the Strand.

In or near Leicester Square, a little to the N. of Charing Cross, a quarter much frequented by French visitors: — *Queen's Hotel*, Leicester Square, R., A., & B. from 5s., L. 3s. 6d., D. 5s. (with band); *Challis's Royal Hotel*, 59-64 Rupert Street, Coventry Street, R., A., & B. from 5s. 6d., L. 2s., D. 4s.; *Hôtel Suisse (Swiss Hotel)*, 53 Old Compton Street, unpretending, well spoken of, R. from 2s., B. from 1s.

The stranger is cautioned against going to any unrecommended house near Leicester Square, as there are several houses of doubtful reputation in this locality.

b. Hotels in or near Piccadilly.

The hotels in this group are convenient for those who wish to be near St. James's Park, the Green Park, Hyde Park (E. end), the principal clubs, St. James's Palace, Marlborough House, Burlington House (Royal Academy), and the most fashionable shops. They include some of the most aristocratic and expensive hostelries in London, all well equipped with electric light, lifts, etc.

In Piccadilly itself: — *Albemarle Hotel* (Pl. 22, R; *IV*), at the corner of Albemarle Street, largely patronized by royalty, the diplomatic corps, and the nobility; excellent wine and cuisine; R. & A. from 7*s.*, L. 4*s.*, D. 7*s.* 6*d.* — *Berkeley* (No. 77), at the corner of Berkeley Street, with a frequented restaurant; R. & A. from 7*s.*, B. 2-4*s.*, L. 4-5*s.*, D. 7*s.* 6*d.* or 10*s.* — *Walsingham House* (No. 152), overlooking the Green Park, R. from 7*s.* 6*d.*, B. from 2*s.*, D. 7*s.* 6*d.* — *Avondale* (No. 68A), at the corner of Dover Street, with restaurant; R. & A. from 7*s.*, B. from 2*s.*, L. 3*s.* 6*d.*, D. from 6*s.* — *Bath*, at the corner of Arlington Street (S. side of Piccadilly).

To the N. of Piccadilly: — *Claridge's*, Brook Street, Grosvenor Square, long the leading West End hotel, rebuilt in 1898 and luxuriously fitted up, R. & A. from 10*s.*, L. 5*s.*, D. 8*s.* (charges lower out of the Season). — *Buckland's*, 43 Brook Street. — *Coburg*, Carlos Place, Grosvenor Square, R. from 6*s.*, D. 7*s.* 6*d.* — *Sackville Hotel*, 28 Sackville Street, near Regent Street, R. & A. from 5*s.*, D. 6*s.*, pens. from 10*s.* 6*d.* — *Long's Hotel*, 15 New Bond Street, R. & A. from 6*s.*, L. 3*s.* 6*d.*, D. 7*s.* 6*d.*; *Burlington* (130 beds), 19 Cork Street, near Bond Street, an old-established house, R. & A. from 4*s.* 6*d.*, D. 6*s.*, pens. (out of the Season) 16*s.*; *Schlette's Hotel*, 14 Cork Street, R. from 4*s.*; *Bristol*, Burlington Gardens, a high-class house, similar to the Albemarle. — *Almond's*, 6 Clifford Street. — *Limmer's Hotel*, George Street, Hanover Square, R. & A. from 5*s.* 6*d.*, D. from 4*s.* — *Brown's & St. George's Hotel*, Albemarle Street and Dover Street, quiet, good cuisine, R. & A. from 6*s.*, D. 6*s.*; *York Hotel*, 9-11 Albemarle Street, R. & A. from 5*s.*, D. 4*s.* 6*d.*; *Carter's*, 14 Albemarle Street; *Krebs' Private Hotel*, 18 Albemarle Street, suites 7-13*gs.* in the Season, 4-6*gs.* out of the Season. — *Thomas's Hotel*, 25 Berkeley Square, a high-class house with apartments let 'en suite'; no tariff or public rooms. — *Fleming's Hotel*, 41 Clarges Street (no public rooms). — *Harvey's Hotel*, Curzon Street, Mayfair, pens. from 10*s.* 6*d.*

To the S. of Piccadilly: — *Carlton*, a huge and handsome establishment at the corner of the Haymarket and Pall Mall, R. from 7*s.* 6*d.*, L. 5*s.*, D. 7*s.* 6*d.* — In Jermyn Street, parallel to Piccadilly: *Waterloo* (No. 85), R. & A. from 3*s.* 6*d.*, L. 2*s.*, D. 3*s.* 6*d.*, pens. from 9*s.* 6*d.*; *Cavendish* (No. 81), an old family hotel, well spoken of, R. & A. from 5*s.* 6*d.*, D. from 5*s.*, reduced terms in winter; *British* (No. 82); *Brunswick* (No. 52); *Cox's* (No. 55); *Morle's* (No. 102). These hotels are all comfortable houses for single gentlemen. *Princes' Hotel*, 36 Jermyn Street, a high-class family hotel, R. from 6*s.*, L. 4*s.* 6*d.*, D. 7*s.* 6*d.* or 10*s.* 6*d.* (restaurant, see p. 16). — *Park Hotel*, Park Place, St. James's Street, R. from 5*s.*, D. from 5*s.*, well spoken of; *Payne's Private Hotel*, 12 Park Place. — *Hôtel Dieudonné*, 11 Ryder Street, St. James's (French).

3. HOTELS.

c. Hotels in or near Westminster.

Convenient for the Houses of Parliament, the Ministerial Offices, Westminster Abbey, the Tate Gallery, St James's Park, Lambeth Palace (across the river), Victoria Station, the United States Embassy, and the offices of the High Commissioner of Canada and the Agents General of the chief British Colonies

Westminster Palace Hotel (Pl. R, 25; *IV*), Victoria Street, opposite Westminster Abbey, with 250 beds, R. & A. from 5*s.*, B. 3*s.* 6*d.*, L. 3*s.* 6*d.*, D. 5*s.*, pens. from 12*s.* 6*d.*; *Hôtel Windsor* (Pl. R, 25; *IV*), also in Victoria Street, with 212 beds, well spoken of, R. & A. from 4*s.*, D. 5*s.*, pens. from 12*s.* — *Buckingham Palace Hotel* (Pl. R, 21; *IV*), Buckingham Palace Gate, a large hotel, R. from 5*s.* 6*d.*, D. 6*s.* — *Grosvenor Hotel*, at Victoria Station (Pl. R, 21; *IV*), a large railway-hotel, R. from 5*s.*, D. from 3*s.* — *Belgravia Residential Hotel*, 72 Victoria Street, pens. from 10*s.* 6*d.* — *St. Ermin's Hotel*, Caxton Street, R., B., & bath 6*s.*, D. 3*s.* or 5*s.*, pens. from 10*s.* 6*d.*

d. Hotels in Kensington and Neighbourhood.

The objects of interest in this district include Hyde Park (W. end), Kensington Gardens and Palace, the Albert Hall, South Kensington Museum, the Natural History Museum, and the Imperial Institute.

*Hans Crescent Hotel, Hans Crescent, Sloane Street (Pl. R, 13), R. from 6*s.*, D. 6*s.*, pens. 16*s.* — *Alexandra Hotel*, 16-21 St. George's Place, Hyde Park Corner (Pl. R, 17). — *Cadogan Hotel*, 75 Sloane Street, Cadogan Place (Pl. R, 17). — *South Kensington Hotel*, Queen's Gate Terrace (Pl. R, 5), 150 bedrooms, R. & A. from 5*s.*, D. 5*s.* — *Royal Palace Hotel* (350 beds), Kensington High Street, overlooking the grounds of Kensington Palace (Pl. R, 6); R. & A. from 4*s.* 6*d.*, B. 2*s.*-3*s.*, L. 3*s.*, D. 5*s.* — The *Maisonettes* (Nos. 28-30), *De Vere Hotel, Prince of Wales Hotel* (Nos. 16, 18), *Broadwalk Hotel* (Nos. 9-13), all residential hotels in De Vere Gardens (Pl. R, 5), provide suites of rooms, with meals (if desired) in the general diningroom; terms from 3*l.* 3*s.* per week upwards. — *Imperial Private Hotel*, 121 Queen's Gate.

Great Western Hotel, Paddington Station (Pl. R, 11), a railway terminal hotel. — *Norfolk Square Hotel*, London St., opposite Paddington Station, R., A., & B. from 6*s.*, D. 4*s.*

*Bailey's Hotel, opposite Gloucester Road Station (Pl. G, 5), with about 250 beds, R. & A. from 4*s.* 6*d.*, D. 5*s.*, pens. from 12*s.* — *Norfolk*, Harrington Gardens (Pl. G, 5), pens. 10*s.* 6*d.* — *Bolton Mansions* (residential), 11 Bolton Gardens (Pl. G, 5), R., A., & B. 5*s.* 6*d.*, L. 2*s.* 6*d.*, D. 3*s.* 6*d.*, pens. from 7*s.* 6*d.* — **Norris's Hotel*, 48-53 Russell Road, Kensington, facing Addison Road Station (beyond Pl. G, 1), a family hotel, R. & A. from 3*s.*, D. 3*s.*, pens. from 2*l.* 12*s.* 6*d.* per week. — *Barkston Gardens Hotel*, 40 Barkston Gardens, South Kensington.

e. Hotels between Oxford Street and Regent's Park.

The *Wallace Gallery* is in this district.

*Hôtel Great Central, Marylebone Station (Pl. R, 16), an enormous and excellently equipped railway hotel with 700 beds; R.

from 3s. 6d., B. 3s., L. 3s., D. 3-5s., pens. from 10s. 6d. — *Langham Hotel* (Pl. R, 24; *I*), Portland Place, a large and centrally situated house, with 450 beds, electric light, lifts, etc.; R. & A. from 4s. 6d., B. 3s., L. 2s. 6d.-3s. 6d., D. 5s., pens. 15s. — *Portland Hotel*, Great Portland Street, less pretending, R. & B. 6s. — *Marshall Thompson's Hotel*, 28 Cavendish Square. — *Ford's Hotel*, 14 Manchester Street, Manchester Square (Pl. R, 19; *I*), R. & A. from 5s., L. 2s. 6d., D. 4s. 6d., pension from 12s. 6d. (except in the Season), an old house and well spoken of. — *Granville Private Hotel*, 24 Granville Place, Portman Square, pens. from 8s. 6d. per day or 2l. 10s. a week. — *Clifton Hotel*, Welbeck Street, pens. 10s. 6d. — *Tudor Hotel*, 87 Oxford Street, cor. of Dean Street, pens. 10s. 6d.

f. Hotels in Bloomsbury and Neighbourhood.

This district includes the large terminal hotels of the northern railways and an immense number of small unpretending h tels and boarding-houses at moderate prices. Its centre of interest is the British Museum.

Midland Grand Hotel, St. Pancras Station (Pl. B, 28), a handsome Gothic building by Sir G. G. Scott and one of the best of the large terminal hotels, with 400 beds; R. & A. from 4s., B. 3s., D. 5s., pens. 12s. — *Euston Hotel*, Euston Station (Pl. B, 24, 28). — *Great Northern Railway Hotel*, King's Cross Station (Pl. B, 31, 32).

In High Holborn (Pl. R, 32; *II*): *First Avenue Hotel*, a large hotel (300 beds) with electric light, lifts, etc., R. & A. from 4s., B. 3s., L. 2s. 6d., D. 5s., well spoken of; *Inns of Court Hotel*, another large house, with a second entrance in Lincoln's Inn Fields.

Hôtel Russell, Russell Square, corner of Guilford Street, a huge new house with 500 rooms, R. & A. from 4s. 6d., B. from 2s., D. 5s.

In Queen Square (Pl. R, 32; *II*): *Shirley's Temperance Hotel* (No. 37), pens. from 5s. 6d. — *West Central Hotel*, 75-79 and 97-105 Southampton Row (Pl. R, 32; *II*), an excellent temperance hotel, R. & A. from 2s. 3d., pens. 6s. 8d.; *Bedford Hotel*, 93 Southampton Row, R. & A. from 2s. 6d., pens. 8s. — *Thackeray Temperance Hotel*, Great Russell St., facing the British Museum, new, well spoken of, R. & A. from 3s., D. 2s. 6d.; *Montague Mansion* (private hotel), adjoining the last, well spoken of, R. from 3s. 6d., D. 3s. 6d., pens. from 53s. per week. — *Philp's Cockburn Hotel* (temperance), 9 Endsleigh Gardens; *Woburn House Hotel*, 12 Upper Woburn Place, corner of Endsleigh Gardens (Pl. B, 28), R. & A. from 2s. 9d., D. 2s. 6d., pens. 5s.-8s. 6d. — *Gower House Hotel* (temperance), Gower Street Station, R. from 2s. 6d.; *London Temperance Hotel*, 70 Euston Square, R. & A. from 2s. 6d., B. 2s. — *Mann's Private Temperance Hotel*, 48 Torrington Square (Pl. R, 28), largely patronized by vegetarians; R., A., & B. from 3s. 9d. — *Morton Temperance Hotel*, 2 Woburn Place.

In Tottenham Court Road (Pl. R, 28): *The Horseshoe* (No. 264) and the *Bedford Head* (No. 235; R., A., & B. 5s., D. 3s.), two commercial houses, suited for gentlemen.

g. Hotels in the City.

These hotels are convenient for those visiting London on business, while the City also contains numerous objects of wider interest such as St. Paul's Cathedral, the Guildhall, the Tower, St. Bartholomew's, and the Charterhouse. The Fleet Street hotels are near the Inns of Court and the Law Courts.

De Keyser's Royal Hotel (Pl. R, 35; *II*), well situated on the Victoria Embankment, Blackfriars, and largely patronized by Germans, Frenchmen, and other foreigners; 400 rooms, electric light, lifts; inclusive terms 12-20s. per day.

Cannon Street Hotel (Pl. R, 39; *III*), R. & A. from 4s., D. 2s. 6d.-5s. — *Holborn Viaduct Hotel* (Pl. R, 35; *II*), R. & A. from 5s., B. 3s., L. 3s. 6d., D. 5s., pens. from 12s. — *Great Eastern Hotel* (Pl. R, 44; *III*), largely frequented by German and other visitors to the great wool sales; R. & A. from 4s. 6d., B. 3s., L. 3s. 6d., D. 4s. 6d. These are large railway hotels.

Castle and Falcon, 5 Aldersgate Street, near St. Martin's le Grand (General Post Office), R. & A. 5s., B. 3s., D. 3s. 6d. — *Manchester Hotel*, 136-145 Aldersgate Street and Long Lane. — *The Albion*, 172 Aldersgate Street. — *Metropolitan Hotel*, South Place, Moorgate St., near the Great Eastern Railway Station. — *Klein's Hotel*, 38 Finsbury Square, R. & A. from 2s., D. 3s. 6d., frequented by Germans, well spoken of; *Seyd's Hotel*, 39 Finsbury Square, R. & B. from 4s., D. 2s. 6d.-3s., well spoken of; *Bücker's Hotel*, Christopher Street, Finsbury Square, R. & B. 5-6s., D. 3s., a favourite foreign hotel. — In Charterhouse Square (Pl. R, 40; *II*) quietly situated: *Cocker's* (No. 18); *Allison's* (No. 13).

In or near FLEET STREET: — *Anderton's Hotel*, 162 Fleet Street, a favourite resort of many dining clubs and masonic lodges, R. & A. from 4s.; *Peele's Hotel*, 177 Fleet Street; *Salisbury Hotel*, Salisbury Square, Fleet Street.

Temperance Hotels in the City: *Devonshire House*, 12 Bishopsgate Without, near Liverpool Street Station (Pl. R, 44; *III*), R. & A. from 3s. 6d., B. 2s. 6d., L. 2s. 6d. — *Wild's*, 34-40 Ludgate Hill (Pl. R, 35; *II*), R. & A. from 2s. 6d., B. 2s. — *Tranter's*, 6-9 Bridgewater Square, Barbican (Pl. R, 40), in a quiet situation, R., A., & B. from 3s. 6d., pens. from 6s. — *Temperance Hotel*, 42 Wood Street, Cheapside, for gentlemen only, R. & A. from 2s.

h. Hotels to the South of the Thames.

There are few hotels of importance on this side of the river, and neither London Bridge Station nor Waterloo Station is provided with a terminal hotel. Fair accommodation may be obtained at the houses mentioned below.

Bridge House Hotel, 4 Borough High Street, London Bridge (Pl. R, 42; *III*), R. & A. from 4s. 6d., B. 2s. to 3s. 6d., D. 2s. 6d to 5s. — *Booth's Hotel*, 166 Westminster Bridge Road (Pl. R, 29). — *York Hotel*, corner of Waterloo Road and York Road, close to Waterloo Station (Pl. R, 30), R., A., & B. from 4s. 6d.; *Waterloo Hotel*, 2-16 York Road, Waterloo, R. & A. from 3s. 6d. — *Queen's Hotel*, Upper Norwood, near the Crystal Palace.

Boarding Houses. The visitor will generally find it more economical to live in a *Boarding House* than at a hotel. For a sum of 30-40s. per week or upwards he will receive lodging, breakfast, luncheon, dinner, and tea, taking his meals and sharing the sitting rooms with the other guests. It is somewhat more difficult to give a trustworthy selection of boarding-houses than of hotels, but the Editor has reason to believe that those noted below are at present (1900) fairly comfortable.

In the West End: *Mrs. Phillips*, 10 Duchess Street, Portland Place, near Langham Hotel (p. 11), 7-9s. per day, 2l. 2s. to 3l. 13s. 6d. per week; *Miss Edwards*, 44 L ngridge Road, Earl's Court, 1l. 7s. to 2l. 2s. per week; *Pension Durham*, 48 St. George's Road, S.W., near Victoria Station, from 5s. per day and 30s. per week; *Dr. Oliver Speer*, 26 Kennet Road, Westbourne Park; *Langham House*, 14 St. Stephen's Road, Ba\swater, from 4s. 6d. per day and 25s. per week; *Mrs. Craston*, 8 Talbot Road, Bayswater, from 5s. 6d. per day or 25s. per week; *Miss Usher*, 42 Cambridge Gardens, North Kensington, W.

Near the British Museum: *Misses Wright*, 15 Upper Woburn Place, Tavistock Square, 6-8s. per day; *Mrs. Jane Hawgood*, 33 Guilford Street, 30-42s. per week; *Miss Watson*, 57 Guilford Street, from 6s. per day or 1l. 10s. per week; *Mrs. Holt*, 10 Bedford Place, Russell Square, from 6s. a day and 34s. 6d. a week; *Miss Smyth*, 3 Bedford Place, Russell Square; *C. Parkinson*, 36 Gower Street, from 2l. 10s. per week; *Mrs. Robinson*, 82 Gower Street, from 25s. 6d. per week; *Mrs. Rosenbarm*, 80 Gower Street, from 6s. per day and 35s. per week; *Mrs. Kellu*, 34 Woburn Place, from 5s. 6d. per day and 30s. per week; *Mrs. Snell*, 21-23 Bedford Place, 6s.-7s. 6d. per day, 42s.-52s. 6d. per week; also at No. 31., 4s. 6d. per day (R. & B. only); *Mrs. Cory*, 23 Torrington Square.

The arrangements of boarding-houses are, however, more suitable for persons making a prolonged sojourn in London than for those who merely intend to devote two or three weeks to seeing the lions of the English Metropolis. To a visitor of the latter class the long distances between the different sights of London make it expedient that he should not have to return for dinner to a particular part of the town at a fixed hour. This independence of action is secured, more cheaply than at a hotel, by taking —

Private Apartments, which may be hired by the week in any part of London. Notices of '*Apartments*', or '*Furnished Apartments*', are generally placed in the windows of houses where there are rooms to be let in this manner, but it is safer to apply to the nearest house-agent. Rooms in the house of a respectable private family may often be obtained by advertisement or otherwise, and are generally much more comfortable than the professed lodging-houses. The dearest apartments, like the dearest hotels, are at the West End, where the charges vary from 2l. to 15l. a week. The best are in the streets leading from Piccadilly (Dover Street, Half Moon Street, Clarges Street, Duke Street, and Sackville Street), and in those leading out of St. James's Street, such as Jermyn Street,

Bury Street, and King Street. Good, but less expensive lodgings may also be obtained in the less central parts of the West End, and in the streets diverging from Oxford Street and the Strand. In Bloomsbury (near the British Museum) the average charge for one room is 15-21s. per week, and breakfast is provided for 1s. a day. Fire and light are usually extras, sometimes also boot-cleaning and washing of bed-linen. It is advisable to have a clear understanding on all these points. Still cheaper apartments, varying in rent according to the amenity of their situation and their distance from the centres of business and pleasure, may be obtained in the suburbs. The traveller who desires to be very moderate in his expenditure may even procure a bedroom and the use of a breakfast parlour for 10s. a week. The preparation of plain meals is generally understood to be included in the charge for lodgings, but the sight-seer will probably require nothing but breakfast and tea in his rooms, taking luncheon and dinner at one of the pastrycooks' shops, oyster-rooms, or restaurants with which London abounds.

Though attendance is generally included in the weekly charge for board and lodging, the servants expect a small weekly gratuity, proportionate to the trouble given them.

Money and valuables should be securely locked up in the visitor's own trunk, as the drawers and cupboards of hotels and boarding-houses are not always inviolable receptacles. Large sums of money and objects of great value, however, had better be entrusted to the keeping of the landlord of the house, if a person of known respectability, or to a banker in exchange for a receipt. It is hardly necessary to point out that it would be unwise to make such a deposit with the landlord of private apartments or boarding-houses that have not been specially recommended.

4. Restaurants. Dining Rooms. Oyster Shops.

English cookery, which is as inordinately praised by some epicures and *bons vivants* as it is abused by others, has at least the merit of simplicity, so that the quality of the food one is eating is not so apt to be disguised as it is on the Continent. Meat and fish of every kind are generally excellent in quality at all the better restaurants, but the visitor accustomed to Continental fare may discern a falling off in the soups, vegetables, and sweet dishes. At the first-class restaurants the cuisine is generally French; the charges are high, but everything is sure to be good of its kind.

The dinner hour at the best restaurants is 4-8 p.m., after which some of them are closed. At less pretentious establishments dinner 'from the joint' is obtainable from 12 or 1 to 5 or 6 p.m. Beer, on draught or in bottle, is supplied at almost all the restaurants, and is the beverage most frequently drunk. The *Grill Rooms* are devoted to chops, steaks, and other dishes cooked on a gridiron. *Dinner from the Joint* is a plain meal of meat, potatoes, vegetables, and cheese. At many of the following restaurants, particularly those in the City, there are luncheon-bars, where from 11 to 3 a chop or small plate of hot meat with bread and vegetables may be obtained for 6-8d. Customers usually take these 'snacks' standing at the bar. In dining *à la carte* at any of the foreign restaurants, one portion will often be found sufficient for two persons. A small fee for attendance is often made; and at the more fashionable restaurants a charge of from 3d. to 1s. for 'table-money' or the 'couvert' must generally be added to the prices as given below.

Many of the larger drapery and outfitting establishments have Luncheon and Tea Rooms, which are convenient for ladies while shopping. The bill-of-fare is usually excellent and the charges moderate. Among these may be mentioned those at *Swan & Edgar's, Shoolbred's, Owen's, Derry & Toms', Evans's* and *Whiteley's* (see p. 26).

Good wine in England is expensive. *Claret* (Bordeaux) is most frequently drunk, but *Port, Sherry*, and *Hock* (a corruption of Hochheimer, used as a generic term for Rhenish wines) may also be obtained at most of the restaurants. Some of the Italian restaurants have good Italian wines.

The traveller's thirst can at all times be conveniently quenched at a *Public House*, where a glass of bitter beer, ale, stout, or 'half-and-half (*i. e.* ale or beer, and stout or porter, mixed) is to be had for $1\frac{1}{2}$-2d. (6d. or 8d. per quart). Good German *Lager Bier* (3-6d. per glass) is now very generally obtainable at the larger restaurants, in some of which it has almost entirely supplanted the heavier English ales Genuine *Munich Beer* ('Pschorr') and *Bohemian Beer* ('Bürgerliches Bräuhaus, Pilsen') from the cask may be obtained at the *Gambrinus Restaurant*, 3 Glasshouse Street, Piccadilly Circus; also German sausages, smoked eel, and similar 'whets'. English-made lagerbeer is supplied in an establishment in the basement of the Café Monico, Piccadilly Circus, fitted up in the 'old German' style. Many of the more important streets contain *Wine Stores* or '*Bodegas*', where a good glass of wine may be obtained for 3d.-6d., a pint of Hock or Claret for 8d.-1s. 6d., and so on. A few taverns have also acquired a special reputation for their wines, but as a rule public house wine cannot be recommended.

The distinguishing features of many of the chief restaurants of London are described in 'Dinners and Diners', by *Lieut.-Col. Newnham-Davis* (Grant Richards; 1899).

Restaurants at the West End.

In and near the STRAND and CHARING CROSS: —

Restaurants of the **Hôtel Cecil* (p. 7) and the **Savoy Hotel* (p. 7), two high-class establishments with charges to correspond, both with open-air terraces and views of the river.

Charing Cross Station Restaurant (Charing Cross Hotel; p. 8).

Adelphi Restaurant (Gatti), at the Adelphi Theatre, 410 Strand, table-d'hôte 3s. 6d.

Romano, 399 Strand, table d'hôte (upstairs) 5s. 6d.

Simpson's Dining Rooms, in the busiest part of the Strand (Nos. 101-103); ladies' room upstairs; dinner from the joint 2s. 6d., fish-dinner 2s. 9d.

Imperial Café-Restaurant (Gatti & Rodesano), 161A & 166 Strand.

*Gaiety Restaurant (Spiers & Pond), at the Gaiety Theatre, 343 and 344 Strand; table-d'hôte from 5.30 till 8 p.m., 3s. 6d.

Tivoli Grand Restaurant, 65 Strand, adjoining the Tivoli Music Hall (German beer), D. 3s.

*Gatti's Restaurant and Café, 436 Strand, with another entrance in Adelaide Street, and a third in King William Street, moderate.

Tavistock Hotel Restaurant, Covent Garden.

Ship Restaurant, 45 Charing Cross, unpretending, L. 2s., D. 3s.

The dining-rooms of the *Victoria, Métropole*, and *Grand Hotels* (see p. 8) are also open to visitors not residing in the hotels. The

Grand also has a buffet and an excellent grill-room (entr. in the Strand; hot luncheon 2s. 6d.).

In and near LEICESTER SQUARE: —

Queen's Hotel, see p. 8; *Hôtel de Provence*, 17 & 18 Leicester Square, German cuisine and Munich beer, D. (5-9 p.m.) 3s.; *Grand Hôtel et Brasserie de l'Europe*, 10-15 Leicester Square, with grill-room and German Bierhalle; *The Cavour*, 20 Leicester Square, hotel and café, French cuisine and attendance, D. (6-9) 3s.; *Monte Carlo Restaurant*, 2 Leicester Street; *Grand Vienna Café-Restaurant*, 8 New Coventry Street; *Globe*, Coventry Street, L. 2s., D. 3s.; *Previtali*, Arundell Street, Coventry Street, D. 3s. 6d.-5s. 6d.

Kettner's Restaurant du Pavillon, French house, 28-31 Church Street, Soho; *Wedde*, 12 Greek Street, Soho; *Hôtel d'Italie (Molinari)*, 52 Old Compton Street, Soho, Italian house (table-d'hôte 2s. 6d.); *Roche*, 16 Old Compton Street, French cuisine, D. 1s. 6d.; *Pinoli*, 17 Wardour Street, Italian, D. 2s.; *Restaurant des Gourmets*, 6 Lisle Street, off Wardour Street, French, unpretending.

Hôtel de Florence, 57 Rupert Street, Italian house (table-d'hôte 3s., luncheon 1s. 6d.).

There are many cheap foreign restaurants in Soho.

In and near PALL MALL: — *Carlton Hotel* (p. 9), with winter-garden, S. after the theatre 5s. — *Epitaux*, 9 Haymarket, L. 2s. 6d., D. 5s., S. 3s. — *Willis's*, 26 King Street, St. James's, L. 4s. 6d., D. à la carte. — *Dieudonné*, Ryder St., St. James's, L. 3s. 6d., D. 6-8s., S. 4s. 6d.

In WESTMINSTER: — *Victoria Mansions Restaurant*, Victoria Street, with dining-room (D. 3s.) and buffet; *Lucas*, 7 Broadway, Westminster. — *Overton*, 3a Victoria Buildings, opposite Victoria Station (fish dinners).

Near HYDE PARK CORNER: — *Hans Crescent Hotel* (p. 10), with winter-garden and music.

In PICCADILLY, REGENT STREET, and the vicinity: —

Princes' Restaurant, one of the handsomest and most fashionable restaurants in London, L. 4s. 6d., S. 5s., D. à la carte (good orchestra).

The Criterion (Spiers and Pond), Regent Circus, Piccadilly, adorned with decorative paintings by eminent artists; theatre, see p. 66. — Table-d'hôte D. in the Grand Hall 3s. 9d., in the W. Room 5s., in the E. Room 10s. 6d., accompanied by music; dinner from the joint 2s. 6d. Grill-room, café, and American bar, etc.

Trocadero, corner of Great Windmill St. and Shaftesbury Avenue, handsomely fitted up, D. 5s., 7s. 6d., 10s. 6d., wine table-d'hôte 3s. 6d., 5s. 6d., 7s. 6d., also à la carte; music during dinner.

Piccadilly Restaurant, in the building of the Pavilion Music Hall, Piccadilly Circus (Munich beer on draught).

Slater's Luncheon and Tea Rooms, 212 Piccadilly.

Monico's, 19 Shaftesbury Avenue, with restaurant, grill-room, café, luncheon-bar, and concert-room (see p. 70), D. 5*s*.

Berkeley Hotel, 77 Piccadilly, with good French cuisine; L. 4-5*s*., D. 7*s*. 6*d*.-10*s*. 6*d*.; also à *la carte*; no suppers served.

Walsingham House, 152 Piccadilly, see p. 9.

Avondile, 68 A Piccadilly, see p. 9.

The Burlington (Blanchard's), 169 Regent Street, corner of New Burlington Street; dinners on first and second floors, ground-floor reserved for luncheons. Ladies' rooms. Dinners at 5*s*., 7*s*. 6*d*., and 10*s*. 6*d*. ; also à *la carte*.

Formaggia (Ital.), 109 Regent Street.

Kühn (Alcock), 21 Hanover Street (café downstairs, p. 19).

Verrey, 229 Regent Street, French cuisine (bouillabaisse to order); open on Sun. evenings.

Grand Café Royal, 68 Regent Street; French dinner 5*s*.

Blanchard's Restaurant, 1-7 Beak Street, Regent Street (ladies not after 5 p.m.); dinner 2*s*. 6*d*.-5*s*. or à *la carte*. Good wines.

Old Blue Posts, 13 Cork Street, dinner from the joint 2*s*. 6*d*.

In and near Oxford Street and Holborn : —

The Pamphilon, 17 Argyll Street, Oxford Street, near Regent Circus, with ladies' rooms; unpretending, moderate charges.

Pagani, 44 & 48 Great Portland Street, with the interesting Artists' Room upstairs, containing drawings and autographs by artists and actors (reserved for private parties); good coffee.

Circus Restaurant (Gianella), 213 Oxford Street, near Regent Circus; *Star and Garter (Pecorini)*, 98 New Oxford Street. — *Buszard* (pastry-cook), 197 Oxford Street (recommended for ladies).

Frascati, 26-32 Oxford Street, a large and handsome establishment, with winter-garden, café, and grill-room; D. 5*s*.

Torino, 45 Oxford St., D. 2*s*. 6*d*., L. 1*s*. 6*d*. & 2*s*. 6*d*.

The Horseshoe, 264-267 Tottenham Court Road, not far from the British Museum, luncheon-bar, grill-room, and dining-rooms; table-d'hôte 5.30 to 8.30 p.m., 2*s*. 6*d*.

Vienna Café (see p. 19), near the British Museum.

Inns of Court Restaurant, in Lincoln's Inn Fields, N. side.

The Holborn Restaurant, 218 High Holborn, an extensive and elaborately adorned establishment, with grill-room, luncheon buffets, etc.; table-d'hôte at separate tables in the Grand Salon from 5.30 to 9 p.m., with music, 3*s*. 9*d*.; L. 2*s*. 6*d*.

City of New York, Hand Court, Holborn, handsomely fitted up.

The Radnor, 73 Chancery Lane and 311-312 High Holborn.

Spiers and Pond's Buffet, Holborn Viaduct Station.

Table-d'hôte at the *First Avenue Hotel* (p. 11) from 5.30 to 8.30 p.m., 5*s*.; also restaurant, grill-room, and luncheon-buffet.

Hotel Great Central, see p. 10.

Table-d'hôte at the *Midland Grand Hotel* (p. 11).

Veglio, 314 Euston Road, near the end of Tottenham Court Road.

Restaurants in the City.

In FLEET STREET : —

The Cock, 22 Fleet Street (chops, steaks, kidneys; good stout); with the fittings of the Old Cock Tavern, pulled down in 1886.

*The Rainbow, 15 Fleet Street (good wines); dinner from the joint, chops, steaks, etc.

Old Cheshire Cheese, 16 Wine Office Court, Fleet Street (steak and chop house; beefsteak pudding on Wednesdays, 2*s.*). Comp. p. 173).

Near ST. PAUL'S : — *Spiers and Pond's Restaurant*, Ludgate Hill Station.

Salutation Restaurant, 17 Newgate Street.

Grand Restaurant de Paris (Schüller), 74 Ludgate Hill, table-d'hôte from 5 to 9, with ½ bottle of claret, 3*s.* 6*d.*

Slater's, 72 Aldersgate Street; *Thomas's, Shannon's*, two chop-houses in Maidenhead Court, Aldersgate Street.

Near the BANK : —

The Palmerston, 34 Old Broad Street. — *Auction Mart (Spiers & Pond), Tokenhouse Yard, Lothbury. — *Charley's Fish Shop* (snacks of fish), 20 Coleman St.

In Gresham Street : — *The Castle* (No. 40); *Guildhall Tavern* (Nos. 81-83).

Ruttermann (Herrmann), 41 and 42 London Wall.

Goldstein ('kosher' cooking), 5 Blomfield Street, London Wall.

In Cheapside: — *Read's* (No. 94), moderate charges; *Queen Anne* (No. 27); *Sweeting's* (No. 158; fish).

Mullen's Hotel Restaurant, Ironmonger Lane, Cheapside (luncheon 2*s.*).

City Restaurant, 34 Milk Street (table-d'hôte 12-3, 1*s.* 3*d.*).

In the Poultry : — *Pimm's (Nos. 3, 4, 5).

In Bucklersbury, near the Mansion House : *Lake & Turner* (No. 21), moderate.

Spiers and Pond's Buffet, Mansion House (Metropolitan) Station.

The Bay Tree, 33 St. Swithin's Lane. — *Windmill*, 151 Cannon Street.

In or near Cornhill : — *Birch's (Ring & Brymer)*, 15 Cornhill, the principal purveyors to civic feasts; *Baker's*, 1 Change Alley, a well-known chop-house.

In Gracechurch Street: *The Grasshopper* (No. 13); *Half Moon* (No. 88); *Woolpack* (No. 4, and 6 St. Peter's Alley).

Ship and Turtle, 129 Leadenhall Street, noted for its turtle.

*London Tavern, formerly *King's Head*, 53 Fenchurch Street. Queen Elizabeth here took her first meal after her liberation from the Tower.

*Crosby Hall (p. 142), 32 Bishopsgate Within (waitresses). These last two are very handsomely fitted up and contain smoking and chess rooms.

Ye Olde Four Swans, 82 Bishopsgate Street Within.

Great Eastern Hotel Restaurant, at the corner of Liverpool Street and Bishopsgate Within.

The George, 86 Fenchurch Street.

Three Nuns, 10 Aldgate High Street, adjoining Aldgate Metropolitan Station.

New Corn Exchange Restaurant, 58 Mark Lane, near the Tower.

Waiters in restaurants expect a gratuity of about 1*d.* for every shilling of the bill, but 6*d.* per person is the most that need ever be given. If a charge is made in the bill for attendance, the visitor is not bound to give anything additional, though even in this case it is customary to give the waiter a trifle for himself.

Among the chief VEGETARIAN RESTAURANTS in London are the *St. George's Café*, 37 St. Martin's Lane, W.C.; *Forster & Hazell*, 8 Queen St., Cheapside, and 100 Bishopsgate Within; *Ideal Café*, 185 Tottenham Court Road; *Central*, 16 St. Bride's Street, Ludgate Circus, E.C.; *Garden*, 24 Jewin Street, E.C.; *Alpha*, 23 Oxford Street.

Oyster Shops.

*Scott (Edwin), 18 Coventry Street, exactly opposite the Haymarket (also steaks); *Blue Posts*, 14 Rupert Street (American specialties, clams, etc.; also grill), these two in the evening for gentlemen only; *Lunn*, 357 Strand; *Pimm*, 3 Poultry, City; *Sweeting*, 158 Cheapside and 70 Fleet Street, City; **Lightfoot*, 3 Arthur Street East and 22 Lime Street, City.

The charge for a dozen oysters is usually from 2*s.* to 4*s.* 6*d.*, according to the season and the rank of the house. Small lobster 1*s.* 6*d.*; larger lobster 2*s.* 6*d.* and upwards. Snacks of fish 2-6*d.* Oysters, like pork, are supposed to be out of season in the months that have no R in their name, *i.e.* those of summer.

5. Cafés. Tea Rooms. Confectioners. Billiard Rooms. Chess.

Cafés at the West End.

Gatti's Café, 436 Strand, good ices (also a restaurant, p. 15); *Carlo Gatti*, Villiers Street, Strand; *Grand Café Royal*, 68 Regent Street (restaurant, p. 17); **Kühn*, 21 Hanover Street, Regent Street (restaurant, p. 17); *Verrey*, corner of Regent Street and Hanover Street, noted for ices (restaurant, p. 17); *Gunter*, 15 Lowndes Street and 23 Motcomb Street, Belgrave Square; *Simpson's Cigar Divan*, 101-103 Strand, second floor, café for gentlemen; *Gentlemen's Café*, Criterion (p. 16); *Monico*, 19 Shaftesbury Avenue (p. 16); *Frascati*, 32 Oxford St. (restaurant, p. 17); **Vienna Café*, corner of Oxford Street and Hart Street, near the British Museum (also restaurant); *Brasserie de l'Europe*, Leicester Square (p. 15); *Appenrodt's Vienna Café*, 8 New Coventry Street, Leicester Square.

Cafés in the City.

Peele's, 177 Fleet Street; *White*, 16 Ludgate Hill; *Café de Paris*, 74 Ludgate Hill; *Karo* (library, chess, etc.), 139 Cannon Street; *Collard's Café Nero*, Wool Exchange, Coleman Street. The shops of *Ye Mecca Company*, in the City, are much frequented in the afternoon for coffee.

Tea Rooms.

Mrs. Robertson, 161 New Bond Street; *Ladies Own Tea Association*, 90 New Bond Street; *Bungalow*, 21 Conduit Street, W.; *Callard*, 65 Regent Street; *Fuller's*, 358 Strand and 31 Kensington High Street; also *Buzzard's* and other confectioners' (see below); and the numerous shops (often crowded), in the principal thoroughfares, of *Lyons & Co.*, *Slater*, and the *Aërated Bread Co.* Light luncheon may be obtained at most of these.

Confectioners.

Charbonnel & Walker, 173 New Bond Street; *Bonthron*, 50-52 Glasshouse Street, Regent Street; *Duclos*, 2 Royal Arcade, Old Bond Street; *Blatchley*, 167, *Buzzard*, 197, both in Oxford Street; *Fuller*, 206 Regent Street, 358 Strand, 31 Kensington High Street, 28 St. Swithin's Lane, City, 113 Victoria Street, S.W., and 131 Queen's Road, Bayswater (American confectionery); *Beadell*, 8 Vere Street; *Gunter & Co.*, 7 Berkeley Square (good ices).

Billiard Rooms.

Bennett, 94 New Bond Street; *Roberts*, Egyptian Hall, Piccadilly; *Peall*, Brighton Chambers, Denman Street, London Bridge; *Carlo Gatti*, Villiers Street; *Courtney*, 191 Piccadilly. Billiard-tables will also be found in almost every hotel and large restaurant or public house. The usual charge is 1s. per hour (1s. 6d. by gas-light), or 6d. per game of fifty. The chief matches are played at the Egyptian Hall (p. 68), the Argyll Billiard Hall, the Westminster Aquarium (p. 68), the Gaiety Restaurant (p. 15), and the rooms of the leading billiard-table makers, comfortable accommodation being provided in each case for spectators.

Chess.

Chess is played at the *London Tavern* (p. 18), *Crosby Hall* (p. 18), *Simpson's Divan*, 101 Strand (p. 19), *Gatti's Café*, 436 Strand (p. 19), and many other cafés. London contains numerous first-class chess-clubs, the chief being the *City of London Chess Club*, Grocers' Hall Court, Poultry, E.C.; the *Divan Chess Club*; and the *St. George's*, 87 St. James's Street, S.W.

6. Libraries, Reading Rooms, and Newspapers.

Public Libraries. London and its suburbs now contain up-wards of fifty free public libraries, where visitors may freely enter and consult the books and magazines. They are open from 8, 9, or 10 a.m. to 9, 10, or 11 p.m., and many of them are also open on Sun. evening. All have free news-rooms, reading-rooms, and reference-libraries; but books are, as a rule, lent out only to residents of the district on a rate-payer's recommendation.

Some sort of an introduction is generally necessary for those who wish to use the books in the following great libraries, at which, however, no fees are charged.

British Museum Library. see p. 326; *Sion College Library*, on the Thames Embankment, 66,000 vols., the most valuable theological library in London, containing portraits of Laud and other bishops; *Dr. Williams' Library*, University Hall, Gordon Square, with 40,000 vols., containing a large collection of Puritan theology and fine portraits of Baxter and other divines; *Lambeth Palace Library*, p. 369; *Allan Library*, Wesleyan Conference Office, 2 Castle St., Finsbury, with a fine collection of Bibles and theological works (p. 132); *Guildhall Library*, p. 136; *Patent Office Library*, 25 Southampton Buildings, Chancery Lane, especially rich in scientific journals and transactions of learned societies (open free, 10-10).

Circulating Libraries. *Mudie's Select Library (Limited)*, 30-34 New Oxford Street, a gigantic establishment possessing hundreds of thousands of volumes (minimum quarterly subscription, 7s.); branches at 241 Brompton Road and 48 Queen Victoria Street, E.C. *W. H. Smith & Son*, 183 Strand, branch at 2 Arundel Street, W.C.; *London Library*, 14 St. James's Square, with 150,000 vols. (annual subs. 3l., introduction by a member necessary); *London Institution Library*, Finsbury Circus, with 100,000 vols. (annual subs. 2l. 12s. 6d.); *Rolandi*, 20 Berners Street, Oxford Street, for foreign books (300,000 vols.; monthly subs. 4s. 6d., yearly 2l. 2s.); *Cawthorn*, 24 Cockspur St.; *Mitchell's Royal Library (Limited)*, 33 Old Bond St., 16 Gloucester Road, S.W., 5 Leadenhall St., and 7 Palmerston Buildings, Old Broad St., E.C.; *Grosvenor Gallery Library*, 137 New Bond St.

Reading Rooms. Besides those at the free libraries (see above) the following reading-rooms, most of which are supplied with English and foreign newspapers, may be mentioned: *Anglo-American Exchange*, 3 Northumberland Avenue, also with American newspapers (4s. per month); *Colonial Institute*, Northumberland Avenue (subs. 1-2 guineas per annum; comp. p. 103); *Guildhall Free Library*; *Central News Agency*, 5 New Bridge Street, Ludgate Circus (adm. 2d.); *Walker*, Ludgate Circus Buildings (adm. 1d.); *Karo*, 139 Cannon Street; *Commissioners of Patents Library*, 25 Southampton Buildings, Chancery Lane; *Street's Colonial & General Newspaper Offices*, 30 Cornhill, 164 Piccadilly, and 5 Serle Street, Lincoln's Inn; *Brown, Gould, & Co.*, 54 New Oxford Street (adm. 2d.).

Newspapers. About 570 newspapers are published in London
and its environs. Among the principal morning papers are the *Times*
(3*d*.), in political opinion nominally independent of party (printing-
office, see p. 153); then the *Daily News* (1*d*.; a leading Liberal
journal), *Daily Telegraph* (1*d*.), *Standard* (1*d*.; a strong Conservative organ), *Morning Post* (1*d*.; organ of the court and aristocracy), *Morning Advertiser* (1*d*.; the organ of the licensed vic-
tuallers), *Daily Chronicle* (1*d*.), *Financial News* (1*d*.), *Financial
Times* (1*d*.), *Morning Leader* (1/2*d*.; Radical), and *Daily Express*
(1/2*d*.). The *Daily Graphic* (1*d*.) is illustrated. The leading evening
papers include the *Westminster Gazette* (1*d*.), the *Pall Mall Gazette*
(1*d*.), the *St. James's Gazette* (1*d*.), *Evening Standard* (1*d*.), *Globe*
(1*d*.; the oldest evening paper, dating from 1803), *Star* (1/2*d*.), and
Echo (1/2*d*.). All of these are sold at the principal railway-stations,
at newsmen's shops, and in the streets by newsboys. The oldest
paper in the country is the *London Gazette*, the organ of the
Government, established in 1642 and published twice weekly.
The *City Press* (bi-weekly; 2*d*.) contains city and antiquarian notices; *London* (weekly; 1*d*.) and the *London Argus* (weekly; 1*d*.) also
deal with local government topics. Among the favourite weekly
journals are the comic paper *Punch* (3*d*.); the illustrated papers
(6*d*. each), *Sphere*, *Graphic*, *Black and White*, *Illustrated London
News*, *King*, *Sporting and Dramatic News*, *Sketch*, *Lady's Pictorial*,
Lady, *Gentlewoman*, and *Queen* (for ladies); and the superior literary journals and reviews, *Athenaeum*, *Academy*, *Outlook* (3*d*. each),
Spectator, *Speaker*, *Saturday Review*, *Literature* (6*d*. each), *Lon-
doner* (2*d*.), and *Review of the Week* (1*d*.). The *Weekly Dispatch*,
the *Observer* (2*d*.), *Lloyd's News* (circulation of over 1,000,000),
the *People*, *Reynolds'*, the *Sunday Times*, the *Weekly Sun*, and the
Referee (a sporting and theatrical organ) are Sunday papers. The
Guardian (weekly; 6*d*.) is the chief organ of the Church of England,
and the *Tablet* (weekly; 5*d*.) that of the Roman Catholics. *Truth*,
The World, and *Vanity Fair* (6*d*. each) are mainly 'society' papers.

    The *Field* (weekly; 6*d*.) is the principal journal of field-sports and
other subjects interesting to the 'country gentleman'; and next is *Land
and Water*, also weekly (6*d*.). The *Sportsman* (daily; 1*d*.), *Sporting Life*
(daily; 1*d*.), and the *Sporting Times* (weekly; 2*d*.) are the chief organs of
the racing public, and the *Era* (weekly; 6*d*.) and *Stage* (weekly; 2*d*.) of
the theatrical world.

    Science and Art Journals: *Journal of the Society of Arts* (6*d*.), *Nature*
(6*d*.), *Knowledge*, *The Electrician* (weekly; 4*d*.), *Chemical News* (weekly;
4*d*.) *Inventors' Review* (weekly; 3*d*.). The *Lancet* (weekly; 7*d*.) and the *British
Medical Journal* (6*d*.) are the leading medical papers. — Journals and
Transactions of the Geological, Astronomical, and other learned societies.

    Commercial and Professional Journals (weekly): The *Economist* (8*d*.),
the leading commercial and financial authority; *Agricultural Gazette* (2*d*.);
Board of Trade Journal (monthly; 6*d*.); *Farmer* (1*d*.); *Mark Lane Express*
(3*d*.), mainly relied upon for market-prices; *Engineer*, *Engineering* (each
6*d*.), for mechanics, surveyors, and contractors; *Builder* (4*d*.) and *Builders'
Journal* (1*d*.), devoted to building, designs, sanitation, and domestic comfort; *Architect* (4*d*.); *Colliery Guardian* (5*d*.); *Mining Journal* (6*d*.); *Gar-*

deners' Chronicle (3d.); *Bullionist* (6d.); *Railway Times* (6d.); *Money Market Review* (6d.); *The Educational Times* (6d.) and *The Schoolmaster* (1-2d.), for teachers.

The *London American* (1d.; 151 Fleet Street) is a weekly American paper, published in London, while the *Canadian Gazette* (3d.) is a London weekly dealing with Canadian matters. ~everal of the leading American papers have representatives and advertising offices in London. The address of the *Associated Press* is 24 Old Jewry, E.C.

7. Baths.

(Those marked † are or include Turkish baths; those marked § have swimming basins.)

Hot and cold baths of various kinds may be obtained at the baths mentioned below at charges varying from 6d. upwards. The usual charge for a Turkish bath is 2s. 6d. to 3s. 6d.; some establishments have reduced charges in the evening. The Public Baths, which are plainly but comfortably fitted up, were instituted chiefly for the working classes, who can obtain cold baths here for as low a price as 1d., from which the charges rise to 6d. or 8d. They are now to be found in every quarter of London, and many of them include swimming baths. Many of the private baths have most elegant appointments.

† *Argyll Baths*, 10 a Argyll Place, Regent Street.

† *Bell's Baths*, 24 & 26 Basinghall Street, E.C.

† *Bartholomew's Turkish Baths*, 23 Leicester Square, W.C.

§ *Bloomsbury and St. Giles Baths* (public), Endell Street.

† *Charing Cross Baths*, Northumberland Avenue. For ladies, in Northumberland Passage, Craven Street. Adm. 3s. 6d., after 7 p.m. 2s.

Chelsea Baths, 171 King's Road, Chelsea.

§ *Crown Swimming Baths*, Kennington Oval; 6d.

† *Earl's Court Baths*, 25 A Earl's Court Gardens, S.W.

† *Edgware Road Turkish Baths*, 16 Harrow Road.

† *Electropathic and Turkish Baths*, 24 Railway Approach, London Bridge, S.E.

Faulkner's Baths, 26 Villiers Street, by Charing Cross Station; † 50 Newgate Street, E.C.; 4 Panyer Alley, E.C.; at Fenchurch Street Station. These establishments, with lavatories, hair-cutting rooms, etc, are convenient for travellers arriving by railway.

† *Haley's*, 182 and 184 Euston Road.

§ *Kensington Baths* (public), Lancaster Road, W.

† *King's Cross Turkish Baths*, 9 Caledonian Road, King's Cross.

† *London and Provincial Turkish Baths* ('The Hammam'), 76 Jermyn Street, bath 4s, after 7 p.m. 2s.

§ *Metropolitan Baths*, 89 Shepherdess Walk, City Road.

† *Royal York Baths*, 54 York Terrace, Regent's Park.

§ *St. George's Baths* (public), 8 Davies Street, Berkeley Square, and 88 Buckingham Palace Road.

St. James's Baths (public), 14-18 Marshall Street, Golden Square.

§ *St. Margaret's Baths* (public), 34 Great Smith Street, Westminster.

St. Martin's Baths (public), Orange Street, Leicester Square.

§ *St. Marylebone Baths* (public), 181 Marylebone Road.

† *Savoy Turkish Baths*, Savoy Street, Strand.

8. Shops, Bazaars, and Markets.

The Co-operative System.

Shops abound everywhere. In the business-quarters usually visited by strangers it is rare to see a house without shops on the groundfloor. Prices are almost invariably fixed, so that bargaining is unnecessary. Some of the most attractive shops are in Regent Street, Oxford Street, Piccadilly, Bond Street, the Strand, Fleet Street, Cheapside, St. Paul's Churchyard, and Ludgate Hill.

The following is a brief list of some of the best (and, in many cases, the dearest) shops in London; it is, however, to be observed that other excellent shops abound in all parts of London, in many cases no whit inferior to those here mentioned. Besides shops containing the articles usually purchased by travellers for their personal use, or as presents, we mention a few of the large depôts of famous English manufactures, such as cutlery, china, and water-colours.

ARTISTS' COLOURMEN: — *Ackermann*, 191 Regent Street (water colours); *Newman*, 24 Soho Square; *Rowney & Co.*, 64 Oxford Street and 190 Piccadilly; *Winsor & Newton*, 37 Rathbone Place.

BOOKBINDERS: — *Rivière*, 33 Heddon Street, Regent Street; *Zaehnsdorf*, 144 Shaftesbury Avenue, Cambridge Circus; *Kelly*, 7 Water Street, Strand; *Burn & Co.*, 36 Kirby St., E. C.; *Bookbinders' Co-operative Society*, 17 Bury Street, Bloomsbury, W. C.

BOOKSELLERS: — *Hatchards*, 187 Piccadilly; *Bumpus*, 350 Oxford Street; *Harrison & Sons*, 59 Pall Mall; *Griffith & Farran*, 35 Bow Street; *Burleigh*, 370 Oxford Street; *Stanford*, 26 Cockspur Street, Charing Cross (maps, etc.); *Bain*, 1 Haymarket; *Bickers & Son*, 1 Leicester Square; *Gilbert & Field*, 67 Moorgate Street; *Stoneham*, 79 & 129 Cheapside, 129 Fenchurch Street, 39 Walbrook, etc.; *Sotheran & Co.*, 37 Piccadilly and 140 Strand; *Wilson*, 18 Gracechurch Street; *Dunn*, 23 Ludgate Hill and 4A Cheapside; *Cornish*, 297 High Holborn; *Jones & Evans*, 77 Queen St., Cheapside; *Kelly Law Book Co.*, Lincoln's Inn Gate, Carey Street; *Reeves & Turner*, 100 Chancery Lane; *Stevens*, 119 Chancery Lane (the last three for law-books). — FOREIGN BOOKSELLERS: *Dulau & Co.*, 37 Soho Square (general agents for Baedeker's Handbooks); *Williams & Norgate*, 14 Henrietta Street, Covent Garden; *Hachette*, 18 King William Street, West Strand; *Nutt*, 57 Long Acre; *Roques*, 97 New Oxford Street; *Rolandi*, 20 Berners Street; *Siegle*, 30 Lime Street; *Haas & Co.*, 2 Langham Place; *Luzac*, 46 Great Russell Street. — SECONDHAND BOOKSELLERS: *Quaritch* (many rare books), 15 Piccadilly; *Ellis & Elvey*, Bond Street; *Francis Edwards*, 83A High Street, Marylebone, W.; *Sotheran*, see above; *Stevens*, 39 Great Russell Street, W.C.; *Pickering & Chatto*, 66 Haymarket; *C. & E. Brown*, 13 Bishop's Road, Paddington.

CARPETS: — *Gregory & Co.*, 19 Old Cavendish Street, W.;

Hampton & Sons, 8-10 Pall Mall East; *Liberty*, 142 and 218 Regent Street; *Shoolbred & Co.*, 150-162 Tottenham Court Road; *Maple*, 141-149 Tottenham Court Road; *Debenham & Freebody*, 27 Wigmore Street, Cavendish Square; *Marshall & Snelgrove*, 334-354 Oxford Street; *Cardinal & Harford* (Turkish carpets), 108 and 109 High Holborn; *Goodyer* (Oriental), 174 and 198 Regent Street; *Bontor & Co.*, 406 Oxford Street; *Treloar*, 68 Ludgate Hill.

CHEMISTS : — *Prichard*, 10 Vigo Street, Regent Street; *Cooper*, 66 Oxford Street; *Squire & Sons*, 413 Oxford Street; *Bell & Co.*, 225 Oxford Street; *Challice*, 34 Villiers Street, Strand; *Corbyn, Stacey, & Co.*, 96 Leadenhall Street; *Pond*, 68 Fleet Street; *Nurthen & Co.*, 390 Strand; *Savory & Moore*, 143 New Bond Street; *Thomas*, 7 Upper St. Martin's Lane (moderate prices). — HOMŒOPATHIC CHEMISTS: *Armbrecht, Nelson, & Co.*, 13 Duke Street, Grosvenor Square, W.; *Heath & Co.*, 114 Ebury Street, S.W.; *Keene & Ashwell*, 74 New Bond Street, W.; *Leath & Ross*, 58 Duke Street, Grosvenor Square, and 27 Old Jewry; *Cruttenden*, 67 Wigmore Street; *Gould & Son*, 59 Moorgate Street, E. C.

Messrs. *Burroughs, Wellcome. & Co*, Manufacturing Chemists. Snow Hill Buildings, Holborn Viaduct, prepare portable drugs in the form of tabloids, which will be found exceedingly convenient by travellers. Their small and light pocket-cases contain a selection of the most useful remedies in this form. These tabloid drugs may be obtained of all chemists.

CHINA, see Glass.

CUTLERY : — *Asprey & Son*, 166 New Bond Street and 22 Albemarle Street; *Holtzapffel & Co.*, 64 Charing Cross; *Lund*, 56-57 Cornhill; *Mappin Brothers*, 66 Cheapside and 220 Regent Street; *Mappin & Webb*, 158-162 Oxford Street and 2 Queen Victoria Street; *Verinder*, 17A Ludgate Hill; *Rodgers & Sons*, 60 Holborn Viaduct; *Weiss & Son*, 287 Oxford Street. Travelling-bags, writing-cases, dispatch-boxes, etc., are also sold at most of these shops.

CYCLES : — *Swift Cycle Co.*, *Humber & Co.*, *Rudge - Whitworth*, *Singer*, all on Holborn Viaduct (Nos. 15, 32, 23, and 17); *Marriott Cycle Co.*, 71 Queen Street, E. C.; *Quadrant Cycle Co.*, 119 Newgate Street, E.C.; *Bayliss*, 103 Newgate Street; and many others.

DENTISTS : — *A. A. Goldsmith* (American), 53 Harley Street, W.; *K. A. Davenport* (Amer.), 7 Wimpole Street, Cavendish Square; *G. H. Jones*, 57 Great Russell Street; *Coffin* (Amer.), 94 Cornwall Gardens; *Pierrepoint*, 2 Cockspur Street, W.; *Spokes*, 4 Portland Place, W.; *Duncan*, 9 Charles Street, St. James's, W.; *Gabriel*, 7 Portland Place; *Milliken* (Amer.), 23 Henrietta Street, Cavendish Square; *Flemming*, 41 Queen Anne Street, Cavendish Square, W.; *R. C. Moritz*, 130 Cromwell Road, S.W. (the last two somewhat less expensive).

DRAPERS : — *Marshall & Snelgrove*, 334-354 Oxford Street; *Lewis & Allenby*, 193-197 Regent Street; *Russell & Allen*, 17 Old Bond Street; *Liberty* (Oriental fabrics), 142 and 218 Regent Street; *Goodyer* (Oriental goods), 174 and 198 Regent Street; *Howell*,

James, & Co., 5 Regent Street; *Debenham & Freebody*, 27 - 33 Wigmore Street, Cavendish Square, W.; *Owen*, 12A Westbourne Grove, Bayswater, W.; *Jay* (mourning warehouse), 243-253 Regent Street; *Redmayne & Co.*, 19 New Bond Street; *Shoolbred & Co.*, 151-158 Tottenham Court Road, W. C.; *Swan & Edgar (Waterloo House)*, 39-53 Quadrant, Regent Street, and 9-12 Piccadilly; *Peter Robinson*, 216-226 Oxford Street and 256-262 Regent Street; *Derry & Toms*, 99-119 Kensington High Street; *Capper*, 63 Gracechurch Street, City; *Dickins & Jones*, 232 Regent Street; *Robinson & Cleaver* (Irish linen). 170 Regent Street; *Walpole Brothers* (Irish linen), 89 New Bond Street; *Whiteley*, 31-55 Westbourne Grove, Bayswater, W.; *Hitchcock & Co.*, 69-74 St. Paul's Churchyard, City; *Wallis & Co.*, 7 Holborn Circus, E. C.; *Evans*, 292-320 Oxford Street; *Jaeger's Sanitary Woollen System Co.*, 85 Cheapside, E.C., 156 Victoria Street, S.W.. 30 Sloane Street, S.W., 456 Strand, W.C., and 126 Regent Street, W.

DRESSMAKERS: — *Viola*, 27 Albemarle Street, W.; *Liberty* (art costumes), 142 and 218 Regent Street; *Mme. Swaebe*, 9 New Burlington Street, W.; *Durrant*, 116 New Bond Street; *Régy*, 39 Baker Street, W.; *Mrs. Nettleship*, 58 Wigmore St.; *Carey & Wall*, 3 Brook Street, Hanover Square, W. See also Drapers and Ladies' Tailors.

DRY GOODS, see Drapers.

ENGRAVINGS: — *Colnaghi & Co.*, 13 and 14 Pall Mall East; *Graves*, 6 Pall Mall; *Boussod, Valadon, & Co.* (successors of *Goupil & Co.*), 5 Regent Street, Pall Mall, and 10 Charles Street, St. James's, S.W.; *Maclean*, 7 Haymarket and 5 St. James's Street; *Tooth*, 5 Haymarket; *Lefèvre*, 1A King Street, St. James's Square; *Ackermann*, 191 Regent Street; *Leggatt*, 62 Cheapside; *Agnew & Son*, 39b Old Bond Street; *Deighton*, 4 Grand Hôtel Buildings, Trafalgar Square.

FURNITURE: — *Liberty*, 142 and 218 Regent Street; *Smee & Cobay*, 139 New Bond Street; *Gillow*, 406 Oxford Street; *Storey*, 49-53 Kensington High Street; *Shoolbred*, 150-162, *Maple*, 141-149 Tottenham Court Road; *Cooper*, 8 Great Pulteney Street; *Graham & Biddle*, 463 Oxford Street; *Hampton & Sons*, 8-10 Pall Mall East; *Waring & Son*, 175-181 Oxford Street; *Goodyer* (Oriental goods), 198 Regent Street.

FURRIERS: — *Imperial Fur Store (Victory)*, 162 Regent Street; *International Fur Store*, 163 Regent Street; *Jeffs & Harris*, 244 Regent Street; *Ince*, 156, *Marshall & Snelgrove*, 334-354, *Poland*, 190, *Peter Robinson*, 216-226, all in Oxford Street; *Russ*, 70 New Bond Street; *Debenham & Freebody*, 33 Wigmore Street.

GAMES, REQUISITES FOR: — *Wisden & Co.*, 21 Cranbourn Street, W. C.; *Feltham & Co.*, 47 Wilson Street. Finsbury Square; *Ayres*, 111 Aldersgate Street, E. C.; *Hovenden*, 30 Berners Street, W., and 85 City Road, E. C.; *Park* (golf), 115 Cannon Street, E. C.; *Tate*, 18 Princes Street, Cavendish Square (tennis rackets); *Slazenger*,

Laurence Pountney Hill, E. C.; *Holden*, 10 Upper Baker Street, N.W. (tennis rackets); *Jaques*, 102 Hatton Garden, E. C.; *Lilly-white*, 24 Haymarket, W., and 2 Newington Causeway, S. E.; *Piggott*, 117 Cheapside, E. C.; *Parkins & Gotto*, 54-62 Oxford Street.

GLASS AND PORCELAIN: — *Phillips*, 175 Oxford Street; *Copeland & Sons*, 12 Charterhouse Street; *Mortlock & Sons*, 466 Oxford Street; *Daniell & Co.*, 42 Wigmore Street; *Pellatt & Co.*, 21 Northumberland Avenue; *Standish*, 58 Baker Street; *Osler*, 100 Oxford Street; *Goode*, 17-21 South Audley Street; *Green*, 107 Queen Victoria Street; *Venice and Murano Glass Co.*, 30 St. James's Street; *Salviati*, 213 Regent Street (mosaics).

GLOVES: — *Dent*, *Allcroft*, *& Co.* (celebrated firm, wholesale only; Dent's gloves are obtainable at all the retail shops), 97-99 Wood Street, E.C.; *Wheeler*, 16 Poultry and 8 Queen Victoria Street, City; *Penberthy*, 390 Oxford Street (French gloves); *Jugla*, 4 Prince's Buildings, Coventry Street, W.; *Swears & Wells*, 190 Regent Street; *London Glove Co.*, 83 New Bond Street (1st floor) and 45a Cheapside. Also at all the haberdashers' and hosiers' shops.

GOLDSMITHS AND JEWELLERS: — *Gass & Co.*, 166 Regent Street; *Garrard & Co.*, 25 Haymarket; *Lambert & Co.*, 10-12 Coventry Street, Haymarket; *Hancocks & Co.*, 38 and 39 Bruton Street and 152 New Bond Street; *Hunt & Roskell*, 156 New Bond Street; *Streeter & Co.*, 18 New Bond Street; *Tiffany*, 221 Regent Street; *Elkington & Co.*, 22 Regent Street and 42 Moorgate Street (electro-plate); *Packer*, 76 Regent Street; *Mrs. Newman*, 10 Savile Row, W.; *Goldsmiths' & Silversmiths' Co.*, 112 Regent Street; *Watherston & Son*, 12 Pall Mall East; *Liberty* and *Goodyer* (Oriental jewelry), see under Drapers.

GUN AND RIFLE MAKERS: — *Westley Richards*, *Lancaster*, 178 and 151 New Bond Street; *Rigby & Co.*, 72 St. James's Street; *Purdey*, Audley House, South Audley Street; *Grant*, 67A St. James's Street; *Jeffery & Co.*, 60 Queen Victoria Street, E.C.; *Reilly*, 277 Oxford Street; *Winchester Repeating Arms Co.*, 114 Queen Victoria Street, E.C.; *Colt's Fire Arms Company*, 26 Glasshouse Street, W.

HATTERS: — *Lincoln & Bennett*, 40 Piccadilly; *Heath*, 105-109 Oxford Street and 47 Cornhill; *Cater & Co.*, 88 St. James's Street; *Christy & Co.*, 35 Gracechurch Street, City; *Woodrow*, 42 Cornhill and 46 Piccadilly; *Truefitt*, 13 Old Bond Street and 20 Burlington Arcade; *Scotts*, 1 Old Bond Street; *Preedy*, 12a Regent Street. — LADIES' HATTERS: — *Mrs. Heath*, 24 St. George's Place, Hyde Park Corner, S.W.; *Fletcher & Lockwood*, 36 South Audley Street; *Lincoln & Bennett*, 3 Sackville Street, W.; *Henry Heath*, see above. Comp. Milliners.

HOSIERS AND SHIRTMAKERS: — *Hamilton Shirt Making Society*, 41 Poland Street, W.; *Poole & Lord*, 322 Oxford Street; *Hope Brothers*, 44 Ludgate Hill, E. C., 35 Poultry, E. C., 223 and 281 High Holborn, W. C., 84 Regent Street, W., etc.; *Capper, Son*,

& Co., 29 Regent Street; *Harborows.* 6 New Bond Street, W. — Ladies' Hosiery, etc.: *Penberthy*, 390 Oxford Street; *Edmonds, Orr. & Co.* (also children's outfitters), 47 Wigmore Street.

LACE: — *Haywards*, 11 Old Bond Street; *Steinmann*, 185 Piccadilly; *Marshall & Snelgrove*, 334-354 Oxford Street; *Dickins & Jones*, 232 Regent Street.

LADIES' UNDERCLOTHING: — *Mrs. Addley-Bourne*, 174 Sloane Street; *Swears & Wells* (children), 190 Oxford Street.

LEATHER GOODS (dressing-cases, dispatch-boxes, etc.): — *Fisher*, 188 Strand; *John Pound & Co.*, 67 Piccadilly, 211 Regent Street, 378 Strand, and 177 Tottenham Court Road; *Leuchars*, 38 Piccadilly; *Thornhill & Co.*, 144 New Bond Street. Comp. Cutlery and Trunk Makers.

MAP SELLERS (also guidebooks, etc.): — *E. Stanford* (agent for the Ordnance Survey Maps), 26 Cockspur Street, Charing Cross; *C. Smith & Son*, 63 Charing Cross; *Bacon & Co.*, 127 Strand; *Philip & Sons*, 32 Fleet Street.

MILLINERS: — *Michard*, 2 Hanover Square; *Worth et Cie.*, 56 Brook Street; *Colman*, 172 Regent Street; *Louise*, 210 and 266 Regent St.; *Pauline*, 259 Regent St.; *Maison Nouvelle*, Oxford Circus, 237 Regent Street, 85 Kensington High Street, and 9 Brompton Road, S.W.; *Durrant*, 116 New Bond Street; *White*, 63 Jermyn Street; *Maison de Cram*, 41 Chester Square, S.W.

MUSIC SELLERS: — *Boosey & Co.*, 295 Regent Street; *Chappell & Co.*, 49-52 New Bond Street; *Cocks & Co.*, 6 New Burlington Street; *Cramer & Co.*, 207 Regent Street, W., and 40 Moorgate Street, E.C.; *Novello & Co.*, 1 Berners Street, Oxford Street; *Breitkopf & Haertel*, 54 Great Marlborough Street; *Hammond & Co.*, 5 Vigo Street, Regent Street; *Metzler & Co.*, 40-43 Great Marlborough Street; *Augener*, 199 Regent Street and 22 Newgate Street, E.C.; *Keith, Prowse, & Co.*, 48 Cheapside, E.C., Grand Hotel Buildings, W.C., 48 Victoria Street, S.W., First Avenue Hôtel Buildings, High Holborn, W.C., 148 Fenchurch Street, E.C., and 167 New Bond Street, W.; *Woolhouse*, 174 Wardour Street, W.

OPTICIANS: — *Elliott Brothers*, 101 St. Martin's Lane, W.C.; *Dallmeyer*, 25 Newman Street, W.; *Negretti & Zambra*, 38 Holborn Viaduct, 45 Cornhill, and 122 Regent Street; *Callaghan*, 23a New Bond Street; *Dollond & Co.*, 35 Ludgate Hill and 62 Old Broad Street, E.C., and 5 Northumberland Avenue, W.C.; *Cox*, 98 Newgate Street.

PERFUMERS: — *Atkinson*, 24 Old Bond Street; *Piesse & Lubin*, 2 New Bond Street; *Rimmel*, 96 Strand, 180 Regent Street, and 64 Cheapside; *Breidenbach*, 48 Greek Street, Soho (wholesale); *Bayley*, 94 St. Martin's Lane.

PHOTOGRAPHERS: — *Mendelssohn*, 14 Pembridge Crescent, Notting Hill Gate, W.; *Cameron*, 31 George Street, Hanover Square; *Hollyer*, 9 Pembroke Square, Kensington, W. (sitters on Monday only, pictures on other days); *Mayall & Co. (Barraud)*, 126 Piccadilly, W.; *Barrauds*, 263 Oxford Street, W.; *Elliot & Fry*, 55 Baker Street, W.; *Ellis & Walery*, 51 Baker Street, N.W.; *Fradelle & Young*, 283 Regent Street; *London Stereoscopic Co.*, 106 Regent Street, W., and 54 Cheapside, E.C.; *Lyddell Sawyer*, 230 Regent Street; *Van der Weyde*, 182 Regent Street; *Fall*, 9 Baker Street (children).

PHOTOGRAPH SELLERS: — *Autotype Fine Art Gallery*, 74 New Oxford Street; *Mansell*, 405 Oxford Street; *London Stereoscopic Company*, 54 Cheapside and 108 Regent Street; *Spooner*, 379 Strand; *Erdmann & Schanz*, 116 Bedford Hill, Balham Junction, S.W. (photographs of persons, pictures, or places sent on view; catalogue sent on application); *Photocrom Co.*, 121 Cheapside; *Hanfstaengel*, 16 Pall Mall East; *Deighton*, 4 Grand Hôtel Buildings, Trafalgar Square. — PHOTOGRAPHIC MATERIALS: *Fallowfield*, 140 Charing Cross Road; *Marion*, 22 Soho Square; *Kodak Limited*, 115 Oxford Street, 171 Regent Street, and 60 Cheapside; *Negretti & Zambra*, 38 Holborn Viaduct, 45 Cornhill, and 122 Regent Street; *Piggott*, 117 Cheapside.

PIANOFORTE MANUFACTURERS: — *Broadwood & Sons*, 33 Great Pulteney Street, Golden Square; *Collard & Collard*, 16 Grosvenor Street, 26 Cheapside, and Oval Road, Regent's Park; *Erard*, 18 Great Marlborough Street; *Bechstein, Blüthner, Brinsmead, Ibach*, 40, 7, 18, and 54 Wigmore Street, W.; *Hopkinson*, 34 Margaret Street, Cavendish Square, W.; *Pleyell, Wolff, & Co.*, 79 Baker Street; *Steinway*, 15 Lower Seymour Street, W.

PRESERVES, etc. ('Italian Warehouses'): — *Crosse & Blackwell*, 20 and 21 Soho Square and 77 Dean Street (noted firm for pickles; wholesale); *Fortnum, Mason, & Co.*, 181-183 Piccadilly; *Morel Brothers*, 210 Piccadilly; *Jackson*, 172 Piccadilly (American groceries and canned goods); *Cadbury, Pratt, & Co.*, 24 New Bond Street; *Stembridge* (Indian condiments), 18 Green St., Leicester Square.

PRINTSELLERS, see Engravings.

SHOEMAKERS. For gentlemen: — *Thierry*, 70 Regent Street; *Deroy*, 74 Regent Street and 7 Air Street, W.; *Dowie & Marshall*, 455 Strand; *Fuchs*, 54 Conduit Street; *Bowley & Co.*, 53 Charing Cross; *Parker*, 145 Oxford Street; *Peal*, 487 Oxford Street; *Medwin*, 41 Sackville Street and 67 St. James's Street; *Hoby*, 20 Pall Mall; *Tuczek*, 39 Old Bond Street; *Waukenphast*, 60 Haymarket and 37 King William Street, E. C.; *Francis*, 40 Maddox Street; *Holden Brothers* ('nature true' boots), 223 1/2 Regent Street; *Manfield & Son*, 376 Strand, 307 High Holborn, 228 Piccadilly, 67 Cheapside, etc.; *American Shoe Co.*, 169 Regent Street. 373 Strand, and 113 Westbourne Grove; *Lilley & Skinner*, 275 High Holborn, 63 Westbourne Grove, etc. — For ladies: — *Hook, Knowles, & Co.*, 65 New Bond Street (also for gentlemen); *Bird*, 180 Oxford Street; *Gundry & Sons*, 187 Regent Street; *Thierry & Sons*, 292 Regent Street; *Thierry*, 70 Regent Street; *Yapp*, 200 Sloane Street.

SILK MERCERS, see Drapers.

STATIONERS : — *Macmichael*, 42 South Audley Street ; *Parkins & Gotto*, 54-62 Oxford Street ; *Webster & Co.*, 60 Piccadilly ; *Waterlow & Co.*, 49 Parliament Street, S.W., and 52 New Broad Street, E.C. ; *Spiers & Pond*, 35 New Bridge Street, Blackfriars, E.C.

TAILORS : — *Poole & Co.*, 36-39 Savile Row, Regent Street (introduction from former customer required) ; *Henry Walker*, 47 Albemarle Street (ready-money tailor, moderate charges) ; *E. George*, 87 Regent Street ; *Miles*, 4 Sackville Street ; *Parfitt, Roberts, & Parfitt*, 75 Jermyn Street ; *Kerslake & Co.*, 12 Hanover Street, Hanover Square ; *Radford, Jones, & Co.*, 32 George Street, Hanover Square ; *Blamey & Co.*, 62 Charing Cross ; *Ralph & Norton*, 150 Strand ; *Meyer & Mortimer*, 36 Conduit Street ; *Brown, Son, & Long*, 11 Princes Street. Hanover Square ; *Stohwasser & Co.*, 39 Conduit Street ; *Stulz, Papé, & Son*, 10 Clifford Street ; *Phillips & Son*, 58 Regent Street ; *Hoare & Sons*, 251 High Holborn ; *Lionel*, 14 Sloane Street ; *J. W. Doré*, 31 St. James's Street ; *West End Clothiers Co.* (ready money), 171 Strand, 66 Regent Street, 37 Ludgate Hill, and other addresses ; *Wray & Roby*, 78 Queen Street. Cheapside ; *Henry Keen*, 114 High Holborn ; *Piggott*, 117 Cheapside and Milk Street (also general outfitter) ; *Samuel Brothers*, 65 Ludgate Hill, E.C. (boys' outfitters, etc.) ; *Jaeger Sanitary Woollen System Co.*, 42 Conduit Street, W. — CLERICAL TAILORS : *Pratt*, 22 Tavistock Street, Covent Garden ; *Seary*, 13 New Oxford Street. — LADIES' TAILORS : *Redfern*, 26 Conduit Street ; *Goodman & Davis*, 200 Oxford Street ; *Fisher, Nicoll*, Regent Street, Nos. 217 and 114-120 ; *Phillips & Son*, 58 Regent Street ; *Scott Adie* (Scotch goods), 115 Regent Street ; *Pile*, 288 Regent Street. — Ready-made clothes may be obtained very cheaply in numerous large shops (prices usually affixed).

TEA MERCHANTS : — *Ridgways*, 6 and 7 King William Street, City, and 182 Oxford Street ; *Twining & Co*, 216 Strand ; *Dakin & Co.*, 1 St. Paul's Churchyard and 14 Glasshouse Street, Regent Street ; *Law*, 102 & 104 New Oxford Street ; *Cooper, Cooper, & Co.*, 71 Tooley Street, 268 Oxford Circus, and 35 Strand ; *Barber*, 274 Oxford Circus and 102 Westbourne Grove.

TOBACCONISTS : — *Cigar Divan*, 102 Strand ; *Carreras*, 7 Wardour Street (sellers of the Craven mixture, said to be the 'Arcadia' of 'My Lady Nicotine') ; *Fribourg & Treyer*, 34 Haymarket and 3 Leadenhall Street ; *Ponder*, 48 Strand ; *Benson*, 40 St. James's Street ; *Benson & Hedges*, 13 Old Bond Street ; *Carlin*, 189 Regent Street ; *Wolff, Phillips, & Co.*, 18 Great Portland Street, W. ; *Amber & Co.*, 238 and 536 Oxford Street, 52 Regent Street, 2 Coventry Street, and 6 Charing Cross.

TOYS : — *Burlington Arcade*, Piccadilly ; *Lowther Arcade*, Strand ; *Kindergarten Emporium*, 57 Berners Street ; *Mrs. Peck* (dolls), 131 Regent Street ; *Morrell*, 368 Oxford Street ; *Parkins & Gotto*, 54-62 Oxford Street ; *Jaques*, 102 Hatton Garden, E.C. ; *Hamley*, 64 Regent Street, 512 Oxford Street, and 230 High Holborn.

TRUNK MAKERS: — *Allen*, 37 Strand; *Asprey & Son*, 166 New Bond Street and 22 Albemarle Street; *Drew*, 33 Piccadilly Circus, W., and 156 Leadenhall Street, E.C.; *Southgate*, 75 and 76 Watling Street. — (Strangers should be on their guard against the temptation of purchasing trunks and portmanteaus in inferior leather marked 'second hand' — a common form of fraud in houses of a lower class.)

UMBRELLAS AND PARASOLS: — *Sangster & Co.*, 75 Fleet Street, 140 Regent Street, and 10 Royal Exchange; *Martin*, 64-65 Burlington Arcade; *Brigg*, 23 St. James's Street; *Smith*, 57 New Oxford Street, W.C., and 1 Savile Place, Regent Street, W.

UPHOLSTERERS, see Furniture.

WATCHMAKERS: — *Bennett*, 65 Cheapside; *Barraud & Lunds*, 14 Bishopsgate Within, E.C.; *Benson*, 25 Old Bond Street and 62 and 64 Ludgate Hill; *E. Dent & Co.*, 61 Strand; *M. F. Dent & Co.*, 33 Cockspur Street, S.W.; *Chas. Frodsham & Co.*, 115 New Bond Street, W.; *G. E. Frodsham & Co.*, 31 Gracechurch Street, E.C.

WATERPROOF GOODS: — *Matthews & Son*, 58 Charing Cross; *Cording & Co.*, 19 Piccadilly; *George Cording*, 125 Regent Street and 28 Cockspur Street; *Walkley*, 5 Strand; *Piggott*, 117 Cheapside; *Cow*, 46 Cheapside.

WINE MERCHANTS. — There are about 2500 wine merchants in London, most of whom can supply fairly good wine at reasonable prices. Visitors who occupy private apartments should procure their wine from a dealer. The wines at hotels are generally dear and indifferent. The following are good houses: — *Cockburn & Co.* (established 1796; specialty, Scotch whiskey), 8 Lime Street, City; *Hedges & Butler*, 155 Regent Street; *Gilbey*, Pantheon, 173 Oxford Street, besides other offices (with an extensive trade in low-priced wines); *Fortnum & Mason*, 181-183 Piccadilly; *Carbonell & Co.*, 182 Regent Street; *G. Tanqueray & Co.*, 5 Pall Mall East; *Basil Woodd & Sons*, 34 New Bond Street; *Morel Bros. & Cobbett*, 210 Piccadilly, 18 Pall Mall, and 39 Whitcomb Street; *Hatch, Mansfield, & Co.*, 1 Cockspur Street, S.W.; *Payne & Sons*, 61 St. James's Street; *Domecq*, 6 Great Tower Street, E.C. — The *Victoria Wine Co.* (head office, 6 Osborn Street, E., with about 90 branch-offices in London and its suburbs) does a large business in moderate-priced wines, from single bottles upwards. — Most of the best-known continental wine-firms have agencies in London, the addresses of which may be ascertained from the Post Office Directory. Claret and other wines may also be obtained from most of the grocers.

Bazaars. These emporiums afford pleasant covered walks between rows of shops abundantly stocked with all kinds of attractive and useful articles. The most important are the *Royal Arcade*, 28 Old Bond Street; *Opera Colonnade*, Haymarket; *Burlington Arcade*, Piccadilly; *Ludgate* or *Imperial Arcade*, Ludgate Circus; *Baker Street Bazaar*, 58 Baker Street; *Soho Bazaar*, 58 Oxford

Street; *Lowther Arcade*, Strand (chiefly for toys and other articles at moderate prices).

Markets. The immense market traffic of London is among the most impressive sights of the Metropolis, and one with which no stranger should fail to make himself acquainted. The chief markets are held at early hours of the morning, when they are visited by vast crowds hastening to supply their commissariat for the day.

The chief *Vegetable, Fruit, and Flower Market* is *Covent Garden* (p. 232). The best time to visit this market is about sunrise.

Billingsgate (p. 149), the great fish-market, as interesting in its way as Covent Garden, though pervaded by far less pleasant odours, is situated in Lower Thames Street, City, near London Bridge. The market commences daily at 5 a. m.

At *Smithfield* (Pl. R, 36), to the N. of Newgate Street, City, are the *Central Meat, Poultry*, and *Fish Markets*, the chief centres of the food-supply of London. In Farringdon Road, close by, is the new *Farringdon Vegetable Market*. Comp. p. 128.

The *Metropolitan Cattle Market* (Pl. B, 25, 29), Copenhagen Fields, between Islington and Camden Town, is the largest in the world, covering 30 acres of ground and accommodating 8-10,000 cattle, 35,000 sheep, and 1000 pigs. The principal markets are held on Mondays and Thursdays, but on other days the traffic is also very considerable. The great day is the Monday of the week before Christmas. 'Pedlars' Market' on Friday afternoon, see pp. 292, 293. — At *Deptford* (p. 389) is a great *Foreign Cattle Market*, for cattle imported from the Continent and elsewhere.

Among the other important markets of London are *Leadenhall Market* (p. 144), Leadenhall Street, on a site where poultry and game have been sold for at least 400 years; the *Borough Market*, beside St. Saviour's Church (p. 376), one of the largest wholesale fruit and vegetable markets; *Spitalfields Market*, Commercial Street, E., for vegetables, etc., the chief emporium for East London; and the *Shadwell Market*, East of London Docks, for fish. *Columbia Market* (Pl. B, 48), Bethnal Green, was erected by the munificence of the Baroness Burdett Coutts, at a cost of 200,000*l.*, for supplying meat, fish, and vegetables to one of the poorest quarters of London.

The largest Horse Market is *Tattersall's* (Pl. R, 13), Knightsbridge Green, where auction-sales take place every Monday at 11.30 a.m., and in spring on Thursdays also. The horses are on view on Sat. and Sun. (11-5). Tattersall's is the centre of all business relating to horse-racing and betting throughout the country, — the Englishman's substitute for the Continental lotteries. *Aldridge's*, St. Martin's Lane, is another important horse-mart.

The Co-operative System. The object of this system may be described as the furnishing of members of a trading association, formed for the purpose, with genuine and moderately-priced goods on the principle of ready-money payments, the cheapness being secured by economy of management and by contentment with small profits. Notwithstanding the opposition of retail and even of wholesale dealers it has of late years made astonishingly rapid progress in London, where there are now about thirty 'co-operative stores', carrying on an immense trade. The chief companies are the *Army and Navy Co-operative Society*, 105 Victoria Street, Westminster, the *Civil Service Supply Association*, the *Junior Army and Navy Stores*, 15 Regent Street and 39 King Street, Covent Garden, and the *Civil Service Co-operative Society*, 28 Haymarket.

The Civil Service Supply Association Limited consists of shareholders, of members belonging to the Civil Service, and of outsiders (who, however, must be friends of members or shareholders), who pay a subscription of 2s. 6d. per annum. The association now employs nearly 1400 persons, who receive salaries amounting in all to about 104,000l. annually. The cost of the string, paper, and straw used in packing goods for customers amounts to 10,000l. a year, and more than 30,000l. is annually spent for carriage and booking. The total value of the sales in 1899 amounted to 1,741,770l., the net profit being about 2½ per cent. The articles sold comprise groceries, wines, spirits, provisions, tobacco, clothing, books, stationery, fancy goods, drugs, and watches. The chief premises of the association are in Queen Victoria Street, while it has others in Bedford Street and Chandos Street, Strand. — The sales of the Army and Navy Stores reach a still higher total, amounting to about 3,000,000l. per annum.

Strangers or visitors to London are, of course, unable to make purchases at a co-operative store except through a member.

Co-operative Working Societies. Another application of the co-operative system is seen in the various associations established on the principle of the *Co-Partnership of the Workers*.

Among meritorious societies of this kind the following may be mentioned: *Bookbinders' Co-operative Society*, 17 Bury Street, Bloomsbury; *Hamilton Shirt-Making Society*, 41 Poland Street, W.; *Women's Printing Society*, 66 Whitcomb Street, W.C.; *Co-operative Printers*, Tudor Street, New Bridge St., E.C.; *Co-operative Depôt*, 19 Southampton Row, W.C. (tailoring, etc.).

9. Cabs. Omnibuses. Tramways. Coaches.

Cabs. When the traveller is in a hurry, and his route does not coincide with that of an omnibus, he had better at once engage a cab at one of the numerous cab-stands, or hail one of those passing along the street. The '*Four-wheelers*', which are small and uncomfortable, hold four persons inside, while a fifth can be accommodated beside the driver. The two-wheeled cabs, called *Hansoms* from the name of their inventor, have seats for two persons only (though often used by three), and drive at a much quicker rate than the others. Persons without much luggage will therefore prefer a hansom. The driver's seat is at the back, so that he drives over the heads of the passengers sitting inside. Orders are communicated to him through a small trap-door in the roof. A small number of *Electric Cabs*, plying at the same fares as the horse-cabs, were placed on the streets in 1897. — There are now over 11,000 cabs in London, employing nearly 20,000 horses.

Cab Fares from the chief railway-stations to	Broad Street & Liverpool Street	Charing Cross	Euston Square	Fenchurch Street	King's Cross and St. Pancras	London Bridge	Paddington	Victoria	Waterloo
	s. d.	s. d.	s. d.	s. d.	s. d.	s. d.	s. d.	s. d.	s. d.
Bank of England	1 -	1 -	1-6	1 -	1-6	1 -	2-6	2 -	1 -
Bond Street, Piccadilly	1-6	1 -	1 -	1-6	1-6	1-6	1-6	1 -	1 -
British Museum	1-6	1 -	1 -	1-6	1 -	1-6	1-6	1-6	1 -
Covent Garden	1-6	1 -	1 -	1-6	1 -	1-6	1-6	1 -	1 -
Grosvenor Square	2 -	1 -	1 -	2 -	1-6	2 -	1 -	1 -	1-6
Hyde Park Corner	2 -	1 -	1-6	2 -	2 -	2 -	1-6	1 -	1-6
Leicester Square	1-6	1 -	1 -	1-6	1-6	1-6	1-6	1 -	1 -
London Bridge	1 -	1-6	2 -	1 -	1-6		2-6	1-6	1 -
Ludgate Hill	1 -	1 -	1-6	1 -	1 -	1 -	2 -	1-6	1 -
Marble Arch	2 -	1 -	1-6	2 -	1-6	2 -	1 -	1 -	1-6
Oxford Circus	1-6	1 -	1 -	1-6	1 -	2 -	1 -	1 -	1 -
Piccadilly, Haymarket	1-6	1 -	1 -	1-6	1-6	1-6	1-6	1 -	1 -
Post Office	1 -	1 -	1-6	1 -	1 -	1 -	2 -	2 -	1 -
Regent Street, Piccadilly . . .	1-6	1 -	1 -	1-6	1-6	1-6	1-6	1 -	1 -
St. Paul's	1 -	1 -	1-6	1 -	1 -	1 -	2 -	1-6	1 -
South Kensington Museum . .	2-6	1-6	2 -	2-6	2-6	2-6	1-6	1-6	2 -
Strand (Wellington Street) . .	1-6	1 -	1 -	1-6	1 -	1 -	2 -	1 -	1 -
Temple Bar	1 -	1 -	1 -	1 -	1 -	1 -	2 -	1-6	1 -
Tower	1 -	1-6	2 -	1 -	2 -	1 -	2-6	2 -	1-6
Trafalgar Square	1-6	1 -	1 -	1-6	1-6	1-6	1-6	1 -	1 -
Westminster Palace	1-6	1 -	1-6	1-6	1-6	1-6	1-6	1 -	1 -
Zoological Gardens	2 -	1-6	1 -	2-6	1 -	2-6	1-6	2 -	2 -

FARES are reckoned by distance, unless the cab is expressly hired by time. The charge for a drive of 2 M. or under is 1s.; for each additional mile or fraction of a mile 6d. For each person above two, 6d. additional is charged for the whole hiring. Two children under 10 years of age are reckoned as one adult. For each large article of luggage carried outside 2d. is charged; smaller articles are free. The cabman is not bound to drive more than 6 miles. Beyond the 4-mile radius from Charing Cross the fare is 1s. for every mile or fraction of a mile. The charge for waiting is 6d. for each completed 1/4 hr. for four-wheelers, and 8d. for hansoms. The fare by time for the first hour or part of an hour is 2s. for four-wheelers, and 2s. 6d. for hansoms. For each additional 1/4 hr., 6d. and 8d. Beyond the 4-mile radius the fare is 2s. 6d. for the first hour, for both 2-wheel and 4-wheel vehicles, and for each additional 1/4 hr. 8d. The driver may decline to drive for more than one full hour, or to be hired by time between 8 p. m. and 6 a. m.

Whether the hirer knows the proper fare or not, he is recommended to come to an agreement with the driver before starting.

Each driver is bound to possess a copy of the authorised Book of Distances, and to produce it if required.

Some of the London cabmen are apt to be insolent and extortionate. The traveller, therefore, in his own and the general interest, should resist all attempts at overcharging, and should, in case of persistency, demand the cabman's number, or order him to drive to the nearest police court or station.

The driver is bound to deposit any articles left in the cab at the nearest police station within twenty-four hours, to be claimed by the owner at the Head Police Office, New Scotland Yard (p. 237).

The *Fly* is a vehicle of a superior description and is admitted to the parks more freely than the cabs. Flys must be specially ordered from a livery stable keeper, and the charges are of course higher. The tariff of the *Coupé & Dunlop Brougham Company* (14 Regent Street, S.W.) is as follows: coupé with one horse, 7s. 6d. first 2 hrs., 3s. 6d. each additional hr.; coupé with two horses, not quite double these rates, with minimum of 15s.

Omnibuses, of which there are about 150 lines, cross the Metropolis in every direction from 8 a.m. till midnight. The destination of each vehicle (familiarly known as a 'bus), and the names of some of the principal streets through which it passes, are usually painted on the outside. As they always keep to the left in driving along the street, the intending passenger should walk on that side for the purpose of hailing one. To prevent mistakes, he had better mention his destination to the conductor before entering.

The first omnibuses plying in London were started by Mr. George Shilibeer in 1829. They were drawn by three horses yoked abreast, and were much heavier and clumsier than those now in use. At first they were furnished with a supply of books for the use of the passengers. The London service of omnibuses is now mainly in the hands of the *London General Omnibus Co.* and the *London Road Car Co.* The first of these employs 1300 buses, 15,000 horses, and 5000 men; it carries nearly 200 million passengers annually at an average fare of 1½d. The vehicles have been considerably improved of late years; the 'garden seats' on the top are pleasant enough in fine weather and are freely patronized by ladies.

The principal points of intersection of the omnibus lines are (on the N. of the Thames) the Bank, Charing Cross, Piccadilly Circus, Oxford Circus, the Marble Arch, Hyde Park Corner, and the junction of Tottenham Court Road and Oxford Street. The chief point in Southwark is the hostelry called the Elephant and Castle.

Those who travel by omnibus should keep themselves provided with small change to prevent delay and mistakes. The fare varies from 1/2d. to 6d. or 7d. For a drive to Richmond, the Crystal Palace, and other places several miles from the City the usual fare is 1s. A table of the legal fares is placed in the inside of each omnibus.

A special service of small omnibuses, owned and managed by the railway companies, connects the chief stations on the N. side (Euston, etc.) with the chief stations on the S. side (Charing Cross, Waterloo, etc.). These buses, which meet the mail trains, start from inside the stations and carry luggage on the roof. Fare 3d.; each article of luggage carried outside 2d. Passengers with through-tickets to points in the south are conveyed free (reasonable luggage included).

Motor Omnibuses (fares 1/2-2d.) are now running from the Polytechnic (p. 287) viâ Oxford Circus, Regent Street, Piccadilly Circus, Charing Cross, Westminster Bridge, and Kennington Road, to Kennington Gate, Kennington Park (Pl. R, 34; near the Oval, p. 279).

OMNIBUS LINES. The following is a list of the principal routes, with a brief
at which the sections below (a, b, o, etc.) intersect are printed in italics. Some
ed by an asterisk do

a. From

Termini	Name	Colour	Time	Fare
1. **Burdett Road** (Pl. R, 60)-**Shepherd's Bush Green.**	Bayswater	Light Green	Every 4 min.	1*d.*-6*d.*
*2. **City-Camberwell.**	—	Dark Green	Every 12 min.	1*d.*-3*d.*
3. **City-Streatham.**	City Paragon	Green	Every 6 min.	1*d.*-5*d.*
4. **Liverpool St.** (Pl. R, 44)-**Camberwell.**	—	Green	Every 6-8 min.	1*d.*-2*d.*
5. **Liverpool St.-Fulham.**	Walham Green	White	Every 6-7 min.	1*d.*-5*d.*
5a. **Liverpool St.-Fulham High Street.**	Fulham	White	Every 6-7 min.	1*d.*-6*d.*
*6. **Liverpool St.-Hammersmith.**	—	Red	Every 4 min.	1*d.*-5*d.*
7. **Liverpool St.-Kilburn.**	Kilburn	Dark Green	Every 4 min.	1*d.*-5*d.*
8. **Liverpool St.-Lancaster Road.**	John Bull	Dark Green	Every 2 min.	1*d.*-5*d.*
9. **Liverpool St.-Peckham Rye.**	Peckham	Dark Green	Every 1/4 hr.	1*d.*-4*d.*
10. **Liverpool St.-Putney.**	Putney.	White	Every 2 or 3 min.	1*d.*-6*d.*
11. **Liverpool St.-Rotherhithe.**	—	Dark Green	Every 7-8 min.	1*d.*-2*d.*
*12. **Liverpool St.-St. Paul's Station.**	—	Green	Every 5 min.	1*d.*
13. **Liverpool St.-Shepherd's Bush and Starch Green.**	Bayswater	Light Green	Every 10 or 12 min.	1*d.*-6*d.*
*14. **Liverpool St.-Waterloo Station.**	—	Chocolate	Every 4 or 5 min.	1*d.*-2*d.*

indication of the points of interest on or near each. **Termini and the points
of the lines have different time-tables on Sundays. The omnibuses mark-
not ply at all upon Sunday.**

the City.

Route	Points of interest on route
*(1.) Mile End Road, Whitechapel Road, Leadenhall St., Cheapside, Holborn, *Oxford St.*, *Oxford Circus*, Uxbridge Road, *Shepherd's Bush* (beyond Pl. R, 2).	People's Palace, Mansion House, Exchange, Bank, St. Paul's, Guildhall, British Museum, Hyde Park, Kensington Gardens.
(2.) *Gracechurch St.* (Pl. R, 43), King William St., *London Bridge*, Borough High St., 'Elephant & Castle', Walworth Road, *Camberwell Green* (Pl. G, 39).	Monument.
(3.) To *'Elephant & Castle'*, see No. 2. Then Kennington Park Road, Brixton Road, Streatham Hill, London Road, *Streatham Common* (beyond Pl. G, 32).	Monument, Kennington Oval.
(4.) Houndsditch, Minories, Tower Bridge, Tooley St., Spa Road, Grange Road, *Camberwell Green* (Pl. G, 39).	Tower, Mint, Tower Bridge.
(5.) Broad Street (in the reverse direction, Princes St., Moorgate St., Blomfield St.), Queen Victoria St., Cannon St., Ludgate Circus, Fleet St., Strand, *Charing Cross*, Whitehall, *Westminster*, Victoria St., *Victoria Station*, Buckingham Palace Road, Sloane Square, King's Road, Harwood Road, Broadway, Walham Green, *Dawes Road* (Pl. G, 3).	Bank, Exchange, Mansion House, St. Paul's, Temple, Law Courts, Nat. Gallery, Nat. Portr. Gallery, Houses of Parliament, Westminster Abbey, Chelsea Hospital.
(5a.) To Walham Green, see No. 5. Then by Fulham Road to King's Head, *Fulham High Street* (beyond Pl. G, 3).	See No. 5.
(6.) To *Charing Cross*, see No. 5. Then Pall Mall, Regent St., *Piccadilly Circus*, Piccadilly, Knightsbridge, Kensington High St., *Hammersmith Broadway* (beyond Pl. R, 1).	See No. 5. Burlington House, Green Park, Hyde Park, Imperial Institute.
(7.) Old and New Broad St., Cheapside, Holborn, *Oxford St.*, *Oxford Circus*, Edgware Road, *Kilburn High Road* (Pl. B, 2).	Bank-Hyde Park, see No. 1.
(8.) To Edgware Road, see No. 7. Then Praed St., Eastbourne Terrace, Bishop's Road, Westbourne Grove, *Lancaster Road* (beyond Pl. R, 3).	See No. 7.
(9.) Houndsditch, Minories, Tower Bridge, Tooley St., Jamaica Road, St. James's Road, Ilderton Road, Canterbury Road, Loder St., St. Mary's Road, Evelina Road, Nunhead Lane, *Peckham Rye* (beyond Pl. G, 52).	Tower, Mint, Tower Bridge.
(10.) To Knightsbridge, see No. 6. Then Brompton Road, Fulham Road, Walham Green, Putney Bridge, High St. Putney, *Chelverton Road* (beyond Pl. G, 4).	See Nos. 5, 6. South Kensington Museum, Natural History Museum, Hurlingham, Fulham Palace.
(11.) To Jamaica Road, see No. 9. Then *Rotherhithe* (Pl. R, 53).	Southwark Park.
(12.) New and Old Broad St. (returning Moorgate St. and London Wall), Queen Victoria St., *St. Paul's Station* (Pl. R, 35).	Bank, Mansion House, Exchange.
(13.) To *Oxford Circus*, see No. 7. Then Notting Hill, Uxbridge Road, *Shepherd's Bush* (beyond Pl. R, 2). Thence viâ Goldhawk Road to *Starch Green*.	Bank - British Museum, see No. 1. Kensington Gardens.
(14.) To St. Paul's Station, see No. 12. Then Blackfriars Bridge, Stamford St., *Waterloo Station* (Pl. R, 30, 34).	Bank, Mansion House, Exchange.

Termini	Name	Colour	Time	Fare
15. **Shoreditch-West Kensington.**	W. Kensington	Brown	Every 10 min.	1d.-5d.
16. **Liverpool St.-Westminster.**	Westminster	Chocolate	Every 3 or 4 min.	1d.-3d.
17. **Royal Exchange-South Hackney.**	S. Hackney	Red	Every 8-10 min.	1d.-2d.
18. **Royal Exchange-Old Ford.**	Old Ford	Yellow	Every 4 min.	1d.-2d.
19. **Shoreditch - Bayswater.**	Bayswater	Dark Green	Every 10-11 min.	1d.-5d.
20. **South Hackney-Battersea.**	Chelsea	Chocolate	Every 14 min.	1d.-6d.

From the City to: —

Baker St., Nos. 26, 63.
Barnsbury, No. 97.
Bayswater, Nos. 1, 8, 13, 19.
Blackwall, No. 60.
Bow, No. 53.
Brixton, No. 3.

Camberwell ('*Elephant & Castle*'), Nos. 63, 69, 71, 72, 73.
Charing Cross, Nos. 5, 5a, 6, 10, 15, etc.
Chelsea, No. 20.

Clapton, No. 69.
Finsbury Park, No. 22.
Fulham, No. 21.
Highgate, No. 22.
Islington, Nos. 22, 71, 90, 97.

b. From London Bridge

Termini	Name	Colour	Time	Fare
21. **London Bridge-Fulham.**	—	White	Every 6-7 min.	1d.-6d.
22. **London Bridge-Highgate or Tollington Park.**	Favorite	Dark Green	Every 10 min.	1d.-3d.
23. **London Bridge-Kensal Green.**	Paddington	Yellow	Every 5 min.	1d.-6d.
24. **London Bridge-Ladbroke Grove.**	Westbourne Grove and London Bridge.	Red	Every 6 min.	1d.-6d.
*25. **London Bridge-Moorgate St.**	—	Chocolate	Every 5 min.	1d.

Route	Points of interest on route
(15.) 'The Bell', Shoreditch High Street, Norton Folgate, Bishopsgate. Then Liverpool Street to Brompton Road, see No. 10. Then Thurloe Road, South Kensington Station, Old Brompton Road, Lillie Road, 'Cedars Hotel', North End Road (Pl. G, 2).	Bank, etc. South Kensington Museum, etc., see Nos. 6, 10.
(16.) To Westminster, see No. 5. Then Great Smith St., Regency St., Moreton St., Lupus St., WinchesterSt. (Pl. G, 21).	Bank, National Gallery, Westminster Abbey, etc., see No. 5.
(17.) Threadneedle St., Bishopsgate St.,Shoreditch, Hackney Road, Mare St., Victoria Park Road (Pl. B, 55).	Bank, Mansion House, Victoria Park.
(18.) Threadneedle St., Bishopsgate St., Shoreditch High St., Bethnal Green Road, Green St., Roman Road, Armagh Road (Pl. B, 63).	Bank, Mansion House, Bethnal Green Museum, Victoria Park.
(19.) To Liverpool St., see No. 15. Thence to Westbourne Grove, see No. 8. Then Norfolk Terrace, Kensington Park Road, Elgin Crescent, 'The Clarendon', Clarendon Road (beyond Pl. R, 2).	Bank, Guildhall, St. Paul's, Brit. Museum, etc., see No. 8.
(20.) Victoria Park Road, Cambridge Road, Bethnal Green Road, Shoreditch High St., Liverpool St. Thence to Knightsbridge, see No. 6. Then Sloane St., King's Road (Pl. G, 10), Cheyne Walk, Battersea Bridge Road (Pl. G, 15).	Bethnal Green Museum, Bank, St. Paul's, Nat. Gallery, Burlington House, etc., see Nos. 5, 6. Green Park-Hyde Park.

From the City to: —

Kennington, Nos. 63, 97.	Oxford Circus, Nos. 7, 8, 13, 19, 24, etc.	Shoreditch, Nos. 19, 20, 48, 66.
Kensal Green, No. 23.	Paddington, Nos. 63, 23.	Stamford Hill, No. 73.
Kentish Town, No. 72.	Piccadilly Circus, Nos. 6, 10, 15, 20, etc.	Victoria Station, Nos. 5, 48.
Ladbroke Grove, Nos. 19, 24, 29.	St. John's Wood, No. 26.	West Kilburn, No. 28.
		Wormwood Scrubs, No. 29.

Station (Pl. R, 42).

Route	Points of interest on route
(21.) King William St., Cheapside, Holborn, Oxford Street, Charing Cross Road, Shaftesbury Avenue, Piccadilly Circus, Piccadilly, Knightsbridge, Brompton Road, Thurloe Road, S. Kensington Station, Fulham Road, Broadway, Walham Green, 'Salisbury Hotel', Dawes Road (Pl. G, 3).	Monument, Bank, Mansion House, Exchange, Guildhall, British Museum, Burlington House, Hyde Park, South Kensington Museum, Nat. Hist. Museum.
(22.) King William St., Moorgate St., Finsbury Square, City Road, Upper St., Islington, Holloway Road. Thence either to Highgate (Archway Tavern; beyond Pl. B, 29) or viâ Seven Sisters' Road to Tollington Park (beyond Pl. B, 29).	Monument, Bank, Exchange, Mansion House, Agricultural Hall.
(23.) To Oxford St., see No. 21. Then Oxford Circus, Edgware Road, Harrow Road, Bishop's Road, Porchester Road, Harrow Road, Kensal Green (beyond Pl. B, 4).	Monument-Brit.Museum, see No. 21. Hyde Park.
(24.) King William St., Cannon St., Ludgate Circus, Fleet St., Strand, Charing Cross, Pall Mall, Piccadilly Circus, Oxford Circus. Then to Westbourne Grove, see No. 8. Then Richmond Road, Talbot Road, Cornwall Road (Pl. R, 4), Ladbroke Grove.	Monument, Temple, Law Courts, Nat. Gallery, Nat. Portrait Gallery, Hyde Park.
(25.) King William St., Princes St., Moorgate St. Station (Pl. R, 40).	Monument, Bank, Mansion House, Exchange.

Termini	Name	Colour	Time	Fare
*26. **London Bridge-St. John's Wood.**	City Atlas	Dark Green	Every 10 min.	1d.-5d.
26a. **London Bridge-Kilburn.**	—	Green, with Red Band	Every 8-9 min.	1d.-5d.
*27. **London Bridge-West Kensington.**	West Kensington	Brown	Every 10-11 min.	1d.-5d.
28. **London Bridge-West Kilburn.**	Paddington	Yellow	Every 8-10 min.	1d.-6d.
29. **London Bridge-Wormwood Scrubs.**	Bayswater	Dark Green	Every 11-12 min.	1d.-5d.

From London Bridge to : —
Baker St., No. 26.   *Charing Cross*, Nos. 21, 23,   *Holloway*, No. 22.
Camberwell, Nos. 2, 3, 66,   24, etc.   *Islington*, Nos. 22, 71, 90.
   69, 71.   *Clapton*, No. 69.   *Ladbroke Grove*, No. 29.

c. From Charing

Termini	Name	Colour	Time	Fare
*30. **Charing Cross-Baker St.**	—	Chocolate	Every 6 min.	1d.-2d.
30a. **Charing Cross-Fulham.**	Greyhound	Brown	Every 9-10 min.	4d.-4d.
31. **Charing Cross-Cricklewood.**	Cricklewood	Red	Every 4-5 min.	1d.-5d.
31a. **Charing Cross-Child's Hill.**	Child's Hill	Blue and White	Every 8-10 min.	1d.-5d.
32. **Charing Cross-Hammersmith.**	Walham Green viâ Victoria	White	Every 6-7 min.	1d.-4d.
33. **Charing Cross-Harlesden Green.**	Kensal Green and Charing Cross	Red	Every 8-10 min.	1d.-6d.
34. **Charing Cross-Highgate.**	Camden Town	Yellow	Every 3-4 min.	1d.-3d.
35. **Charing Cross-Kilburn.**	—	Red	Every 4-5 min.	1d.-4d.
36. **Charing Cross-West Kilburn.**	—	Red	Every ¼ hr.	1d.-4d.

From Charing Cross to : —
Baker St., Nos. 26, 62, 82.   *Chelsea*, No. 20.   *Kennington*, Nos. 54, 55.
Blackwall, No. 60.   *City*, Nos. 5, 6, 10, 15, etc.   *Kentish Town*, Nos. 34, 44, 50.
Bow, No. 53.   *Euston Station*, No. 52.   *King's Cross*, Nos. 76, 77.
Brixton, No. 54.   *Fulham*, No. 5.   *Ladbroke Grove*, No. 24.
Camberwell, Nos. 64, 65, 82.   *Hackney*, No. 20.   *London Bridge*, Nos. 23, 24,
Camden Town, Nos. 38, 39,   *Hampstead*, No. 39.   26, etc.
   41, 44, 50, 64, 74, 87.   *Holloway*, No. 41.
Chalk Farm, Nos. 39, 44.   *Islington*, No. 49.

Route	Points of interest on route
(26.) To *Oxford St.*, see No 21. Then *Oxford Circus*, Orchard St., *Baker St.*, Park Road, Wellington Road. Thence either viâ Finchley Road to *Swiss Cottage* (Pl. B, 10) or viâ Marlborough Road and Abbey Road to '*Princess of Wales*' (Pl. B, 6).	See No. 21. **Madame Tussaud's**, Regent's Park, Lord's Cricket Ground.
(26a.) To Edgware Road, see No. 23. Then to *High Road*, *Kilburn* (Pl. B, 2).	See No. 21. **Marble Arch.**
(27.) To S. Kensington Station, see No. 21. Then Old Brompton Road, Lillie Road, '*Cedars' Hotel*', *North End Road* (Pl. G, 2).	Monument-South Kensington Museum, see No. 21.
(28.) To Harrow Road, see No. 23. Then Warwick Road, Sutherland Avenue, Shirland Road, *Malvern Road* (Pl. B, 3).	Monument-Brit. Museum, see No. 21. Hyde Park.
(29.) To *Oxford St.*, see No. 21. From *Oxford Circus* to Elgin Crescent, see No. 19. Then Ladbroke Grove (Pl. R, 3), Cambridge Gardens, St. Mark's Road, St. Quintin's Avenue, '*North Pole*', *North Pole Road.*	Monument-British Museum, see No. 21. Hyde Park.

From London Bridge to : —

Oxford Circus, Nos. 21, 24, 26, etc.	*Paddington*, Nos. 23, 24, 29.	*Shoreditch*, Nos. 66, 69.
Old Kent Road, No. 90.	*Piccadilly Circus*, Nos. 21, 24, 27, etc.	*Stamford Hill*, No. 73.
		Streatham, No. 3.

Cross (Pl. R, 26).

Route	Points of interest on route
(30.) Pall Mall, *Piccadilly Circus*, *Oxford Circus*, Regent St., Cavendish Place, Wigmore St., High St. Marylebone, Nottingham Place, *Baker St. Station* (Pl. R, 20).	National Gallery, Nat. Portrait Gallery, St. James's Hall, Queen's Hall, Wallace Gallery, Madame Tussaud's.
(30a.) To Lillie Road (Pl. G, 2), see No. 15. Thence by *Fulham Palace Road* to '*The Greyhound*'.	See No. 15.
(31.) Pall Mall, *Piccadilly Circus*, *Oxford Circus*, Oxford St., Edgware Road, *Kilburn*, Shoot-up Hill, *Cricklewood* (beyond Pl. B, 1).	St. James's Park, St. James's Hall, Hyde Park.
(31a.) Regent Street, Oxford Circus, *Baker Street Station*, St. John's Wood, Finchley Road, FortuneGreen Road, West End Lane, *Child's Hill* (beyond Pl. B, 1).	See No. 26.
(32.) On Sundays only; route, see No. 6.	See No. 6.
(33.) To Edgware Road, see No. 31. Praed St., Eastbourne Terrace, Bishop's Road, Porchester Road, Harrow Road, *High St. Harlesden* (beyond Pl. B, 4).	See No. 31. Kensal Green Cemetery.
(34.) Charing Cross Road, *Oxford St.*, Tottenham Court Road, Hampstead Road, Camden High St., Kentish Town Road, Fortess Road, Junction Road, *Archway Tavern* (beyond Pl. B, 21).	National Gallery, National Portrait Gallery, Zoological Gardens.
(35.) To High Road, *Kilburn* (corner of Palmerston Road, Pl. B, 2), see No. 31.	See No. 31.
(36.) To Edgware Road, see No. 31. Then Harrow Road, and thence to *Malvern Road* (Pl. B, 3), see No. 28.	See No. 31.

From Charing Cross to : —

Old Kent Road, Nos. 82, 87.	*St. John's Wood*, Nos. 26, 65, 82.	*Walham Green*, No. 10.
Oxford Circus or *St.*, Nos. 24, 26, 27, 38, 50, 53, etc.	*St. Pancras Station*, No. 77.	*Waterloo*, Nos. 62, 64, 65, 74.
Paddington, Nos. 24, 33.	*Shoreditch*, Nos. 5, 48.	*West Kensington*, Nos. 15, 27.
Peckham, No. 56.	*Stoke Newington*, No. 49.	*Westminster*, Nos. 5, 16, 52, 54, 55.
Piccadilly Circus, Nos. 6, 20, 21, 56, etc.	*Tufnell Park*, No. 50.	*Wormwood Scrubs*, No. 29.
Putney, No. 10.	*Victoria*, Nos. 38, 39, 41.	

9. OMNIBUSES.

Termini	Name	Colour	Time	Fare
37. **Victoria-Bays- water.**	Victoria Station	Red	Every 3-4 min.	1*d.*-3*d.*
38. **Victoria-Camden Road.**	Camden Town	Yellow	Every 10 min.	1*d.*-4*d.*
39. **Victoria-Chalk Farm.**	Adelaide	Yellow	Every 8 min.	1*d.*-3*d.*
40. **Victoria-Chelsea Bridge.**	—	Brown	Every 5-8 min.	1*d.*-1¹/₂*d.*
41. **Victoria-Holloway Road.**	Camden Town	Yellow	Every 7-8 min.	1*d.*-5*d.*
42. **Sloane Square- Hornsey.**	Hornsey Rise	Dark Green	Every 9-10 min.	1*d.*-6*d.*
42a. **Victoria-Tolling- ton Park.**	Favourite	Dark Green	Every 10 min.	1*d.*-5*d.*
43. **Victoria-Hornsey.**	Holloway	Dark Green	Every 8-9 min.	1*d.*-5*d.*
43a. **Victoria-Hornsey Rise.**	Favourite	Dark Green	Every 10 min.	1*d.*-5*d.*
44. **Victoria-Kentish Town.**	Camden Town	Yellow	Every 8 min.	1*d.*-4*d.*
45. **Victoria-Kilburn.**	Victoria Station	Red	Every 5-6 min.	1*d.*-4*d.*
46. **Victoria - King's Cross.**	—	Light Green	Every 2 min.	1*d.*-3*d.*
*47. **Victoria-King's Cross.**	Royal Blue	Blue	Every 4-6 min.	1*d.*-3*d.*
48. **Victoria-Shore- ditch.**	Victoria and Liverpool St. Favorite	Brown	Every 5-6 min.	1*d.*-3*d.*
49. **Victoria-Stoke Newington.**		Dark Green	Every 5-6 min.	1*d.*-5*d.*
50. **Victoria-Tufnell Park.**	Camden Town	Yellow	Every 10 min.	1*d.*-4*d.*
51. **Victoria-West Kil- burn.**	—	Red	Every 7 min.	1*d.*-5*d.*

and Westminster (Pl. R, 25).

Route	Points of interest on route
(37.) Grosvenor Place, Hamilton Place, Park Lane, Edgware Road, Praed St., Eastbourne Terrace, Bishop's Road, '*Royal Oak*' (Pl. R, 7).	Hyde Park, Green Park.
(38.) Victoria St., *Westminster*, Whitehall, *Charing Cross*, St. Martin's Lane, *Oxford St.*, Tottenham Court Road, Hampstead Road, High St, *Camden Town*, Camden Road, *Brecknock Arms* (Pl. B, 25).	Westminster Abbey, Houses of Parliament, Nat. Gallery, Nat.Portr.Gallery, Regent's, Park, Zoological Gardens.
(39.) Viâ *Westminster* to High St., *Camden Town*, see No. 38. Then Chalk Farm Road, '*Adelaide Tavern*' (Pl. B, 18).	See No. 38.
(40.) Buckingham Palace Road, Commercial Road, *Chelsea Bridge* (Pl. G, 18).	For Battersea Park.
(41.) Viâ *Westminster* to *Charing Cross*, see No. 38. Thence to Hampstead Road, see No. 34. Then *Camden Town*, Camden Road (Pl. B, 25), Parkhurst Road, *Holloway Road*.	See No. 38.
(42.) *Sloane Square* (Pl. G, 17), Sloane St., Park Lane, Oxford St., Orchard St., *Baker St.*, Marylebone Road, Euston Road, King's Cross, Caledonian Road, Holloway Road (Pl. B, 33), Seven Sisters' Road, *Hornsey Road*.	Hyde Park, Marble Arch Regent's Park.
(42a.) Victoria Street, *Charing Cross*, Strand, Chancery Lane, Holborn, Rosebery Avenue, Holloway Road (Pl. B, 33), Stroud Green Road, *Tollington Park*.	Houses of Parliament, Westminster Abbey, Law Courts.
(43.) Grosvenor Place, Piccadilly, Old Bond Street, New Oxford Street, *Oxford Circus*, Regent Street, Mortimer Street, Great Portland Street, Euston Road, King's Cross, 'Angel', *Islington*, Upper St., *Holloway Road* (Pl. B, 33), Seven Sisters' Road, Hornsey Road, Tollington Park Road, '*Stapleton Hall Tavern*', *Stroud Green Road*.	Green Park, Burlington House, St. James's Hall, Regent's Park.
(43a.) As No. 42a to Holloway Road, *Hornsey Road*.	See No. 42a.
(44.) To Chalk Farm Road, see No. 39. Then Ferdinand St., *Malden Road* (Pl. B, 17), *Lismore Road*. [See also No. 50.]	See No. 39.
(45.) To Edgware Road, see No. 37. Then Maida Vale, High Road, *Kilburn* (*Palmerston Road*; Pl. B, 2).	See No. 37.
(46.) To *Piccadilly Circus*, see No. 43. Then Coventry St., Leicester Square, Long Acre, Great and Little Queen St., Southampton Row, Guilford St., Judd St., *King's Cross Station* (Pl. B, 32).	Green Park, Hyde Park, Burlington House, St. James's Hall, Foundling Hospital.
(47.) Grosvenor Place, Piccadilly, Old and New Bond St., Oxford St., *Oxford Circus* (Pl. R, 23), Tottenham Court Road, Euston Road, *King's Cross* (Pl. B, 32).	Green Park, Hyde Park, Burlington House, Grosvenor Gallery.
(48.) To *Liverpool St.* and Bank, see No. 5. Then Threadneedle Street, Bishopsgate Street, and to '*The Bell*', *Shoreditch High Street* as in No. 15.	See No. 5.
(49.) To *Islington* ('Angel'), see No. 43. Then Essex Road, Newington Green Road, Albion Road (Pl. B, 41), *Stoke Newington*.	See No. 43.
(50.) Viâ *Westminster* to *Camden Town*, see No. 38. Then Kentish Town Road, Fortess Road, *Boston Tavern* (beyond Pl. B, 21).	See No. 38.
(51.) To Edgware Road, see No. 37. Then Harrow Road, and thence to *Malvern Road* (Pl. B, 3), see No. 28.	Hyde Park, Green Park.

From Victoria Station to: —

Baker St., No. 61.
Camberwell, No. 61.

CamdenTown, Nos.41, 39, 50.
Chalk Farm, No. 39.

Charing Cross, Nos. 38, 39, 41, etc.
Fulham, No. 5.

From Westminster to: —

Baker St., Nos. 62, 65, 82.
Brixton, No. 54.
Camberwell, Nos. 56, 65, 82.

CamdenTown, Nos.41, 39, 50.
Charing Cross, Nos. 5, 16, 52, 54, 55, etc.
City, Nos. 5, 16.

Fulham, No. 5.
Hammersmith, No. 32.
Islington, Nos. 43, 49.
Kennington, Nos. 54, 55.

e. From Oxford Circus (Pl. R, 23)

Termini	Name	Colour	Time	Fare
53. **Oxford Circus-Bow Church.**	—	Dark Green	Every 8 min.	$1d.$-$4d.$
54. **Oxford Circus-Brixton Church.**	Brixton	Light Green	Every 5 min.	$1/2d.$-$4d.$
54a. **Oxford-Circus-Old Ford.**	—	Yellow, with Red Band	Every 8 min.	$1d.$-$4d.$
55. **OxfordCircus-Brixton (Loughboro Hotel).**	—	Red	Every 7-8 min.	$1/2d.$-$31/2d.$
56. **Oxford Circus-Peckham.**	Times	Light Green	Every $1/4$ hr.	$1d.$-$4d.$
57. **Oxford St.-Acton or Ealing-Hanwell.**	Hanwell	Red	Every $1/4$ hr.	$1d.$-$7d.$
*58. **Gower Street-Edgware Road.**	—	Blue & White	Every 5 min.	$1d.$-$2d.$

From Oxford Circus or Oxford St. to: —

Baker St., Nos.26, 30, 65, 82.
Barnsbury, No. 79.
Bayswater, Nos. 1, 8, 13, 19.
Burdett Road, No. 1.
Camberwell, Nos. 64, 65, 82.
Camden Road, No. 38.
Camden Town, Nos. 34, 38, 44, 50, 64, 74, 87, etc.

Chalk Farm, Nos. 39, 81.
Charing Cross, Nos. 24, 53, 64, 82, etc.
City, Nos. 1, 7, 8, 13, 19, 24, etc.
Cricklewood, No. 31.
Fulham, No. 21.
Hammersmith, No. 79.

Hampstead, Nos. 81, 39.
Harlesden, No. 33.
Highbury, Nos. 93, 94, 95, 96.
Highgate, No. 34.
Holloway, Nos. 41, 43, 88.
Hornsey, No. 43.
Islington, Nos. 43, 91, 94, 95, 96.

f. From Piccadilly

*59. **Piccadilly Circus-Baker St.**	—	Chocolate	Every 4 min.	$1d.$-$2d.$
60. **Piccadilly Circus-Blackwall.**	Blackwall	Blue	Every 6 min.	$1d.$-$4d.$

From Victoria Station to: —

Hammersmith, No. 32.
Islington, Nos. 43, 49.
Liverpool St., No. 5.

Oxford Circus, Nos. 38, 41, 44, 50, 54, etc.
Paddington, No. 37.

Piccadilly Circus, Nos. 43, 46.

From Westminster to: —

Oxford Circus, Nos. 38, 41, 44, 50, 54, etc.
Peckham, No. 56.

Piccadilly Circus, Nos. 43, 54, 62, 65.
Pimlico, No. 61.

St. John's Wood, Nos. 65, 82.
Waterloo Station, No. 62.

& Oxford St. (Tottenham Court Road; Pl. R, 27).

Route	Points of interest on route
(53.) To Cannon St., see No. 24. Then Queen Victoria St., Cornhill, Aldgate, Whitechapel Road, Mile End Road, Bow Road, *Bow Church* (Pl. B, 68).	See No. 24. **Mansion House, Bank, Exchange, People's Palace.**
(54.) Regent St., *Piccadilly Circus*, Pall Mall, *Charing Cross*, Whitehall, *Westminster*, Westminster Bridge Road, Kennington Road, Kennington Park Road, Brixton Road (Pl. G, 31, 32).	**St. James's Hall, National Gallery, Nat. Portrait Gallery,** Westminster Abbey, Houses of Parliament, Kennington Oval.
(54a.) Oxford Street, Holborn, Cheapside, Liverpool Street, Shoreditch, Bethnal Green Road, *Old Ford* (Pl. B, 59).	**General Post Office, Mansion House.**
(55.) Nearly same route as No. 54.	See No. 54.
(56.) To Westminster Bridge Road, see No. 54. Then St. George's Road, '*Elephant & Castle*', Walworth Road, Camberwell Road, Peckham Road, *Rye Lane* (Pl. G, 48).	See No. 54.
(57.) *Oxford Circus*, Uxbridge Road, Shepherd's Bush, Acton Vale, High St., *Acton;* thence to *Ealing Broadway* and *Hanwell.*	**Hyde Park, Kensington Gardens.**
(58.) Euston Road, Tottenham Court Road, *Oxford Circus*, Oxford St., *Edgware Road Station* (Pl. B, 16).	**Hyde Park.**

From Oxford Circus or Oxford St. to: —

Kensal Green, No. 23.
Kentish Town, Nos. 34, 44, 50.
Kilburn, Nos. 7, 31, 35.
Ladbroke Grove, Nos. 19, 24.
Lancaster Road, No. 8.
London Bridge, Nos. 24, 26, 21, etc.
Old Kent Road, Nos. 82, 87.

Paddington, Nos. 8, 24, 29, 33.
Peckham, No. 56.
Putney, No. 95.
St. John's Wood, Nos. 26, 65, 82.
Shepherd's Bush, Nos. 1, 13.
Shoreditch, No. 19.

Walham Green, Nos. 91, 96.
Waterloo, Nos. 64, 74, 87.
W. Kensington, Nos. 27, 88.
Westminster, Nos. 38, 41, 44, 50, 54, etc.
W. Kilburn, Nos. 28, 36.
Wormwood Scrubs, No. 29.

Circus (Pl. R, 26).

(59.) Piccadilly, Bond St., Oxford St., Orchard St., Baker St. (Pl. R, 20). [See also Nos. 62, 65, 82.]	Burlington House, Grosvenor Gallery, Madame Tussaud's.
(60.) To Cannon St., see No. 24. Thence to Whitechapel Road, see No. 53. Then Commercial Road, East India Dock Road, '*Aberfeldy Tavern*' (Pl. R, 71).	See No. 24. **E. & W. India Docks.**

From Piccadilly Circus to : —

Barnsbury, No. 79.	*Charing Cross*, Nos. 6, 10,	*Hammersmith*, Nos. 6, 32, 79.
Bow, No. 53.	15, 21, 27, etc.	*Harlesden Green*, No. 31.
Brixton, No. 54.	*Chelsea*, No. 20.	*Highbury*, Nos. 93, 94, 95, 96.
Camberwell, Nos. 56, 64, 65.	*City*, Nos. 6, 10, 15, 20, etc.	*Holloway*, Nos. 43, 88.
	Cricklewood, No. 31.	*Hornsey*, No. 43.
Camden Town, Nos. 64, 74, 87.	*Fulham*, No. 21.	*Islington*, Nos. 43, 91, 94, 95, 96.
	Hakney, No. 20.	

g. From Baker St.

Termini	Name	Colour	Time	Fare
61. **Baker St.-Pimlico.**	—	Chocolate	Every 4-5 min.	1*d*.-3*d*.
62. **Baker St.-Waterloo Station.**	—	Chocolate,	Every 4-5 min.'	$^1/_2 d$.-$2^1/_2 d$.
63. **Paddington-Brixton.**	King's Cross	Light Green	Every 4 min.	$^1/_2 d$.-5*d*.

From Baker Street Station to : —

Camberwell (Elephant & Castle'), Nos. 63, 65, 82.	*City*, Nos. 26, 63.	*Kennington*, No. 63.
Charing Cross, Nos. 26, 30, 62, 65, 82.	*Hornsey*, No. 42.	*King's Cross*, Nos. 42, 63, 92, 93.
	Hyde Park, No. 42.	
	Islington, Nos. 92, 93.	*London Bridge*, No. 26.

h. From Camberwell (Pl. G, 38, 39)

	Name	Colour	Time	Fare
64. **Camberwell Gate-Camden Town.**	Waterloo	Dark Blue	Every 4 min.	$^1/_2 d$.-4*d*.
65. **Camberwell Gate-St. John's Wood.**	Atlas	Light Green	Every 8-10 min.	$^1/_2 d$.-5*d*.
66. **Camberwell Gate-Shoreditch.**	Hackney Road	Orange	Every 3-4 min.	$^1/_2 d$.-$3^1/_2 d$.
67. **Camberwell Green-Clapham.**	—	Green	Every 10 min.	1*d*.-2*d*.
68. **Camberwell Green-King's Cross.**	Waterloo	Dark Blue	Every 4-5 min.	1*d*.-3*d*.
69. **'Elephant & Castle'-Clapton.**	Clapton	Dark Green	Every 5-6 min.	1*d*.-4*d*.

From Piccadilly Circus to: —

Kennington, Nos. 54, 55.
Kilburn, Nos. 31, 35.
King's Cross, Nos. 46, 79, 88, 91.
Ladbroke Grove, Nos. 24, 29.
London Bridge, Nos. 21, 24, 27.

Old Kent Road, Nos. 82, 87.
Paddington, Nos. 24, 33.
Peckham, No. 56.
Putney, Nos. 10, 95.
St. John's Wood, Nos. 65, 82.
Victoria & Westminster, Nos. 43, 54, 62, 82, etc.

Walham Green, Nos. 10, 91, 96.
Waterloo, Nos. 62, 64, 74, 87.
West Kensington, Nos. 15, 27, 88.
West Kilburn, No. 36.

Station (Pl. R, 20).

Route	Points of interest on route
(61.) *Great Central Station* (Pl. R, 16), Marylebone Road, Baker St., Orchard St., N. & S. Audley St., Grosvenor Square, Hamilton Place, Grosvenor Place, *Victoria Station*, Buckingham Palace Road, *Ebury Bridge* (Pl. G, 17).	Madame Tussaud's, Hyde Park, Green Park.
(62.) Baker St., Orchard St., Oxford St., Bond St., *Piccadilly Circus*, Pall Mall, *Charing Cross*, Whitehall, *Westminster*, Westminster Bridge, York Road, *Waterloo Station* (Pl. R, 34).	Madame Tussaud's, Grosvenor Gallery, Burlington House, Nat. Gallery, Nat. Portrait Gallery, Westminster Abbey, Houses of Parliament.
(63.) *Praed St.* (Pl. R, 11), Chapel St., Marylebone Road, *Baker St. Station*, Euston Road, King's Cross, Gray's Inn Road, Holborn, St. Andrew St., Ludgate Circus, Blackfriars Bridge & Road, Kennington Park Road, 'White Horse', Brixton (Pl. G, 31).	Madame Tussaud's, St. Paul's, Kennington Oval.

From Baker Street Station to: —

Oxford Circus, Nos. 26, 30, 65, 82.
Piccadilly Circus, Nos. 59, 62, 65, 82.

Sloane Square, No. 42.
St. John's Wood, Nos. 26, 65, 82.
Victoria, No. 61.

Walham Green, No. 92.
West Kensington, No. 93.
Westminster, Nos. 62, 82.

and 'Elephant & Castle' (Pl. G, 33, 37).

(64.) *Old Kent Road*, Walworth Road, 'Elephant & Castle', London Road, Waterloo Station, Waterloo Bridge, Strand, *Charing Cross*, Pall Mall, *Piccadilly Circus*, *Oxford Circus*, Regent St., Great Portland St., Albany St., Park St., 'Britannia' (Pl. B, 22). [See also No. 87.]	Nat. Gallery, Nat. Portrait Gallery, St. James's Hall, Queen's Hall, Regent's Park, Zoological Gardens.
(65.) Walworth Road, 'Elephant & Castle', London Road, Westminster Bridge Road. Thence to *Oxford Circus*, see No. 54; and thence to *Swiss Cottage* (Pl. B, 10), see No. 26. [See also No. 82.]	See Nos. 54, 26.
(66.) Walworth Road, 'Elephant & Castle', Borough High St., *London Bridge*, Gracechurch St., Bishopsgate St., Shoreditch, Hackney Road, *Shoreditch Church*.	Monument, Leadenhall Market.
(67.) Denmark Hill (Pl. G, 40), Coldharbour Lane, Acre Lane, Clapham Park Road, *Clapham Common*.	
(68.) To Waterloo Bridge, see No. 64. Then Fleet St., Chancery Lane, Holborn, Gray's Inn Road, *King's Cross Station* (Pl. B, 31, 32).	Temple, Law Courts.
(69.) Borough High St., *London Bridge*, Gracechurch St., Bishopsgate St., Shoreditch, Kingsland Road, Dalston Lane, Pembury Road (Pl. B, 49), Clapton Road, *Lea Bridge Road*.	Monument, Leadenhall Market.

Termini	Name	Colour	Time	Fare
70. **'Elephant & Castle'-Earl's Court.**	—	Green	Every 4-5 min.	$\frac{1}{2}d.$-4$d.$
71. **'Elephant & Castle'-Islington.**	—	Red	Every 3 min.	1$d.$-2$d.$
72. **'Elephant & Castle'-Kentish Town.**	King's Cross	Light Green	Every 10 min.	$\frac{1}{2}d.$-4$d.$
73. **'Elephant & Castle'-Stamford Hill.**	Stamford Hill	Light Green	Every 5-6 min.	1$d.$-3$d.$

From Camberwell to: —
Baker St., Nos. 63, 65, 82. | *City*, Nos. 2, 3, 63, 68, etc. | *London Bridge*, Nos. 2, 3
Charing Cross, Nos. 56, 64, 65, 82. | *Kennington*, Nos. 63, 70. | 69, 72.
| | *Oxford Circus*, Nos. 56, 64, 82

i. From Waterloo

*74. **Waterloo - Camden Town.**	Waterloo Station	Dark Blue	Every 4 min.	$\frac{1}{2}d.$-3$d.$
75. **Waterloo-Euston Station.**	L. & N.W. Rail. 'Bus	—	irreg. intervals	2$d.$-3$d.$
76. **Waterloo-King's Cross Station.**	Gt. N. Railway 'Bus	—	irreg. intervals	3$d.$
77. **Waterloo -St - Pancras.**	Midland Railway 'Bus	—	irreg. intervals	2$d.$-3$d.$

From Waterloo Station to: — *Baker St.*, No. 62. | *Charing Cross*, Nos. 62, 64,
Camberwell, Nos. 64, 68. | 74, etc.
| *City*, No. *14.

j. From

*78. **Hammersmith-Barnes.**	—	Chocolate	Every few min.	1$d.$-2$d.$
79. **Hammersmith-Barnsbury.**	Hammersmith	Red	Every 2-3 min.	1$d.$-5$d.$
*80. **Hammersmith-Wandsworth.**	—	White and Green	Every 5-6 min.	1$d.$-3$d.$

From Hammersmith to — *Charing Cross*, Nos. 32, *6. | *Liverpool St.*, No. *6.

Route	Points of interest on route
(70.) Lower and Upper Kennington Lane, Vauxhall Bridge, Vauxhall Bridge Road, Buckingham Palace Road, Pimlico Road, Lower Sloane St., Sloane St., Brompton Road, Cromwell Road, *Earl's Court* (Pl. G, 1).	Kennington Oval, Tate Gallery, South Kensington Museum, Natural History Museum.
(71.) Borough High St., *London Bridge*, King William St., Cheapside, Aldersgate St., Goswell Road, '*Angel*' (Pl. B, 35).	Monument, Mansion House, Bank, Guild Hall, St. Paul's, General Post Office.
(72.) London Road, Blackfriars Bridge Road, Blackfriars Bridge, Ludgate Circus, St. Bride St., Holborn, Gray's Inn Road, King's Cross, Pancras Road, Great College St., Kentish Town Road, Prince of Wales Road, '*Mother Shipton*' (Pl. B, 17).	St. Paul's.
(73.) To Kingsland Road, see No. 69. Then Stoke Newington Road, *Stamford Hill* (beyond Pl. B, 45).	Monument, Leadenhall Market.

From Camberwell to: —

Peckham, No. 56.	*Pimlico*, No. 70.	*Victoria* or *Westminster*, Nos. 61, 56, 65.
Piccadilly Circus, Nos. 56, 64, 65.	*Shoreditch*, No. 69.	
	Streatham, No. 3.	*Waterloo*, Nos. 64, 68.

Station (Pl. R, 30, 34).

Route	Points of interest on route
(74.) Same Route (reversed) as No. 64. [See also No. 87.]	See No. 64.
(75.) Waterloo Bridge, Strand, Chancery Lane, Holborn, Red Lion St., Judd St., *Euston Station* (Pl. B, 24, 28).	Temple, Law Courts, Foundling Hospital.
(76.) Waterloo Bridge, Strand, *Charing Cross*, St. Martin's Lane, Long Acre, Great Queen St., Southampton Row, Russell Square, Judd St., *King's Cross Station* (Pl. B, 31, 32).	Nat. Gallery, Nat. Portrait Gallery, Foundling Hospital.
(77.) Same Route as No. 76. *St. Pancras Station* (Pl. B, 28).	See No. 76.

From Waterloo Station to: —

Oxford Circus, Nos. 64, 74, 87.	*Piccadilly Circus*, Nos. 62, 64, 74, 87.
King's Cross, No. 68.	*Westminster*, No. 62.

Hammersmith.

Route	Points of interest on route
(78.) Broadway, Bridge Road, Hammersmith Bridge, Castlenau, Upper Bridge Road, *Barnes*.	
(79.) Broadway, Hammersmith Road, Kensington Road (Pl. R, 1), Knightsbridge, Piccadilly, *Piccadilly Circus*, Shaftesbury Avenue, Charing Cross Road, *Oxford St.*, Tottenham Court Road, King's Cross, Caledonian Road, '*Pocock Arms*' (Pl. B, 30).	Kensington Gardens, Imperial Institute, Hyde Park, Green Park, Burlington House.
(80.) Broadway, Queen St., Fulham Palace Road, Lillie Road, Dawes Road, Walham Green, *Wandsworth Bridge and High Street* (beyond Pl. G, 4).	

From Hammersmith to: —   *Oxford Circus*, No. 79.   *Piccadilly Circus*, Nos. 79, *6, 32.

Termini	Name	Colour	Time	Fare
81. **Hampstead-Oxford Street.**	Hampstead	Yellow	Every 8-10 min.	1d.-4d.
82. **St. John's Wood-Old Kent Road.**	Atlas	Light Green	Every 10 min.	1/2d.-51/2d.
83. **Kilburn-Fulham Road.**	Kilburn	Light Blue	Every 3 min.	1d.-5d.
84. **West Hampstead-Fulham Road.**	Kilburn and Fulham Road	Light Blue	Every 10 min.	1d.-5d
84a. **Finchley Road-Fulham Road.**	Kilburn	Light Blue	Every 10 min.	d.-5d.
85. **Kilburn-Harlesden.**	—	Light Green	Every 25 min.	1d.-4d.

From Hampstead (Chalk Farm) to : —   *Charing Cross*, Nos. 39, 44.
                                   Oxford Circus, Nos. 39, 81.
From Highgate to : —   *Charing Cross*, No. 34. } *Islington*, No. 22.
From St. John's Wood to : —
Baker Street, Nos. 26, 65, 82. } *Charing Cross*, Nos. 26, 65, } *London Bridge*, No. *26.
Camberwell, Nos. 63, 65, 82. }   82.
From Kilburn (or West Kilburn) to : —
Charing Cross, Nos. 31, 35, } *City*, No. 7.   } *London Bridge*, No. 28.
    36.

86. **Holloway - Bayswater.**	—	Chocolate	Every 10 min.	1d.-4d.
87. **Camden Town - Old Kent Road.**	Waterloo	Dark Blue	Every 4 min.	1d.-4d.
88. **Holloway-Fulham.**	Favorite	Blue	Every 10 min.	1d.-6d.

From Camden Town to : —
Charing Cross, Nos. 38, 39, } '*Elephant & Castle*' No. 64. } *Oxford Circus*, Nos. 34, 38.
  41, 44, 50, 74, etc.   44, 50, 64, etc.
From Kentish Town (Pl. B, 17, 21) to : —
                   Charing Cross, Nos. 34, 44, } *City*, No. 72.
                    50   } '*Elephant & Castle*', No. 72.

St. John's Wood, and Kilburn.

Route	Points of interest on route
(81.) *High St.* (beyond Pl. B, 13), Haverstock Hill, Chalk Farm Road, *Camden Town*, Hampstead Road, Tottenham Court Road, *Oxford St.*, *St. Giles' Church* (Pl. R, 27).	Hampstead Heath, Regent's Park, Zoological Gardens.
(82.) '*Swiss Cottage*' (Pl. B, 10). Thence to *Oxford Circus*, see No. 26. Thence to Westminster Bridge Road, see No. 54. Then London Road, '*Elephant & Castle*', *Old Kent Road* (Pl. G, 41).	See Nos. 26, 54.
(83.) *Priory Road* (Pl. B, 6), Kilburn High Road, Cambridge Road, Walterton Road, Great Western Road, Richmond Road, Pembridge Villas, Notting Hill, Church St., Kensington High St., Earl's Court Road, Redcliffe Gardens, *Fulham Road (Redcliffe Arms;* Pl. G, 6).	Earl's Court Exhibition.
(84.) *West End Lane* (Pl. B, 5), Priory Road, and thence as No. 83.	See No. 83.
(84a.) '*North Star*', *Finchley Road* (Pl. B, 10), Broadhurst Gardens, Priory Road, and thence as No. 83.	See No. 83.
(85.) High Road, Palmerston Road (Pl. B, 2), Christ Church Road, Willesden Lane, High Road Willesden, Craven Park, Harrow Road, *Harlesden*.	

From Hampstead (Chalk Farm) to: —   *Victoria* and *Westminster*, Nos. 39, 44.

From Highgate to: —   *London Bridge*, No. 22.   *Oxford St.*, No. 34.

From St. John's Wood to: —
Oxford Circus, Nos. 26, 65, 82.   *Piccadilly Circus*, Nos. 65, 82.   *Westminster*, Nos. 65, 82.

From Kilburn (or West Kilburn) to: —
Oxford Circus, Nos. 7, 28, 31, 33, 36.   *Piccadilly Circus*, Nos. 31, 35, 36.   *Victoria*, Nos. 45, 51.

Kentish Town, & Holloway.

Route	Points of interest on route
(86.) '*Nag's Head*', *Holloway*, Camden Road (Pl. B, 25), Park St., Regent's Park Road, Albert Road, St. John's Wood Road, Clifton Gardens, Warwick Road, Harrow Road, Porchester Road, Queen's Road, *Uxbridge Road* (Pl. R, 7).	Regent's Park, Zoological Gardens, Lord's Cricket Ground, Kensington Gardens.
(87.) Same Route (reversed) as No. 64 to '*Elephant & Castle*'. Then New and Old Kent Road.	See No. 64.
(88.) *Seven Sisters' Road*, Holloway Road (Pl. B, 33), Caledonian Road, King's Cross, Great Portland St., Regent St., *Oxford Circus*, *Piccadilly Circus*, Piccadilly, Knightsbridge, Brompton Road. Thence to West Kensington as in No. 15 and to *Greyhound Road*, *Fulham* (beyond Pl. G, 2).	Burlington House, Hyde Park, Imperial Institute.

From Camden Town to: —
Piccadilly Circus, Nos. 64, 74, 87.   *Victoria* and *Westminster*, Nos. 39, 41, 50.   *Waterloo Station*, No. 64.

From Kentish Town (Pl. B, 17, 21) to: —
   Oxford Circus Nos. 31, 44, 50.   *Victoria* and *Westminster*, Nos. 44, 50.

Termini	Name	Colour	Time	Fare
*89. Islington-Holborn Viaduct.	—	Red	Every 5 min.	1d.
90. Finsbury Park-Peckham Park Road.	—	Dark Green	Every 5-7 min.	1d.-4d.
91. Islington-Walham Green.	—	Blue and White	Every 4-5 min.	1d.-5d.
92. Islington-Walham Green.	—	Blue	Every 9-10 min.	1d.-6d.
93. Highbury-West Kensington.	—	Blue	Every 9-10 min.	1d.-6d.
94. Highbury-Piccadilly.	—	Light Green	Every 4 min.	1d.-3d.
94a. Highbury-Paddington Station.	—	White	Every 10 min.	1d.-4d.
95. Highbury-Putney.	—	Light Blue	Every 16 min.	1d.-6d.
96. Highbury-Walham Green.	—	Blue	Every 8-9 min.	1d.-6d.
97. Barnsbury-Brixton.	Islington	Chocolate	Every 5 min.	1/2d.-41/2d.

From Islington to: —
Baker St., Nos. 92, 93.   *City*, Nos. 22, 71, 90, 97.   *London Bridge*, Nos. 22, 71, 90.
Charing Cross, No. 49.   '*Elephant & Castle*', No. 71.
Hornsey, No. 43.

Termini	Colour	Time	Fare
98. Acton-Hanwell.	Red	Every 1/2 hr.	1d.-4d.
99. Blackheath-Eltham.	Dark Green	Every hr.	3d. & 6d.
*100. Blackheath-Shooters' Hill.	Light Green	irreg.	3d.
*101. Blackheath-Vanbrugh Park.	Red	Every 1/2 hr.	3d.
102. Beckenham-Catford.	Light Green	Every 1/2 hr.	2d.-4d.
103. Brixton-West Norwood.	Green	Every 1/4 hr.	1d.-3d.
104. Chelsea Bridge-Knightsbridge.	Red	Every 7-10 min.	1/2d.-2d.
105. Clapham-Putney.	Light Green	Every 1/4 hr.	1d.-4d.
106. ClaphamJunction-Knightsbridge.	Light Blue	Every 1/4 min.	1d.-3d.
107. Clapham Jct.-Montholme Road.	Green	Every 12 min.	1d.
108. Clapham Junction-Tooting.	Red	Every few min.	1d.-2d.

Highbury, & Barnsbury.

Route	Points of interest on route
(89.) '*Angel*' (Pl. B, 35), St. John's Street Road, West Smithfield, Giltspur St., *Holborn Viaduct* (Pl. R, 35).	Smithfield.
(90.) *Hornsey Wood Tavern* (beyond Pl. B, 37), Blackstock Road, Essex Road, New North Road, City Road, Finsbury Square, Moorgate St., *London Bridge*, Borough High St., Great Dover St., *Old Kent Road* ('*Shard Arms*').	Bank, Exchange, Mansion House, Monument.
(91.) '*Angel*' (Pl. B, 35), King's Cross. Thence to Brompton Road, see No. 88. Then Old Brompton Road, Fulham Road, Walham Green (Pl. G, 3), *Wandsworth Bridge Road* (beyond Pl. G, 4).	See No. 88.
(92.) '*Hare & Hounds*', *Upper St.* (Pl. B, 34), '*Angel*', Pentonville Road, King's Cross, *Baker St.*, Orchard St., Oxford St., Park Lane, Knightsbridge, Brompton Road, S. Kensington Station, Fulham Road, '*Red Lion*', *Broadway*, *Walham Green* (Pl. G, 3).	Hyde Park, South Kensington Museum, Natural History Museum.
(93.) To *Piccadilly Circus*, see No. 94. Then Piccadilly, Old Brompton Road, Lillie Road, *North End Road*.	Agricultural Hall, St. James's Hall, Hyde Park.
(94.) *Highbury Barn* (beyond Pl. B, 37), Highbury Grove, Upper St., '*Angel*', *Islington*, St. John's Street Road, Rosebery Avenue, Theobald's Road, *Oxford St.*, Charing Cross Road, *Piccadilly Circus* (Pl. R, 26).	Agricultural Hall, St. James's Hall.
(94a.) *Highbury Barn* (beyond Pl. B, 37) to 'Angel' as above, then King's Cross, Euston Road, *Baker Street Station*, Marylebone Road, *Praed Street*, *Paddington* (Pl. R, 11).	
(95.) To *Piccadilly Circus*, see No. 94. Then Piccadilly, Knightsbridge, Sloane St., King's Road, Chelsea, Parson's Green, Hurlingham Lane, *Putney Bridge*.	See No. 94. Burlington House, Hyde Park.
(96.) To Knightsbridge, see Nos. 94, 95. Thence to *Walham Green*, see No. 92.	See Nos. 94, 95, 92.
(97.) *Offord Road* (Pl. B, 30), Thornhill Road, Richmond Road, Liverpool Road, 'Angel', *Islington*, Goswell Road, Aldersgate St., Ludgate Circus, Blackfriars Bridge, Kennington Park Road, *Brixton Road* (Pl. G, 32).	Agricultural Hall, St. Paul's.

From Islington to: —
Oxford Circus, Nos. 43, 91, 94-96.   *Piccadilly Circus*, Nos. 43, 91, 94-96.   *Victoria & Westminster*, Nos. 43, 49.
Putney, No. 95.

Omnibus Lines.

Termini	Colour	Time	Fare
108a. Cricklewood-Hendon.	Red	Every 20-30 min.	1*d.*-2*d.*
*108b. Crystal Palace-Norwood.	Green	Every hr.	3*d.*-4*d.*
*109. Finsbury Park-Clapton.	Brown	Every 10 min.	1*d.*-2*d.*
110. Lee Green-Grove Park.	Light Green	Every hr.	2*d.*-4*d.*
111. Lee Green-New Cross.	Light Green	Every 7 min.	1*d.*-2*d.*
112. Peckham-East Dulwich.	Light Green	Every 8 min.	1*d.*-2*d.*
113. Peckham-Forest Hill.	Green	Every 1/4 hr.	1*d.*-2*d.*
114. Peckham-Lordship Lane.	Light Green	Every 20 min.	1*d.*-3*d.*
115. Peckham-Old Kent Road.	Light Green	Every 7 min.	1*d.*
116. Shepherd's Bush-Walham Green.	Green	Every 1/4 hr.	1*d.*-4*d.*
117. Highgate-Barnet.	Red	Every hr.	4*d.*

Tramways. About 130 miles of tramways, with over 1200 cars, and carrying 150 million passengers annually, are in operation, and are convenient for visiting the outlying districts of London (fares ¹/₂d.-5d.). Horses are still the chief motive power. Most of the lines on the S. side of the Thames (fare ¹/₂d.-3d.) are now managed by the London County Council. The cars are comfortable and run every few minutes. In many cases transfer-tickets are issued between tramway and bus lines. The following are among the chief lines: —

N. SIDE OF THE THAMES.

1. From **Aldgate** (Pl. R, 47; *III*): *a*. To *Well St.* (Pl. B, 54) viâ Bethnal Green Museum; *b*. To *Poplar* (Pl. R, 67); *c*. To *Stratford* (Pl. B, 70). — *d*. From STRATFORD to *Leytonstone*; *e*. To *Manor Park*. — *f*. From VICTORIA PARK (Cassland Road; Pl. B, 54) to the *West India Docks* (Pl. R, 62).

. From **Moorgate St.** (Pl. R, 44; *III*): *a*. To *Finsbury Park* (beyond Pl. B, 33) viâ Islington; *b*. To *Finsbury Park* viâ Canonbury; *c*. To *Finsbury Park* (Manor House) viâ Southgate Road; *d*. To *Upper Clapton*; *e*. To *Dalston* and *Stamford Hill*; *f*. To *Highgate* viâ Holloway Road (Pl. B, 33). — *g*. From BISHOPSGATE ST. (Pl. R, 44) to *Stoke Newington*. — *h*. From FINSBURY PARK to *Edmonton*; *i*. To *Wood Green*.

3. From **Aldersgate St.** (Pl. R, 40): *a*. To *Hackney* (Mare St.; Pl. B, 49); *b*. To *Highgate*.

4. From **Holborn** (Pl. R, 36): *a*. To *Dalston* and *Stamford Hill*; *b*. To *Holloway* viâ King's Cross; *c*. To *Parliament Hill* viâ King's Cross. — From BLOOMSBURY (Theobald's Road; Pl. R, 32): *d*. To *Lea Bridge Road*; *e*. To *Poplar*. — *f*. From CLERKENWELL ROAD (Pl. R, 36) to *Holloway Road* viâ King's Cross.

5. From **King's Cross** (Pl. B, 32): *a*. To *Hampstead Heath*; *b*. To *Islington* (Angel; Pl. B, 35). See also No. 4.

6. From **Euston Road** (Pl. B, 24): *a*. To *Hampstead Heath*; *b*. To *Highgate* viâ Kentish Town (Pl. B, 21); *c*. To *Holloway* (Nag's Head) viâ Camden Road (Pl. B, 25).

7. From **Harrow Road** (Lock Bridge) to *Harlesden* viâ Kensal Green.

8. From **Uxbridge Road Station**: *a*. To *Acton*; *b*. To *Goldhawk Road*.

9. From **Victoria Station** (Pl. G, 21) to *Vauxhall Bridge* (Pl. G, 26).

S. SIDE OF THE THAMES.

10. From **Kew Bridge**: *a*. To *Hammersmith Broadway*; *b*. To *Richmond*.

11. From **Chelsea Bridge** (Pl. G, 18): *a*. To *Lavender Hill*; *b*. To *Clapham Junction*.

12. From **Vauxhall Bridge** (Pl. G, 26) to *Camberwell*.

13. From **Westminster Bridge** (Pl. R, 29): *a*. To *Wandsworth* (North St.) viâ Battersea Park Road; *b*. To *Wandsworth* (East Hill) viâ Lavender Hill; *c*. To *Lower Tooting*; *d*. To *Streatham Hill* (cable); *e*. To *Peckham* and *New Cross*; *f*. To *Greenwich*.

14. From **Waterloo Station** (Pl. R, 34): *a*. To *Clapham* and *Tooting*; *b*. To *Peckham* (Rye Lane); *c*. To *Greenwich*.

15. From **Blackfriars Bridge** (Pl. R, 34): *a*. To *Tooting*; *b*. To *Streatham Hill* (cable); *c*. To *Peckham* and *New Cross*; *d*. To *Greenwich*.

16. From **Old Kent Road**: *a*. To *Streatham*; *b*. To *Camberwell Green*.

17. From **London Bridge** (Hop Exchange; Pl. R, 38): *a*. To *Wandsworth* (North St.) viâ Battersea Park Road; *b*. To *Wandsworth* (East Hill) viâ Lavender Hill.

18. From **Plumstead Church** to *Greenwich*, viâ Woolwich.

The **Highgate Cable Tramway**, the first of the kind in Europe, opened in 1884, ascends *Highgate Hill* from the *Archway Tavern* (p. 374); the cars start every 5 min. (fare 1*d*.). The motive power is supplied by an endless wire rope, placed in a tube below the surface of the road and kept in motion by a stationary engine. Connection between the car and the rope is effected by means of a 'gripping attachment', passing through a slit in the middle of the track. The rope runs between the jaws of the 'gripper', which the driver closes when he wishes to start the car, reversing the operation and applying the brakes when he wishes to stop.

Coaches. During the summer-months well-appointed stage coaches run from London to various places in the vicinity, usually starting from Northumberland Avenue between 10 and 11.45 a.m. The fares vary from 2*s.* 6*d.* to 15*s.*; return-fares one-half or two-thirds more; box-seats usually 2*s.*6*d.* extra. Some of these coaches are driven by the gentlemen who own them. They afford better opportunities in many respects for viewing the scenery than railway-trains, and may be recommended in fine weather. On the more popular routes seats have often to be booked several days in advance. The whole coach may generally be engaged for seven to ten guineas. A few of these coaches now ply in winter also. Particulars may be obtained on application at Cook's Office, in the Victoria Hotel, or at Gaze's Office, 4 Northumberland Avenue.

Among the places to which coaches usually run are *Virginia Water* (29 M.; return-fare 18*s.* 6*d.*), *Box Hill* (27 M.; 10*s.*, return 15*s.*), *Brighton* (53 M.; fare 15*s.*), *Ascot* (30 M.; 10*s.*, return 15*s.*), *Bushey* ('The Hall'; 16 M.; 6*s.*), *Ockham* (22 M.; 10*s.* 6*d.*, return 15*s.* 6*d.*), *St. Albans* (25 M.; return-fare 15*s.*), *Dorking* (26 M.; 10*s.*, return 15*s.*), *Hampton Court* (16 M.; return-fare 10*s.* 6*d.*), *Windsor* (30 M.; 12*s.* 6*d.*, return 17*s.* 6*d.*), and *Guildford* (28 M.; 10*s.*, return 15*s.*).

See 'Coach Drives from London' by *B. Hounsell* ('Sportsman' Office, 139 Fleet Street, E. C.).

10. Railways.

The following are the chief Terminal Railway Stations in London, besides which there are about 300 small stations for local and suburban traffic.

I. **Euston Square Station** (Pl. B, 24, 28), the terminus of the LONDON AND NORTH WESTERN RAILWAY, Euston Square, near Euston Road and Tottenham Court Road. An additional station has been opened a little to the W. Trains for *Rugby, Crewe, Chester, Bangor, Holyhead* (whence steamers to *Ireland*); *Birmingham, Shrewsbury, Stafford, Leicester, Derby, Nottingham, Lincoln, Leeds, Hull; Liverpool, Manchester; Carlisle, Glasgow, Edinburgh,* etc. — SUBURBAN TRAINS to *Chalk Farm, Loudoun Road, Kilburn & Maida Vale, Queen's Park, Willesden Junction, Sudbury & Wembley, Harrow, Stanmore, Pinner, Bushey, Watford, Rickmansworth,* and *St. Albans.*

II. **St. Pancras Station** (Pl. B, 28), Euston Road, to the W. of King's Cross Station, the terminus of the MIDLAND RAILWAY. Trains for *Bedford, Leicester, Nottingham, Derby, Manchester, Liverpool, Blackburn, Chesterfield, Sheffield, Hull, York, Leeds, Bradford, Newcastle; Glasgow, Edinburgh,* etc. — SUBURBAN TRAINS for *Camden Road, Kentish Town, Haverstock Hill, Finchley Road, West End, Child's Hill, Welsh Harp,* and *Hendon; Highgate Road, Junction Road, Upper Holloway, Hornsey Road, Crouch Hill,*

*Harringay Park, St. Ann's, South Tottenham; Walthamstow, Ley-
tonstone, East Ham, Barking, Upminster; Southend*, etc.

III. **King's Cross Station** (Pl. B, 31, 32), Euston Road, terminus of the GREAT NORTHERN RAILWAY. Trains for the N. and
N.E.: *York, Newcastle, Edinburgh; Hull, Leeds, Sheffield, Manchester, Liverpool; Cambridge, Luton, Hertford, Lincoln.* — SUB-
URBAN TRAINS to *Holloway, Finsbury Park, Highgate, Finchley, Mill
Hill,* and *Edgware; Harringay, Hornsey, Barnet,* and *Enfield; Hatfield, Knebworth,* and *Hitchin*, etc.

IV. **Marylebone Station** (Pl. R, 16), the London terminus of
the GREAT CENTRAL RAILWAY, for the N., N.W., & N.E. of England
and for Scotland (trains start from the W. side of the station).
Trains to *Brackley, Rugby, Lutterworth, Leicester, Loughborough,
Nottingham, Chesterfield, Sheffield, Doncaster, Rotherham, Barnsley,
Huddersfield, Halifax, Bradford, York, Darlington, Newcastle,
Scarborough, Worksop, Gainsborough, Lincoln, Retford, Grimsby,
Cleethorpes, Hull, Manchester, Warrington, Liverpool, Stockport,
Oldham, Ashton-under-Lyne, Staleybridge, St. Helens, Wigan,
Chester, Southport, Glasgow,* and *Edinburgh.*

V. **Paddington Station** (Pl. R, 11, 12), terminus of the GREAT
WESTERN RAILWAY for the W. and S.W. of England (trains start
from the W. side of the station). Trains to *Cheltenham, Gloucester, Bath, Bristol, Exeter; Plymouth, Falmouth; Newport, Car-
diff, Swansea, New Milford; Oxford, Leamington, Warwick, Stratford-on-Avon, Birmingham, Wolverhampton, Shrewsbury, Chester,
Liverpool, Manchester,* etc. — SUBURBAN TRAINS to *Westbourne
Park, Acton, Ealing, Hanwell, Brentford, Uxbridge; Staines; Maidenhead, Henley; Great Marlow, High Wycombe; Aylesbury; Windsor; Reading,* etc

VI. **Liverpool Street Station** (Pl. R, 44; *III*), near Bishopsgate
Street, terminus of the GREAT EASTERN RAILWAY (18 platforms,
20 lines, nearly 1000 trains per day). Trains to *Southend, Chelms-
ford, Colchester, Harwich, Ipswich, Norwich, Cromer, Lowestoft, Yarmouth; Cambridge, Ely, Lynn, Wisbech, Peterborough, Lincoln, Doncaster, York,* etc. — SUBURBAN TRAINS to *Bethnal Green, Hackney,
Stoke Newington, Stamford Hill, Seven Sisters, Palace Gates; Edmonton, Enfield; Clapton, Tottenham, Enfield Lock, Waltham Cross,
Cheshunt, Broxbourne, Rye House, Hertford; Walthamstow, Chingford; Coborn Road (Old Ford), Stratford, Leytonstone, Epping Forest,
Ongar; Forest Gate, Ilford, Romford, Southend; Canning Town, Victoria and Albert Docks, Woolwich; Shoreditch, Whitechapel, Shadwell,
Wapping, Rotherhithe, Deptford Road, New Cross, Croydon,* etc.

VII. **Broad Street Station** (Pl. R, 44; *III*), terminus of the
NORTH LONDON RAILWAY. Trains to *Shoreditch, Haggerston,* and
Dalston, where the line forks. The rails to the W. run to *Mildmay
Park, Canonbury, Islington & Highbury, Barnsbury, Camden Town,
Kentish Town, Gospel Oak* (for Highgate; to *Chingford,* see p. 57),

Hampstead Heath, Finchley Road, West End Lane, Brondesbury, Kensal Rise, Willesden Junction (an important station for North London, stopped at by all the express trains of the L. N.W. railway), *Acton, South Acton* (branch to *Hammersmith Broadway*, for *Bedford Park*), *Hammersmith, Gunnersbury, Kew Bridge, Kew Gardens, Richmond,* and *Kingston.* The line to the E. goes to *Hackney, Homerton, Victoria Park, Old Ford, Bow,* and *Poplar.* Trains also run every $1/4$ hr. from Broad Street to *Camden Town* (as above) and *Chalk Farm,* on the L. N. W. railway; and every $1/2$ hr. to *Dalston, Highbury, Camden Town, Kentish Town;* thence as above to *Willesden Junction,* and thence to *St. Quintin Park & Wormwood Scrubs, Uxbridge Road* (for *Shepherd's Bush*), *Kensington* (*Addison Road;* p. 58), *Earl's Court, South Kensington,* and thence by the 'inner circle' (p. 60) to *Mansion House.* — Gospel Oak is also the terminus of a line viâ *Highgate Road, Junction Road, Upper Holloway, Hornsey Road, Crouch Hill, Harringay Park, St. Ann's Road, South Tottenham, St. James's Street, Hoe Street, Wood Street,* and *Hale End,* to *Chingford.*

VIII. **Charing Cross Station** (Pl. R, 26, 30; *IV*), close to Trafalgar Square, one of the West End termini of the SOUTH EASTERN AND CHATHAM RAILWAY to *Tunbridge Wells, Hastings; Dorking, Guildford, Reading; Canterbury, Ramsgate, Margate, Folkestone, Dover; Rochester, Maidstone,* etc. — SUBURBAN TRAINS to *Chislehurst, Sevenoaks, Croydon; Spa Road, Deptford, Greenwich, Woolwich, Dartford, Gravesend, Chatham; New Cross, Lewisham, Beckenham, Bromley, Bickley; Blackheath, Bexley Heath; Lee, Eltham, Sidcup,* etc.

IX. **Cannon Street Station** (Pl. R, 39; *III*), near the Bank, City terminus for the same lines as Charing Cross. Trains from Charing Cross to Cannon Street, and *vice versâ,* every 10 minutes.

X. **Victoria Station** (Pl. R, G, 21), in Victoria Street, the terminus of the LONDON, BRIGHTON, AND SOUTH COAST RAILWAY, and also one of the West End termini of the SOUTH EASTERN AND CHATHAM RAILWAY.

1. The CHATHAM RAILWAY (MAIN LINE), to *Clapham, Brixton, Herne Hill, Dulwich, Sydenham Hill, Beckenham, Bromley, Bickley, Rochester, Chatham, Faversham, Canterbury, Dover, Deal; Queenborough, Sheerness; Herne Bay, Margate, Broadstairs, Ramsgate; Swanley, Sevenoaks, Maidstone,* and *Ashford.*

2. The CRYSTAL PALACE branch of the S. E. & C. R.: stations *Wandsworth Road, Clapham, Brixton, Denmark Hill, Peckham Rye, Nunhead, Honor Oak, Lordship Lane, Upper Sydenham, Crystal Palace (High Level Station).*

3. The METROPOLITAN EXTENSION, to *Ludgate Hill* and *Holborn Viaduct Station,* viâ *Grosvenor Road, Battersea Park Road, Wandsworth Road, Clapham & North Stockwell, Brixton & South Stockwell, Loughborough Junction, Camberwell New Road, Walworth Road, Elephant and Castle,* and *Borough Road;* also through-trains to *King's Cross* (G.N.R.) and *Kentish Town* (Mid. Railway).

4. The West London Extension, viâ *Battersea, Chelsea, West Brompton*, to *Kensington (Addison Road)*, where there are connections for *Ealing, Southall*, and *Windsor*, for *Euston*, and for the N. London Railway (see p. 56) to *Ealing* and *Southall* (G.W.R.).

5. The Brighton and South Coast Railway, viâ *Clapham Junction* (a most important station for South London, through which 1200 trains pass daily), *Wandsworth Common*, *Balham*, *Streatham Hill*, *West Norwood*, *Gipsy Hill*, and *Crystal Palace (Low Level Station)*, to *Norwood Junction* (see below), or by *Clapham Junction*, *Wandsworth Common*, *Balham*, *Streatham Common*, *Norbury*, *Thornton Heath*, and *Selhurst* to *Croydon* (see below). At Norwood Junction and Croydon the line joins the London Bridge and Brighton Line.

6. The South London Line, viâ *Grosvenor Road*, *Battersea Park Road*, *Wandsworth Road*, *Clapham Road*, *East Brixton*, *Denmark Hill*, *Peckham Rye*, *Queen's Road*, *Old Kent Road*, and *South Bermondsey*, to *London Bridge*.

XI. **Ludgate Hill Station** (Pl. R, 35; *II*), near St. Paul's Cathedral and Blackfriars Bridge, City station of the Metropolitan Extension of the South Eastern and Chatham Railway (p. 57).

XII. **Holborn Viaduct Station** (Pl. R, 35; *II*), Holborn Viaduct, City terminus for the main line trains of the South Eastern and Chatham Railway.

XIII. **St. Paul's Station** (Pl. R, 35; *II*), Queen Victoria Street, another terminus of the South Eastern and Chatham Railway, for the *Main Line*, *Catford*, and *Crystal Palace* trains.

XIV. **Fenchurch Street Station** (Pl. R, 43; *III*), near the Bank (S. side of Fenchurch St.), terminus of the Blackwall Railway to *Shadwell, Stepney, Limehouse, West India Docks, Poplar*, and *Blackwall*, and of the Tilbury, Gravesend, and Southend Railway.

XV. **Baker Street Station** (Pl. R, 20), of the Metropolitan Railway (p. 60), practically ranks among the London termini since the extension of the St. John's Wood branch to *Harrow, Northwood, Rickmansworth, Chesham*, and *Aylesbury* (comp. R. 43).

On the right (S.) bank of the Thames: —

XVI. **London Bridge Station** (Pl. R, 42), the City terminus of the Brighton and South Coast Railway, viâ *Norwood Junction* (see above), *Croydon* (see above), *Purley* (junction for *Caterham*), *Red Hill Junction* (branch W. for *Reigate, Box Hill*, and *Dorking*; E. for *Dover*), *Three Bridges* (for *Arundel*), and *Hayward's Heath* (junction for *Lewes* and *Newhaven*), to *Brighton*. Also to *Chichester* and *Portsmouth* for the *Isle of Wight*. — Suburban Trains to *New Cross, Brockley, Honor Oak Park, Forest Hill, Sydenham (Crystal Palace), Penge*, and *Anerley*; to *Victoria Station*, see p. 57.

XVII. **Waterloo Station**, Waterloo Road, Lambeth (Pl. R, 30), terminus of the South Western Railway, consists of three parts —

1. The NORTHERN (entrance on the E. and N.E.), for the line to *Reading* by *Vauxhall*, *Queen's Road*, *Clapham Junction*, *Wandsworth*, *Putney*, and *Barnes*. At Barnes the line forks; the branch to the right (N.) forms a loop-line viâ *Chiswick*, *Kew Bridge*, *Brentford*, *Isleworth*, and *Hounslow*, beyond which it rejoins the main line; that to the left (the main line) passes *Mortlake*, *Richmond*, *Twickenham* (branch to *Strawberry Hill*, *Shepperton*, *Teddington*, *Kingston*, and *Combe & Malden*) and *Staines* (junction for *Windsor*).

2. The CENTRAL (entrance on the E. and W.), for the main line to *Southampton*, *Bournemouth*, *Weymouth*, *Portsmouth (Isle of Wight)*, *Salisbury*, *Exeter*, *Plymouth*, *Ilfracombe*, *North Cornwall*, etc.

3. The SOUTHERN (same entrances as the Central), for local trains to *Guildford* viâ *Earlsfield*, *Wimbledon* (an important junction), and *Raynes Park*. At Raynes Park a loop-line, to the left, runs viâ *Epsom* and *Leatherhead*, rejoining the older line at *Effingham Junction*. The latter line proceeds viâ *Combe-Malden* and *Surbiton*. The trains for *Surbiton*, *Thames Ditton*, and *Hampton Court* also start from the Southern station; and also a service to *Kingston* and *Twickenham* (see above).

[*Waterloo Junction*, adjoining Waterloo terminus on the E., is a distinct station belonging to the South Eastern & Chatham Railway.]

On all the English lines the first-class passenger is entitled to carry 112lb. of luggage free, second-class 80lb., and third-class 60lb. The companies, however, do not always charge for overweight unless the excess is exorbitant. On all inland routes the traveller should see that his luggage is duly labelled for his destination, and put into the right van, as otherwise the railways are not responsible for its transport. Travellers to the Continent require to book their luggage and obtain a ticket for it, after which it gives them no farther trouble. The railway-porters are nominally forbidden to accept gratuities, but it is a common custom to give 2d.-6d. to the porter who transfers the luggage from the cab to the train or vice versâ.

Travellers accustomed to the formalities of Continental railway-officials may perhaps consider that in England there are too much left to themselves. Tickets are not invariably checked at the beginning of a journey, and travellers should therefore make sure that they are in the proper compartment. The names of the stations are not always so conspicuous as they should be (especially at night); and the way in which the porters call them out, laying all the stress on the last syllable, is seldom of much assistance. The officials, however, are generally civil in answering questions and giving information. In winter foot-warmers with hot water are usually provided. It is 'good form' for a passenger quitting a railway carriage where there are other travellers to close the door behind him, and to pull up the window if he has had to let it down.

SMOKING is forbidden in all the carriages except in the compartments marked 'smoking' under a penalty of 40s.

Bradshaw's Railway Guide (monthly; 6d.) is the most complete; but numerous others (the *ABC Railway Guide*, etc.), claiming to be easier of reference, are also published. Each of the great railway-companies publishes a monthly guide to its own system (price 1-2d.).

Metropolitan or Underground Railways.

An important artery of 'intramural' traffic is afforded by the *Metropolitan* and *Metropolitan District Railways*. These lines,

which for the most part run under the houses and streets by means
of tunnels, and partly also through cuttings between high walls,
form a complete belt (the 'inner circle') round the whole of the
inner part of London, while various branch-lines diverge to the
outlying suburbs. The Midland, Great Western, Great Northern,
and other railways run suburban trains in connection with the Metropolitan lines. The Metropolitan Railway was constructed at a
cost of 1,000,000*l.* per mile. The Underground Railways convey
over 150 million passengers annually, or nearly 3 million per week,
at an average rate of about twopence per journey. Over the quad-
ruple part of the line, at Farringdon Street, 1200 trains run every
week-day. Experiments in the use of electrical traction have been
successfully made on a section of the line, and it is hoped that this
method of haulage will soon supersede steam locomotive power on
the 'inner circle'. The stations on the underground lines are the
following (see Railway Map) : —

Mark Lane, for the Tower of London, the Mint, Corn Exchange,
Billingsgate, and the Docks.

Aldgate, Houndsditch, corner of Leadenhall and Fenchurch
Streets, for Mincing Lane, Whitechapel, Minories, and the East End.

From Aldgate the line is extended to *Aldgate East* and *St. Mary's*
(Whitechapel), whence the trains run on to *Shadwell, Wapping, Rotherhithe,
Deptford Road,* and *New Cross,* on the East London Railway. Through-
trains now run between New Cross and many of the District and Metropolitan stations.

Bishopsgate, near the Liverpool Street (Great Eastern; subway) and Broad Street (North London) stations.

Moorgate Street, close to Finsbury Circus, 5 min. from the
Bank, chief station for the City.

Aldersgate Street, Long Lane, near the General Post Office
and Smithfield Market; change for Ludgate Hill, Crystal Palace,
and South Eastern and Chatham Railway.

Farringdon Street, in Clerkenwell, $1/4$ M. to the N. of Holborn
Viaduct, connected with *Holborn Viaduct* and *Ludgate Hill* stations
(see p. 58); trains to and from the latter (South Eastern and
Chatham Railway) every 10 minutes.

King's Cross, corner of Pentonville Road and Gray's Inn Road,
connected with the Great Northern and Midland Railways.

Gower Street, near Euston Square (North Western) Terminus
and about $1/2$ M. from the British Museum. Omnibus (2*d.*) to Edgware Road Station (p. 61) in connection with the trains.

Portland Road, Park Square, at the S.E. angle of Regent's
Park, $1/2$ M. from the S. entrance of the Zoological Gardens.

Baker Street (comp. p.58), corner of York Place, another station
for the Botanic and Zoological Gardens. A little to the E., in Marylebone Road, is Madame Tussaud's (p. 68). Railway-omnibuses to
Oxford Circus (1*d.*), Piccadilly Circus (1*d.*), and Charing Cross (2*d.*).

BRANCH LINE to *St. John's Wood, Rickmansworth,* and *Aylesbury,* see R. 43

Edgware Road, Chapel Street. Omnibus to Gower St. (p. 60).

BRANCH LINE to *Bishop's Road, Royal Oak, Westbourne Park, Notting Hill* (the last two stations are both near Kensal Green Cemetery), *Latimer Road, Shepherd's Bush, Hammersmith* (trains every ¼ hr.); also to *Turnham Green* (Bedford Park), *Gunnersbury, Kew Gardens, Richmond* (trains every half-hour, from Bishop's Road to Richmond in 28 min.). — From Latimer Road branch-line to the left to *Uxbridge Road, Addison Road (Kensington;* for Olympia, p. 69), *Earl's Court,* and *Brompton (Gloucester Road),* see below; trains every ½ hr.

Praed Street (Paddington), opposite the Great Western Hotel and the Paddington Station, with which it is connected by a subway.

Queen's Road (Bayswater), near N. side of Kensington Gardens.

Notting Hill Gate, Notting Hill High Street, for the E. part of Notting Hill, Campden Hill, etc.

Kensington High Street, Kensington, ⅓ M. from Holland House and Park, and ¾ M. from the Albert Hall.

Gloucester Road (Brompton).

BRANCH LINES: To *Earl's Court, West Brompton, Walham Green* (for Stamford Bridge Athletic Grounds), *Parson's Green* (for Hurlingham Park), *Putney Bridge, East Putney, Southfields, Wimbledon Park,* and *Wimbledon;* to *Earl's Court, West Kensington, Hammersmith, Ravenscourt Park, Turnham Green, Gunnersbury, Kew Gardens,* and *Richmond;* to *Earl's Court, Addison Road, Latimer Road,* etc. (see above); to *Earl's Court, Addison Road, Willesden Junction, Broad Street* (see p. 57). From Turnham Green a branch runs to *Chiswick Park, Mill Hill Park, Ealing Common,* and *Ealing* (Broadway).

South Kensington, Cromwell Road, for South Kensington Museum (3 min. to the N.), Natural History Museum, Albert Hall, Albert Memorial, and the Imperial Institute.

Sloane Square, near Chelsea Hospital, station for Battersea Park.

Victoria, opposite Victoria Terminus (p. 57), with which it is connected by a subway, and ¼ M. from Buckingham Palace.

St. James's Park, York Street, to the S. of St. James's Park.

Westminster Bridge, Victoria Embankment, at the W. end of Westminster Bridge, station for the Houses of Parliament, Westminster Abbey, etc. From Westminster to Blackfriars the line runs below the Victoria Embankment (p. 150).

Charing Cross, for Charing Cross, Trafalgar Square, National Gallery, National Portrait Gallery, and West Strand.

Temple, between Somerset House and the Temple, below Waterloo Bridge, station for the Law Courts, Somerset House, and the London School Board Office.

Blackfriars, Bridge Street, adjacent to Blackfriars Bridge, connected by a covered way with the St. Paul's Station of the South Eastern and Chatham Railway, and near Ludgate Hill Station (p. 58).

Mansion House, corner of Cannon Street and Queen Victoria Street, station for St. Paul's. Omnibus to Liverpool Street Station.

Cannon Street, below the terminus of the South Eastern Railway (covered way), the station nearest the Bank and the Exchange.

The Monument, at the corner of Eastcheap, station for the Monument, London Bridge, and the Coal Exchange.

Trains run on the 'inner circle' in both directions from 5.30 a.m.
to nearly midnight, at intervals of 3-10 min. during the day, and of
20 min. before 7 a.m. or after 9 p.m. On Sundays the train-service
is suspended during the 'church interval' (11 a.m.-1 p.m.).

The stations generally occupy open sites, and are lighted from above,
many of them being roofed with glass. The carriages are lighted with gas.
The booking-office is generally on a level with the street, at the top of
the flight of stairs leading down to the railway. The official who checks
the tickets points out the right platform, while the tickets themselves
are marked with a large red O or I (for 'outer' and 'inner' line of rails),
corresponding with notices in the stations. After reaching the platform,
the traveller had better enquire whether the train for his destination is
the first that comes up or one of those that follow, or consult the somewhat
inconspicuous telegraph-board on which the destination of the 'next train'
is indicated. It may, however, be useful to know that the trains of the
'inner circle' have one white light on the engine; trains between Hammersmith and New Cross have two white lights to the left in front of
the engine, between Hammersmith and Aldgate two white lights to the
right in front, and between Richmond and Aldgate two white lights. The
terminus towards which the train is travelling is also generally placarded
on the front of the engine. Above the platforms hang boards indicating
the points at which the different classes of carriage are drawn up; the
first-class carriages are in the middle of the train. The names of the
stations are called out by the porters, and are always painted at different
parts of the platform and on the lamps and benches, though frequently
difficult to distinguish from the surrounding advertisements. As the stoppages are extremely brief, no time should be lost either in taking seats
or alighting. Passengers leave the platform by the 'Way Out', where
their tickets are given up. Those who are travelling with through-tickets
to a station situated on one of the branch-lines show their tickets at the
junction where carriages are changed, and where the officials will indicate
the proper train. — Comp. the time-tables of the companies.

The carriages are of three classes; the third class is apt to be incon-
veniently crowded between 8 and 10 a.m. and 5 and 7 p.m. by passengers
going to or returning from their daily work. The fares are extremely
moderate, seldom exceeding a shilling even for considerable distances.
Return-tickets are issued at a fare and a half. At first, in order to make
himself acquainted with the Metropolis, the stranger will naturally prefer
to make use of omnibuses and cabs, but when his early curiosity is satisfied
he will probably often avail himself of the easy, rapid, and economical
mode of travelling afforded by the Underground Railway.

Electric Railways.

The City and South London Electric Railway, opened in 1890, passes
under the Thames just above London Bridge by means of two separate
tunnels for the 'up' and 'down' traffic. This underground electric railway,
4¼ M. in length, runs from *Moorgate Street* (Pl. R, 40; *III*) to *Clapham
Common* (beyond Pl. G, 28), with intermediate stations at the *Bank*, *Denman Street* (London Bridge), the *Borough*, *Elephant and Castle*, *New Street*
(Kennington), *Kennington Oval*, *Stockwell* (Pl. G, 32), and *Clapham Road*.
The entire journey is performed in 22 min., by trains running every
3-5 minutes, a uniform fare of 2d. for any distance being paid on entering
the stations. At each station powerful hydraulic lifts convey the passengers
between the streets and the platforms, while there are also broad and
convenient staircases. The total cost was 200,000l. per mile. An extension
to Islington is in course of construction.

The Waterloo and City Railway, opened in 1898, connects the ter-
minus of the London & South-Western Railway with the City. It begins at
Waterloo Station (low level), crosses the Thames in two tunnels just above
Blackfriars Bridge, and ends, near the Mansion House, at the *City Station*,

which is connected by means of tunnel footpaths with the Bank Station of the Central London Railway (see below). The total length is 1½ M., and there are no intermediate stations; the journey occupies 4 or 5 minutes (fare 2*d*.).

The **Central London Railway**, opened in 1900, runs eastwards from *Shepherd's Bush* (beyond Pl. R, 2) in two parallel tunnels, under Uxbridge Road, Oxford Street, Holborn, and Cheapside to the *Bank* (Pl. R, 39, 43; *III*), a distance of 6 M., with intermediate stations at *Holland Park, Notting Hill Gate, Lancaster Gate, Westbourne, Marble Arch. Bond Street, Oxford Circus, Tottenham Court Road, British Museum, Chancery Lane*, and *General Post Office*. At the Bank Station, immediately in front of the Royal Exchange, the line is connected with the two preceding electric railways. Trains run every few minutes, taking about ½ hr. for the entire journey (uniform fare 2*d*.).

Various other underground electric railways are projected, authorised, or in construction.

11. Steamboats.

On the Thames between Hampton Court towards the west and Southend and Sheerness on the east there are about 45 piers or landing-places, the larger half of which are on the north or left bank. At *London Bridge* there are two piers, *Old Swan Pier*, on the N. bank, immediately above the bridge, and *Surrey Side Pier*, on the S. bank, immediately below. Between the bridges, as the reach between Vauxhall Bridge on the west and London Bridge on the east is sometimes called, are the piers at *All Hallows, Blackfriars, Temple, Charing Cross, Westminster, Lambeth*, and *Vauxhall*. Above Vauxhall Bridge are *Nine Elms, Pimlico, Battersea Park, Cadogan (Chelsea), Carlyle Pier (Chelsea), Battersea Square, Wandsworth, Putney, Hammersmith, Kew, Richmond, Teddington,* and *Hampton Court*. Below London Bridge ('below bridge') are *Cherry Gardens* (in no sense corresponding with its name), *Thames Tunnel, Globe Stairs, Limehouse, West India Docks, Commercial Docks, Greenwich, North Greenwich, Blackwall, South Woolwich, North Woolwich, Rosherville, Gravesend, Southend,* and *Sheerness*, where the Nore light-ship is reached, and the estuary of the Thames expands into the German Ocean.

The Thames has never been adequately made use of as a water-highway for passenger-service, and at present it seems not unlikely that the service will be still farther curtailed unless the City or the County Council take it in hand. The steamers ply in summer only. Comp. the advertisements in the daily papers.

THAMES STEAMBOAT COMPANY. Above bridge steamers of this company have hitherto plied between *London Bridge* (Old Swan Pier) and *Chelsea* (Cadogan Pier), calling at intermediate stations (fares 1*d*.-2*d*. according to distance); between *Chelsea* (Cadogan Pier) and *Kew* (fare 6*d*.), every ½ hr.; and once daily between *London Bridge* (ca. 9.30 a.m.) and *Hampton Court* (22 M. in 2-3 hrs.; fare 1*s*., return-fare 1*s*. 6*d*.). Below bridge steamers of this company have hitherto plied between *Old Swan Pier* and *Greenwich* (fare 3*d*.) and *Woolwich* (fare 5*d*.), every 20-30 min.; and once daily between *London Bridge* and *Gravesend* (1*s*., return 1*s*. 6*d*.). On Sundays and holidays the fare is raised for most of the shorter trips. The steamers may also be hired for excursion-parties at prices ranging from 6*l*. to 35*l*. per day.

'BELLE' STEAMERS. From *London Bridge* (Fresh Wharf) daily (except Frid.) at 9.15 a.m. for *Gravesend, Southend* (fares 2*s*. 6*d*., 2*s*.), *Walton-on-the-Naze* (4*s*. 6*d*., 3*s*. 6*d*.), and *Clacton* (4*s*. 6*d*., 3*s*. 6*d*.). At Clacton steamers are changed (daily except Friday) for *Felixstowe, Harwich*, and *Ipswich*

(5s. 6d., 4s.), and for *Yarmouth* (7s. 6d., 5s.). Another steamer plies daily (except Frid.) at 9.35 a.m. to *Margate* (4s. 6d., 3s. 6d.).

NEW PALACE STEAMERS CO. The 'Royal Sovereign' plies daily to *Margate* and *Ramsgate*, and the 'Kohinoor' daily to *Southend* and *Margate*, both starting from *Old Swan Pier*. From *Tilbury* 'La Marguerite' runs on alternate days to *Boulogne* (3-4 hrs. on shore), and *Ostend* (2 hrs. on shore). Return-fares: to Margate, saloon 6s., fore-cabin 5s.; to Boulogne (including third-class railway to Tilbury) 14s.; to Ostend 14s. 6d.

The 'Queen Elizabeth' of the QUEENS or THE RIVER STEAMSHIP CO. ascends the river daily (except Frid.) from *Old Swan Pier* to *Kew* (9d.; return 1s. 3d.), *Richmond* (1s. 3d., return 2s.), and *Hampton Court* (1s. 10 d., return 2s. 6d.). Luncheon on board 2s. 6d.

12. Theatres, Music Halls, and other Entertainments.

The performance at most of the London theatres begins about 7.30, 8, or 8.30, and lasts till 11 p.m. The ticket-office is usually opened half-an-hour before the performance. Many theatres also give so-called 'morning performances' or 'matinées', beginning about 2.30 or 3 p.m. For details consult the notices 'under the clock' (*i.e.* immediately before the summaries and leaders) in the daily papers.

London possesses about 50 theatres and about 500 music-halls, which are visited by 325,000 people nightly or nearly 100,000,000 yearly. A visit to the whole of the theatres of London, which, however, could only be managed in the course of a prolonged sojourn, would give the traveller a capital insight into the social life of the people throughout all its gradations. Copies of the play are often sold at the theatres for 6d. or 1s. At some of the better theatres all extra fees have been abolished, but many of them still maintain the objectionable custom of charging for programmes, the care of wraps, etc. Opera-glasses may be hired for 1s. or 1s. 6d. from the attendants; in some theatres the glasses are placed in automatic boxes attached to the backs of the seats and opened by dropping a sixpenny piece or a shilling in the slot. *French* (late *Lacy*), 89 Strand, is the chief theatrical bookseller.

The best seats are the *Stalls*, next to the Orchestra, and the *Dress Circle*. On the occasion of popular performances tickets for these places are often not to be had at the door on entering, but must be secured previously at the *Box Office* of the theatre. The office always contains a plan of the theatre, showing the positions of the seats. Tickets for the opera and for most of the theatres may also be obtained from *Lacon & Ollier*, 168A New Bond Street; *Hays*, 26 Old Bond Street, 82 Cornhill, and 4 Royal Exchange Buildings; *Keith*, *Prowse*, *& Co.*, 48 Cheapside, 148 Fenchurch Street, Grand Hôtel Buildings, 48 Victoria Street, First Avenue Hotel Buildings, High Holborn, and 167 New Bond Street; *Cramer*, 207 Regent Street and 40-46 Moorgate Street, City; *Newman*, Queen's Hall, Langham Place; *Ashton*, 38 Old Bond Street, 35 Sloane Street, and Stock Exchange; *Mr. Louis A. Back*, 200 Piccadilly; *Mitchell's Royal Library*, 33 Old Bond Street, 5 Leadenhall Street, and 16 Gloucester Road; *Cecil Roy*, 17 Wigmore Street, 11 Pont Street, 53 St. George's Place, 38 Sloane Street, 59 South Audley Street, and 68 Regent Street, and elsewhere, at charges somewhat higher as a rule than at the theatres themselves, but occasionally lower. Single box-seats can generally be obtained at the door as well as at the box-office, except when the boxes are let for the season.

Those who have not taken their tickets in advance should be at the door 1/2 hr. before the beginning of the performance, with, if possible, the exact price of their ticket in readiness. All the theatres are closed on Good Friday and Christmas Day, and many throughout Passion Week.

Evening-dress is not now compulsory in any of the London theatres, but is customary in the stalls and dress circle and *de rigueur* in most parts of the opera-house during the opera season.

The chief London theatres are the following (many of them closed in August and September).

ROYAL ITALIAN OPERA, or COVENT GARDEN THEATRE, on the W. side of Bow Street, Long Acre, the third theatre on the same site, was built in 1858 by Barry. It accommodates an audience of 3500 persons, being nearly as large as the Scala at Milan, and has a handsome Corinthian colonnade. This house was originally sacred to Italian opera, but is now also used for promenade concerts in autumn and for fancy dress balls, etc., in winter. Boxes 3–10 guineas, orchestra stalls 21s., balcony 15s., amphitheatre 10s., 7s., and 5s., gallery 2s. 6d. Performance commences at 8 or 8.30 p.m. Operas have also been given here at 'theatre' prices — i.e. about 50 per cent lower than those just mentioned. In winter, stalls 6s., stage stalls 4s., grand circle 2s. 6d., balcony stalls 2s., promenade 1s.

DRURY LANE THEATRE, between Drury Lane and Brydges St., near Covent Garden, where Garrick, Kean, the Kembles, and Mrs. Siddons used to act. Shakspeare's plays, comedies, spectacular plays, English opera, etc. Pantomime in winter. Stalls 10s. 6d., grand circle 7s. and 6s., first circle 5s. and 4s., balcony 2s., pit 2s. 6d., gallery 1s. No fees. The vestibule contains a statue of Kean as Hamlet, by Carew, and others.

LYCEUM THEATRE, Strand, corner of Wellington Street. Shakspearian pieces, comedies, etc. (Sir Henry Irving and Miss Ellen Terry). Stalls 10s. 6d., dress circle 7s., upper circle 4s., amphitheatre 2s. 6d., pit 2s. 6d., gallery 1s. No fees.

HAYMARKET THEATRE, at the S. end of the Haymarket. English comedy and drama. Stalls 10s. 6d., balcony stalls 7s., balcony 5s., pit-circle 2s. 6d., upper boxes 2s. 6d., gallery 1s. No fees.

HER MAJESTY'S THEATRE, in the Haymarket, opposite the preceding. English comedy and drama (Mr. Beerbohm Tree). Stalls 10s. 6d., dress circle 7s. 6d., balcony 5s., upper circle 2s., 3s., and 4s., pit 2s. 6d., gallery 1s.

ST. JAMES'S THEATRE, King Street, St. James's Square. Comedies and society plays (Mr. George Alexander). Stalls 10s. 6d., dress circle 7s., upper circle 4s., pit 2s. 6d., gallery 1s. No fees.

SAVOY THEATRE, Savoy Place, Strand (electric light). English comic operas and operettas. Stalls 10s. 6d., balcony 7s. 6d. and 6s., first circle 4s., pit 2s. 6d., amphitheatre 2s., gallery 1s. No fees.

WYNDHAM'S THEATRE, Charing Cross Road, with a roof-garden and elevator. Comedies, society pieces, etc. (Mr. Charles Wyndham and Miss Mary Moore). Prices from 1s. to 10s. 6d.

ROYAL ADELPHI THEATRE, 411 Strand (N. side), near Bedford Street. Melodramas and farces. Stalls 10s. 6d., dress circle 6s., upper circle 4s. and 3s., pit 2s. 6d., gallery 1s.

STRAND THEATRE, 168 Strand, near Somerset House. Comedies, opera-bouffes, and burlesques. Stalls 10s. 6d., dress circle 6s., boxes 4s., pit 2s., gallery 1s.

GAIETY THEATRE, 345 Strand (rebuilding). Musical comedies, burlesques, farces. Orchestra stalls 10s. 6d., balcony stalls 6s. and 7s. 6d., upper boxes 5s. and 4s., pit 2s. 6d., gallery 1s. No fees.

VAUDEVILLE THEATRE, 404 Strand. Comedies, farces, and burlesques. Stalls 10s. 6d., dress circle 7s. 6d. and 6s., lower circle 5s., upper circle 4s., pit 2s. 6d., gallery 1s.

GLOBE THEATRE, Newcastle Street, Strand. Comedies, etc. (Mr. John Hare). Prices as at the Strand Theatre.

ROYAL COURT THEATRE, Sloane Square, Chelsea. Comediettas, farces, etc. Stalls 10s. 6d., dress circle 7s. 6d., upper circle 4s., pit 2s. 6d., gallery 1s. No fees.

CRITERION THEATRE, Piccadilly East. Comedies, society plays, farces, etc. Stalls 10s. 6d., dress circle 7s., family circle 3s., pit 2s. 6d., gallery 1s.

GARRICK THEATRE, Charing Cross Road. Comedies and dramas. Stalls 10s. 6d., dress circle 7s. 6d. and 6s., upper boxes 4s., pit 2s. 6d., gallery 1s.

SHAFTESBURY THEATRE, Shaftesbury Avenue. Comedies, etc. Stalls 10s. 6d., dress circle 7s. 6d. and 6s., upper circle 4s., pit 2s. 6d., amphitheatre 1s. 6d., gallery 1s.

LYRIC THEATRE, Shaftesbury Avenue. Comedy-operas, romantic drama, etc. Stalls 10s. 6d., balcony stalls 7s. 6d. and 6s., circle 4s., pit 2s. 6d., gallery 1s.

GREAT QUEEN STREET THEATRE, Great Queen Street, Lincoln's Inn Fields. Light comedy (Mr. W. S. Penley). Stalls 10s. 6d., dress circle 6-7s., upper circle 4s., pit 2s. 6d., gallery 1s.

DALY'S THEATRE, Cranbourn St., Leicester Square. Shakspearian pieces, comedies, etc. (Daly Company, with Miss Ada Rehan, in the season). Stalls 10s. 6d., balcony 7s., upper circle 4s., pit 2s. 6d., gallery 1s.

TERRY'S THEATRE, 105 Strand. Comedies, domestic dramas, etc. (Mr. Edward Terry). Stalls 10s. 6d., dress circle 7s. 6d. and 6s., upper boxes 4s., pit 2s. 6d., gallery 1s.

AVENUE THEATRE, Northumberland Avenue. Light comedy (Mr. Chas. Hawtrey). Stalls 10s. 6d., balcony stalls 7s. 6d., dress circle 6s., upper circle 4s. and 3s., pit 2s., gallery 1s.

DUKE OF YORK'S THEATRE, St. Martin's Lane, near Trafalgar Square. Comedies, dramas, etc. Stalls 10s. 6d., balcony 7s. 6d. and 6s., upper boxes 4s., pit 2s. 6d., gallery 1s.

PRINCE OF WALES THEATRE, Coventry Street, Haymarket. Comedies, operettas, etc. Stalls 10s. 6d., dress circle 7s. 6d. and 6s., upper circle 4s., pit 2s. 6d., gallery 1s.

NEW OLYMPIC THEATRE, Wych Street, Strand. Comedies, melodramas, and extravaganzas.

ROYALTY THEATRE, 73 Dean Street, Soho. Comedies, burlesques, and opera-bouffes. Stalls 10s. 6d., dress circle 7s. 6d. and 6s., upper circle 4s., pit 2s. 6d., gallery 1s.

ROYAL COMEDY THEATRE, Panton Street, Haymarket. Comedies, musical comedies, etc. Stalls 10s. 6d., balcony 6s.-7s., pit 2s. 6d.

PRINCESS'S THEATRE, 150 Oxford Street, to the E. of Oxford Circus. Melodramas, musical comedies, etc. Stalls 6s., grand circle 4s. and 3s., first circle 2s., pit stalls 1s. 6d., pit 1s., gallery 6d.

IMPERIAL THEATRE, Royal Aquarium, Westminster (see p. 273). Comedies, burlesques, and farces. Stalls 7s., dress circle 5s., boxes 3s., pit 2s., amphitheatre 1s.

GRAND THEATRE, High Street, Islington. Comedies, melodramas, operettas, etc.; pantomime in winter. Stalls 4s., dress circle 3s., balcony 2s., pit stalls 1s. 6d., pit 1s., gallery 6d.

NATIONAL STANDARD THEATRE, 204 Shoreditch High Street. Popular pieces. Balcony 3s., stalls 2s., pit stalls 1s., gallery 4d.

WEST LONDON THEATRE, Church Street, near Edgware Road Station. Stalls and boxes 2s., pit 6d., gallery 4d.

PAVILION THEATRE, Whitechapel, holding nearly 4000 persons. Nautical dramas, melodramas, farces. Admission 3d.-1s.

ROYAL SURREY THEATRE, 124 Blackfriars Road. Melodramas and farces. Admission 2s. 6d., 2s., 1s., 6d., 4d.

BRITANNIA THEATRE, Hoxton Street, in the N.E. of London, holding nearly 3400 persons. Melodramas. Prices 3d. to 2s.

ELEPHANT AND CASTLE THEATRE, New Kent Road. Popular performances. Prices 4d. to 2s. 6d.

SUBURBAN THEATRES. Within the last few years a number of theatres have been built in the suburbs of London, where very fair performances are frequently to be seen (sometimes metropolitan companies). Among these are the *Métropole*, Camberwell Green; *Terriss*, Rotherhithe; *Kennington Theatre*; *Crown Theatre*, Peckham; *Royal Duchess*, Balham; *Shakspeare*, Lavender Hill, Battersea; *Marlborough*, Holloway Road; *Shakspeare*, near Clapham Junction; *Lyric Opera House*, Hammersmith; *Brixton*, Brixton Oval; *Grand*, Fulham Road; *Coronet*, Notting Hill Gate; and theatres at Kilburn, Camden Town, Dalston, Stratford, Mile End, Lewisham, Croydon, Richmond, etc. Adm. 6d.-5s.

Music Halls and Variety Entertainments.

The objectionable custom of charging 6d. for a programme, often consisting mainly of advertisements, is also rife at the music halls.

PALACE THEATRE OF VARIETIES, Cambridge Circus, Shaftesbury Avenue. Begins at 8 p.m. Prices 7s. 6d., 5s., 3s., 2s., 1s., 6d.

ALHAMBRA, Leicester Square (elaborate ballets). Begins at 7.30 p.m. Fauteuils and grand circle stalls 7s. 6d., stalls and promenade 5s., grand balcony 3s., pit stalls 2s., pit 1s.

EMPIRE THEATRE OF VARIETIES, Leicester Square (also with good ballets). Prices 7s. 6d., 5s., 3s., 2s., 1s., 6d.

LONDON PAVILION, Piccadilly Circus. Begins at 7.30 p.m. Prices 1s., 1s. 6d., 3s., 4s., 5s.

HIPPODROME, Cranbourn Street, corner of Charing Cross Road. Performances at 2 and 8 p.m. Prices 7s. 6d., 5s., 3s., 2s., 1s.

THE OXFORD, 14 Oxford Street. Begins at 7.15 p.m. Adm. from 1s.

Tivoli Theatre of Varieties, Strand. Begins at 7.30 p.m Prices 5s., 3s., 2s., 1s. 6d., 1s.

Metropolitan Music Hall, 267 Edgware Road. Begins at 8 p.m. Adm. 6d. to 2l. 2s.

Royal Music Hall, 242 High Holborn. Begins at 7.30 p.m. Prices 3s., 2s., 1s., 6d.

Canterbury Theatre of Varieties, 143 Westminster Bridge Road. Entertainment begins at 7.40 p.m. Adm. from 6d.

Middlesex Music Hall, Drury Lane. Begins at 7.30 p.m. Prices from 6d. upwards.

Sadler's Wells Theatre, Rosebery Avenue, St. John Street Road, Clerkenwell. Begins at 7.30 p.m. Prices 4d. to 1s. 6d.

Royal Victoria Coffee Music Hall, 131 Waterloo Road, Lambeth, formerly the Victoria Palace Theatre. Open at 7 p.m. Prices from 3d. to 10s. 6d. (private box).

Paragon Theatre of Varieties, 95 Mile End Road. Begins at 7.30 p.m. Admission from 6d. upwards.

Foresters' Hall, 93 Cambridge Road, E.

Collins's Music Hall, Islington Green, near the Royal Agricultural Hall. Admission 6d.-3s.

South London Palace of Amusements, 92 London Road, St. George's Fields, near the Elephant and Castle, a large hall with 5000 seats. Concerts, ballets, etc. Admission 2s., 1s. 6d., 1s., and 6d.

Exhibitions and Entertainments. Public Gardens.

Madame Tussaud's Waxwork Exhibition, Marylebone Road, near Baker Street Station, a collection of wax figures of ancient and modern notabilities. The best time for visiting it is in the evening, by gaslight. Admission 1s. — At the back (6d. extra) are a room with various memorials of Napoleon I. and the '*Chamber of Horrors*', containing the guillotine which decapitated Louis XVI. and Marie Antoinette, and other articles of a ghastly nature.

Egyptian Hall, Piccadilly, opposite Burlington Arcade. Maskelyne and Cooke's conjuring and illusionary performances (at 3 and 8 p.m.; 5s., 3s., 2s., 1s.), concerts, art-exhibitions, etc.

Moore and Burgess Minstrels, St. James's Hall, Regent Street and Piccadilly. Adm. 5s., 3s., 2s., and 1s. At 8 p.m. daily; and on Mondays, Wednesdays, and Saturdays at 3 p.m. also.

Royal Aquarium and Summer and Winter Garden, Broad Sanctuary, Westminster (p. 273). Theatre, concerts, ballets, acrobatic, pantomimic, and conjuring performances. Adm. 1s. Various side-shows extra.

Agricultural Hall, Liverpool Road, Islington. Cattle shows, military tournaments (notably the Royal Military Tournament in June), lectures, dioramas, concerts, etc. — The *Mohawk Minstrels* (Christy Minstrels) also give their entertainments here.

NIAGARA HALL, York Street, Westminster (near St. James's Park Station). Skating-rink of real ice (adm. in the morning or evening 3s., in the afternoon 5s.).

CRYSTAL PALACE, Sydenham (p. 396). Occasional exhibitions, dog-shows, cat-shows, poultry-shows, etc.; pantomime in winter.

OLYMPIA, opposite the Addison Road Station, Kensington, a huge amphitheatre, holding 10,000 people, for spectacular performances, sporting and military shows, bicycling contests, promenade concerts, etc. (see daily papers; adm. 1-5s.).

EARL'S COURT EXHIBITION GROUNDS (Pl. G, 1, 2), with (1900) the Women's Exhibition, a gigantic wheel (300 ft. high), a belvedere tower 200 ft. high, a captive balloon, a panorama of Hungary, and the huge Empress Theatre (adm. 1s.).

ROSHERVILLE GARDENS, Gravesend. Music, dancing, theatre, zoological collection. Admission 6d. Reached by rail or steamer. Open in summer only.

WEMBLEY PARK, to the N.W. of London. Music, boating on artificial lake, athletic contests, balloon ascents, various outdoor amusements, and occasionally fireworks. Wembley Tower. Admission 6d.; tower 6d. extra. Reached by train from Baker St. Station (see R. 43).

ALEXANDRA PALACE, Muswell Hill (p. 375). Music, boating, switchback railway, café chantant, waxwork exhibition, fireworks, and various side-shows. Also special shows. Admission 1s.

13. Concerts and Exhibitions of Pictures.

Concerts.

ST. JAMES'S HALL (p. 285), with entrances from the Regent Street Quadrant and Piccadilly, used for concerts, balls, and public meetings. Among the concerts given here are the favourite *Monday and Saturday Popular Concerts*, held every Monday evening at 8 o'clock and every Saturday afternoon at 3 o'clock during the winter season, at which classical music is performed by eminent artistes. Admission to these concerts: stalls 5s., front gallery 3s., other seats 1s.

QUEEN'S HALL (p. 288), Langham Place, W., a large hall with 3000 seats. Among the concerts given here are the *Philharmonic Concerts*, in May and June, and the *Sunday Afternoon Concerts* (Mr. Henry J. Wood, conductor), in winter.

ROYAL ALBERT HALL, South Kensington (p. 343). Sunday afternoon concerts (seats 3d.-2s.) in winter, and musical fêtes and concerts on a large scale at uncertain intervals.

CRYSTAL PALACE, Sydenham (p. 396); occasional concerts.

AGRICULTURAL HALL, Islington (p. 68). Occasional concerts, which are advertised in the daily papers.

STEINWAY HALL, 15 Lower Seymour Street, Portman Square. Mr. Clifford Harrison gives his recitals here.

St. George's Hall (p. 287), 4 Langham Place, W.

Princess's Concert Room, at the back of the Princess's Theatre (p. 67); occasional concerts.

Grafton Gallery, Grafton Street, Bond Street.

International Hall, above the Café Monico (p. 17).

The Panel Concert Date List, obtained free on application (enclosing stamped envelope) to Mr. Louis A. Back (see p. 61), contains all the forthcoming concert-engagements of importance.

Exhibitions of Pictures.

Royal Academy of Fine Arts, Burlington House, Piccadilly (p. 283). Exhibition of the works of living British painters and sculptors, from first Monday in May to first Monday in August. Open daily 8-7; admission 1s., catalogue 1s. During the last week open also from 7.30 to 10.30 p.m.; admission 6d. Exhibition of the works of Ancient Masters in January and February. Diploma and Gibson galleries, open throughout the year (see p. 283; entrance to the right of the main entrance).

The New Gallery, 121 Regent Street. Summer and winter exhibitions. Admission 1s.

Royal Society of Painters in Water Colours, 5a Pall Mall East. Open from Easter to the end of July, and from December to March; admission 1s., catalogue 1s.

Royal Institute of Painters in Water Colours, Piccadilly Galleries, 191 Piccadilly. Exhibitions from March to the end of June (9-6; 1s.).

Society of British Artists, 6½ Suffolk Street, Pall Mall. Exhibitions from 1st April to 1st Aug. (9-6) and from 1st Dec. to 1st March (9-5). Admission 1s.

Royal Society of Painter-Etchers. Spring exhibitions at 5a Pall Mall East.

Society of Oil Painters. Exhibition at 191 Piccadilly from Nov. to Jan. (10-4; 1s.).

Society of Lady Artists. Summer exhibition at the Suffolk Street Galleries (see above); admission 1s., catalogue 6d.

Doré Gallery, 35 New Bond Street, containing large paintings by *Gustave Doré*. Daily, 10-6; 1s.

Grafton Gallery, Grafton Street, Bond Street; occasionally.

Princes Club Skating Rink, Knightsbridge; occasionally.

There are also in winter and spring various exhibitions of French, Belgian, German, Dutch, and other paintings at 120 Pall Mall (French Gallery), 39 Old Bond Street (Agnew's), 47 New Bond Street (Hanover Gallery), 5 Regent Street (Goupil Gallery), 235a Regent Street (Holland Gallery), 148 New Bond Street (Fine Art Society), 160 New Bond Street (Dowdeswell Galleries), 157 New Bond Street (Continental Gallery), 5 Haymarket (Mr. Tooth), 7 Haymarket (McLean's), the St. James's Gallery, 4a King Street (Mr. Mendoza), etc. Usual charge 1s.

14. Races, Sports, and Games.

Horse Racing. The principal race-meetings taking place within easy distance of London are the following: —

1. The *Epsom Summer Meeting*, at which the *Derby* and *Oaks* are run. The former invariably takes place on a Wednesday, and the latter on a Friday, the date being generally within a fortnight before or after Whitsuntide (end of May or beginning of June).

The Derby was instituted by the Earl of Derby in 1780, and the value of the stakes now sometimes exceeds 6000l. The length of the course is 1½ M., and it was gone over by Persimmon in 1896 and by Diamond Jubilee in 1900 in 2 min. 42 sec., the shortest time on record. Both horses and mares are allowed to compete for the Derby (mares carrying 3lb. less weight), while the Oaks is confined to mares. In both cases the age of the horses running must be three years. To view these races London empties itself annually by road and rail, though Parliament no longer suspends its sitting on Derby Day, once its almost invariable custom. The London and Brighton Railway Company (London Bridge and Victoria stations) has a station at Epsom close to the course, and this is the most convenient route. It may also be reached by the London and South Western Railway from Waterloo. The increased facilities of reaching Epsom by train have somewhat diminished the popularity of the road; but the traveller who would see the Derby Day and its characteristic sights thoroughly will not regret his choice if he select the latter. A decently appointed open carriage and pair, holding four persons, will cost 8-10l., everything included. A hansom cab can be had for rather less than half that amount, but an arrangement should be made with the driver on the previous day. A seat on a coach or brake may usually be secured for about 2l., luncheon included. The appearance of Epsom Downs on Derby Day, crowded with myriads of human beings, is one of the most striking and animated sights ever witnessed in the neighbourhood of London, and will interest the ordinary visitor more than the great race itself.

2. The *Ascot Week* is about a fortnight after the Derby. The Gold Cup Day is on Thursday, when some members of the Royal Family usually drive up the course in state, attended by the master and huntsmen of the Royal Buckhounds. The course is reached by train from Waterloo; or the visitor may travel by the Great Western Railway (Paddington Station) to Windsor and drive thence to Ascot.

3. At *Sandown*, near Esher, at *Kempton Park*, Sunbury, and at the *Hurst Park Club*, Hampton, races and steeple-chases are held several times during the year.

4. The *Epsom Spring Meeting*, lasting for three days, on one of which the City and Suburban Handicap is decided.

Besides the above there are numerous smaller race-meetings near London, but with the exception of that at *Croydon* they will hardly repay the trouble of a visit, as they are largely patronised by the 'rough' element. The stranger should, if possible, attend races and other public gatherings in company with a friend who is well acquainted with the best method of seeing the sport. Much trouble and disappointment will be thereby avoided.

Newmarket, the headquarters of racing, and *Goodwood Races*, see *Baedeker's Great Britain.*

Hunting. This sport is carried on throughout England from autumn to spring. Cub-hunting generally begins in September and continues until 31st October. Regular fox-hunting then takes its place and lasts till about the middle of April. Hare-hunting lasts from 28th Oct. to 27th Feb., and buck-hunting begins on 14th September. Should the traveller be staying in the country he will probably have but little difficulty in seeing a meet of a pack of foxhounds. The Surrey fox-hounds are the nearest to London. There is a pack of harriers at Brighton. The Royal Buckhounds often meet in the vicinity of Windsor, and when this is the case the journey can be easily made from London. The quarry is a stag, which is allowed to escape from a cart. The huntsmen and whippers-in wear a scarlet and gold uniform. The followers of the hounds wear scarlet, black, and indeed any colour, and this diversity, coupled with the large attendance in carriages, on foot, and on horseback, makes the scene a very lively one. For meets of hounds, see the *Field*.

Fishing (roach, perch, gudgeon, pike, barbel, dace, and trout) can be indulged in at all places on the *Thames* between Richmond and Wallingford. No permission is required, except in private waters. The services of a fisherman, with punt and tackle, can be secured at a charge of about 10*s.* per day, the hirer providing him with dinner and beer. The *Lea* (p. 416), *Darent, Brent, Colne*, etc., also afford good opportunities for the London angler. See the *Anglers' Diary* (Field Office, 346 Strand; 1*s.* 6*d.*), and compare p. 416.

Cricket. *Lord's* at St. John's Wood (p. 299), the headquarters of the Marylebone Club (sec., Mr. F. E. Lacey), is the chief cricket ground in London. Here are played, in June and July, the Eton and Harrow, the Oxford and Cambridge, and many others matches. The *Kennington Oval* (p. 379), the headquarters of the Surrey County Club, is also an important cricket-centre. See also pp. 401, 414.

Golf. Golf, which is in season all the year round, has become exceedingly popular in England within the last few years. Near London there are golfing-courses at *Blackheath* (Royal Blackheath Club, founded in 1608), *Richmond, Wimbledon, Tooting, Wembley, Northwood, Eltham, Cassiobury Park, West Drayton, Ealing, Mitcham, Stanmore*, and a score of other places.

Football. Football is in season from about September to April. The chief matches under the Rugby Football Union rules are played at the *Rectory Field, Blackheath* (headquarters of the Blackheath Football Club); *Richmond Old Deer Park* (London Scottish Club); and *Richmond Athletic Ground* (Richmond Club). The *Crystal Palace* and the *Essex County Ground* at Leyton are the scenes of the best matches under the Football Association rules. The Oxford and Cambridge matches (both Rugby and Association) are decided at *Queen's Club, West Kensington* (p. 103).

Athletics. The chief scene of athletic sports of all kinds is *Stamford Bridge*, on the Fulham Road, where the *London Athletic Club* has its headquarters. The Amateur Championships of the

United Kingdom are decided here when these sports are held in London (every third year). The University Sports, between Oxford and Cambridge, take place at Queen's Club, in the Boat Race week (see p. 74). The card now comprises ten 'events'. It was at Queen's Club that the International contest between Oxford and Cambridge on the one side and Harvard and Yale on the other took place in 1899. The *German Gymnastic Society*, 26 Pancras Road, King's Cross, takes the lead among all gymnastic clubs; about half of its 7-800 members are English. The *Amateur Athletic Association* consists of representatives of the leading athletic clubs.

Boxing. Among the chief boxing clubs in London are the *West London Boxing Club* and the *Cestus Boxing Club*, and there are also boxing clubs in connection with the German Gymnastic Society, the London Athletic Club, etc. Most of these are affiliated to the *Amateur Boxing Association*. A competition for amateur boxers is held yearly, the prizes being handsome challenge cups presented by the Marquis of Queensberry.

Lawn Tennis. The governing and controlling body for this pastime is the *Lawn Tennis Association* (sec., Mr. W. H. Collins), established in 1888. The Lawn Tennis Championship of the World is competed for early in July on the ground of the *All England Lawn Tennis Club*, Wimbledon, and the Covered Court Championship and other important competitions take place at Queen's Club. Courts open to strangers are found at the Crystal Palace, Battersea Park, and other public gardens, drill-halls, etc., but this game cannot be enjoyed to perfection except in club or private grounds.

Rackets and **Court Tennis** are played at Lord's (p. 299), Prince's Club, and Queen's Club. The Amateur Championship in tennis and the Public Schools and University Rackets Competitions are decided at Queen's Club.

Cycling. There are now a great many cycling clubs in London, the oldest of which was founded in 1870. The chief bicycle race-meetings are held at Catford, Putney, Herne Hill, the Crystal Palace, and Wood Green.

The English 'rule of the road' is the reverse of that on the Continent and in America; keep to the *left* in meeting, to the *right* in overtaking vehicles. Lamps must be lit at dusk.

The headquarters of the *National Cyclists' Union* are at 27 Chancery Lane (sec. Mr. Sam. R. Noble), and those of the *Cyclists' Touring Club* are at 47 Victoria Street, Westminster (sec., Mr. E. R. Shipton). The chief consul for the foreign district of the latter club is Mr. E. A. Tafel, 162 Cecil Street, Manchester; the representative for the United States of America is Mr. Joseph Pennell, 14 Buckingham Street, Strand. All cyclists touring in Great Britain will find it advantageous to join the C. T. C. Exhibitions of bicycles, tricycles, and their accessories are held in London annually. Compare the *Monthly Gazette* of the Cyclists' Touring Club.

Hockey is rapidly growing in popularity, and there are over thirty clubs in or near London affiliated to the *Hockey Association*.

Baseball, though played extensively in the Midland Counties, has not taken root in or near London.

Lacrosse is now played by about a score of clubs in or near London, and the chief authority in this part of the country is the *South of England Lacrosse Association.* The final ties of the International and North v. South matches are generally played either on the Richmond Athletic Ground or at the Crystal Palace.

Archery. The focus of this sport in London is in the grounds of the *Royal Toxopholite Society,* Regent's Park (see p. 294).

Croquet has of late come again into favour and is played at the Crystal Palace, Wimbledon, and elsewhere.

Aquatics. The chief event in the year is the *Oxford and Cambridge Boat Race,* usually rowed on the second Saturday before Easter. The course is on the Thames, from Putney to Mortlake; the distance is just over $4^{1}/_{4}$ M., and the time occupied in rowing it varies from just under 20 min. to 23 min., according to the state of the wind and tide. The Londoners pour out to see the boat-race in almost as great crowds as to the Derby, sympathetically exhibiting in some portion of their attire either the dark-blue colours of Oxford or the light-blue of Cambridge. — There are also several regattas held upon the Thames. The best are those at *Henley* (at the end of June or the beginning of July), *Marlow, Staines,* and *Walton.* To Henley crews are usually sent from the universities of Oxford, Cambridge, and Dublin, by Eton College, and by the London Rowing Club, the Leander, the Thames Club, and other clubs of more or less note. Crews from American universities sometimes take part in the proceedings. On Aug. 1st a boat-race takes place among young Thames watermen for *Doggett's Coat and Badge,* a prize founded by Doggett, the comedian, in 1715. The course is from Old Swan Pier, London Bridge, to the site of the Old Swan at Chelsea, about 5 miles. — Yacht-races are held at the mouth of the Thames in summer, under the auspices of the *Royal Thames Yacht Club,* the *Royal London Yacht Club,* and the *New Thames Yacht Club.* See the *Rowing Almanack* (1s.; Field Office).

Swimming. London contains nearly 100 swimming clubs, with their headquarters at the Public Baths (p 23). Most of them are affiliated to the *Life Saving Society* (8 Bayley Street, Bedford Square, W.C.), established in 1891. The *Amateur Swimming Association* conducts various championship competitions, swum in the Thames and elsewhere. *Water Polo* is also very popular.

Skating. Among the chief skating resorts in or near London are the Welsh Harp (p. 417), Ruislip Reservoir (p. 420), Wembley Park (p. 420), the Serpentine (p. 331), Regent's Park (p. 294), Hampstead Heath (p. 372), and (indoors) Niagara (p. 69). The headquarters of the *London Skating Club* are in the gardens of the Toxopholite Society (p. 294); the secretary of the *National Skating Association* is Mr. H. Ellington, 6 Suffolk Street, Pall Mall East.

15. Embassies and Consulates. Colonial Representatives. Bankers.

Embassies.

America, United States of. Embassy, 123 Victoria Street, S.W. (office-hours 11-3); ambassador, *Hon. Joseph H. Choate.* Consulate, 12 St. Helen's Place, Bishopsgate, E. C.; consul-general, *William M. Osborne, Esq.;* vice-consul-general, *Richard Westacott, Esq.*

Austria. Embassy, 18 Belgrave Square. Consulate, 22 Laurence Pountney Lane, E.C.

Belgium. Legation, 18 Harrington Gardens, S.W. Consulate, 29 Great St. Helen's, E.C.

Brazil. Legation, 55 Curzon Street, W. Consulate, 6 Great Winchester Street, E.C.

China. Legation, 49 Portland Place, W.

Denmark. Legation, 24 Pont Street, S.W. Consulate, 1 Muscovy Court, Tower Hill, E.C.

France. Embassy, Albert Gate House, Hyde Park. General Consulate, 4 Christopher Street, Finsbury, E.C.

Germany. Embassy, 9 Carlton House Terrace. General Consulate, 49 Finsbury Square, E.C.

Greece. Chargé d'Affaires, 31 Marloes Road, Cromwell Road, S.W. Géneral Consulate, 19 Eastcheap, E.C.

Italy. Embassy, 20 Grosvenor Square, W. General Consulate, 44 Finsbury Square, E.C.

Japan. Legation, 4 Grosvenor Gardens, S.W. Consulate, 84 Bishopsgate Street Within, E. C.

Netherlands. Legation, 8 Grosvenor Gardens, S.W. Consulate, 4 Coleman Street, E.C.

Persia. Legation, 30 Ennismore Gardens, S.W. Consulate, 165 Fenchurch Street, E.C.

Portugal. Legation, 12 Gloucester Place, Portman Square, W. Consulate, 6 South Street, Finsbury, E.C.

Russia. Embassy, Chesham House, Belgrave Square, S.W. Consulate, 17 Great Winchester Street, E.C.

Spain. Embassy, 1 Grosvenor Gardens, S.W. Consulate, 20 Mark Lane, E.C.

Sweden and Norway. Legation, 52 Pont Street, S.W. Consulate, 24 Great Winchester Street, E.C.

Switzerland. Legation and Consulate, 52 Lexham Gardens, W.

Turkey. Embassy, 1 Bryanston Square. Consulate, 29 Mincing Lane, E.C.

Representatives of British Colonies.

Canada, Dominion of. High Commissioner, *Lord Strathcona and Mountroyal,* 17 Victoria Street, S.W.

Cape Colony. Agent General, *Sir David Tennant*, 112 Victoria Street, S.W.

Natal. Agent General, *Sir Walter Peace*, 64 Victoria Street, S.W.

New South Wales. Agent General, *Hon. Henry Copeland*, 9 Victoria Street, S.W.

New Zealand. Agent General, *Hon. W. Pember Reeves*, 13 Victoria Street, S.W.

Queensland. Agent General, *Sir Horace Tozer*, 1 Victoria Street, S.W.

South Australia. Agent General, *Hon. Dr. J. A. Cockburn*, 1 Crosby Square, E. C.

Tasmania. Agent General, *Sir Philip Oakley Fysh*, 5 Victoria Street, S.W.

Victoria. Agent General, *Sir Andrew Clarke*, 15 Victoria Street, S.W.

West Australia. Agent General, *Hon. Edw. H. Wittenoom*, 15 Victoria Street, S.W.

Bankers.

PRIVATE BANKS : — Messrs. *Barclay & Co.*, 54 Lombard Street and 1 Pall Mall East; *Child*, 1 Fleet Street; *Coutts*, 59 Strand; *Drummond*, 49 Charing Cross; *Glyn, Mills, & Co.*, 67 Lombard Street; *Hoare & Co.*, 37 Fleet Street; *Robarts, Lubbock, & Co.*, 15 Lombard Street; *Smith, Payne, & Smiths*, 1 Lombard Street, etc.

JOINT STOCK BANKS : — *London and County*, 21 Lombard Street; *London Joint Stock*, 5 Prince's Street, Mansion House, E. C.; *London and Provincial*, 7 Bank Buildings; *London and South Western*, 170 Fenchurch Street; *London and Westminster*, 41 Lothbury; *Union Bank of London*, 2 Prince's Street, Mansion House, E.C.; *Lloyds*, 72 Lombard Street and 222 Strand; *Williams, Deacon, & Manchester & Salford Bank*, 20 Birchin Lane, etc.

AMERICAN BANKS : — *Brown, Shipley, & Co.*, Founders' Court, Lothbury, E. C., and 123 Pall Mall, S.W.; *Baring Brothers*, 7-9 Bishopsgate Street Within, E.C.; *J. S. Morgan & Co. (Drexel & Co.)*, 22 Old Broad Street, E. C.; *Knauth, Nachod, & Kühne*, at the Alliance Bank, Bartholomew Lane, E.C.; *London, Paris, & American Bank*, 40 Threadneedle Street, E.C.; *Bank of British North America*, 3 Clement's Lane, Lombard Street, E. C.

All the banking companies have branch-offices in different parts of London, some as many as fifteen or twenty.

MONEY CHANGERS. *Cook's Tourist Offices*, Ludgate Circus, 445 Strand, 33 Piccadilly, 13 Cockspur Street, 82 Oxford Street, Euston Road (in front of St. Pancras Station), and at the corner of Gracechurch Street and Leadenhall Street; *Gaze's Tourist Offices*, 142 Strand, 4 Northumberland Avenue, 150 Piccadilly, 53 Queen Victoria Street, and 32 Westbourne Grove ; *Davison*, 264 & 318 Strand; *Whiteley*, 31-61 Westbourne Grove; *Smart*, 72 Westbourne Grove; *Anglo-American Exchange* (p. 21); *Lady Guide Association* (p. 83).

16. Divine Service.

To enable visitors belonging to different religious denominations to attend their respective places of worship, a list is here given of the principal churches in London. The denominations are arranged in alphabetical order. The chief edifices of the Church of England are noticed throughout the Handbook.

There are about 700 churches of the Church of England in London or its immediate vicinity, of which about 70 are parish-churches in the City, 50 parish-churches in the Metropolitan district beyond, and 550 ecclesiastical parish or district churches or chapels, some connected with asylums, missions, etc. Of the Nonconformist churches, which amount to about 800 in all, 240 are Independent, 130 Baptist, 150 Wesleyan, and 50 Roman Catholic. — The hours named after each church are those of divine service on Sundays; when no hour is specified it is understood that the hours of the regular Sunday services are 11 a.m. and 6.30 p.m. Many of the Saturday morning and evening papers give a list of the principal preachers on Sunday.

BAPTIST CHAPELS: — *Metropolitan Tabernacle*, Newington Butts, close to the Elephant and Castle (p. 379), the church of the late Rev. C. H. Spurgeon; services at 11 and 6.30. — *Westbourne Park Chapel (Dr. Clifford)*; services at 11 and 7. — *Bloomsbury Chapel*, Shaftesbury Avenue; services at 11 and 7. — *Park Square Chapel*, Regent's Park; services at 11 and 7.

CATHOLIC APOSTOLIC CHURCHES: — Gordon Square, Euston Road; services at 6, 10, 2, and 5. — Mare Street, Hackney. — College Street, Chelsea. — Duncan Street, Islington, and others. — Services various, but almost always, *inter alia*, at 6 a.m. and 5 p.m.

CONGREGATIONALISTS or INDEPENDENTS: — *City Temple*, Holborn Viaduct *(Dr. Parker)*; services at 11 and 7 (lecture on Thurs. at noon). — *Union Chapel*, Islington. — *Westminster Chapel*, James Street, Westminster. — *Weigh House Chapel*, Duke Street, Grosvenor Square; 11 and 7. — *Kensington Chapel*, Allen Street, Kensington. — *Christ Church*, Westminster Bridge Road; the tower and spire of this church were built by Americans in London as a memorial of Abraham Lincoln. — *Whitefield's Tabernacle*, Tottenham Court Road; 11 and 7.

FRIENDS or QUAKERS: — Meeting-houses at 52 St. Martin's Lane, Trafalgar Square (service at 11), and Devonshire House, 12 Bishopsgate Street (services at 11 and 6.30). There are in all 25 meeting-houses in the London District.

INDEPENDENTS, see Congregationalists.

IRVINGITES, see Catholic Apostolic Churches.

JEWS: — *Great Synagogue*, St. James' Place, Aldgate. — *New Synagogue*, Great St. Helen's, Leadenhall Street. — *West London Synagogue*, 34 Upper Berkeley Street, Edgware Road. — *Central Synagogue*, Great Portland Street. — *Bayswater Synagogue*, Chichester Place, Harrow Road. — *West End Synagogue*, St. Petersburg Place, Bayswater Road. — *Spanish & Portuguese Synagogues*, Bevis Marks, E. C., and Lauderdale Road, Maida Vale. — Service begins at sunset on Fridays. The office of the Chief Rabbi is at 22 Finsbury Square, E.C.

METHODISTS. a. Wesleyan Methodists: — *Wesley's Chapel*, 47 City Road; *Great Queen Street Chapel*, Lincoln's Inn Fields; *Finsbury Park Chapel*, Wilberforce Road; *Hinde Street Chapel*, Manchester Square; *Mostyn Road Chapel*, Brixton Road; *Peckham Chapel*, Queen's Road, Peckham; *Welsh Wesleyan Chapel*, 45 Almorah Road, Islington. — b. Other Methodists: — *Brunswick Chapel* (New Connexion), 156 Great Dover Street, Southwark; *Surrey Chapel* (Primitive Methodists), Blackfriars Road, S. E.; *United Methodist Free Chapel*, Willow Street, Tabernacle Square, Moorgate; *United Free Chapel*, Queen's Road, Bayswater.

NEW JERUSALEM or SWEDENBORGIAN CHURCHES: — Palace Gardens Terrace, Kensington. — Argyle Square, King's Cross. — Camden Road, Holloway. — *College Chapel*, Devonshire Street, Islington. Services at 11 and 7.

PRESBYTERIANS: — *Scottish National Church* (Church of Scotland), Pont Street, Belgravia (*Dr. Donald Macleod*); 11 and 6.30. — *Regent Square Church*, Regent's Square, Gray's Inn Road; services at 11 and 7. — *Marylebone Church*, Upper George Street, Bryanston Square, Edgware Road. — *St. John's Wood Presbyterian Church*, Marlborough Place, St. John's Wood (*Dr. Munro Gibson*). — *Trinity Church*, Clapham Road (*Dr. MacEwan*). — *Welsh Calvinist Chapel*, Cambridge Circus, Charing Cross Road. — Office of the English Presbyterian Church, 7 East India Avenue, E. C.

ROMAN CATHOLICS: — *St. George's Cathedral*, St. George's Road, Southwark; various services. — *Pro-Cathedral*, High Street, Kensington; services at 7, 8, 9, 10, 11, 4, and 7. — *Oratory*, South Kensington; services at 6.30-11, 3.30, and 7. — *Jesuit Church*, Farm Street, Berkeley Square. — *St. Mary's*, Moorfields, close to Liverpool Street Station; services at 7, 8, 9.30, 10, 11, 3.30, and 7. — *St. Mary of the Angels*, Westmoreland Road, Bayswater. — *St. Etheldreda's*, Ely Place, Holborn; principal services at 11.15 and 7. — *St. Patrick's*, Soho Square. — *St. Joseph's*, Highgate Hill. — *St. Dominic*, Maitland Park, Haverstock Hill. — *New Priory*, Quex Road, Kilburn. — *St. Mary's*, Cadogan Street, Chelsea. — *St. John of Jerusalem*, Great Ormond Street, W.C. — High Mass usually begins at 11 a.m., and Vespers at 7 p.m. The Low Masses are at 7 or 8 a.m., and there is usually an afternoon service also.

SWEDENBORGIANS, see New Jerusalem Churches.

UNITARIANS: — *Little Portland Street Chapel* (Rev. P. H. Wicksteed). — *Rosslyn Hill Chapel*, Hampstead (*Dr. Brooke Herford*). — *Essex Church*, Notting Hill Gate. — *Effra Road Chapel*, Brixton. — *Wandsworth Chapel*, East Hill. — Offices, Essex Hall, Essex Street, Strand.

WESLEYANS, see Methodists.

The services of the *South Place Ethical Society* are held at the

South Place Institute at 11.15 a.m.; the lectures of the *West London Ethical Society (Dr. Stanton Coit)* are given at the Royal Palace Hotel (p. 10), at 11 a.m. — The *Positivists (Mr. Fred. Harrison)* meet in Newton Hall, Fetter Lane, at 7.30 p.m. — *Theistic Church (Rev. Charles Voysey)*, Swallow Street, Piccadilly; 11 and 7. — *Ethical Religion Society (Dr. Washington Sullivan)*, Steinway Hall, 15 Lower Seymour Street; 11.15 a.m.

The headquarters of the *Salvation Army* are at 101 Queen Victoria Street, E. C.; of its Social Wing at 20 Whitechapel Road, E. C. — The *Church Army* has its headquarters at 130 Edgware Road.

Foreign Churches: — *Danish Church* (Lutheran), King Street, Poplar; service at 11 a.m. Danish service also at the German Chapel Royal (see below) at 4.30 p.m. — *Dutch Church* (Reformed Calvinist), 6 Austin Friars, near the Bank; service at 11.15 a.m. — *French Protestant*, Soho Square; services at 11 and 7. — *French Protestant Evangelical Church*, Monmouth Road, Westbourne Grove, Bayswater; services at 11 and 7. — *French Anglican Church*, 233 Shaftesbury Avenue; services at 11 and 3.30. — *French Roman Catholic Chapels*, Little George Street (French & Portuguese Embassies), and at 5 Leicester Place, Leicester Square; various services. — *German Chapel Royal* (Lutheran), St. James's Palace; service at 11.45 a.m. — *German Lutheran Church* (lately in the Savoy), 46 Cleveland Street, Fitzroy Square; services at 11 and 6.45. — *German Lutheran Churches*, in Little Alie Street, Whitechapel, and at Dalston. — *German Reformed Church*, Goulston Street, Aldgate. — *German Evangelical Church*, Fowler Road, Islington. — *German Methodist Church (Böhlerkirche)*, Commercial Road; services at 11 and 6.30. — *German Roman Catholic Chapel*, 47 Union Street, Whitechapel; services at 9, 11, 3, and 7. — *German Synagogue*, see Jews. — *Greek Chapel* (Russian), 32 Welbeck Street, Cavendish Square; service at 11 a.m. — *Greek Church* (St. Sophia), Moscow Road, Bayswater; service at 11.15 a.m. — *Italian Roman Catholic Church (St. Peter's)*, Hatton Garden, Clerkenwell Road, E.C.; services at 11, 4, and 7. — *Norwegian Lutheran Church (Ebenezer)*, Bickley Road, Rotherhithe, S.E.; services at 11 and 5. — *Swedish Protestant Church*, Prince's Square, St. George's Street, Shadwell; service at 11 a.m (p. 167). — *Swiss Protestant Church*, 78 Endell Street, Long Acre; service at 11 a.m.

17. Post and Telegraph Offices. Parcels Companies. Commissionnaires. Messengers. Lady Guides.

Post Office. The General Post Office is in St. Martin's le Grand (p. 122). The *Poste Restante Office* is on the S. (right) side of the portico (p. 122), and is open from 8 a.m. to 9 p.m. There are also Poste Restante Offices at all the branch-offices. Letters to be called for, which should have the words 'Poste Restante' added to the address, are delivered to applicants on the production of their passports or other proof of identity, but it is better to give correspondents a private address. Letters addressed to persons who have not been found are kept for 2–8 weeks (according to their place of origin), and then sent to the *Dead Letter Office* for return to the writer, or for destruction. Such letters, however, will be returned within a specified time to the writer, if a request to that effect appear on the envelope.

Unprepaid letters are charged double postage, but may be refused by the addressee. The postage for the whole of Great Britain, Ireland, and the islands in the British seas is 1d. for *Letters* not exceeding 4 oz., and ¹/₂d. for every additional 2 oz.; for *Newspapers* ¹/₂d. each, irrespective of weight. The fee for registration for a letter or other packet is 2d.; special registered-letter envelopes are supplied at 2¹/₄-3d. each (postage extra). For letters to any British colony, except Australia and Cape Colony, the rate is 1d., to any other part of the world 2¹/₂d. for every ¹/₂ oz. For *Book Packets* ¹/₂d. per 2 oz. is charged for Great Britain and the countries of the postal union. No inland book-packet may exceed 2 ft. in length, 1 ft. in width, and 1 ft. in depth, or 5lbs. in weight. Newspapers for abroad pay book-post rates. *Post Cards* for use in the British Islands are issued at 5¹/₂d. or 6d. per packet of ten (thin and thick); for countries included in the postal union and some others, at 1d. each; reply post-cards may be had at double these rates. Inland post-cards are transmissible abroad with an additional ¹/₂d. stamp. Private post-cards, conforming in size and thickness to the official cards and prepaid by means of adhesive stamps, may also be used; those for abroad must have the words 'Post Card' on the address side (sold by most stationers). *Letter Cards*, the communication on which is concealed from view, are sold at 1¹/₄d. each or eight for 9d. Envelopes of two sizes, with embossed ¹/₂d. stamps, of three sizes, with embossed 1d. stamps, and of two sizes, with embossed 2¹/₂d. stamps, and newspaper wrappers with impressed ¹/₂d. or 1d. stamps, are also sold.

The number of daily deliveries of letters in London varies from six to twelve according to the distance from the head office at St. Martin's le Grand. On Sundays there is no delivery, but letters posted in the pillar boxes within the town limits and in some of the nearer suburbs are collected in time for the general day mails and for the first London district delivery on the following day. Letters for the evening mails must be posted in the pillars before 5 p.m., in the central district before 6 p.m., or at the General Post Office, with an additional ¹/₂d. stamp, up to 7.30 p.m. Foreign letters may be posted at the General Post Office till 7 p.m. with an additional 1d. stamp; till 7.15 with 2d. extra; till 7.30 with 3d. extra; and at the termini for Continental trains till 8 p.m. with 4d. extra. Most of the head district offices are open on Sunday from 8 a.m. to 8 p.m. Full official information will be found in the *Post Office Guide* (quarterly; 6d.), or the *Post Office Handbook* (half-yearly; 1d.).

EXPRESS LETTERS. About 270 of the chief post-offices in London receive letters and parcels to be delivered in London and its suburbs by special messenger at a charge of 3d. per mile or part of a mile. Parcels over 1lb. are charged an extra fee of 1d. for every additional lb. or part of a lb. Express letters handed in at other post-offices are forwarded in the ordinary course of post to the nearest Express Delivery Office, whence they are sent on by special messenger.

London is divided into eight POSTAL DISTRICTS, — the Eastern, Northern, North Western, Western, South Western, South Eastern, East Central, and West Central, — which are designated by the capital letters E., N., N.W., etc. Each has its district post-office, from which letters are distributed to the surrounding district. At these chief district offices letters may be posted about $1/2$ hr. later than at the branches or pillars. The delivery of London letters is facilitated by the addition to the address of the initials of the postal district. The number of offices and pillars in London is upwards of 3600 and the number of people employed is about 17,000.

PARCEL POST. The rate of postage for an inland parcel is 3d. for a weight not exceeding 1lb.; each additional pound 1d. The maximum length allowed for such a parcel is 3 ft. 6 in., and the length and girth combined must not exceed 6 ft.; the maximum weight is 11lbs. Registration and insurance (up to 120l.) are allowed. Such parcels must be handed in at a post-office, not posted in a letter-box. — A *Parcel Post Service*, at various rates, is also established between the United Kingdom and most foreign countries (not including the United States) and British colonies. A 'Customs Declaration' and a 'Despatch Note' (forms to be obtained at a post-office) must be filled up for each foreign parcel.

POST OFFICE MONEY ORDERS are issued for sums not exceeding 10l. at the numerous *Money Order Offices* connected with the post-office, at least one of which is to be found in every post town in the United Kingdom. For sums under 1l. the charge for transmission is 2d.; over 1l. and under 3l., 3d.; over 3l., 4d. *Foreign Money Orders*, payable in the countries of the postal union, are issued at a charge of 6d. up to 2l., 1s. up to 6l., and 1s. 6d. up to 10l.

POSTAL ORDERS, of the value of 1s., 1s. 6d., 2s., 2s. 6d., 3s., 3s. 6d., 4s., 4s. 6d., 5s., 7s. 6d., 10s., 10s. 6d., 15s., and 20s., are issued at a small charge varying from $1/2$d. to $11/2$d. They are payable at any Money Order Office in the United Kingdom. If not presented for payment within three months from the last day of the month of issue, a fresh commission is charged equal to the original cost. By the use of not more than five 1d. stamps, affixed to the face of the order, any broken amount may be made up.

TELEGRAPH MONEY ORDERS are issued for sums not exceeding 10l. by all post-offices transacting telegraph and money order business. A charge of not less than 6d. is made for the official telegram of advice, in addition to which a commission of 4d. is charged for sums not exceeding 3l., and 6d. for sums over 3l. Telegraph money orders may also be sent to a few foreign countries (not including the United States of America).

Telegraphs. The whole telegraph system of Great Britain, with the sole exception of wires for the private use of the railway-companies, belongs to Government (p. 122). The tariff for inland telegrams is $1/2$d. per word, with a minimum charge of 6d.; the addresses are counted as part of the telegram. Replies up to 48 words may be prepaid. Telegraph-forms with embossed stamps may be purchased singly (6d.) or in books of 20 (10s. 2d.). Telegrams are received at all railway-stations and almost all post-offices throughout the country. They may also be posted in any pillar box or post-office and are in that case, if properly prepaid, despatched as soon as possible after the box is cleared. London and its suburbs contain more than 300 telegraph-offices, open from 8 a.m. to 8 p.m. Always open are: Central Station, St. Martin's le Grand (corner of Newgate Street); London Bridge Station; Liverpool St. Station; St. Pancras Station; Victoria Station; Waterloo

Station; West Strand; Willesden Junction Station; Stratford Railway Station. The office at King's Cross Station is open always except 1.30 to 2.30 on Sunday.

Foreign Telegrams. The tariff per word for telegrams to *Belgium, Holland, France,* or *Germany* is 2*d.*; *Italy, Austria, Hungary, Denmark, Norway,* or *Switzerland* 3*d.*; *Spain, Portugal,* or *Sweden* 3½*d.*; *Russia in Europe* 5½*d.*; *Turkey* or *Greece* 6½*d.*; *Canada* 1*s.* - 1*s.* 6*d.*; *United States* 1*s.*-1*s.* 6*d.*; *India* 3*s.* 8*d.* to 4*s.*; *Cape Colony* or *Natal* 4*s.*; *Australia* 4*s.* 7*d.* to 5*s.* 1*d.*; *West Indies* 1*s.* 8*d.* to 7*s.* 5*d.*; *South America* 3*s.* 1*d.* to 7*s.* 7*d.* The minimum in any case is 10*d.*

Telephones. The telephonic communication of London is mainly in the hands of the *National Telephone Co.,* the head office of which is in Oxford Court, Cannon Street, City. There are numerous call-rooms throughout London and district, open to the public at the rate of 3*d.* for each three minutes' conversation. — Telephonic communication with Paris was established in 1891. The public call-offices are at the General Post Office West (p. 122; always open), West Strand Office (always open), and Threadneedle Street Post Office (open on week-days from 8 a.m. to 8 p.m.). Charge 8*s.* per three minutes. [Paris time is 10 min. in advance of London time, a fact to be taken into account in arranging for conversations with Paris correspondents.]

Parcels Companies. Parcels for London and the environs are transmitted by the *London Parcels Delivery Company* (head-office, Rolls Buildings, Fetter Lane, Fleet Street), and by *Carter, Paterson, & Co.* (126 Goswell Road, E.C.), both with numerous receiving offices distributed throughout London, usually in shops indicated by notices. Within a radius of 3 M. a parcel under 4lbs. is sent for 3*d.*, under 14lbs., 6*d.*, under 28lbs., 9*d.*, and so on up to 112lbs. for 1*s.* 2*d.*; beyond 3 M. the charges are from 4*d.* upwards. [A card with C. P. in large letters, conspicuously exhibited in the window, will arrest the first of Carter and Paterson's vans which happens to pass the house.] Parcels for all the chief towns of England are conveyed by *Pickford & Co.* (57 Gresham Street, E.C.), but the Post Office is the best carrier for packages not exceeding 11lbs. in weight. Parcels for the Continent are forwarded by the *Continental Daily Parcels Express* (53 Gracechurch Street) and the *Globe Parcels Express* (20 St. Paul's Churchyard and 9 Blenheim Street, New Bond Street), which work in connection with the continental post-offices. Parcels for America are forwarded by *Staveley & Co.'s American European Express,* 45a Jewin Street, E.C., the *American Express,* 3 Waterloo Place, S.W., and the *American Line Steamship Co.* (p. 3). *Pitt & Scott* (25 Cannon Street, City, and 69 Shaftesbury Avenue) and *G. W. Wheatley & Co.* (10 Queen Street, Cheapside, and 23 Regent Street) are general shipping and parcel agents for all parts of the world.

Commissionnaires. These are a corps of retired soldiers of good character, organised in 1859 by Captain Sir Edward Walter of the 'Times' newspaper, and form convenient and trustworthy messengers for the conveyance of letters or small parcels. Their head-office is at Exchange Court, 419a Strand, but they are also to be found in most of the chief thoroughfares, where they may be recognised by their green uniform and metal badge. Their charges are 3*d.* per mile or 6*d.* per hour; the rate is a little higher if the parcel to be carried weighs more than 14lbs. The charge for a day is about 4*s.* 6*d.*, and they may also be hired by special arrangement for a week or a longer period. — The *Army and Navy Pensioners Employment Society,* 1a Craig's Court, Charing Cross, is a similar organisation.

District Messenger Service Co. Messengers of this company charge 4*d.* per half-mile, 6*d.* per mile, 8*d.* per hr., fares extra. Letters are posted or cabs called at 2*d.*, or 4*d.* after 10 p.m. and on Sundays. Head-office: 100 St. Martin's Lane, W.C.; numerous branch-offices, open always.

The **Lady Guide Association,** 20 Haymarket, S.W. (Foundress and Manageress, Miss Davis), established in 1888, provides ladies qualified to act as guides to the sights of London, as interpreters, as travelling companions, as aids in shopping, etc. (not for gentlemen unaccompanied by ladies). It also keeps a register of boarding and lodging houses, engages rooms at hotels, exchanges money, provides railway and other tickets, and generally undertakes to give all the information and assistance required by a stranger in London. Tickets are issued for the services of the lady guides at rates ranging from 5s. to 10s. per day, and proportionately by the week, month, or year. Other tickets include lodgings, etc., in London or on the Continent. The fee for meeting at railway-stations is 5s. 6d. — The *Ladies' Matinée Club* (entry fee 5s., annual subs. 10s. 6d.), at the same address, is intended for the convenience of ladies living in the suburbs or the country.

18. Outline of English History.

The visitor to the Metropolis of Great Britain, whether from the western hemisphere, from the antipodes, or from the provinces of that country itself, will at almost every step meet with interesting historical associations; and it is to a great extent on his acquaintance with these that the enjoyment and instruction to be derived from his visit will depend. We, therefore, give a brief table of the chief events in English history, which the tourist will often find convenient as an aid to his memory. In the following section will be found a sketch of the rise and progress of London itself.

B.C. 55-449 A.D.	ROMAN PERIOD.
B.C. 55-54.	Of Britain before its first invasion by **Julius Cæsar** in B.C. 55 there is no authentic history. Cæsar repeats his invasion in B.C. 54, but makes no permanent settlement.
43 A.D.	**Emp. Claudius** undertakes the subjugation of Britain.
78-85.	Britain, with part of Caledonia, is overrun by the Roman general **Agricola,** and reduced to the form of a province.
412.	Roman legions recalled from Britain by **Honorius.**
449.	The Britons, deprived of their Roman protectors, are unable to resist the attacks of the *Picts,* and summon the *Saxons,* under *Hengist* and *Horsa,* to their aid.
449-1066.	ANGLO-SAXON PERIOD.
449-585.	The Saxons, re-inforced by the *Angles, Jutes,* and other Germanic tribes, gradually overcome Britain on their own account, until the whole country, with trifling exceptions, is divided into the seven kingdoms of the Saxon **Heptarchy** (585). To this period belong the semi-mythical exploits of *King Arthur* and his knights.
	Christianity re-introduced by *St. Augustine* (597). The *Venerable Bede* (d. 735). *Caedmon* (about 680).

827.	**Egbert** unites all England in one kingdom.
835-871.	Contests with the *Danes* and *Normans*, who repeatedly invade England.
871-901.	**Alfred the Great** defeats the Danes, and compels them to make peace. Creates navy, establishes militia, revises laws, reorganises institutions, founds schools at Oxford, is a patron of learning, and himself an author.
979-1016.	**Ethelred the Unready** draws down upon England the vengeance of the Danes by a massacre of those who had settled in England.
1013.	The Danish king *Sweyn* conquers England.
1017-1035.	*Canute the Great*, the son of Sweyn, reigns over England.
1035-1040.	*Harold Harefoot*, illegitimate son of Canute, usurps the throne.
1040-1042.	*Hardicanute*, son of Canute. — The Saxon line is restored in the person of —
1042-1066.	**Edward the Confessor**, who makes London the capital of England, and builds Westminster Abbey (see p. 247). His brother-in-law and successor —
1066.	**Harold** loses his kingdom and his life at the *Battle of Hastings*, where he opposed the invasion of the Normans, under William the Conqueror.

1066-1154.	NORMAN DYNASTY.
1066-1087.	**William the Conqueror,** of Normandy, establishes himself as King of the English. Introduction of Norman (French) language and customs.
1087-1100.	**William II.**, surnamed *Rufus*, after a tyrannical reign, is accidentally shot by Sir Walter Tyrrell while out hunting.
1100-1135.	**Henry I.**, *Beauclerc*, defeats his elder brother Robert, Duke of Normandy, at the battle of *Tenchebrai* (1106), and adds Normandy to the possessions of the English crown. He leaves his kingdom to his daughter *Matilda*, who, however, is unable to wrest it from —
1135-1154.	**Stephen,** *of Blois*, grandson of the Conqueror. David, King of the Scots, and uncle of Matilda, is defeated and captured
1138.	at the *Battle of the Standard*. Stephen appoints as his successor Matilda's son, Henry of Anjou or Plantagenet (from the *planta genista* or broom, the badge of this family).

1154-1399.	HOUSE OF PLANTAGENET.
1154-1189.	**Henry II.** Strife with *Thomas Becket*, Archbishop of Canterbury, over the respective spheres of the civil and ecclesiastical powers. The Archbishop excommunicates the
1170.	King's followers, and is murdered by four knights at Can-
1172.	terbury. The E. part of Ireland is conquered by Strongbow and De Courcy. *Robin Hood*, the forest outlaw, flourishes.

1189-1199.	**Richard I.**, *Coeur de Lion*, takes a prominent part in the Third Crusade, but is captured on his way home, and imprisoned in Germany for upwards of a year. He carries on war with Philip II. of France.
1199-1216.	**John**, surnamed *Lackland*, is defeated at *Bouvines* by Philip II. of France, and loses Normandy. *Magna Charta*, the groundwork of the English constitution, is extorted from him by his Barons (comp. pp. 240, 410).
1216-1272.	**Henry III.**, by his misrule, becomes involved in a war with his Barons, headed by *Simon de Montfort*, and is defeated at *Lewes*. His son Edward gains the battle of *Evesham*, where De Montfort is slain. *Hubert de Burgh* defeats the French at sea. *Roger Bacon*, the philosopher.
1272-1307. 1305.	**Edward I.**, *Longshanks*, vanquishes the Welsh under *Llewelyn*, and completes the conquest of Wales. The heir apparent to the English throne thenceforward bears the title of *Prince of Wales*. *Robert Bruce* and *John Baliol* struggle for the crown of Scotland. Edward espouses the cause of the latter (who swears fealty to England), and overruns Scotland. The Scots, led by *Sir William Wallace*, offer a determined resistance. Wallace executed at London. The Scots defeated at *Falkirk* (1297) and *Methven* (1306), and the country subdued. Establishment of the English Parliament in its modern form.
1307-1327. 1314.	**Edward II.** is signally defeated at *Bannockburn* by the Scots under *Robert Bruce* the third, and is forced to retire to England. The Queen and her paramour *Mortimer* join with the Barons in taking up arms against the King, who is deposed, and shortly afterwards murdered in prison.
1327-1377. 1364.	**Edward III.** defeats the Scots at *Halidon Hill* and *Neville's Cross*. Lays claim to the throne of France, and invades that country, thus beginning the hundred years' war between France and England. Victories of *Sluys* (naval), *Crécy* (1346), and *Poitiers* (1356). John the Good of France, taken prisoner by the *Black Prince*, dies in captivity. After the death of the Black Prince England loses all her French possessions, except Calais and Gascony. Order of the Garter founded. Movement against the pretensions and corruption of the clergy, headed by the early reformer *John Wycliffe*. House of Commons holds its meetings apart from the House of Lords.
1377-1399.	**Richard II.** Rebellion of *Wat Tyler*, occasioned by increase of taxation (see p. 128). Victory over the Scots at *Otterburn* or *Chevy Chase*. *Henry of Bolingbroke, Duke of Lancaster*, leads an army against the King, takes him captive, and according to popular tradition starves him to death in

Pontefract Castle. *Geoffrey Chaucer*, the father of English poetry, flourishes.

<table>
<tr><td>1399-1461.</td><td></td></tr>
</table>

HOUSE OF LANCASTER.

1399-1413. **Henry IV.**, *Bolingbroke*, now secures his election to the crown, in right of his descent from Henry III. Outbreak of the nobility, under the *Earl of Northumberland* and his son
1403. *Henry (Percy Hotspur)*, is quelled by the victory of *Shrewsbury*, at which the latter is slain.

1413-1422. **Henry V.** renews the claims of England to the French crown, wins the battle of *Agincourt*, and subdues the N. of France. Persecution of the *Lollards*, or followers of Wycliffe.

1422-1461. **Henry VI.** is proclaimed King of France at Paris. The *Maid of Orleans* defeats the English and recovers French possessions. Outbreak of the civil contest called the 'Wars of the Roses', between the houses of Lancaster (red rose) and York (white rose). Henry becomes insane. *Richard, Duke of York*, great-grandson of Edward III., lays claim to the throne, joins himself with *Warwick*, the 'King-Maker', and wins the battle of *Northampton*, but is defeated and slain at *Wakefield*. His son *Edward*, however, is appointed King. Rebellion of *Jack Cade*.

1461-1485. HOUSE OF YORK.

1461-1483. **Edward IV.** wins the battles of *Towton*, *Hedgley Moor*, and *Hexham*. Warwick takes the part of *Margaret of Anjou*, wife of Henry VI., and forces Edward to flee to Holland, whence, however, he soon returns and wins the victories of *Barnet* and *Tewkesbury*. Henry VI. dies sud-
1471. denly in the Tower. Edward's brother, the *Duke of Clarence*, is said to have been drowned in a butt of malmsey.

1483. **Edward V.**, the youthful son of Edward IV., is declared illegitimate, and murdered in the Tower, along with his brother (p. 159), by his uncle, the *Duke of Gloucester*, who takes possession of the throne as —

1483-1485. **Richard III.**, but is defeated and slain at *Bosworth* by *Henry Tudor*, *Earl of Richmond*, a scion of the House of Lancaster.

1485-1603. HOUSE OF TUDOR.

1485-1509. **Henry VII.** marries *Elizabeth*, daughter of Edward IV., and so puts an end to the Wars of the Roses. The pretenders *Lambert Simnel* and *Perkin Warbeck*.

1509-1547. **Henry VIII.**, married six times (to *Catherine of Aragon*, *Anne Boleyn*, *Jane Seymour*, *Anne of Cleves*, *Catherine Howard*, and *Catherine Parr*). Battles of the *Spurs* and

Flodden. Separation of the Church of England from that of Rome. Dissolution of monasteries and persecution of the Papists. *Cardinal Wolsey* and *Thomas Cromwell*, all-powerful ministers. Whitehall and St. James's Palace built.

1547-1553. **Edward VI.** encourages the Reformed faith.

1553-1558. **Mary I.** causes *Lady Jane Grey*, whom Edward had appointed his successor, to be executed, and imprisons her own sister *Elizabeth* (pp. 161, 234). Marries *Philip of Spain*, and restores Roman Catholicism. Persecution of the Protestants. Calais taken by the French.

1558-1603. **Elizabeth.** The Reformed faith re-established. Flourishing state of commerce. *Mary, Queen of Scots*, executed after a
1587. long confinement in England. Destruction of the Spanish
1588. 'Invincible Armada'. *Sir Francis Drake*, the celebrated circumnavigator. Foundation of the East India Company. Golden age of English literature : *Shakspeare*, *Bacon*, *Spenser*, *Jonson*, *Beaumont*, *Fletcher*, *Marlowe*, *Drayton*.

1603-1714. HOUSE OF STUART.

1603-1625. **James I.**, King of Scots, and son of Mary Stuart, unites by his accession the two kingdoms of England and Scotland. Persecution of Puritans and Roman Catholics. Influence of *Buckingham*. Gunpowder Plot. Execution of *Sir Walter Raleigh*.

1625-1649. **Charles I.** imitates his father in the arbitrary nature of his rule, quarrels with Parliament on questions of taxation, dissolves it repeatedly, and tyrannically attempts to arrest five leading members of the House of Commons (*Hampden*, *Pym*, etc.). Rise of the *Covenanters* in Scotland. *Long Parliament.* Outbreak of civil war between the King and his adherents *(Cavaliers)* on the one side, and the Parliament and its friends *(Roundheads)* on the other. The King defeated by *Oliver Cromwell* at *Marston Moor* and *Naseby*. He takes refuge in the Scottish camp, but is given up to the Parliamentary leaders, tried, and executed at Whitehall (p. 234).

1649-1653. **Commonwealth.** The Scots rise in favour of Charles II., but are defeated at *Dunbar* and *Worcester* by Cromwell.

1653-1660. **Protectorate.** Oliver Cromwell now becomes Lord Protector of England, and by his vigorous and wise government makes England prosperous at home and respected abroad. *John Milton*, the poet, *Thomas Hobbes*, the philosopher, and *George Fox*, the founder of the Quakers, live at this period.
1658. On Cromwell's death he is succeeded by his son **Richard**, who, however, soon resigns, whereupon Charles II. is restored by *General Monk* or *Monck*.

1660-1685. **Charles II.** General amnesty proclaimed, a few of the regicides only being excepted. Arbitrary government. The

Cabal. Wars with Holland. Persecution of the Papists after the pretended discovery of a *Popish Plot.* Passing of the *Habeas Corpus Act.* Wars with the Covenanters. Battle of *Bothwell Bridge. Rye House Plot.* Charles a pensioner of France. Names *Whig* and *Tory* come into use. *Dryden* and *Butler,* the poets; *Locke,* the philosopher.

1685-1688.	**James II.**, a Roman Catholic, soon alienates the people by his love for that form of religion, is quite unable to resist the invasion of *William of Orange,* and escapes to France, where he spends his last years at St. Germain.
1688-1702.	**William III. and Mary II.** William of Orange, with his wife, the elder daughter of James II., now ascends the throne. The *Declaration of Rights.* Battles of *Killiecrankie* and *The Boyne. Sir Isaac Newton.*
1702-1714.	**Anne,** younger daughter of James II., completes the fusion of England and Scotland by the union of their parliaments. *Marlborough's* victories of *Blenheim, Ramilies, Oudenarde,* and *Malplaquet,* in the Spanish War of Succession. Capture of *Gibraltar.* The poets *Pope, Addison, Swift, Prior,* and *Allan Ramsay.*

1714 to the present day.	HANOVERIAN DYNASTY.
1714-1727.	**George I.** succeeds in right of his descent from James I. Rebellion in Scotland (in favour of the *Pretender*) quelled. *Sir Robert Walpole,* prime minister. *Daniel Defoe.*
1727-1760.	**George II.** Rebellion in favour of the Young Pretender, *Charles Edward Stuart,* crushed at *Culloden.* Canada taken from the French. *William Pitt, Lord Chatham,* prime minister; *Richardson, Fielding, Smollett, Sterne,* novelists; *Thomson, Young, Gray, Collins, Gay,* poets; *Hogarth,* painter.
1760-1820.	**George III.** American War of Independence. War with France. Victories of *Nelson* at *Aboukir* and *Trafalgar,* and of *Wellington* in Spain and at *Waterloo.* The younger *Pitt,* prime minister; *Shelley* and *Keats,* poets.
1820-1830.	**George IV.** Roman Catholic Emancipation Bill. *Daniel O'Connell.* The English aid the Greeks in the War of Independence. Victory of *Navarino. Byron, Sir Walter Scott, Wordsworth, Coleridge, Southey.*
1830-1837.	**William IV.** Abolition of slavery. Reform Bill.

The present sovereign of Great Britain is —

Victoria, born 24th May, 1819; ascended the throne in 1837; married, on 10th Feb., 1840, her cousin, Prince Albert of Saxe-Coburg-Gotha (d. 14th Dec., 1861).

The children of this marriage are: —

(1) Victoria, born 21st Nov., 1840; married to the Crown Prince of Germany, 25th Jan., 1858.

(2) Albert Edward, Prince of Wales, Heir Apparent to the throne, born 9th Nov., 1841; married Alexandra, Princess of Denmark, 10th Mar., 1863.

(3) Alice, born 25th April, 1843; married to the Grand-Duke of Hessen-Darmstadt, 1st July, 1862; died 14th Dec., 1878.

(4) Alfred, Duke of Edinburgh, born 6th Aug., 1844; married the Grand Duchess Marie of Russia, 23rd Jan., 1874.

(5) Helena, born 25th May, 1846; married to Prince Christian of Schleswig-Holstein-Sonderburg-Augustenburg, 5th July, 1866.

(6) Louise, born 18th March, 1848; married to the Marquis of Lorne, now the Duke of Argyll, 21st March, 1871.

(7) Arthur, Duke of Connaught, born 1st May, 1850; married Princess Louise Margaret of Prussia, daughter of Prince Frederick Charles, 13th March, 1879.

(8) Leopold, Duke of Albany, born 7th April, 1853; married Princess Helen of Waldeck-Pyrmont, 27th April, 1882; died 28th March, 1884.

(9) Beatrice, born 14th April, 1857; married Prince Henry of Battenberg, 23rd July, 1885 (died 20th Jan., 1896).

19. Historical Sketch of London.

The most populous city in the world (which London unquestionably is) cannot fail to have had an eventful history, in all that concerns race, creed, institutions, culture, and general progress. At what period the Britons, one branch of the Celtic race, settled on this spot, there is no authentic evidence to shew. The many forms which the name assumes in early records have led to much controversy; but it is clear that 'London' is derived from the Latin *Londinium*, the name given it in Tacitus, and that this is only an adaptation by the Romans of the ancient British name *Llyn* or *Lin*, a pool, and *din* or *dun*, a high place of strength, a hill-fort, or city. The 'pool' was a widening of the river at this part, where it makes a bend, and offered a convenient place for shipping. Whether the 'dun' or hill was the high ground reached by Ludgate Hill, and on which St. Paul's now stands, or Cornhill, near the site of the Mansion House, it is difficult to decide †. Probably both these elevations were on the 'pool'. The etymology of the first syllable of London is the same as that of 'Lin' in Lincoln, which was called by Ptolemy Lindon (Λίνδον), and by the Romans Lindum, the second syllable of the modern form of the name representing the word 'Colonia'. The present British or Welsh name of London is *Llundain;* but it was formerly also known to the Welsh as *Caer-ludd*, the City of Lud, a British king said to have ruled here just before the Roman period, and popularly supposed to be commemorated in Lud-gate†, one of the gates of the old walled city, near the junction of Ludgate Hill and Farringdon Street.

† The latter alternative is that of the Rev. W. J. Loftie, one of London's best historians (see p. 104).

†† In reality from the Anglo-Saxon *Lydgeaat*, a postern (Loftie).

London, in the days of the Britons, was probably little more than a collection of huts, on a dry spot in the midst of a marsh, or in a cleared space in the midst of a wood, and encompassed by an artificial earthwork and ditch. That there was much marsh and forest in the immediate vicinity is proved by the character of the deep soil when turned up in digging foundations, and by the small subterranean streams which still run into the Thames, as at Dowgate, formerly *Dourgate* ('water gate', from Celtic *dwr*, water), at the Fleet Ditch, at Blackfriars Bridge, etc.

After the settlement of the Romans in Britain, quite early in the Christian era, London rapidly grew in importance. In the time of the Emperor Nero (62 A.D.), the city had become a resort of merchants from various countries and the centre of a considerable maritime commerce, the river Thames affording ready access for shipping. It suffered terribly during the sanguinary struggle between the Romans and the British queen Boadicea, and was in later centuries frequently attacked and plundered by piratical bands of Franks, Norsemen, Danes, and Saxons, who crossed the seas to reap a ruthless harvest from a city which doubtless possessed much commercial wealth; but it speedily recovered from the effects of these visitations. As a Roman settlement London was frequently named *Augusta*, but it was never raised to the dignity of being a municipium like *Verulamium* (p. 418) or *Eboracum* (York) and was not regarded as the capital of Roman Britain. It extended from the site of the present Tower of London on the E. to Newgate on the W., and inland from the Thames as far as the marshy ground known in later times as Moorfields. Relics are still found almost annually of the foundations of Roman buildings of a substantial and elegant character. Fragments of the Roman wall are also discernible.

This wall was maintained in parts until modern times, but has almost entirely disappeared before the alterations and improvements which taste and the necessities of trade have intr duced The most prominent remaining piece of the Roman walls is in London Wall, between Wood Street and Aldermanbury. where an inscribed tablet calls attention to it. Another fragment may be seen in the adjacent churchyard of St. Giles, Cripplegate (see p. 129); while a third, 8 ft thick, forms the north boundary of the New Post Office buildings (p 122) from Aldergate Street to King Edward Street. The Roman wall seems to have been 9-12ft. thick and 20 ft. high and to have consisted of a core of rubble with a facing of stone and bonding courses of brick.

The gates of Roman London, whose walls are believed to have been first built on such an extended scale as to include the above-mentioned limits by the Emperor Constantine in the fourth century, were Newgate, Bishopsgate, and a gate on the river. In after-times we find Lud-gate, Dour-gate, Billings-gate, Postern-gate, Ale-gate or All-gate (Aldgate), Bishops-gate, Moor-gate, Cripple-gate, Alders-gate, and New-gate, all of which are still commemorated in names of streets, etc., marking the localities. Roman London from the Tower to Ludgate was about a mile in length, and from the

Thames to 'London Wall' about half-a-mile in breadth. Its remains at Cheapside and the Mansion House are found at about 18 feet below the present surface. The Roman city at first enclosed must, however, have been smaller, as Roman sepulchres have been found in Moorgate Street, Bishopsgate, and Smithfield, which must then have lain beyond the walled city. The Saxons, who seldom distinguished themselves as builders, contributed nothing to the fortification of London; but King Alfred refounded the city and restored the walls (886) as a rampart against the Danes, who never took London afterwards. The Normans also did much, beginning with the erection of the Tower. During the earlier ages of Saxon rule the great works left here by the Romans — villas, baths, bridges, roads, temples, statuary — were either destroyed or allowed to fall into decay, as was the case, indeed, all over Britain.

London became the capital of one of the Anglo-Saxon kingdoms, and continued to increase in size and importance. The sites of two of modern London's most prominent buildings — Westminster Abbey and St. Paul's Cathedral — were occupied as early as the beginning of the 7th cent. by the modest originals of these two stately churches. Bede, at the beginning of the 8th cent., speaks of London as a great market frequented by foreign traders, and we find it paying one-fifth of a contribution exacted by Canute from the entire kingdom. From William the Conqueror London received a charter† in which he engaged to maintain the rights of the city, but the same monarch erected the White Tower to overawe the citizens in the event of disaffection. At this time the city probably contained 30-40,000 inhabitants. A special promise is made in Magna Charta, extorted from King John, to observe all the ancient privileges of London; and we may date the present form of its Corporation, consisting of Mayor, Aldermen, and Common Councilmen, from a somewhat earlier period ††. The 13th and 14th centuries are marked in the annals of London by several lamentable fires, famines, and pestilences, in which many thousands of its inhabitants perished. The year 1381 witnessed the rebellion of Wat Tyler, who was slain by Lord Mayor Walworth at Smithfield. In this outbreak, and still more in that of Jack Cade (1450), London suffered severely, through the burning and pillaging of its houses. During the reigns of Henry VIII. (1509-47) and his daughter Mary (1552-58), London acquired a terrible familiarity with the fires lighted to consume unfortunate 'heretics' at the stake, while under the more beneficent

† The following is the text of this charter as translated by Bishop Stubbs: — 'William king greets William bishop and Gosfrith portreeve, and all the burghers within London, French and English, friendly; and I do you to wit that I will that ye be all lawworthy that were in King Edward's day. And I will that every child be his father's heir after his father's day; and I will not endure that any man offer any wrong to you. God keep you'.

†† A deed among the archives of St. Paul's mentions a 'Mayor of the City of London' in 1193.

reign of Elizabeth (1558-1603) the capital showed its patriotic zeal by its liberal contributions of men, money, and ships, for the purpose of resisting the threatened attack of the Armada.

A map of London at this time would show the Tower standing on the verge of the City on the E., while on the W. the much smaller city of Westminster would still be a considerable distance from London. The Strand, or river-side road connecting the two cities, would appear bordered by numerous aristocratic mansions, with gardens extending into the fields or down to the river. Throughout the Norman period, and down to the times of the Plantagenets and the Wars of the Roses, the commonalty lived in poor and mean wooden dwellings; but there were many good houses for the merchants and manufacturers, and many important religious houses and hospitals, while the Thames was provided with numerous convenient quays and landing-stages. The streets, even as lately as the 17th cent., were narrow, dirty, full of ruts and holes, and ill-adapted for traffic. Many improvements, however, were made at the period we have now reached (the end of the 16th cent.), though these still left London very different from what we now see it.

In the Civil Wars London, which had been most exposed to the exactions of the Star Chamber, naturally sided with the Roundheads. It witnessed Charles I. beheaded at the Palace of Whitehall in 1649, and Oliver Cromwell proclaimed Lord Protector of England in 1653; and in 1660 it saw Charles II. placed on the throne by the 'Restoration'. This was a period when England, and London especially, underwent dire suffering in working out the problem of civil and religious liberty, the successful solution of which laid the basis of the empire's greatness. In 1664-66 London was turned into a city of mourning and lamentation by the ravages of the Great Plague, by which, it is calculated, it lost the enormous number of 100,000 citizens. Closely treading on the heels of one calamity came another — the Great Fire — which, in September, 1666, destroyed 13,000 houses, converting a great part of the eastern half of the city into a scene of desolation. This disaster, however, ultimately proved very beneficial to the city, for London was rebuilt in a much improved form, though not so advantageously as it would have been if Sir Christopher Wren's plans had been fully realised. Among the new edifices erected after the fire was the present St. Paul's Cathedral. Of important buildings existing before the fire Westminster Abbey and Hall, the Temple Church, the Tower, and a few of the City churches are now almost the only examples.

Wren fortunately had his own way in building the fifty odd City churches, and the visitor to London should not fail to notice their great variety and the skill with which they are grouped with St. Paul's — though this latter feature has been somewhat obscured by recent demolitions and erections. A good panorama of the entire group is obtained from the tower of St. Saviour's, Southwark; the general effect is also visible from Blackfriars Bridge (p. 152).

It was not, however, till the reign of Queen Anne (1702-14) that London began to put on anything like its present appearance. In 1703 it was visited by a fearful storm, by which houses were overthrown, the ships in the river driven on shore, churches unroofed, property to the value of at least 2,000,000l. destroyed, and the lives of several hundreds of persons sacrificed. The winter of 1739-40 is memorable for the Great Frost, lasting from Christmas to St. Valentine's Day, during which a fair was held on the frozen Thames. Houses were first numbered in 1767. Great injuries were inflicted on the city by the Gordon No-Popery Riots of 1780. The prisons were destroyed, the prisoners released, and mansions burned or pillaged, thirty-six conflagrations having been counted at one time in different quarters; and the rioters were not subdued till hundreds of them had paid the penalty of their misdeeds with their lives.

Many of the handsomest streets and finest buildings in London date from the latter half of last century. To this period belong the Mansion House, the Horse Guards, Somerset House, and the Bank. During the 19th cent. the march of improvement has been so rapid as to defy description. The Mint, the Custom House, Waterloo Bridge, London Bridge, Buckingham Palace, the Post Office, the British Museum, the Athenæum Club, the York Column, the National Gallery, the Houses of Parliament, the new Law Courts, and the whole of Belgravia and the West End beyond, have all arisen during the last 90 years. An important event in the domestic history of the city was the commencement of gas-lighting in 1807. (Before 1716 the provisions for street-lighting were very imperfect, but in that year an act was passed ordering every householder to hang out a light before his door from six in the evening till eleven.) From that time to the present London has been actively engaged, by the laying out of spacious thoroughfares and the construction of handsome edifices, in making good its claim to be not only the largest, but also one of the finest cities in the world. Among the most important achievements of the past decade have been the construction of the Tower Bridge (p. 165) and of the Blackwall and electric railway tunnels under the Thames (pp. 168, 62). The Thames Embankment and many other thoroughfares are now lighted by electricity.

No authentic estimate of the population of London can be traced farther back than two centuries. Nor is it easy to determine the area covered by buildings at different periods. At one time the 'City within the Walls' comprised all; afterwards was added the 'City without the Walls'; then the city and liberties of Westminster; then the borough of Southwark, S. of the river; then numerous parishes between the two cities; and lastly other parishes forming an encircling belt around the whole. All these component elements at length came to be embraced under the name of 'London'. The population was about 700,000 in the year 1700, about 900,000 in 1800, and 1,300,000 in 1821. Each subsequent decennial census included a larger area than the one that preceded it. The original 'City' of London, covering little more than 1 square mile, has in this way expanded to a great metropolis of fully 120 square miles, containing, in 1898, a population of 4,504,766 persons (see p. 96). Extension of commerce has accompanied the growth of population. Statistics of trade in past centuries are wanting; but at the present time London supplies half the total customs-revenue of the kingdom. The vessels entering and clearing at the port of London comprize one-sixth of the total tonnage of the British and foreign vessels trading between the United Kingdom and foreign countries and British colonies. Comp. also p. 96.

20. Topography and Statistics.

Topography. The city of London is built upon a tract of un-
dulating clay soil, which extends irregularly along the valley of
the Thames from a point near Reading to Harwich and Herne Bay
at the mouth of the river, a distance of about 120 miles. It is divided
into two portions by the river *Thames*, which, rising in the Cotswold
Hills in Gloucestershire, is from its source down to its mouth in
the German Ocean at Sheerness 230 M. in length, and is navigable
by sea-going vessels for a distance of 50 M. — The southern and
less important part of London (*Southwark*, *Lambeth*, *Greenwich*, etc.)
lies in the counties of *Surrey* and *Kent;* the northern and principal
portion in *Middlesex*. The latter part of the immense city may be
divided, in accordance with its general characteristics, into two great
halves (not taking into account the extensive outlying districts on
the N. and the N.E., which are comparatively uninteresting to
strangers) : —

I. The *City* and the *East End*, consisting of that part of London
which lies to the E. of the Temple, form the commercial and
money-making quarter of the Metropolis. It embraces the Port, the
Docks, the Custom House, the Bank, the Exchange, the innumerable counting-houses of merchants, money-changers, brokers,
and underwriters, the General Post Office, the printing and publishing offices of The Times, the legal corporations of the Inns of Court,
and the Cathedral of St. Paul's, towering above them all.

II. The *West End*, or that part of the town to the W. of the
Temple, is the quarter of London which spends money, makes laws,
and regulates the fashions. It contains the Palace of the Queen, the
Mansions of the aristocracy, the Clubs, Museums, Picture Galleries,
Theatres, Barracks, Government Offices, Houses of Parliament, and
Westminster Abbey; and it is the special locality for parks, squares,
and gardens, for gorgeous equipages and powdered lackeys.

Besides these great divisions the following districts are distinguished by their population and leading occupations: —

I. On the LEFT BANK of the Thames: —

(a) To the E. of the City is the so-called *Long Shore*, which
extends along the bank of the Thames, and is chiefly composed of
quays, wharves, storehouses, and engine-factories, and inhabited
by shipwrights, lightermen, sailors, and marine store dealers.

(b) *Whitechapel*, with its Jewish tailoring workshops.

(c) *Houndsditch* and the *Minories*, the quarters of the Jews.

(d) *Bethnal Green* and *Spitalfields* to the N., and part of *Shoreditch*, form a manufacturing district, once occupied to a large extent by silk-weavers, partly descended from the French Protestants
(Huguenots) who took refuge in England after the Revocation of
the Edict of Nantes in 1685. Furniture-making and boot-making
are now the chief industries.

(e) *Clerkenwell*, between Islington and Hatton Garden, the district of watch-makers and metal-workers.

(f) *Paternoster Row*, near St. Paul's Cathedral, the focus of the book-trade.

(g) *Chancery Lane* and the *Inns of Court*, the headquarters of barristers, solicitors, and law-stationers.

II. In *Surrey* and *Kent*, on the RIGHT BANK of the Thames: —

(a) *Southwark* and *Lambeth*, containing numerous potteries, glass-works, machine-factories, breweries, and hop-warehouses.

(b) *Bermondsey*, famous for its tanneries, glue-factories, and wool-warehouses.

(c) *Rotherhithe*, farther to the E., chiefly inhabited by sailors, ship-carpenters, coal-heavers, and bargemen.

(d) *Deptford*, with its great cattle-market, on the river, to the S.E. of Southwark.

(e) *Greenwich*, with its hospital, park, and observatory.

(f) *Woolwich*, with its arsenal and dockyards.

By the Redistribution Bill of 1885 London is divided for parliamentary purposes into the City Proper, returning two members of parliament, and 27 metropolitan boroughs comprising 57 single member districts. London University also returns one member.

The *City Proper*, which strictly speaking forms a county of itself and is not included in Middlesex, is bounded on the W. by the site of Temple Bar and Southampton Buildings; on the N. by Holborn, Smithfield, Barbican, and Finsbury Circus; on the E. by Bishopsgate Without, Petticoat Lane, Aldgate, and the Minories; and on the S. by the Thames.

The City is divided into 26 *Wards* (or 27, including that of Bridge Without or Southwark) and 112 parishes, has a separate administration and jurisdiction of its own, and is presided over by the Lord Mayor. At the census of 1896 it consisted of 456 inhabited houses with 31.0·3 inhabitants (43,687 less than in 1871). The *resident* population is steadily decreasing on account of the constant emigration to the West End and suburbs, the ground and buildings being so valuable for commercial purposes as to preclude their use merely as dwellings. More than 5000 houses are left empty every night under the guardianship of the 930 members of the City police force. The *day* population of the City in 1891 was 301,381, and the number of houses or separate tenements in which persons were actively employed during the day was 25,143. The rateable value of property in 1900 was 4.571,454*l.* or about 1,500,000*l.* more than that of Liverpool. Sites for building in the City sometimes realise no less than 20-70*l.* per square foot. The annual revenue of the City of London is over 1,000,000*l.* In 1891 an attempt was made to estimate the number of persons and vehicles entering the City precincts within 24 hours. Enumerators were stationed at 80 different inlets, and their returns showed the enormous totals of 1,121,708 persons and 92,488 vehicles.

Westminster, to the W. of the City, bounded on the N. by Bayswater Road and Oxford Street, on the W. by Chelsea, Kensington, and Brompton, and on the S. by the Thames, comprises three of the parliamentary boroughs (Westminster Proper or the Abbey District, the Strand District, and the District of St. George's, Hanover

Square), each returning one member to the House of Commons. It
contains 23,104 houses and 193,465 inhabitants. Though a city
constituted by royal charter, Westminster had no municipality until
the vestries for the three districts were replaced by a borough council under the London Government Act of 1899.

The remaining parliamentary boroughs are *Battersea* (including
Clapham), *Bethnal Green*, *Camberwell*, *Chelsea*, *Deptford*, *Fins-*
bury, *Fulham*, *Greenwich*, *Hackney*, *Hammersmith*, *Hampstead*,
Islington, *Kensington*, *Lambeth*, *Lewisham*, *Marylebone*, *Newington*,
Paddington, *St. Pancras*, *Shoreditch*, *Southwark* (including Bermondsey and Rotherhithe), *Tower Hamlets*, *Wandsworth*, and *Wool-*
wich. The population, area, and boundaries of these new boroughs
are given in a map published by Philip, 32 Fleet Street (6*d.*)

Statistics. The City, the West End, and the Borough, together
with the suburban villages which have been gradually absorbed,
form the great and constantly extending Metropolis of London —
a city which, in the words of Tacitus (*Ann.* 14, 33), was and still
is 'copiâ negotiatorum et commeatuum maxime celebre'. It has
doubled in size within the last half-century, being now, from Stratford and Blackwall on the E. to Kew Bridge and Acton on the W.,
14 M. in length, and, from Clapham and Herne Hill on the S. to
Hornsey and Highgate on the N., 8 M. in breadth, while it covers an
area of 122 square miles. This area is, at a rough estimate, occupied
by 8000 streets, which if laid end to end would form a line 3000 M.
long. The 600,000 buildings of this gigantic city include 1500
churches of various denominations, 7500 public houses, 1700 coffee-
houses, and 500 hotels and inns. The Metropolitan and City Police
District, which extends 12-15 M. in every direction from Charing
Cross, embraces an area of 690 sq. M., with 7000 M. of streets and
roads and 900,000 inhabited houses. The annual rateable value of
house property in the County of London (see p. 97) in 1900 was
37,549,521*l.* According to the census of 1896, the population of London consisted of 4,433,018 souls (or within the bounds of the Metropolitan Police District 5,633,332 in 1891), an increase of 599,824
over that of 1881. The number of paupers was 106,670. In 1898
the population was 4,504,766. Within the last forty years the population of London has been almost doubled (pop. in 1851, 2,363,274),
and about 2000 M. of new streets have been constructed. There are
in London more Scotsmen than in Aberdeen, more Irish than in
Dublin, more Jews than in Palestine, and more Roman Catholics than
in Rome. The number of Americans resident in London has been
estimated by a competent authority at 15,000, while perhaps 100,000
pass through it annually. In Paris the Americans number about 8000.

The total cost of the government of London is 13,100,000*l.* annually, and its debt amounts to 45,‘00,000*l.*

When London overflowed the old City boundaries the areas outside the limits of the Corporation (see p. 95) were administered

under a medley of some 200 private Acts. The needs of traffic and sanitary reform produced the Metropolis Management Act, 1855, under which (and some amending Acts) local government was handed over to 42 Vestries and District Boards, which again elected a central authority, the *Metropolitan Board of Works*. The last body lost public confidence and in 1889 was superseded by the LONDON COUNTY COUNCIL, created by the Local Government Act, 1888, and entrusted with several new powers. The 'County of London' includes the City and parts of the counties of Middlesex, Surrey, and Kent. There are 118 Councillors, two being elected triennially by the borough franchise for each parliamentary division, and 19 Aldermen appointed by the Council. The office of the County Council is in Spring Gardens, Charing Cross (Pl. R, 26, IV). Its annual income is about 4,000,000*l.* and its debt 35,600,000*l.* By the London Government Act, 1899, coming into operation on Nov. 1st, 1900, the vestries, etc., are amalgamated into 28 *Metropolitan Boroughs*, to whose councils are transferred the powers and duties of the existing bodies and of various boards for baths, libraries, and cemeteries.

The most important work of the Metropolitan Board of Works was the *Main Drainage System*, begun in 1859 under Sir Joseph Bazalgette, and carried out at a cost of 6,500,000*l.* New works now undertaken by the County Council will cost ultimately over 3,000,000*l.* Every year 60,000,000 tons of sewage are conveyed through 87$\frac{1}{2}$ M. of main sewers to Barking Creek and Crossness at the mouth of the Thames, where are works for deodorising and precipitating. The *Thames Embankment* (described at p. 150), *Queen Victoria Street*, *Shaftesbury Avenue*, and *Charing Cross Road* are scarcely less important undertakings of the Board of Works, which also freed the bridges from tolls at a cost of 1,500,000*l.*, and established a free ferry across the Thames at Woolwich. The County Council has also carried out large schemes for the facilitation of traffic. *Blackwall Tunnel*, opened in 1897, cost 1,400,000*l.*, and is 6300 ft. in length and 24 ft. in diameter. Two new tunnels are being undertaken between Poplar and Greenwich and at Rotherhithe at a cost of about 2,250,000*l.* A new bridge is being built at *Vauxhall*, and *Highgate Archway* has been reconstructed. *Rosebery Avenue* is the largest new street so far built by the Council, but a gigantic scheme is now in progress for widening the Strand at Holywell Street and cutting a new thoroughfare to Holborn. This will cost about 4,500 000*l.*, and entails the building of large blocks of working-class dwellings on the site of the old Millbank prison to rehouse about 4000 persons displaced. About 20 per cent of the population live in overcrowded conditions, and much has been done, though much remains to do, to remedy this evil. In *Boundary Street*, Bethnal Green, the Council has cleared 15 acres of slums, the largest municipal undertaking of the kind, and rehoused in handsome new dwellings 4100 persons, at a total cost of 630 000*l.* Schemes completed and in progress involve over 42,000 persons and 2,000,000*l.* The Council is the authority for administering the Building Acts in London. It also controls in all 3814 out of the 6051 acres of royal parks and open spaces in London and has made ample provision for games and so forth. Five asylums are maintained at an annual cost of 400,000*l.* for nearly 15,000 lunatics. The Council also owns over two-thirds of the tramway mileage in London. Its income from the lines is about 1 200,000*l.*, paid by 225,000,000 passengers, and the capital invested is 3,900,000*l.*

The Council controls the *London Fire Brigade*, a force of 1200 men costing 197,000*l.* a year. To deal with about 3500 fires annually there are 91 land fire-engines and 8 river engines. The headquarters are in Southwark Bridge Road; chief officer, Commander Wells, R.N. — The *London Salvage Corps* (63 Watling Street, E.C.) is a body of about 100 men maintained by the principal Fire Insurance Companies to assist in saving property in fires.

Eight private companies supply *Water* to London and the neighbouring districts, including a population of 6,000,000 persons. In 1898 the daily supply was 205½ million gallons, of which 168½ million gallons or 28 gallons per head of the population were for domestic purposes. Over 82 per cent of the supply is drawn from the Thames and Lea. The gross income of the companies is 2,172,000*l*.

There are five great *Gas Companies*, which supply over 35,000 million cubic feet of gas, from the sale of which they derive over 4,000,000*l*., besides 1,000,000*l*. from residual products.

The new *Borough Councils* will have as their main duties the care of the public health, the provision of local drainage, and the maintenance of the streets. Public baths, libraries, and electric lighting works, many of which are already instituted, will also come within their purview, as well as the clearing of unhealthy areas. The total expenditure by vestries in 1896-97 was 2,762,000*l*.

The *Poor Law* in London is administered by 30 Boards of Guardians, 6 Boards of Managers of School Districts, and two Boards of Managers for Sick Asylum Districts. There is also a central body, the Metropolitan Asylums Board, partly elected by the Boards of Guardians and partly nominated by the Local Government Board; it maintains 11 fever hospitals, a smallpox convalescent hospital, 3 hospital-ships, an ambulance service for all London, 4 imbecile hospitals, and a training ship. The total yearly expenditure by poor law authorities is over 3,000,000*l*., and the number of paupers relieved is about 120,000 daily.

The elementary education (free since 1891) of London is attended to by the **London School Board**, consisting of 55 members, elected by the City and the ten other districts into which London is divided for the educational franchise. In the City the electors are the voters for Common Councilmen, in the other divisions the rate-payers. The annual income of the Board, exclusive of loans, is about 2,800,000*l*. The 430 schools provided by the board accommodate 525,000 children, out of a total of 782,000 upon the roll of efficient schools. There are also 280 evening schools and 590 centres for training in cookery and other special subjects. The number of teachers is over 9,700, besides about 1700 pupil-teachers. The office of the board is on the Victoria Embankment, near the Temple Station (see p. 152).

Technical Education in London is chiefly managed by the *City and Guilds of London Institute* (Gresham College; p. 137) and the *Technical Education Board* of the London County Council (St. Martin's Place, W. C.). The latter body consists of 20 members of the County Council, 3 from the School Board, and 12 from other bodies.

With the former are connected the *Guilds Central Technical College* (p. 346). *Finsbury Technical College* (Leonard St., E. C.), the *Technical Art School* (122 Kennington Park Road), and the *Leather Trades School* (42 Bethnal Green Road). The Technical Education Board, which spends about 180,000*l*. a year, has opened a *Central School of Arts and Crafts* (316 Regent St.), but its main activity is directed towards developing existing Polytechnics and technical schools by grants for technical classes and by providing 634 annual scholarships for pupils from elementary schools. A visit to any of the following will be of interest to the educationist (previous arrangement with the secretary desirable): *Northampton Institute* (p. 131), *City of Lon-*

don College (White St., Moorfields), *Birkbeck Institution* (p. 174; these three constitute the *City Polytechnic*); *People's Palace* (p. 169); *Regent Street Polytechnic* (p. 287). Several of the polytechnics have social and recreative, as well as educational sides. There are also many special technical and art schools in London. Several of the great City Guilds (p. 100) have found a worthy outlet for some of their wealth in the development of technical education.

21. General Hints.

Some of the following remarks may be deemed superfluous by many readers of this Handbook; but a few observations on English or London peculiarities may not be unacceptable to the American, the English-speaking foreigner, or the provincial visitor.

In England Sunday, as is well known, is observed as a day of rest and of public worship. Shops, places of amusement, and the City restaurants are closed the whole day, while other restaurants are open from 1 to 3, and from 6 to 11 p.m. only. Many museums and galleries, however, are now opened on Sun. (p. 108). Many places of business are closed from 1, 2, or 3 p.m. on Saturday till Monday morning. Among these are all the banks and insurance-offices and practically all the wholesale warehouses.

Like '*s'il vous plaît*' in Paris, '*if you please*' or '*please*' is generally used in ordering refreshments at a café or restaurant, or in making any request. The English forms of politeness are, however, by no means so minute or ceremonious as the French. For example, the hat is raised to ladies only, and is worn in public places, such as shops, cafés, music-halls, and museums. It should, however, be removed in the presence of ladies in a lift (elevator).

The fashionable hour for paying visits in London is between 4 and 6 p.m. The proper mode of delivering a letter of introduction is in person, along with the bearer's visiting-card and address; but when this is rendered inconvenient by the greatness of distance or other cause, the letter may be sent by post, accompanied by a polite explanation.

The usual dinner hour of the upper classes varies from 6 to 8 or even 9 p.m. It is considered permissible for guests invited to a dinner-party to arrive a few minutes late. A common form of invitation is 'eight, for half-past eight', in which case the guest should arrive not later than the latter hour. Gentlemen remain at table, over their wine, for a short time after the ladies have left.

Foreigners may often obtain, through their ambassadors, permission to visit private collections which are not open to the ordinary English tourist.

We need hardly caution newcomers against the artifices of pickpockets and the wiles of impostors, two fraternities which are very numerous in London. It is even prudent to avoid speaking to strangers in the street. All information desired by the traveller may be obtained from one of the policemen, of whom about 15.550 (about 900 mounted) perambulate the streets of the Metropolis. If a policeman is not readily found, application may be made to a postal letter carrier, to a commissionnaire, or at a neighbouring shop. A considerable degree of caution and presence of mind is often requisite in crossing a crowded thoroughfare, and in entering or alighting from a train or omnibus. The 'rule of the road' for foot-passengers in busy streets is to keep to the right. Poor neighbourhoods should be avoided after nightfall. Strangers are also warned against *Mock Auctions*, and indeed should neither buy nor sell at any auction without the aid of an experienced friend or a trustworthy broker. 'Rule of the road' for vehicles, see p. 73.

ADDRESSES of all kinds may be found in *Kelly's Post Office Directory*, a thick volume of 3000 pages, which may be seen at all the hotels and cafés and at most of the principal shops. The addresses of residents at the West End and other suburbs may also be obtained from *Boyle's Court Guide*,

Webster's Royal Red Book, the *Royal Blue Book*, or *Kelly's Suburban Directory*, and those of city men and firms in *Collingridge's City Directory*.

A useful adjunct to most houses in the central parts of London is a *Cab Whistle*, one blast upon which summons a four-wheeler, two a hansom.

Among the characteristic sights of London is the *Lord Mayor's Show* (9th Nov.), or the procession in which — maintaining an ancient and picturesque, though useless custom — the newly-elected Lord Mayor moves, amid great pomp and ceremony, through the streets from the City to the Courts of Justice, in order to take the oath of office. It is followed by the great dinner in the Guildhall (p. 135).

22. Guilds, Charities, Societies, Clubs.

Guilds. The City Companies or Guilds of London were once upwards of one hundred in number, about eighty of which still exist, though few exercise their ancient privileges. About forty of them possess halls in which they transact business and hold festivities; the others meet either in rooms lent to them at Guildhall, or at the offices of the respective clerks. Nearly all the companies are called *Livery Companies*, and the members are entitled, on ceremonial occasions, to wear the liveries (gowns, furs, etc.) of their respective guilds. Many of the companies are extremely wealthy, while others possess neither halls nor almshouses, neither estates nor revenues, — nothing but ancient charters to which they reverentially cling. Some of the guild-houses are among the most interesting buildings in London, and are noticed throughout the Handbook. The Twelve Great Companies, wealthier and more influential than the rest, are the *Mercers*, *Grocers*, *Drapers*, *Fishmongers*, *Goldsmiths*, *Skinners*, *Merchant Taylors*, *Haberdashers*, *Salters*, *Ironmongers*, *Vintners*, and *Clothworkers*. Some of the companies represent trades now quite extinct, and by their unfamiliar names strikingly illustrate the fact how completely they have outlived their original purpose. Such are the *Bowyers*, *Broderers*, *Girdlers*, *Horners*, *Loriners* (saddler's ironmongers), *Patten Makers*, and *Scriveners*.

Charities. The charities of London are on a scale commensurate with the vastness of the city, being no fewer than 2000 in number. They comprise hospitals, dispensaries, asylums; bible, tract, missionary, and district visiting societies; provident homes, orphanages, etc. A tolerably complete catalogue will be found in *Fry's Guide to the London Charities* (1s. 6d.), *Howe's Classified Directory of Metropolitan Charities* (1s.), or *Low's Handbook to the Charities of London* (1s.). The total voluntary subscriptions, donations, and bequests to these charities amount to about 5,000,000l. annually, or more than 1l. for each man, woman, and child in the capital. The institution of 'Hospital Sunday', on which collections are made in all the churches for the hospitals, produces a yearly revenue of about 45,000l. Non-churchgoers have a similar opportunity afforded them on 'Hospital Saturday', when about 750 ladies station themselves at street-corners to receive contributions; this produces about 7000l., while collections made at the same time in workshops add 13,000*l.* or more. The following is a brief list of the chief general hospitals, besides which there are numerous special hospitals for cancer, small-pox, fever, consumption, eye and ear diseases, and so forth.

Charing Cross, Agar Street, Strand. — *French Hospital*, 172 Shaftesbury Avenue. — *German*, Dalston Lane, Dalston. — *Great Northern*, Holloway Road. — *Guy's*, St. Thomas Street, Southwark. — *Italian*, 40 Queen Square. — *King's College*, Portugal Street, Lincoln's Inn Fields. — *London*, 209 Whitechapel Road. — *London Homeopathic*, Great Ormond Street. — *Metropolitan*, Kingsland Road, E. — *Middlesex*, Mortimer Street, Berners Street. — *North-West London*, 18 Kentish Town Road. — *University College*, or *North London*, Gower Street. — *Royal Free*, 256 Gray's Inn Road. — *St. Bartholomew's*, Smithfield. — *St. George's*, Hyde Park Corner. — *St. Mary's*, Cambridge Place, Paddington. — *St. Thomas's*, Albert Embankment. — *Temperance*, Hampstead Road. — *Vegetarian*, at Loughton (p. 415). — *West London*, Hammersmith Road. — *Westminster*, Broad Sanctuary.

The following are HOSPITALS FOR LADIES, in which patients are received for a moderate charge: — *Establishment for Invalid Ladies*, 90 Harley Street (1*l.*-2*l.* 5*s.* 6*d.* per week); *New Hospital for Women*, 144 Euston Road, with lady-doctors; *Chelsea Hospital for Women*, Fulham Road.

University Settlements. These residential colonies, which are intended to bring the knowledge and culture of the educated classes into direct contact with the needs and problems of the poor, for the benefit of both, are interesting to the student of social questions.

The oldest and perhaps most characteristic example is *Toynbee Hall* (p. 169). Institutions of a similar kind, some of which are connected with particular religious bodies and more or less missionary in their aims, are: *Oxford House*. Mape St., Bethnal Green Road (Church of England); *Robert Browning Hall*, York Road, Walworth (Congregational); *Mansfield House*, 143 Barking Road, Canning Town; *Bermondsey Settlement*, Farncombe St., Jamaica Road (Methodist); *Passmore Edwards Settlement*, Tavistock Place, Bloomsbury. *Mayfield House*, Shoreditch, *St. Margaret's House*, Bethnal Green, the *Women's Settlement*, Canning Town, etc., are similar institutions for women.

Societies. The societies for the encouragement of industry, art, and science in London are extremely numerous, and many of them possess most ample endowments. The names of a few of the most important may be given here, some of them being described at length in other parts of the Handbook: —

Royal Society, Royal Academy, Society of Antiquaries, Geological Society, Royal Astronomical Society, Linnaean Society, Chemical Society, British Association for the Advancement of Science, all in Burlington House, Piccadilly. — *Royal Archaeological Institute*, 20 Hanover Square. — *Royal College of Physicians*, Pall Mall East. — *Royal College of Surgeons*, 40 Lincoln's Inn Fields. — *Royal Geographical Society*, 1 Savile Row, Burlington Gardens. — *Royal Agricultural Society*, 13 Hanover Square. — *Royal Asiatic Society*, 22 Albemarle Street, Piccadilly. — *Royal Society of Literature*, 20 Hanover Square, W. — *Royal College of Science*, Exhibition Road, South Kensington. — *Society for the Encouragement of Arts, Manufactures, and Commerce*, generally known as the *Society of Arts*, John Street, Adelphi, Strand. — *Royal Academy of Music*, 4 Tenterden Street, Hanover Square. — *Royal College of Music*, Prince

Consort Road, South Kensington. — *Trinity College* (music and arts), 13 Mandeville Place, Manchester Square. — *Guildhall School of Music*, John Carpenter Street, Victoria Embankment. — *Heralds' College*, Queen Victoria Street. — *Institution of Civil Engineers*, 25 Great George Street, Westminster. — *Institute of Mechanical Engineers*, Storey's Gate. — *Royal Institute of British Architects*, 9 Conduit Street, W. (good collection of books on architecture). — *Sanitary Institute of Great Britain* (Museum of Hygiene), 74a Margaret Street, Cavendish Square. — *Royal Institution*, 21 Albemarle Street, Piccadilly. Popular lectures on science, art, and literature are delivered here on Friday evenings during the Season (adm. by a member's order). Six lectures for children, illustrated by experiments, are given after Christmas. — *London School of Economics and Political Science*, 10 Adelphi Terrace. — *London School of Ethics and Social Philosophy*, Passmore Edwards Settlement, Tavistock Place, Bloomsbury. — *Society of Authors*, 4 Portugal Street, Lincoln's Inn Fields, W. C.

The **Clubs** are chiefly devoted to social purposes. Most of the club-houses at the West End, particularly those in or near Pall Mall, are very handsome, and admirably fitted up, affording every possible comfort. To a bachelor in particular his 'club' is a most serviceable institution. Members are admitted by ballot, but candidates are rejected by a certain small proportion of 'black balls' or dissentient votes. The entrance fee varies from 2*l*. 2*s*. to 40*l*., and the annual subscription is from 3*l*. 3*s*. to 15*l*. 15*s*. The introduction of guests by a member is allowed in some, but not in all of the clubs. The cuisine is usually admirable. The wine and viands, which are sold at little more than cost price, often attain a pitch of excellence unequalled by the most elaborate and expensive restaurants.

We append a roughly classified list of the most important clubs:—

Political. — Conservative: *Carlton*, 94 Pall Mall, the premier Conservative Club (1800 members); *City Carlton*, 24 St. Swithin's Lane; *Conservative Club*, 74 St. James's Street (1300 members); *Constitutional*, Northumberland Avenue (6500 members); *Junior Carlton*, 30-35 Pall Mall (2100 members); *Junior Conservative*, 43 Albemarle Street (5500 members); *Junior Constitutional*, 101 Piccadilly (5500 members); *Primrose*, 4 Park Place, St. James's (5000 members); *St. Stephen's*, 1 Bridge Street, Westminster. — Liberal: *Brooks's*, 60 St. James's Street (Whig club); *City Liberal Club*, Walbrook; *Devonshire*, 50 St. James's Street (1200 members); *National Liberal*, Whitehall Place (5500 members); *New Reform Club*, St. Ermin's Hotel (p. 10); *Reform*, 104 Pall Mall, the premier Liberal Club (1400 members). — The *St. James's Club*, 106 Piccadilly, is for the diplomatic service (650 members).

Military and Naval and University Clubs. — *Army and Navy Club*, 36 Pall Mall (2400 members); *Cavalry*, 127 Piccadilly; *East India United Service*, 16 St. James's Square (2500 members); *Guards' Club*, 70 Pall Mall; *Junior Army and Navy*, 10 St. James's Street (2000 members); *Junior Naval and Military*, 96 Piccadilly; *Junior United Service*, 11 Charles Street (2000 members); *Naval and Military*, 94 Piccadilly (2000 members); *New Oxford and Cambridge*, 68 Pall Mall; *New University*, 57 St. James's Street; *Oxford and Cambridge*, 71-76 Pall Mall; *United Service*, 116 Pall Mall (1600 members; members must not hold lower rank than major in the army or commander in the navy); *United University*, 1 Suffolk Street.

Literary, Dramatic, Artistic Clubs, etc. — *Arts Club*, 40 Dover Street, Piccadilly; *Arundel*, 1 Adelphi Terrace. — *Athenaeum Club*, 107 Pall Mall, the club of the *literati*; 1200 members. (Distinguished strangers visiting London may be elected honorary members of the Athenæum during their temporary residence in London.) — *Authors'*, 3 Whitehall Court, S.W.; *Burlington Fine Arts Club*, 17 Savile Row; *Caledonian*, 30 Charles St., S.W.; *Camera*, 28 Charing Cross Road; *Crichton*, 39 King St., Covent Garden; *Garrick Club*, 13 and 15 Garrick Street, Covent Garden, for literary men and actors (650 members); *Press Club*, Wine Office Court, Fleet Street; *Royal Societies' Club*, 63 St. James's Street (1500 members); *Savage Club*, 6 Adelphi Terrace.

Sporting Clubs. — *Alpine Club*, 23 Savile Row; *Automobile*, 4 Whitehall Court; *Badminton*, 100 Piccadilly (1000 members; sporting and coaching); *Baths Club*, 34 Dover Street (for swimming, etc.; 2000 members, including 500 ladies); *Golfers'*, 3 Whitehall Court; *Isthmian*, 105 Piccadilly; *Kennet Club*, 27 Old Burlington Street; *Ladies' Kennel Association; National Sporting Club*, 43 King Street, Covent Garden; *Nimrod*, 12 St. James's Square; *Prince's*, Knightsbridge (rackets and tennis); *Queen's*, West Kensington (tennis, rackets, etc.); *Sports Club*, 8 St. James's Square; *Turf Club*, 85 Piccadilly (whist and other card games); *Victoria*, 18 Wellington Street, Strand. — *Hurlingham Club*, see p. 386; *Ranelagh Club*, see p. 386. — Comp. pp. 71-74.

Social and General Clubs. — *Albemarle*, 13 Albemarle Street, for ladies and gentlemen (800 members); *Arthur's*, 69 St. James's Street; *Bachelors'*, 8 Hamilton Place; *Boodle's*, 28 St. James's Street (chiefly for country gentlemen); *City Athenaeum*. Angel Court, E.C.; *City of London*, 19 Old Broad Street, City; *Cocoa Tree*, 64 St. James's Street; *Colonial Club*, Whitehall Court, Charing Cross; *Eccentric*, 21 Shaftesbury Avenue; *German Athenaeum*, 93 Mortimer Street; *Gresham*, 1 Gresham Place, City; *Grosvenor*, 135 New Bond Street (3000 members); *Hyde Park*, Albert Gate; *Junior Athenaeum*, 116 Piccadilly; *Marlborough*, 52 Pall Mall; *National*, 1 Whitehall Gardens; *New*, 4 Grafton Street; *New Lyric*, Coventry Street. W.; *Oriental*, 18 Hanover Square; *Orleans*, 29 King Street, St. James's; *Piccadilly*, 123 Piccadilly; *Portland*, 9 St. James's Square (whist); *Raleigh*, 16 Regent Street; *Savile Club*, 107 Piccadilly; *Thatched House*, 86 St. James's Street; *Travellers'*, 106 Pall Mall (800 members; each member must have travelled at least 1000 miles from London); *Union Club*, Trafalgar Square, corner of Cockspur Street; *Wellington*, 1 Grosvenor Place; *White's Club*, 38 St. James's Street; *Whitehall Club*, 47 Parliament Street; *Windham Club*, 13 St. James's Square.

Ladies' Clubs. — *Alexandra*, 12 Grosvenor Street (900 members); *Sandringham*, 38 Dover Street; *Pioneers'*, 5 Grafton St.; *Writers'*, Hastings House, Norfolk Street, Strand; *New County*, 21 Hanover Square (300 members); *Empress*, 32 Dover St.; *Green Park*, 10 Grafton St.; *Grosvenor Crescent*, 15 Grosvenor Crescent. — The *Albemarle* (see above), the *Sesame*, 28 Dover Street, and the *Denison*, 15 Buckingham Street, Strand (for social discussions). are for ladies and gentlemen.

The *Royal Colonial Institute*, Northumberland Avenue, founde i 1868 for the purpose of 'providing a place of meeting for all gentlemen connected with the Colonies and British India' (3800 members), offers many of the advantages of a good club. — The *American Society in London* (114 Southampton Row, W. C.) has for its object 'the promotion of patriotic and social life amongst Americans residing in London, and the fostering of the sentiments of mutual resj ect and affection, which bind together the peoples of America and Great Britain'. — The *Foreign Missions Club*, 149 Highbury New Park, is intended for missionaries and those interested in their work.

23. Books relating to London.

The following are some of the best and latest works on London and its neighbourhood.

*London Past and Present, by *Henry B. Wheatley* (based upon *Peter Cunningham's Handbook of London*); 3 vols.; 1891 (an invaluable storehouse of information, arranged in alphabetical order).

*London: its Celebrated Characters and Remarkable Places, by *J. Heneage Jesse;* 3 vols., illustrated; 1871.

Memorials of London and London Life in the 13th, 14th, and 15th Centuries, by *H. T. Riley;* **1868** (a series of extracts from early chronicles).

John Stow's Survey of London (1598); cheap reprint, edited by *Prof. Henry Morley,* in the 'Carisbrooke Library' (Routledge; 1890).

London (Historic Towns Series), by *W. J. Loftie;* 1887.

In and out of London, by *W. J. Loftie;* illustrated; 1876.

A History of London, by *W. J. Loftie;* 2 vols., illus.; 2nd ed., **1884.**

London City, by *W. J. Loftie* ; illustrated; 1891.

Round about London (12 miles), by a *Fellow of the Society of Antiquaries;* 6th ed., 1893.

Walks in London, by *Aug. J. C. Hare;* 2 vols., illus.; 6th ed., 1894.

London, by *Sir Walter Besant;* illustrated; 1893.

Westminster, by *Sir Walter Besant;* illustrated; 1895.

South London, by *Sir Walter Besant;* illustrated; 1898.

Northern Heights of London, by *Wm. Howitt;* illustrated; 1869.

Thorne's Handbook to the Environs of London; 2 vols., 1877.

Knight's London; 2 vols.; illustrated.

Cassell's Old and New London, by *W. Thornbury* and *E. Walford;* 6 vols., illustrated; new ed., 1898.

Cassell's Greater London (15 miles), by *E. Walford;* 2 vols., illustrated; new ed.. 1893-95.

London City Churches, by *A. E. Daniell;* 1895.

London Riverside Churches, by *A. E. Daniell;* 1897.

Dickens's London, by *T. E. Pemberton;* 1876.

Thackeray's London, by *W. H. Rideing;* 1885.

In the Footprints of Charles Lamb, by *B. E. Martin;* ill.; 1891.

Old London Street Cries and the Cries of To-day, by *A. W. Tuer;* illustrated; 1885.

Literary Landmarks of London, by *Laurence Hutton;* 8th ed., 1892.

The Highway of Letters (Fleet Street), by *Thomas Archer;* ill.; 1893.

Memorable London Houses, by *Wilmot Harrison;* 3rd ed., 1890.

Literary London, by *W. P. Ryan;* 1898.

Stories of the Streets of London, by *H. Barton Baker;* 1899.

London in the Jacobite Times, by *Dr. Doran;* 2 vols., 1877.

The Romance of London, by *J. Timbs;* 2nd ed., 1869.

Curiosities of London, by *J. Timbs;* 1876.

Clubs and Club Life in London, by *J. Timbs;* illustrated; 1872.

Haunted London, by *W. Thornbury,* edited by *E. Walford;* 1880.

The Town, by *Leigh Hunt;* illustrated; last ed., 1893.

The Old Court Suburb (Kensington), by *Leigh Hunt;* 1860.

Saunter through the West End, by *Leigh Hunt;* 1861.

London City Suburbs, by *Percy Fitzgerald;* illustrated; 1893.

London up to Date, by *George Augustus Sala;* 1895.

Belcour's London in my Pocket and *Massey's* Streets of London (each 1*s.*) are intended to help in ascertaining the position of any street in London.

Little's London Pleasure Guide (annual; 1*s.*) gives convenient information as to theatres (plans), race-meetings, regattas, shows, etc.

The *London Manual* (1*s.* annually) explains the functions of the public bodies of the Metropolis.

Whitaker's Almanack (1*s.* and 2*s.* 6*d.*) gives a large amount of useful information in a condensed form.

The most detailed plan of London is that of the *Ordnance Survey,* on a scale of 5 ft. per mile (in course of publication; several hundred sheets at 2*s.* 6*d.* each; index map 4*d.;* Edward Stanford, 26 Cockspur Street, S.W.). — Stanford's excellent *New Map of the County of London* consists of 20 sheets (4 inches to a mile) at 1*s.* each (complete, in portfolio, 16*s.*).

24. Preliminary Ramble.

Nothing is better calculated to afford the traveller some insight into the labyrinthine topography of London, to enable him to ascertain his bearings, and to dispel the first oppressive feeling of solitude and insignificance, than a drive through the principal quarters of the town.

The outside of an omnibus affords a much better view than a cab (fares, see p. 34), and, moreover, has the advantage of cheapness. If the driver, beside whom the stranger should sit, happens to be obliging (and a small gratuity will generally make him so), he will afford much useful information about the buildings, monuments, and other sights on the route; but care should be taken not to distract his attention in crowded parts. Even without such assistance, however, our plan of the city, if carefully consulted, will supply all necessary information. If ladies are of the party, an open *Fly* (see p. 34) is the most comfortable conveyance.

Taking *Hyde Park Corner*, at the W. end of Piccadilly, as a convenient starting-point, we mount one of the numerous omnibuses which ply to the Bank and London Bridge and traverse nearly the whole of the quarters lying on the N. bank of the Thames. Entering Piccadilly, we first pass, on the right, the Green Park, beyond which rises Buckingham Palace (p. 329). A little farther to the E., in the distance, we descry the towers of Westminster Abbey (p. 247) and the Houses of Parliament (p. 237). In Regent Street on the right, at some distance off, rises the York Column (p. 280). Passing Piccadilly Circus with the Shaftesbury Memorial (p. 286), we drive to the right through the Haymarket, near the end of which are the Haymarket Theatre (p. 65) on the left, and Her Majesty's Theatre (p. 65) on the right. We now come to Trafalgar Square, with the Nelson Monument (p. 186) and the National Gallery (p. 188). On the right, in the direction of Whitehall, we observe the old statue of Charles I. Passing Charing Cross, with the large Charing Cross Hotel (p. 8) on the right, we enter the Strand, where the Adelphi, Lyceum, Gaiety, and other theatres lie on our left, and the Savoy, Terry's, and Strand theatres on our right (pp. 65, 66). On the left is Southampton Street, leading to Covent Garden (p. 232), and on the right Wellington Street, with Somerset House (p. 182) near the corner, leading to Waterloo Bridge (p. 183). Near the middle of the Strand we reach the church of St. Mary le Strand (p. 182), and farther on is St. Clement Danes (p. 181). On the left we see the extensive new Law Courts (p. 179). Passing the site of Temple Bar (see p. 179), we now enter the City proper (p. 95). On the right of Fleet Street are several entrances to the Temple (p. 176), while on the left rises the church of St. Dunstan in the West (p. 173). At the end of Farringdon Street, diverging on the left, we notice the Holborn Viaduct Bridge (p. 125); on the right, in New Bridge Street, is the Ludgate Hill Station. We next drive up Ludgate Hill, pass St. Paul's Cathedral (p. 111) on the left, and turn to the left to Cheapside, noticing the monument of Sir Robert Peel (p. 121), to the N. of which is the General Post Office (p. 122). In Cheapside we observe Bow Church (p. 134) on the right, and near it the Guildhall (p. 134) at the end of King Street on the left. Quitting Cheapside, we enter the Poultry, in which the Mansion House (p. 138) rises on the right. Opposite the Mansion House is the Bank of England (p. 139), and before us is the Royal Exchange (p. 140), with Wellington's Statue in front. We then drive through King William Street, with the Statue of William IV., observing the Monument (p. 148) on the left.

We now quit the omnibus, and walk along Lower Thames Street, passing Billingsgate (p. 149) and the Custom House (p. 149), to the Tower (p. 155). We then cross the new Tower Bridge (p. 165) and walk back along Tooley Street, on the S. side of the river, to St. Saviour's Church (p. 376) and London Bridge (p. 147). Hence we may return to Hyde Park Corner by omnibus, or ascend the river by steamer (see p. 63), passing under the Cannon Street Station Railway Bridge, Southwark Bridge (with St. Paul's rising on the right), the Chatham and Dover Bridge, and Blackfriars Bridge. Between Blackfriars Bridge and Westminster runs the Victoria Embankment (p. 150). On the right are the Temple (p. 176) and Somerset House (p. 182). The steamer then passes under Waterloo Bridge (p. 183), beyond which, to the right, on the Embankment, stands Cleopatra's Needle (p. 151), with the huge Savoy and Cecil Hotels (p. 7) rising behind. We alight at Charing Cross Pier, adjacent to the Charing Cross Railway Bridge, and re-embark in a *Chelsea Boat*, which will convey us past Montague House (p. 237), New Scotland Yard (p. 237), Westminster Bridge (p. 246), and the Houses of Parliament (p. 237), behind which is Westminster Abbey (p. 247). On the left is the Albert Embankment, with St. Thomas's Hospital (p. 380); and, farther on, Lambeth Palace (p. 380) with the Lollards' Tower. Passing under Lambeth Bridge, we see the Tate Gallery (p. 274) on the left, in front of which is a temporary bridge. We then reach Vauxhall Bridge. From Vauxhall the traveller may walk or take a tramway-car to Victoria Station, whence an omnibus will convey him to Oxford Street.

Those who have time for a longer excursion may proceed from the Tower up Seething Lane to the Fenchurch St. Station of the *London & Blackwall Railway*, whence a train carries them to Blackwall. Thence after inspecting *Blackwall Tunnel* (p. 168) we return by steamer (p. 63) to London Bridge, and proceed as above.

In order to obtain a view of the quarters on the right (S.) bank of the Thames, or Surrey side, we take a light-green *Atlas* omnibus (*not* a City Atlas) in Regent Circus, Oxford Street (Plan R, 23), and drive through Regent Street, Regent's Quadrant, Piccadilly Circus, Regent Street (continued), Waterloo Place (with the Crimean Monument and the York Column), Pall Mall East, and Charing Cross to (right) Whitehall. Here we observe, on the left, Whitehall Banqueting Hall (p. 233), and on the right the Admiralty, the Horse Guards (p. 236), and the Government Offices. Our route next lies through Parliament Street, beyond which we pass Westminster Abbey (p. 247) and the Houses of Parliament (p. 237) on the right. The omnibus then crosses Westminster Bridge (p. 246), with the Victoria Embankment on the left, and the Albert Embankment and St. Thomas's Hospital on the right. Traversing Westminster Bridge Road, we observe, on the right, Christ Church (p. 382) and Hawkstone Hall. In Lambeth Road we perceive the Church of St. George (p. 382), the Roman Catholic Cathedral of Southwark, and, opposite to it, Bethlehem Hospital (p. 381). On the W. side of St. George's Circus, with its obelisk, rises the Blind Asylum. A little to the S. of this point, we arrive at the Elephant and Castle (on the right), where we alight, to resume our journey on a blue Waterloo omnibus. This takes us through London Road to Waterloo Road, to the right of which are the Surrey Theatre (Blackfriars Road), Magdalen Hospital, and the Victoria Music Hall (p. 68), and on the left the South Western Railway Station. We then cross Waterloo Bridge (p. 182), drive along Wellington Street, passing Somerset House (p. 181), and turn to the left into the Strand, which leads us to Charing Cross.

Our first curiosity having thus been gratified by a general survey of London, we may now devote our attention to its collections, monuments, and buildings in detail.

25. Disposition of Time.

The most indefatigable sight-seer will take at least three weeks to obtain even a superficial acquaintance with London and its objects of interest. A plan of operations, prepared beforehand, will aid him in regulating his movements and economising his time. Fine days should be spent in visiting the docks, parks, gardens, and environs. Excursions to the country around London, in particular, should not be postponed to the end of one's sojourn, as otherwise the setting in of bad weather may altogether preclude a visit to the many beautiful spots in the neighbourhood. Fuller particulars of many excursions which can be made from London in the course of a long day, though hardly included in its environs, will be found in *Baedeker's Handbook to Great Britain*. Rainy days had better be devoted to the galleries and museums.

The following list shows the days and hours when the principal collections and other sights are accessible. In winter (Oct. to April inclusive) the collections close at the earlier hours shown in the ac-

	Sunday	Monday	Tuesday	Wednesday
Carlyle Museum (p. 370) . . .	—	10 till dusk	10 till dusk	10 till dusk
Charterhouse (p. 129)	services	10-4, 5, 6	10-4, 5, 6	10-4, 5, 6
Chelsea Hospital (p. 369) . . .	services	10-1, 2-7	10-1, 2-7	10-1, 2-7
*Crystal Palace (p. 396)	—	10 till dusk	10 till dusk	10 till dusk
*Dulwich Gallery (p. 401) . . .	—	1-4, 5, 6	10-4, 5, 6	10-4, 5, 6
*Foundling Hospital (p. 293) . .	11-1, 5-6	10-4		
Greenwich Hospital (p. 392) . .	2-4, 5, 6	10-4, 5, 6	10-4, 5, 6	10-4, 5, 6
Guildhall, Picture Gallery (p. 136).	3-8	10-4, 5	10-4, 5	10-4, 5
—, Museum (p. 136)	—	10-4, 5	10-4, 5	10-4, 5
°Hampton Court Palace (p. 406)	2-4, 6	10-4, 6	10-4, 6	10-4, 6
Imperial Institute (p. 345) . .	—	11-5	11-5	11-5
*Kensington Palace (p. 334) . .	2-6, 6	10-4, 6	10-4, 6	—
°Kew Gardens (p. 413)	1-6	10(12)-6	10(12)-6	10(12)-6
Leighton House (p. 337) . . .	—	2-5.30	2-5.30	2-5.30
Monument (p. 148)	—	8-6, 9-4	8-6, 9-4	8-6, 9-4
Museum, Bethnal Green (p. 170)	2 till dusk	10-10	10-4, 5, 6	10-4, 5, 6
—, **British (p. 299)	2.30 till dusk	10-6	10-6	10-6
—, Geological (p. 285)	2 till dusk	10-10	10-5	10-5
—, *Natural History (p. 346) .	2.30 till dusk	10-4, 4.30, 5, 5, 5.30, 6	10-4, 4.30, 5, 5.30, 6	10-4, 4.30, 5, 5.30, 6
—, Soane (p. 230).	—	—	11-5	11-5
—, **South Kensington (p. 349)	2 till dusk	10-10	10-10	10-4, 5, 6
—, United Service (p. 235) . .	—	11-4, 6	11-4, 6	11-4, 6
**National Gallery (p. 188) . .	2-4, 6	10-4, 5, 6	10-4, 5, 6	10-4, 5, 6
*— — of British Art (p. 274) .	2-4, 6	10-4, 5, 6	10-4, 5, 6	10-4, 5, 6
**— Portrait Gallery (p. 220) .	2.30-5.30	10-4, 5, 6	10-4, 5, 6	10-4, 5, 6
*Parliament, Houses of (p. 237)	—	—	—	—
Royal Academy, Summer Exhib. (p. 283)	—	8-7	8-7	8-7
—, Winter Exhib. (p. 283) . .		9 till dusk	9 till dusk	9 till dusk
—, Gibson and Diploma Gal. (p. 283).	—	11-4	11-4	11-4
Royal College of Surgeons(p.229)	—	11-4, 5	11-4, 5	11-4, 5
**St. Paul's Cathedral (p. 111)	services	9-5	9-5	9-5
Society of Arts (p. 185)	—	10-4	10-4	—
*Temple Church (p. 177) . . .	services	10-4, 5	10-4, 5	10-4, 5
*Tower (p. 155).	—	10-4, 6	10-4	10-4
**Wallace Collection (p. 283) .	2-5, 6	2-6	11-6	10-6
**Westminster Abbey (p. 247) .	services	9 till dusk	9 till dusk	9 till dusk
*Zoological Gardens (p. 294) .	(see p. 295)	9 till dusk	9 till dusk	9 till dusk

Thursday	Friday	Saturday	Admission free except when otherwise stated.
10 till dusk	10 till dusk	10 till dusk	Admission 1*s.*, on Sat. 6*d.*
10-4, 5, 6	10-4, 5, 6	10-4, 5, 6	Great Hall closed 3-4.
10-1, 2-7	10-1, 2-7	10-1, 2-7	
10 till dusk	10 till dusk	10 till dusk	Adm. 1*s.*; on Sat. sometimes 2*s.* 6*d.*
10-4, 5, 6	10-4, 5, 6	10-4, 5, 6	
—	—	—	Donation expected.
10-4, 5, 6	10-4, 5, 6	10-4, 5, 6	
10-4, 5	10-4, 5	10-4, 5	Closed on alternate Sundays.
10-4, 5	10-4, 5	10-4, 5	
10-4, 6	—	10-4, 6	
11-5	11-5	11-5	Free before 1 p.m.; 1*s.* after.
10-4, 6	10-4, 6	10-4, 6	Closed Good Friday, Christmas Day.
10(12)-6	10(12)-6	10(12)-6	Hothouses open from 1 p.m.
2-5.30	2-5.30	2-5.30	Adm. 1*s.*; free on Tues & Sat.
8-6, 9-4	8-6, 9-4	8-6, 9-4	Adm. 3*d.*
10-10	10-4, 5, 6	10-10	Adm. 6*d.* on Wed.; other days free.
10-6	10-6	10-6	Some galleries close at 4 or 5 p.m.
10-5	—	10-10	Closed from 10th Aug. to 10th Sept.
10-4, 4.30, 5,	10-4, 4.30, 5,	10-4, 4.30, 5,	Also on Sat. and Mon. till 8 p.m. from
5.30, 6	5.30, 6	5.30, 6	May 1st to July 15th, and till 7 p.m. from July 16th till Aug. 31st.
11-5	11-5	—	From March to Aug. inclusive; from Sept. to Feb. on application.
10-4, 5, 6	10-4, 5, 6	10-10	Adm. 6*d.* Wed., Thurs., Frid.; other days free. Exhib. Gall. always free.
11-4, 6	11-4, 6	11-4, 6	Adm. 6*d.*
11-4, 5, 6	11-4, 5, 6	10-4, 5, 6	Adm. 6*d.* on Thurs. & Frid.; closed on Sun. in winter.
11-4, 5, 6	11-4, 5, 6	11-4, 5,	Adm. 6*d.* on Thurs. & Frid.; closed on Sun. in winter.
10-4, 5	10-4, 5	10-4, 5, 6	Adm. 6*d.* on Thurs. & Frid.; closed on Sun. in winter.
—	—	10-3.30	Tickets gratis.
8-7	8-7	8-7	From 1st Mon. in May to 1st Mon. in Aug. Adm. 1*s.*
9 till dusk	9 till dusk	9 till dusk	From 1st Mon. in Jan. to 1st Mon. in Mar. Adm. 1*s.*
11-4	11-4	11-4	
11-4, 5	—	—	By special permission.
9-5	9-5	9-5	Crypt 6*d.*; Whispering Gallery 6*d.*
10-4	10-4	10-4	
10-4, 5	10-4, 5	10-12	
10-4	10-4	10-4, 6	Adm. free (Armoury and Crown Jewels 6*d.* each, except on Mon. & Sat.).
10-6	11-6	10-6	Adm. 6*d.* on Tues. & Frid.; closed on Sun. in winter.
9 till dusk	9 till dusk	9 till dusk	Adm. to chapels 6*d.*; free on Mon. & Tues.
9 till dusk	9 till dusk	9 till dusk	Adm. 1*s.*; on Mon. 6*d.*

companying table; in summer at the later hours. The early forenoon and late afternoon hours may be appropriately spent in visiting the principal churches, many of which are open the whole day, or in walking in the parks or in the Zoological and the Botanical Gardens, while the evenings may be devoted to the theatres. The best time for a promenade in Regent Street or Hyde Park is between 5 and 7 o'clock, when they both present a remarkably busy and attractive scene. When the traveller happens to be near London Bridge (or the Tower Bridge) he should take the opportunity of crossing it in order to obtain a view of the Port of London and its adjuncts, with its sea-going vessels arriving or departing, the innumerable river-craft of all sizes, and the vast traffic in the docks. A trip to Gravesend (see p. 389) should by all means be taken in order to obtain a proper view of the shipping, no other port in the world presenting such a sight.

The data in the accompanying table (pp. 108, 109), though carefully revised down to 1900, are liable to frequent alteration. The traveller is, therefore, recommended to consult one of the principal London newspapers with regard to the sights of the day. Our list does not include parks, gardens, and other places which, on all week-days at least, are open to the public gratis. The doubleasterisks indicate those sights which should on no account be omitted, while those next in importance are denoted by single asterisks. These indications, in conjunction with the special tastes and interests of each individual, will help the hurried visitor to make good use of his time. The movement for the Sunday opening of museums, galleries, and other large public collections has recently made great strides in London; and that day need no longer count as practically a *dies non* in the traveller's itinerary.

I. THE CITY.

1. St. Paul's Cathedral.

The *City*, already noticed in the Introduction as the commercial centre of London, has sometimes also been not unaptly termed its capital. In the very heart of it, conspicuously situated on a slight eminence, stands London's most prominent building, ***St. Paul's Cathedral** (Pl. R, 39; *III*).

Some authorities maintain that in pagan times a temple of Diana occupied the site of St. Paul's, but Sir Christopher Wren rejected this idea. Still the spot must at least have been one of some sanctity, to judge from the cinerary urns and other vessels found here, and Wren was of opinion, from remains discovered in digging the foundations of the present edifice, that there had been a church on this spot built by Christians in the time of the Romans, and demolished by the Pagan Saxons. It is believed to have been restored by Ethelbert, King of Kent, about A.D. 610. This building was burned down in 961, and rebuilt within a year. It was again destroyed by fire in 1087, but a new edifice was at once begun, though not completed for about 200 years. This church, Old St. Paul's, was 590 ft. long (30 ft. longer than Winchester cathedral, now the longest church in England), and in 1315 was furnished with a timber spire, covered with lead, 460 ft. high according to Wren's estimate, though earlier authorities state it to have been 520 ft. in height (*i.e.* 8 ft. higher than Cologne Cathedral). The spire was injured by lightning in 1445, but was restored, and it continued standing till 1561, when it fell a prey to the flames. The church itself was damaged by this fire, and fell into a very dilapidated condition. The S.W. tower was called the Lollards' Tower (comp. p. 380). Before the building of the Lady Chapel in 1225 the choir was adjoined by the church of St. Faith, the name of which was afterwards applied to the crypt beneath the cathedral-choir, which was used by the congregation on the demolition of their church. Near the cathedral once stood the celebrated Cross of St. Paul (Powle's Cross), where sermons were preached, papal bulls promulgated, heretics made to recant, and witches to confess, and where the Pope's condemnation of Luther was proclaimed in the presence of Wolsey. The cross and adjacent pulpit were at length removed by order of parliament in 1643. The platform on which the cross stood was discovered in 1879, at a depth of about 6 ft., by workmen engaged in laying out the garden on the N.E. side of the church (comp. Plan).

The subterranean portions of the half-ruined church were used as workshops and wine-cellars. A theatre was erected against one of the outer walls, and the nave was converted into a public promenade, the once famous *Paul's Walk*. The Protector Somerset (in the reign of Edward VI.) went so far as to employ the stones of the ancient edifice in the construction of his palace (Somerset House, p. 181). In the reign of Charles I. an extensive restoration was undertaken, and a beautiful portico built by *Inigo Jones*. The Civil War, however, put an end to this work. After the Restoration, when the church was about to be repaired, its remains were destroyed by the Great Fire of 1666 (p. 148), though the ruinous nave was used for service until 1673. — Among the numerous historical reminiscences attaching to Old St. Paul's, we may mention that it was the burial-place of a long series of illustrious persons, and the scene of Wycliffe's citation for heresy in 1337, and of the burning of Tyndale's New Testament in 1527. — The farm of Tillingham in Essex has belonged to St. Paul's since the 7th cent., representing perhaps the most ancient tenure in the country.

The present church, designed by *Sir Christopher Wren*, and begun in 1675, was opened for divine service on Sun., Dec. 5th,

1697, and completed in 1710. The ordinary statement that the whole building was completed by one architect, Sir Christopher Wren, and by one master mason, Thomas Strong, under one bishop, Dr. Compton, is correct only as far as Wren is concerned. The greater part of the cost of construction (747,954l.) was defrayed by a tax on coal. Sir Christopher Wren received during the building of the cathedral a salary of 200l. a year.

The church, which resembles St. Peter's at Rome, though much smaller, is in the form of a Latin cross. It is 500 ft. in length and 118 ft. broad, and the transept is 250 ft. long. The inner dome is 225 ft., the outer, from the pavement to the top of the cross, 364 ft. in height. The diameter of the drum beneath the dome is about 112 ft., of the dome itself 102 ft. (37 ft. less than that of St. Peter's at Rome). In the original model the plan of the building was that of a Greek cross, having over the centre a large dome, supported by eight pillars; but the court party, which was favourable to Roman Catholicism, insisted, notwithstanding Wren's opposition, on the erection of the cathedral with a long nave and an extensive choir, suitable for the Romish ritual.

The church is so hemmed in by streets and houses that it is difficult to find a point of view whence the colossal proportions of the building can be properly realised. The best idea of the majestic dome, allowed to be the finest known, is obtained from a distance, e.g. from the Thames below Blackfriars Bridge (view from the bridge itself now somewhat interfered with). St. Paul's is the fifth largest church in Christendom, being surpassed by St. Peter's at Rome, and the Cathedrals of Milan, Seville, and Florence.

EXTERIOR. It is interesting to note the union of classic details and style with the essentially Gothic structure of St. Paul's. It has aisles lower than the nave and surmounted by a triforium, just as in regular Gothic churches. But the triforium, though on a large scale, is not shown from the nave; while the lowness of the aisles is concealed on the outside by masking-walls, so as to preserve the classical appearance and cover what would be, in a Gothic church, the flying buttresses. The *West Façade*, towards Ludgate Hill, was brought better to view in 1873 by the removal of the railing, though on the three other sides the church is still surrounded by high and heavy railings. In front of this façade rises a *Statue of Queen Anne*, with England, France, Ireland, and America at her feet; the present statue, erected in 1886, is a replica of the original by *Bird* (1712). The façade, 180 ft. in breadth, is approached by a flight of 22 marble steps, and presents a double portico, the lower part of which consists of 12 coupled Corinthian columns, 50 ft. high, and the upper of 8 Composite columns, 40 ft. high. On the apex of the pediment above the second row of columns, which contains a relief of the Conversion of St. Paul by *Bird*, rises a statue of St. Paul 15 ft. in height, with St. Peter

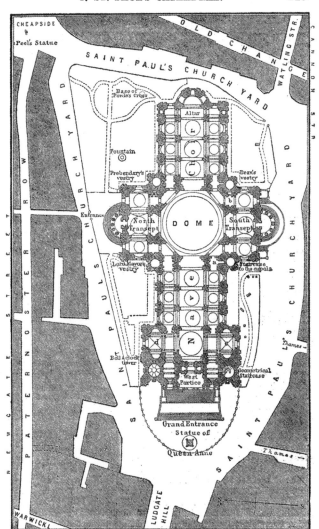

and St. James on his right and left. On each side of the façade is
a *campanile* tower, 222 ft. in height, with statues of the four Evangelists at the angles. The one on the N. side contains a fine peal of
12 bells, hung in 1878, and the other contains the largest bell in
England ('Great Paul'), hung in 1882 and weighing more than 16
tons. Each arm of the transept is terminated by a semicircular portico, crowned with five statues of the Apostles, by *Bird* (those on
the S. are copies erected in 1900). Over the S. portico is a phœnix,
with the inscription 'Resurgam', by *Cibber*; over the N. portico, the
royal arms. In reference to the former it is related, that, when the
position and dimensions of the great dome had been marked out, a
labourer was ordered to bring a stone from the rubbish of the old
cathedral to be placed as a guide to the masons. The stone which
he happened to bring was a piece of a gravestone with nothing of
the inscription remaining save the one word 'Resurgam' in large
letters. This incident was regarded as a favourable omen, and the
word accordingly adopted as a motto. At the E. end the church
terminates in a circular projection or apse. The balustrade, about
9 ft. high, on the top of the N. and S. walls was erected contrary to the
wishes of Wren, and is considered by modern architects a mistake.
A drum in two sections, the lower embellished with Corinthian, the
upper with Composite columns, bears the finely-proportioned double
Dome, the outer part of which consists of wood covered with lead.
The *Lantern* above it is supported by a hollow cone of brickwork
resting upon the inner dome. On the top of the lantern is a ball, surmounted by a cross, the ball and cross together weighing 8960 pounds.
The ball is 6 ft. in diameter, and can hold ten or twelve persons.

The church is open daily from 9 a.m. to 5 p.m. The usual ENTRANCES
are on the W. and N. The monuments in the nave and transepts may be
inspected, free of charge, at any time, except during divine service,
which takes place daily at 10 a.m. (choral) and 4 p.m. (choral) in the
choir, and on Sundays at 8 a.m., 10.30 a.m. (fine music), 3.15 p.m., and
7 p.m. On week-days daily services are also held at 8 a.m. in the chapel
in the crypt, and at 8 p.m. in the N.W. chapel; Holy Communion is celebrated at 8 a.m. and a short sermon preached at 1.15 p.m. in the N.W.
chapel. The choir is open to visitors (free) between 11 and 3.30 and after
evening-service, the entrance being by the gate of the S. ambulatory.
Tickets admitting to the Library, Clock, the Whispering Gallery, and the
Stone Gallery (6d.) and to the *Crypt and Vaults (6d.) are obtained in the
S. transept. Tickets admitting to the Golden Gallery (1s.) and to the Ball
(1s.) are obtained from the keeper in the Stone Gallery.

The INTERIOR is imposing from the beauty and vastness of its
proportions, but strikes one as somewhat bare. Though it is evi-
dent from the care with which the carved stone enrichments are
executed that Wren did not contemplate decorating the entire in-
ateior in the rich style of the Italian churches of the day, it is prob-
brle that he intended some portions to be adorned in colour. But
with the exception of Thornhill's grisailles (see p. 115), practically
nothing was done in this direction until about 1860, when a Decoration Completion Fund was founded, mainly through the exertions

of Dean Milman (p. 116), for the embellishment of the interior with marble, gilding, mosaics, and stained glass. The decoration of the dome was completed in 1863-94, that of the choir (see p. 117) in 1891-97. The dome is adorned with eight scenes from the life of St. Paul in grisaille by *Thornhill*, restored in 1854, but hardly visible from below (see p. 119). In the niches above the Whispering Gallery are marble statues of the Fathers of the Church. The eight large mosaics in the spandrels of the dome, executed by *Salviati*, represent St. Matthew and St. John, designed by *G. F. Watts*, St. Mark and St. Luke, by *Brittan*, and Isaiah, Jeremiah, Ezekiel, and Daniel, by *A. Stevens*. On the lower quarter-domes at the shorter sides of the octagon supporting the dome are mosaics by *Richmond* (comp. p. 117): N.E. the Crucifixion; S.E. the Resurrection; S.W. the Entombment. On the last pier (N. side) in the nave is an allegorical painting representing 'Time, Death, and Judgment', painted and presented by *G. F. Watts*. — The *Organ*, which is one of the finest in Great Britain, is divided into two parts, one on each side of the choir, with connecting mechanism under the choir flooring. The builder, *Mr. Willis*, in constructing it, used some of the pipes of the old organ by *Father Smith* or *Schmitz*, which dated back to 1694. — Above the N. door is a copy of the celebrated inscription in memory of Sir Christopher Wren (original, see p. 119).

The numerous monuments of celebrated Englishmen (chiefly naval and military officers), which make the church a kind of national Temple of Fame (though second to Westminster Abbey, p. 247), are very rarely of artistic value, while many are remarkable for egregiously bad taste.

The GRAND ENTRANCE (W.) is a favourable point for a survey of the whole length of the nave. The N.W. or Morning Chapel, to the left, is handsomely decorated with marble. The mosaic, representing the Three Maries at the Sepulchre on Easter Morn, was executed by *Salviati*, and commemorates Archdeacon Hale. The stained-glass window is a memorial of *Dean Mansel* (1868-71). Then to the left, in the N. AISLE : —

L. *The Crimean Cavalry Monument*, in memory of the officers and men of the British cavalry who fell in the Crimean war (1854-56).

L. *Major-General Sir Herbert Stewart*, who died in 1885 of wounds received at the battle of Abu-kru, in the Sudan; bronze medallion and reliefs by *Boehm*.

L. *Major-General Charles George Gordon*, killed at Khartoum 1885; sarcophagus-tomb, with bronze effigy by *Boehm*.

R., beneath the central arch of the aisle : *Monument to the *Duke of Wellington* (d. 1852), by *Stevens*. The bronze figure of Wellington rests on a lofty sarcophagus, overshadowed by a rich marble canopy, with 12 Corinthian columns. Above are colossal groups of Valour and Cowardice, Truth and Falsehood. The monument still wants the equestrian effigy with which the sculptor intended it to be crowned. Though originally designed for its present position, this monument stood in the Consistory Court (p. 118) until 1893.

L. *William, Lord Melbourne* (d. 1848) and *Frederick, Lord Melbourne* (d. 1853), by *Marochetti.* Two angels guard the closed entrance to the tomb.

In the N. TRANSEPT: —

L. *Sir Joshua Reynolds* (d. 1792), the celebrated painter, statue by *Flaxman.* Upon the truncated column to his left is a medallion portrait of Michael Angelo.

L. *Admiral Lord Rodney* (d. 1792), by *Rossi.* At his feet is History listening to the Goddess of Fame (on the right), who recounts the Admiral's exploits.

L. *Lieutenant-General Sir Thomas Picton* (killed at Waterloo in 1815), by *Gahagan.* In front of his bust is a Goddess of Victory presenting a crown of laurels to a warrior, upon whose shoulder leans the Genius of Immortality.

R. *Admiral Earl St. Vincent* (d. 1823), the victor at Cape St. Vincent; statue by *Baily.*

L. *General William Francis Patrick Napier* (d. 1860), the historian of the Peninsular War, by *Baily.*

L. *Sir Charles James Napier* (d. 1853); statue by *Adams*, 'a prescient General, a beneficent Governor, a just Man' (comp. p. 186).

R. *Admiral Lord Duncan* (d. 1804), who defeated the Dutch in the naval battle of Camperdown; statue by *Westmacott.*

L. *General Sir William Ponsonby* (d. 1815), 'who fell gloriously in the battle of Waterloo', by *Baily;* a nude dying hero, crowned by the Goddess of Victory, with a falling horse in the rear.

L. *Admiral Charles Napier* (d. 1860), commander of the English Baltic fleet in 1854, with portrait in relief, by *Adams.*

L. *Henry Hallam* (d. 1859), the historian; statue by *Theed.*

L. *Dr. Samuel Johnson* (d. 1784), statue by *Bacon.*

We have now arrived at the CHOIR (adm., see p. 114), the entrance to which, however, is on the other side, beyond the handsome pulpit of coloured marbles, erected in memory of *Captain Fitzgerald.* In the *S. Ambulatory* are the following monuments: —

Henry Hart Milman, Dean of St. Paul's (d. 1868); sarcophagus and recumbent figure, by *Williamson.* — On the wall at each end of this monument are fragments of stone believed to have belonged to the Temple at Jerusalem.

Dr. Donne, the poet, Dean of St. Paul's from 1621 till his death in 1631, a sculptured figure in a shroud, in a niche in the wall, by *Nicholas Stone* (the only uninjured monument from old St. Paul's).

Charles J. Blomfield, Bishop of London (d. 1857); sarcophagus with recumbent figure, by *G. Richmond.*

John Jackson, Bishop of London (d. 1884); by *Woolner.*

Reginald Heber, Bishop of Calcutta (d. 1826); a kneeling figure in episcopal robes, by *Chantrey*. The relief on the pedestal represents the prelate confirming converted Indians.

The *Apse*, behind the reredos, is fitted up as the Jesus Chapel; the altar-piece, in a marble frame, is a copy of the Doubting of St. Thomas, by Cima da Conegliano, in the National Gallery (p. 198). To the right is the recumbent marble statue of *Canon Liddon* (d. 1890), on an altar-tomb by *Bodley & Garner*.

The *Reredos*, behind the main altar, is an elaborate white Parian marble structure in the Italian Renaissance style, designed by *Messrs. Bodley & Garner* and unveiled in 1888. The sculptures, by *Guellemin*, represent the chief events in the life of Christ; at the top are statues of the Risen Saviour, the Virgin and Child, St. Paul, and St. Peter. The two latten candlesticks on the altar are copied from four old ones, formerly in England, but now in St. Bavon's, Ghent (see *Baedeker's Belgium and Holland*). The Choir Stalls are by *Grinling Gibbons*, and some of the iron work by *Tijou* (p. 398).

The vaulting and walls of the choir have been decorated in glass (smalto) mosaic from designs by *Sir W. B. Richmond*. On the central panel on the roof of the apse is Christ enthroned; to the right and left are Recording Angels. On the panels below the stone ribs of the roof in the apse and the adjoining bay are six figures of Virtues, *viz.* (beginning to the N.), Hope, Fortitude, Charity, Truth, Chastity, and Justice. The upper windows of the Apse represent the Four and Twenty Elders of the Revelation, with angels. In the adjoining bay are panels with Noah's Sacrifice (S.) and Melchizedek blessing Abraham (N.); the larger panels above these represent the Sea giving up its Dead. — In the choir proper the chief features of the mosaic decoration are the saucer-domes above each of the three bays. That in the easternmost bay represents the Creation of the Birds, while the subjects of the other two are the Creation of the Fishes and the Creation of the Beasts. On the four pendentives in each bay are Herald Angels, with extended arms. In the spaces between the clerestory windows on the N. side are the Delphic and Persian Sibyls, Alexander the Great, Cyrus, Abraham and the Angels, and Job and his three Friends; on the S. side are David, Solomon, Aholiab, Bezaleel, Moses, and Jacob. On the spandrels of the arches of the E. bay are Angels with the Instruments of the Passion; on the spandrels of the central bay, the Temptation (S.) and the Annunciation (N.); on the spandrels of the W. bay, Expulsion from Paradise (S.) and Creation of the Firmament (N.). The rectangular panels above the organ represent Adam and Eve in the Garden of Eden. The clerestory windows were also designed by Sir W. B. Richmond.

The mosaics are executed in the style of the early mosaicists, and not after the smooth modern method. Their general effect certainly adds largely to the richness and warmth of the choir; but comparatively few of their details can be satisfactorily distinguished from below under ordinary conditions of light. It is hoped that arrangements may be made by which they can be viewed from the top of the cornice. The glass tesseræ were furnished by *Messrs. Powell* of Whitefriars, and the whole work was executed by British workmen.

Leaving the passage round the choir, we turn to the left. Close by is the entrance to the Crypt (see p. 119). Then —

In the S. TRANSEPT : —

L. *John Howard* (d. 1790), the philanthropist; statue by *Bacon*. On the scroll in the left hand are written the words '*Plan for the improvement of prisons and hospitals*'; the right hand holds a key. He died at Cherson in the S. of Russia, while on a journey which he had undertaken 'to ascertain the cause of and find an efficacious remedy for the plague'. This monument was the first admitted to new St. Paul's.

L. *Admiral Earl Howe* (d. 1799), by *Flaxman*. Behind the statue of the hero is Britannia in armour; to the left Fame and Victory; on the right reposes the British lion. — Adjoining —

L. *Admiral Lord Collingwood* (d. 1810), Nelson's companion in arms (p. 120), by *Westmacott*.

L. *Joseph Mallord William Turner* (d. 1851), the celebrated painter; statue by *Macdowell*.

Opposite the door of the S. transept, in the passage to the nave, against the great piers: —

L. *Admiral Lord Nelson* (d. 1805), by *Flaxman*. The want of the right arm, which Nelson lost at Cadiz, is concealed by the cloak; the left hand leans upon an anchor supported on a coiled-up cable. The cornice bears the inscription 'Copenhagen — Nile — Trafalgar', the names of the Admiral's chief victories. The pedestal is embellished with figures in relief representing the German Ocean, the Baltic Sea, the Nile, and the Mediterranean. At the foot, to the right, couches the British lion; while on the left is Britannia inciting youthful sailors to emulate the great hero.

R. *Marquis Cornwallis* (d. 1805), first Governor-General of India, in the dress of a knight of the Garter; at the base, to the left, Britannia armed, to the right two fine Indian river-gods, by *Rossi*.

In the S. transept to the W. of the door: —

L. *Sir Astley Paston Cooper* (d. 1842), the surgeon, by *Baily*.

L. *Lieutenant-General Sir John Moore* (d. 1809), by the younger *Bacon*. The general, who fell at Corunna, is being interred by allegorical figures of Valour and Victory, while the Genius of Spain erects his standard over the tomb.

L. *Lieutenant-General Sir Ralph Abercromby* (d. 1801), by *Westmacott*. The general, mortally wounded, falls from his rearing horse into the arms of a Highland soldier. The sphinxes at the sides are emblematical of Egypt, where Sir Ralph lost his life.

L. *Sir William Jones* (d. 1794), the orientalist, who, in Dean Milman's words, 'first opened the poetry and wisdom of our Indian Empire to wondering Europe'; statue by *Bacon*.

In the S. AISLE: —

L. *Thomas Fanshaw Middleton* (d. 1822), the first English bishop in India, by *Lough*. The prelate is represented in his robes, in the act of blessing two young heathen converts.

Farther on is a chapel, formerly used as the Ecclesiastical or Consistory Court of the Diocese and now as the Baptistery. The bas-reliefs on the walls, referring to Wellington, are by *Calder Marshall* (E. end) and *Woodington* (W. end). The wooden screen between the chapel and the nave was carved by *Grinling Gibbons*.

At the end of the nave is the *Crimean Monument*, to the memory of the officers of the Coldstream Guards who fell at Inkerman in 1854, a relief by *Marochetti*, with the colours of the regiment hung above.

In the S. aisle, near the S. transept (Pl. a), is the entrance to the UPPER PARTS of the church (admission, see p. 114). Ascending about 110 steps, we reach a gallery (above the S. aisle), a room at the end of which contains the *Library* (12,000 volumes; portrait of the founder, Bishop Compton; autographs of Wren, Laud, Cranmer, etc.). The flooring consists of artistically executed mosaic in wood. The large, self-supporting, winding staircase, called the *Geometrical Staircase*, is interesting only on account of its age. The *Great Bell* (cast in 1716; 88 steps) and the large *Clock* (constructed in 1708; 13 steps more), in the S.W. tower, scarcely repay the fatigue of ascending to them. The minute hand of the clock is nearly 10 ft. long.

The *Whispering Gallery*, in the interior of the cupola, reached by a flight of steps from the library (260 steps from the floor of the church), is remarkable for a curious echo, which resembles that of the Salle d'Echo in the Conservatoire des Arts et Métiers at Paris. A slight whisper uttered by the wall on one side of the gallery is distinctly audible to an ear near the wall on the other side, a distance of 108 ft. in a direct line, or 160 ft. round the semicircle. This is the best point of view for Thornhill's ceiling-paintings, and from it we also obtain a fine survey of the interior of the church.

The subjects of Thornhill's paintings are as follows: — 1. Conversion of St. Paul; 2. Elymas the sorcerer; 3. Paul at Lystra; 4. The Gaoler at Philippi; 5. St. Paul preaching at Athens; 6. Books of magic burned at Ephesus; 7. St. Paul before Agrippa; 8. Shipwreck at Malta.

From this point a flight of 118 steps leads to the *Stone Gallery*, an outer gallery, enclosed by a stone parapet, which runs round the foot of the outer dome. This gallery commands an admirable view of the city. The survey is still more extensive from the outer *Golden Gallery* above the dome and at the foot of the lantern, to which a winding staircase ascends in the inside of the roof. The *Ball* (p. 114) on the lantern is 45 ft. higher (616 steps from the tesselated pavement of the church).

On the E. side of the S. transept is the door (Pl. b) leading down into the *CRYPT*, which extends under the entire church. In a straight direction from the staircase, at the foot of which are busts of *Sir John Macdonald* (1815-91), premier of Canada, and *Sir Harry Parkes* (d. 1885), is the S. choir-aisle, in the last window-recess of which is the plain, flat, tombstone of *Sir Christopher Wren*, the architect of St. Paul's. On the wall above is the original tablet with the inscription containing the celebrated words '*Lector, si monumentum requiris, circumspice*'. This tablet formerly stood at the entrance to the choir, in the upper church. In the flooring are the memorial slabs of many celebrated artists, which have earned the name of 'Painters' Corner' for this part of the crypt. Among these are *Benjamin West*; *Sir Joshua Reynolds*; *Sir Thomas Lawrence*; *Sir Edwin Landseer*; *John Opie*; *J. M. W. Turner* (buried, at his own dying request, near Reynolds); *Sir Edgar Boehm*; *Lord Leighton*; and *Sir John Millais*. *John Rennie*, builder of Waterloo Bridge; *Robert Milne*, who built several other London bridges; *Dean Newton*, *Dean Milman*, *William Babington*, *Sir Astley Cooper*, *Sir William Jones*, and *Canon Liddon* also repose here. — The E. end of the crypt, used as a morning chapel (Church of St. Faith; p. 111), contains a few mutilated monuments from the earlier building (*i.e.* prior to 1666). The window above the altar is a copy of Reynolds's window at New College, Oxford (see *Baedeker's Great Britain*). The fine mosaic pavement, like that in other parts of the crypt, was executed by female convicts from Woking. — The W. portion of the crypt is usually shown by an attendant (no fee). Beneath the chancel-arch, in a space lighted by four candelabra of polished granite, stands the sarcophagus of *Wellington* (d. 1852), consisting of a huge block of porphyry, resting on a granite base. Adjacent is the sarcophagus of *Sir Thomas Picton* (see p. 116), who fell at Waterloo in 1815. Farther on, exactly under the centre of the dome, is the black marble sarcophagus of *Nelson* (d. 21st Oct., 1805), containing an inner coffin made of part of the mainmast of the French flag-ship L'Orient, which was blown up at Aboukir. This sarcophagus, said, but probably erroneously, to be the work of Torregiano (p. 264), was originally ordered by Card. Wolsey for himself (comp. p. 414). The smaller sarcophagus on the S. is that of Nelson's comrade, *Admiral Collingwood* (d. 1810), while on the N. is that of the *Earl of Northesk* (d. 1831). At the extreme W. end of the crypt is the car used at the Duke of Wellington's funeral. It was cast from guns captured in the victories of the 'Iron Duke'.

The crypt also contains memorials to the *Rt. Hon. William Dalley* (d. 1888), Attorney General of New South Wales; *Lord Napier of Magdala* (d. 1890); *Sir Bartle Frere*; and *George Cruikshank*.

In May an annual festival is held in St. Paul's for the benefit of the sons of deceased clergymen. Adm. by tickets, procured at the Corporation House, 2 Bloomsbury Place, Bloomsbury Square, W.C. On St. Paul's Day (Jan. 25th) a selection from Mendelssohn's 'St. Paul' is performed with orchestra and choir; and Bach's Passion Music is given on the Tuesday of Holy Week.

The Charity School Festivals, formerly held in St. Paul's, but discontinued for some years, have recently been resumed.

The clerical establishment of the cathedral consists of the Dean, four Canons, 30 Prebendaries, 12 Minor Canons, and 6 Vicars Choral. *Sydney Smith* and *R. H. Barham*, author of the 'Ingoldsby Legends', were canons of St. Paul's. — For a full account of this noble church, see Dean Milman's 'Annals of St. Paul's' and Dr. W. Sparrow Simpson's 'St. Paul's Cathedral and Old City Life' (1895).

The street round the cathedral, called *St. Paul's Churchyard* was in the 16th cent. open to Paternoster Row, with a few intervening buildings, all belonging to the precincts. These disappeared in the Great Fire.

Dean's Yard, near the S.W. corner of the cathedral, leads to the S., past the *Deanery*, to the *Choir House*, with a choristers' school, in Great Carter Lane. A tablet on the W. wall of the archway leading from Carter Lane into Bell Yard commemorates Shakspeare's association with the Bell Tavern, formerly on this site. On the E., to the N. of Knightrider Street, lay *Doctors' Commons* (cleared away in 1862-67), where marriage licenses used to be issued. The *Doctors' Commons Will Office* was removed in 1874 from St. Bennet's Hill to Somerset House in the Strand (p. 181).

Celebrated coffee-houses in the Churchyard, where authors and booksellers used to meet, were St. Paul's Coffee House, near the archway leading to Doctors' Commons; Child's Coffee House, a great resort of the clergy and *literati*; and the Queen's Arms Tavern, often visited by Dr. Johnson. Among the famous eighteenth century publishers of St. Paul's Churchyard may be mentioned Johnson, Hunter, and Rivington. At the corner next Ludgate Hill is the site of the shop (rebuilt in 1885) of John Newbery, the bookseller, immortalized by Goldsmith, Johnson, and W. Irving. Newbery was the first publisher to issue books for children, and Goldsmith is said to have written 'Goody Two Shoes' for him, as well as to have shared in the preparation of the original 'Rhymes of Mother Goose'.

2. General Post Office. Christ's Hospital. Newgate. Holborn.

Paternoster Row. Peel's Statue. Central Criminal Court. St. Sepulchre's.

Leaving *St. Paul's Churchyard*, on the N. side of the church, we enter **Paternoster Row** (so called from the prayer-books or rosaries formerly sold in it), the chief seat of the publishers and booksellers. To the W., in Stationers' Hall Court, off Ludgate Hill, is situated *Stationers' Hall*, the guildhouse of the booksellers and stationers.

This company is one of the few London guilds the majority of whose members actually practise their nominal craft. The society lost its monopoly of publishing almanacks in 1771, but still carries on this business extensively. The company distinguished itself in 1631 by printing a Bible with the word 'not' omitted in the seventh commandment. Every work published in Great Britain must be registered at Stationers' Hall to secure the copyright. The registers go back to 1557. The hall contains portraits of Richardson, the novelist (Master of the Company in 1754), and his wife, Prior, Steele, Bunyan, and others; also *West's* painting of King Alfred sharing his loaf with the pilgrim St. Cuthbert, and a stained-glass window in memory of Caxton, placed here in 1894.

At the E. end of Paternoster Row, at the entrance to *Cheapside* (p. 133), rises the **Statue of Sir Robert Peel** (d. 1850), by *Behnes*.

Immediately to the N., on the E. side of St. Martin's le Grand, is the **General Post Office East** (Pl. R, 39, and *III*; comp. p. 79), built in the Ionic style in 1825-29, from designs by *Smirke*. In this building, 390 ft. in length, *Letters* and *Newspapers* are dealt with and all the ordinary business of a post-office carried on. *Parcels* are received here, but are at once sent on to the Parcel Post Office at Mount Pleasant, Farringdon Road. To the S. of the portico is the 'Poste Restante' Office. This is the headquarters of the London Postal District, and the vast City correspondence is all dealt with here. The *Returned Letter Office* is at Mt. Pleasant, where boards are exhibited with lists of persons whose addresses have not been discovered, and the provincial mails are also to be hereafter dealt with in a new building there.

POSTAL TRAFFIC. The number of *letters* delivered by post in the United Kingdom in the year ending March 31st, 1899, was 2,186,800,000, or 54,3 letters per head of population. Besides letters, 855,600,000 *book-packets* and *newspapers*, and 382,200,000 *post-cards* were delivered in that year. About 20-25 per cent of the letters and other postal packets from or to foreign lands come from or are addressed to the United States. In the same year the Parcel Post forwarded 71,913,000 parcels within the United Kingdom. In 1898-99 there were issued 9,721.647 inland *post-office orders*, representing a sum of 28,604,078*l*., and 76,755,217 *postal orders*, amounting in value to 27,217,436*l*. The *Post Office Savings Banks* (see p. 154), established in 1861, hold at present about 123,000,000*l*. on deposit. The profits of the English Post Office Department in 1898-99 amounted to 3,637,000*l*.

Opposite to the General Post Office East stands the **General Post Office West**, containing the *Telegraph Department*. This imposing building was erected in 1870-73 at a cost of 485,000*l*. The large Telegraph Instrument Galleries, measuring 300 by 90 ft., should be visited (admission by request from a banker or other well-known citizen). They contain 500 instruments with their attendants. On the sunk-floor are four steam-engines of 50 horse-power each, by means of which messages are forwarded through pneumatic tubes to the other offices in the City and Strand district. The number of telegrams conveyed annually exceeds 85 millions.

The vast and ever-growing business of the General Post Office found itself straitened for room even in these huge buildings, and the **General Post Office North** was built in 1890-95 to the N. of Angel Street. The building, which is connected with the Telegraph Office by a covered bridge, is designed in the classic style by *Henry Tanner*, and accommodates the Office of the Postmaster General, and the staffs of the Secretary, the Solicitor, and the Receiver and Accountant General of the post-office. On the roof is a lawn-tennis court for the use of the employees. The site and building cost 571,660*l*.

To the N. of this building, at the beginning of *Aldersgate Street* (p. 132), is the church of *St. Botolph Without Aldersgate* (Pl. R 39, 40; *III*), the small cemetery of which has been laid out as a public garden, familiarly known as the 'Postmen's Park'. It is proposed to decorate the arcade here (presented by Mr. G. F. Watts) with scenes illustrative of heroism in humble life.

To the W. of the General Post Office is the busy NEWGATE

Street, leading to Holborn and Oxford Street. This neighbourhood was long the quarter of the butchers. In *Panyer Alley*, the first cross-lane to the left, once inhabited by basket-makers, is an old relief of a boy sitting upon a 'panier'. with the inscription:

'When ye have sought the citty round,
Yet still this is the highest ground.
August the 27th, 1688'.

Farther on, King Edward Street, at the corner of which is the *Post Office Station* of the Central London Railway (p. 63), leads to the right past *Christ Church*, built by Wren in 1687-1704 and containing the remains of Richard Baxter (d. 1691). The interior was re-arranged in 1896. The 'Spital Sermon', preached here annually on Easter Tuesday, is attended in state by the Lord Mayor and aldermen. — Behind the church, and reached also by a passage from Newgate Street, is —

Christ's Hospital (Pl. R, 39; *III*), a school for 820 boys and 350 girls, founded by Edward VI. (1553), with a yearly income from land and funded property of about 60,000*l.*, in addition to funds devoted to non-educational purposes. It occupies the site of an ancient monastery of the Grey Friars, founded in the 13th cent., and once the burial-place of many illustrious persons. The general government of the school is in the hands of a large 'Council of Almoners', consisting of noblemen and other gentlemen of position nominated by the Governors, the Universities, certain learned societies, the Corporation of the City of London, and other bodies. The original costume of the boys is still retained, consisting of long blue gowns, yellow stockings, and knee-breeches. No head-covering is worn even in winter. The pupils *(Blue Coat Boys)*, who are admitted between the ages of nine and thirteen, must be the children of parents whose income is insufficient for their proper education and maintenance. 'Presented' children (*i.e.* those nominated by Governors for direct admission on the Foundation) are first sent to the Preparatory School at Hertford, whence they are transferred according to their progress to the Boys' School. Their education, which is partly of a commercial nature, is continued until the age of sixteen or seventeen. A few of the more talented pupils are, however, prepared for a university career, and form the two highest classes of the school, known as the *Grecians* and *Deputy-Grecians*. About six of these are annually preferred to the university, with an exhibition of 70*l.* a year. There are also 40 *King's Boys*, forming the mathematical school founded by Charles II. in 1672. An excellent high-class education is also given in the Girls' School. The school possessed many ancient privileges, some of which it still retains. From time to time the Mathematical Boys appear at Court; and on Easter Tuesday the entire school is presented to the Lord Mayor, at the Mansion House, when each boy receives the gift of a coin fresh from the Mint. A line in the swimming-bath marks the junction of three parishes. In the *Hall*, which was erected by *Shaw* in 1825-29, the head-pupils annually deliver a number of public orations. The 'public suppers' on four Thursdays in Lent, at 7 p.m., are worth attending (tickets from the Clerk). Among the pictures on the walls are the Founding of the Hospital by Edward VI.; Presentation of the King's Boys at the Court of James II., a very large work by *Verrio;* Boy attacked by a shark, by *Copley;* Portraits of the Queen and Prince Albert, by *Grant.* Among the celebrated men who were educated here we may mention William Camden, Stillingfleet, Middleton, Dyer, Samuel Richardson (?), S. T. Coleridge, Charles Lamb, Leigh Hunt, Cavagnari, Sir Henry Cole, and Sir Henry Sumner Maine (d. 1888).

Considerable changes have been introduced into the management of the school by a scheme of the Charity Commissioners, approved by Her Majesty in Council (1890). The principal school is to be removed from London to Horsham in Sussex, where the foundation-stone of the new buildings was laid in 1897. Copies of this scheme and other particulars relating to the Foundation generally may be obtained on application at the Clerk's Office.

Opposite Christ's Hospital is *Warwick Lane*, leading from Newgate Street to Paternoster Row (p. 121). On the wall of the first house on the right is a curious relief of 1668, representing Warwick, the 'King-maker'. Farther on is the *Cutlers' Hall* (1887).

At the W. end of Newgate St., at the corner of Old Bailey, stands **Newgate Prison** (Pl. R, 35; *II*), once the principal prison of London, now used as a temporary house of detention for prisoners awaiting trial at the Old Bailey Court. The present building, which was begun in 1770 by *George Dance*, was partly destroyed in 1780, before its completion, by the Gordon rioters, but was restored in 1782. The principal façade, looking towards the Old Bailey, is 300 ft. in length. The interior was rebuilt in 1858 on the separate cell system. Permission to inspect the prison, which has accommodation for 192 prisoners, is granted by the Secretary of State for the Home Department, the Lord Mayor, and the Sheriffs. The public place of execution, which was formerly at Tyburn near the Marble Arch (p. 294), was from 1783 till 1868 in front of Newgate. The condemned went to the scaffold through the small door, next the governor's house, on the W. front. Executions now take place within the prison. Among the famous or notorious prisoners once confined in old Newgate were George Wither, Anne Askew, Daniel Defoe, Jack Sheppard, Titus Oates, Lord George Gordon (who died here of the gaol distemper in 1793), and William Penn. Old London Wall had a gateway at the bottom of Newgate Street.

Adjoining Newgate is the **Central Criminal Court** (to be rebuilt), consisting of two divisions; *viz.* the *Old Court* for the trial of grave offences, and the *New Court* for petty offences. The trials are public, but as the courts are often crowded, a fee of 1-5*s.*, according to the interest of the case, must generally be given to the door-keeper to secure a good seat. At great trials, however, tickets of admission are usually issued by the aldermen and sheriffs.

No. 68 Old Bailey, near Ludgate Hill, was the house of the infamous thief-catcher Jonathan Wild, himself hanged in 1725.

A little to the W. of Newgate begins the ***Holborn Viaduct** (Pl. R, 35, 36; *II*), a triumph of the art of modern street-building, designed by *Haywood*, and completed in 1869. Its name is a reminiscence of the '*Hole-Bourne*', the name given to the upper course of the *Fleet* (p. 172), from its running through a deep hollow. This structure, 465 yds. long and 27 yds. broad, extending from Newgate to Hatton Garden, was constructed in order to overcome the serious obstruction to the traffic between Oxford Street and the City caused by the steep descent of Holborn Hill. Externally the viaduct, which is constructed almost entirely of iron, is not visible, as rows of new buildings extend along either side. Beneath the roadway are vaults for commercial purposes, and subways for gas and water pipes, telegraph-wires, and sewage, while at the sides are the cellars of the houses. At the E. extremity, to the right, stands *St. Sepulchre's Church* (practically rebuilt in modern times), with its square tower, where a knell is tolled on the occasion of an execution at Newgate. At one time a nosegay was presented at this church to every criminal on his way to execution at Tyburn. On the S. side of the choir lie the remains of the gallant *Captain John Smith* (d. 1631). 'Sometime Governour of Virginia and Admirall of New England'. The position of his vanished monument is indicated by a brass plate bearing a replica of the original inscription, beginning : —

'Here lyes one conquer'd that hath conquer'd kings !'

Roger Ascham (d. 1568), author of 'The Scholemaster' and teacher of Lady Jane Grey, is also buried here. A recital on the fine organ is usually given after Sun. evening-service.

Obliquely opposite, to the left, is the *Holborn Viaduct Station* of the South Eastern and Chatham Railway (p. 58), and near it is the *Holborn Viaduct Hotel* (p. 12). The iron *Bridge over Farringdon Street (which traverses Holborn Valley, p. 172) is 39 yds. long and is supported by 12 columns of granite, each 4 ft. in diameter. On the parapet are bronze statues of Art, Science, Commerce, and Agriculture; on the corner-towers, statues of famous Lord Mayors. Flights of steps descend in the towers to Farringdon Street.

To the left, beyond the bridge, are the *City Temple* (Congregational church; Dr. Joseph Parker; see p. 77) and *St. Andrew's Church*, the latter erected in 1686 by Wren. Col. Hutchinson was married at St. Andrew's to Lucy Apsley in 1638; Richard Savage was baptized here on Jan. 18th, 1696-97; William Hazlitt was married here (May 1st, 1808), with Charles Lamb as best man; and Benjamin Disraeli (Lord Beaconsfield) was christened here on July 31st, 1817, at the age of twelve years.

A little farther on is Holborn Circus, embellished with an *Equestrian Statue of Prince Albert*, by *Bacon*, with allegorical figures and

reliefs on the granite pedestal. The new and wide *Charterhouse Street*
leads hence in a N.E. direction to *Smithfield* (p. 128) and *Charterhouse Square* (p. 129), while *Hatton Garden* (so named from Sir
Christopher Hatton, Queen Elizabeth's Lord Keeper) leads to the
N. towards *Clerkenwell Road*.

Near the beginning of Charterhouse Street is the entrance to **Ely Place**,
formerly the site of the celebrated palace of the bishops of Ely, where John
of Gaunt, brother of the Black Prince and father of Henry IV., died in 1399.
The chapel of the palace, known as °**Ely Chapel** (*St. Etheldreda's;* see p. 78),
escaped the fire of 1666 and has been recently restored. It is a good
specimen of 14th cent. architecture and retains its original oaken roof.
The noble E. and W. windows are splendid examples of tracery, and the
former is filled with fine stained glass. The crypt is also worth visiting,
and the quaint cloister, planted with fig-trees, forms a strangely quiet
nook amid the roar of Holborn.

On the W. side of Holborn Circus begins *Holborn*, leading to
Oxford Street and Bayswater; see p. 293. On the N. side of Holborn is *Furnival's Inn*, formerly an inn of chancery (comp. p. 175),
entirely rebuilt in 1818 and recently again restored for the new
offices of the Prudential Assurance Co. (see below). Charles Dickens
was living at Furnival's Inn when he began the 'Pickwick Papers'.
The statue here is of Henry Peto (1830). *Leather Lane*, on the E.
side of Furnival's Inn, is largely inhabited by Italians of the poorer
classes. In Brooke Street, to the W. of the Inn, stood the house
(No. 39; rebuilt) in which *Chatterton* killed himself in 1770. At the
corner of Brooke Street is the office of the *Prudential Assurance Co.*,
a Gothic building in red brick, by A. Waterhouse. Opposite the N.
end of Brooke Street is *St. Alban's Church* (Pl. *III*; R. 36), the
scene of the labours of the Rev. A. H. Makonochie (d. 1887) and
still noted for its extremely ritualistic services. The interior is
adorned with painting, alabaster, and coloured marble. On the S.
side of Holborn, opposite Furnival's Inn, is *Barnard's Inn*, an old
inn of chancery, purchased by the Mercers' Company, which in 1894
here erected two large red brick buildings for the *Mercers' Schools*,
with accommodation for 300 pupils. The old hall of the inn has
been preserved as a dining-room for the boys. The Mercers' Schools
claim to have been established about the middle of the 15th cent.,
and number John Colet, Dean of St. Paul's (p. 137), and Sir Thomas Gresham (p. 137) among their distinguished scholars. A little
farther to the W., opposite Gray's Inn Road, is °*Staple Inn*, a quaint
and picturesque old inn of chancery (comp. p. 175), celebrated
like Barnard's Inn, by Dickens. The hall of Staple Inn has been
recently restored. Dr. Samuel Johnson wrote 'Rasselas' here.

3. St. Bartholomew's Hospital and Church. Smith-
field. St. Giles. Charterhouse.

St. Bartholomew's Hospital (Pl. R, 40; *II*), in Smithfield, to
the N. of Christ's Hospital, is the oldest and one of the wealthiest

benevolent institutions in London. In 1123 Rahere, a favourite of Henry I., founded here a priory and hospital of St. Bartholomew, which were enlarged by Richard Whittington, Lord Mayor of London. The hospital was refounded by Henry VIII. on the suppression of the monasteries in 1547. The present large quadrangular edifice was erected by *Gibbs* in 1730-33, and has two entrances. Above the W. gate, towards Smithfield, built in 1702, is a statue of Henry VIII., with a sick man and a cripple at the sides. An inscription on the external wall commemorates the burning of three Protestant martyrs in the reign of Queen Mary (p. 128). Within the gate is the church of *St. Bartholomew the Less*, originally built by Rahere, but re-erected in 1823. The hospital enjoys a yearly revenue of 50,000*l.*, and contains 678 beds, in which about 6500 patients are annually attended. Relief is also given to about 16,000 out-patients and about 144,000 casual patients. Cases of accident are taken in at any hour of the day or night, and receive immediate and gratuitous attention. The famous Medical School connected with the hospital has numbered among its teachers Harvey, the discoverer of the circulation of the blood, Abernethy, and other renowned physicians. The medical school was rebuilt and enlarged in 1876-81 at a cost of 50,000*l.* It includes *Anatomical, Medical*, and *Chemical Theatres*, a large *Dissecting Room*, various *Laboratories, Museums of Anatomy* and *Botany*, and a well-furnished *Library*.

The great hall contains a few good portraits, among which we notice an old portrait of Henry VIII. (*not* by Holbein); Dr. Radcliffe, physician to Queen Anne, by *Kneller*; Perceval Pott, for 42 years surgeon to the Institution, by *Sir Joshua Reynolds*; Abernethy, the physician, by *Sir Thomas Lawrence*. The paintings on the grand staircase (the Good Samaritan, the Pool of Bethesda, Rahere as founder of the Hospital, and a Sick Man borne by monks) are the work of *Hogarth*, who executed them gratuitously, and was in return made a Governor for life.

The neighbouring ***Church of St. Bartholomew the Great,** chiefly in the Anglo-Norman style, restored in 1863-66 and again in 1886 et seq., merits attention (open daily, 9.30-5). With the exception of the chapel in the Tower (p. 159), which is 20 years earlier, this is the oldest church in the City of London. Like the Hospital (see above) it was founded by Rahere in 1123, sixty years before the foundation of the Temple Church (p. 177).

The existing church, consisting merely of the choir, the crossing, and one bay of the nave of the original Priory Church, is mainly pure Norman work as left by Rahere. Other portions of the church were alienated or destroyed by Henry VIII. From Smithfield we pass through an arched gateway, richly ornamented with fine dog-toothed moulding, which formed the entrance either to the nave, now the graveyard, or to an inner court. Here may be seen some remains of the E.E. piers of the nave, which was somewhat later than the choir. Early in the 15th cent. the apsidal end of the choir was replaced by a square ending, with two Perpendicular windows, the jambs of which still remain. The clerestory was rebuilt at the same time and a fine Lady Chapel thrown out to the E. of the high-altar. This chapel was long used as a fringe manufactory, being mutilated almost beyond recognition; it was, however, repurchased in 1886 for 6500*l.* and has been restored. Below it is an interesting crypt (adm. 6*d.*). *Prior Bolton* made farther alterations in the 16th cent. and his rebus (a 'bolt' through a 'tun') may be seen at the base of the beautiful oriel on the S. side of the choir and on the doorway at the E. end of the S. ambulatory. The present apse was built in the recent restoration, from a design by Mr. Aston Webb, and has restored the choir to something of its original beauty. The blacksmith's forge which occupied the N. transept has been removed and the transept has been restored, while the S. transept has also been recently thrown open. Doors in the transepts lead respectively to the N. triforium, containing a collection of stones found during the restoration, and to the S. triforium with Bolton's oriel (adm. to each 6*d.*). Photographs of the church are sold by the verger (prices 6*d.*-2*s.;* description of the church 1*s.*).

The *Tombs* are worthy of attention. That of the founder, on the N. side of the sanctuary, with its rich canopy, is much later than the effigy of Rahere resting upon it. In the S. ambulatory is the handsome tomb, in alabaster, of Sir Walter Mildmay (d. 1589), Chancellor of the Exchequer to Queen Elizabeth and founder of Emmanuel College, Cambridge. Many of the epitaphs are curious; that of John and Margaret Whiting (1680-81) in a window-recess, in the N. aisle, ends: —

'Shee first deceased, Hee for a little Tryd
To live without her, likd it not and dyd'.

The last line in the epitaph of Edward Cooke (1652), to the E. of Mildmay's tomb, refers to the fact that it is inscribed on a kind of 'weeping marble' which frequently exuded moisture. The modern heating arrangements of the church have put an end to the phenomenon. — At the W. end of the church is a tasteful oaken organ-screen, erected in 1889.

Among the notable men who have lived in Bartholomew Close are Milton, Franklin (working in a printing-office), Hogarth (who was baptized in the existing font), Dr. Caius, and Washington Irving.

The adjoining market-place of **Smithfield** (Pl. R, 36, 40; *II*), a name said to have been originally *Smooth-field*, was formerly a tournament ground, and lay outside the walls of London. Here Bartholomew Fair, with its revels, was held for many ages. Shamfights, tilts, tricks of acrobats, and even miracle-plays were exhibited. Wat Tyler was slain here in 1381 by the then Lord Mayor, Sir William Walworth; and here, in the reign of 'Bloody Mary', many of the persecuted Protestants, including Anne Askew, Rogers, Bradford, and Philpot, suffered death at the stake, while under Elizabeth several Nonconformists met with a similar fate. Smithfield was the place of public execution before Tyburn, and in 1305 witnessed the beheading of the Scottish patriot, William Wallace. Subsequently, during a long period, Smithfield was the only cattle-market of London. The space having at length become quite inadequate, the cattle-market was removed to Copenhagen Fields (p. 32) in 1855, and in 1862-68 the ***London Central Meat Market** was erected here. The building, designed by *Sir Horace Jones*, is in a pleasing Renaissance style, with four towers at the corners. It is 630 ft. long, 245 ft. broad, and 30 ft. high, and covers an area of 3½ acres. The roof is of glass and iron. A broad carriage-road intersects the market from N. to S.

Below the building is an extensive Railway Depôt, connected with several underground railways, from which the meat is conveyed to the market by a lift. In the centre of Smithfield is a small garden, with a handsome fountain. The road winding round the garden leads down to the subterranean area below the market, which is a sufficiently curious specimen of London underground life to repay the descent.

To the W. of the Meat Market is the *London Central Poultry and Provision Market*, which was opened for business in 1876. It is by the same architect and in the same style as the Meat Market, and measures 260 by 245 ft. Still farther to the W. (on the E. side of Farringdon Street) stands the *London Central General Market*, erected in 1885-92, comprizing sections for poultry and provisions, fish, and fruit, vegetables, and flowers.

At the corner of Giltspur Street and Cock Lane, opposite the S. part of St. Bartholomew's Hospital, is an inscription to the effect that this was *Pye Corner*, where the Great Fire of 1666 stopped, having begun in Pudding Lane (p. 148). In 1762 Cock Lane was the scene of the famous imposture known as the 'Cock Lane Ghost', which so interested Dr. Johnson, Horace Walpole, and other eminent men of the time.

Charterhouse Street, a broad and handsome thoroughfare, leads to the W. from Smithfield to Holborn (p. 125).

A little to the E. of Smithfield is the late-Perpendicular church of **St. Giles** (Pl. R, 40), Cripplegate, built at the end of the 14th cent., and much injured by a fire in 1545; open 10-4, Sat. 10-1 (entered by the N. door in Fore Street; W. front approached by an archway of 1660 in Red Cross Street).

It contains the tombs of John Milton (d. 1674), who wrote 'Paradise Lost' in a house in this parish (comp. p. 132), now pulled down; Foxe (d. 1587), the martyrologist; Frobisher (d. 1594), the voyager; and Speed (d. 1629; effigy under the clock), the topographer. Oliver Cromwell was married in this church (Aug. 22nd, 1620), and the parish-register contains an entry of the burial of Daniel Defoe (d. 1731). Milton is commemorated by a good bust, by *Bacon* (1793), now placed on a cenotaph of 1862; and his supposed resting-place is marked by a stone in front of the chancel-rail. The monument of Constance Whitney (d. 1628; N. wall) has given rise to a baseless legend that she was buried alive and resuscitated by the attempt of a thief to steal her ring. The wooden pulpit, screen, and font-cover were carved by *Grinling Gibbons*. The window at the W. end of the S. aisle commemorates Edward Alleyn, founder of Dulwich College (p. 401). Comp. *J. J Baddeley's* 'Church and Parish of St. Giles' (1888).

In the churchyard is an old bastion of London Wall, and close by, in *London Wall*, is a small part of the churchyard of St. Alphage, containing another large and interesting fragment of the old wall (p. 91).

To the E. of St. Giles, running N. from Fore Street to Chiswell Street, is *Milton Street*, better known as the 'Grub Street' of Pope and his contemporaries. A little farther to the E., at the corner of London Wall and Throgmorton Avenue, is *Carpenters' Hall*, rebuilt in 1876 and containing some old portraits and plate.

To the N.E. of Smithfield we traverse Charterhouse Square to the **Charterhouse** (corrupted from Chartreuse; Pl. R, 40), once a Carthusian monastery, or priory of the Salutation (whence the name of the old Salutation Tavern in Newgate Street), founded in 1371 on the site of a burying-field for persons dying of the plague. After its dissolution by Henry VIII. in 1537 the monastery passed through various hands, including those of Lord North and Thomas Howard,

Duke of Norfolk, who made it the town-house of the Howards.
Queen Elizabeth made a stay of five days at the Charterhouse awaiting her coronation, and her successor James I. kept court here for
several days on entering London. The property was purchased in
1611 by *Thomas Sutton*, a wealthy merchant, for his 'Hospital', *i.e*
a school for 40 'poor boys' and a home for 80 'poor men'. A curfew,
tolled every evening at 8 or 9 o'clock, proclaims the number of the
'poor brethren'. These are not former pupils of the school; the
fictitious instance of Thackeray's Col. Newcome, who was both a
pupil and a poor brother, is one which has very rarely occurred
in the real history of the institution. The school was transferred
in 1872 to Godalming in Surrey, where large and handsome buildings were erected for it. The part of the property thus vacated
was sold to the Merchant Taylors' Company for their ancient school,
now containing 500 boys. The Charterhouse School, which is attended by 440 boys besides 60 on the foundation, boasts among its
former scholars the names of Barrow, Crashaw, Lovelace, Steele,
Addison, Blackstone, Wesley, Thomas Day (author of 'Sandford and
Merton'), Grote, Thirlwall, Leech, Havelock, and Thackeray; while
among the famous pupils of the Merchant Taylors' School are Edmund
Spenser, James Shirley, and Lord Clive. Visitors are shown over
the buildings by the porter any day except Sun.; but the Great Hall
is closed between 3 and 4. Visitors may attend service in the chapel
on Sun. at 11 and 2.30 and on Wed. at 9.30 and 6.

The ancient buildings date chiefly from the early part of the 16th
cent., but have been modified and added to by Lord North, the Duke of
Norfolk, and others. The *Great Hall* is considered one of the finest specimens of a 16th cent. room in London. The *Great Staircase* and the
Great Chamber upstairs are, with the exception of the W. window of the
latter, just as the Duke of Norfolk left them three centuries ago. Part
of the original *Chapel* (1371) remains, but it was altered by the monks
about 1500 and greatly enlarged by the Trustees of Thomas Sutton in
1612, when it received its present Jacobean appearance. It is approached
by a cloister with memorials of Thackeray, Leech, Havelock, John Hul-
lah, etc., and contains a fine alabaster monument of Sutton (1611) and the
monuments of the first Lord Ellenborough by Chantrey and of Dr. Raine
by Flaxman. The altar-piece is a copy of Francia's Pietà in the National
Gallery (p. 195; No. 180). The initials of Prior Houghton, who was head
of the priory at the dissolution, may be seen on the outer wall of the
Washhouse Court. The two quadrangles in which the Pensioners and some
of the officials reside were built about 1825-40.

The *Master's Lodge* contains several portraits: Sutton, the founder of
the institution; Charles II.; George Villiers, second Duke of Buckingham
(one of *Kneller's* best portraits); Duke of Monmouth; Lord Chancellor
Shaftesbury; Lord Chancellor Somers; William, Earl of Craven; Archbishop Sheldon; Talbot, Duke of Shrewsbury; and the fine portrait of
Dr. Burnet, also by *Kneller*.

A little to the W. of the Charterhouse is *St. John's Lane*, in
which is situated **St. John's Gate** (Pl. R, 36), an interesting relic
of an old priory of the knights of St. John, with lateral turrets,
erected in the late-Gothic style in 1504, by *Prior Docwra*. On the
N. side of the gateway are the arms of the priory and of Docwra;
and on the S. side those of England and of France. The knights

of St. John were suppressed by Henry VIII., restored by Mary, and finally dispersed by Elizabeth. The rooms above the gate were once occupied by Cave, the founder of the 'Gentleman's Magazine' (1731), to which Dr. Johnson contributed and which had a representation of St. John's Gate on the cover; they contain some interesting historical relics. The building is now occupied by the Order of St. John, a benevolent association engaged in ambulance and hospital work, etc. Visitors are admitted on week-days 10-5, Sat. 10-1. — In St. John's Square, to the N. of the gate, is *St. John's Church* (care-taker, Mrs. Toms, 111 Clerkenwell Road). The Norman crypt, now being restored, dates from the 12-13th cent., and formed part of the old priory church. It was in this crypt that the exposure of the 'Cock Lane Ghost' (p. 129) was consummated. In the little graveyard, behind the church, are buried the grandfather and other relatives of Wilkes Booth, the murderer of President Lincoln. — Clerkenwell Road runs to the W. from St. John's Square to Gray's Inn Road, with Gray's Inn. The considerable district of *Clerkenwell*, now largely inhabited by watch-makers, goldsmiths, and opticians, derives its name from the 'Clerks' Well' once situated here, to which the parish clerks of London annually resorted for the celebration of miracle plays, etc.

A little to the N., at the corner of St. John Street Road and Ashby Street, is the *Martyrs' Memorial Church* (*St. Peter's*; Pl. B, 36), a fantastic French Gothic edifice erected about 1870, with statues of the Smithfield Protestant martyrs. Close by are *Northampton Square* and *Northampton Institute* (Pl. B, 36), occupying what was once the garden of the London house of the Marquis of Northampton. The institute, opened in 1897, is probably the largest polytechnic in London (p. 98). — A little to the E. runs *Goswell Road*, the S. part of which, formerly named Goswell Street, is familiar to all readers of 'Pickwick'. — *Swedenborg* died in 1772 at 26 Great Bath Street, Clerkenwell.

Clerkenwell Road is continued to the E. by Old Street, from which, on the right, diverges Bunhill Row, with the **Bunhill Fields Cemetery** (Pl. R, 40, 44), also known for a time as *Tindall's Burial Ground*, once the chief burial-place for Nonconformists, but disused since 1852. It contains the tombs of John Bunyan (d. 1688; sarcophagus with recumbent figure, to the S. of the central walk), Daniel Defoe (d. 1731; obelisk to the N. of the central walk), Dr. Isaac Watts (d. 1748; altar-tomb to the E. of Defoe), Susannah Wesley (d. 1742; mother of John and Charles Wesley), William Blake (d. 1827), Dr. John Owen (1616-83), Henry, Richard, and William Cromwell (descendants, but not sons, of the Protector), Thomas Stothard, R. A. (d. 1834), etc.

A little to the W. of this cemetery is the *Friends' Burial Ground*, with the grave of George Fox, founder of the Society of Friends or Quakers.

Immediately to the S. of Bunhill Fields are the headquarters and drill-ground of the **Honourable Artillery Company**, the oldest military body in the kingdom.

The H. A. C., as it is generally called, received its charter of incorporation, under the title of the Guild or Fraternity of St. George, from

Henry VIII. in 1537, and its rights and privileges have been confirmed by upwards of 20 royal warrants, the last dated March, 1889. The officers of the Trained Bands and the City of London Militia were formerly always selected from members of this Company. Since 1660 the Captain-General and Colonel has always been either the King or the Prince of Wales. The names of John Milton, Christopher Wren, and Samuel Pepys are on the roll of former members. The Company, which has occupied its present ground since 1642, consists of two batteries of field-artillery and a battalion of infantry. It is the only volunteer corps which includes horse-artillery. Since 1883 the H. A. C. takes precedence next after the regular forces. The Ancient and Honourable Artillery Company of Boston (Mass.), the oldest military body in America, was founded in 1638 by some members of the H. A. C. who had emigrated. The two corps are associated on the friendliest terms. See the History of the Company, by *Lt. Col. Raikes*.

In City Road, facing the E. entrance of Bunhill Fields, is **Wesley's Chapel** (Pl. R, 44). John Wesley (1703-91) is buried in the graveyard behind the chapel, and in front of it is his *Statue*, unveiled in 1891. His mother (d. 1742) and his brother Charles (d. 1788) are commemorated in the chapel. *Wesley's House* (No. 47 City Road), adjoining the chapel on the S., is now partly fitted up as a WESLEY MUSEUM (daily, 10-4, 3d.). Wesley's sitting-room, the bedroom in which he died, and the small adjoining room which was the scene of his private devotions are shown, containing furniture belonging to Wesley, books, autographs, portraits, and personal relics. — In Castle Street, the first street running E. to the S. of the chapel, is the *Allan Wesleyan Library* (p. 21), containing one of the finest collections of Biblical and theological works in England. At No. 14 Blomfield Street, London Wall (Pl. R, 43, 44), are the offices of the **London Missionary Society**, containing a small *Museum* (open daily, 9.30-6, on application). — The vestry of the small *Church of All Hallows-on-the-Wall* (Pl. R, 43; III), in London Wall, is believed to occupy the site of a bastion of the Roman city wall. The entrance to the pulpit, by a flight of steps leading direct from the vestry through the wall of church, is unique in London. — In *Finsbury Circus* (Pl. R, 44; *III*) is the *London Institution* (p. 21).

In Curtain Road (Pl. R, 44), reached viâ Castle Street and Scrutton Street, is the *Church of St. James* which probably stands on or near the site of the old *Curtain Theatre*, where, according to tradition, 'Hamlet' was first performed. It is not unlikely that Shakspeare acted here in his own plays. To commemorate this association a stained-glass window was erected in 1886 at the W. end of the church by Mr. Stanley Cooper.

To the S.E. of the Charterhouse is the *Aldersgate Street Station* (Metropolitan; p. 60). *Aldersgate Street* leads hence to St. Martin's le Grand and St. Paul's (p. 111).

The old residences in this street, including Shaftesbury House and Lauderdale House, have all disappeared. Milton lived for a time in Lamb Alley (now Maidenhead Court), Aldersgate Street, and afterwards in Jewin Street, a side-street to the E. John Wesley 'found assurance of salvation' at a meeting in Aldersgate Street (May 24th, 1738).

4. Cheapside. Guildhall. Mansion House.

Goldsmiths' Hall. St. Mary le Bow. Gresham College. Mercers' Hall. Armourers' Hall. St. Stephen's, Walbrook.

From St. Paul's Churchyard (p. 120), **Cheapside** (Pl. R, 39, and *III;* from the Anglo-Saxon *ceapian,* 'to sell', 'to bargain'), beginning at *Peel's Statue* (p. 121), runs to the E. and is continued to the Mansion House (p. 138) by the *Poultry.* Cheapside, one of the busiest streets in the city, rich in historical reminiscences, is now lined with handsome shops. Its jewellers and mercers have been famous from a time even earlier than that of honest John Gilpin, under whose wheels the stones rattled 'as if Cheapside were mad'. Cheapside Cross, one of the memorials erected by Edward I. to Queen Eleanor, stood here, at the end of Wood St. (p. 134), till destroyed by the Puritans in 1643; and the neighbourhood was frequently the scene of conflicts between the apprentices of the various rival guilds. To the right and left diverge several cross-streets, the names of which probably preserve the position of the stalls of the different tradespeople in the far back period when Cheapside was an open market. Land here is worth 1,000,000*l.* per acre.

From the W. end of Cheapside, Foster Lane, behind the General Post Office, leads to the N., passing *St. Vedast's Church* (rebuilt by Wren after the Great Fire; Robert Herrick baptized here in 1591; singular relief over the W. door), **to Goldsmiths' Hall,** re-erected in the Renaissance style by *Hardwick* in 1835 (visitors must be introduced by a member). Chief objects of interest in the interior: Grand Staircase, with portraits of George IV., by *Northcote;* William IV., by *Hayter;* George III. and his consort Charlotte, by *Ramsay;* in the Committee Room (first floor), the remains of a Roman altar found in digging the foundations of the present hall; portrait of Lord Mayor Myddelton, who provided London with water by the construction of the New River (1613), by *Jansen;* portrait of Lord Mayor Sir Martin Bowes (1545), with the goblet which he bequeathed to the Goldsmiths' Company (out of which Queen Elizabeth is said to have drunk at her coronation, and which is still preserved); portraits of Queen Victoria, by *Hayter;* Prince Albert, by *Smith;* Queen Adelaide, by *Shee;* busts of George III., George IV., and William IV., by *Chantrey;* statues of Cleopatra and the Sibyl, by *Story.* — The Company, incorporated in 1327, has the privilege of assaying and stamping most of the gold and silver manufactures of England, for which it receives a small percentage.

Opposite Foster Lane, to the left, is Old Change, leading to Cannon Street (p. 154). In this street, at the corner of Watling Street, is the *Church of St. Augustine* (Pl. R, 39; *III*), rebuilt by Wren in 1683-95. The Rev. R. H. Barham, author of the 'Ingoldsby Legends', was rector here from 1842 till his death in 1845.

To the left, a little farther on in Cheapside (No. 143), is *Sad-*

dlers' Hall, with a fine large hall and a good gateway. Near the
corner of Wood Street, on the left, still stands the plane-tree mentioned by Wordsworth in his 'Poor Susan'; it is specially protected
in the leases of the adjoining houses. Between Friday Street and
Bread Street, on the right, once stood the Mermaid Tavern †, rendered
famous by the social meetings of Shakspeare, Beaumont, Fletcher,
Dr. Donne, and other members of the club founded here by Ben
Jonson in 1603. John Milton was born in Bread Street in 1608,
and a tablet on the house at the corner of Bread Street and Watling Street commemorates his birth and his baptism in the church
of All Hallows, formerly on this site. Sir Thomas More (b. 1480)
was born in Milk Street, on the opposite side.

On the right (S.) side of Cheapside, farther on, is the church of
St. Mary le Bow, or simply *Bow Church* (so named after an earlier
church on the same site borne by stone *arches*), one of *Wren's* best
works, with a tower 235 ft. high. The tower, at the top of which
is a dragon 9 ft. long, is especially admirable; 'no other modern
steeple', says Fergusson, 'can compare with this, either for beauty
of outline or the appropriateness with which classical details are
applied to so novel a purpose'. The church has a fine old Norman
crypt. Persons born within the sound of Bow-bells are popularly
called *Cockneys, i.e.* true Londoners.

A curious old rhyming couplet foretold that: —
    'When the Exchange grasshopper and dragon from Bow
    Shall meet — in London shall be much woe.'

This improbable meeting actually took place in 1832, when the two
vanes were sent to the same yard for repairs.

The ecclesiastical *Court of Arches* takes its name from having originally met in the vestry of this church.

On the W. wall of the church is an inscription referring to Milton,
removed from the church of All Hallows (see above) on its destruction.

To the E. of St. Mary le Bow, *Queen Street*, on the right (S.),
leads to *Southwark Bridge* (p. 155); while *King Street*, on the left
(N.), leads to the Guildhall (see below). In King Street, to the left,
at the corner of Gresham Street, stands the *Church of St. Lawrence
Jewry* (open daily, 11-4), built by Wren in 1671-80 and containing
the tomb and monument of Archbp. Tillotson (d. 1694), who was
lecturer here for 30 years. The Lord Mayor and Corporation attend
service at this church on Michaelmas Day, before electing the new
Lord Mayor. The fountain to the N. of the church, with sculptures
by *Joseph Durham* (1866), commemorates the pious benefactors of
the parishes of St. Lawrence Jewry and St. Mary Magdalen from
1375 to 1765.

The present **Guildhall** (Pl. R, 39; *III*), or Council Hall of the city,
was originally erected in 1411-39 for the sittings of the magistrates
and municipal corporation, on the site of an older hall used for a

---

† Some authorities believe this stood to the N. of Cheapside, adjoining Saddlers' Hall.

similar purpose. It was seriously injured by the great fire of 1666, but immediately restored. The unpleasing front towards King Street was erected in 1789 from designs by the younger *Dance*, with the exception of the porch, which dates from 1425. Above the latter are the arms of the city, with the motto, *Domine dirige nos.* — The *Great Hall* (open all day), 152 ft. long, 49$\frac{1}{2}$ ft. broad, and 89 ft. high, is now used for various municipal meetings, the election of the Lord Mayor and members of parliament, and public meetings of the citizens of London to consider questions of great social or political interest. The open timber roof is very handsome; it dates from a restoration of the hall in 1864-70. The stained-glass window at the E. end was presented by the Lancashire operatives in acknowledgment of the City of London's generosity during the Cotton Famine (1862-65); that at the W. end is a memorial of the late Prince Consort. The subjects of the other windows are taken from the history of the city. The two fanciful wooden figures (14$\frac{1}{2}$ ft. high) on the W. side, carved by *Saunders* in 1708, are called *Gog* (on the left) and *Magog* (on the right). Their predecessors, made of wickerwork, were formerly carried in the Lord Mayor's procession. By the N. wall are monuments to Lord Chatham, by *Bacon*; Wellington, by *Bell*; and Nelson, by *Smith*. On the S. wall are monuments to William Pitt, by *Bubb*, and Lord Mayor Beckford, by *Moore* (bearing on the pedestal the mayor's famous address to George III., which some writers affirm was never actually delivered). — Every 9th of November the Lord Mayor, on the occasion of his accession to office, gives a great public dinner here to the members of the Cabinet, the chief civic dignitaries, and others, which is generally attended by nearly 1000 guests. The speeches made by the Queen's Ministers on this and other civic occasions are scanned attentively, as often possessing no little political significance. The expense of this banquet is shared jointly by the Lord Mayor and the Sheriffs. — In this hall took place the trials of Anne Askew (burned at Smithfield in 1546), the Earl of Surrey (1547), Lady Jane Grey (1554), and others.

On the N. side of the Great Hall is the entrance to the council chambers. Visitors apply for admission at the keeper's office, on the left. The vestibules contain busts of Cobden, Gladstone, Beaconsfield, Granville Sharp (by *Chantrey*), etc. The *Common Council Chamber*, erected from the plans of Sir Horace Jones in 1884, is a handsomely decorated twelve-sided apartment, 54 ft. in diameter, covered with a dome surmounted by an oak lantern, 81$\frac{1}{2}$ ft. above the floor. The clerestory windows of the dome represent the cardinal virtues; above are frescoes depicting the crafts of 24 of the livery companies, surmounted by their arms. The chamber proper is separated from a surrounding corridor by richly carved screens, glazed with the arms of the 53 remaining companies. Above the corridor is the public gallery. The chamber contains a statue of

George III., by *Chantrey*, and several royal busts. The *Aldermen's Room* (17th cent.) contains a ceiling painted by *Thornhill*, and carved panels and stained-glass windows exhibiting the arms of various Lord Mayors. The royal arms above the Lord Mayor's chair are believed to be unique in including the arms of Hanover ensigned with the 'electoral bonnet'. The *Old Council Chamber*, now used for the sittings of the Lord Mayor's Court, dates from 1777. It contains portraits, by *Jos. Wright*, of the judges who settled the various claims arising from the great fire in 1666. — The interesting old *Crypt*, borne by clustered columns of Purbeck marble, is now, with the porch, almost the sole relic of the original Guildhall of 1411-31 (apply to beadle in the great hall).

The Guildhall Library, or *Free Library of the Corporation of the City of London* (open in summer, *i.e.* May-Aug. inclusive, daily, 10-6; in winter, Mon.-Frid. 10-8, Sat. 10-6), contains in its handsome hall, built in the Tudor style in 1871-72, above 112,000 volumes, including several good specimens of early printing, and a large and valuable collection of works on or connected with London, its history, antiquities, and famous citizens. The special collections include the library of the old Dutch church in Austin Friars (p. 140; with valuable MSS. and original letters of Reformers), a carefully selected Hebrew library (catalogue, 1891), etc. It also possesses a very fine collection of maps and plans of London, a series of English medals, and a number of London tradesmen's tokens of the 16th century. In 1899 the Library, Reading Room, and Museum were visited by 337,263 persons. On the right is the *Reading Room*. The leading English newspapers may be consulted in the *Directory Room*. In the room at the head of the staircase to the museum are a cabinet of Italian mosaics, lent by the Rev. *H. L. Nelthropp*, and an interesting collection of ancient chronometers, clocks, watches, and watch-movements, made by members of the Clockmakers' Company, whose library is also deposited at the Guildhall. Comp. 'The Guildhall Library and its Work', by *Charles Welch*, F. S. A. (1893).

The *Museum (adm., see p. 108), on the sunk floor, contains a collection of Roman antiquities found in London: a group of the Deæ Matres, found at Crutched Friars; hexagonal funeral column, from Ludgate Hill; Roman tesselated pavement, from Bucklersbury (1869); sarcophagus of the 4th cent., from Clapton; statue of a Roman warrior and some architectural antiquities found in a bastion of the old Roman wall in Bishopsgate; a curious collection of old London shop and tavern signs (17th cent.), including (at the foot of the staircase) that of the Boar's Head in Eastcheap (dated 1668; the tavern is mentioned by Shakspeare; comp. p. 146); a large collection of smaller antiquities, terracotta figures, lamps, vases, dishes, goblets, trinkets, spoons, pins, needles, etc. There are also two sculptured slabs from Nineveh. Two glass-cases in the centre contain autographs, including those of Cromwell, Wellington, and Nelson. [One of Shakspeare, dated 10th Mar., 1613 (purchased for 147*l*.), is now preserved in the Library.]

The **Corporation Art Gallery** (adm., see p. 108), on the right of the entrance to the Guildhall, contains the chief historical portraits and other paintings belonging to the Corporation, collected here from the old council chamber and committee-rooms, and also a number of paintings by *Sir John Gilbert*, presented by the artist, and a few other recent donations. Loan exhibitions are occasionally held.

The numerous pigeons which congregate in the nooks and crannies of the Guildhall, or fly about the yard, will remind the traveller of the famous pigeons of St. Mark at Venice. They are fed daily ab ut 11 a.m.

Comp. 'Descriptive Account of the Guildhall of the City of London', by *John E. Price* (folio, 1886). Guide to the Guildhall, 6*d*. (1898).

In Aldermanbury, to the W. of the Guildhall, is the *Church of St. Mary*, Aldermanbury, containing the tomb of Lord Jeffreys

(d. 1689), of the 'Bloody Assizes'. Milton was married here to his second wife in 1656. Heminge and Condell, Shakspeare's brother actors, who published the first folio edition of his plays (1623), are commemorated by a monument in the churchyard (unveiled in 1896).

Love Lane leads hence to the W. to *St. Alban's* (open 1-2), a small church by Wren (1685), with a curious old hour-glass fixed above the pulpit. — In Addle Street, to the N. of Love Lane, is *Brewers' Hall*, containing an ancient kitchen and a curiously decorated leaden cistern. — Silver Street continues Addle Street to Monkswell Street, in which is situated the *Barber-Surgeons' Court Room* (Pl. R. 40; *III*). Among the curiosities preserved here are a valuable work by Holbein (at least in part), representing Henry VIII. renewing the company's charter in 1541, and a portrait of Inigo Jones by Van Dyck.

At the corner of Basinghall Street, to the E. of the Guildhall, stands **Gresham College**, founded by *Sir Thomas Gresham* (p. 140) in 1579 for the delivery of lectures by seven professors, on law, divinity, medicine, rhetoric, geometry, astronomy, and music.

The lectures were delivered in Gresham's house in Bishopsgate Street until 1768, when it was taken down and the lectures were transferred to the Royal Exchange. The present hall was erected in 1843 out of the accumulated capital of Gresham's bequest. The lecture theatre can hold 500 persons. According to Gresham's will, some of the lectures were to be delivered in the middle of the day, and in Latin, but the speakers now deliver their courses of four lectures each in English, at 6 p.m. (free). — The Royal Society held its meetings at Gresham College from 1660 to 1710. It now contains the head-office of the *City and Guilds of London Institute* (see p. 98).

From Gresham College we return to Cheapside by Ironmonger Lane, in which is the entrance to **Mercers' Hall**, the guildhouse of the silk mercers, rebuilt in 1884, the façade of which is in Cheapside. The interior contains portraits of Dean Colet, founder of St. Paul's School, and Sir Thomas Gresham, founder of the Exchange, as well as a few relics of Sir Richard Whittington. The 'Legh Cup' (1499), used at the Company's banquets, is one of the finest pieces extant of English mediæval plate. The chapel, which is adorned with modern frescoes of Becket's Martyrdom and the Ascension, occupies the site of the house in which Thomas Becket was born in 1119, and where a hospital and chapel were erected to his memory about the year 1190. Henry VIII. afterwards granted the hospital to the Mercers, who had been incorporated in 1393.

Old Jewry, to the E. of Mercers' Hall, derives its name from the synagogue which stood here prior to the persecution of the Jews in 1291. On its site, close to the Bank, now stands the *Grocers' Hall*, the guildhouse of the Grocers, or, as they were once called, the 'Pepperers', with a fine stained-glass window. This company is one of the oldest in London (incorporated 1345). At No. 26 Old Jewry are the headquarters of the *City Police*. Old Jewry is continued towards the N. by *Coleman Street*, in which, on the right, is situated the *Armourers' Hall* (Pl. R, 39; *III*), founded about 1450, spared by the fire of 1666, and rebuilt in 1840. It contains an interesting and valuable collection of **armour** and old plate, including a tilting gauntlet made to lock fast over the spear.

The continuation of Cheapside towards the E. is called the Poultry, once the street of the poulterers. The modern terracotta panels on No. 14 refer to royal processions that passed through the street in 1546, 1561, 1660, and 1844. At the farther end of the Poultry, on the right, rises the **Mansion House** (Pl. R, 39; *III*), the official residence of the Lord Mayor during his year of office, erected by *Dance* in 1739-52. Lord Burlington sent in a design by the famous Italian architect Palladio, which was rejected on the naïve question of one of the aldermen — 'Who was Palladio — was he a freeman of the city?' The building is preceded by a Corinthian hexastyle portico. The tympanum contains an allegorical group in relief by *Sir Robert Taylor*.

In the interior, to the left of the entrance, is the Lord Mayor's police-court, open to the public daily from 12 to 2. The long suite of state and reception rooms are shown only by the special permission of the Lord Mayor. The principal room is the *Egyptian Hall*, in which the Lord Mayor gives his banquets and balls, said to be a reproduction of the hall described under that name by Vitruvius. It is 90 ft. long and 60 ft. wide and the vaulted ceiling is supported by fluted columns. The large windows are filled with stained glass, and the hall contains several pieces of modern English sculpture: °Caractacus and the nymph Egeria, by *Foley*; Genius and the Morning Star, by *Baily*; Comus, by *Lough*; Griselda, by *Marshall*. Other rooms are the *Saloon*, adorned with tapestry and sculpture; the *State Drawing Rooms*; the *Long Parlour*; the *Venetian Parlour* or Lord Mayor's business room; the *Old Ball Room*; etc.

The interior of **St. Stephen's Church**, *Walbrook* (open 1-3 daily, except Sat.) behind the Mansion House, with its graceful dome supported by Corinthian columns, is considered one of *Wren's* masterpieces, but has recently been somewhat marred by alterations. On the N. walls hangs the Stoning of St. Stephen, one of the best works of Benjamin West, formerly over the altar. Walbrook leads direct to Cannon Street Station (p. 57).

Queen Victoria Street (p. 153) leads directly from the Mansion House to Blackfriars Bridge (see p. 152).

5. The Bank of England. The Exchange.

Stock Exchange. Merchant Taylors' Hall. Crosby Hall. St. Helen's Church. Cornhill. Leadenhall Market. St. Andrew's Undershaft. Corn Exchange.

The space (Pl. R, 39, 43; *III*) enclosed by the Mansion House, the Bank, and the Exchange, is the centre from which radiate the most important streets of 'the City'. It is also the chief point of convergence of the London omnibus traffic, which during business hours is enormous. The subways in connection with the Central London Railway (p. 63) enable foot-passengers to cross the street in ease and safety.

Opposite the Mansion House, and bounded on the S. by Threadneedle Street, on the W. by Prince's Street, on the N. by Lothbury, and on the E. by Bartholomew Lane, stands the **Bank of England** (Pl. R, 39, 43 ; *III*), an irregular and isolated building of one story. The central nucleus of the building was designed by *Mr. George Sampson* and opened in 1834, but the edifice as now seen is mainly the work of *Sir John Soane*, who was architect to the Bank from 1788 to 1827. The external walls are entirely devoid of windows, the Bank being, for the sake of security, lighted from interior courts. The only attractive portion of the architecture is at the N.W. angle, which was copied from the Temple of the Sibyl at Tivoli. The garden-court in the interior was formerly the churchyard of St. Christopher-le-Stocks. The edifice covers an area of about four acres.

The Bank was founded in 1694, the first suggestion of it apparently emanating from William Paterson, a Scotsman, though, perhaps, his importance in the matter has been over-estimated. It is a joint stock bank, and was the first of the kind established in the kingdom. Having exclusive privileges, secured by Royal Charter, it continued to be the only joint-stock bank in London till 1834, when the London and Westminster Bank, soon to be followed by many others, was established. The Bank of England is the only bank in London which has the power of issuing paper money. Its original capital was 1,200,000*l.*, which has since been multiplied more than twelvefold. The number of persons employed within its walls is about 1000. The vaults usually contain at least 20 million pounds sterling in gold and silver, while there are over 25 millions of pounds sterling of the Bank's notes in circulation. The Bank acts as the agent of Government in all business transactions connected with the national debt (now amounting to about 650,000,000*l.*), receives and registers transfers of stock, and pays the quarterly dividends on the various kinds of stock ; it also carries on business like other banks in discounting bills, receiving deposits, and lending money. It is bound to buy all gold bullion brought to it, at the rate of 3*l.* 17*s.* 9*d.* per oz. The government of the Bank is vested in a Governor, a Deputy-Governor, and twenty-four Directors.

The business offices of the Bank are open to the public daily from 9 to 4; the Printing, Weighing, and Bullion Offices are shown only under special circumstances by permission of the Governor or Deputy-Governor, to whom an introduction must be obtained.

The whole of the printing for the Bank is done within its walls, and upwards of 50,000 new bank-notes are produced daily, their value ranging from 5*l.* to 1000*l.* The note printing-presses are exceedingly interesting. Postal orders and Indian bank-notes are also printed here. All notes paid into the Bank are at once cancelled, so that in some cases the active life of a bank-note may not be longer than a single day. The cancelled notes, however, are kept for five years in the *Old Note Office*, in case they may be required as testimony in a court of law. Every week or so the notes received in the corresponding week five years ago are burned; and the furnace provided for this purpose, 5 ft. in height and 10 ft. in diameter, is said to be filled on each occasion. The stock of paid notes for five years amounts to about 80 millions, weighs 90 tons, and represents a value of 1750 millions of pounds sterling; if the notes were joined end to end they would form a ribbon 13,000 M. long, while their superficial extent would almost equal that of Hyde Park. The *Bank-Note Autograph Books* contain the signatures of various royal and distinguished personages. A bank-note for 1,000,000*l.* is also exhibited to the curious visitor. The *Weighing Office* contains machines for weighing sovereigns (33 per minute), which throw those of full weight into one compartment and the light ones into another. A daily average of gold to the value of 80,000*l.* is thus tested. The *Bullion Office* is the treasury for the precious metals. The Bank is protected at night by a small guard of soldiers, in addition to a large staff of superintendents and warders.

In Post Office Court, Lombard Street, is the *Bankers' Clearing House*, a useful institution through which bankers obtain the amount of cheques and bills in their hands without the trouble of collecting them at the various banks on which they are drawn. The bills and cheques received by the various bankers during the day are here compared, and the difference settled by a cheque on the Bank of England. The amount changing hands here is enormous, reaching in the year ending Dec. 31st, 1898, the sum of 8,097,291,000*l.*, or 606,010,000*l.* more than in 1897.

In Capel Court, opposite the Bank, is the **Stock Exchange**, the headquarters of the *Stock-brokers* (about 1300 in number) and *Stock-jobbers* (about 2000), each of whom pays a large entrance-fee and an annual subscription of 30 guineas. Strangers are not admitted. The Stock Exchange (familiarly known in the City as 'the house') has recently been much enlarged.

In Throgmorton Street, to the N. of the Stock Exchange, is the *Drapers' Hall*, dating originally from 1667 but in great part rebuilt in 1866-70. It contains a portrait of Nelson by *Sir William Beechey*, and a picture of Mary, Queen of Scots, and her son James I., attributed to *Zucchero*. Adjoining is the *Drapers' Garden*, containing one or two old mulberry-trees.

The *Dutch Church* in Austin Friars, behind the Drapers' Hall, dates from the 14th cent. and is one of the few ecclesiastical edifices which escaped the fire of 1666. It was restored in 1863-65, after a fire, and contains numerous tombs of the 14-16th centuries.

The **Royal Exchange** (Pl. R, 43; *III*), built in 1842-44 by *Tite*, is the third building of the kind on the same site. The first Exchange, erected in 1564-70 by Sir Thomas Gresham, was destroyed in the Great Fire (1666), and its successor, by Jarman, was also burned down in 1838. The present building, which cost about 150,000*l.*, is preceded by a Corinthian portico, and approached by a broad flight of steps. The group in the tympanum is by *Westmacott*: in the centre is Commerce, holding the charter of the Exchange in her hand; on the right the Lord Mayor, municipal officials, an Indian, an Arab, a Greek, and a Turk; on the left English merchants, a Chinese, a Persian, a Negro, etc. On the architrave below is the inscription: 'The Earth is the Lord's and the fulness thereof'.

The interior of the Exchange forms a quadrangular covered court surrounded by colonnades. The tesselated pavement of Turkey stone is the original one of Gresham's Exchange. In the centre is a statue of Queen Victoria, by *Hamo Thornycroft*; in the N.E. and S.E. corners are statues of Queen Elizabeth, by *Watson*, and

Charles II. The 22 panels of the walls of the colonnades are to be filled with historical paintings typifying Liberty, Commerce, and Education.

Seven of these are completed: Phœnicians bartering with the Ancient Britons in Cornwall, by *Lord Leighton*; London receiving its charter from William the Conqueror, by *Seymour Lucas*; Queen Elizabeth opening Gresham's Exchange in 1571, by *Ernest Crofts*; Charles I. demanding the five members at Guildhall, by *S. J. Solomon*; The Fire of London, by *Stanhope Forbes*; Queen Victoria opening the present Exchange, by *R. W. Macbeth*; Crown offered to Richard III. at Baynard's Castle, by *S. Goetze*.

The chief business-hour is from 3.30 to 4.30 p.m., and the most important days are Tuesdays and Fridays. On the front (E.) of the campanile (180 ft. in height) is a statue of Sir Thomas Gresham, and at the top is a large gilded vane in the shape of a grasshopper (Gresham's crest). The shops on the outside of the Exchange greatly disfigure the building. Nearly opposite the Exchange is No. 15 Cornhill, occupied by Messrs. Birch, confectioners, and said to be the oldest shop in London.

At the E. end of the Exchange a staircase, adorned with a statue of Prince Albert by *Lough*, ascends to *Lloyd's Subscription Rooms*, the central point of every kind of business connected with navigation, maritime trade, marine insurance, and shipping intelligence. The name is derived from a coffee-house kept by Edward Lloyd towards the close of the 17th century and frequented by men interested in shipping. 'Lloyd's List' has been published regularly since 1721. The vestibule is adorned with a statue of Huskisson by *Gibson*. On the wall is a tablet to the 'Times' newspaper, erected in recognition of the public service it rendered by the exposure of a fraudulent financial conspiracy of gigantic character. The first room is used by Underwriters and contains huge ledgers in which the most detailed information as to the merchant-shipping of the world is carefully posted from day to day; the second is the Merchants' or Reading Room, with a huge collection of provincial and foreign newspapers; the third or 'Captains' Room' is a restaurant accessible only to the 700 members of 'Lloyd's' and their friends. Lloyd's has an annual income of about 50,000*l*. It keeps a staff of about 1500 agents in all parts of the world.

Lloyd's Register of British and Foreign Shipping (2 White Lion Court, Cornhill; new building being erected in Lloyd's Avenue) was established in 1834 by a society of merchants and ship-owners, quite distinct from 'Lloyd's'. Its object is to secure an accurate description of the seaworthiness of mercantile vessels. Vessels of the best description are classed as A 1.

In front of the Exchange is an *Equestrian Statue of Wellington*, by *Chantrey*, erected in 1844, beside which is a handsome fountain with a female figure. On the S.E. side of the Exchange is a statue (erected in 1882) of *Sir Rowland Hill*, the inventor of the cheap postal system. Behind the Exchange is a seated statue of *Peabody* (d. 1869), by *Story*, erected in 1871 by public subscription.

George Peabody, an American merchant, who carried on an extensive business and spent much of his time in London, gave at different times upwards of half a million of money for the erection of suitable dwellings for the working classes of the Metropolis. The property is managed by a body of trustees. The number of persons accommodated in the Peabody Buildings is about 20,000, each family paying an average weekly rent of about 5s. 2d., which includes the use of baths and wash-houses. The capital of the fund now amounts to about 1,290,000l. Mr. Peabody declined a baronetcy offered by the Queen, but accepted a miniature portrait of Her Majesty. He spent and bequeathed still larger sums for educational and benevolent purposes in America, the grand total of his gifts amounting to nearly 2,000,000l. sterling. — The *Guinness Trust*, a similar fund established by Lord Iveagh in 1889 with a gift of 200,000l., has provided about 1900 model dwellings, at an average weekly rent of 2s. 1d. per room.

Farther along Threadneedle Street, beyond Finch Lane, is the **Merchant Taylors' Hall,** the largest of the London Companies' halls, erected, after the Great Fire of 1666, by *Jarman* (admission on application to a member). The company received its first charter in 1327. The handsome hall contains some good portraits : Henry VIII., by *Paris Bordone ;* Duke of York, by *Lawrence ;* Duke of Wellington, by *Wilkie ;* Charles I. ; Charles II. ; James II. ; William III. ; Queen Anne ; George III. and his consort ; Lord Chancellor Eldon, by *Briggs ;* Pitt, by *Hoppner.* There is also a valuable collection of old plate. The small but interesting *Crypt* was spared by the Fire. It is said that eighteen haunches of venison are cooked in the kitchen at one time for the annual banquet in July.

Threadneedle Street ends at Bishopsgate Street Within, in which, near the point of junction, is the *National Provincial Bank of England* (No. 112), which is worth visiting for the beautiful interior of its large hall, a remarkable specimen of the Byzantine-Romanesque style, with polished granite columns and polychrome decoration. Immediately opposite is the *Wesleyan Centenary Hall.* Farther to the E. stands ***Crosby Hall,** built in 1466 by Alderman Sir John Crosby, and once occupied by the notorious Duke of Gloucester, afterwards Richard III. The building subsequently belonged to Sir Thomas More, and it is mentioned by Shakspeare in his 'Richard III.' For a long time it was used for the reception of ambassadors, and was considered the finest house in London. During the Protectorate it was a prison ; and it afterwards became in turn a meeting-house, a warehouse, and a concert and lecture room. It has been lately restored, and is now used as a restaurant (p. 18). Crosby Hall deserves a visit as being one of the few existing relics of the domestic architecture of mediæval London, and the only one in the Gothic style. The present street front and many parts of the interior do not belong to the ancient structure. The *Banqueting Hall* has a fine oaken roof.

*St. Helen's Church (open daily, except Sat., 11.30-4), near Crosby Hall, the 'Westminster Abbey of the City', was originally founded at a very early date and afterwards became connected with a nunnery established about 1212 on the site now occupied by St. Helen's Place. The present building, dating mainly from the 13-15th cent., was restored in 1891-93 under the superintendence of Mr. John L. Pearson. It consists of two parallel naves, 122 ft. long, together with a S. transept, adjoined on the E. by two chapels. The S. nave was used for parochial purposes, while that on the N. was the 'nuns' choir' or church. In the N. wall of the latter may still be seen the arched entrance from the nunnery and (near the E. end) a curious hagioscope or squint, originally connected with the cloisters. Over the hagioscope is an inscription (1877) to Alberico Gentile (d. 1611), the Italian jurist, and professor of civil law at Oxford, who was buried near it. Close by are the flat tombs of Sir Thomas Gresham (p. 140) and Sir Julius Cæsar (d. 1636), Master of the Rolls in the reign of James I. The Latin inscription on the latter is to the effect that Cæsar had given his bond to Heaven to yield up his soul willingly when God should demand it. The handsomest memorial is perhaps that of Sir William Pickering (d. 1574), on the N. side of the chancel. On the S. side is the tomb of Sir John Crosby (d. 1475; see p. 142). In the E. chapels are tombs removed from the church of St. Martin Outwich and several brasses. The stained-glass windows are modern; the fourth from the W. end of the nuns' choir was erected in 1884 to the memory of Shakspeare, who was a parishioner in 1598 and is rated in the parish books for 5l. 13s. 4d. — In St. Helen's Place is the modern *Hall of the Leathersellers*, a company incorporated at the end of the 14th century. The building is erected over the old crypt of St. Helen's Nunnery. Here also (No. 12) is the Consulate General of the United States. — The *Church of St. Ethelburga*, in Bishopsgate (entrance between Nos. 52 and 53), just to the N. of St. Helen's Place, also escaped the Great Fire.

Bishopsgate Street Within is continued to the N. by Bishopsgate Street Without (*i.e.* outside the walls), and the site of the gate which gave name to both is indicated by a tablet on the house at the corner of Camomile Street (Pl. R, 43; *III*). On the left side of Bishopsgate Without, opposite Houndsditch, is the *Church of St. Botolph without Bishopsgate* (Pl. R, 43; *III*), rebuilt in 1725-29. John Keats was baptized here on Oct. 31st, 1795. Farther on Bishopsgate Without passes (on the left) Liverpool Street (station, see p. 56). On the opposite side of the street, a little farther on, is the *Bishopsgate Institute*, opened in 1894, with a library, reading-room, etc. *Shoreditch*, the continuation of Bishopsgate Street, leads to the chief goods-depôt of the Great Eastern Railway, beneath which is a fish, fruit, and vegetable market. The churchyard of *St. Leonard's*, Shoreditch, now opened in summer as a public garden, is the burial-place of many actors, including Shakespeare's contemporary Richard Burbage (d. 1618). The present church dates from 1740, but incorporates a chancel window of the 13th cent.; it was restored in 1899. To the E. lies *Spitalfields*, with its shoemakers (see p. 94) and bird-fanciers, beyond which is *Bethnal Green* (p. 94). At No. 204 High Street, Shoreditch, is the *Standard*

Theatre (Pl. R, 44), a characteristic 'East End' place of amusement (see p. 67). The *Britannia Theatre* (Pl. B, 44), in Hoxton Street, lies to the N.W., in the crowded district of *Hoxton*. Shoreditch High Street is continued due N. by Kingsland Road to *Kingsland* and to *Dalston*, where the *German Hospital* is situated. Farther to the N. are *Stoke Newington* and *Clapton* (tramway No. 2 g; p. 54).

The open spaces in Stoke Newington include *Clissold Park* (55 acres), intersected by the New River (p. 138) and acquired for the public in 1889, and *Stoke Newington Common* (5¼ acres). *Abney Park Cemetery* was formerly the estate of Sir Thomas Abney, with whom Dr. Isaac Watts spent the last thirty years of his life, and contains a statue of the hymn-writer by Baily. Mrs. Booth, wife of Gen. Booth of the Salvation Army, is buried near the upper end of the cemetery. Other famous names connected with Stoke Newington are those of Edgar Allan Poe, who was at school here in 1817-19 (comp. his 'William Wilson'); Daniel Defoe; Thomas Day, author of 'Sandford and Merton'; John Howard, the philanthropist; and Bridget Fleetwood, eldest daughter of Oliver Cromwell. — In *Hornsey*, to the N.W. of Stoke Newington, is *Finsbury Park* (115 acres).

In **Cornhill**, the street which leads to the E. straight past the S. side of the Exchange, rises on the right (S.) *St. Michael's Church*, with a large late-Gothic tower, built by *Wren*, and restored by *Sir G. G. Scott*. Farther on is *St. Peter's Church*, which, according to an ancient tablet preserved in the vestry, was originally founded in 179 A.D. by 'Lucius, the first Christian king of this land, then called Britaine'. The present structure was built by Wren in 1680-81. The organ is by Father Smith (p. 115), and its old key-board, now in the vestry, was used by Mendelssohn on Sept. 30th, 1840. Both churches are open daily (except Sat.), 12-2. Gray, the poet (1716-71), was born in the house which formerly occupied the site of No. 41 Cornhill.

In *Leadenhall Street*, which continues Cornhill, stands, on the right and near the corner of Gracechurch Street, **Leadenhall Market**, one of the chief marts in London for poultry, game, and hides (see p. 32). The old *House of the East India Company*, in which Charles Lamb (for 33 years), James Mill, and John Stuart Mill were clerks, stood at the corner of Leadenhall Street and Lime Street. On the opposite side of Leadenhall Street, at the corner of St. Mary Axe, is the small church of **St. Andrew Undershaft** (*i. e.* under the maypole, as the maypole which used to be erected here was higher than the tower of the church), a Perpendicular building of 1520-32, with a turreted tower (daily, 12-2). At the end of the N. aisle is the tomb of Stow, the antiquary (d. 1605). Near this tomb is the monument of Sir Hugh Hammersley (d. 1636), with two fine figures of attendants, by Thomas Madden. Still farther on, on the same side, is the *Church of St. Catherine Cree* (daily, 12-2), with an interior by Inigo Jones, being the successor of an older church in which Holbein (d. 1543) is said to have been interred. The character of the services held here by Archbp. Laud in 1631 at the consecration of the church formed one of the charges in his trial. The *New Zealand Chambers* (No. 34) are one of Norman Shaw's reproductions of mediæval architecture. Leadenhall Street is joined at its E. end by Fenchurch Street (see below).

Lombard Street and *Fenchurch Street*, forming a line on the S. nearly parallel to Cornhill and Leadenhall Street, are also among the busiest thoroughfares of the city. Lombard Street has been for ages the most noted street in London for banking and finance, and has inherited its name from the 'Lombard' money-dealers from Genoa and Florence, who, in the 14th and 15th centuries, took the place of the discredited and persecuted Jews of 'Old Jewry' as money-lenders. Alexander Pope (1688-1744) was born in Plough Court, on the right (S.) side of Lombard Street, in a house demolished in 1872. On the N. side of Lombard Street is the *Church of St. Edmund King and Martyr* (open 10-4), completed by Wren in 1690, in which Addison was married to the Countess of Warwick on Aug. 9th, 1716. Fenchurch Street reminds us by its name of the fenny character of the district when the old church was built (drained by the little stream of 'Lang bourne' running into the 'Walbrook')[†]. On the N. side of the street was the *Elephant Tavern* (rebuilt), where Hogarth lodged for some time, and which was once adorned with several of his works. Adjacent is the *Ironmongers' Hall*, whose company dates from the reign of Edward IV., with an interesting interior, portraits of Izaak Walton and Admiral Hood, etc. Fenchurch Street is connected with Great Tower Street by *Mincing Lane* (so called from the 'minchens', or nuns of St. Helen's, to whom part of it belonged), which is the central point of the colonial wholesale trade. The *Clothworkers' Hall*, in Mincing Lane, was built in 1860; the company, of which Samuel Pepys was master in 1677, was incorporated in the 15th century. A little to the E., in *Mark Lane* (originally *Mart Lane*), is the **Corn Exchange** (Pl. R 43, *III*; chief market on Mon., 11-3), and near it is *Fenchurch Street Station* (for the railway to Blackwall, p. 58). The fine *Tower of All Hallows Staining*, behind the warehouses at the N. end of this lane, reached viâ Star Alley, is one of the oldest of the relics which have survived the Great Fire. On the E. side of Mark Lane is Hart Street, with the *Church of St. Olave* (open 12.30 to 3), interesting as having survived the Great Fire, and as the church once frequented by Samuel Pepys (d. 1703). The picturesque interior contains a number of curious old tombs, including those of Pepys and his wife. A bust of Pepys was placed on the S. wall in 1884. The skulls over the gate of the churchyard in Seething Lane are said to commemorate the fact that many persons who died of the plague in 1665 are buried here, but this tradition is not supported by the burials-register of the church. In the same street once stood a monastery of the 'Crossed Friars', a reminiscence of whom still exists in the

---

[†] **Mr. Loftie** thinks 'fen' may be a corruption of the Anglo-Saxon *foin* (hay), as 'grace' in Gracechurch Street is of *grass*.

adjoining street of Crutched Friars. — At the junction of Fenchurch Street and Leadenhall Street stands *Aldgate Pump*, disused since 1876; a 'draught (draft) on Aldgate Pump' used to be a cant term for a bad bill. From this point Aldgate High Street runs E. to the *Aldgate Station* of the Metropolitan Railway, passing the *Church of St. Botolph Aldgate* (Pl. R, 47; *III*). The supposed head of the Duke of Suffolk (beheaded 1554) is preserved in this church in a glass-case (removed from the Trinity Church, see below).

In Great Alie Street (Pl. R, 47), a litt'e to the S.E. of Aldgate Station, once stood *Goodman's Fields Theatre*, in which Garrick made his first appearance on a London stage in the character of Richard III. (Oct. 19th, 1741).

On the E. margin of the City proper lies HOUNDSDITCH, the quarter of Jew brokers and second-hand dealers, whence the *Minories* lead southwards to the Tower and the Thames. In the Minories rises the old *Church of the Holy Trinity* (Pl. R, 47; *III*), once belonging to an abbey of Minoresses, or nuns of the order of St. Clare, and containing several curious old monuments, on one of which are the arms (stars and stripes) of the Washington family. The church has been closed (keys at No. 6, The Crescent, Minories), and the living amalgamated with that of St. Botolph, Aldgate.

From Aldgate Station *Whitechapel High Street* runs E. to *Whitechapel*, see R. 10.

6. London Bridge. The Monument. Lower Thames Street.

Fishmongers' Hall. St. Magnus the Martyr's. Billingsgate. Custom House. Coal Exchange.

King William Street, a wide thoroughfare with handsome buildings, leads S.E. from the Bank to London Bridge. Immediately on the left, at the corner of Lombard Street, is the church of *St. Mary Woolnoth*, erected in 1716, by *Hawksmoor*. It contains a tablet to the memory of Newton, the friend of Cowper the poet and once rector of the parish, with an epitaph by himself. Newton's remains, however, were removed to Olney in 1893. The fine organ was originally built by *Father Schmitz* (1681; comp. p. 115). Beneath the church is the *Bank Station* of the City and S. London Electric Railway (p. 62). — In St. Clement's Lane, to the left, is *St. Clement's Church* (open 12-3), built by Wren in 1686 and containing a stained-glass window and brass tablets commemorating Thomas Fuller (d. 1661), Bishop Pearson (d. 1686), author of the 'Exposition of the Creed', and Bishop Walton (d. 1661), editor of the 'Biblia Polyglotta'. Purcell was organist in this church. Farther on, at the point where King William Street, Gracechurch Street, Eastcheap, and Cannon Street (p. 154) converge, on a site once occupied by Falstaff's 'Boar's Head Tavern', rises the *Statue of William IV.*, by Nixon. Adjacent is the *Monument Station* of the Underground Railway (p. 61). To the left, in Fish Street Hill, is the *Monument* (see p. 148). On each side of the first arch of London Bridge, which crosses *Lower Thames Street* (p. 149), are flights of stone steps descending to the street below.

London Bridge (Pl. R, 42; *III*), until a century ago the only bridge over the Thames in London, and still the most important, connects the City, the central point of business, with the *Borough*, on the Surrey (S.) side of the river (see p. 376).

The Saxons, and perhaps the Romans before them, erected various wooden bridges over the Thames near the site of the present London Bridge, but these were all at different periods carried away by floods or destroyed by fire. At length in 1176 Henry II. instructed *Peter*, chaplain of the church of St. Mary Cole, to construct a stone bridge at this point, but the work was not completed till 1209, in the reign of Henry's son, John. A chapel, dedicated to St. Thomas of Canterbury, was built upon the bridge, and a row of houses sprang up on each side, so that the bridge resembled a continuous street. It was terminated at both banks by fortified gates, on the pinnacles of which the heads of traitors used to be exposed.

In one of the houses dwelt Sir John Hewitt, Lord Mayor in the time of Queen Elizabeth, whose daughter, according to the romantic story, fell into the river, and was rescued by Edward Osborne, his apprentice. The brave and fortunate youth afterwards married the young lady and founded the family of the present Duke of Leeds.

The present London Bridge, about 60 yds. higher up the river than the old bridge (removed in 1832), was designed by *John Rennie*, a Scottish engineer, begun in 1825 under the superintendence of his sons, *Sir John* and *George Rennie*, and completed in 1831. The total outlay, including the cost of the approaches, was about 2,000,000*l.* The bridge, 928 ft. long and 54 ft. broad, is borne by five granite arches, of which that in the centre has a span of 152 ft. The lamp-posts on the bridge are cast of the metal of French cannon captured in the Peninsular War.

It is estimated that, in spite of the relief afforded by the Tower Bridge, 22,000 vehicles and about 110,000 pedestrians cross London Bridge daily, a fact which may give the stranger some idea of the prodigious traffic carried on in this part of the city. New-comers should pay a visit to London Bridge on a week-day during business-hours to see and hear the steady stream of noisy traffic. Stoppages or 'blocks' in the flow of vehicles, of course, sometimes take place; but, thanks to the skilful management of the police, such interruptions are seldom of long duration. One of the police regulations for this and other busy bridges is that slow-moving vehicles travel at the sides, and quick ones in the middle. London Bridge divides London into 'above' and 'below' bridge. Looking *down* the river we survey the *Port of London* (p. 165), the part immediately below the bridge being called the *Pool*. Sea-going vessels of the largest size may ascend the river to this point, but the busiest and most crowded part of the port now lies below the Tower Bridge, of which a good view is obtained hence. *Above* bridge the traffic is carried on chiefly by penny steamboats and coal barges. Among the buildings visible from the bridge are, on the N. side of the river, the Tower, the Custom House, Billingsgate Market, the Monument, St. Paul's, a great number of other churches, and the Cannon Street Station, while on the Surrey side lie St. Saviour's Church, Barclay and Perkins's Brewery, and numerous great warehouses. Near the S. end of the bridge lies *London Bridge Station* (p. 58).

An admirable survey of the traffic on the bridge as well as on the river is obtained from **The Monument** (Pl. R, 43; *III*), in Fish Street Hill, a little to the N. This consists of a fluted column, 202 ft. in height, designed by *Wren*, and erected in 1671-77 in commemoration of the Great Fire of London, which, on 2nd-7th Sept., 1666, destroyed 460 streets with 89 churches and 13,200 houses, valued at 7,335,000*l.* The height of the column is said to equal its distance from the house in *Pudding Lane* in which the fire broke out. A winding staircase of 345 steps (adm. 3*d.*) ascends the column to a platform enclosed by an iron cage (added to put a stop to suicides from the monument), above which rises a gilt urn with blazing flames, 42 ft. in height. The pedestal bears inscriptions and allegorical reliefs.

Just above London Bridge are the tunnels by which the *City and South London Electric Railway* passes under the Thames (see p. 62).

Immediately to the W. of London Bridge, at the lower end of *Upper Thames Street*, stands **Fishmongers' Hall**, a guildhouse erected in 1831 on the site of an older building. The Company of Fishmongers existed as early as the time of Edward I. It originally consisted of two separate trades, that of the *Salt-Fishmongers* and that of the *Stock-Fishmongers*, which were united to form the present body in the reign of Henry VIII. The guild is one of the richest in London, possessing an annual revenue of 50,000*l.* In politics it has usually been distinctively attached to the Whig party, while the Merchant Taylors are recognised as the great Tory company. On the landing of the staircase is a statue of Lord Mayor Walworth (a member of the company), who slew the rebel Wat Tyler (p. 128). Among the objects of interest in the interior are the dagger with which that rebel was slain; a richly embroidered pall used at Walworth's funeral; a chair made out of part of the first pile driven in the construction of Old London Bridge, supposed to have been submerged in the Thames for 650 years; portraits of William III. and his queen by *Murray*, George II. and his consort by *Shackleton*, and Queen Victoria by *Herbert Smith*.

Vintners' Hall (Pl. R, 39; *III*), 68 Upper Thames Street, was built by Wren in 1671 but almost entirely rebuilt in 1820-23. The old Council Chamber contains good oak-carving. The company was incorporated in 1436-37. — Near the W. end of Upper Thames St. is *St. Benet's Church*, built by Wren in 1683, now used as a Welsh Church.

LOWER THAMES STREET runs eastwards from London Bridge to the Custom House and the Tower. Chaucer, the 'father of English poetry', is said to have lived here in 1379-85. Close to the bridge, on the right, stands the handsome church of *St. Magnus the Martyr* (open 12-2), with a cupola and low spire, built by *Wren* in 1676. Miles Coverdale, Bishop of Exeter, author of the first complete printed English version of the Bible (1535), was once rector of St. Magnus and his remains were transferred hither in 1840 from St. Bartholomew by the Exchange, when that church was pulled down.

Farther to the E., on the Thames, is **Billingsgate** (Pl. R, 42, *III*; so called from a gate of old London, named, as an improbable tradition says, after Belin, a king of the Britons), the chief fish-market of London, the bad language used at which has become proverbial. In the reign of Elizabeth this was a market for all kinds of provisions, but since the reign of William III. it has been used for fish only. Fish has been landed and sold here from time immemorial, though now by far the largest part of the fish-supply comes by railway: salmon from Scotland, cod and turbot from the Doggerbank, lobsters from Norway, soles from the German ocean, eels from Holland, and oysters from the mouth of the Thames and the English Channel. Oysters and other shell-fish are sold by measure, salmon by weight, and other fish by number. The best fish is bought at the beginning of the market by the regular fishmongers. After them come the costermongers, who are said to sell a third of the fish consumed in London. Billingsgate wharf is the oldest on the Thames. The present market, with a figure of Britannia on the apex of the pediment, was designed by *Sir Horace Jones*, and opened in 1877. The market begins daily at 5 a.m., and is one of the sights of London (see p. 32).

Adjacent to the fish-market is the **Custom House** (Pl. R, 42; *III*), built by *Laing* in 1814-17, with an imposing façade towards the Thames, 490 ft. in length, by *Sir R. Smirke*. The customs-duties levied at the port of London amount to nearly 10,000,000*l.* a year, being about equal to those of all the other British seaports put together. The London Custom House employs about 2000 officials; in the *Long Room* (190 ft. in length by 66 in breadth) nearly 80 clerks are at work. Confiscated articles are stored in a warehouse reserved for this purpose, and are disposed of at annual sales by auction, which take place in Mincing Lane, and yield 2000*l.* per annum. Between the Custom House and the Thames is a broad quay, which affords a fine view of the river and shipping.

The **Coal Exchange,** opposite, at the corner of St. Mary at Hill, erected in 1849 from plans by *Bunning*, is in the Italian style, and has a tower 106 ft. in height. Adjoining it on the E. is a *hypocaust,* or stove of masonry belonging to a Roman bath, discovered when the foundations were being dug (shown on application to one of the attendants). The circular hall, with glass dome and triple gallery, is adorned with frescoes by *F. Sang*, representing the formation of coal and process of mining. The flooring is inlaid with 40,000 pieces of wood, arranged in the form of a mariner's compass. The sword in the municipal coat-of-arms in the centre is said to be formed of the wood of a mulberry-tree planted by Peter the Great in 1698, when he was learning the art of ship-building at Deptford. A collection of fossils, etc., is shown in cases in the galleries. — The amount of coal annually consumed in London alone at present averages upwards of 6,000,000 tons.

To the N. of the Custom House and to the E. of the Coal Exchange, at the convergence of St. Dunstan's Hill and Idol Lane, is the *Church of St. Dunstan's in the East* (Pl. R, 42; *III*), rebuilt in 1671 by Wren and again in 1817-21; the square tower, ending in a kind of lantern-steeple, is Wren's work (1699). The church contains a number of monuments and stained glass windows. In the vestry is a model of Wren's church, carved in oak and chestnut. — The *Church of St. Mary at Hill*, a little to the W. of St. Dunstan's, was built by Wren in 1672-77 (tower modern). Its present rector, the Rev. W. Carlile, is the founder of the Church Army, and the services include many popular features. Adjacent is the *City Samaritan Office*, a kind of club for the destitute.

Lower Thames Street debouches at its E. end upon Tower Hill (p. 163). — The *Tower*, see p. 155.

7. Thames Embankment. Blackfriars Bridge. Queen Victoria Street. Cannon Street.

Cleopatra's Needle. The Times' Publishing Office. Bible Society. Heralds' College. London Stone. Southwark Bridge.

The *Victoria Embankment*, which leads from Westminster Bridge (Pl. R, 29; *IV*) towards the E. along the N. bank of the Thames as far as Blackfriars Bridge (Pl. R, 35; *II*), offers a pleasant approach to the City and the Tower to those who have already explored the Strand and Fleet Street. It was constructed in 1864-70, under the supervision of *Sir Joseph W. Bazalgette* (p. 97), at a cost of nearly 2,000,000*l.* It is about 2300 yds. in length, and consists of a macadamised carriage-way 64 ft. wide, with a foot pavement 16 ft. broad on the land-side, and one 20 ft. broad on the river-side. The whole of this area was once covered by the tide twice a day. It is protected on the side next the Thames by a granite wall, 8 ft. thick, for which a foundation was made by sinking iron cylinders into the river-bed as deeply as possible and filling them with concrete. Under the Embankment run three different tunnels. On the inland side is one traversed by the Metropolitan District Railway, while on the Thames side there are two, one above the other, the lower containing one of the principal intercepting sewers (p. 97), and the upper one holding water and gas pipes and telegraph-wires. Rows of trees have been planted along the sides of the Embankment, which in a few years will afford a shady promenade. At intervals are large openings, with stairs leading to the floating steamboat piers (p. 63), which are constructed of iron, and rise and fall with the tide. Part of the land reclaimed from the river has been converted into tasteful gardens.

The principal approaches to the Victoria Embankment are from Blackfriars Bridge and Westminster Bridge (p. 246), from Horseguards Avenue, leading off Whitehall, from Charing Cross (p. 187), and from Arundel, Norfolk, Surrey, Savoy, and Villiers Streets, all leading off the Strand.

Beginning at Westminster Bridge (p. 246), we see *St. Stephen's Club* to the left, and a little farther on pass *New Scotland Yard* (p. 237) and *Montague House* (p. 237). Immediately above Charing Cross Bridge rises a lofty block of buildings containing the *National Liberal Club* (p. 187). The public gardens (band on summer evenings, except Thurs. & Sat.) in front of these are embellished with bronze statues of *William Tyndale*, the translator of the New Testament, *Sir Bartle Frere*, and *General Outram*. Below the bridge is another public garden, with statues of *Robert Burns* and *Robert Raikes*, the founder of Sunday schools, and with a memorial fountain bearing a bronze medallion of *Henry Fawcett*, *M. P.* The ancient level of the river is indicated by the beautiful old **Watergate* of York House, a palace begun by Inigo Jones for the first Duke of Buckingham (in the N.W. corner of this garden). No. 15 Buckingham Street, behind the Watergate, formed part of York House and contains old ceilings adorned with stucco and paintings (comp. p. 185). Above is the *Adelphi Terrace* (p. 185). On the right of the Embankment, by the Adelphi Steps, rises **Cleopatra's Needle** (Pl. R, 30; *II*), an Egyptian obelisk erected here in 1878.

This famous obelisk was presented to the British Government by Mohammed Ali, and brought to this country by the private munificence of Dr. Erasmus Wilson, who gave 10,000*l.* for this purpose. Properly speaking Cleopatra's Needle is the name of the companion obelisk now in New York, which stood erect at Alexandria till its removal, while the one now in London lay prostrate for many years. Both monoliths were originally brought from Heliopolis, and is referred to in the inscription on the London obelisk as the 'house of the Phœnix'. The obelisk, which is of reddish granite, measures 68½ ft. in height, and is 8 ft. wide at the base. Its weight is 180 tons. The pedestal of grey granite is 18⅔ ft. high, including the steps; the inscriptions on it summmarize the ancient and modern history of the Obelisk. The Obelisk of Luxor at Paris is 76 ft. in height, and weighs 240 tons.

Two large bronze *Sphinxes*, designed by Mr. G. Vulliamy, have been placed at the base of the Needle.

A little farther on, near Waterloo Bridge, rises the *Cecil Hotel* (p. 7), an enormous new building by Perry and Reed, occupying the site of one of the most ambitious enterprizes of the notorious Liberator Society. It is adjoined by the *Savoy Hotel* (p. 7; at the back of the Savoy, p. 184), beyond which stands the *Medical Examination Hall*. The latter, a building of red brick and Portland stone in the Italian style, erected in 1886, contains a statue of the Queen by Williamson, unveiled in 1889. Below the bridge are the river-façade and terrace of *Somerset House* (p. 182). Farther on,

near the Temple Station, is a statue of *Isambard Brunel;* and in
the adjoining gardens are statues of *W. E. Forster*, erected in 1890,
and of *John Stuart Mill*, erected in 1878. Behind Forster's statue
is the tasteful *Office of the London School Board*, the weekly meetings of which are held here on Thursday at 3 p.m. (public admitted
to the gallery; p. 98). Then follows the *Temple* (p. 176), with its
modern Gothic *Library* and its *Gardens*. Farther to the E., beyond
two palatial blocks of offices, are the buildings of the *Metropolitan
Asylums Board* and the *Thames Conservancy;* immediately adjoining the latter is the Gothic building of *Sion College and Library*
(see p. 21), opened in 1886, beyond which is the handsome building of the *City of London School*, completed in 1883, of which Sir
J. R. Seeley was an alumnus. To the N., in Tudor Street, is the
Guildhall School of Music (3600 pupils), a building in the Italian
style, erected by the Corporation of London in 1886 at a cost of
22,000*l*. The Embankment ends at Blackfriars Bridge, at the N.
end of which is a statue of *Queen Victoria*, by Birch, erected in
1897. Adjacent is *De Keyser's Royal Hotel* (p. 12).

Albert Embankment, see p. 380; *Chelsea Embankment*, see p. 368.

Blackfriars Bridge (Pl. R, 34, 35; *II*), an iron structure, built
by *Cubitt*, and opened in 1869, occupies the site of a stone bridge
dating from 1769, the piers of which had given way. The bridge,
which consists of five arches (the central having a span of 185 ft.)
supported by granite piers, is 1272 ft. in length, including the
abutments, and 80 ft. broad. The cost of construction amounted to
320,000*l*. The dome of St. Paul's is seen to advantage from this bridge
(comp., however, p. 112), which also commands an excellent view
otherwise. Just below Blackfriars Bridge the Thames is crossed by
the *South Eastern and Chatham Railway Bridge*, and just above is
the tunnel by which the *Waterloo and City Railway* (p. 62) passes
under the river.

The bridge derives its name from an ancient Monastery of the Black
Friars, situated on the bank of the river, and dating from 1276, where
several parliaments once met, and where Cardinals Wolsey and Cam-
peggio pronounced sentence of divorce against the unfortunate Queen
Catharine of Aragon in 1529 ('King Henry VIII.' ii. 4). Shakspeare once
lived at Blackfriars, and in 1599 acted at a theatre which formerly occupied part of the site of the monastery, and of which the name *Playhouse
Yard* is still a reminiscence. In 1607 Ben Jonson was also a resident
here, and Van Dyck lived at Blackfriars from 1632 till his death in 1641.

In *New Bridge Street*, which leads straight to the N. from Blackfriars Bridge, immediately to the right, is the *Blackfriars Station*
of the Metropolitan District Railway (p. 61); and farther on, beyond
Queen Victoria Street (see p. 153), is the large *Ludgate Hill
Station* of the South Eastern and Chatham Railway (p. 58), opposite which, on the left, the prison of *Bridewell* (so called from the
old 'miraculous' Well of St. Bride or St. Bridget) stood down to
1864. The site of the prison was once occupied by Bridewell

Palace, in which Shakspeare lays the 3rd Act of his 'Henry VIII.' New Bridge Street ends at *Ludgate Circus*, at the E. end of *Fleet Street* (p. 172), the prolongation to the N. being called *Farringdon Street* (see p. 125). To the E., opposite Fleet Street, diverges *Ludgate Hill*, leading to St. Paul's Cathedral, and passing under the viaduct of the South Eastern and Chatham Railway (p. 58).

QUEEN VICTORIA STREET, a broad and handsome thoroughfare, 1/3 M. in length, constructed at vast expense, leads straight from Blackfriars Bridge, towards the E., to the Mansion House and the Bank. To the right, at its W. end, is the large *St. Paul's Station* of the South Eastern and Chatham Railway. In Water Lane, to the left, stands *Apothecaries' Hall*, built in 1670, and containing portraits of James I., Charles I., and others. The company, most of whose members really are what the name implies, grants licenses to dispense medicines and to give medical advice; and pure drugs are prepared in the chemical laboratories at the back of the Hall. On the left side of Queen Victoria Street, farther on, is the **Office of The Times** (Pl. R, 35; *II*), a handsome building of red brick. The tympanum bears an allegorical device with allusions to times past and future. Behind the Publishing Office, in Printing House Square (so called from the former office of the king's printers), is the interesting *Printing Office*. Tickets of admission are sometimes issued on written application to the Manager, enclosing a note of introduction or reference. Visitors should be careful to attend at the hour named in the order, when the second edition of the paper is being printed. No fewer than 20,000 copies can be struck off in an hour by the wonderful mechanism of the *Walter* press, and perhaps 50,000 are issued daily. The continuous rolls or webs of paper, with which the machine feeds itself, are each 4 miles in length, and of these 28 to 30 are used in one day. The finished and folded copies of *The Times* are thrown out at the other end of the machine. The type-setting machines are also of great interest. The guide explains all the details (no gratuity). *The Times* celebrated its centenary in 1888.

Printing House Square stands on a corner of old London which for many ages was occupied by frowning Norman fortresses. Part of the castle of Mountfitchet, a follower of the Conqueror, is said to have stood here; and the ground between the S. side of Queen Victoria Street, or Earl Street, and the Thames was the site of *Baynard's Castle* (mentioned in 'Richard III.') with its extensive precincts, which replaced an earlier Roman fortress, and probably a British work of defence. Baynard's Castle was presented by Queen Elizabeth to the Earls of Pembroke, and continued to be their residence till its destruction in the Great Fire †.

---

† This is the ordinary account, but it is disputed by Mr. Loftie, who maintains that the later house known as Baynard's Castle did not occupy

Farther on in Queen Victoria Street is the church of *St. Andrew by the Wardrobe* (open 12–2), built by Wren in 1692, adjacent to which, on the E., rises the large building occupied by the **British and Foreign Bible Society**, erected in 1868. The number of Bibles and Testaments issued by this important society now amounts to about four millions a year. The total number of copies issued since its foundation in 1804 is over 151,000,000, printed in 339 different languages and dialects. The annual income of the society from subscriptions and the sale of Bibles is about 220,000*l.* Visitors (daily, except Sat. and Mon.) are shown the library, containing an extensive and probably unique collection of Bibles in different languages. The board-room contains a portrait of Lord Shaftesbury, by *Millais*; and on the staircase is a large painting by *E. M. Ward:* Luther's first study of the Bible. — Farther to the E., on the same side of the street, are the large buildings of the *Savings Bank Department* of the Post Office (new building, see p. 387).

To the left, farther on in Queen Victoria Street, is **Heralds' College,** or the **College of Arms** (rebuilt in 1683), anciently the town house of the Earls of Derby. The library contains a number of interesting objects, including a sword, dagger, and ring belonging to James IV. of Scotland, who fell at Flodden in 1513; the Warwick roll, a series of portraits of the Earls of Warwick from the Conquest to the time of Richard III. (executed by *Rous* at the end of the 15th cent.); genealogy of the Saxon kings, from Adam, more curious than trustworthy, illustrated with drawings of the time of Henry VIII.; portrait of the celebrated Talbot, Earl of Shrewsbury, from his tomb in old St. Paul's. The college also contains the official records of the nobility and gentry of England and other valuable genealogical collections. Visitors require an introduction.

The office of Earl-Marshal, president of Heralds' College, is hereditary in the person of the Duke of Norfolk. The college consists of three kings-at-arms, Garter, Clarenceux, and Norroy — six heralds, Lancaster, Somerset, Richmond, York, Windsor, and Chester — and four pursuivants, Rouge Croix, Bluemantle, Portcullis, and Rouge Dragon. The main duty of the corporation is to make out and preserve the pedigrees and armorial bearings of noble families and to conduct such royal ceremonials as are in the department of the Earl-Marshal. It also grants arms and records royal warrants of precedency and changes of name.

On the N. side of Queen Victoria Street, farther on, are the churches of *St. Nicholas Cole Abbey* and *St. Mary Aldermary*, two of Wren's reconstructions. Nearly opposite the latter of these, in which Milton was married to his third wife (Feb. 24th, 1663), Queen Victoria Street intersects CANNON STREET, the most direct route between St. Paul's Churchyard and London Bridge, and *Queen Street* (p. 134), leading from Cheapside to Southwark Bridge (p. 155). Near the intersection, facing Bread Street, is *St. Mildred's Church*, built by Wren (1683) and containing, like many others of the City churches,

the site of the original fortress of that name. See his 'London' (in the 'Historic Towns Series'; 1887).

some very handsome woodwork. Shelley married Mary Godwin at
this church on Dec. 30th, 1816. Cannon Street, which is $^2/_3$ M.
long, was constructed at a cost of 589,470*l.*, and opened in 1854.
This street contains the *Cannon Street* (p. 61) and *Mansion House*
(p. 61) stations of the Metropolitan District Railway, and also the
extensive *Cannon Street Station*, the City Terminus of the South
Eastern and Chatham Railway (p. 57; hotel, see p. 12). Opposite the
last stands the church of *St. Swithin*, popularly regarded as the saint
of the weather, rebuilt by Wren in 1678; into its S. wall is built the
London Stone, an old Roman milestone, supposed to have been the
milliarium of the Roman forum in London, from which the distances
along the various British highroads were reckoned. Against this
stone, which is now protected by an iron grating, Jack Cade once
struck his staff, exclaiming 'Now is Mortimer lord of the city'. In
St. Swithin's Lane stands the large range of premises known as
'*New Court*', occupied by Messrs. Rothschild. — Close by is *Salters'
Hall*, and near it was Salters' Hall Chapel, begun by the ejected
minister Richard Mayo in 1667, and long celebrated for its
preachers and theological disputations. — Down to 1853 the *Steel
Yard*, at one time a factory or storehouse of the Hanseatic League,
established in 1250, stood on the site now occupied by the Cannon
Street Terminus. — Adjacent to the station, on the W., is Dowgate Hill, with the *Hall of the Skinners*, who were incorporated in
1327. The court (with its wooden porch) and interior were built
soon after the Fire; the staircase and the wainscoted 'Cedar Room'
are interesting. The fine plate of this company includes the curious
'Cockayne Cups' of 1565. Cannon Street ends at the Monument,
beyond which it is continued by *Eastcheap* and *Great Tower Street*
to *Tower Hill* (p. 163).

Southwark Bridge (Pl. R, 38; *III*), erected by *Sir John Rennie*
in 1815-19, at a cost of 800,000*l.*, is 700 ft. long, and consists of
three iron arches, borne by stone piers. The span of the central
arch is 240 ft., that of the side ones 210 ft. The traffic is comparatively small on account of the inconvenience of the approaches,
but has of late greatly increased. In Southwark, on the S. bank,
lies *Barclay and Perkins's Brewery* (p. 378). The river farther down
is crossed by the imposing five-arched railway-bridge of the *South
Eastern Railway* (terminus at Cannon Street Station, see above).

8. The Tower.

Trinity House. Royal Mint. Tower Bridge.

The Tower is conveniently reached by the Underground Railway to
Mark Lane Station (Pl. R, 42; *III*); or by omnibus from Liverpool Street
(Nos. 9, 11; p. 36).

The **Tower** (Pl. R, 46; *III*), the ancient fortress and gloomy
state-prison of London, and historically the most interesting spot in

England, is an irregular mass of buildings erected at various periods, surrounded by a battlemented wall and a deep moat, which was drained in 1843. It stands on the bank of the Thames, to the E. of the City, and outside the bounds of the ancient city-walls. The present external appearance of the Tower is very unlike what it originally was, perhaps no fortress of the same age having undergone greater transformations. Though at first a royal palace and stronghold, the Tower is best known in history as a prison. It

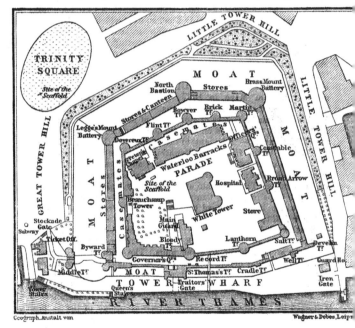

is now a government arsenal, and is still kept in repair as a fortress. The ground-plan is in the form of an irregular pentagon, which covers an area of 13 acres, and is enclosed by a double line of circumvallation (the *outer* and *inner ballium* or *ward*), strengthened with towers. The square White Tower rises conspicuously in the centre. A broad quay, with a gun-park, lies between the moat and the Thames.

It is possible, though very doubtful, that a fortification of some kind stood on this site in Roman times; but the Tower of London properly originated with William the Conqueror (see p. 91). The oldest part of the fortress is the *White Tower* (p. 158), begun about 1078 on a site previously occupied by two bastions built by King Alfred in 885. The architect was Gundulf, Bishop of Rochester. It is said to owe its name to the fact that its walls were whitewashed in 1240. Under William II. (1087-1100) the inner ward was surrounded by a wall, while the moat was made by Richard I. (1189-99), but the most extensive additions were due to Henry III. (1216-72), from whose reign dates the greater part of the present fortifications. The *Chapel* in the White Tower is mentioned for the first time in 1189, the *Church of St. Peter* in 1210. The *Royal Residence*, which stood to the S.E. of the White Tower, was probably erected by the beginning of the 13th cent.; most of it, including the great hall in which Anne Boleyn was tried, was pulled down by Cromwell (1649-58), and the remainder has since disappeared. Charles II., who here spent the night before his coronation (1661), was the last monarch who has resided in the Tower.

The Tower (adm., see p. 108) is provided with four entrances, viz. the *Iron Gate*, the *Water Gate*, and the *Traitors' Gate*, all on the side next the Thames; and on the W., the principal entrance, or *Lions' Gate*, so called from the royal menagerie formerly kept here. (The lions were removed to the Zoological Gardens in Regent's Park in 1834.) To the right is the *Ticket Office*, where tickets are procured for the Armoury (6d.) and the Crown Jewels (6d.). Free days should be avoided on account of the crowd. A simple *Refreshment Room* adjoins the ticket office. The quaintly-attired *Warders* or *Beef-eaters*, who are stationed at different parts of the building, are all old soldiers of meritorious service. The term Beef-eater is commonly explained as a corruption of *Buffetiers*, or attendants at the royal *Buffet*, but is more probably a nickname bestowed upon the ancient Yeomen of the Guard from their well-fed appearance or the fact that rations of beef were regularly served out to them when on duty. The names of the different towers, gates, etc., are now indicated by placards, and the most interesting objects in the armouries also bear inscriptions. The *Guides to the Tower* (1d. and 6d.; both by W. J. Loftie) are almost unnecessary, except to those who take a special interest in old armour.

We here describe the parts usually open to visitors in the prescribed order. Visitors really interested may sometimes obtain an order from the Constable of the Tower admitting them to parts not shown to the general public.

To the left of the entrance, opposite the Ticket Office, is a Turkish cannon, presented by Sultan Abdul Medjid Khan in 1857. A stone bridge, between two towers (*Middle Tower* and *Byward Tower*), leads across the moat (which can still be flooded by the garrison) into the *Outer Bail* or anterior court. On the left is the *Bell Tower*, adjacent to which is a narrow passage, leading round the fortifications within the outer wall. Farther on, to the right, is the *Traitors' Gate*, a double gateway on the Thames, by which state-prisoners were formerly admitted to the Tower; above it is *St. Thomas's Tower*. A gateway opposite leads under the *Bloody Tower* (p. 161), with its portcullis, to the *Inner Bail*. Immediately to the right is the round *Wakefield Tower* (p. 161), also called *Record Tower* from the fact that it contained the public records until 1856. Here are now preserved the —

CROWN JEWELS, or *Regalia*. During the confusion that prevailed after the execution of Charles I. the royal ornaments and part of the Regalia, including the ancient crown of King Edward, were sold. The crowns and jewels made to replace these after the Restoration retain the ancient names. The Regalia now consist of the following articles, which are preserved in a glass-case, protected by a strong iron cage: —

St. Edward's Crown, executed for the coronation of Charles II. This was the crown stolen in 1671 by Col. Blood and his accomplices, who overpowered and gagged the keeper. The bold robbers, however, did not succeed in escaping with their booty. *Queen Victoria's Crown*, made in 1838, a masterpiece of the modern goldsmith's art, is adorned with no fewer than 2783 diamonds and 310 other gems. The uncut ruby ('spinel') in front, said to have been given to the Black Prince in 1367 by Don Pedro of Castile, was worn by Henry V. on his helmet at the battle of Agincourt. The large sapphire in the cross at the top is said to have belonged to Edward the Confessor. The *Prince of Wales's Crown*, of pure gold, without precious stones. The *Queen Consort's Crown*, of gold, set with jewels. The *Queen's Crown*, a golden circlet, embellished with diamonds and pearls, made for Queen Maria d'Este, wife of James II. *St. Edward's Staff*, made of gold, 4¹/₂ ft. long and about 90 lbs. in weight. The orb at the top is said to contain a piece of the true cross. The *Royal Sceptre* with the Cross, 2 ft. 9 in. long, richly adorned with precious stones. The *Sceptre of the Dove*, or *Rod of Equity*. Above the orb is a dove with outspread wings. *Queen Victoria's Sceptre*, with richly gemmed cross. The *Ivory Sceptre* of Queen Maria d'Este, surmounted by a dove of white onyx. The *Sceptre of Queen Mary*, wife of William III. The *Orbs* of the King and Queen. Model of the *Koh-i-Noor* (Mountain of Light), one of the largest diamonds known, weighing 162 carats. The original, now at Windsor Castle, was formerly in the possession of Runjeet Singh, Rajah of Lahore, and came into the hands of the English in 1849, on their conquest of the Punjâb. The *Curtana*, or pointless *Sword of Mercy*. The *Swords of Justice*. The *Coronation Bracelets*. The *Royal Spurs*. The *Coronation Oil Vessel* or *Ampulla*, in the form of an eagle. The *Spoon* belonging to the ampulla, thought to be the only relic of the ancient regalia. The *Salt Cellar of State*, in the form of a model of the White Tower. The silver-gilt *Baptismal Font* for the royal children. A silver *Wine Fountain* given by the Corporation of Plymouth to Charles II. Gold *Basin* used in the distribution of the Queen's alms on Maundy Thursday. The total value of the Regalia is estimated at 3,000,000*l*.

The cases at the side contain the insignia of the *Orders of the Garter, Star of India, the Bath, St. Michael and St. George, Thistle, St. Patrick, Crown of India, Royal Victorian Order*, etc.; also the *Victoria Cross*, the *Distinguished Service Order*, and others.

On quitting the Wakefield Tower, close to which a singularly incongruous block of red brick buildings has been erected (1900), we proceed to the Inner Bail. In the centre of this court, upon slightly rising ground, stands the *WHITE TOWER, or *Keep*, the most ancient part of the fortress (p. 157). It measures 107 ft. from N. to S. and 118 ft. from E. to W., and is 92 ft. high. The walls are 13-15 ft. thick, and are surmounted with turrets at the angles. The original Norman windows, with the exception of four on the S. side, were altered in the classical style by Sir

Christopher Wren in 1663-1709. Among the many important scenes enacted in this tower may be mentioned the abdication of Richard II. in favour of Henry of Bolingbroke in 1399. We enter on the S. side and ascend to the second floor by a winding staircase passing through the massive wall. It was under this staircase that the bones conjectured to be those of the two young princes murdered by their uncle Richard III. (see p. 161) were found. On the first floor are two apartments, said to have been those in which Sir Walter Raleigh was confined and wrote his History of the World (1605-17; closed). The *Chapel of St. John*, on the second floor, with its massive pillars and cubical capitals, its wide triforium, its apse borne by stilted round arches (somewhat resembling those of St. Bartholomew's, p. 127), and its barrel-vaulted ceiling, is one of the finest and best-preserved specimens of Norman architecture in England. The other rooms contain the armoury.

The *COLLECTION OF OLD ARMOUR, in the two upper floors of the White Tower, though not equal to the best Continental collections of the kind, is yet of great value and interest. The rooms on the second floor contain Eastern arms and armour, the more modern European arms, and a number of personal relics. The main portion of the collection is in the Council Chamber, including a series of equestrian figures in full equipment, as well as numerous figures on foot, affording a faithful picture, in approximately chronological order, of English war-array from the time of Edward I. (1272) down to that of James II. (1688). In the Norman period armour consisted either of leather, cut into small pieces like the scales of a fish, or of flat rings of steel sewn on to leather. Chain mail was introduced from the East in the time of Henry III. (1216-72). Plates for the arms and legs were introduced in the reign of Edward II. (1307-27), and complete suits of plate armour came into use under Henry V. (1413-22). The glass-cases contain various smaller objects of interest. — On quitting St. John's Chapel we enter the —

EAST ROOM on the second floor. The walls and ceilings of this and the next room are adorned with trophies of arms in the form of stars, flowers, coats-of-arms, and the like. In the cases and on the walls are armour and weapons from Asia, America, Africa, and the South Sea Islands. To the right, near the end of the room, suit of Japanese armour presented to Charles II. by the Mogul. In the middle of the room are two models of the Tower at different periods; and at the end is a large Burmese bell. — We now enter the —

BANQUETING HALL. In the cases are British and other European weapons of the 19th century. At the head of the room, between two grotesque wooden figures, known as 'Gin' and 'Beer', is a case containing instruments of torture. To the right, two chased brass guns made for the Duke of Gloucester, son of Queen Anne, who died in 1700 at the age of eleven. By the window-wall is an equestrian figure of Queen Elizabeth on her way to return thanks at St. Paul's for the destruction of the Spanish Armada (1588). Adjacent is a beautiful Maltese cannon, captured from the French by a British frigate. By the opposite wall is the block on which Lord Lovat, the last person beheaded in England, suffered the penalty of high treason on Tower Hill in 1747. Beside it is a heading-axe, which has been in the Tower since 1687. In the centre of the room: Model of the Tower

in 1882; model for a Wellington monument, designed by John Bell. At
the end of the room are two cases containing the uniform worn by the
Duke of Wellington as Constable of the Tower and the cloak upon which
General Wolfe died before Quebec in 1759. To the left are early cannon
and shot; also part of the pump of the 'Mary Rose', sunk in 1545 and recovered in 1840. To the right, beside the lift, two drums captured at Blenheim (1704). — We now ascend the winding-stair beside the lift to the —

COUNCIL CHAMBER, in which the abdication of Richard II. took place.
To the left of the entrance are specimens of metal-quilted garments of
the 15-16th cent.; to the right, cases with Eastern chain-mail, bronze swords,
and primitive weapons. We turn to the left. In the first cases are Roman,
Greek, British, Anglo-Saxon, and other early arms and armour. In the stands
and on the walls of this and the next room are European staff-weapons of the
15-17th cent. (halberds, partizans, bills, boar-spears, etc.). The finest suits of
armour are displayed on a series of equestrian figures, interspersed among
which are numerous weapons of the periods illustrated by the suits of armour.
1 (to the left), Plate armour of the 15th cent.; 3 (to the right), Early
16th cent. suit, made in Nuremberg; the horse-armour shows the Burgundian
cross; 2 (to the left), Modern copy of a knight's suit of the time of
Richard III. (14·3-85), worn by the Marquis of Waterford at the Eglinton
tournament in 1839; two suits of the same period, one ornamented with
engraving; 4. Fluted suit of the time of Henry VII. (1485-1509). — The
following suits of armour belonged to Henry VIII. (1509-47): to the right,
28. Foot-armour, 29. Armour known as a tonlet; to the left, 6, 7. Equestrian
suits, one partly gilt; to the right, *5. Magnificent suit, of German workmanship, said to have been presented by the Emperor Maximilian to
Henry VIII. on his marriage with Catharine of Aragon. Among the numerous ornaments inlaid in gold the rose and pomegranate, the badges of
Henry and Catharine, are of frequent recurrence; the other cognisances
of Henry, the portcullis, fleur-de-lys, and dragon, and the initials of the
royal pair connected by a true-lover's knot, also appear. On the armour of
the horse are engraved scenes of martyrdom. Opposite (left) is a helmet with
ram's horns and a mask, also presented by Maximilian to Henry VIII. —
In the corner by the window are a German tilting-saddle (1470), several
tilting-lances (including one said to have belonged to the Duke of Suffolk), and
other equipments for the lists. The armour at the end of the room dates
chiefly from the 16th cent.; the damascened suit in the centre is of the
17th cent.; No. 30 is a suit for a man 7 ft. in height. — We now follow
the other side of the room. To the left: 9. Suit of the Earl of Worcester (d. 1589); behind, bowman and musketeer of the same period;
8. Suit of the 16th cent., formerly said to belong to Sir Henry Lee, Master
of the Armouries to Queen Elizabeth (1570). 10. Suit actually worn by
Robert Dudley, Earl of Leicester (1580), the favourite of Queen Elizabeth;
the armour bears his initials and crest. 12. Tournament-suit of Robert
Devereux, Earl of Essex, worn by the king's champion at the coronation
of George I. At the end of the room are electrotype reproductions of
shields, pieces of armour, etc., including a copy of the shield at Windsor
ascribed to Cellini. — We turn to the left and enter the —

EAST ROOM on the third floor. To the left of the entrance is a case
with maces and axes and specimens illustrating the evolution of the bayonet.
In the case to the right are cross-bows, and two English long-bows of yew
recovered from the wreck of the 'Mary Rose' (see above). On the left side
of the room are figures of horsemen and pikemen of the 17th cent., and at
the end of the room are wall-cases containing helmets, morions, etc.
Returning by the opposite side of the room we notice: 17. Suit, richly
inlaid with gold, belonging to Henry, Prince of Wales (1612), eldest son
of James I.; 18. Suit of French workmanship, worn by Charles I. as Prince
of Wales; 19. Gilt suit presented to Charles I. by the City of London; 24.
Mounted figure with slight suit of armour that belonged to James II. (1685),
after whose time armour was rarely worn. The cases at the top of the
room contain rapiers and bucklers and early firearms, some of which are
breechloaders. The table-cases contain portions of armour, daggers,
swords, etc. In the case to the right of the exit, at the left end of the

third shelf, is a helmet (modern), worn by Louis Napoleon (Napoleon III.) at the Eglinton Tournament in 1839.

At the foot of the staircase by which we leave the White Tower are some fragments of the old *State Barge* of the Master-General of the Ordnance (broken up in 1859), with the arms of the Duke of Marlborough and other decorations in carved and gilded oak.

Outside the White Tower is an interesting collection of old cannon, some of very heavy calibre, chiefly of the time of Henry VIII., but one going back to the reign of Henry VI. (1422–61). — We now cross the 'Tower Green' to the Beauchamp Tower, on the W. side, the only other part of the Tower shown to ordinary visitors. On the way we pass the site of the scaffold, marked by a railing.

The BEAUCHAMP TOWER, built by Edward III. (1327–77), consists of three stories, which are connected by a narrow winding staircase. The walls of the room on the first floor are covered with inscriptions by former prisoners, including some transferred hither from other parts of the Tower. The inscription of John Dudley, Earl of Warwick, eldest brother of Lord Guildford Dudley, is on the right side of the fire-place, and is a well executed family coat-of-arms with the following lines : —

'Yow that these beasts do wel behold and se,
May deme with ease wherefore here made they be
Withe borders wherein . . . .
4 brothers' names who list to serche the grovnd'.

Near the recess in the N.W. corner is the word IANE (repeated in the window), supposed to represent the signature of Lady Jane Grey as queen, but not inscribed by herself. Above the fire-place is a Latin inscription left by Philip Howard, Earl of Arundel, eldest son of the Duke of Norfolk who was beheaded in 1573 for aspiring to the hand of Mary, Queen of Scots. The earliest inscription is that of Thomas Talbot, 1462. The inscriptions in the upper chamber (not shown) are less interesting.

The thirteen TOWERS of the Inner Ward, at one time all used as prisons, were afterwards employed in part for the custody of the state archives. The names of several of them are indissolubly associated with many dark and painful memories. In the *Bloody Tower* (freed in 1900 from its disfiguring coat of stucco) the sons of Edward IV. are said to have been murdered, by order of Richard III. (comp. pp. 159, 265); others ascribe the name to the suicide of Henry, 8th Duke of Northumberland, in 1585. In the *Bell Tower* the Princess Elizabeth was confined by her sister Queen Mary, and Arabella Stuart was imprisoned for four years; Lady Jane Grey is said to have been imprisoned in *Brick Tower;* Lord Guildford Dudley, husband of Lady Jane Grey, was confined, with his father and brothers, in *Beauchamp Tower* (see above) ; in the *Bowyer Tower*, the Duke of Clarence, brother of Edward IV., is popularly supposed to have been drowned in a butt of malmsey; and Henry VI. was commonly believed to have been murdered in *Wakefield (Record) Tower*. The *Salt Tower* contains a curious drawing of the zodiac, by Hugh Draper of Bristol, who was confined here in 1561 on a charge of sorcery. The *Lanthorn Tower* was entirely rebuilt in 1882.

At the N.W. corner of the Tower Green is the chapel of St. Peter ad Vincula (interior sometimes accessible for a fee), built in its present form by Henry VIII., and restored in 1877. The original church, probably built by Henry II., was burned in 1512. The chapel preserves its open oak roof of the 16th cent. and contains various monuments chiefly connected with governors of the Tower. The organ, originally constructed by Father Schmitz (p. 115), was brought hither in 1893 from the old Chapel Royal at Whitehall (p. 234). On the wall, to the N. of the exit, we notice the leaden inscribed plates found interred with the coffinless remains of Lords Kilmarnock, Balmerino, and Fraser of Lovat, executed in 1746-7. Adjoining the chapel is a small burial-ground.

'In truth, there is no sadder spot on earth than this little cemetery. Death is there associated, not, as in Westminster Abbey and St. Paul's, with genius and virtue, with public veneration and with imperishable renown; not, as in our humblest churches and churchyards, with everything that is most endearing in social and domestic charities; but with whatever is darkest in human nature and in human destiny, with the savage triumph of implacable enemies, with the inconstancy, the ingratitude, the cowardice of friends, with all the miseries of fallen greatness and of blighted fame'. — *Macaulay.*

The following celebrated persons were buried in this chapel : Sir Thomas More, beheaded 1535 (but comp. p. 371); Anne Boleyn, beheaded 1536; Thomas Cromwell, Earl of Essex, beheaded 1540; Margaret Pole, Countess of Salisbury, beheaded 1541; Queen Catharine Howard, beheaded 1542; Lord Admiral Seymour of Sudeley, beheaded 1549; Lord Somerset, the Protector, beheaded 1552; John Dudley, Earl of Warwick and Duke of Northumberland, beheaded 1553; Lady Jane Grey and her husband, Lord Guildford Dudley, beheaded 1554; Robert Devereux, Earl of Essex, beheaded 1601; Sir Thomas Overbury, poisoned in the Tower in 1613; Sir John Eliot, died as a prisoner in the Tower 1632; James Fitzroy, Duke of Monmouth, beheaded 1685; Simon, Lord Fraser of Lovat, beheaded 1747. The executions took place in the Tower itself only in the cases of Anne Boleyn, Catharine Howard, the Countess of Salisbury, Lady Jane Grey, and Devereux, Earl of Essex; in all the other instances the prisoners were beheaded at the public place of execution on Tower Hill (see p. 163).

The list of those who were confined for a longer or shorter period in the Tower comprises a great number of other celebrated persons : John Baliol, King of Scotland, 1296; William Wallace, the Scottish patriot, 1305; David Bruce, King of Scotland, 1347; King John of France (taken prisoner at Poitiers, 1356); Duke of Orleans, father of Louis XII. of France, 1415; Lord Cobham, the most distinguished of the Lollards (burned as a heretic at St. Giles in the Fields, 1416); King Henry VI. (who is said to have been murdered in the Wakefield Tower by the Duke of Gloucester, 1471); Anne

Askew (tortured in the Tower, and burned in Smithfield as a heretic, 1546); Archbishop Cranmer, 1553; Sir Thomas Wyatt (beheaded on Tower Hill in 1554); Earl of Southampton, Shakspeare's patron, 1562; Sir Walter Raleigh (see p. 159; beheaded at Westminster in 1618); Earl of Strafford (beheaded 1641); Archbishop Laud (beheaded 1645); Viscount Stafford (beheaded 1680); Lord William Russell (beheaded 1683); Lord Chancellor Jeffreys, 1688; Duke of Marlborough, 1692, etc.

The large modern buildings to the E. (right) of St. Peter's Church are the *Wellington* or *Waterloo Barracks*, erected in 1845 on the site of the Grand Storehouse and Small Armoury, which had been destroyed by fire in 1841. The armoury at the time of the conflagration contained 150,000 stand of arms.

On *Tower Hill*, N.W. of the Tower, formerly stood the scaffold for the execution of traitors (see p. 162), on a site now within Trinity Square gardens. William Penn (comp. p. 164) was born, and Otway, the poet, died on Tower Hill, and here too Sir Walter Raleigh's wife lodged while her unfortunate husband languished in the Tower. On the N. side rises **Trinity House**, a plain building, erected in 1793-95 from designs by *Wyatt*, the façade of which is embellished with the arms of the corporation, medallion portraits of George III. and Queen Charlotte, and several emblems of navigation. This building is the property of 'The Master, Wardens, and Assistants of the Guild, Fraternity, or Brotherhood, of the most glorious and undividable Trinity', a company founded by Sir Thomas Spert in 1515, and incorporated by Henry VIII. in 1529. The society consists of a Master, Deputy Master, 24 Elder Brethren, and an unrestricted number of Younger Brethren, and was founded with a view to the promotion and encouragement of English navigation. Its rights and duties, which have been defined by various acts of parliament, comprise the regulation and management of lighthouses and buoys round the British coast, and the appointment and licensing of efficient pilots. Two elder brethren of Trinity House assist the Admiralty Court in deciding all cases relating to collisions at sea. Its surplus funds are devoted to charitable objects connected with sailors. The interior of Trinity House contains busts of Admirals St. Vincent, Howe, Duncan, and Nelson; and portraits of James I. and his consort Anne of Denmark, James II., Sir Francis Drake, and others. There are also a large picture of several Elder Brethren by *Dupont*, a small collection of models (including one of the old stage barge of the Elder Brethren), and various naval curiosities. In the visitors' book is an interesting series of autographs. The Duke of York, son of the Prince of Wales, is the present Master of Trinity House, while the Prince of Wales himself is an 'Elder Brother'. The annual income of Trinity House is said to be above 300,000*l*. Visitors are usually admitted on written application.

At the end of Great Tower Street, to the W. of the Tower, is the church of **All Hallows, Barking** (Pl. R, 42; *III*), founded by the nuns of Barking Abbey (p. 390), in Essex, 7 M. distant. Several times altered, the church had a very narrow escape from the Great Fire (see Pepy's Diary, Sept. 5th, 1666) and since 1883 has undergone an extensive restoration, especially in the interior. The tower dates from the 17th cent.; the principal porch is modern. Upon the latter are statues of St. Ethelburga, first abbess of Barking Abbey, and Bishop Lancelot Andrewes (b. 1555), who was baptised in the church. The parish register records also the baptism of William Penn (Oct. 23rd, 1644). Archbishop Laud was buried in the graveyard after his execution on Tower Hill (1645), but his body was removed in 1663 to the chapel of St. John's College, Oxford, of which he was an alumnus. John Quincy Adams was here married to Louisa Catherine Johnson on July 26th, 1797. All Hallows is noted for its brasses, the oldest of which (1389) is that of William Tonge in the S. aisle, while the finest is a Flemish brass of 1530, immediately in front of the Litany desk. Rubbings of the brasses may be purchased from 6d. upwards. — The *Czar's Head*, opposite the church, is said to occupy the site of a tavern frequented by Peter the Great (see p. 182).

The *Tower Subway*, an iron tube 400 yds. long and 7 ft. in diameter, constructed in 1870 for 20,000l., passing under the Thames from the S. side of Great Tower Hill, was closed to passengers in 1897. The gloomy and unpleasant passage is now occupied by a gas-main.

On the E. side of Tower Hill stands the **Royal Mint,** erected in 1811, from designs by *Johnson* and *Smirke*, on the site of the old Cistercian Abbey of St. Mary of the Graces (see p. 247), and so extensively enlarged in 1881-82 as to be practically a new building. The Mastership of the Mint (an office abolished in 1869) was once held by Sir Isaac Newton (1699-1727) and Sir John F. W. Herschel (1850-55). Permission to visit the Mint (for not more than six persons) is given for a fixed day and hour by the Deputy-Master of the Mint, on written application. The various processes of coining are extremely interesting, and the machinery used is of a most ingenious character. Each of the improved presses can stamp and mill 120 coins per minute. The cases in the museum contain a large number of coins and commemorative medals, including specimens of Maundy money, and gold pieces of 2l. and 5l., never brought into general circulation.

In 1898 the value of the money coined at the Mint was 6,260,670l., including 3,334,065 sovereigns; 2,946,605 half-sovereigns; 317,599 crowns; 2,148,505 half-crowns; 2,914,416 florins; 9,264,551 shillings; 6,651.699 sixpences; 4,607,418 threepences; 24,147,156 pence; 9,142,500 half-pence; and 3,668,610 farthings; besides Maundy money (p. 236), value 396l., and colonial money, value 504,098l. In 1887-96 there were here prepared for issue 46,743,772 sovereigns. 31,874,154 half-sovereigns, 22,217,624 half-crowns, 17,839,800 florins, 66,191,400 shillings, etc.; of copper or bronze coins over 2c6.000,000 were issued. The average annual value of the Imperial coinage issued by the Mint in 1886-95 was 7,008,928l. The average profit of the Mint is about 146,730l. — There are branches of the Mint at Melbourne, Sydney, and Perth in Australia; and there are mints also at Calcutta and Bombay.

Immediately below the Tower the Thames is spanned by the huge *Tower Bridge (Pl. R, 46; *III*), built by the Corporation in 1886-94. This bridge, designed by *Sir Horace Jones* and *Mr. Wolfe Barry*, comprizes a permanent footway, 142 ft. above high-water level, reached by means of lifts and stairs in the supporting towers, and a carriage-way, 29 1/2 ft. above high-water, the central span of which (200 ft. long) is fitted with twin bascules or draw-bridges, which can be raised in 1 1/2 min. for the passage of large vessels. The bascules and footway are borne by two massive Gothic towers, rising upon huge piers, which are connected with the river-banks by permanent spans (each 270 ft. long), suspended on massive chains hanging between the central towers and smaller castellated towers on shore. The substantial framework of the bridge, including the central towers, which are cased in stone, is of steel. Including the approaches, the bridge is 1/2 M. long, and has already cost 1,200,000*l*., though the S. approach (to be made by the County Council) is not yet completed. The annual cost of maintenance is 14,000*l*. An enumeration made in 1897 showed that about 10,000 vehicles and 25,000 pedestrians crossed the Tower Bridge daily. See 'History of the Tower Bridge', by Chas. Welch, F. S. A.

9. The Port and Docks.

St. Katharine Docks. London Docks. Thames Tunnel. Commercial Docks. Regent's Canal. West and East India Docks. Millwall Docks. Blackwall Tunnel. Royal Victoria and Albert Docks.

The Docks may be reached by *Steamer* from London Bridge (p. 63); by *Omnibus* (No. 60; p. 44); or by *Railway*. Trains from Fenchurch St. Station (Pl. R, 43) every 1/4 hr. to *Leman St., Shadwell, Stepney, Limehouse, West India Docks, Millwall Junction, Poplar*, and *Blackwall* (1/4 hr.; fares 6*d*., 4*d*.,3*d*.); and every 1/2 hr. (Sat. every 1/4 hr.) from Millwall Junction to *South Dock, Millwall Docks*, and *North Greenwich* (25 min.; fares from London 10*d*., 7*d*., 5*d*.), whence there is a steam-ferry to *Greenwich* (p. 391). Also about thrice an hour from Fenchurch St., and once an hour from Liverpool St. Station (Pl. R, 44) to the *Victoria and Albert Docks* (to Gallion's Station, 25-35 min.; fares 11*d*., 8*d*., 6*d*.).

One of the most interesting sights of London is the **Port**, with its immense warehouses, the centre from which the commerce of England radiates all over the globe. The *Port of London*, in the wider sense, extends from London Bridge to the mouth of the Thames, opposite the *Isle of Sheppey*, and it is actually occupied by shipping all the way to Tilbury Docks. In 1898 the aggregate burden of vessels from foreign ports entering and clearing at London amounted to 15,003,187 tons.

Immediately below London Bridge begins the *Pool* (p. 147), which is held to end at Limehouse Reach. Ships bearing the produce of every nation under the sun here discharge their cargoes, which, previous to their sale, are stored, subject to customs, in large bonded warehouses mostly in the **Docks**. Below these warehouses, which form small towns of themselves, and extend in long rows along the banks of the Thames, are extensive cellars for wine, oil, etc., while above ground are huge magazines, landing-stages, packing-yards, cranes, and every kind of apparatus necessary for the loading, unloading, and custody of goods. The docks are not municipal or public property, but are owned by various private joint-stock dock companies. The principal docks (London, St. Katharine, East and West India, Royal Victoria and Albert, and Tilbury) are under the management of the *London and India Docks Joint Committee*.

To the E. of the Tower, and separated from it by a single street, called *Little Tower Hill*, are the **St. Katharine Docks** (Pl. R, 46 ; *III*), opened in 1828, and covering an area of 23 acres, on which 1250 houses with 11,300 inhab. formerly stood. The old St. Katharine's Hospital once stood on this site. The engineer was *Telford*, and the architect *Hardwick*. The docks admit vessels up to 250 ft. in length and 24 ft. of draught. The warehouses can hold 110,000 tons of goods.

St. Katharine's Steamboat Wharf, adjoining the Docks, is mainly used as a landing-stage for steamers from the continent.

London Docks (Pl. R, 50), lying to the E. of St. Katharine Docks, were constructed in 1805 at a cost of 4,000,000*l.*, and cover an area of 100 acres. They have three entrances from the Thames, and contain water-room for about 400 vessels, exclusive of lighters. Their warehouses can store from 170,000 to 260,000 tons of goods (according to description), and their cellars 121,000 pipes of wine. At times upwards of 3000 men are employed at these docks in one day. Every morning at 6 o'clock there may be seen waiting at the principal entrance a large and motley crowd of labourers, to which numerous dusky visages and foreign costumes impart a curious and picturesque air. The capital of the London & St. Katharine Docks Co. amounts to 11,000,000*l.* The door in the E. angle of the docks, inscribed '*To the Kiln*', leads to a furnace in which adulterated tea and tobacco, spurious gold and silver wares, and other confiscated goods, used to be burned. The long chimney is jestingly called the *Queen's Tobacco Pipe*.

Nothing will convey to the stranger a better idea of the vast activity and stupendous wealth of London than a visit to these warehouses, filled to overflowing with interminable stores of every kind of foreign and colonial products; to these enormous vaults, with their apparently inexhaustible quantities of wine; and to these extensive quays and landing-stages, cumbered with huge stacks of hides, heaps of bales, and long rows of casks. — Permission to visit the warehouses and vaults may be obtained from the secretary of the London and India Docks Joint Committee, at 109 Leadenhall Street, E.C. Those who wish to taste the wines must procure a *tasting-order* from a wine-merchant. Ladies are not admitted after 1 p.m. Visitors should be on their guard against the insidious effects of 'tasting' in the heavy, vinous atmosphere.

St. George Street, to the N. of the docks, was formerly the notorious *Ratcliff Highway*. No. 179 is the shop of Jamrach, the well-known dealer in wild animals. Swedenborg (1688-1772) is buried in a vault beneath the *Swedish Church* in Prince's Square (Pl. R, 51).

To the S. of the London Docks, and about 2 M. below London Bridge, lies the quarter of the Metropolis called *Wapping*, from which the **Thames Tunnel** leads under the river to Rotherhithe on the right bank. The tunnel was begun in 1824, on the plans and under the supervision of *Sir Isambard Brunel*, and completed in 1843, after several accidents occasioned by the water bursting in upon the works. Seven men lost their lives during its construction. It consists of two parallel arched passages of masonry, 14 ft. broad, 16 ft. high, and 1200 ft. long, and cost 468,000*l*. The undertaking paid the Thames Tunnel Company so badly, that their receipts scarcely defrayed the cost of repairs. The tunnel was purchased in 1865 by the East London Railway Company for 200,000*l*., and is now traversed daily by about 40 trains (terminus at Liverpool Street Station, p. 56). — A *Steam Ferry* (1*d*.) crosses the Thames between Wapping and Rotherhithe.

At *Rotherhithe* (see p. 95), to the E. of the tunnel, are situated the numerous large basins of the **Surrey Commercial Docks** (Pl. R, 53, etc.), covering together an area of about 350 acres, and chiefly used for timber. The *Grand Surrey Canal* extends hence to Camberwell and Peckham. On the N. bank of the river, to the E. of Wapping, lie *Shadwell* and *Stepney*. It is proposed to construct a tunnel between Rotherhithe and Shadwell resembling the Blackwall Tunnel (p. 168). The old church of *St. Dunstan* (Pl. R, 59) in Stepney, $1/2$ M. to the N. of the river, contains the tomb of Sir Thomas Spert (p. 163) and several quaint monuments. In the wall of the W. porch is a stone with an inscription (1663) stating it to have been brought from Carthage. There is a popular but erroneous belief that every British subject born on the high seas belongs to Stepney parish. At *Limehouse*, opposite the Commercial Docks, is the entrance to the **Regent's Canal,** which runs N. to Victoria Park, then turns to the W., traverses the N. part of London, and unites with the Paddington Canal, which forms part of a continuous water-route as far as Liverpool. *Limehouse Cut* is another canal joining the river Lea (p. 172). *St. Anne's Church* (Pl. R, 63), with its conspicuous tower, was built by Hawksmoor (1730). The **West India Docks** (Pl. R, 62, etc.), about 350 acres in area, lie between Limehouse and Blackwall, to the N. of the *Isle of Dogs*, which is formed here by a sudden bend of the river. Several of the chief lines of steamers load and discharge their cargoes in these docks. The three principal basins are called the *Import Dock*, the *Export Dock*, and the *South Dock*. There is a dry dock in the *Blackwall Basin*, and pumps have been erected to maintain the water in the docks at or above high-water level. The warehouses are on a most capacious scale, including refrigerating chambers with accommodation for 100,000 carcases of sheep. The cranes and other machinery are adapted for handling the largest logs of furniture wood; and the floating derrick 'Elephant' can lift a weight of 20 tons. The smaller **East India Docks** (Pl. R, 70, 71) are at *Blackwall*, a little lower down. Some of the chief lines of sailing ships use these, and many passenger-steamers call at the adjoining *Brunswick Pier*. The **Millwall Docks**, 100 acres in extent (35 water), are in the Isle of Dogs, to the S. of the West India Docks. At the S. extremity of the Isle of Dogs is *North Greenwich Railway Station*, in Cubitt Town, whence there is a railway steam-ferry to Greenwich, on the S. bank of the Thames. Above Greenwich lies *Deptford*, with the Corporation *Market for Foreign Cattle*, occupying 30 acres, on the site of the old Admiralty dockyard.

The **Blackwall Tunnel** (Pl. R, 70), begun for the County Council in 1892 and opened in 1897, affords a free passage for pedestrians and vehicles beneath the Thames, from Blackwall, 6 M. below London Bridge, to E. Greenwich. The N. approach begins at East India Dock Road (Pl. R, 71), the S. at Blackwall Lane (Pl. R, 69); and there are also staircases for pedestrians in vertical shafts near the river on each bank. The tunnel is lighted with electricity. The work was designed by *Sir A. R. Binnie*.

The total length, including the open approaches on both banks, is 2070 yds., of which 1490 yds. form the actual tunnel, 407 yds. being sub-aqueous. The tunnel is a tube, 27 ft. in external diameter, formed of cast iron 2 in. thick, lined within with cement concrete, faced with glazed tiles. The headway in the centre of the roadway is $17\frac{1}{2}$ ft. At one point the top of the tunnel is only $5\frac{1}{2}$ ft. below the river-bed. The tunnel was excavated by means of a shield driven by hydraulic jacks, and it is the largest shield-driven tunnel ever constructed. The total cost of the work was 1,265,000*l.*, of which 871,000*l.* were spent on the tunnel proper.

Still lower down than the East India Docks, between Bow Creek, North Woolwich, and Gallion's Reach, lie the magnificent **Royal Victoria and Albert Docks**, $2\frac{3}{4}$ M. in length, lighted by electricity and provided with every convenience and accommodation for sailing-vessels and steamers of the largest size. Their area is about 500 acres, of which 180 are water. The steamers of the Peninsular and Oriental, the British India, the Allan, the National, and other important companies put in at these docks. The hydraulic machinery includes a crane with a lifting capacity of 55 tons; and the warehouses have accommodation for 350,000 refrigerated sheep and 250,000 tons of miscellaneous goods. All the tobacco imported into London is stored at the Royal Victoria Dock. In the Royal Albert Dock are two graving docks, 502 and 410 ft. in length.

We may regain London by train from *Gallion's Station* (Hotel, small but first-class) at the E. end of the Royal Albert Dock (comp. p. 165); or we may take the *Woolwich Free Ferry* from *North Woolwich*, immediately S. of the dock, to Woolwich (p. 394). The ferry is used annually by 4,000,000 passengers and 300,000 vehicles.

The large docks at *Tilbury* a e described at p. 391.

10. Bethnal Green Museum. Victoria Park.

Toynbee Hall. People's Palace.

Adjoining the City proper on the E. lies WHITECHAPEL, a district chiefly inhabited by artisans, the main thoroughfare traversing which is *Whitechapel Road*, continued by *Mile End Road*, leading to Bow and Stratford (comp. p. 170). To the left, about ¼ M. beyond Aldgate Station (p. 60), diverges *Commercial Street*, in which stands *St. Jude's Church* (Pl. R, 47; *III*), open daily, 10-5, containing copies of four of the principal works of *Mr. G. F. Watts*, finished off by that artist himself ('Love and Death', 'Messenger of Death', 'Death crowning Innocence', 'The Good Samaritan'). The exterior is adorned with a fine mosaic ('Time, Death, and Judgment'), after *Watts*.

Adjoining the church is Toynbee Hall, founded in 1885 and named after *Arnold Toynbee*, who died in the prime of youth (in 1883), while actively engaged in lecturing on political economy to the working-men of London. The hall, which is a 'hall' in the academic sense, contains rooms for about 20 residents, chiefly Oxford and Cambridge graduates desirous of sharing the life and experiences of the E. end poor (comp. p. 101). It also contains drawing, dining, reading, and lecture rooms, a library, etc., in which numerous social meetings are held for the people of the neighbourhood. The warden is the Rev. Canon S. Barnett, late vicar of St. Jude's. Those interested in work of this kind should write to the secretary for cards of admission. Toynbee Hall is also one of the centres of the 'University Extension Lectures' scheme.

In Whitechapel Road, a little farther on, on the left, is *Whitechapel Free Library and Museum*, built in 1892, adjoined on the W. by a public *Art Gallery*, opened in 1900.

The gallery is the direct outcome of the *Loan Exhibition of Pictures*, established by Mr. and Mrs. Barnett and held for a fortnight or three weeks every Easter from 1880 till 1898 in the schoolrooms adjoining St. Jude's. The exhibition generally contained some of the best works of modern English artists, and ranked among the artistic 'events' of the year. The new building, designed by *Mr. Harrison Townsend*, is adorned with a mosaic frieze by *Mr. Walter Crane*, illustrating the 'Sphere and Message of Art'.

On the opposite side of the road, ½ M. farther on, stands the *London Hospital* (Pl. R, 52; 800 beds; p. 101), behind which is the church of *St. Philip Stepney*, with a fine Gothic interior.

In Commercial Road (Pl. R, 51), to the S. of this point, are *Dr. Barnardo's Homes for Destitute Children*.

About 300 yds. farther on *Cambridge Road* diverges to the left, leading to *Bethnal Green Museum* (p. 170).

To the left, in Mile End Road, ¼ M. beyond the London Hospital, is *Trinity Hospital* or *College* (Pl. R, 52, 56), a picturesque group of almshouses established by the Trinity House (p. 163) for master mariners or mates and their wives or widows. The chapel has some interesting stained glass. In the quadrangle is a statue of Capt. Sandes, a former benefactor. — About ½ M. beyond Trinity Hospital is the **People's Palace for East London** (Pl. R, 60), a large institution for the 'recreation and amusement, the intellectual and material advancement of the vast artisan population of the East End'.

The form of the People's Palace was suggested by the 'Palace of Delight' described in Sir Walter Besant's novel, 'All Sorts and Conditions of Men'; and the nucleus of the 100,000l. required for its erection was furnished by an endowment of *Mr. J. E. Barber Beaumont* (d. 1841). This was largely supplemented by voluntary public subscriptions, including 60,000l. from the Drapers' Company, which finally, in 1892, endowed the Palace with an annual contribution of 7000l. for educational purposes, to which 3500l. is annually added from the City Parochial Charities' Fund. The large *Queens' Hall*, adorned with statues of the queens of England, etc., by F. Verheyden, was opened in 1887, a *Free Public Library* and a *Swimming Bath* in 1888, a *Winter Garden* in 1892, and large *Engineering Workshops* in 1894. The Palace also comprizes a gymnasium, reading-rooms, well-equipped chemical and physical laboratories, a school of art, and numerous class-rooms.

The educational work of the Palace, carried on under the name of the *East London Technical College*, includes a Technical Day School, attended by 400 boys between the ages of 12 and 16; a Day College for older students of either sex, with courses in engineering, chemistry, and art; and Evening Classes in scientific, technical, and general subjects, attended by about 4000 students annually. — Popular exhibitions are annually held in the grounds; and concerts and entertainments of various kinds are given in the Queens' Hall on Mon., Thurs., and Sat. evenings (adm. 1d.-6d.).

Mile End Road is continued to the E. by Bow Road to Bow and Stratford (p. 414). About 1/4 M. beyond the People's Palace *Grove Road* diverges to the N., leading to Victoria Park (p. 174), and *Burdett Road* diverges to the S., leading to the West India Docks (p. 167; tramway No. 1f, p. 54).

The **Bethnal Green Museum** (Pl. B, 52), a branch of South Kensington Museum, opened in 1872, occupies a red brick building in Victoria Park Square, Cambridge Road, Bethnal Green. It was established chiefly for the benefit of the inhabitants of the poorer East End of London. The chief permanent contents are collections of specimens of food and of animal products, but loan collections of various kinds are also always on view. Admission, see p. 108 (catalogues on sale). The number of visitors in 1899 was 440,917. There is a plain refreshment-room in the N. basement.

The Museum may be conveniently reached by an Old Ford omnibus from the Bank (No. 18; p. 38); by the Metropolitan Railway to Aldgate, and thence by a Well Street tramway-car (a red car; fare 2d.), which passes the Museum; or by train from Liverpool Street Station to Cambridge Heath (about every 10 min.; through-booking from Metropolitan stations). In returning we may traverse Victoria Park to the (20 min.) Victoria Park Station of the N. London Railway, whence there are trains every 1/4 hr. to Broad Street, City.

The space in front of the Museum is adorned with a handsome majolica *Fountain*, by Minton (1862). The interior of the Museum, entirely constructed of iron, consists of a large central hall, surrounded by a double gallery. To the right and left as we enter are busts of *Garibaldi* and *Cromwell*, both by M. Noble.

The extensive and well-arranged *Collection of Articles used for Food* occupies the N. side of the lower gallery. It comprises specimens of various kinds of edibles, models of others, analyses, diagrams, drawings, and so forth. On the S. side is the collection of *Animal Products*, largely consisting of clothing materials (wool, silk, leather, etc.) at different stages of their manufacture. Here also is the *Doubleday Collection of Butterflies and Moths*, shown on application to an attendant. — The area of the central hall is occupied by an interesting *Collection of Pottery and Porcelain* (lent by Mr. Henry Willett, of Brighton), showing how British history may be illustrated by the homely pottery used as cottage ornaments, etc. In the middle are a marble statue of Diana, by *Benzoni*, and a copy in marble of *Canova's* Venus. On the sides of the hall, near the end, are drawings of Old London (on the S.) and the Arundel Society's reproductions of the works of old masters (on the N.). The mosaic flooring, formed from refuse chippings of marble, was executed by female convicts in Woking Prison. The S. basement contains a collection of sketches by George Cruikshank, the caricaturist, a collection of painted and enamelled tiles, terracotta, earthenware, and porcelain, and a collection of Coleoptera. In the N. basement are a number of Japanese, Chinese, and Indian works of art, etc.

The N. side of the upper gallery, well lighted from the roof, now contains a *Collection of Works of Ornamental Art* in gold, silver, bronze, and china, French furniture, etc., lent by Mr. and Mrs. Massey-Mainwaring and others. At the E. end is a *Collection of European Porcelain*, lent by the late Sir A. Wollaston Franks. The S. side is mainly occupied by mediæval and modern art objects, including sumptuous furniture, jewellery, modern tapestry, glass, iron and bronze work, etc. Near the E. staircase is a fine collection of war and other medals given by the late Surgeon-Major Fleming. On screens on the N. side and on the walls of the S. side of the gallery is the *Dixon Collection* of water-colours and oil-paintings, bequeathed to the Museum in 1885. The former include examples of De Wint, Cooper, Birket Foster, David Cox, etc.; the latter are less interesting.

————————

The large building in Green Street, to the S. of the Museum, is an *Insane Asylum*. — From Old Ford Road, which diverges to the E. immediately to the N. of the Museum, *Approach Road*, in which is the *City of London Consumption Hospital*, leads to the N.E. to **Victoria Park** (Pl. B, 55, 58, 59). This park, covering 217 acres of ground, laid out at a cost of 130,000l., forms a place of recreation for the poorer (E.) quarters of London. The eastern and larger portion is unplanted, and is used for cricket and other games. The W. side is prettily laid out with walks, beds of flowers, and two sheets of water, on which swans may be seen disporting themselves, and pleasure-boats hired. Near the centre of the park is the *Victoria Fountain*, in the form of a Gothic temple, erected by Baroness Burdett Coutts (comp. p. 32) in 1862. The park also contains open-air gymnasiums. The most characteristic time to see Victoria Park is on a Sat. or Sun. evening or on a public holiday. On the N.W. side of the park, near *Hackney Common*, is the large and

handsome *Hospice for the Descendants of French Protestants*. To the
N.E. of Victoria Park are *Hackney Marshes* (Pl. B, 61, 62, 65, 66), a
large area (337 acres) of flat meadow-land, intersected by the river
Lea, and opened as a public park in 1894. The *White Hart Inn* here,
said to date from 1513, was a resort of Dick Turpin, the highwayman.

Victoria Park is most easily reached by the *North London Railway;*
trains start from *Broad Street Station*, City (p. 56), every ¹/₄ hr., and reach
Victoria Park Station, at the N.E. extremity of the park, in 18 min. (fares
6d., 4d., 2¹/₂d.; return-tickets 9d., 6d., 4d.).

11. Fleet Street. The Temple. Chancery Lane. Royal Courts of Justice.

*St. Bride's. Church of St. Dunstan in the West. New Record Office.
Lincoln's Inn. Gray's Inn. Temple Church. Temple Bar.*

Fleet Street (Pl. R, 35; *II*), one of the busiest streets in London,
leads from Ludgate Circus to the Strand and the West End. It derives
its name from the *Fleet Brook*, which, now in the form of a main
sewer, flows through *Holborn Valley* (p. 125) and under Farringdon
Street, reaching the Thames at Blackfriars Bridge. On the E. side
of the brook formerly stood the notorious *Fleet Prison* for debtors,
which was removed in 1846. Prisoners condemned by the Star Chamber were once confined here, and within its precincts were formerly
celebrated the clandestine 'Fleet marriages' (see 'The Fleet: its
River, Prison, and Marriages', by *John Ashton;* 1888). Its site (in
Farringdon Street, on the right) is now occupied by the handsome
Gothic *Congregational Memorial Hall*, opened in 1874, at a total
cost of 93,450*l.*, and so named in memory of the 2000 ministers
ejected from the Church of England by Charles II.'s Act of Uniformity, 1662.

Fleet Street itself contains few objects of external interest,
though many literary associations cluster round its courts and
byways. It is still celebrated for its newspaper and other printing
and publishing offices. To the left (entrance in St. Bride's Passage,
adjoining the office of *Punch*) is **St. Bride's,** a church built by *Wren*
in 1680 (steeple 1701), with a handsome tower 223 ft. in height.
In the central aisle is the grave of Richardson, the author of 'Clarissa
Harlowe' (d. 1761), who lived in Salisbury Square in the neighbourhood. The old church of St. Bride, destroyed in the Fire, was
the burial-place of Sackville (1608), Lovelace (1658), and the printer
Wynkin de Worde. In a house in the adjacent churchyard Milton
once lived for several years. In St. Bride's Lane is the *St. Bride's
Foundation Institute*, a polytechnic for the printers of London, opened
in 1894, with a fine technical library, a gymnasium, a swimming
bath, and equipments for technical instruction in the art of printing.
Shoe Lane, nearly opposite the church, leads to Holborn; while a
little farther on, on the same side, are *Wine Office Court*, in which

is still the famous old hostelry of the *Cheshire Cheese* (p. 18), where Dr. Johnson (whose alleged chair is shown here) and Goldsmith so often dined, and Boswell so often listened and took notes; *Gough Square*, at the top of the Court (to the left), where Johnson laboured over his Dictionary and other works (house marked by a tablet); *Bolt Court*, where Johnson spent the last years of his life (1776-84), and where Cobbett afterwards toiled and fumed; and *Crane Court*, once the home of the Royal Society, its president being Sir Isaac Newton, and now the seat of the Scottish Corporation, whose ancient Hall, burnt down in 1877, is replaced by a modern erection of 1879-80. On the other side is Bouverie Street, leading to what was once the lawless *Alsatia*, immortalised by Scott in the 'Fortunes of Nigel'. In 1883 a part of the ancient Carmelite monastery of White-friars was discovered in this street, including a fragment of a stone tower of great thickness and strength, while in 1895 a small crypt (14th cent.) was found below a house in Britton's Court, opening off the adjacent Whitefriars Street. Fetter Lane (see below), and Chancery Lane (p. 174) farther to the W., on the N. side, also lead to Holborn. Izaak Walton, the famous angler, once occupied a shop as a hosier (1624-43; comp. p. 174) at the corner of Chancery Lane. Between Fetter Lane and Chancery Lane rises the church of **St. Dunstan in the West,** erected by *Shaw* in 1832 on the site of a more ancient building; it has a fine Gothic tower. Over the vestry door (on the E. side of the church) is a statue of Queen Elizabeth from the old Lud Gate, once a city-gate at the foot of Ludgate Hill. The old clock of St. Dunstan had two wooden giants to strike the hours, which still perform that office at St. Dunstan's Villa, Regent's Park (p. 294). A stained-glass window at the W. end of the N. aisle and a tablet on the E. wall commemorate Izaak Walton, who was warden of the church. Near St. Dunstan's Church, at No. 183 Fleet Street, was Cobbett's book-shop and publishing office, where he issued his 'Political Register'; and on the opposite side, now No. 56, was the house of William Hone, the free-thinking publisher of the 'Every-day Book'. No. 184, Fleet Street (rebuilt in 1892) was once oc-cupied by Drayton, the poet (d. 1631). Opposite Fetter Lane is *Mitre Court*, with the tavern once frequented by Johnson, Gold-smith, and Boswell.

FETTER LANE (Pl. R, 35, 36 ; *11*) is said to derive its name from the 'faitours' or beggars that once infested it. To the left, a few yards from Fleet Street, is an entrance to *Clifford's Inn* (p. 175), once the residence of *Robert Paltock* (1697-1767), author of that strange and fascinating book 'The Life and Adventures of Peter Wil-kins'. Farther on is the *New Record Office* (p. 174), the main en-trance of which is in Chancery Lane. The *Moravian Chapel*, opposite the Record Office, escaped the great fire in 1666. In Fleur-de-Lis Court, off Fetter Lane, is *Newton Hall*, the meeting-place of the

Positivists under Mr. Frederic Harrison (p. 79). In Breams Buildings, which runs from Fetter Lane to Chancery Lane, is the *Birkbeck Literary and Scientific Institute* (p. 99), with about 13,000 students.

Chancery Lane (Pl. R, 32, 31, 35; *II*) leads through the quarter chiefly occupied by barristers and solicitors. Izaak Walton occupied a shop on the right near Crown Court, after removing from Fleet Street (p. 173). On the right is *Old Serjeants' Inn*, opening into *Clifford's Inn* (p. 175). Farther up, on the same side, is the **New Record Office** (Pl. R, 35; *II*), for the custody of legal records and state-papers, a huge fire-proof edifice in the Tudor style, the E. part of which was erected in 1851-66 by *Sir J. Pennethorne*, while the W. part, facing Chancery Lane, was added by *Mr. John Taylor* in 1891-96. The latter covers what used to be *Rolls Yard*; and the former Court of the Master of the Rolls and also the Rolls Chapel have been taken down. A portion of the chapel, however, has been incorporated with the new building, and is to be arranged as a museum. The fine monument it contained to *Dr. John Young*, Master of the Rolls, by *Torregiano* (1516), is still *in situ*. A fragment of the old chancel-arch has been re-erected against the S.E. wall of the new building.

The interior of the Record Office is arranged so as to be as nearly fire-proof as possible. The rooms have no communication with each other but open on narrow corridors paved with brick. Each room or compartment is about 25 ft. long, 17 ft. broad. and 15³/₄ ft. high. The floor, door-posts, window-frames, and ceilings are of iron, and the shelves of slate. Since the completion of the structure the state papers, formerly kept in the Tower, the Chapter House of Westminster Abbey, the Rolls Chapel in Chancery Lane, at Carlton Ride, and in the State Paper Office in St. James's Park, have been deposited here. Here, for instance, are preserved the *Domesday Book*, in two parchment volumes of different sizes, containing the results of a statistical survey of England made in 1086 by order of William the Conqueror; the deed of resignation of the Scottish throne by David Bruce in favour of Edward III.; a charter granted by Alphonso of Castile on the marriage of Edward I. with Eleanor of Castile; the treaty of peace between Henry VIII. and Francis I., with a gold seal; various deeds of surrender of monasteries in England and Wales in favour of Henry VIII.; and an innumerable quantity of other records. The business-hours are from 10 a.m. to 4.30 p.m. (on Sat. 2 p.m.), during which the Search Rooms are open to the public. Documents down to 1760 may be inspected gratis; the charge for copying is 6d.-1s. (according to date) per folio of 72 words, the minimum charge being 2s.

Near the Holborn end of Chancery Lane, on the right, are Southampton Buildings, in which is situated the Government **Patent Office** (Pl. R, 35, 36), recently rebuilt and extended into Staple Inn. Here all applications for the protection of inventions and designs are dealt with, as well as most of those for the protection of trademarks. In 1898 there were nearly 28,000 applications for patents (700 by women), over 20,000 for designs, and over 9700 for trademarks. Adjacent, in Quality Court, is the 'Sale Branch', where specifications of English patents from the 17th cent. onwards may be purchased. For the *Patent Office Library*, see p. 21.

To the barristers belong the four great *Inns of Court*, viz. the

Temple (Inner and *Middle)* on the S. of Fleet Street (see p. 176),
Lincoln's Inn in Chancery Lane, and *Gray's Inn* in Holborn. These
Inns are incorporations for the study of law, and possess by common law the exclusive privilege of calling to the Bar. Each is
governed by its older members, who are termed *Benchers.*

Formerly subsidiary to the four Inns of Court were the nine *Inns of
Chancery,* which now, however, have little beyond local connection with
them, and are let out in chambers to solicitors, barristers, and the general public. These are *Clifford's Inn, Clement's Inn,* and *Lyon's Inn* (now
the site of the Globe Theatre), attached to the Inner Temple; *New Inn*
and *Strand Inn,* to the Middle Temple; *Furnival's Inn* and *Thavies' Inn,*
to Lincoln's Inn; *Staple Inn* and *Barnard's Inn* (p. 126), to Gray's Inn.
Serjeants' Inn. Chancery Lane, was originally set apart for the use of the
serjeants-at-law, whose name is derived from the 'fratres servientes' of the
old Knights Templar; but the building is now used for other purposes.
See 'The Inns of Court and Chancery', by W. J. Loftie.

Lincoln's Inn (Pl. R, 31, 32; *II*), the third of the Inns of Court
in importance, is situated without the City, on a site once occupied
by the mansion of the Earl of Lincoln and other houses. The *Gate-
house* (restored in 1899) in Chancery Lane was built in 1518 by *Sir
Thomas Lovell,* whose coat-of-arms it bears. Ben Jonson is said to
have been employed as a bricklayer in constructing the adjacent
wall about a century later (1617); but the truth of this tradition
may well be doubted, since in 1617 Jonson was 44 years old and
had written some of his best plays. The *Chapel* was erected by *Inigo
Jones* in 1621-23, and contains good wood-carving and stained glass.
Like the Round Church of the Temple, this chapel was once used
as a consultation-room by the barristers and their clients.

The *New Hall,* the handsome dining-hall of Lincoln's Inn, in
the Tudor style, was completed in 1845 under the supervision of
Mr. Hardwick, the architect. It contains a large fresco of the School
of Legislation, by *G. F. Watts* (1860), and a statue of Lord Eldon,
by *Westmacott.* The *Library,* founded in 1497, is the oldest in
London, and contains 25,000 vols. and numerous valuable MSS.;
most of the latter were bequeathed by Sir Matthew Hale, a member
of the Inn. Among its most prized contents is the fourth volume
of Prynne's Records, for which the society gave 335*l.* — Sir Thomas
More, Shaftesbury, Selden, Oliver Cromwell, William Pitt, Lord
Erskine, Lord Mansfield, Lord Brougham, Canning, Benjamin Disraeli, and W. E. Gladstone were once numbered among its members.
Thurloe, Cromwell's secretary, had chambers at No. 24 Old Square
(to the left, on the groundfloor) in 1645-59, and the Thurloe papers
were afterwards discovered here in the false ceiling (commemorative
tablet on the wall towards Chancery Lane). Among the preachers
of Lincoln's Inn were Usher, Tillotson, Warburton, Heber, and
Frederick Denison Maurice. — The *Court of Chancery,* or, more
correctly, under the Judicature Act of 1873, the 'Equity Division
of the High Court of Justice', formerly held some of its sittings in
Lincoln's Inn (comp. p. 180). *Lincoln's Inn Fields,* see p. 228.

Chancery Lane ends at Holborn, at a point a little to the N. of which is **Gray's Inn** (Pl. R, 32; *II*), which formerly paid a ground-rent to the Lords Gray of Wilton and has existed as a school of law since 1371. The Elizabethan Hall, built about 1560, contains fine wood-carving. Shakspeare's 'Comedy of Errors' was acted here in 1594. The Archbishops' Window in the chapel, completed in 1899, shows a group of Becket, Whitgift, Juxon, Laud, and Wake. During the 17th cent. the garden, in which a number of trees were planted by Francis Bacon, was a fashionable promenade; but it is not now open to the public. The name of Lord Chancellor Bacon is the most eminent among those of former members of Gray's Inn; others are Sir William Gascoigne, who committed the Prince of Wales (Henry V.) to prison, Thomas Cromwell, Lord Burleigh, Laud, and Sir Samuel Romilly. Comp.'Chronicles of an Old Inn', by *Andrée Hope*.

Gray's Inn Road, an important but unattractive thoroughfare to the E. of Gray's Inn, runs to the N., passing *Holborn Town Hall* and the *Royal Free Hospital*, from Holborn to Euston Road (King's Cross Station, p. 56). Elm Street leads to the E. from this road to the *Parcel Post Office* (p. 122), on the site of the old *Cold-bath House of Correction*.

The **Temple** (Pl. R, 35; *II*), on the S. side of Fleet Street, formerly a lodge of the Knights Templar, — a religious and military order founded at Jerusalem, in the 12th century, under Baldwin, King of Jerusalem, to protect the Holy Sepulchre, and pilgrims resorting thither, and called Templars from their original designation as 'poor soldiers of the Temple of Solomon' — became crown-property on the dissolution of the order in 1313, and was presented by Edward II. to Aymer de Valence, Earl of Pembroke. After Pembroke's death the Temple came into the possession of the Knights of St. John, who, in 1346, leased it to the students of common law. From that time to the present day the building, or rather group of buildings, which extends down to the Thames, has continued to be a school of law. The Temple property passed into the hands of the Crown on the dissolution of the religious houses in the reign of Henry VIII. (1541); but in 1609 it was declared by royal decree the free, hereditary property of the corporations of the *Inner* and the *Middle Temple* subject only to a rent-charge of 10*l.*, which was extinguished in 1873.

The Inner Temple is so called from its position within the precincts of the City; the Middle Temple derives its name from its situation between the Inner and the Outer Temple, the last of which was afterwards replaced by Exeter House (and later by Essex House). The name Outer Temple is now appropriated by a handsome block of offices and chambers directly opposite the new Law Courts (p. 179). Middle Temple Lane separates the Inner Temple on the east from the Middle Temple on the west. The Inner and

the Middle Temple possess in common the *Temple Church, or
St. Mary's Church, situated within the bounds of the Inner Temple.
Adm., see p. 108; visitors knock at the door.

This church is divided into two sections, the *Round Church* and
the *Choir*. The Round Church, about 58 ft. in diameter, a Norman
edifice with a tendency to the transition style, and admirably enriched, was completed in 1185. The choir, in the Early English
style, was added in 1240. During the Protectorate the ceiling
paintings were whitewashed; and the old church afterwards became
so dilapidated, that it was necessary in 1840-42 to subject it to a
thorough restoration, a work which cost no less than 70,000*l*. The
lawyers used formerly to receive their clients in the Round Church,
each occupying his particular post like merchants 'on change'. The
incumbent of the Temple Church is called the Master of the
Temple. The present Master is the Rev. Canon Ainger.

A handsome Norman archway leads into the interior, which is
a few steps below the level of the pavement. The choir, at the end
of which are the altar and stalls (during divine service open to
members of the Temple corporations and their friends only), and
the Round Church (to which the public is admitted) are both
borne by clustered pillars in marble. The ceiling is a fine example
of Gothic decorative painting, carefully restored on the original
lines. The pavement consists of tiles, in which the lamb and the
cross (the *Agnus Dei*), the heraldic emblem of the Templars, and
the Pegasus, the arms of the Inner and Middle Temple respectively,
continually recur. Most of the stained-glass windows are modern.
In the Round Church are nine *Monuments of Templars* of the 12th
and 13th centuries, consisting of recumbent figures of dark marble
in full armour. One of the four on the S. side, under whose pillow
is a slab with foliage in relief, is said to be that of William Marshal,
Earl of Pembroke (d. 1219), brother-in-law of King John, who filled
the office of Regent during the minority of Henry III. The monuments are beautifully executed, but owe their fresh appearance to
a 'restoration' by Richardson in 1842. At the S.W. corner of the
choir are a black marble slab in memory of *John Selden* (d. 1654),
'the great dictator of learning to the English nation', and a bust of
Richard Hooker (d. 1600), formerly Master. In a recess in the S.
wall of the choir, near the E. end, is a fine recumbent effigy of a
mitred ecclesiastic, discovered during the restoration in 1840. The
triforium, which encircles the Round Church, contains some uninteresting old monuments, but is not now open to the public. On
the stair leading to it is a small penitential cell, prisoners in which
could hear the service in the church by means of slits in the wall.

Oliver Goldsmith (d. 1774), author of the 'Vicar of Wakefield',
is buried in the *Churchyard* to the N. of the choir. — See 'The
Temple Church and Chapel of St. Ann', by *H. T. Baylis, Q. C.*
(2nd ed., London, 1895).

The well-kept *Temple Gardens*, once immediately adjacent to
the Thames, but now separated from it by the Victoria Embankment, are open to the public on days and hours determined from
time to time by the Benchers (ascertainable by enquiry at the gates
or lodges). Here, according to Shakspeare, were plucked the *white*
and *red roses* which were assumed as the badges of the houses of
York and Lancaster, in the long and bloody civil contest, known as
the 'Wars of the Roses'.

Plantagenet.	Great lords, and gentlemen, what means this silence?
	Dare no man answer in a case of truth?
Suffolk.	Within the Temple hall we were too loud;
	The garden here is more convenient.
	. . . .
Plantagenet.	Since you are tongue-tied and so loath to speak,
	In dumb significants proclaim your thoughts:
	Let him that is a true-born gentleman,
	And stands upon the honour of his birth,
	If he suppose that I have pleaded truth,
	From off this brier pluck a white rose with me.
Somerset.	Let him that is no coward, nor no flatterer,
	But dare maintain the party of the truth,
	Pluck a red rose from off this thorn with me.
	. . . .
Warwick.	— This brawl to-day,
	Grown to this faction in the Temple Garden,
	Shall send, between the red rose and the white,
	A thousand souls to death and deadly night.

Henry VI., Part I; Act ii. Sc. 4.

The Temple Gardens used to be famous for their *Chrys-
anthemums*, a brilliant show of which was held in November. The
figure of a Moor (Italian; 17th or 18th cent.), bearing a sun-dial,
was brought from the garden of St. Clement's Inn.

The fine Gothic *HALL of the Middle Temple, built in 1572, and
used as a dining-room, is notable for its handsome open-work ceiling
in old oak. The walls are embellished with the armorial bearings of
the Knights Templar, and five large full-length portraits of princes,
including an equestrian portrait of Charles I. The large windows
contain the arms of members of the Temple who have sat in the
House of Peers. Shakspeare's 'Twelfth Night' was acted in this hall
during the dramatist's lifetime (Feb. 2nd, 1601-2). — The *Library*
(40,000 vols.) is preserved in a modern Gothic building on the side
next the Thames, which contains a hall 85 ft. long and 62 ft. high.
— The new *Inner Temple Hall*, opened in 1870, is a handsome
structure, also possessing a fine open-work roof. It is adorned with
statues of Templars and Hospitallers by *Armstead*. The *Library*
(50,000 vols.) occupies a commodious suite of rooms overlooking
the terrace so lovingly described by Charles Lamb.

Oliver Goldsmith lived and died on the second floor of 2 Brick
Court, Middle Temple Lane; Blackstone, the famous commentator
on the law of England, lived in the rooms below him; and Dr. Johnson occupied apartments in Inner Temple Lane, in a house now
taken down. Charles Lamb was born in Crown Office Row (within

the Temple) in 1775; from 1801 to 1809 he lived at 16 Mitre Court Buildings and from 1809 to 1817 at 4 Inner Temple Lane, but both houses have been torn down.

The list of eminent members of the Inner Temple includes the names of Littleton, Coke, Selden, Francis Beaumont, Lord Mansfield, and William Cowper. On that of the Middle Temple are the names of Raleigh, Pym, Clarendon, Ireton, Wycherley, Shadwell, Congreve, Burke, Sheridan, Blackstone, and Moore.

At the W. end of Fleet Street rises the *Temple Bar Memorial*, with statues of the Queen and the Prince of Wales at the sides and surmounted by the City Griffin and arms. This was erected in 1880 to mark the site of **Temple Bar**, a gateway formerly adjoining the Temple, between Fleet Street and the Strand, built by *Wren* in 1670. Its W. side was adorned with statues of Charles I. and Charles II., its E. side with statues of Anne of Denmark and James I. The heads of criminals used to be barbarously exhibited on iron spikes on the top of the gate. When the reigning sovereign visited the City on state occasions, he was wont, in accordance with an ancient custom, to obtain permission from the Lord Mayor to pass Temple Bar. The heavy wooden gates were afterwards removed to relieve the Bar of their weight, as it had shown signs of weakness; and the whole erection was finally demolished early in 1878, to permit of the widening of the street and to facilitate the enormous traffic. In 1888 the gate was re-erected near one of the entrances of Theobalds Park, Waltham Cross, Herts, the seat of Sir H. B. Meux (see p. 416).

Adjoining the site of Temple Bar, on the S. side of Fleet Street, stands the large new building of Child's Bank, which was in high repute in the time of the Stuarts, and is the oldest banking-house in London but one. Dryden, Pepys, Nell Gwynne, and Prince Rupert were early customers of this bank. The Child family is still connected with the business. Next door to this house was the 'Devil's Tavern', noted as the home of the Apollo Club, of which Ben Jonson, Randolph, and Dr. Kenrick were frequenters. The tavern was in time absorbed by Child's Bank, which also used the room over the main arch of Temple Bar as a storehouse.

Immediately to the W. of Temple Bar, on the N. side of the Strand (p. 181), rise the **Royal Courts of Justice**, a vast and magnificent Gothic pile, forming a whole block of buildings, with a frontage towards the Strand of about 500 ft. The architect was *Mr. G. E. Street*, who unfortunately died shortly before the completion of his great work; a statue of him, by Armstead, has been placed on the E. side of the central hall. The Courts were formally opened on Dec. 4th, 1882, by Queen Victoria, in presence of the Lord Chancellor, the Prime Minister, and the other chief dignitaries of the realm. The building cost about 750,000*l.* and the site about 1,450,000*l.* The principal internal feature is the large central hall, 238 ft. long, 48 ft. wide, and 80 ft. high, with a fine mosaic flooring designed by Mr. Street. The building contains in all 19 court rooms and about 1100 apartments of all kinds. When the courts are sitting, the general public are admitted to the galleries only, the central hall and the court-rooms being reserved for members of the Bar and persons connected with the cases. During the vacation the central hall is open to the public from 11 to 3, and tickets of admission to the courts may be obtained gratis at the superintendent's office.

For about a century and a half after the Norman Conquest the royal court of justice, which included the Exchequer and the 'Curia Regis', followed the King from place to place; but one of the articles of Magna Charta provided that the Common Pleas, or that branch of the court in which disputes between subjects were settled, should be fixed at Westminster. The accession of Edward I. found the Courts of King's Bench, Common Bench, and Exchequer all sitting in Westminster Hall. The Court of Chancery sat regularly in Westminster Hall as early as the reign of Edward II., but was afterwards removed to Lincoln's Inn. This separation of common law and equity proved very inconvenient to the attorneys and others, and the Westminster courts became much too small for the business carried on in them. It was accordingly resolved to build a large new palace of justice to receive all the superior courts, and the site of the present Law Courts was fixed upon in 1867. The work of building actually began in 1874. The Judicature Act of 1873 provided that the same rule of law should be enforced in the historically independent Courts of Common Law and Equity, and united all the superior tribunals of the country into a Supreme Court of Judicature, subdivided into a court of original jurisdiction (the High Court of Justice, with the two divisions of 'Queen's Bench' and 'Chancery') and a court of appellate jurisdiction (the Court of Appeal). The House of Lord still remains the ultimate Court of Appeal, exercising its jurisdiction through its legal members — the Lord Chancellor, peers who have held the position of Lord Chancellor, and certain law-lords holding life-peerages.

II. THE WEST END.

12. Strand. Somerset House. Waterloo Bridge.

St. Clement Danes. The Roman Bath. King's College. St. Mary le Strand. Savoy Chapel. Savoy Palace. Society of Arts. National Life Boat Institution. Eleanor's Cross.

The **Strand** (Pl. R, 26, 31, and *II*; so named from its skirting the bank of the river, which is now concealed by the buildings), a broad street containing many handsome shops, is the great artery of traffic between the City and the West End, and one of the busiest and most important thoroughfares in London. It was unpaved down to 1532, and about this time it was described as 'full of pits and sloughs, very perilous and noisome'. At this period many of the mansions of the nobility and hierarchy stood here, with gardens stretching down to the Thames (comp. p. 92). The names of several streets and houses still recall these days of bygone magnificence, but the palaces themselves have long since disappeared or been converted to more plebeian uses. Ivy Bridge Lane and Strand Bridge Lane commemorate the site of bridges over two water-courses that flowed into the Thames here, and there was a third bridge farther to the E. The Strand contains a great many newspaper-offices and theatres.

Just beyond the site of Temple Bar (p. 179), to which its name will doubtless long attach, on the (N.) right, rise the new *Law Courts* (p. 179). The church of **St. Clement Danes,** in the centre of the Strand, was erected in 1681 from designs by *Wren* and restored in 1898. The tower, 115 ft. in height, was added by *Gibbs* in 1719. Dr. Johnson used to worship in this church, a fact recorded by a tablet on the back of the pew. The church is said to bear its name from being the burial-place of Harold Harefoot and other Danes. To the N. of St. Clement Danes is *Clement's Inn* (p. 175), now connected with the Temple, and named after St. Clement's Well, once situated here, but removed in 1874. Shallow (Henry IV., Part II) reminds us that he 'was once of Clement's Inn', when he was known as 'mad Shallow' and 'lusty Shallow'. From this point *Wych Street,* containing the *Olympic Theatre* (p. 66) and an entrance to *New Inn* (p. 175), leads to Drury Lane. — In *Newcastle Street* is the *Globe Theatre* (p. 66).

The Strand between St. Clement Danes and Newcastle Street is being widened by the removal of the block of houses (including the Opera Comique) separating it from *Holywell Street* on the N. At No. 36 Holywell Street is a survivor of the ancient signs with which every shop in London used to be provided (a crescent moon with a face in the centre).

Essex Street, Arundel Street, Norfolk Street, and *Surrey Street,* diverging to the S. of the Strand, mark the spots where stood the mansions of the Earl of Essex (Queen Elizabeth's favourite) and the Earl of Arundel and Surrey (Norfolk); and they all lead to the Thames Embankment. Peter the Great resided in Norfolk Street during his visit to London in 1698, William Penn once lived at No. 21, and Mrs. Lirriper's famous lodgings were in the same street. In Devereux Court, to the E. of Essex Street, is a bust of Lord Essex said to be by Colley Cibber and to mark the site of the Grecian Coffee House. George Sale (1680-1736), the translator of the Koran, as well as Congreve (d. 1729), the dramatist, lived and died in Surrey Street. Beyond Surrey Street, on the left, is the *Strand Theatre* (p. 66). At No. 5 Strand Lane, the narrow opening to the W. of the Strand Theatre, is an ancient **Roman Bath**, about 13 ft. long, 6 ft. broad, and $4\frac{1}{2}$ ft. deep, one of the few relics of the Roman period in London (open to visitors on Sat., 11-12). The bricks at the side are laid edgewise, and the flooring consists of brick with a thin coating of stucco. At the point where the water, which flows from a natural spring, has washed away part of the stucco covering, the old pavement below is visible. The clear, cold water probably flows from the old '*Holy Well*', situated on the N. side of the Strand, which lent its name to Holywell Street (p. 177). The Roman antiquities found here are preserved in the British Museum (p. 323). Close by, on the right of the passage, is another bath, said to have been built by the Earl of Essex about 1588; it is supplied by a pipe from the Roman bath.

King's College, the large pile of buildings adjoining Strand Lane on the W., built by *Smirke* in 1828, forms the E. wing of Somerset House (see below). It includes a *School* for boys as well as a *College* with departments for theology, literature, medicine, etc. Among its distinguished students were Sir James Fitzjames Stephen, Prof. Cayley, Prof. Thorold Rogers, and Dean Farrar. The *Museum* contains a collection of models and instruments, including apparatus used by Daniell, Faraday, and Wheatstone.

In the Strand we next reach, on the N. side, the church of **St. Mary le Strand**, built by *Gibbs* in 1717, on the spot where stood in olden times the notorious Maypole, the May-day and Sunday delight of youthful and other idlers. It was called St. Mary's after an earlier church which had been demolished by Protector Somerset to make room for his mansion of Old Somerset House (see below). Thomas Becket was rector of this parish in the reign of King Stephen (1147). — Drury Lane, a street much in need of improvement, and containing the theatre of the same name (p. 65), leads N. from this point to Oxford Street and the British Museum.

Farther on, on the S. side of the Strand, rises the stately façade of **Somerset House** (Pl. R, 31 ; *II*), 150 ft. in length. The present large quadrangular building was erected by *Sir William Chambers* in 1776-86, on the site of a palace which the Protector Somerset began to build in 1549. The Protector, however, was beheaded

(p. 162) before it was completed, and the palace fell to the Crown. It was afterwards the residence of Anne of Denmark, consort of Jrames I., of Henrietta Maria, the queen of Charles I., and of Cath aoine of Braganza, the neglected wife of the second Charles. Inig-Jnes died here in 1652. The old building was taken downo in 1766, and the present edifIce, now occupied by various public offIces, erected in its stead. The imposing principal façade towards the Thames, 780 ft. in length, rises on a terrace 50 ft. broad and 50 ft. high, and is now separated from the river by the Victoria Embankment. The quadrangular court contains a bronze group by *Bacon*, representing George III. leaning on a rudder, with the English lion and Father Thames at his feet. The two wings of the building were erected during the 19th cent.: the eastern, containing King's College (p. 182), by *Smirke*, in 1828; the western, towards Wellington Street, by *Pennethorne*, in 1854-56. The sum expended in constructing the latter alone was 81,000*l.*; and the cost of the whole building amounted to 500,000*l.* At Somerset House no fewer than 1600 officials are employed, with salaries amounting in the aggregate to 350,000*l.* The building is said to contain 3600 windows. The public offIces established here include the *Audit Office*; the *Inland Revenue Office*, in the new W. wing, where stamps are issued and public taxes and excise duties received; the *Office of the Registrar-General of Births, Deaths, and Marriages*; and the *Probate Registry*. The last, to which *Doctors' Commons Will Office* (p. 121) was transferred in 1874, is the great repository of testamentary writings of all kinds. The Central Hall (open daily, 10-3) contains an interesting collection of wills, including those of Shakspeare, Holbein, Van Dyck, Newton, and Samuel Johnson. The will of Napoleon I., executed at St. Helena, used to be kept here, but was handed over to the French in 1853. The registers of wills go back to the 14th century. The lowest recorded amount of personalty is 1*s.* 7*d.*, in a will of 1882. Visitors are allowed to read copies of wills previous to 1700, from which also pencil extracts may be made. For showing wills of a later date a charge of 1*s.* is made. A fee of 1*s.* is also charged for searching the calendars. No extracts may be made from these later wills, but official copies may be procured at 8*d.* per folio page.

On the W. side of Somerset House is Wellington Street, leading to *****Waterloo Bridge.** This bridge, one of the finest in the world, was built by *John Rennie* for a company in 1811-17, at a cost of over 1,000,000*l.* It is 460 yds. long and 42 ft. broad, and rests upon 9 arches, each of 120 ft. span and 35 ft. high, and borne by granite buttresses. It commands an admirable view of the W. part of London between Westminster and St. Paul's, of the Thames Embankment, and of the massive but well-proportioned façade of Somerset House. In 1878 the bridge was sold to the

Metropolitan Board of Works for 475,000*l.* and opened to the public toll-free. — Waterloo Bridge Road, on the S. side of the river, leads to *Waterloo Station* (p. 58).

On the N. side of the Strand we next observe the *Gaiety Theatre* (p. 66) and the *Lyceum Theatre* (p. 65). Beyond these, between Burleigh Street and Exeter Street (commemorating Exeter House, the residence of Queen Elizabeth's Lord Chancellor), is *Exeter Hall*, marked by its Corinthian portico, and capable of containing 5000 persons. It is the property of the Young Men's Christian Association and used for the advocacy of religious and philanthropic movements. The large annual 'May Meetings' of various religious societies held here begin in April and sometimes extend into July.

To the left is Savoy Street, leading to the **Savoy Chapel**, dedicated to St. John the Baptist, and built in the Perpendicular style in 1505-11, during the reigns of Henry VII. and Henry VIII., on the site of the ancient *Savoy Palace*.

The chapel, created one of the Chapels Royal by George III. and now a 'Royal Peculiar' attached to the Duchy of Lancaster, was seriously injured by fire in 1864, but restored at the expense of Queen Victoria. The handsome wooden ceiling is modern. Bishop Gavin Douglas of Dunkeld (d. 1522), the poetical translator of Virgil, is buried in the chancel (with brass), and George Wither (d. 1667), the poet, was also buried here. Fine stained glass. Savoy Palace was first built in 1245, and was given by Henry III. to Peter, Count of Savoy, the uncle of his queen, Eleanor of Provence. The captive King John of France died here in 1364, and Chaucer was probably married here when the palace was occupied by John of Gaunt. It lay between the present chapel and the river, but has entirely disappeared. At the Savoy, in the time of Cromwell, the Independents adopted a Confession of Faith, and here the celebrated 'Savoy Conference' for the revision of the Prayer Book was held, when Baxter, Calamy, and others represented the Nonconformists. The German chapel which used to stand contiguous to the Savoy Chapel was removed in widening Savoy Street, which now forms a thoroughfare to the Thames Embankment. The French Protestants who conformed to the English church had a chapel here from the time of Charles II. till 1737. See *Memorials of the Savoy*, by the Rev. W. J. Loftie (Macmillan; 1878).

Farther on, to the left, is *Terry's Theatre* (p. 66), beyond which Beaufort Buildings leads to the *Savoy Theatre* (p. 65).

At No. 13 Cecil Street, to the left (now almost wholly engulfed by the Hôtel Cecil), Sir W. Congreve (d. 1828), the inventor of the Congreve Rocket, resided and made his experiments, firing the rockets across the Thames. Edmund Kean (1787-1833) lived at No. 21 in the same street.

A little to the N. of this part of the Strand lies *Covent Garden Market* (p. 232). On the right, between Southampton Street and Bedford Street, is the *Vaudeville Theatre* (p. 66); beyond it, the *Adelphi Theatre* (p. 65). In Bedford Street is a store of the *Civil Service Supply Association* (p. 33).

To the S. of the Strand, opposite the Adelphi Theatre, is the region known as **'The Adelphi'**, built by four brothers called Adam, whose names are commemorated in Adam St., John St., Robert St., James St., and William St., and in the Adelphi Terrace. In John St.

rises the building of the *Society of Arts* (Pl. R, 30; *II*), an association established in 1754 for the encouragement of arts, manufactures, and commerce, which took a prominent part in promoting
the Exhibitions of 1851 and 1862. The large hall (open daily,
10-4, except Saturday) contains six paintings by *Barry* (1777-83),
representing the progress of civilisation. No. 14 in the same street
is the headquarters of the *Royal National Life Boat Institution*,
founded in 1824 and supported entirely by voluntary contributions.
This society now possesses a fleet of 290 life-boats stationed round
the British coasts, and in 1899 was instrumental in saving 609
lives and 20 vessels. The total number of lives saved through the
agency of the Institution from its foundation down to 1900 was
41,842. The expenditure of the society in 1899 was 85,143*l*. The
average cost of establishing a life-boat station is 1050*l*., and the
annual expense of maintaining it 100*l*. — Adelphi Terrace, overlooking the Thames and the Embankment, contains the house
(No. 5) in which David Garrick died in 1779 (tablet). Nos. 6 and
7 in this terrace are occupied by the *Savage Club*; No. 8 by the
Irish Literary Society; No. 9 by the *Royal Statistical Society*; and
No. 10 by the *School of Economics and Political Science* (founded
in 1896). The arches below the terrace were once a resort of bad
characters of various kinds, but are now enclosed as wine-cellars. —
On the right, where King William Street joins the Strand, stands
the *Charing Cross Hospital*; and in King William Street is the
Ophthalmic Hospital. A little farther on, to the right, is the *Lowther
Arcade* (p. 32), and on the left is *Coutts's Bank*, a very noted firm,
with which the royal family has banked for 200 years. The names
of several streets on the S. side of the Strand here (George, Villiers,
Duke, Buckingham) refer to George Villiers, Duke of Buckingham,
who once owned their site (comp. p. 151). 'Of' Lane has disappeared.

At the W. end of the Strand, on the left, is **Charing Cross
Station** (with a large *Hotel*, p. 8), a West End terminus of the
South Eastern Railway (p. 57), built by *Barry* on the site of
Hungerford Market, where the mansion of Sir Edward Hungerford
stood until it was burned down in 1669. In front of it stands a mod-
ern copy of *Eleanor's Cross*, a Gothic monument erected in 1291 by
Edward I. at Charing Cross, near the spot where the coffin of his
consort was set down during its last halt on the way to Westminster
Abbey. The original was removed by order of Parliament in 1647.
The river is here crossed by the *Charing Cross Railway Bridge*, on
one side of which is a footway (freed from toll in 1878; the most
direct route to Waterloo Station). — To the E. of the station is
Villiers Street, which descends to the *Embankment Gardens* (p. 151)
and to the *Charing Cross Station* (p. 61) of the Metropolitan District
Railway. — Benjamin Franklin lived at No. 7 *Craven Street* (denoted
by a memorial tablet), to the W. of the station.

13. Trafalgar Square.

Nelson Column. St. Martin's in the Fields. Charing Cross.

*Trafalgar Square (Pl. R, 26; *II, IV*), one of the finest open places in London and a great centre of attraction, is, so to speak, dedicated to *Lord Nelson*, and commemorates his glorious death at the battle of Trafalgar (22nd Oct., 1805), gained by the English fleet over the combined armaments of France and Spain. By this victory Napoleon's purpose of invading England was frustrated. The ambitious Emperor had assembled at Boulogne an army of 172,000 infantry and 9000 cavalry, and also 2413 transports to convey his soldiers to England, but his fleet, which he had been building for many years at an enormous cost, and which was to have covered his passage of the Channel, was destroyed by Nelson at this famous battle. The Admiral is, therefore, justly revered as the saviour of his country.

In the centre of the square rises the massive granite **Column**, 145 ft. in height, to the memory of the hero. It is a copy of one of the Corinthian columns of the temple of Mars Ultor, the avenging god of war, at Rome, and is crowned with a *Statue of Nelson*, by *Baily*, 17 ft. in height. The pedestal is adorned with reliefs in bronze, cast with the metal of captured French cannon. On the N. face is a scene from the battle of Aboukir (1798); Nelson, wounded in the head, declines to be assisted out of his turn by a surgeon who has been dressing the wounds of a common sailor. On the E. side is the battle of Copenhagen (1801); Nelson is represented as sealing upon a cannon the treaty of peace with the conquered Danes. On the S. is the death of Nelson at Trafalgar (21st Oct., 1805); beside the dying hero is Captain Hardy, commander of the Admiral's flag-ship. Below is Nelson's last signal: 'England expects every man will do his duty'. On the W. side is a representation of Nelson receiving the sword of the Spanish commander after the battle of St. Vincent (1797).—Four colossal bronze lions, modelled by *Sir Edwin Landseer* (d. 1871) in 1867, couch upon pedestals running out from the column in the form of a cross. — The monument was erected in 1843 by voluntary contributions at a total cost of about 45,000*l*.

Towards the N. side of the square, which is paved with asphalt, are two fountains. A *Statue of Sir Henry Havelock*, the deliverer of Lucknow (d. 1857), by *Behnes*, stands on the E. (Strand) side of the Nelson Column, and a *Statue of Sir Charles James Napier*, the conqueror of Scinde (d. 1853), by *Adams*, on the other. The N.E. corner of the square is occupied by an *Equestrian Statue of George IV.*, in bronze, by *Chantrey*. Between the fountains is a *Statue of General Gordon* (d. 1885), by *Hamo Thornycroft*, erected in 1888.

On the terrace on the N. side of the square rises the *National Gallery* (p. 188), adjoined by the *National Portrait Gallery* (p. 220). Near it, on the E., is the church of **St. Martin in the Fields**, with a noble Grecian portico, erected in 1721-26 by *Gibbs*, on the site of an earlier church. The tower and spire are 185 ft. high. In the church, at the W. end of the nave, is a bust of Gibbs, by *Rysbrack*. Nell Gwynne (d. 1687), Farquhar the dramatist (d. 1707), Roubiliac the sculptor (d. 1762), and James Smith (d. 1839), one of the authors of 'Rejected Addresses', were buried in the churchyard.

Adjoining Morley's Hotel, on the E. side of the square, is the building of the *Royal Humane Society*, founded in 1774 for the rescue of drowning persons. This valuable society possesses a model house on the N. bank of the Serpentine in Hyde Park, containing models of the best appliances for saving life, and apparatus for aiding bathers and skaters who may be in danger. It also awards prizes and medals to persons who have saved others from drowning.

Down to 1874 *Northumberland House*, the noble mansion of the Duke of Northumberland, with the lion of the Percies high above the gates, rose on the S.E. side of Trafalgar Square. It was purchased in 1873 by the Metropolitan Board of Works for 497,000*l.*, and was removed to make way for Northumberland Avenue, a broad new street from Charing Cross to the Thames Embankment (comp. p. 151). The *Grand Hôtel* (p. 8) occupies part of the site. Two other large hotels, the *Hôtel Métropole* and the *Hôtel Victoria*, have been built on the opposite side of Northumberland Avenue. Next door to the Grand Hôtel is the *Constitutional Club*, a handsome building of red and yellow terracotta in the style of the German Renaissance, by Edis, erected in 1886. At the corner of Northumberland Avenue and Whitehall Place, facing the Thames, is the magnificent building of the *National Liberal Club*, by Waterhouse, opened in 1887. One of the most attractive features of this imposing edifice is the spacious flagged terrace overlooking the Embankment Gardens and the river; another is the grand staircase.

On the W. side of Trafalgar Square, between Cockspur Street and Pall Mall East, is the *Union Club* (p. 103), adjoining which is the *Royal College of Physicians*, built by *Smirke* in 1825, and containing a number of portraits and busts of celebrated London physicians.

Charing Cross (Pl. R, 26, and *IV*; probably so called from the village of *Cherringe* which stood here in the 13th cent.), on the S. side of Trafalgar Square, between the Strand and Whitehall, is the principal point of intersection of the omnibus lines of the West End, and the centre of the 4 and 12 miles circles on the Post Office Directory Map. The *Equestrian Statue of Charles I.*, by *Le Sueur*, which stands here, is remarkable for the vicissitudes it has undergone. It was cast in 1633, but had not yet been erected when the Civil War broke out. It was then sold by the Parliament to a brazier, named John Rivet, for the purpose of being melted down, and this worthy sold pretended fragments of it both to friends and foes of the Stuarts. At the Restoration, however, the statue was produced uninjured, and in 1674 it was erected on the spot where *Eleanor's*

Cross (p. 185) had stood down to 1647. In *Hartshorn Lane*, an adjoining street, Ben Jonson, when a boy, once lived with his mother and her second husband, a bricklayer.

CHARING CROSS ROAD (Pl. R, 27), a great and much needed thoroughfare from Charing Cross to Tottenham Court Road, cuts through a number of low streets and alleys to the N. of St. Martin's Church. At the S. end of this street, to the left, is the new *National Portrait Gallery* (p. 220), and to the right are a *Savings Bank*, the *St. Martin's Vestry Hall and Public Library*, the *Garrick Theatre*, and *Wyndham's Theatre*, opened in 1899 (p. 65). To the left are the back of the *Alhambra* (p. 67), the *Hippodrome* (p. 67), some large blocks of *Industrial Dwellings*, and a *Welsh Presbyterian Chapel*. The road then expands into *Cambridge Circus*, in which is the handsome façade of the *Palace Music Hall* (p. 67), erected as the Royal English Opera House in 1891. In the section of Charing Cross Road to the N. of the Circus is the church of *St. Mary the Virgin*, Soho, on the site of the first Greek church in London (1677). — SHAFTESBURY AVENUE, another wide street opened in 1886, runs from Piccadilly Circus, past the *Lyric* and the *Shaftesbury Theatres* (p. 66), to meet Charing Cross Road at Cambridge Circus, and is prolonged to New Oxford Street opposite Hart Street, Bloomsbury.

14. The National Gallery.

Among the buildings round Trafalgar Square the principal in point of size, although perhaps not in architectural merit, is the ****National Gallery** (Pl. R, 26; *II*), situated on a terrace on the N. side, and erected in 1832-38, at an original cost of 96,000*l.*, on the site of the old King's Mews. The building, designed by *Wilkins*, is in the Grecian style, and has a façade 460 ft. in length. The Gallery was considerably altered and enlarged in 1860; an extensive addition (including the central octagon) was made by Mr. E. M. Barry in 1876; and five other rooms, including a gallery 85 ft. long, were opened in 1887. At the back of the National Gallery is the new *National Portrait Gallery* (p. 220).

The nucleus of the National Gallery, which was formed by Act of Parliament in 1824, consisted solely of the Angerstein collection of 38 pictures. It has, however, been rapidly and greatly extended by means of donations, legacies, and purchases, and is now composed of some 1650 pictures, about 1100 of which are exhibited in the 22 rooms of the Gallery, while the others are either housed in the Tate Gallery (modern British pictures; comp. p. 275) or are lent to provincial collections. Among the most important additions have been the collections presented or bequeathed by Robert Vernon (1847), J. M. W. Turner (1856), and Wynn Ellis (1876); and the Peel collection, bought in 1871. For a long period part of the building was occupied by the Royal Academy of Arts, which, however, was removed to Burlington House (p. 282) in 1869. There are other national collections at South Kensington (p. 358) and at Hertford House (p. 283). — In 1899 the National Gallery was visited on the free days by 420,272 persons, being a daily average of 2040, in addition to 35,229 visitors on 31 Sun.

afternoons, and on the pay-days (Thurs. and Frid.) by 41,473 persons, besides 17,100 students.

From the number of artists represented the collection in the National Gallery is exceedingly valuable to students of the history of art. The older Italian masters are especially important. The catalogues originally prepared by *Mr. Wornum* (d. 1877), and since re-issued with corrections and additions (Foreign Schools 1s., abridgment 6d.. 1898; British School 6d., 1899), comprise short biographies of the different artists. The 'Pall Mall Gazette Guide to the National Gallery' (6d.; sold outside the doors) contains a descriptive catalogue and a scheme for studying the gallery in a series of twelve 'half-holiday visits'. *Mr. E. T. Cook's* 'Popular Handbook to the National Gallery' (Macmillan & Co., 5th ed., 1897) includes an interesting collection of notes on the pictures by Mr. Ruskin and others. *Mr. Cosmo Monkhouse's* 'In the National Gallery' (1895) may also be consulted. 'The National Gallery', edited by *Sir Edward J. Poynter*, is a monumental work in three volumes, with reproductions of every picture in the National and Tate Galleries (1900-1901; price 7l 7s.) Each picture is inscribed with the name of the painter, the year of his birth and death, the school to which he belongs, and the subject represented. In a few instances this Handbook differs from the Catalogue in its ascriptions of authorship. — The present director is *Sir E. J Poynter, P. R. A.*, and the keeper and secretary is *Mr. Hawes Turner.* - Photographs of the paintings, by Morelli, are sold in the gallery at prices ranging from 1s. to 10s. Others, and perhaps better, may be found at *Deighton's*, 4 Grand Hôtel Buildings (on the other side of Trafalgar Square), at *Hanfstaengel's*, 26 Pall Mall East, and at the *Autotype Fine Art Gallery*, 74 New Oxford Street.

Admission to the Gallery, see p. 108. Thursday and Friday are students' days and should be avoided by the ordinary visitor, as the crowds of easels preclude a satisfactory view of the pictures. The Gallery is closed for cleaning on the Thursday, Friday, and Saturday before Easter Sunday. Sticks and umbrellas are left at the entrance (no charge).

The pictures are arranged in schools, with as close adherence as possible to a chronological order. The main staircase facing us as we enter ascends to Room I, in which begins the series of Italian works. The staircase to the left leads to the British Schools; that on the right to the French and Spanish Schools.

The **Hall** contains busts of the painters W. Mulready (d. 1863) and Th. Stothard (d. 1834), by *Weekes*. On the walls are two large landscapes with cattle by *James Ward*, the Battle of the Borodino by *Jones*, a forest-scene by *Salvator Rosa*, a landscape by *Hobbema*, the Battle of Camperdown by *Thos. Whitcombe* (b. ca. 1760), and a cast of a bust of Mantegna by *Sperandio*.

To the left is a staircase descending to a room containing *Water Colour Drawings* from paintings by early Italian and other masters, published and lent by the Arundel Society. Other rooms contain copies of paintings by *Velazquez* at Madrid and by *Rembrandt* at St. Petersburg.

To the right is a flight of steps (with a bronze bust of Napoleon at the top) descending to the collection of *Turner's Water Colours* (catalogue by Ruskin, 1s.), now occupying four rooms. Other drawings of the Arundel Society are also exhibited here.

The **VESTIBULE OF THE MAIN STAIRCASE** is roofed by a glass dome and embellished with marble columns and panelling, of green 'cipollino', 'giallo antico', 'pavonazzetto', etc. Here are hung several large paintings of the **BRITISH SCHOOL**. To the left (W.):

1372. *John J. Halls* (ca. 1790-1830), Admiral Sir George Cockburn; 789. *Thomas Gainsborough* (p. 216), Family group; *Sir Henry Raeburn* (Scottish School; d. 1823), 1435. Portrait of Lieut. Col. McMurdo, 1146. Portrait of a lady; 1228. *Fuseli* (d. 1825), Titania

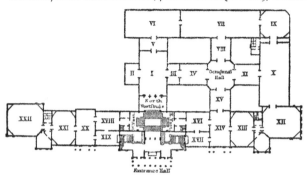

and Bottom; 1102. *Longhi*, Andrea Tron, Procurator of St. Mark's, Venice (placed here temporarily). To the right (E.): 1449. *Philippe de Champaigne* (d. 1674), Cardinal Richelieu; *143. *Sir Joshua Reynolds* (p. 216), Equestrian portrait of Lord Ligonier; 681. *Reynolds*, Capt. Orme; 684. *Gainsborough*, Dr. Schomberg; 144. *Sir Thomas Lawrence* (d. 1830), Benjamin West, the painter; 677. *Sir Martin Shee* (d. 1850), Portrait of the actor Lewis as the Marquis in the 'Midnight Hour'. — The North Vestibule (see Plan), in the centre of which is a Renaissance copy, in porphyry, of the head of the Dying Alexander in the Uffizi, is now devoted mainly to the works of the EARLY TUSCAN SCHOOL, chiefly of historical interest. To the right: 276. *School of Giotto* (d. 1336), Two Apostles; 1456. *Italian School*, Virgin and Child with angels; 564. *Margaritone* (Arezzo; 1216-93), Virgin and Child; 581. *Spinello Aretino* (Tuscan School; d. 1410), Three saints; 568. *School of Giotto*, Coronation of the Virgin; 579. *School of Taddeo Gaddi* (d. 1366; chief scholar of Giotto), Baptism of Christ. To the left: 1437. *Barnaba da Modena* (second half of 14th cent.), Descent of the Holy Ghost; 569. *Andrea Orcagna* (d. 1368), Coronation of the Virgin, with saints (large altar-piece from San Pietro Maggiore in Florence; schoolpiece); *Spinello Aretino*, 1468. Crucifixion, 1216-1216 B. (above), Fragments of frescoes. Also, eleven interesting Greek portraits of the 2nd and 3rd cent. from mummies found in the Fayûm.

Room I is devoted to the TUSCAN SCHOOLS (15-16th cent.). — To the left: 226. *Tuscan School* (copy of Botticelli?), Madonna and Child, with John the Baptist and angels, with a rose-hedge in the background (fine circular frame); 246. *Girolamo del Pacchia* (d. after

1535), Madonna and Child; 218. *Baldassare Peruzzi* (Siena; d. 1536), Adoration of the Magi (said to give portraits of Titian, Michael Angelo, and Raphael); 1124. *Filippino Lippi* (pupil of Botticelli; d. 1504), Adoration of the Magi (school-piece); 1301. *Tuscan School*, Savonarola (on the back, his martyrdom); 645. *Mariotto Albertinelli* (d. 1515), Virgin and Child; 704. *Angelo di Cosimo*, called *Bronzino* (1502-72), Cosimo I., Duke of Tuscany; 1143. *Ridolfo Ghirlandajo* (son of the more famous Domenico Ghirlandajo; 1483-1561), Christ on the way to Golgotha. — *1034. *Sandro Filipepi*, called *Botticelli* (1447-1510), The Nativity; to the left the Magi, to the right the Shepherds, in front shepherds embraced by angels.

The subject is conceived in a manner highly mystical and symbolical. At the top of the picture is a Greek inscription to the following effect: 'This picture I, Alessandro, painted at the end of the year 1500, in the (troubles) of Italy in the half-time after the time during the fulfilment of the eleventh of St. John in the second woe of the Apocalypse, in the loosing of the devil for three years and a half. Afterwards he shall be chained and we shall see him trodden down as in this picture'.

248. *Fra Filippo Lippi* (d. 1469), Vision of St. Bernard; *592. *Botticelli*, Adoration of the Magi; 809. In the manner of *Michael Angelo*, Madonna and Child, with John the Baptist and angels (unfinished); 727. *Pesellino* (d. 1457), Trinità; 790. *Michael Angelo Buonarroti* (1475-1564), Entombment (unfinished and youthful work; in tempera, on wood). — *296. *School of Verrocchio*, Virgin adoring the Infant Christ, with angels.

This painting is executed with great carefulness, but the conception of the forms and proportions is hardly worthy of a master of the first rank, such as Verrocchio, to whom some critics assign the work.

781. *Tuscan School*, Tobias and the Angel; 1194. *Marcello Venusti* (follower of Michael Angelo; d. ca. 1580), Jesus expelling the money-changers from the Temple; 8. After *Michael Angelo*, A dream of human life. — *292. *Ant. Pollajuolo* (d. 1498), Martyrdom of St. Sebastian.

This picture was painted in 1475 for the altar of the Pucci chapel, in the church of San Sebastiano de' Servi at Florence, and according to Vasari is the artist's masterpiece. The head of the saint, which is of great beauty, is the portrait of a Capponi.

1150. Ascribed to *Jacopo da Pontormo* (1494-1557), Portrait of a man; *593. *Lorenzo di Credi* (Florence, pupil of Verrocchio at the same time as Leonardo da Vinci; d. 1537), Madonna and Child; 21. *Cristofano Allori* (1577-1621), Portrait; 648. *Lorenzo di Credi*, Virgin adoring the Infant (in his best style); *293. *Filippino Lippi*, Madonna and Child, with SS. Jerome and Dominic, an altar-piece with predella (rich landscape); 1323. *Bronzino*, Piero de' Medici. 1430. *Beccafumi* (1486-1551), Esther before Ahasuerus; 1131. *Pontormo*, Joseph and his Brethren; according to Vasari, the boy seated on the steps, with a basket, is a portrait of Bronzino. *Bronzino*, 650. Portrait, 670. Knight of St. Stephen; 649. Ascribed to *Pontormo*, Portrait of a boy, in the style of Bronzino (probably a youthful work of the latter); 17. *Andrea del Sarto* (the greatest

master of the school; 1486-1531), Holy Family (school-piece); 589.
Fra Filippo Lippi, Virgin with the Holy Child and an angel; *690.
Andrea del Sarto, Portrait, a masterpiece of chiaroscuro; 782. *Botti-
celli*, Madonna and Child (in tempera, on wood); 698. *Piero di
Cosimo* (pupil of Cosimo Rosselli and teacher of A. del Sarto; d.
ca. 1521), Death of Procris, in a beautiful landscape. — 651.
Bronzino, Venus, Cupid, Folly, and Time, an allegory.

'Bronzino painted a picture of remarkable beauty, which was sent
into France to King Francis. In this picture was pourtrayed a naked
Venus together with Cupid, who was kissing her. On the one side were
Pleasure and Mirth, with other Powers of Love, and on the other Deceit,
Jealousy, and other Passions of Love.' — *Vasari*.

1048. *Italian School* (16th cent.), Portrait of a Cardinal; *915.
Botticelli, Mars and Venus; 1035. *Franciabigio* (d. 1525), A Knight
of Malta; 927. *Filippino Lippi*, Angel; 626. *Botticelli*, Young man.

Room II. SIENESE AND OTHER TUSCAN MASTERS. To the left:
1461. *Matteo di Giovanni* (d. 1495), St. Sebastian; 1406. *Fra Angelico
da Fiesole* (d. 1455), Annunciation (school-piece); 591. *Benozzo
Gozzoli* (pupil of Fra Angelico; 1420-98), Rape of Helen (school-
piece); 573-575 and (farther on) 576-578. *Orcagna*, Small pictures
belonging to the large altar-piece, No. 569 (p. 190); *666. *Fra
Filippo Lippi*, Annunciation, painted like No. 667 for Cosimo de'
Medici and marked with his crest; 1215. *Domenico Veneziano*
(d. 1461), Madonna and Child; 667. *Fra Filippo Lippi*, John the
Baptist and six other saints, seated on a marble bench (painted for
Cosimo de' Medici; 1389-1464); 227. *Cosimo Rosselli* (d. 1507;
school-piece), Various saints (names on the original frame); 766,
767. *Domenico Veneziano* (d. 1461), Saints (in fresco)t — 283.
Benozzo Gozzoli, Virgin and Child enthroned, with saints.

'The original contract for this picture, dated 23d Oct., 1461, is still
preserved. The figure of the Virgin is in this contract specially directed
to be made similar in mode, form, and ornaments to the Virgin Enthroned, in the picture over the high-altar of San Marco, Florence, by
Fra Giovanni (Angelico) da Fiesole, and now in the Academy there'.—
Catalogue.

*663. *Fra Angelico*, Christ with the banner of the Resurrection,
surrounded by a crowd of saints, martyrs, and Dominicans, 'so beautiful', says Vasari, 'that they appear to be truly beings of Paradise';
567. *Segna di Buonaventura* (Sienese school; ca. 1310), Christ on the
Cross; 586. *Zenobio Macchiavelli* (pupil of Benozzo Gozzoli; 1418-
79), Madonna enthroned; 1199. *Florentine School of the 15th cent.*,
Madonna and Child, with John the Baptist and an angel. — *566.
Duccio di Buoninsegna (founder of the school of Siena; d. about
1339), Madonna and Child.

'A genuine picture, which illustrates how well the master could
vivify Byzantine forms with tender feeling'.

1155. *Matteo di Giovanni da Siena* (d. 1495), Assumption, the
Virgin throwing down her girdle as a proof to the incredulous
St. Thomas; 1331. *Bernardino Fungai* (d. 1516), Virgin and

Child surrounded by cherubim; 1682. *Francesco di Giorgio* (1439-1502), Virgin and Child; 909. *Benvenuto da Siena* (d. ca. 1518), Madonna and Child; 582. *Fra Angelico* (school-piece), The Magi.

Room III. TUSCAN SCHOOLS. To the left: *School of Taddeo Gaddi*, 215, 216. Saints; 594. *Emmanuel* (Greek priest; Byzantine School), SS. Cosmas and Damian (one of the earliest pictures in the Gallery in point of artistic development); 701. *Justus of Padua* (School of Giotto; d. 1400), Coronation of the Virgin, dated 1367 (a small triptych, of cheerful, soft, and well-blended colouring); 916. *Botticelli* (school-piece), Venus and Cupid; *583. *Paolo Uccello*, Cavalry Engagement at Sant' Egidio (1416), one of the earliest Florentine representations of a secular subject; **1196.** *Tuscan School*, Amor and Castitas; 1299. *Dom. Ghirlandajo* (?), Portrait of a youth (school-piece, much restored); 598. *Filippino Lippi* (?), St. Francis in glory; 565. *Giov. Cimabue* (1240-1302), Madonna and Child enthroned ('the early efforts of Cimabue and Giotto are the burning messages of prophecy, delivered by the stammering lips of infants' — Ruskin). *Filippino Lippi*, 1033. (more probably Botticelli; comp. No. 592, p. 191). Adoration of the Magi (in a circular frame); 1412. Virgin and Child, with the young John the Baptist. 895. *Piero di Cosimo*, Warrior in armour; 275. *Botticelli*, Virgin and Child (a circular picture in a fine old frame); no number, *Ghirlandajo*, Costanza de' Medici (lent by Mr. Salting); 928. Ascribed to *Antonio Pollajuolo*, Apollo and Daphne. — 1126. *Botticelli* (?), Assumption of the Virgin.

In the centre of the upper part of the picture is the Virgin, kneeling before the Saviour, while around are cycles or tiers of angels, apostles, saints, and seraphim. Below are the apostles gathered round the tomb of the Virgin, with portraits of the Palmieri, the donors of the altar-piece. The picture was probably executed by a pupil from a cartoon by Botticelli. In the background are Florence and Fiesole, with the Villa Palmieri.

580. *Jacopo Landini di Casentino* (d. ca. 1390), St. John the Evangelist lifted up into Heaven.

Those who wish to continue their survey of the Italian schools should omit Room IV for the present and pass on to Room V (p. 195).

Room IV. EARLY FLEMISH SCHOOL. The names of the artists are in many cases doubtful.

To the left: 721. *J. van Schoreel* or *Scorel* (d. 1562), Portrait; 709 *Flemish School*, Virgin and Child; *1432. *Gheerardt David* (early Flemish painter of Bruges; d. 1523), Mystic Marriage of St. Catharine, with the kneeling donor to the left; 945. *Joachim Patinir* (d. ca. 1524), Nun; 1433. *Flemish School* (15th cent.), Portrait of a lady; 720. *J. van Schoreel* or *Scorel* (?), Rest on the Flight into Egypt; 774. *Flemish School* (15th cent.), Virgin and Child enthroned; 715. *Patinir*, Crucifixion; 1419. *Flemish School*, Legend of St. Giles; *1045. *Gheerardt David*, Wing of an altar-piece, representing Canon Bernardino di Salviatis, a Florentine merchant in Flanders, with SS. Martin, Donatian, and Bernardino of Siena, a masterpiece.

*686. *Hans Memling* or *Memlinc* (early Flemish master of Bruges; d. ca. 1495), Virgin and Child enthroned.

This is the only authentic work of this master in the gallery, and is marked by his peculiar tenderness of conception and vividness of tints.

711. Ascribed to *Rogier van der Weyden* (d. 1464), Mater Dolorosa.

*222. *Jan van Eyck* (d. 1440; founder of the early Flemish School), Portrait of a man.

'This is a panel in which minute finish is combined with delicate modelling and strong relief, and a brown depth of colour.' — *C. & C.*

696. *Flemish School*, Marco Barbarigo.

*186. *Jan van Eyck*, Portraits of Giovanni Arnolfini and Jeanne de Chenany, his wife.

'In no single instance has John van Eyck expressed with more perfection, by the aid of colour, the sense of depth and atmosphere; he nowhere blended colours more carefully, nowhere produced more transparent shadows..... The finish of the parts is marvellous, and the preservation of the picture perfect'. — *Crowe and Cavalcaselle*, 'Early Flemish Painters'.

'Without a prolonged examination of this picture, it is impossible to form an idea of the art with which it has been executed. One feels tempted to think that in this little panel Van Eyck has set himself to accumulate all manner of difficulties, or rather of impossibilities, for the mere pleasure of overcoming them. The perspective, both lineal and aërial, is so ably treated, and the truthfulness of colouring is so great, that all the details, even those reflected in the mirror, seem perspicuous and easy; and instead of the fatigue which the examination of so laborious and complicated a work might well occasion, we feel nothing save pleasure and admiration'. — *Reiset*, '*Gazette des Beaux Arts*', 1878 (p. 7).

The signature on this picture is 'Johannes de Eyck fuit hic' ('Jan van Eyck was here'). The inscription on No. 222 (see above) is equally modest: 'Als ich kan' ('As I can').

719. *Henrik met de Bles* ('Henry with the forelock'; Flemish painter of the 16th cent.), Mary Magdalen.

*290. *Jan van Eyck*, Portrait of a man, dated 1432.

'The drawing is careful, the painting blended to a fault.' — *C. & C.*

708. *Flemish School*, Virgin and Child; 747. Attributed to *Memling*, St. John the Baptist and St. Lawrence, 'very minutely and delicately worked'; 712. *Rogier van der Weyden*, Ecce Homo; *Flemish School*, 783. Exhumation of St. Hubert, 1078. Deposition from the Cross, 265. Virgin and Child, 1079. Adoration of the Magi; 713. *Jan Mostaert* (b. 1474), Virgin and Child; 718. *Henrik met de Bles*, Mt. Calvary; 655. *Bernard van Orley* (d. 1542), Reading Magdalen. — *Flemish School*, 1086, 1280. Christ appearing to Mary after his Resurrection, 1063. Portrait; *Patinir*, 717. St. John in Patmos, 716. St. Christopher bearing the Infant Christ, 1298. (in a fine old frame), River-scene; 714. *C. Engelbertsz*, Mother and child; 664. *Rogier van der Weyden*, Deposition in the tomb; 653. *Flemish School*, Man and wife; 1082. *Patinir*, Visitation; *Flemish School*, 1081. Portrait, 1089. Virgin and Child with St. Elizabeth, 264. Count of Hainault with his patron-saint, 947. Portrait; 266. *Lambert Lombard* (1505-66), Deposition from the Cross; 946. *Jan Mabuse* (*Jan*

Gossaert; early Flemish portrait and historical painter; d. 1532), Portrait; 1084. *Patinir,* Flight into Egypt; 1689. *Flemish School* (ca. 1500), Man and wife; *944. *Marinus de Zeeuw or Van Romerswael* (d. ca. 1570; a follower of Q. Matsys), Two bankers or usurers in their office, one inserting items in a ledger, while the other seems to recall with difficulty the particulars of some business-transaction; *656. *Jan Mabuse,* Portrait, drawing and colouring alike admirable; 654. *School of Rogier van der Weyden,* Mary Magdalen; 1083. *Flemish School,* Christ crowned with thorns; 1036. *Flemish School,* Portrait; 710. *Hugo van der Goes* (?), Monk, 'a vivid and truthful portrait'; 657. *Jac. Cornelissen* (Amsterdam; d. ca. 1560), Dutch lady and gentleman, with their patron-saints, Peter and Paul; 295. *Quinten Matsys* (d. 1530), Salvator Mundi and Virgin Mary, replicas of two pictures at Antwerp; *943. *Flemish School,* Portrait; 1042. *Catharine van Hemessen* (portrait-painter at the Spanish court; 16th cent.), Portrait of a man with fair hair.

Room V. SCHOOLS OF FERRARA AND BOLOGNA. To the left: *Cosimo Tura* (Ferrara; 1420-95), 773. St. Jerome in the wilderness, 772. Madonna and Child, with angels; 597. *Fr. Cossa* (end of 15th cent.), St. Vincent Ferrer; 82. *Mazzolino da Ferrara* (1480-1528), Holy Family. — *1119. *Ercole di Giulio Grandi* (Ferrara; d. 1531), Madonna enthroned, with John the Baptist and St. William; the throne is adorned with sculptural panels (a masterpiece). — *Benvenuto Tisio,* surnamed *Garofalo* (d. 1559), *81. Vision of St. Augustine; 170. Holy Family; *671. Madonna and Child enthroned, surrounded by SS. William, Clara, Francis, and Anthony (altarpiece, destitute of the charm of colouring seen in his smaller works). — 590. *Marco Zoppo* (Bologna; d. after 1498), Dead Christ, with John the Baptist and Joseph of Arimathea; 1127. *Ercole de' Roberti* (d. 1496), Last Supper; 638. *Francesco Francia (Raibolini,* early school of Bologna, also a goldsmith; d. 1517), Madonna and Child, with saints; *629. *Lorenzo Costa* (teacher of Francia; d. 1535), Madonna enthroned, dated 1505; 770. *Giovanni Oriolo* (Ferrara; d. after 1461), Leonello d'Este, Marquis of Ferrara (d. 1450); *Francia,* *179. Virgin enthroned and St. Anne, *180. Pietà (the lunette of No. 179; these are the finest specimens of the school in the collection); 169. *Mazzolino* (Ferrara; d. ca. 1528), Holy Family; 752. *Lippo di Dalmasio* (end of the 14th cent.), Madonna and Child; 641. *Mazzolino,* The Woman taken in adultery; 669. *Ortolano* (Ferrara; d. ca. 1525), SS. Sebastian, Rochus, and Demetrius; 1234. *Dosso Dossi* (?), Allegorical group; 1217. *Ercole de' Roberti*, Israelites gathering manna.

Room VI. UMBRIAN SCHOOL. To the left: *Melozzo da Forli* (?; d. 1494), 756. Music, 755. Rhetoric (similar representations at Berlin); 249. *Lorenzo da San Severino* (second half of the 15th cent.), Marriage of St. Catharine; *1282. *Jacopo da Empoli* (ca.

1554-1640), San Zenobio resuscitating a dead child; 1107. *Niccolò da Foligno* (*Alunno*; end of the 15th cent.), The Passion, a triptych; 1103. *Fiorenzo di Lorenzo* (end of 15th cent.), Madonna and saints (lucid colouring); 910. Ascribed to *Signorelli* (more probably by *Genga da Urbino*), Triumph of Chastity, a fresco; 1441. *Pietro Vannucci* (called *Perugino*, the master of Raphael; 1446-1523), Adoration of the Shepherds (a large fresco); 911. *Bernardino Pinturicchio* (d. 1513), Return of Ulysses; 1104. *Giannicola Manni* (a pupil of Perugino; d. 1544), Annunciation; 1051. *Umbrian School*, Our Lord, St. Thomas, and St. Anthony of Padua, the donor kneeling to the right; 1032. *Lo Spagna* (*Giovanni di Pietro*, a Spanish pupil of Perugino; d. after 1530), Agony in the Garden; *288. *Perugino*, Madonna adoring the Infant, with the archangel Michael on the left and Raphael with Tobias on the right (a masterpiece); 693. *Pinturicchio*, St. Catharine of Alexandria; 691. Ascribed to *Lo Spagna*, Ecce Homo; 1431. *Perugino*, Baptism of our Lord; *Umbrian School*, 702. Madonna and Child, 1304. Marcus Curtius (?); 703. *Pinturicchio*, Madonna and Child.

**213. *Raphael* (*Sanzio*; 1483-1520), Vision of a knight (a youthful work, as fine in its execution as it is tender in its conception).

This little gem reveals the influence of Raphael's early master Timoteo Viti, without a trace of the later manner learned from Perugino. The original *Cartoon hangs beneath.

'Two allegorical female figures, representing respectively the noble ambitions and the joys of life, appear to a young knight lying asleep beneath a laurel, and offer him his choice of glory or pleasure'. — *Passavant.*

**1171. *Raphael*, Madonna degli Ansidei, bought from the Duke of Marlborough in 1884 for 70,000*l.*, the largest sum ever given for a picture.

This Holy Family was painted by Raphael in 1506 for the chapel of the Ansidei family in the Servite church at Perugia. In 1764 it was purchased by Lord Robert Spencer, brother of the third Duke of Marlborough. The two figures flanking the Virgin are those of John the Baptist and St. Nicholas of Bari, the latter represented in his episcopal robes. The small round loaves at his feet refer to his rescue of the town of Myra from famine. In the background is a view of the Tuscan hills. From the canopy hangs a rosary. — This great work, the most important example of Raphael in the country, was executed under the influence of Perugino and is in admirable preservation.

*744. *Raphael*, Madonna, Infant Christ, and St. John (the 'Aldobrandini' or 'Garvagh Madonna').

'The whole has a delicate, harmonious effect. The flesh, which is yellowish in the lights, and lightish brown in the shadows, agrees extremely well with the pale broken rose-colour of the under garment, and the delicate bluish grey of the upper garment of the Virgin. In the seams and glories gold is used, though very delicately'. — *Waagen*, '*Treasures of Art in Great Britain*'.

This work belongs to Raphael's later period, and some authorities believe he painted it with the aid of his pupils.

*168. *Raphael*, St. Catharine of Alexandria, painted in the master's Florentine period.

'In form and feeling no picture of the master approaches nearer to it than the Entombment in the Borghese Palace, which is inscribed 1507.' — *W.*

181. *Perugino*, Madonna and Child; 751. *Giovanni Santi* (Umbrian painter and poet, Raphael's father; d. 1494), Madonna; *1075. *Perugino*, Virgin and Child, with SS. Jerome and Francis; 27. *Raphael*, Pope Julius II. (an old copy of the original in Florence); 596. *Palmezzano* (pupil of Melozzo; d. after 1537), Entombment; 646. *Unknown Master* (15th cent.), St. Catharine; 929. After *Raphael*, Madonna and Child, old copy of the Bridgewater Madonna (original, see p. 340); *1128. *Signorelli* (d. 1523), Circumcision, a dramatic composition (the figure of the child has been altered by repainting); 647. *Unknown Master* (15th cent.), St. Ursula; 1220. *L'Ingegno* (*Andrea di Luigi;* ca. 1484), Madonna and Child; 769. *Piero della Francesca* (ca. 1460), St. Michael and the serpent; 1133. *Signorelli*, Adoration of the Holy Child (schoolpiece?); 1092. *Zaganelli* (*Bernardino da Cotignola;* ca. 1505-27), Martyrdom of St. Stephen; 665. *Piero della Francesca*, Baptism of Christ; 912-914. *Pinturicchio* (Umbrian school-pieces), Illustrations of the story of Griselda (the last in Boccaccio's Decameron); 1218, 1219. *Francesco Ubertini*, surnamed *Bacchiacca* (Florence; d. 1557), History of Joseph; 758. Ascribed to *P. della Francesca* (?), Portrait of a lady; *P. della Francesca*, 908. Nativity (injured), 585. Portrait; 282. *Umbrian Master* (probably *Bertucci of Faenza*, belonging to the Eclectic School), Madonna and Child enthroned.

Room VII. VENETIAN AND BRESCIAN SCHOOLS. To the left: *735. *P. Morando* (*Cavazzola*, the most important master in Verona before Paolo Veronese; d. 1522), St. Rochus with the angel, an excellent specimen of his work; *625. *Moretto* (*Alessandro Bonvicino*, the greatest painter of Brescia; d. 1555), Madonna and Child, with saints; *748. *Girolamo dai Libri* (Verona; d. 1556), Madonna and Child, with St. Anne, clear in colour and harmonious in tone, heralding the style of Paolo Veronese; 1203. *Cariani* (*Giovanni de' Busi;* ca. 1480-1541), Madonna and Child with saints; *Giambattista Moroni* (portrait-painter at Bergamo, pupil of Moretto; d. 1578), 1023. Portrait of a lady, *1316. Portrait of an Italian nobleman; 287. *Bart. Veneziano* (rare Venetian master, first half of the 16th cent.), Portrait, painted in 1530 (rich in colour); 595. *Venetian School*, Portrait; 26. *Paolo Veronese* (d. 1588), Consecration of St. Nicholas; 1041. *Paolo Veronese* (?), St. Helena; 34. *Titian* (*Tiziano Vecellio;* 1477-1576), Venus and Adonis (an early copy of the original in Madrid); *1022. *Moroni*, Nobleman; 224. *Titian*, The Tribute Money (school-piece). — *4. *Titian*, Holy Family, with adoring shepherd. This brilliantly coloured picture is an early work of the master and is painted in the manner afterwards adopted by his pupil Palma Vecchio.

*1. *Sebastian del Piombo* (of Venice, follower of Michael Angelo; d. 1547), Raising of Lazarus.

'The transition from death to life is expressed in Lazarus with wonderful spirit, and at the same time with perfect fidelity to Scripture. The grave-clothes, by which his face is thrown into deep shade, vividly excite the idea of the night of the grave, which but just before enveloped him; the eye looking eagerly from beneath this shade upon Christ, his Redeemer, shows us, on the other hand, in the most striking contrast, the new life in its most intellectual organ. This is also expressed in the whole figure, which is actively striving to relieve itself from the bonds n which it was fast bound'. — *W.*

The picture was painted in 1517-19 in competition with Raphael's Trans- figuration. The figure of Lazarus is quite in the spirit of Michael Angelo.

20. *Sebastian del Piombo*, Portraits of the painter with his seal ('piombo') of office in his hand, and Cardinal Ippolito de' Medici, painted after 1531; *635. *Titian*, Madonna and Child, with SS. John the Baptist and Catharine (the latter probably the portrait of an aristocratic lady); 1025. *Moretto*, Portrait of an Italian noble- man (1526); 32. *School of Titian*, Rape of Ganymede. — *35. *Titian*, Bacchus and Ariadne, painted in 1514 for Alphonso, Duke of Ferrara.

'This is one of the pictures which once seen can never be forgotten .... Rich harmony of drapery tints and soft modelling, depth of shade and warm flesh all combine to produce a highly coloured glow; yet in the midst of this glow the form of Ariadne seems incomparably fair. Nature was never reproduced more kindly or with greater exuberance than it is in every part of this picture. What splendour in the contrasts of colour, what wealth and diversity of scale in air and vegetation; how infinite is the space — how varied yet mellow the gradations of light and shade!' — *C. & C.*

*16. *Tintoretto* (*Jacopo Robusti*, Venice; d. 1594), St. George and the Dragon (an early work); 816. *Cima da Conegliano* (Venice, contemporary of Bellini; d. 1517), Christ appearing to St. Thomas; 1309. *Bernardino Licinio* (Venice; flor. 1524-41), Portrait of a young man; *697. *Moroni*, Portrait of a tailor ('Tagliapanni'), a masterpiece praised by contemporary poets; 1377. *Giovanni Giro- lamo Savoldo* (Brescia, about 1480-1548), Adoration of the Shep- herds; 234. *Catena* (Treviso, d. 1531 at Venice; a follower of Giov. Bellini), Warrior adoring the Infant Christ; 1214. *Michele da Verona* (d. after 1523), Coriolanus meeting Volumnia and Veturia. 1455. *Giovanni Bellini*, often shortened into Giambellino (ca. 1428-1516; the greatest Venetian painter of the 15th cent., described by Mr. Ruskin as 'the mighty Venetian master who alone of all the painters of Italy united purity of religious aim with perfection of artistical power'), Circumcision. 24. *Sebastian del Piombo*, Portrait of a lady as St. Agatha; 277. *Bassano* (*Jacopo da Ponte*, Venetian painter of the late Renaissance; d. 1592), Good Samaritan; 930. *School of Giorgione*, Garden of Love; *1450. *Sebastian del Piombo*, Holy Fam- ily; 1031. *Giov. Gir. Savoldo*, Mary Magdalen at the Sepulchre.

*270. *Titian*, Christ and Mary Magdalen after the Resurrection ('Noli me tangere').

A youthful work of the master. The slenderness of the figures, which are conceived in a dignified but somewhat mundane spirit, and the style of the landscape reveal the influence of Giorgione.

1213. *Gentile Bellini* (d. 1507), Portrait of a mathematician; 636. *Palma Vecchio* (d. 1528; pupil of Titian), Portrait of a poet; 623. *Girolamo da Treviso* (a follower of Raphael; d. 1544), Madonna and Child (mentioned by Vasari as the painter's masterpiece); *280. *Giovanni Bellini*, Madonna of the Pomegranate.

*300. *Cima da Conegliano*, Madonna and Child; 1105. *Lorenzo Lotto* (1480-1555), The apostolic prothonotary Juliano; *777. *Paolo Morando*, Madonna and Child, with John the Baptist and an angel, a masterpiece of this 'Raphael of Verona'; 1165. *Moretto*, Virgin and Child, with saints; 1202. *Bonifazio Veronese* (d. 1540), Madonna and Child, with saints; 750. *Vittore Carpaccio* (Venice, contemporary of Giov. Bellini; d. after 1522), Madonna and Child, with the Doge Giovanni Mocenigo in adoration; 699. *Lotto*, Portraits of Agostino and Niccolò della Torre (1515); 742. *Moroni*, Lawyer; 1123. *Venetian School* (16th cent.), Venus and Adonis; *268. *Paolo Veronese* (*Caliari*, 1528-88), Adoration of the Magi, painted in 1573 for the church of St. Sylvester at Venice. *Giovanni Bellini*, *726. Christ in Gethsemane, an early work revealing the influence of Mantegna, who has treated the same subject (comp. No. 1417, p. 200); 812. Death of St. Peter Martyr (a late work). 694. *Catena* (d. 1531), St. Jerome in his study; 1130. Ascribed to *Tintoretto*, Christ washing the feet of his disciples; 1490 and (farther on) 1489. *Venetian School* (14th cent.), Venetian senators; *299. *Moretto*, Italian nobleman; 3. *School of Titian*, Concert. — 1313. *Tintoretto*, Origin of the Milky Way (ceiling-decoration).

Jupiter, descending through the air, bears the infant Hercules towards Juno, while the milk escaping from the breasts of the goddess resolves itself into the constellation known as the Via Lactea or Milky Way.

674. *Paris Bordone* (Treviso, celebrated for his female portraits; d. 1571), A lady of Genoa. — *294. *Paolo Veronese*, Family of Darius at the feet of Alexander the Great, bought for 13,650*l*.

'In excellent condition; perhaps the only existing criterion by which to estimate the genuine original colouring of Paul Veronese. It is remarkable how entirely the genius of the painter precludes criticism on the quaintness of the treatment. Both the incident and the personages are, as in a Spanish play, romantically travestied'. — *Rumohr* (MS. notes).

Mr. Ruskin calls this picture 'the most precious Paul Veronese in the world' ... 'The possession of the Pisani Veronese will happily enable the English public and the English artist to convince themselves how sincerity and simplicity in statements of fact, power of draughtmanship, and joy in colour were associated in a perfect balance in the great workmen in Venice'.

637. *Paris Bordone*, Daphnis and Chloë; 1024. *Moroni*, Italian ecclesiastic; 778. *Martino da Udine*, surnamed *Pellegrino da San Daniele* (Friuli, pupil of Bellini; d. 1547), Madonna and Child; *1047. *Lotto*, Family group; 173. *Bassano*, Portrait of a nobleman; *297. *Il Romanino* (*Girolamo Romani*, Brescia, a rival of Moretto; d. 1566), Nativity (an altar-piece in five compartments).

On Screens: 634. *Cima da Conegliano*, Madonna and Child; *Giovanni Bellini*, *1440. St. Dominic, 1233. Blood of the Redeemer (an early, symbolical work, recalling the fancies of mediæval mysticism). — 631. *Francesco Bissolo* (d. about 1530), Portrait of a woman; 695. *Andrea Previtali* (d. 1528), Monk adoring the Holy

Child; 736. *Bonsignori* (Verona; d. 1519), Portrait of a senator, dated 1487; 1476. *A. Meldolla*, surnamed *Schiavone* (1522-82), Jupiter and Semele. — 1418. *Antonello da Messina* (said to have imported painting in oil from Flanders into Italy; d. after 1493), St. Jerome. — 673. *Ant. da Messina*, Salvator Mundi, 1465.

'The earliest of his pictures which we now possess. It is a solemn but not an elevated mask; half Flemish, half Italian'. — *C. & C.*

Antonello da Messina, 1166. Crucifixion (in a mountainous landscape), 1141. Portrait of a young man (painted in 1474). — 1409. *Cordelle Agii* (*Andrea Cordegliaghi*; pupil of Giov. Bellini), Marriage of St. Catharine. — 808. *Giovanni Bellini*, St. Peter Martyr (with very delicate gradations in the flesh tones).

*189. *Giov. Bellini*, The Doge Leonardo Loredano.

This masterly portrait is remarkable alike for its drawing, its colouring, and its expression of character. Loredano, who held office from 1501 to 1521, was one of the most powerful of the Venetian Doges. His face is that of a born ruler — 'fearless, faithful, patient, impenetrable, implacable — every word a fate' *(Ruskin).*

599. *Giov. Bellini*, Madonna and Child; 1478. *Giov. Mansueti* (about 1500), Symbolic representation of the Crucifixion; *Franc. Mantegna* (son of Andrea; d. after 1517), 1106. Resurrection, 1381. Holy Women at the Sepulchre, 639. Christ and Mary Magdalen in the Garden; 907. *Carlo Crivelli* (d. ca. 1493; Venice), St. Catharine and the Magdalen; *281. *Marco Basaiti* (Venetian School; ca. 1520), St. Jerome reading; 1173. *School of Giorgione*, Unknown subject; 1310. *School of Bellini (Cima da Conegliano?)*, Ecce Homo.

*269. After *Giorgione* (*Giorgio Barbarelli*, a fellow-pupil of Titian under Giov. Bellini; d. 1511), Knight in armour.

A slightly altered and admirable repetition of the knight in Giorgione's altar-piece at Castelfranco. Mr. Ruskin speaks of the original altar-piece at Castelfranco as one of the two best pictures in the world.

1160. *Venetian School of the 15th cent.*, Adoration of the Magi; 1120. *Cima da Conegliano*, St. Jerome in the wilderness (on panel).

Room VIII. PADUAN AND EARLY VENETIAN SCHOOLS. To the left: 668. *Carlo Crivelli*, The Beato Ferretti; 1145. *Andrea Mantegna* (d. 1506; School of Padua), Samson and Delilah (on the tree is the motto 'foemina diabolo tribus assibus est mala peior'); 804. *Marco Marziale* (Venetian painter; flor. ca. 1492-1507), Virgin and Child.

771. *Bono da Ferrara* (15th cent.), St. Jerome in the desert. — 776. *Vittore Pisano of Verona*, often called *Vittore Pisanello* (founder of the Veronese school, painter and medallist; d. 1451), SS. Anthony and George, with a vision of the Virgin and Child.

In the frame are inserted casts of two of Pisano's medals. The one above represents Leonello d'Este, his patron; the other, the painter himself.

*1436. *Pisano*, Vision of St. Eustace; *Antonio Vivarini* (d. ca. 1470), 768. SS. Peter and Jerome, 1284. SS. Francis and Mark; 1417. *A. Mantegna*, The Agony in the Garden, an early work, from the Northbrook Gallery (comp. No. 726, p. 199, by Bellini); 807. *Crivelli*, Madonna and Child enthroned; *274. *A. Mantegna*,

Virgin and Child with the Baptist and the Magdalen (conscientiously minute in execution and of plastic distinctness in the outlines); 803. *Marziale*, Circumcision (1500), with fine portrait-heads.

*902. *Andrea Mantegna*, Triumph of Scipio, or the reception of the Phrygian mother of the gods (Cybele) among the publicly recognised divinities of Rome.

In obedience to the Delphic oracle, the 'worthiest man in Rome' was selected to receive the goddess, and the choice fell upon Publius Cornelius Scipio Nasica (B.C. 204). The picture was painted for a Venetian nobleman, Francesco Cornaro, whose family claimed to be descended from the Roman *gens Cornelia*. It was finished in 1506, a few months before the painter's death, and is 'a tempera', in chiaroscuro. It is not so important a work of Mantegna as the series at Hampton Court (p. 409), but also exhibits Mantegna's wonderful feeling for the antique and his share in 'that sincere passion for the ancient world which was the dominating intellectual impulse of his age.'

284. *Bartolommeo Vivarini* (Venice; end of the 15th cent.), Virgin and Child, with SS. Paul and Jerome; 1125. Ascribed to *Mantegna*, Two allegorical figures of the Seasons, in grisaille; 602. *Crivelli*, Dead Christ supported by angels; 904. *Gregorio Schiavone* (the 'Slavonian', a native of Dalmatia; ca. 1470), Madonna and Child.

*724. *Carlo Crivelli*, Madonna and Child, with saints.

This picture is known, from the swallow introduced, as the 'Madonna della rondine'. 'It may be said of the predella, which represents St. Catharine, St. Jerome in the wilderness, the Nativity of our Lord, the Martyrdom of St. Sebastian, and St. George and the Dragon, that Crivelli never concentrated so much power on any small composition'. — *C. & C.*

Above, 749. *Niccolo Giolfino* (Verona; ca. 1465-1520), Portraits; *Crivelli*, 788. Madonna and saints (large altar-piece in 13 sections, painted in 1476), 739. Annunciation, dated 1486 (the heads are pleasing and the motions graceful), 906. Madonna in prayer.

Central Octagon. VARIOUS SCHOOLS. In the angles of the octagon: *Paolo Veronese*, 1324. Scorn, 1325. Respect, 1326. Happy Union, 1318. Unfaithfulness, a series of allegorical groups from the decoration of a ceiling. To the left (on entering from R. VIII): 1240 and (farther on) 1239. *Girolamo Mocetto* (Venice, painter and engraver; ca. 1490-1514), Massacre of the Innocents; 1211, 1212. *Domenico Morone* (Veronese school; b. 1442), Tournament scenes; 1135, 1136. *Veronese School* (15th cent.), Legend of Trajan and the widow; *Liberale da Verona* (1451-1535), 1336. Death of Dido, 1134. Madonna and Child with angels; 97. *School of P. Veronese*, Rape of Europa; 1121. *Venetian School*, Young man; 41. *Giov. Cariani*(?), Death of St. Peter Martyr; 285. *Francesco Morone* (early Veronese painter; d. 1529), Madonna and Child; 1241. *Pedro Campaña* (b. 1503), Martha bringing Mary Magdalen to hear Christ (temporarily placed here). — 1098. *Bart. Montagna* (d. 1523), Madonna and Child, 802. Madonna and Child; 931. *P. Veronese*, Mary Magdalen laying aside her jewels. — 632, 633. *Girolamo da Santacroce* (flourished 1520-49), Saints; 630. *Gregorio Schiavone*, Madonna and Child enthroned, with saints (altar-piece).

Room IX, adjoining Room VII. Schools of Lombardy and Parma. To the left: 806. *Boccaccio Boccaccino* (Cremona; d. 1525), Procession to Calvary; 1337. *Giov. Antonio Bazzi,* surnamed *Sodoma* (Siena, pupil of Leon. da Vinci; d. 1549), Head of Christ. *Ambrogio Borgognone* (architect and painter, Milanese School; ca. 1455-1523), 1410. Virgin and Child; 1077. Christ bearing the Cross, Virgin and Child, Agony in Gethsemane, a triptych, one of the master's earlier works; 298. Marriage of St. Catharine of Alexandria, to the right St. Catharine of Siena. Above, 1465. *Gaudenzio Ferrari* (d. after 1547), Resurrection; 286. *Francesco Tacconi* (Cremona; d. after 1490), Virgin and Child enthroned (the only signed work of this master extant); 729. *Vincenzo Foppa* (d. 1492), Adoration of the Magi; 1416. *Filippo Mazzola* (d. 1505), Virgin and Child; 700. *Lanini* (d. ca. 1578), Holy Family, with Mary Magdalen, Pope Gregory, and St. Paul (dated 1543); 33. *Parmigiano (Francesco Maria Mazzola;* d. 1540), Vision of St. Jerome; *15. *Correggio (Antonio Allegri;* d. 1534), Ecce Homo; 1052. *Lombard School,* Portrait of a young man; 76. After *Correggio,* Christ's Agony in the Garden; 1661, 1662. *Ambrogio de Predis* (ca. 1500), Angels making music.

*1093. *Leonardo da Vinci* (1452-1519), Madonna and Child, with John the Baptist and an angel, resembling 'La Vierge aux Rochers' in the Louvre, bought from the Earl of Suffolk in 1881 for 9000*l.* The nimbi and cross are later additions.

1300. *Milanese School,* Virgin and Child; *23. *Correggio,* 'La Madonna della Cesta', or 'La Vierge au Panier'.

*10. *Correggio,* Mercury instructing Cupid in the presence of Venus, of the master's latest period.

This picture has passed through the hands of numerous owners, chiefly of royal blood. It was bought by Charles I. of England with the rest of the Duke of Mantua's collection in 1630. From England it passed to Spain, Naples, and then to Vienna, where it was purchased by the Marquis of Londonderry, who sold it to the National Gallery. It has suffered considerable damage during its wanderings.

Mr. Ruskin, who describes Correggio as 'the captain of the painter's art as such, the master of the art of laying colour so as to be lovely' couples this picture with Titian's Bacchus (p. 198), as one of the two paintings in the Gallery he would last part with.

1295. *Girolamo Giovenone* (Vercelli; early 16th cent.), Madonna and Child with saints; 1665. *A. de Predis,* Portrait; *923. *Andrea da Solario* (Milan; d. after 1515), Venetian senator (recalling Anton. da Messina); 1438. *Milanese School,* Head of John the Baptist; 1200, 1201. *Macrino d'Alba* (ca. 1500), Saints; *734. *Solario,* Portrait, a work of much power and finish (1505); 779, 780. *Ambrogio Borgognone,* Family portraits, painted on two fragments of a silken standard, attached to wood; *728. *Giov. Ant. Boltraffio* (pupil of Leonardo at Milan; d. 1516), Madonna and Child (an effective, though simple and quiet composition, suffused in a cool light); 753. *Altobello Melone* (Cremona; 15th cent.), Christ and the Disciples on the way to Emmaus; 1152. *Martino Piazza* (16th cent.),

John the Baptist; 1149. *Marco da Oggiono* (Milanese School, pupil of Leonardo; d. 1540), Madonna and Child; 219. *Lombard School* (16th cent.), Dead Christ; 1466. *Lelio Orsi* (1511-86), The road to Emmaus; *1144. *Sodoma*, Madonna and Child, with St. Catharine of Siena, St. Peter, and a monk; *18. *Bernardino Luini* (Milan; pupil of Leonardo da Vinci; ca. 1475-1535), Christ disputing with the doctors

Visitors who wish to make an unbroken survey of Italian art should now pass on to R. XIII (p. 211), with works of the later Italian schools.

Room X. DUTCH AND FLEMISH SCHOOLS. Besides works of Rubens and Van Dyck, the chiefs of the Flemish school of the 17th cent., this room contains good examples of Rembrandt, their great Dutch contemporary, principally of his later period. His pupils, Nicolas Maas or Maes and Pieter de Hooghe, are also well represented. The small pictures by Flemish masters of the 15th cent., though neither usually of the first class, nor always to be attributed to the painters whose names they bear, are yet of great interest, as affording a varied survey of the realistic manner of the school.

To the left: 1305. *G. Donck* (17th cent.), Jan van Hensbeeck and his wife; 237. *Rembrandt van Ryn* (*Harmensz* or *Hermanszoon*, Amsterdam; 1607-69), Portrait of a woman (one of his latest works, dated 1666); 1168. *Van der Vliet* (Delft; d. 1642), Portrait of a Jesuit; *775. *Rembrandt*, Old lady (1634); 223. *L. Bakhuizen* (1631-1708), Dutch shipping; 239. *A. van der Neer* (1603-77; Amsterdam), River by moonlight; *1248. *Bart. van der Helst* (one of the best Dutch portrait-painters; b. at Haarlem in 1611 or 1612; d. 1670), Portrait of a girl (dated 1645); *1247. *Nicolas Maes* or *Maas* (1632-93; figure-painter at Dort, a pupil of Rembrandt), The card-players (an exceedingly graphic group of lifesize figures); *53. *Aelbert Cuyp* (Dort; 1605-91), Landscape with cattle and figures (with masterly treatment of light and great transparency of shadow); above, 981. *W. van de Velde the Younger* (1633-1707), Storm at sea; 51. *Rembrandt*, Jewish merchant; 954. *Cornelis Huysmans* (1648-1727; Malines and Antwerp), Landscape; 38. *Peter Paul Rubens* (Antwerp; 1577-1640), Rape of the Sabine women; 901. *Jan Looten* (Dutch landscape-painter in the style of Van Everdingen; d. ca. 1681), Landscape.

*672. *Rembrandt*, His own portrait (1640).

'If Rembrandt has often chosen to represent himself in more or less eccentric costumes, he has here preferred to pose as a man of quiet and dignified simplicity .... The portrait is admirable in design and tone. A delicate and warm light shines from above on part of the forehead, cheek, and nose, and imparts a golden hue to the shirt collar, while a stray beam brings the hand into like prominence. The execution is excellent, the effect of light delicate and vigorous'. — *Vosmaer*.

*243. *Rembrandt*, Portrait of a man, dated 1659.

'This picture is one of those darkly coloured pieces which Rembrandt meant to be strongly lighted. The head alone is in the full light, the

hands are in the half-light only. The most conspicuous colours are vivid
brown and red. The features, with the grey beard and moustache,
though heavily painted, are well defined, and look almost as if chiselled
by the brush, while the effect is enhanced by the greenish tint of the
colouring. The face, and the dark eyes in particular, are full of ani-
mation. The whole work is indeed a marvel of colouring, expression, and
poetry'. — *Vosmaer.*

Rembrandt, *1674. Burgomaster; *1675 (farther on), Old woman.
These two fine portraits were purchased from Lord de Saumarez in
1899 for 15,050*l*. The former seems to be in the nature of a study.

49. *Sir Anthony van Dyck* (1599-1641), Portrait.

*1172. *Van Dyck*, Charles I. mounted on a dun horse and
attended by Sir Thomas Morton.
This fine specimen of Van Dyck was acquired at the sale of the
Blenheim Collection in 1884 for 17,500*l*. It was originally in Somerset
House and was sold by Cromwell for 150*l*. The great Duke of Marl-
borough discovered and bought it at Munich.

679. *Ferd. Bol* (pupil of Rembrandt; d. 1680), Astronomer
(1652); 732. *A. van der Neer*, Canal scene (daylight scenes and
canvases of so large a size as this were rarely executed by Van der
Neer); 190. *Rembrandt*, Jewish Rabbi; *52. *Van Dyck*, Portrait
(probably Cornelius van der Geest); 146. *A. Storck* (d. 1710?),
Shipping on the Maes. — 194. *Rubens*, Judgment of Paris.
Smaller repetitions exist in the Louvre and at Dresden. The London
picture, though possibly not painted entirely by Rubens' own hand, was
certainly executed under his guidance and supervision.

71. *Jan Both* (Utrecht, painter of Italian landscapes in the style
of Claude; d. after 1662), Landscape with figures.

*45. *Rembrandt*, The Woman taken in adultery, dated 1644.
'The colouring of the 'Woman taken in adultery' is in admirable
keeping. A subdued light, an indescribable kind of glow, illumines the
whole work, and pervades it with a mysterious harmony. The idea of
the work is most effectively enhanced by the magic of chiaroscuro . . . .
The different lights, the strongest of which is thrown on the yellow robe
of the woman, on the group on the stairs, and on the gilded altar, are
united by means of very skilful shading. The whole of the background
is bathed in dark but warm shades'. — *Vosmaer.*

*47. *Rembrandt*, Adoration of the Shepherds (1646); *1252.
Frans Snyders (animal and fruit painter, Antwerp; 1579-1657),
Fruit; *66. *Rubens*, Autumnal landscape, with a view of the Château de Stein, the painter's house, near Malines; 1137. *Jac. van
Oost* (d. 1671), Portrait of a boy; 166. *Rembrandt*, Capuchin friar;
1222. *Melchior d'Hondecoeter* (animal-painter at Utrecht; d. 1695),
Foliage, birds, and insects. — 289. *Gerrit Lundens* (1622-77; Amsterdam), Amsterdam Musketeers.
'This picture, although but a greatly reduced copy of the renowned
work by Rembrandt in the State Museum at Amsterdam, has a unique
interest as representing the pristine condition of its great original before
it was mutilated on all four sides and shorn of some of its figures . . . .
in order to suit the picture to the dimensions of a room to which it was
at that time (early part of last century) removed'. — *Official Catalogue.*

238. *Jan Weenix the Younger* (Amsterdam; d. 1719), Dead game;
*207. *Nicholas Maas*, The idle servant, a masterpiece, dated 1655;

*794. *P. de Hooghe* (1632–81), Courtyard of a Dutch house; 140. *Bart. van der Helst*, Portrait of a lady; 685. *Meindert Hobbema* (Amsterdam, pupil of Ruysdael; 1638–1709), Landscape; *J. van Ruysdael* (Haarlem; 1628–82), 989. Water-mills, 628, *627. Landscapes with waterfalls; *Van Dyck*, 877. Portrait of himself, 50. Emp. Theodosius refused admission to the Church of Sant' Ambrogio at Milan by St. Ambrose (copied, with slight alterations, from Rubens's picture at Vienna); 948. *Rubens*, Landscape (sketch); 1096. *Jan Weenix*, Hunting scene; 1053. *Emanuel de Witte* (d. 1692; Amsterdam), Interior of a church; *680. *Van Dyck* (after Rubens), Miraculous Draught of Fishes. *David Teniers the Younger* (genre-painter in Antwerp, pupil of A. Brouwer and Rubens; 1610–90), *805. Old woman peeling a pear; 817. Château of the painter at Perck, with portraits of himself and his family. 986. *Ruysdael*, Water-mills; 137. *J. van Goyen* (1596–1656), Landscape; 1289. *A. Cuyp*, Landscape with cattle; *Rubens*, 59. Brazen Serpent, 279. Horrors of War, coloured sketch for a large picture in the Pitti Palace at Florence; 242. *Teniers*, Players at tric-trac or backgammon; *Rubens*, 157. Landscape, 67. Holy Family; 1327. *J. van Goyen*, Winter-scene; 1008. *Pieter Potter* (?; father of Paul Potter; d. 1652), Stag-hunt; 152. *Van der Neer*, Evening-scene, with figures and cattle by *Cuyp*, whose name is inscribed on the pail; 1012. *Matthew Merian* (b. at Bâle in 1621, d. 1687; painted portraits at Nuremberg and Frankfort), Portrait of a man; 1050. *L. Bakhuizen*, Sea-piece.

*278. *Rubens*, Triumph of Julius Cæsar, freely adapted from Mantegna's famous cartoons, now in Hampton Court Palace.

The Flemish painter strives to add richness to the scene by Bacchanalian riot and the sensuality of imperial Rome. His elephants twist their trunks, and trumpet to the din of cymbals; negroes feed the flaming candelabra with scattered frankincense; the white oxen of Clitumnus are loaded with gaudy flowers, and the dancing maidens are dishevelled Mænads. But the rhythmic procession of Mantegna, modulated to the sounds of flutes and soft recorders, carries our imagination back to the best days and strength of Rome. His priests and generals, captives and choric women are as little Greek as they are modern. In them awakes to a new life the spirit-quelling energy of the Republic. The painter's severe taste keeps out of sight the insolence and orgies of the Empire; he conceives Rome as Shakspeare did in '*Coriolanus*' (*Symonds*).

57. *Rubens*, Conversion of St. Bavon; 737. *Ruysdael*, Landscape with waterfall; 46. *Rubens*, Peace and War (presented by the painter to Charles I. in 1630); 955. *Corn. van Poelenburg* (d. 1667; Utrecht, imitator of the Roman School), Ruin, with women bathing; 1061. *Egbert van der Poel* (d. 1664; Delft), View of Delft after the explosion of a powder-mill in 1654; 970. *Gabriel Metsu* (Amsterdam; 1630–67), The drowsy landlady; *963. *Isaac van Ostade* (landscape and figure painter, pupil of his elder brother Adriaen; d. 1649), Frozen river (glowing with light, very transparent in colour, and delicate in treatment); 1005. *Nic. Berchem* (1620–83), Landscape; 1352. *Fréd. de Moucheron* (d 1686), Land-

scape; *B. Fabritius* (flourished 1650-72), 1339. Birth of John the Baptist, 1338. Adoration of the Shepherds; *757. *School of Rembrandt*, Christ blessing little children; 1221. *A. de Pape* (d. 1666), Interior; 1255. *Jan Jansz van de Velde* (a rare Amsterdam painter; ca. 1622-56), Still-life; 1256. *Herman Steenwyck* (Delft), Still-life; 156. *Van Dyck*, Study of horses; 72. *Rembrandt*, Landscape; 151. *Jan van Goyen*, River-scene; *1277. *Nic. Maas*, Portrait (dated 1666); 1060. *Philip Wouverman* (Haarlem; 1619-68), Vedettes, an early work; 154. *Teniers the Younger*, Musical party; 1095. *Jan Lievens* (1607-74), Portrait; *797. *A. Cuyp*, Portrait, dated 1649; 924. *P. Neeffs* (d. ca. 1660), Church-interior; 1000. *Bakhuizen*, Shipping; 158. *Teniers*, Boors regaling; 221. *Rembrandt*, The artist at an advanced age.

On SCREENS: 1446, 1445. *Rachel Ruysch* (1664-1750), Studies of flowers; 1442. *L. Bakhuizen*, Ships in a gale; 968. *Gerard Dou* (Leyden; 1613-75), Portrait of his wife; 199. *Godfried Schalcken* (Dutch genre - painter, famed for his candle-light effects, and a pupil of Gerard Dou; d. 1706), Lesbia weighing jewels against her sparrow (Catullus, Carmen iii).

*896. *Gerard Terburg* or *Ter Borch* (Deventer, the greatest Dutch painter of conversation-pieces; d. 1681), Peace of Münster.

'This picture represents the Plenipotentiaries of Philip IV. of Spain and the Delegates of the Dutch United Provinces assembled in the Rath-haus at Münster, on the 15th of May, 1648, for the purpose of ratifying and confirming by oath the Treaty of Peace between the Spaniards and the Dutch, signed on the 30th of January previous'. (*Catalogue*). It is one of the master's very finest works.

Gerard Dou, 1415. Portrait of Anna Maria van Schurman, 192. Portrait of himself; 796. *Jan van Huysum* (1682-1749), Flowers.

*54. *Rembrandt*, Woman wading, dated 1654.

'Her eyes are cast down, her head inclined. Is she hesitating to enter the water in which she is mirrored? .... The charm and value of this painting lie in the brillant touch and impasto, the warm and forcible colouring, the middle tints, and the admirable modelling'. — *Vosmaer*, '*Rembrandt, sa Vie et ses Œuvres*'.

Rembrandt, 43. Descent from the Cross, 1400. Christ before Pilate; *1114-1118. *Gonzales Coques* (Antwerp; d. 1684), The five senses, allegorical and finely executed half-lengths; *H. Sorgh* (Rotterdam, pupil of Teniers the Younger; d. 1682), 1056. Man and woman drinking, 1055 (farther on), Card-players; 1132. *Hendrick Steenwyck the Younger* (b. at Frankfort, worked at Antwerp and at London, where he supplied architectural backgrounds to Van Dyck's portraits; 1580-1649), Interior; 1011. *Coques*, Portrait.

Room XI. DUTCH AND FLEMISH SCHOOLS. To the left: 202. *M. d'Hondecoeter*, Poultry ('this cock was Hondecoeter's favourite bird, which he is said to have taught to stand to him in a fixed position as a model'); 1312. *Jan Victors* or *Victoors* (b. at Amsterdam in 1620), Village cobbler; 1390. *J. van Ruysdael*, View near Scheveningen; 1423. *J. van Ravesteyn* (1572-1657), Portrait of a lady; 1420. *G. A. Berckheyde* (Haarlem; 1638-98), View in Haarlem; 1341. *Cornelius Gerritz Dekker* or *Decker* (Haarlem; d. 1678), Landscape; 1231. *Sir Anthony More* or *Moro* (b. at Utrecht in 1512; painted portraits in England), Portrait; 1243. *Dutch School*, Portrait; 1462. *Hendrik Dubbels* (Amsterdam; d. 1676), Sea-piece; 1346. *H. van Avercamp* (d. after 1663), Winter-scene; 1469. *Willem K. Heda* (d. ca. 1680). Still-life; 1397. *Dutch School*, Old woman sewing; 44. *J. van Ruysdael*, Bleaching ground; 1293. *J. M. Molenaer* (d. 1668), Musical party; 1001. *J. van Huysum* (d. 1740), Flowers; 1251 and (farther on) 1021. *Frans Hals* (ca. 1580-1666), Portraits; 1015. *Jan van Os* (1744-1808), Still-life; 1680. *Dutch School* (17th cent.; attributed to K. Dujardin), Portrait; 1002. *Jac. Walscappelle* (d. after 1717), Flowers and fruit; 78. *N. Berchem*, Landscape; 1447. *A. F. van der Meulen* (1632-90; painted for Louis XIV.; d. at Brussels), Hunting party; 1007. *Jan Wils* (d. before 1670), Landscape; 1094. *Sir A. More* (?), Portrait; 1010. *Dirck van Delen* (architectural painter in Zeeland; 17th cent.), Extensive palatial buildings of Renaissance architecture, with figures by *A. Palamedesz*; *1292. *Jan van Bylert* (Utrecht; 1603-71), Family group; 155. *D. Teniers the Younger*, The misers; 1348. *Adriaen van de Velde* (1635-72), Landscape, 1380. *Jan van Os*, Fruit and flowers; 1329. *Q. Brekelenkam* (d. 1668), Interior; 1342. *J. de Wet* (17th cent.), Landscape; 959. *Jan Both*, River-scene; 746. *Jac. van Ruysdael*, Landscape; 1439. *Salomon van Ruysdael* (uncle of J. van Ruysdael; d. 1670), River-scene; *G. Schalcken*, 997. Old woman, 998. The duet; 1287. *Dutch School*, Interior of an artgallery; 1278. *Hendrik Gerritz Pot* (d. ca. 1656), Convivial party; 1074. *Dirck Hals* (younger brother of Frans; d. 1656), Merry party; 1399. *G. Terburg*, Portrait of a gentleman; 1383. *Jan Vermeer of Delft* (1632-75), Young lady at a spinet; 1004. *N. Berchem*, Italian landscape; 1387. *Willem C. Duyster* (Amsterdam; 1599-1635), Players at tric-trac; 1443. *H. Steenwyck the Younger*, Churchinterior; *C. Janssens* (b. at Amsterdam, ca. 1594; painted in England), 1320. Aglonius Voon, 1321 (farther on), Cornelia Remoens; *1459. *Gerbrand van den Eeckhout* (1621-74), The wine-contract; *Jan Both*, 956. Italian scene, 209. Landscape (figures by *Poelenburg*); 1386. *Willem C. Duyster*, Soldiers quarrelling; 1345. *Jan Wouverman* (landscape-painter at Haarlem), Landscape; *1660. *A. van der Werff* (1659-1722). Portrait of the artist; 1311. *Jan Beerstraaten* (1622-66), Winter-scene; *212. *Thos. de Keyser* (Amsterdam; about 1660), Merchant and clerk; 1294. *W. de Poorter* (d. after 1645), Allegorical subject; 1481. *C. P. Bega*, The philosopher; 1444. *Ger. van Honthorst* (1590-1656), Peasants warming themselves; 1451. *G. A. Berckheyde*, Church-interior; 1353. *M. Ryckaert* (1587-1631), Landscape with satyrs; 953. *Teniers*, Toper; 1401. *Pieter Snyers* (1681-1752), Still-life; 1479. *Avercamp*, Ice-scene.

We now again pass through Room X in order to reach —

Room XII. PEEL COLLECTION. This is a collection of Flemish and Dutch cabinet-pieces, chiefly works of the very first rank.

819. *Bakhuizen*, Off the mouth of the Thames; *W. van de Velde*, 872. Shipping, 876. Gale.

*873. *W. van de Velde*, Coast of Scheveningen.
'The numerous figures are by Adriaen van de Velde. The union of these two great masters makes this one of the most charming pictures of the Dutch school'. — *W.*

*834. *P. de Hooghe*, Dutch interior (broad, full sunlight effect); 818. *Bakhuizen*, Coast-scene; 865. *Jan van de Cappelle* (marine painter of the 17th cent., at Amsterdam; under the influence of Rembrandt), Coast-scene. — *864. *Gerard Terburg*, Guitar-lesson.
'Terburg may be considered as the creator of what are called conversation-pieces, and is at the same time the most eminent master in that line. In delicacy of execution he is inferior to none; nay in a certain delicate blending he is superior to all. But none can be compared to him in the magical harmony of his silver tones, and in the gradations of the aërial perspective'. — *W.*

853. *Rubens*, Triumph of Silenus; *839. *Metsu*, Music-lesson; 884. *Wynants* (d. ca. 1680), Landscape (figures by *A. van de Velde*).
*852. *Rubens*, Portrait, known as the 'Chapeau de paille'.
'The chief charm of the celebrated 'Chapeau de Paille' (chapeau de poil) consists in the marvellous triumph over a great difficulty, that of painting a head entirely in the shadow cast by the hat, and yet in the clearest and most brilliant tones'. — '*Kugler*', edited by *Crowe.*

*856. *Jan Steen* (painter of humorous conversation-pieces; Delft and the Hague; d. 1679), The music-master (an early and very carefully finished work).

*869. *Adriaen van de Velde* (brother of Willem and pupil of Wynants at Haarlem; 1639-72), Frost-scene.
'Admirably drawn, touched with great spirit, and of a very pleasing, though, for the subject, perhaps too warm a tone'. — *W.*

829. *Jan Hackaert* (Amsterdam; 17th cent.), Stag-hunt; *870, 871. *W. van de Velde*, Sea-pieces; *849. *Paul Potter* (The Hague; 1625-54), Landscape with cattle; 833. *Hobbema*, Forest-scene. — *868. *A. van de Velde*, Ford.
'The composition is very tasteful, and the contrast between the concentrated mass of light and the clear half-shadow, which is repeated in soft broken tones upon the horizon, is very attractive'. — *W.*

*826. *K. du Jardin* (1622-78), Figures and animals reposing. — *835. *Pieter de Hooghe*, Court of a Dutch house (1658).
'Excites a joyful feeling of summer. In point of fulness and depth of tone and execution one of the best pictures of the master'. — *W.*

875. *W. van de Velde*, Light breeze; 882. *Wouverman*, Landscape; 827. *K. du Jardin*, Fording the stream, dated 1657.

*830. *Hobbema*, The Avenue, Middelharnis.
'From simple and by no means beautiful materials a picture is formed which, by the feeling for nature and the power of art, makes a striking impression on the intelligent spectator. Such daylight I have never before seen in any picture. The perspective is admirable, while the gradation, from the fullest bright green in the foreground, is so delicately observed, that it may be considered a masterpiece in this respect, and

is, on the whole, one of the most original works of art with which I am acquainted'. — *W.*

866. *Van der Heyde*, Street in Cologne, with figures by *A. van de Velde;* 880. *Wouverman*, On the sea-shore, selling fish (supposed to be his last work); 874. *W. van de Velde*, Calm at sea; 828. *K. du Jardin*, Landscape, with cattle. — *846. *Adriaen van Ostade* (figure-painter at Haarlem, pupil of Frans Hals; d. 1685), The alchymist.

'The effect of light in the foreground, the predominant golden tone of extraordinary brightness and clearness, the execution equally careful and spirited, and the contrast of the deep cool chiaroscuro in the background have a peculiar charm'. — *W.*

*822. *Cuyp*, Horseman and cows in a meadow.

'Of exquisite harmony, in a bright cool light, unusual with him'. — *W.*

867. *A. van de Velde*, Farm cottage; 861. *Teniers*, River-scene. 883. *Wynants*, Landscape, with accessories by *Lingelbach* (dated 1659).

'This landscape has, in a rare degree, that serene, cool freshness of tone which so admirably expresses the character of northern scenery, and in which Wynants is quite unrivalled'. — *W.*

*832. *Hobbema*, Village, with water-mills (in a warm, summer-like tone); *836. *Phil. de Koninck* (pupil of Rembrandt; d. 1688), Landscape, figures by *A. van de Velde.* — *825. *Gerard Dou*, Poulterer's shop.

'Besides the extreme finish, in which he holds the first place, it surpasses many of his other pictures in its unusual clearness and in the agreeable and spirited heads'. — *W.*

850. *Rembrandt*, Portrait; 841. *Willem van Mieris* (d. 1747), Fish and poultry shop (1713); 855. *Ruysdael*, Landscape with a waterfall.

*878. *Wouverman*, 'La belle laitière'.

'This picture combines that delicate tone of his second period with the great force which he adopted especially toward the end of it. The effect of the dark figures relieved against the landscape is extraordinary'. — *W.*

*879. *Wouverman*, Interior of a stable (very delicately finished). — 831. *Hobbema*, Ruins of Brederode Castle.

'Strongly illumined by a sunbeam, and reflected in the dark yet clear water which surrounds them'. — *W.*

*847. *Isaac van Ostade*, Village-scene in Holland.

'This delicately drawn picture combines the greatest solidity with the most spirited execution, and the finest impasto with the greatest glow and depth of tone. Paul Potter himself could not have painted the grey horse better'. — *W.*

820. *Berchem*, Landscape, with ruin; 881. *Wouverman*, Gathering faggots; 862. *Teniers*, The husband surprised; 854. *Ruysdael*, Forest-scene; 823. *Cuyp*, River-scene, with cattle; 843. *Caspar Netscher* (pupil of Terburg, settled at The Hague; d. 1684), Children blowing soap-bubbles (1670); 863. *Teniers*, Dives in torment; 951. *David Teniers the Elder* (pupil of Rubens, and also of Elsheimer at Rome; d. 1649), Playing at bowls; 1003. *Jan Fyt* (animal-painter

at Antwerp in the time of Rubens; d. 1661), Dead birds; 957. *Jan Both*, Cattle and figures; 205. *J. W. E. Dietrich* (German School, court-painter at Dresden; d. 1774), Itinerant musicians; 964. *Van der Cappelle*, River-scene; 962, 961. *A. Cuyp*, Cattle and figures; 994. *Jan van der Heyde* (architectural and landscape painter at Amsterdam; 1637-1712), Street; 982. *A. van de Velde*, Landscape; 965. *Van der Cappelle*, River-scene; 949. *Teniers the Elder*, Rocky landscape; 984. *A. van de Velde*, Landscape; 977. *W. van de Velde*, Sea-piece; 1344. *S. van Ruysdael*, Landscape; 969. *A. van der Neer*, Frost-scene; 1421. *Jan Steen*, Terrace-scene with figures; 991. *Ruysdael*, Prostrate tree; *J. van der Heyde*, 993. Landscape, 992. Gothic and classic buildings; 1017. *Unknown Flemish Master*, Landscape (signed D. D. V., 1622); *Willem van de Velde*, 978. River-scene, 980. Dutch vessels saluting, 979. Shipping; 1006. *Berchem*, Landscape; 950. *Teniers*, Conversation; 973. *Philip Wouverman*, Sandbank in a river; 975. *Philip Wouverman*, Stag-hunt; 1683. *A. Cuyp*, Study of a horse; 983. *Adriaen van de Velde*, Bay horse, cow, and goat; 1009. *Paul Potter*, The old grey hunter; *159. *Maas*, The Dutch housewife, dated 1655; 974. *Philip de Koninck*, Hilly, wooded landscape, with a view of the Scheldt and Antwerp Cathedral; *995. *Hobbema*, Forest-landscape, of peculiarly clear chiaroscuro; 988. *Ruysdael*, Old oak; *153. *Maas*, Cradle; *Van der Cappelle*, 966. River-scene, 967. Shipping; 1013. *Hondecoeter*, Geese and ducks. *Ruysdael*, *990. Landscape (a *chef-d'oeuvre*); 987. Rocky landscape. — 952. *Teniers the Younger*, Village-fête, dated 1643.

'An admirable original repetition of the masterly picture in the possession of the Duke of Bedford, though not equal to the Bedford picture in delicacy'. — *W.*

958. *Jan Both*, Outside the walls of Rome.

*976. *Philip Wouverman*, Battle.

'Full of animated action, of the utmost transparency, and executed with admirable precision'. — *W.*

1470. *Jacob Weier* (German school; d. 1670), Battle-scene; 1288. *A. van der Neer*, Frost-scene; 971. *Wynants*, Landscape; 211 *J. van Huchtenburgh* (d. 1733), Battle; 134. *C. G. Dekker* or *Decker*, Landscape; 1347. *I. van Ostade*, Farmyard; 972. *Jan Wynants*, Landscape.

On SCREENS: 845. *Netscher*, Lady at a spinning-wheel (finished with great delicacy; 840 (farther on), *Frans van Mieris* (d. 1681), Lady feeding a parrot (these two figures, of the same size and in the same dress, afford an interesting comparison of the workmanship of the two masters). — 857-860. *Teniers*, The Seasons. — *848. *Isaac van Ostade*, Canal-scene in winter.

'The great truth, admirable treatment, and fresh feeling of a winter's day render it one of the *chefs-d'oeuvre* of the master'. — *W.*

*824. *A. Cuyp*, Ruined castle in a lake ('gilded by the most glowing evening-sun').

*838. *Gabriel Metsu*, The duet.
'Painted in the warm, full tone, which is especially valuable in his pictures'. — *W.*

*821. *Gonzales Coques*, Family portraits, amply justifying the artist's claim to be the 'Little Van Dyck'. — *844. *Netscher*, Maternal instruction.
'The ingenuous expression of the children, the delicacy of the handling, the striking effect of light, and the warm deep harmony render this one of the most pleasing pictures by Netscher'. — *W.*
Above the cupboard at the back there hangs a small copy of Rubens's 'Brazen Serpent' in this collection (No. 59, see p. 205).

999. *G. Schalcken*, Candle-light effect; 187. *P. P. Rubens*, Apotheosis of William the Silent; 1332. *Netscher*, George, 1st Earl of Berkeley (?); 985. *K. du Jardin*, Sheep and goats.
A small corner-room, entered from the passage between RR. XII and XIII, contains *Monochrome Paintings* and *Crayon Drawings*.

Room XIII. Later Italian School. What is known as the Eclectic or Academic School of Painters arose in Italy with the foundation of a large academy at Bologna by the Carracci in 1589. Its aim was to combine the peculiar excellences of the earlier masters with a closer study of nature. The best representatives of the school are grouped together in this room, which also contains examples of the later Venetian masters.

Annibale Carracci (younger brother of Lodovico, and founder along with him of the Bolognese Academy; d. 1609), 93. Silenus gathering grapes; 94. Bacchus playing to Silenus, quite in the style of the ancient frescoes. 228. *Jacopo Bassano*, Christ driving the money-changers out of the Temple; 624. Ascribed to *Giulio Romano* (Roman School, pupil of Raphael; d. 1546), Infancy of Jupiter; 135. *Canaletto* (*Antonio Canale*, of Venice; d. 1768), Landscape with ruins; 1054. *Francesco Guardi* (architectural and landscape painter, closely allied to Canaletto; d. 1793), View in Venice; 1157. *Bernardo Cavallino* (Naples; d. 1654), Nativity; 48. *Domenichino* (*Domenico Zampieri*; d. 1641), Tobias and the Angel; 22. *Guercino* (*Giovanni Francesco Barbieri*; d. 1666), Angels weeping over the body of Christ (a good example of this painter, resembling Caravaggio in the management of the light, and recalling the picture of the same subject by Van Dyck in the Antwerp Museum); 214. Ascribed to *Guido*, Coronation of the Virgin; 198. *Ann. Carracci*, Temptation of St. Anthony, unattractive; 160. *Pietro Francesco Mola* (1612–68), Repose on the Flight into Egypt; 11. *Guido Reni* (d. 1642), St. Jerome; 936. *Ferdinando Bibiena* (Bologna; 1657–1743), Performance of Othello in the Teatro Farnese at Parma.

*942. *Canaletto*, Eton College in 1746, with the Thames in the foreground.
This picture was painted during the artist's visit to England in 1746-48, perhaps, as Mr. Cook points out, in the same year (1747) that Gray published his well-known 'Ode on a distant Prospect of Eton College'.

Pietro Longhi (Venetian genre-painter, sometimes called the 'Italian Hogarth'; 1702-62), 1334. Fortune-teller, 1100. Domestic group, 1101. Masked visitors at a menagerie; 935. *Salvator Rosa* (Neapolitan landscape-painter; d. 1673), River-scene. — 937. *Canaletto*, Scuola di San Rocco, Venice.

The picture represents 'the ceremony of Giovedì Santo or Maundy Thursday, when the Doge and officers of state with the fraternity of St. Rock went in procession to the church of St. Mark to worship the miraculous blood'. — *Catalogue.*

940. *Canaletto*, Ducal Palace and Column of St. Mark, Venice; 1333. *Tiepolo* (1692-1769), Deposition from the Cross; 25. *Ann. Carracci*, St. John in the Wilderness; 939. *Canaletto*, Piazzetta of St. Mark; 851. *Seb. Ricci* (d. 1734), Venus asleep; 1206. *Salv. Rosa*, Landscape; 210. *Guardi*, Piazza of St. Mark, Venice; *Giuseppe Zais* (Venetian; d. 1784), 1296. Landscape, 1297. River-scene; 934. *Carlo Dolci* (Florentine painter of sacred subjects; d. 1686), Virgin and Child; 196. *Guido*, Susannah and the Elders ('a work', says Mr. Ruskin, 'devoid alike of art and decency'); *84. *Salv. Rosa*, Mercury and the woodman; 9. *Ann. Carracci* (?), Christ appearing to St. Peter after his Resurrection (the difficulties of foreshortening have been but partly overcome); 75. *Domenichino*, Landscape with St. George and the Dragon; 200. *Sassoferrato* (*Giov. Batt. Salvi;* d. 1685), Madonna in prayer (crude in colouring, common in form, and lighted for effect); 193. *Guido Reni*, Lot and his daughters; 163. *Canaletto*, Grand Canal, Venice; 138. *Panini* (Roman School; d. 1764), Ancient ruins. — 740. *Sassoferrato*, Madonna and Child.

The composition is not by Sassoferrato, but is from an earlier etching by Cav. Ventura Salembeni (d. 1613). See *Catalogue.*

28. *Lodovico Carracci* (d. 1619), Susannah and the Elders; *643. *Rinaldo Mantovano* (pupil of Giulio Romano), Capture of Carthagena, and the Moderation of Publius Cornelius Scipio, colouring and drawing both excellent (design probably due to Romano). — *56. *Annibale Carracci*, Landscape with figures.

'Under the influence of Titian's landscapes and of Paul Bril, who was so justly esteemed by him, Annibale acquired that grandeur of composition, and beauty of outlines, which had so great an influence upon Claude and Gaspar Poussin.' — *W.*

941. *Canaletto*, Grimani Palace, Venice; 177. *Guido Reni*, Mary Magdalen; 174. *Carlo Maratta* (Roman painter; d. 1713), Portrait of Cardinal Cerri; 172. *Caravaggio* (*Michaelangelo Amerighi*, founder of the naturalistic school of Naples; d. 1609), Christ and the Disciples at Emmaus; 127. *Canaletto*, View of the Scuola della Carità, now the Accademia delle Belle Arti, Venice; 63. *Ann. Carracci*, Landscape. — 29. *Baroccio* (*Federigo Barocci*, a follower of Correggio; 1528-1612), Holy Family ('La Madonna del Gatto', so called from the cat introduced).

'The chief intention of the picture is John the Baptist as a child, who teases a cat by showing her a bullfinch which he holds in his hand. The Virgin, Christ, and Joseph seem much amused by this cruel sport.' — *W.*

933. *Padovanino* (*Alessandro Varotari*, of Venice; d. 1650), Boy with a bird; 271. *Guido Reni*, Ecce Homo; 70. *Padovanino*, Cornelia and her children (children form this artist's favourite subject); *644. Ascribed to *Rinaldo Mantovano*, Rape of the Sabine women, and Reconciliation between the Romans and Sabines (these pictures recall, in many respects, Raphael's frescoes in the Vatican); 77. *Domenichino*, Stoning of St. Stephen; 69. *Pietro Fran. Mola* (d. 1668), St. John in the wilderness; 1059. *Canaletto*, Church of San Pietro di Castello, Venice; 88. *Ann. Carracci*, Erminia taking refuge with the shepherds (from Tasso); 938. *Canaletto*, Regatta on the Canale Grande, Venice; 85. *Domenichino*, St. Jerome and the angel; *191. *Guido Reni*, Youthful Christ embracing St. John, a very characteristic work, and the best picture by Guido in this collection; 1058. *Canaletto*, Canal Reggio, Venice.

On a SCREEN: 1429. *Canaletto* (?), Interior of the Rotunda at Ranelagh (p. 369); 1454. *F. Guardi*, Gondola; 1192, 1193. *Tiepolo*, Sketches for altar-pieces.

Room XIV. SPANISH SCHOOL. To the left: 1376. *Velazquez* (d. 1660), Duel in the Prado near Madrid (sketch); 1286. *Bartolome Esteban Murillo* (influenced by Velazquez and Van Dyck; d. 1682), Boy drinking; *745. *Velazquez*, Philip IV.; 1676. *F. de Herrera* (1576-1656), Christ and the Doctors; *741. *Velazquez*, Dead warrior ('Orlando muerto'); 1457. *Domenico Theotocopuli* (d. 1625), surnamed *Il Greco*, Christ expelling the traders; 1308. *J. B. del Mazo* (1610-87), Portrait; *47. *Murillo*, Spanish peasant boy.

1434. *Velazquez*, A Betrothal (little more than a sketch).

This picture was at one time believed to represent the betrothal of the daughter of Philip IV. to the Emperor Leopold, but it is perhaps more probable that it depicts the less magnificent betrothal of the painter's own daughter to his confrère El Mazo (see above, No. 1308). In this case the knight of Santiago seated at the table is probably a portrait of Velazquez.

*197. *Velazquez*, Philip IV. hunting the wild boar; 1291. *Juan de Valdes Leal* (1630-91), Assumption; 1122. *D. Theotocopuli*, A Cardinal; *Velazquez*, 1375. Christ at the house of Martha; 1129. Philip IV. (bought at the Hamilton sale for 6300 *l.*); *13. *Murillo*, Holy Family; *1315. *Velazquez*, Portrait of Admiral Pulido-Pareja; *Francesco Goya* (1746-1828), 1473. Portrait, 1472. Scene from a play; 1257. *Murillo*, Birth of the Virgin; *Josef Ribera*, surnamed *Lo Spagnoletto*, 235. Dead Christ, 244. Shepherd and lamb; *1148. *Velazquez*, Scourging of Christ; 1471. *Goya*, Picnic: 1229. *Morales* (1509-86; surnamed 'the Divine' from his love of religious subjects), Holy Family, a highly finished little work, recalling the Flemish manner; *Zurbaran* (d. 1662), 230. Franciscan monk, *232. Nativity (formerly considered an early work of Velazquez); *176. *Murillo*, St. John and the Lamb.

Room XV. GERMAN SCHOOL. To the left: *658. *Early German School* (formerly ascribed to Martin Schongauer), Death of the Virgin;

707. *German School* (15th cent.), Two saints; 291. *Lucas Cranach* (1472–1553), Young lady; 1424. *A. Elsheimer* (b. at Frankfort 1578; d. at Rome 1620), Tobias and the angel; 257. Attributed to the *Meister von Liesborn* (ca. 1465), Purification of the Virgin and the Presentation of Christ; 1088. *German School* (16th cent.), Crucifixion; 254, 255 (farther on), 261. *Meister von Liesborn*, Saints; 251 and (farther on) 250. *Meister von Werden*, Saints; 1049. *Westphalian School* (?), Crucifixion; 687. *William of Cologne* (early Cologne painter; 14th cent.), St. Veronica with her napkin; 706. *Master of the 'Lyversberg Passion'* (Cologne; 15th cent.), Presentation in the Temple; 1087. *German School* (15–16th cent.), Mocking of Christ; 259. *Meister von Liesborn*, Head of Christ; 262. *School of the Meister von Liesborn*, Crucifixion; 659. *Rottenhammer* (d. 1623), Pan and Syrinx; 1014. *Elsheimer*, Martyrdom of St. Lawrence; no number, *French* or *Flemish School* (15th cent.), Lady as Mary Magdalen; *Petrus Cristus* (1444–72), Young man; *B. Bruyn* (ca. 1524–55), Portrait; *D. Bouts* (1400–75), Virgin and Child; 195. *German School* (16th cent.), Medical professor; 1232. *H. Aldegrever* (d. after 1555), Portrait; 1085. *Lower Rhenish School*, Virgin and Child (triptych); 1427. *Hans Baldung Grien* (d. 1545), Pietà; no number, *Christoph Amberger*, Portrait.

*1314. *Hans Holbein the Younger* (son and pupil of H. Holbein the Elder; worked much in London; 1497–1543), The Ambassadors.

The picture, along with Nos. 1315 (see p. 213) and 1316 (p. 197), was purchased from Lord Radnor in 1890 for 55,000*l*. The figure on the left is Jean de Dinteville, French ambassador in London in 1533, and that on the other side is George de Selve, Bishop Elect of Lisieux. The curious object in the foreground is the distorted projection of a skull, as will be seen when viewed diagonally from the right.

253. *Meister von Werden*, Mass of St. Hubert; 705. Attributed to *Meister Stephan* (d. 1451), Saints; 184. *Nicolas Lucidel* (ca. 1527–90; b. in Hainault, painted portraits at Nuremberg), Young German lady (formerly ascribed to More); 1080. *Lower Rhenish School*, Head of St. John the Baptist, with mourning angels; 1151. *German School*, Entombment; 722. *German School*, Portrait; no number, **Hans Holbein*, Princess Christina of Denmark, widow of Francesco Sforza, Duke of Milan (lent by the Duke of Norfolk); 245. *Hans Baldung Grien*, Senator (with the monogram of Albrecht Dürer, probably forged).

Room XVI (adjoining R. XIV). FRENCH SCHOOL. The French landscape-painter *Claude Lorrain* (*Claude Gellée*; 1600–1682), who is represented in this collection by several fine examples, is chiefly eminent for his skill in aërial perspective and his management of sunlight. Salvator Rosa and the two Poussins lived and painted at Rome contemporaneously with him. *Nicholas Poussin* (1594–1665), more famed as a painter of figures than of landscapes, was the brother-in-law of *Gaspar Poussin* (properly *Gaspar Dughet*; 1613–75), a follower of Claude.

On the right (N.) wall of this room hang two large landscapes by Claude and two by Turner (p. 219); the two latter bequeathed by the artist on condition that they should be hung beside the Claudes. To the left: *479. *Turner*, Sun rising in a mist. — *12. *Claude*, Landscape with figures (with the inscription on the picture itself, 'Mariage d'Isac avec Rebeca'), a work of wonderfully transparent atmosphere, recalling in its composition the celebrated picture 'Il molino' (the mill) in the Palazzo Doria at Rome, painted in 1648. — 498. *Turner*, Dido building Carthage.

This picture is not considered a favourable specimen of Turner, whose 'eye for colour unaccountably fails him' (Ruskin). Mr. Ruskin comments on the 'exquisite choice' of the group of children sailing toy boats, as expressive of the ruling passion which was to be the source of Carthage's future greatness.

The visitor will scarcely need to be referred to 'Modern Painters' (Vol. I), for Mr. Ruskin's eloquent comparison of Turner with Claude and the other landscape-painters of the old style and for his impassioned championship of the English master.

*14. *Claude*, Embarkation of the Queen of Sheba (1648).

'The effect of the morning sun on the sea, the waves of which run high, and on the masses of building which adorn the shore, producing the most striking contrast of light and shade, is sublimely poetical'. — *W.*

Then, to the right: *J. B. S. Chardin* (d. 1779), 1664. 'La Fontaine', 1258. Still-life. — 40. *Nicholas Poussin*, Landscape, with Phocion.

According to Mr. Ruskin this is 'one of the finest landscapes that ancient art has produced, — the work of a really great and intellectual mind'.

*62. *N. Poussin*, Bacchanalian dance.

This is the best example of Nicholas Poussin in the gallery. The composition is an imitation of an ancient bas-relief.

19. *Claude*, Landscape, with Narcissus and Echo; *N. Poussin*, 42. Bacchanalian festival, 39. Nursing of Bacchus, 65. Cephalus and Aurora; 1154. *Jean Greuze* (painter of fancy portraits; d. 1805), Girl with a lamb. *Claude*, 55. Landscape, with death of Procris; *30. Embarkation of St. Ursula. *Greuze*, 1019. Head of a girl looking upward, 1020. Girl with an apple; 58. *Claude*, Landscape with goats; 161. *Gaspard Poussin*, Italian landscape; 165. *N. Poussin*, Plague among the Philistines at Ashdod; 61. *Claude*, Landscape. — *31. *G. Poussin*, Landscape, with Abraham and Isaac.

This is the finest picture by Poussin here. Seldom, perhaps, have the charms of a plain, as contrasted with hilly forms overgrown with the richest forests, been so well understood and so happily united as here, the effect being enhanced by a warm light, broken by shadows of clouds'. — *W.*

*6. *Claude*, Landscape with figures (David and Saul in the cave of Adullam?).

Room XVII. FRENCH SCHOOL. To the left: 91. *N. Poussin*, Sleeping nymph surprized by satyrs; 95. *G. Poussin*, Landscape with Dido and Æneas, with sky much overcast; 236. *C. J. Vernet* (grandfather of Horace Vernet; 1714-89), Castle of Sant' Angelo at Rome; 206. *Greuze*, Head of a girl; 101-104. *Nicolas Lancret* (painter of 'fêtes galantes'; d. 1743), Ages of man; 1057. *C. J. Vernet*,

River‑scene; 1335. *French School* (15th cent.), Madonna; 660.
Ascribed to *Fr. Clouet* (court‑painter to Francis I.; d. 1572), Por‑
trait; *Simon Marmion* (15th cent.), 1303. Choir of angels, 1302.
Soul of St. Bertin borne to heaven; 1190. Ascribed to *Clouet*, Portrait
of a boy; 1422. *Eustache Le Sueur* (d. 1655), Holy Family; 1425. *Le
Nain* (d. 1648), Portraits; *Claude*, 5. Seaport at sunset, 2. Pastoral
landscape with figures (reconciliation of Cephalus and Procris);
98.·*G. Poussin*, Landscape; 798. *Philip de Champaigne* (d. 1674),
Three portraits of Cardinal Richelieu, painted as a guide in the
execution of a bust (over the profile on the spectator's right are the
words, 'De ces deux profiles ce cy est meilleur'); *G. Poussin*, 1159.
Calling of Abraham, 68. Landscape; *Claude*, 1319. Landscape and
view in Rome, 1018. Classical landscape (dated 1673); 1393. *C. J.
Vernet*, Mediterranean seaport; 1090. *François Boucher* (1704‑70),
Pan and Syrinx; 903. *Hyacinthe Rigaud* (portrait‑painter under
Louis XIV. and Louis XV.; d. 1743), Cardinal Fleury; 36. *G. Pous‑
sin*, Land‑storm; 64. *S. Bourdon* (1616‑71), Return of the Ark from
captivity; 1653. *Mme. Vigée Le Brun* (1755‑1842), Portrait of herself.

To reach the next room, we cross the main staircase.

Room XVIII. OLDER BRITISH SCHOOL. In the doorway, under
glass, are the palettes of John Constable (left) and Ford Madox
Brown (right). To the left: 308. *Thomas Gainsborough* (one of the
most eminent of English portrait‑painters; 1727‑88), Musidora. —
Sir Joshua Reynolds (portrait‑painter and writer on art, founder
and first president of the Royal Academy; 1723‑92), 892. Robinetta,
a study of the Hon. Mrs. Tollemache (painted about 1786), 162.
Infant Samuel, 107. The banished lord, 889. His own portrait,
886. Admiral Keppel, 890. George IV. as Prince of Wales, 307.
Age of Innocence, *1259. Anne, Countess of Albemarle, *182. Heads
of angels, 305. Portrait, 885. The snake in the grass, 888. James
Boswell, the biographer of Johnson. — *Thomas Gainsborough*, 1482.
Daughter of the artist; 925. Landscape; 1044. Portrait; *760. Or‑
pin, parish clerk of Bradford, Wiltshire; *683. Mrs. Siddons. —
1651. *George Romney* (a rival of Reynolds and Gainsborough;
1734‑1802), Portrait of Mrs. Mark Currie; 1670. *Sir William Beechey*
(1753‑1839), Portrait; 725. *J. Wright of Derby* (1734‑97), An ex‑
periment with the air‑pump; 1491. *Allan Ramsay* (son of the poet;
1713‑84), Portrait; 1496. *John Bettes* (portrait‑painter; d. ca. 1573),
Portrait; 1652. *Unknown Painter* (16th cent.), Catherine Parr; 1485,
1486. *Gainsborough*, Landscapes; 1487. *Zoffany* (d. 1810), Portrait
of Gainsborough; 1452. *Stubbs* (1724‑1806), Landscape, with a
gentleman holding his horse; 1483. *Gainsborough*, Two dogs; 106,
754. Reynolds, Portraits; *Romney*, 1667. Lady and child, 1668. Lady
Hamilton (sketch); 79. *Reynolds*, The Graces decorating a terminal
figure of Hymen (portraits of the daughters of Sir W. Montgomery);
Romney, 1068. The parson's daughter, 1669. Lady Craven, *312.
Lady Hamilton as a Bacchante; 111. *Reynolds*, Lord Heathfield, the

defender of Gibraltar in 1779-83 ; 304. *R. Wilson* (1713-82), Lake Avernus, with the Bay of Naples in the distance ; 109. *Gainsborough*, The watering-place ; *Reynolds*, 306. Portrait of himself, 887. Dr. Johnson, 891. Lady and child.

Room XIX. BRITISH SCHOOL. To the left of the door leading from the staircase : 314. *Sam. Scott* (d. 1772), Old Westminster Bridge in 1745 ; 1174. *Gainsborough*, Sketch for No. 109 (see above) ; 1198. *Abbot* (1760-1803), Portrait ; 1153. *Hogarth* (1697-1764), Family group ; 1016. *Sir Peter Lely* (d. 1680), Portrait ; 113-118. *Hogarth*, Marriage à la mode (in 1750 Hogarth received only 126*l.* for the series, which, when sold again in 1794, realised 1381*l.*) ; 108. *Wilson*, Landscape ; *1249. *William Dobson* (1610-46 ; the 'English Van Dyck'), Endymion Porter, Groom of the Bedchamber to Charles I.

*1242. *Alexander Nasmyth* (1758-1840 ; a painter of portraits and landscapes at Edinburgh ; father of Patrick Nasmyth), Stirling Castle.

Sir David Wilkie describes Alex. Nasmyth as 'the founder of the landscape school of Scotland, and the first to enrich his native land with the representation of her romantic scenery'.

1224. *Hudson* (d. 1779), Scott, the painter ; 229. *Gilbert Stuart* (1745-1828), Portrait of Benjamin West, P.R.A. ; *Hogarth*, 1464.Calais Gate, 1374. The painter's servants ; 1681. *British School* (18th cent.), St. Paul's from the river ; 1328. *Sam. Scott*, View of Westminster from the Thames ; no number, attributed to *Hogarth*, Garden-party (lent by Miss Sealy) ; 1076. *Unknown Master*, Portrait, supposed to be the poet Gay ; 1403, 1402. *Henry Morland* (d. 1797), The laundry-maid ; 1064, 302, 1071, 303. 267. *Wilson*, Landscapes ; *Hogarth*, 112. Portrait of himself, 675, 1663. Portraits of his sisters ; 1281. *Francis Cotes* (d. 1770), Portrait of Mrs. Brocas ; *Hogarth*, 1161. Miss Fenton the actress as 'Polly Peachum' in the 'Beggars' Opera', *1046. Sigismonda mourning over the heart of Guiscardo, 1162. Shrimp Girl ; 1453. *Nebot* (18th cent.), Covent Garden Market with St. Paul's Church ; *Sam. Scott*, 313. Old London Bridge, 1223. Old Westminster Bridge.

Room XX. BRITISH SCHOOL. 380, 381. *Patrick Nasmyth* (1786-1831), Landscapes ; 1163. *Thomas Stothard* (1755-1834), The Pilgrimage to Canterbury (after Chaucer) ; 1497. *George Morland* (d. 1804), Rabbiting ; 1384. *Patrick Nasmyth*, View in Hampshire ; 900. *John Hoppner* (1759-1810), Countess of Oxford ; 1307. *Sir Thomas Lawrence* (1769-1830), Miss Caroline Fry ; 1177. *Patrick Nasmyth*, Landscape ; 733. *John S. Copley, R. A.* (b. at Boston, Mass., in 1737 ; d. 1815), Death of Major Peirson ; *Stothard*, 1070. Cupids preparing for the chase , 322. Battle, 320. Diana and her nymphs bathing ; *311. *Gainsborough*, Rustic children ; 1480. *Gilbert Stuart*, Portrait of the painter ; 785. *Lawrence*, Mrs. Siddons ; 1671. *Sir William Beechey*, Portrait ; 1306. *Thomas Barker* (1769-1847), Landscape ; 317. *Stothard*, Greek vintage ; 1272. *John Constable* (one of

the foremost English landscape-painters, who has exercised great
influence on the modern French school of landscape; 1776-1837),
The Cenotaph erected in memory of Sir Joshua Reynolds in Coleorton
Park, Leicestershire; 1158. *James Ward* (d. 1859), Harlech Castle;
110. *Wilson*, Landscape; 129. *Lawrence*, John Angerstein (p. 188);
926. *John Crome* ('Old Crome' of Norwich; d. 1821), Windmill;
1413. *Lawrence*, Portrait. *1273. *Constable*, Flatford Mill; 310.
Gainsborough, Landscape; 1030. *George Morland*, Interior of a
stable; *1396. *Romney*, Mr. and Mrs. William Lindow; 1351. *Morland*, Door of a village inn; 1156. *George Arnald* (d. 1841), On the
Ouse, Yorkshire. *Copley*, 787. Siege of Gibraltar; 100. Last public
appearance of the Earl of Chatham, who fainted in endeavouring to
speak in the House of Peers on April 7th, 1778, and died a month
later; 1072, 1073. Studies for No. 100. 321. *Stothard*, Intemperance
(Cleopatra and Mark Antony); *Crome*, 689. Mousehold Heath near
Norwich, *1037. Slate-quarries; 1254. *Unknown Master* (late 18th
cent.?), Hyde Park Corner; 893. *Lawrence*, Princess Lieven; 1408.
John Opie (d. 1807), Portrait; *Gainsborough*, 1271. Portrait, 309.
The watering-place, 80. The market-cart, 1283. Dedham; 119. *Sir
George Beaumont* (1753-1827), Landscape, with Jaques and the
wounded stag; 301. *R. Wilson*, View in Italy; 1039. *Thomas Barker*,
Landscape; 1460. *Julius Caesar Ibbetson* (1759-1817), Smugglers
on the Irish coast; 897. *Crome*, View at Chapelfields, Norwich;
1658. *George Lambert* (1710-65), Landscape; 1290. *Wilson*, Landscape; 1274. *Constable*, The Glebe Farm.

Room XXI. MODERN BRITISH SCHOOL. To the left: 1208. *John
Opie*, William Godwin; *J. S. Cotman* (d. 1842), 1111. Wherries on
the Yare, *1458. A galiot in a gale; 1175. *James Ward*, Regent's
Park in 1807; 1167. *Opie*, Mary Wollstonecraft (Mrs. Godwin); 316.
Loutherbourg (d. 1812), Lake in Cumberland; *1666. *Sir John Millais* (1829-96), Right Hon. W. E. Gladstone. — *Sir Edwin Landseer*
(1802-73), 409. King Charles spaniels; 1349, 1350. Studies of
lions; 606. Shoeing the bay mare; 603. Sleeping bloodhound (painted in four days). 340. *Sir A. Callcott* (1779-1844), Dutch peasants
returning from market; *621. *Rosa Bonheur* (1822-99), Horse-fair;
1494. *Millais*, Yeoman of the Guard; *Turner* (see p. 219), 494. Dido
and Æneas leaving Carthage, 485. View of Abingdon, 496. Bligh
Sand, 495. Apuleia in search of Apuleius, 483. View of London
from Greenwich, 486. Windsor; 120. *Beechey*, Nollekens, the sculptor; *604. *Landseer*, Dignity and Impudence; *130. *Constable*, Corn-
field; 1404. *Jackson* (1778-1831), Portrait; 899. *Thomas Daniell*
(1749-1840), View in Bengal; *1207. *Constable*, Hay-wain; 183.
Thomas Phillips (d. 1845), Sir David Wilkie; 327. *Constable*, The
valley farm; 346. *Callcott*, Entrance to Pisa from Leghorn; 124.
Jackson, Portrait; 1186. *John Glover* (1767-1849), Landscape with
cattle; 1654. *G. F. Watts* (b. 1817), Russell Gurney, late Recorder
of London; 922. *Lawrence*, Child with a kid; 122. *Sir David Wilkie*

(d. 1841), Village-festival; 784. *Opie*, William Siddons; 1275. *Constable*, View at Hampstead; 99. *Wilkie*, The blind fiddler.

A small corner-room, entered from the passage between RR. XXI and XXII, contains small works by *William Blake* (1757-1827), *Turner* (see below), *Hogarth*, *Stothard*, *Nasmyth*, *Wilkie*, *Callcott*, and others. Among these may be mentioned: *Turner*, 510. Pilate washing his hands, 526. New moon, 561. Glen (unfinished), 551. Tapping the furnace, 482. Garreteer's petition; *Blake*, 1110. Spiritual form of Pitt guiding Behemoth (an 'iridescent sketch of enigmatic dream's symbolising the power of statesmanship in controlling brute force), 1164. Procession from Calvary. — Here also are a few *Miniatures* and Turner's palette.

Room XXII contains an admirable collection of paintings by *J. M. W. Turner* (1775-1851), the greatest English landscape painter (comp. p. 215), chiefly bequeathed by the artist himself. To the left: 535, 370, 544, 534. Four Venetian pieces; 472. Calais pier, English packet arriving; 470. Tenth plague of Egypt; 476. Shipwreck; *530. Snowstorm, steamboat off a harbour making signals; 813. Fishing-boats in a breeze; 490. Snowstorm, with Hannibal crossing the Alps; 480. Death of Nelson; 493. The Deluge; 481. Boat's crew recovering an anchor at Spithead; 488. Apollo slaying the Python; 477. Garden of the Hesperides; 513. Vision of Medea; 516. Childe Harold's Pilgrimage: Italy; *497. Crossing the brook; 512. Caligula's palace and bridge at Baiæ; 558. Fire at sea (unfinished); 458. Portrait of himself; *528. Burial of Sir David Wilkie at sea; 511. Orvieto 501. Shipwreck at the mouth of the Meuse; 559. Petworth Park; 560. Chichester Canal; 506. Dido directing the equipment of the fleet at Carthage; *502. Richmond Hill; 508. Ulysses deriding Polyphemus; 505. Apollo and the Sibyl, Bay of Baiæ; *492. Frosty morning; 520. Apollo and Daphne; *538. Rain, steam, and speed, the Great Western Railway; *524. The 'Fighting Temeraire' towed to her last berth to be broken up (one of the most frequently copied pictures in the whole Gallery); 369. Prince of Orange landing at Torbay; 548. Queen Mab's Grotto; 523. Agrippina landing with the ashes of Germanicus.

15. The National Portrait Gallery.

Adjoining the National Gallery on the N.E., but forming an entirely separate building, is the ****National Portrait Gallery** (Pl. R, 26; *II*), erected in 1890-96. It is a handsome edifice in the Italian palatial style, designed by *Mr. Ewan Christian*, and is adorned externally with busts and carving. The entrance (adm., see p. 108) is on the E. side, facing St. Martin's Place. The entire cost of the building was defrayed by *Mr. W. H. Alexander*. The director is *Mr. Lionel Cust*. Catalogue (1898), 6d.

The collection, which was founded by act of parliament in 1856, now contains upwards of 1100 portraits of men and women eminent in British history, literature, art, and science, and deservedly ranks among the most interesting sights of London. The present building had unfortunately to be built in three stories, and some of its thirty odd exhibition-rooms are small and not too well lighted. The arrangement and numbering of the rooms are also somewhat puzzling; and a careful study of the plan is necessary. The pictures, however, have been hung with great taste and judgment; on the upper floor a chronological order has been adhered to, while downstairs the arrangement is mainly by groups. The following selection of the most interesting works follows a chronological order as far as possible and begins on the top floor. The show-cases scattered throughout the rooms contain engravings, medals, autographs, and the like.

From an artistic point of view the finest paintings are in the earlier rooms, including specimens of Van Dyck, Zucchero, More, Mierevelt, Reynolds, Dobson, Kneller, Gainsborough, Romney, and others. The falling off is particularly noticeable in the royal portraits, those of Queen Victoria and Prince Albert comparing very poorly with those of (*e.g.*) the Tudor period. The fine series of portraits by *Mr. G. F. Watts* (p. 226), however, does something to redeem the mediocrity of the Victorian era.

TOP FLOOR.

Room I (small) contains the earliest portraits of the collection. Portraits of *Richard II.* (1366-1400) and *Henry IV.* (1366-1413), by unknown masters. Facsimile of an ancient diptyoh representing *Richard II.*, at the age of fifteen, kneeling before the Virgin and Child. Portrait of *Geoffrey Chaucer* (1340-1400). Tracings of the portraits of *Edward III.* (1312-77) and his family formerly on the E. wall of St. Stephen's Chapel, Westminster (date, 1356), now destroyed.

Room II, chiefly containing portraits of the Tudor Period (1485-1603). To the left, several portraits of the Plantagenet period, executed at a later date and of little artistic value. The best is that of *Richard III.* (d. 1483), in the act of putting a ring on his finger, probably by a Flemish painter. *Henry VIII.* (1491-1547), at the age of fifty-three, an early-Flemish copy of the portrait by Luke Hornebolt at Warwick Castle; *Catharine Howard* (1520-42), by a pupil of Holbein; *Cardinal Wolsey* (1471-1530), a crude performance, probably after an Italian original; **Thomas Cranmer, Archbishop of Canterbury* (1489-1556), by Gerbarus Flicius; portraits of *Latimer* (d. 1555) and *Ridley* (d. 1555); *Edward VI.* (1537-53), by a pupil of Holbein; *Lady Jane Grey* (1537-54), a small work by Lucas de Heere; *Sir Thomas More* (1478-1535); *Queen Mary I.* (1516-58); two portraits of *Edward VI.*, in the manner of Holbein; *William Herbert, Earl of Pembroke* (1507-69), probably by Sir Anthony More (Moro), a pupil of Schoreel; several portraits of *Queen Elizabeth* (1533-1603); portraits of the *Earl of Essex* (d. 1540), *Sir Walter Raleigh* (d. 1618), and the *Earl of Leicester* (1531-88); *Sir Thomas Gresham* (1519-79), founder of the Royal Exchange

NATIONAL PORTRAIT GALLERY

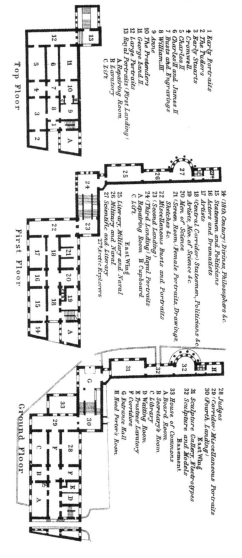

Top Floor

First Floor

Ground Floor

1 Early Portraits
2 The Tudors
3 Early Stuarts
4 Cromwell
5 Charles II
6 Charles II and James II
7 Busts and Engravings
8 William III
9 Anne
10 The Pretenders
11 George I and II
12 Large Portraits
13 Royal Portraits (First Landing)
  A Repairing Room
  B Lavatory
  C Lift

14 (18th Century) Divines, Philosophers &c.
15 Statesmen and Politicians
16 Actors and Dramatists
17 Artists
18 (Central Corridor) Statesmen, Politicians &c.
19 Artists, Men of Science &c.
20 Men of Science
21 (Screen Room) Female Portraits, Drawings.
22 Miscellaneous Busts and Portraits
23 (Second Landing)
24 (Third Landing) Rapid Portraits
  Sketches &c.
25 Literary, Military and Naval
26 Military and Naval
27 Scientific and Literary
27* Arctic Explorers
  A Repairing Room B Cupboard
  C Lift
  East Wing

28 Judges
29 (Corridor) Miscellaneous Portraits
30 (Fourth Landing)
  East Wing
31 Sculpture Gallery, Electrotypes
32 Sculpture and Models
  Basement
33 House of Commons
  A Board Room
  B Secretary's Room
  C Library
  D Waiting Room
  E Trustees' Lavatory
  F Corridors
  G Entrance Hall
  H Head Porter's Room.

(p. 140), by More; *Foxe* (1516-87), author of the 'Book of Martyrs';
Sir Henry Unton (d. 1596), a curious work with scenes from his
life, by an unknown painter; portrait of the '*Judicious Hooker*'
(d. 1600); *Peter Martyr Vermilius* of Florence (d. 1562), preacher of
the Reformation at Oxford, by Hans Asper of Zürich; two portraits
of *Mary, Queen of Scots* (1542-87), one after Janet, the other by
Oudry; *Mary of Lorraine* (1515-60), mother of Mary Stuart, long
supposed to be a portrait of the latter (so-called Fraser-Tytler
portrait); *John Knox* (1505-72), the Scottish Reformer.

Room III (Early Stuarts; 1603-49). *King James I.* (1567-
1625); oil-portrait of *Shakspeare* (the Chandos portrait). In the
case below are an engraving from the first folio edition of the plays
(1623), a photograph of a portrait of Shakespeare in the Memorial
Gallery at Stratford-on-Avon, a photograph of his monument in the
church there, and specimens of his signature. *Ben Jonson* (d. 1637);
James VI. of Scotland at the age of eight, by Zucchero; *James I.*,
in the royal robes, by Van Somer; *Lord Chancellor Bacon* (1561-
1626), by Van Somer; *Michael Drayton*, the poet (d. 1631); *Group
of eleven statesmen, assembled at Somerset House in 1604 to ratify
a commercial treaty between England, Spain, and Austria, by Marcus Gheeraedts, a fine work; *Coke*, the famous legal authority; *Endymion Porter*, confidant of Charles I. (1587-1649), by Dobson;
Countess of Pembroke (d. 1621), by Gheeraedts; *Sir John Suckling*
(1609-42), after Van Dyck; *Francis Quarles* (1592-1644), by
Dobson; *Sir Dudley Carleton, Viscount Dorchester* (1574-1632),
and his wife, by Mierevelt. The adjoining case contains small
portraits of *William Drummond, James VI.,* and *Robert Cecil, First
Earl of Salisbury.* Portraits of *John Fletcher* (d. 1625), *Lord Herbert
of Cherbury* (d. 1648), and *Harrington* (d. 1677). The case in this
corner contains an engraving of *Guy Fawkes* (1560-1606) and other
conspirators of the Gunpowder Plot, with good portraits taken from
life. *Earl of Strafford* (d. 1641), after Van Dyck; *Two Cavaliers*,
by W. Dobson; *Abp. Laud* (1573-1645), after Van Dyck; *Children
of Charles I.*, early copy of a well-known work by Van Dyck (see
p. 428); *Charles I.* (1600-49), by Old Stone, after Van Dyck; *Sir
Kenelm Digby* (d. 1665), by Van Dyck; *George Villiers, First Duke
of Buckingham* (d. 1628), and his family, by Honthorst; *Sir Julius
Caesar* (d. 1636; see p. 143), by Van Somer; *John Selden*, the
antiquary (1584-1654); *William Dobson* (1610-46), a follower of
Van Dyck and the first native English portrait-painter of any
eminence, by himself. In the fourth case is a miniature of Queen
Elizabeth.

Room IV (Commonwealth; 1649-60). *Portraits of *Queen Elizabeth of Bohemia* (d. 1662), by Honthorst and Mierevelt; *Inigo
Jones*, the architect (1573-1652), by Old Stone, after Van Dyck;
Oliver Cromwell (1599-1658), by Robert Walker; case with photographs of portraits of Oliver Cromwell; *Ireton* (1611-51), by Walker;

Oliver Cromwell at the age of fifty-eight, by an unknown painter;
Milton (1608-74), by Van der Plaas; portraits of *Baxter, Marvel,
Cocker* (the arithmetician who lives in the phrase 'according to
Cock er'; comp. p. 379), and *Sir Matthew Hale.*

Room V (Charles II.; 1660-85). Portraits of *Samuel Butler* and
the poet *Waller; Isaac Barrow*, by Claude le Fèvre; *John Owen;
Thomas Hobbes*, the philosopher (d. 1679), by J. M. Wright; *Abp.
Tillotson; Monck, Duke of Albemarle*, by Sir Peter Lely; *Col. Blood*
(see p. 158), by Soest; *William, Lord Russell; Algernon Sidney;
Archbp. Sancroft; Sir Peter Lely*, by himself; *Dr. William Harvey*
(1578-1657), discoverer of the circulation of the blood; *A. A.
Cooper*, first Earl of Shaftesbury; *Prince Rupert*, by Lely; *Charles II.*, by Mrs. Beale; *Wycherley*; several male portraits by Lely;
Pepys, by John Hayls; **George Villiers, Second Duke of Buckingham* (d. 1687), by Lely; *'Old Parr'*, the centenarian (see p. 259),
after Honthorst; *Cowley; Dryden*, by Kneller.

Room VI (Charles II. and James II.; 1660-1688). Portraits of
Nell Gwynne, Mary Davis, the actress, *La Belle Hamilton*, and other
beauties, by Sir Peter Lely; the **Countess of Shrewsbury*, by the
same artist; *Izaak Walton* (1593-1683), by Jacob Huysman; *Locke*,
the philosopher, by Brownover and after Kneller; *Saint Evremond*,
by Parmentier; *Mary of Modena*, second wife of James II., by
Wissing; *James II.*, by Riley; *Duchess of Cleveland*, by Kneller;
Duke of Monmouth, by Lely; *Boyle*, by Kerseboom.

Room VII (Busts and Engravings). Engravings of various worthies
of the 17th century. Busts of *Colley Cibber* (1671-1757), attributed
to Roubiliac (realistically painted), *Cromwell*, by E. Pierce and by
an unknown artist (latter in bronze), and *John Hampden* (terracotta; artist unknown).

Room VIII (William III.; 1688-1702). *Lord Chancellor Jeffreys*,
by Kneller; *Sir Isaac Newton* (1642-1727), by Vanderbank; **Sir
Christopher Wren*, the architect of St. Paul's Cathedral (1632-1723),
by Kneller; *Mary II.*, by Netscher; the *Seven Bishops* (p. 244),
by an unknown artist; *William III.*, by Wyck; *Mary II.*, by Wissing; *Earl of Halifax* (1661-1715), *Earl of Rochester* (d. 1711), by
Kneller.

Room IX (Queen Anne; 1702-14). *Jonathan Swift* (1667-1745),
by C. Jervas; *Congreve*, by Kneller; *Gay*, unfinished sketch by
Kneller; *Joseph Addison* (1672-1719), old copy of the 'kit-cat' portrait by Kneller; *Alexander Pope* (1688-1744), crayon by Hoare;
Pope, by Richardson and by Kneller; *Bentley*, by Thornhill; *Steele*,
by Richardson; *Viscount Bolingbroke*, the statesman (1678-1751),
by H. Rigaud; *William, First Earl Cowper* (1665-1773), by Kneller;
Duke of Marlborough, by Closterman and Kneller (the latter treated
allegorically); portraits of *Queen Anne; Duchess of Marlborough*, by
Kneller; *Admiral Rooke* (1650-1709), by Dahl; *Bishop Berkeley*
(1684-1753), by Smibert; *James Thomson*, the poet (d. 1748), (by

Paton; *Joseph Addison* (see above), by Dahl; *Matt. Prior* (1664-1721), the poet, by Hudson, after Richardson.

Room X (The Pretenders). *President Duncan Forbes of Culloden* (1685-1747); *Prince James*, the Old Pretender (1688-1766), by Belle; *Prince Charles Edward*, the Young Pretender (1720-88), and his wife, the *Countess of Albany*, small portraits by Battoni; his brother, *Cardinal York*, by Rosalba Carriera; other portraits of the Pretenders and Card. York, by Largillière, Battoni, and Raphael Mengs; *Dr. Isaac Watts*, by Kneller; *Edward Young* (1684-1765), author of 'Night Thoughts'.

Room XI (George I. and II.; 1714-60). *Samuel Richardson* (1689-1761), by Highmore; *Charles Boyle*, 4th Earl of Orrery, by Jervas; *Earl of Chesterfield* (1694-1773), by Allan Ramsay, and another by Hoare; *Lord Lyttelton* (1709-73); *Chas. Sackville*, 6th Earl of Dorset, by Kneller; *Robert Harley*, Earl of Oxford, after Kneller; *Thomas Gray*, by Eccardt. An adjoining case has small portraits and autographs of Gray and Horace Walpole. *Horace Walpole*, by Eccardt, and another by Hone; *Sir Robert Walpole*, by Van Loo; *George Washington*, by Gilbert Stuart; *Wm. Hogarth*, the painter (1697-1764), by himself; *Committee of the House of Commons* (1729), by Hogarth; **Simon Fraser*, Lord Lovat, by Hogarth; *Bust of W. Hogarth*, by Roubiliac; *Sir Hans Sloane* (p. 299), by Slaughter; *Roubiliac*, by Carpentiers; *Samuel Richardson* (1689-1761), by Highmore; *Händel*, the composer (d. 1759), by Hudson and (terracotta bust) by Roubiliac.

Room XII (Corridor with large portraits). *Pope and Martha Blount*, by Jervas; *Philip II. of Spain*, by Coello; *James II.*, by Kneller; *Henry, Prince of Wales* (1594-1612), by Van Somer; *Queen Henrietta Maria* (1609-69), in the style of Van Dyck; *Charles I.* (1600-49), by Mytens; *William III.*, by Wyck; *Warren Hastings* (1733-1818), by Devis; *Lord Mansfield*, by Copley; *Sir Wm. Hamilton* (1730-1803), by Sir Joshua Reynolds; *Shenstone*, by Alcock. — *Bust of Thomas Gray*, by Bacon.

Room XIII (Staircase Landing; Royal Portraits). Various royal portraits by Hudson, Jervas, etc. — *Bust of Newton*, by Baily, after Roubiliac.

FIRST FLOOR.

Room XIV (18th century; Divines, Philosophers, etc.). *Benjamin Franklin* (1706-90), by Baricolo; *Dr. Erasmus Darwin* (1731-1802), by Wright of Derby; *Sir Richard Arkwright*, the inventor (1732-92), by the same; *Samuel Johnson* (1709-84), by James Barry (unfinished); *George Whitefield*, the preacher (d. 1770), by Woolaston; *Sir Philip Francis* (1740-1818), by Lonsdale; *William Woodfall* (1745-1808), the printer of the 'Letters of Junius', by Beach; *John Howard* (d. 1790), by Mather Brown; *John Wesley*

(1703-91), at the age of 63, by Hone, and another, at the age of 85 by Hamilton; *Bust of Wesley*, by an unknown artist; *Abp. Secker*, by Reynolds; *Paley*, by Beechey.

Room XV (Statesmen and Politicians). **W. Pulteney*, *Earl of Bath* (1682-1764), by Reynolds, vigorously handled; *J. P. Curran* (1750-1817); *Lord Chancellor Thurlow* (1732-1806), by Lawrence, and another by Phillips; *Sir James Mackintosh* (d. 1832), by Lawrence; *William Pitt the Younger* (1759-1806), by Hoppner; *R. B. Sheridan* (d. 1816), by Russell; **Charles James Fox* (1749-1806), by Hickel; *Edmund Burke* (d. 1797), by Reynolds; *William Pitt*, first Earl of Chatham (d. 1778), by Hoare; *Warren Hastings* (1733-1818), by Sir Thos. Lawrence, and another by Tilly Kettle. — Busts of *William Pitt* and *Charles James Fox*, by Nollekens; of *Canning*, by Chantrey, etc.

Room XVI (Actors and Dramatists). *David Garrick* (1717-79), by Pine; *Kemble* (1757-1823), the tragedian, by Gilbert Stuart; *Peg Woffington* (1720-60), the actress, painted as she lay in bed paralysed, by A. Pond; *Edmund Kean* (1787-1833), by Sam. John Stump; *Mrs. Siddons* (d. 1831), by Beechey; *Oliver Goldsmith* (1728-74), by a pupil of Reynolds, a portrait familiar through engravings; *Joseph Grimaldi*, the famous clown (1779-1837), by Cawse. — Bust of *Garrick* (see above).

Room XVII (Artists) is now divided into two sections by a partition. 1st Section: Busts of *Sir Charles Eastlake* (d. 1865), by Gibson, and *Wm. Etty* (d. 1849), by Noble. Portraits of *John Flaxman* (1755-1826), by Romney and Head; *Lord Leighton* (1830-96), by Watts; *John Opie* (1761-1807), by himself; *William Blake* (d. 1827), by Phillips. — 2nd Section: Busts of *Sir Thos. Lawrence* (d. 1830), by Baily, and *Benjamin West* (d. 1820), by Chantrey. Portraits of *Angelica Kauffmann* (d. 1807), by herself; *Romney* (d. 1802), by himself; *Benjamin West*, by Gilbert Stuart; *Sir John Soane* (p. 230), by Jackson; *Gainsborough* (d. 1788), by himself; *Reynolds, Chambers*, and *Wilton*, group by J. F. Rigaud; *Sir Joshua Reynolds*, by himself; *James Barry* (1741-1806), by himself; *Wright of Derby* (1734-97), by himself; *Sir John Millais* (1829-96), by Keene (pen-and-ink sketch); *Chantrey* (1781-1841), by himself (chalk); *Constable* (1776-1837), by himself (lead-pencil); *Patrick Nasmyth* (1787-1831), by Bewick; *Sir David Wilkie* (1785-1841), by himself; *J. M. W. Turner* (1775-1851), by Chas. Turner; *D. G. Rossetti* (1828-82), drawn in pencil by himself in 1846; *Ford Madox Brown* (1821-93), by Rossetti (pencil); *John Leech* (1817-64), by Millais.

In the centre is a bronze statuette of *Baron Marochetti* (1805-67), by Ambrosio.

XVIII. Central Corridor (Statesmen, Politicians, etc.). *Lord Brougham* (1778-1868), by Lonsdale; *Joseph Hume* (1777-1855), by Walton; *Sir Rowland Hill* (1795-1879), by Vinter; *John Brigh*

(1811-89), by Ouless; *Cobden* (1804-65), by Dickinson; *Benjamin Disraeli* (1804-81), by Millais; *Lord John Russell* (1792-1878), by Grant; *George Grote* (1794-1871), the historian of Greece, by Stewardson.

ROOM XIX (Artists, Men of Science, etc.). Portraits of *Daniel Maclise* (d. 1870), *Bewick, Landseer, Chantrey* (d. 1841), *John Gibson*, the sculptor (1790-1866), and other artists. *Family of Adam Walker*, by Romney; *John Home* (1722-1808), author of 'Douglas', by Raeburn; *Charles Dibdin* (d. 1814), by Phillips; *Macpherson* ('Ossian'; 1736-96), by a pupil of Reynolds; *Henry Mackenzie* (1745-1831), the 'Man of Feeling', by Raeburn; *Tobias Smollett* (1721-71); *John Smeaton* (1724-92), the engineer, by Rhodes; *Sir William Herschel* (1738-1822), by Abbott.

ROOM XX (Men of Science). *Dr. Jenner* (d. 1823), discoverer of the protective properties of vaccination, by Northcote; in front of him lies his work 'On the Origin of Vaccine Inoculation' (1801), with a cow's hoof as letter-weight. **James Watt* (1736-1819), by C. F. de Breda. — In the centre, *Benjamin Disraeli*, statuette by Lord Ronald Gower.

ROOM XXI (Screen Room; Female Portraits, Drawings, Sketches, etc.). 1st Section: *Mrs. Fry*, after Leslie; *Lady Hamilton*, by Romney; *Harriet Martineau*, by Evans; *Mary Mitford*, by Lucas; *Mrs. Trimmer* (1741-1810), by Henry Howard; *Hannah More*, by Pickersgill; *George Eliot (Mrs. Cross*; d. 1880), drawing by Sir F. W. Burton; *E. B. Browning*, the poetess (d. 1861), a chalk drawing by Talfourd; *Mary Shelley; Marian Evans (George Eliot)* and her father, by Mrs. Charles Bray (1842); *Christina Rossetti* (1830-94) and her mother, drawing by Dante Rossetti; *Thos. Hood* (1799-1845) and his wife; *Ann Taylor (Mrs. Gilbert*; 1782-1866) and *Jane Taylor* (1783-1824), by their father, Isaac Taylor; *Mary Somerville* (1780-1872), in crayons, by Swinton; *Jane* and *Anna Maria Porter* (1776-1850 and 1780-1832), by Harlow (crayons); *Mr.* and *Mrs. Piozzi (Mrs. Thrale*; d. 1809 and 1821), by Geo. Dance; *Jane Welsh Carlyle* (1801-66), by Sam. Laurence. — 2nd Section: *Bulwer Lytton* (1803-73), by Chalon; *Southey* (1774-1843), by P. Vandyke; *Wilkie Collins* (d. 1889), by Millais; *Samuel Rogers* (1763-1855), by Dance; *Lamb, Coleridge, Southey*, and *Wordsworth*, four small drawings in one frame, by Hancock; *Tennyson*, by Arnault; *James Hogg* (d. 1833), the 'Ettrick Shepherd', by Denning; *Wm. Cowper* (1731-1800), by Harvey, after Abbot; *Robert Louis Stevenson* (1850-94), by W. B. Richmond (sketch). — 3rd Section: *Wellington*, at the age of thirty-five, *Nelson*, by Edridge; *Wolfe*, facsimile of a sketch made at Quebec in 1759; *Mungo Park* (1771-1806), miniature after Edridge; *Henry Grattan* (1746-1820), by Wheatley; *W. Wilberforce*, the philanthropist (d. 1833), by Sir T. Lawrence (unfinished); *Sir Robert Peel*, by Linnell; *Rev. Ed. Irving* (1792-1834), founder of the Irvingite or Catholic Apostolic Church, drawing by Slater; *David Livingstone* (1813-73), sketch from life by Bonomi;

Lord Palmerston (d. 1865) at the age of eighteen; *Dean Stanley* (1815-81); *Priestley* (1733-1804), by Mrs. Sharples; *John Wilkes* (1727-97), by Earlom; *Daniel O'Connell* (d. 1847), by Mulrenin; *George Washington*, by Mrs. Sharples (crayon). — Busts of *Mrs. Hemans* (1793-1835; Fletcher), *Mrs. Jameson* (1794-1860; Gibson), *Miss Amelia Edwards* (1832-92; Ball), and *Grace Darling* (1815-42; Dunbar).

XXII. CORRIDOR (Miscellaneous Busts and Portraits). Bust of *Sir Robert Peel* (d. 1850), by Noble; *Francis Horner*, the politician and essayist, one of the founders of the 'Edinburgh Review' (1778-1817), by Sir Henry Raeburn; Bust of the *Duke of Wellington* (d. 1852), by Francis; *Sir Wm. Blackstone* (d. 1780), by Reynolds; *David Livingstone* (d. 1873), by F. Havill. — The case in the centre contains clay busts of the *Hon. Mrs. Norton* (by Williamson), *Sir Wm. Stirling Maxwell* (by Williamson), *Abp. Sumner* (1780-1862; by Adams), and *Sir Chas. T. Newton* (d. 1894; by Boehm). On screens: collection of portraits in chalk by George Richmond (*Canon Liddon, Keble, Pusey, Samuel Rogers, Cardinal Newman, Ruskin*, etc.); *Admiral Lord Nelson*, after Guzzardi.

XXIII. LANDING. Full-length portraits of *Kemble* and *Mrs. Siddons*, by Sir Thos. Lawrence. — Busts of *Douglas Jerrold* (d. 1857), by Baily; of *Thomas Moore* (d. 1852), by C. Moore; and of *Charles Knight* (d. 1873), by Durham.

We now descend a few steps to another landing, from which we enter the **East Wing** of the First Floor.

XXIV. LANDING (Royal Portraits). *William, Duke of Cumberland* (d. 1765), by Reynolds; *Prince Albert* (d. 1861), by Winterhalter; *Queen Victoria* at the ages of 56 and 80, both after Angeli; *George III.* (1738-1820), by Allan Ramsay; *Queen Charlotte* (1744-1818), wife of George III., by Ramsay.

The short passage leading from this landing to R. XXV contains busts of *Southey* (Lough), *Tennyson* (Miss Grant), *B. W. Proctor* (Foley), and *Scott* (Chantrey).

ROOM XXV (Literary, Military, and Naval). *Cowper*, by Romney. *Sir Walter Scott* (d. 1832), in his study at Abbotsford, with his deerhound Maida, by Sir Wm. Allan, the last portrait he sat for; another by Landseer. *Robert Burns* (d. 1796), by Nasmyth, well known from engravings; *Shelley* (1792-1821), by Miss Amelia Curran; *John Keats* (d. 1821), by Severn (another, by Hilton, over the door); *Lord Byron* (d. 1824), in Albanian costume, by T. Phillips, and another by Westall; *Leigh Hunt* (d. 1859), by Haydon; *Lord Macaulay* (d. 1859), sketch by Grant; *Charles Dickens* (d. 1870), by Maclise; *Chas. Lamb* (d. 1834), by Hazlitt; *Chas. and Mary Lamb*, by Cary; *Southey* (d. 1843), by Edridge; *S. T. Coleridge* (d. 1834), by Peter Vandyke and by Allston; *Thos. Campbell* (d. 1844), by Lawrence. — Fine series of portraits by G. F. Watts: *Sir Henry Taylor, D. G. Rossetti, Sir Ant. Panizzi, Matt. Arnold, Tennyson, Browning, Card.*

Manning, Lord Lawrence, J. S. Mill, William Morris, Robert Lowe (Lord Sherbrooke), Carlyle, Lord Lytton, the *Earl of Shaftesbury, Lord Lyndhurst, Dr. Martineau, Lord John Russell, Gladstone,* and *Lord Stratford de Redcliffe. — W. S. Landor* (d. 1864), by Fisher; *Robert Browning* (d. 1889), by Lehmann; *W. M. Thackeray* (d. 1863), by S. Laurence; *Charles Dickens,* by Ary Scheffer; *Douglas Jerrold* (d. 1857), by Macnee; *Coventry Patmore* (d. 1896), by J. S. Sargent; *Thomas Carlyle* (d. 1881), by Millais; **Thomas de Quincey* (1785-1859), by Sir John Watson Gordon. — *R. L. Stevenson* (d. 1894), by Richmond; *William Gifford* (d. 1826), by Hoppner; *Sir Richard Burton* (d. 1890), by Lord Leighton; *Fred. Denison Maurice* (d. 1872), by S. Laurence; *Card. Newman* (d. 1890), by Miss E. Deane. — On the W. wall are various military and naval celebrities, including *Lord Clive* (d. 1774), by Dance; *Lord Heathfield* (d. 1790), by J. S. Copley; *General Wolfe* (1726-59), by Schaak; *Lord Nelson* (d. 1805), by L. J. Abbott and H. Füger of Vienna (two portraits). — In the centre are busts of *Porson, Captain Cook, Thackeray* (by Foley), *Carlyle* (by Boehm), *Richard Jefferies,* a medallion of *Lord Stanhope,* the historian, an electrotype bust of *Thackeray* as a boy, and an electrotype mask of *John Keats.*

Room XXVI (Military and Naval). Above the entrance, *Marquis Wellesley* (d. 1842), by J. P. Davies. To the right: *Sir Sidney Smith* (d. 1841), by Eckstein; *Sir James Outram* (d. 1863), by Brigstocke; the *Duke of Wellington,* by the Count d'Orsay; *Admiral Lord Lyons* (d. 1858), by G. F. Watts; *Sir John Moore* (1761-1848), by Lawrence; *Capt. Cook* (1728-79), by Webber; *Thomas Paine* (1737-1809), by Millière, after Romney.

Room XXVII (Scientific and Literary). *Sir David Brewster* (1781-1868), by Watson Gordon; *Capt. Marryatt* (1792-1848), by John Simpson; *Charles Darwin* (1809-82), by Collier; *Sir Chas. Halle* (d. 1895), by Watts; *Professor Huxley* (1825-95), by Collier; *Sir Richard Owen* (d. 1892), by Pickersgill; *Michael Faraday* (d. 1867), by Phillips; *George Stephenson* (1781-1848), by Pickersgill; *Professor John Wilson* (*Christopher North;* d. 1854), by Gordon; **William Roscoe** (d. 1831), by Williamson; *Charles Babbage* (d. 1871), inventor of the calculating machine, by Lawrence. — On a screen: *Sir Henry Halford* (d. 1844), by Sir W. Beechey; *'Father Mathew'* (d. 1856), the 'Apostle of Temperance in Ireland', by Leahy. — Busts of *Faraday* (by Brock), *George Stephenson* (by Pitts), and others. Interesting autographs in the cases.

Room XXVII a (Arctic Explorers). This room contains portraits of *Sir John* and *Lady Franklin* (d. 1847 and 1875) and 20 small portraits of Arctic explorers and others connected with the search for Franklin. Also portraits of *Nares* and *McClintock,* the Arctic navigators. Bronze bust of *Franklin,* by Lucchesi. Arctic Council discussing a scheme for the search for Franklin, by Philips.

We now return to R. XXIV (Landing) and descend thence to the —

GROUND FLOOR.

ROOM XXVIII (Judges). Modern Judges, including *Talfourd*, by Pickersgill.

XXIX. CORRIDOR (Miscellaneous Portraits). *Wordsworth*, by Pickersgill; *Scott*, by Gilbert; *Bishop Colenso* (d. 1883); *Lord Campbell* (d. 1861), by Woolnoth; *Sir George Scharf* (d. 1895), former keeper of the National Portrait Gallery, by Ouless; *Jeremy Bentham, the economist and political writer (d. 1832), by T. Frye and H. W. Pickersgill. — Bust of *Dr. Thos. Arnold* (1795-1842), by Behnes.

XXX. LANDING. *Convention of the Anti-Slavery Society* in 1840, by Haydon, with portraits of Clarkson, Fowell Buxton, Gurney, Lady Byron, etc. — Busts of *Lord Francis Jeffrey* (d. 1850), by Park, and *Samuel Lover* (d. 1868), by Foley.

ROOMS XXXI and XXXII, on the groundfloor of the **E. Wing**, form the Sculpture Gallery. R. XXXI contains electrotype casts of statues and busts, including a series representing *English Monarchs* and their wives; figures of *Lord Darnley* and *Mary, Queen of Scots*; recumbent figures of *Edward II.* and *Robert Curthose, Duke of Normandy*; and a statue of *Francis Bacon*, from his tomb. — R. XXXII contains models of busts of the *Duchess of Sutherland* (1806-68) and *Sir James Scarlett* (1799-1871), by Matthew Noble; and a series of bust-models by Sir J. E. Boehm. By the dividing arch is a bust of *Tennyson*, by F. J. Williamson. In the space beyond the arch is a seated figure of *Edward W. Lane* (1801-76), the Orientalist, in Egyptian costume, by his brother. On the end-wall are a marble half-figure of *Mrs. Siddons* (1755-1831), by T. Campbell, and a medallion of *Henry Fawcett* (d. 1884), by Mary Grant. By the windows are bust-models of *C. S. Parnell* (d. 1891), by Mary Grant, and *Dean Buckland* (d. 1856), by H. Weekes. In the centre, a recumbent figure of *Dean Stanley* (d. 1881), by Boehm.

A staircase to the right (as we enter the Gallery) descends to the **Basement,** with —

ROOM XXXIII. The *House of Commons in 1793*, by Karl Anton Hickel, presented by the Emperor of Austria in 1885. — The *First House of Commons after the Reform Bill of 1832*, with 320 portraits, by Hayter. — The *House of Lords in 1820*, during the discussion of the bill to divorce Queen Caroline, by Hayter (with portraits of the Queen, etc.). — Also a large collection of engraved legal portraits.

16. Royal College of Surgeons. Soane Museum.

Floral Hall. Covent Garden Market. St. Paul's. Garrick Club.

Lincoln's Inn Fields (Pl. R, 31; *II*), to the W. of Lincoln's Inn (p. 175), are surrounded by lawyers' offices and form one of the largest squares in London. The gardens were laid out by Inigo Jones, and before their enclosure in 1735 they were a favourite haunt of thieves and a resort of duellists. They were thrown open to the public in 1895. Lord William Russell (p. 163) was executed here in 1683, and among the other names closely associated with the Fields are those of the Duke of Newcastle, prime minister of George II. (house at the corner of Great Queen Street), Blackstone, Spencer Perceval (No. 59), Lord Erskine, Milton, Nell Gwynne, Tennyson (No. 55), John Forster (No. 58; the house of Mr. Tulkinghorn in 'Bleak House'), Brougham (No. 50), and Thomas Campbell (No. 61). Comp. 'Lincoln's Inn Fields', by *C. W. Heckethorn* (1895).

On the S. side of Lincoln's Inn Fields rises the **Royal College of Surgeons,** designed by *Sir Charles Barry*, and erected in 1835. It contains an admirable Museum, conspicuous for its excellent organization and arrangement. Visitors are admitted, through the personal introduction or written order of a member, on Mon., Tues., Wed., and Thurs. from 10 to 4 in winter, and from 10 to 5 in summer. The Museum is closed during the month of September. Application for orders of admission, which are not transferable, may be made to the secretary.

The nucleus of the museum consists of a collection of 13,000 anatomical preparations formed by John Hunter (d. 1793), which was purchased by Government after his death and presented to the College. It is divided into two chief departments: *viz.* the *Physiological Series*, containing specimens of animal organs and formations in a normal state, and the *Pathological Series*, containing similar specimens in an abnormal or diseased condition. The number of specimens in the Museum has been enormously increased since its foundation, and the building containing it has been several times enlarged. It now consists of five main rooms : the Western, Middle, and Eastern Museums, and the New Large and Small Museums (the last two erected in 1888-91).

The **Human Osteological Collection** occupies the groundfloors of the Western, New Large, and New Small Museums and includes an admirable and extensive collection of the skulls of the different nations of the earth, deformed skeletons, abnormal bone formations, and the like. In the Central Wall Case on the E. side of the New Large Museum is the skeleton of the Irish giant Byrne or O'Bryan, 7 ft. 7 in. high; adjoining it, under a glass-shade, is that of the Sicilian dwarf, Caroline Crachami, who died at the age of 10 years, 20 in. in height. Under the same shade are placed wax models of her arm and foot, and beside it is a plaster cast of her face. The Floor Cases contain various anatomical preparations. In the centre of the Western Museum is hung the skeleton of a Greenland whale; a marble statue of Hunter by Weekes, erected in 1864, stands in the middle of the floor at the S. end of the hall.

The **Comparative Osteological Collection** occupies the Eastern Museum, the Middle Museum, and part of the Western Museum. In the centre of the Eastern Museum are the skeletons of the large mammalia: whales (including a sperm-whale or cachalot, 50 ft. long), hippopotamus, giraffe, rhinoceros, elephant, etc. The elephant, Chunee, was exhibited for many years in England, but becoming unmanageable had at last to be shot. The poor animal did not succumb till more than 100 bullets had been fired into its body. The skeleton numbered 4506 A. is that of the first tiger shot by the Prince of Wales in India in 1876. The skeleton of 'Orlando', a Derby winner, and that of a favourite deerhound of Sir Edwin Landseer, are also exhibited here. The Cases round the room contain smaller skeletons. In the Middle Museum the most interesting objects are the large antediluvian skeletons. Skeleton of a gigantic stag (erroneously called the *Irish Elk*), dug up from a bed of shell-marl beneath a peat-bog at Limerick; giant armadilloes from Buenos Ayres; giant sloth (mylodon), also from Buenos Ayres; the huge megatherium, with the missing parts supplied. In the Wall Cases is a number of smaller skeletons and fossils. Several Floor Cases in the Western Museum contain a collection illustrating the zoology of the invertebrates, such as zoophytes, shell-fish, crabs, and beetles.

The galleries round the rooms contain *Pathological Specimens* (W. Museum and New Large Museum), *Physiological Specimens* (E. and Middle Museums), *Dermatological Specimens* (top gallery of W. Museum), etc. The *Collection of Calculi*, the *Toynbee Collection of Diseases of the Ear*, and the *Collection illustrating Diseases of the Eye* (all in the W. Museum) deserve special mention. The *Histological Collection* now comprises 12,000 specimens. The upper galleries of the new museums contain a collection of drawings and photographs illustrating rare or curious diseases. A room, entered from the staircase of the Eastern Museum, contains a collection of surgical instruments.

The College also possesses a library of about 50,000 volumes. The Council Room contains a good portrait of Hunter by *Reynolds* and several busts by *Chantrey*.

At No. 13, Lincoln's Inn Fields, N. side, opposite the College of Surgeons, is **Sir John Soane's Museum** (Pl. R, 31; *II*), founded by *Sir John Soane* (d. 1837), architect of the Bank of England. During March, April, May, June, July, and August this interesting collection is open to the public on Tues., Wed., Thurs., and Frid., from 11 to 5. During the recess visitors are admitted by tickets obtained from the curator, Mr. George Henry Birch, F. S. A. The collection, which is exceedingly diversified in character, occupies about a score of rooms and cabinets, some of which are very small, and is most ingeniously arranged, every corner being turned to account. Many of the contents are of little general interest, but some of the pictures and other objects of art are of great importance and well repay a visit. There are also many curiosities of historical or personal interest. A *General Description* of the contents, price 6*d.*, may be had at the Museum.

The DINING ROOM AND LIBRARY, which the visitor first enters, are decorated somewhat after the Pompeian style. The ceiling-paintings are by *Henry Howard, R. A.*, the principal subjects being Phœbus in his car, Pandora among the gods, Epimetheus receiving Pandora, and the Opening of Pandora's vase. On the walls are *Reynolds'* Snake in the grass, a replica of the picture at the National Gallery, and a portrait of Sir John Soane, by *Lawrence*. The Italic painted fictile vase at the N. end of the room, 2 ft. 8 in. high, the Greek vase and English chopine on the E. side, and a French clock with a small orrery may be mentioned. A glazed case on a table contains a fine illuminated MS. with a frontispiece by *Giulio Clovio*. The library also contains a large collection of valuable old books, drawings, and MSS., which are accessible to the student.

We now pass through two diminutive rooms, forming a corridor, into the MUSEUM, containing numerous marbles, columns, etc. To the right is the PICTURE GALLERY, a room measuring 13 ft. 8 in. in length, 12 ft. 4 in. in breadth, and 19 ft. 6 in. in height, which, by dint of ingenious arrangement, can accommodate as many pictures as a gallery of the same height, 45 ft. long and 20 ft. broad. The walls are covered with movable shutters, hung with pictures on both sides. Among these are: *Hogarth*, *The Rake's Progress, a celebrated series of eight pictures, and *The Election (four pictures); *Canaletto*, The Rialto at Venice, and The Piazza of St. Mark; a series of drawings by *Piranesi*; a collection of *Sir John Soane's* architectural designs; study of a head from one of Raphael's large cartoons, perhaps by *Giulio Romano*, and a copy by Flaxman of two heads from another cartoon. — When the last shutter of the S. wall is opened we see into a well-lighted recess, with a copy of a nymph by Westmacott, and into a small room called the Monk's Parloir (see below).

From the hall with the columns we descend into a kind of crypt, where we thread our way to the left, through numerous statues, both originals and casts, relics of ancient art, modern works by Flaxman and others, and a collection of cinerary urns, to the SEPULCHRAL CHAMBER, which contains the most interesting object in the whole collection. This is an Egyptian *Sarcophagus, found in 1817 by Belzoni in a tomb in the valley of Bîbân el-Mulûk, near the ancient Thebes, and consisting of one block of alabaster or arragonite, 9 ft. 4 in. long, 3 ft. 8 in. wide, and 2 ft. 8 in. deep at the head, covered both internally and externally with hieroglyphics and figures; it is 2½ inches in thickness. The hieroglyphics are interpreted as referring to Seti I., father of Ramses the Great. The sarcophagus was bought by Sir John Soane in 1824 for 2000*l*. On the S. side of this, the lower part of the Museum, is the MONUMENT COURT.

The MONK'S PARLOIR (see above) contains objects of mediæval art, some Peruvian and other antiquities, and two fine Flemish wood-carvings. The rooms on the groundfloor (to which we now re-ascend) are filled with statuary, architectural fragments, terracottas, and models, among which some fine Roman portrait-busts may be noticed. Behind the cast of the Apollo Belvedere is an additional picture-gallery, containing specimens of *Canaletto* (*Port of Venice), *Turner* (*Adm. Tromp's barge entering the Texel; Kirkstall Abbey), *Callcott* (*Passage Point), *Clerisseau*, *Eastlake*, *Ruysdael*, etc. Adjoining this is a recess with portraits of the Soane family, works by *Ruysdael* and *Watteau* (Les Noces), etc. In the BREAKFAST ROOM are some choice illuminated MSS., and an inlaid pistol which once belonged to Peter the Great. This room, for its arrangement, mode of lighting, the use of mirrors, etc., is, perhaps, unique in London.

The DRAWING ROOMS, on the first floor, contain a carved ivory and gilt table and four chairs from the palace of Tippoo Sahib at Seringapatam; a collection of exquisitely delicate miniature paintings on silk, by *Labelle;* a small but choice collection of antique gems (the 'Capece' collection); many drawings and paintings; and various architectural designs by *Sir John Soane*. In the glass-cases are exhibited the first three folio editions of Shakspeare, an original MS. of Tasso's 'Gerusalemme Liberata', several large illuminated MSS., two sketch-books of Sir Joshua Reynolds, etc. On stands in these rooms are cork models of Pompeii, ancient temples, etc.

On the walls of the STAIRCASE are hung pictures, prints, and sculptures. — A large variety of ancient painted glass has been glazed in the windows throughout the museum.

In Sardinia St., beginning at an archway near the S.W. corner of the square and running to the W., is the *Sardinian Catholic Chapel* (Pl. R, 31; *II*), opposite which Benjamin Franklin lodged while working as a printer in Wild Court, a little to the W. A little to the S.E. is the large *King's College Hospital*, behind which lies the once unsavoury district of *Clare Market*, named from the Earls of Clare (tablet) and now considerably improved.

GREAT QUEEN STREET, running to the S.W. from the N.W. corner of Lincoln's Inn Fields, contains *Freemasons' Hall* and *Freemasons'*

Tavern, the London headquarters of the Masonic Craft. Among former residents in this street were Lord Herbert of Cherbury, Sir Godfrey Kneller, and Sheridan. *Trinity Church*, in Little Queen Street, running to the N. to Holborn, stands on the site of the house in which Mary Lamb killed her mother in a fit of insanity (1796). Beyond Drury Lane (p. 182) Great Queen Street is continued by *Long Acre*, with numerous coach-builders' establishments. To the left (S.) of Long Acre diverges Bow Street, in which is the *Royal Italian Opera*, Covent Garden, adjoined by the *Floral Hall*, now used as a foreign fruit wholesale market. Nearly opposite is the *New Bow Street Police Court*, the most important of the 14 metropolitan police courts of London. At the corner of Bow Street and Russell Street was *Will's Coffee House*, the resort of Dryden and other literary men of the 17-18th centuries. Waller, Fielding, Wycherley, and Grinling Gibbons are among the eminent persons who once resided in Bow Street.

Russell Street leads hence to the E. to *Drury Lane Theatre* (p. 65), and to the W. to **Covent Garden Market** (Pl. R, 31 ; *II*), the property of the Duke of Bedford, the principal vegetable, fruit, and flower market in London. It presents an exceedingly picturesque and lively scene, the best time to see the vegetable-market being about 6 o'clock on the mornings of Tuesdays, Thursdays, and Saturdays, the market-days (comp. p. 32). The show of fruit and flowers is one of the finest in the world, presenting a gorgeous array of colours and diffusing a delicious fragrance; it is seen to full advantage from 7 to 10 a.m. The Easter Eve flower-market is particularly brilliant.

The neighbourhood of Covent Garden is full of historic memories. The name reminds us of the *Convent Garden* belonging to the monks of Westminster, which in Ralph Agas's Map of London (1560) is shown walled around, and extending from the Strand to the present Long Acre (see above), then in the open country. The Bedford family received these lands (seven acres, of the yearly value of 6*l*. 6*s*. 8*d*.) as a gift from the Crown in 1552. The square was planned by Inigo Jones ; and vegetables used to be sold here, thus perpetuating the associations of the ancient garden. In 1831 the Duke of Bedford erected the present market-buildings, which have recently been much improved, though they are still quite inadequate for the enormous business transacted here on market-days. The neighbouring streets, Russell, Bedford, and Tavistock, commemorate the family names or titles of the lords of the soil. In the Covent Garden Piazzas, now nearly all cleared away, the families of Lord Crewe, Bishop Berkeley, Lord Hollis, Earl of Oxford, Sir Godfrey Kneller, Sir Kenelm Digby, the Duke of Richmond, and other distinguished persons used to reside. In this square was the old 'Bedford Coffee house', frequented by Garrick, Foote, and Hogarth, where the Beef-Steak Club was held ; and here was the not over savoury 'Old Hummums Hotel'. Here also was 'Evans's' (so named from a former proprietor), a house once the abode of Sir Kenelm Digby, and long noted as a place for suppers and evening entertainments. It is now occupied by a club. — At No. 4 York Street, to the E. of the Flower Market, Thos. de Quincey wrote the 'Confessions of an English Opium Eater'. Charles and Mary Lamb lived at No. 20 Russell Street (1817-23). Joseph Turner (1775-1851), the son of a hair-dresser, was born at No. 20 Maiden Lane, to the S. of Covent Garden; and in the same street Andrew Marvell (1621-78), the poet, once resided, and Voltaire lodged for some time.

The neighbouring church of **St. Paul**, a plain building erected by *Inigo Jones* at the beginning of the 17th cent., contains nothing of interest. It was the first Protestant church of any size erected in London. In the churchyard are buried *Samuel Butler* (d. 1680), the author of 'Hudibras'; *Sir Peter Lely* (*Vandervaes*, d. 1680), the painter; *W. Wycherley* (d. 1715), the dramatist; *Grinling Gibbons* (d. 1721), the carver in wood; *T. A. Arne* (d. 1778), the composer of 'Rule Britannia'; *John Wolcot* (Peter Pindar; d. 1819), the author; *John Taylor* (d. 1654), the 'Water Poet'; and *Kynaston* (d. 1712), the actor of female parts.

The **Garrick Club**, 13 and 15 Garrick Street, Covent Garden, founded in 1831, possesses an important and valuable collection of portraits of celebrated English actors, shown on Wednesdays only, to visitors accompanied by a member. The fine bust of Shakespeare was discovered in 1845, bricked up in a wall at Lincoln's Inn Fields.

17. Whitehall.

United Service Museum. The Horse Guards. The Government Offices.

The broad and handsome street leading from Trafalgar Square, opposite the National Gallery, to the S., towards Westminster, is called **Whitehall** (Pl. R, 26; *IV*); after the famous royal palace of that name formerly situated here, of which the banqueting-hall only now remains.

At the beginning of the 13th cent. the Chief Justiciary, Hubert de Burgh, who resided here, presented his house with its contents to the Dominican monks of Holborn, who afterwards sold it to Walter Gray, Archbishop of York. Thenceforward it was the London residence of the Archbishops of York, and was long known as York House or York Palace. On the downfall of Wolsey, Archbishop of York, and favourite of Henry VIII., York House became crown-property, and received the name of *Whitehall*: —

> 'Sir, you
> Must no more call it York-place, that is past;
> For, since the cardinal fell, that title's lost;
> 'Tis now the king's, and call'd — Whitehall'.
> *Hen. VIII.* iv. 6.

The palace was greatly enlarged and beautified by its new

owner, Henry VIII., and with its precincts became of such extent
as to reach from Scotland Yard to near Bridge Street, and from the
Thames far into St. James's Park, passing over what was then the
narrow street of Whitehall, which it spanned by means of a beautiful gateway designed by Holbein.

The banqueting-hall of old York House, built in the Tudor
style, having been burned down in 1615, James I. conceived the idea
of erecting on its site a magnificent royal residence, designed by
Inigo Jones, which would have filled the whole space between Westminster and Charing Cross, St. James's Park and the Thames. The
building was begun, but, at the time of the breaking out of the
Civil War, the Banqueting Hall only had been completed. In 1691
part of the old palace was burned to the ground, and the remainder
in 1697; so that nothing remained of Whitehall, except the new
hall, still standing on the E. side of Whitehall (see below).

The reminiscences of the tragic episodes of English history
transacted at Whitehall are much more interesting than the place
itself. It was here that Cardinal Wolsey, the haughty, splendour-
loving Archbishop of York, gave his costly entertainments, and
here he was disgraced. Here, too, Henry VIII. became enamoured
of the unhappy Anne Boleyn, at a ball given in honour of the fickle
and voluptuous monarch; and here he died in 1547. Holbein, the
famous painter, occupied rooms in the palace at that period. It
was from Whitehall that Elizabeth was carried as a prisoner to the
Tower, and to Whitehall she returned in triumph as Queen of
England. From an opening made in the wall between the upper
and lower central windows of the Banqueting Hall Charles I. was
led out to the scaffold erected in the street close by. A little later
the Protector Oliver Cromwell took up his residence here with his
secretary, John Milton, and here he died on 3rd Sept., 1658. Here
Charles II., restored, held a profligate court, and here he died in
1685. After the destruction of Whitehall Palace by fire in 1697
St. James's Palace became the royal residence.

The **Banqueting Hall,** one of the most splendid specimens of
the Palladian style of architecture, is 111 ft. long, $55^1/_2$ ft. wide,
and $55^1/_2$ ft. high. The ceiling is embellished with pictures by
Rubens, on canvas, painted abroad, at a cost of 3000*l.*, and sent
to England. They are in nine sections, and represent the Apotheosis of James I. in the centre, with allegorical representations
of peace, plenty, etc., and scenes from the life of Charles I., the
artist's patron. Van Dyck was to have executed for the sides a
series of mural paintings, representing the history and ceremonies
of the Order of the Garter, but the scheme was never carried out.
George I. converted the banqueting-house into a *Royal Chapel*,
which was dismantled in 1890, and in 1894 the United Service
Museum was removed hither (p. 235). The basement floor or crypt,
previously subdivided into dark cellars, was restored and provided

with a concrete floor, while the wood of the oaken pews was used to panel the bases of the walls and piers.

Adjoining the Banqueting Hall on the S. are the new buildings of the **Royal United Service Institution**, which was founded in 1830 and possesses an interesting collection of objects connected with the military and naval professions, and a library. The institution numbers about 4600 members, each of whom pays an entrance fee of 1l. and a yearly subscription of the same amount or a life-subscription of 10l. The new buildings contain a large *Lecture Hall, Library, Smoking Room*, etc., while the *United Service Museum* is accommodated in the Banqueting Hall (see below). Admission to the Museum, see p. 108. Soldiers, sailors, and policemen in uniform are admitted free.

The BANQUETING HALL contains a large °Model of the battle of Waterloo, by *Captain Siborne*, in which 190,000 figures are represented, giving one an admirable idea of the disposition and movements of the forces on the eventful day; relics of Napoleon, Nelson, and the Duke of Wellington; the skeleton of Napoleon's charger, Marengo; the skull of Shaw, the Lifeguardsman; and numerous memorials of Waterloo. *Hamilton's* model of Sebastopol, showing the position of the troops; a model of the battle of Trafalgar, showing the British fleet breaking the enemy's line; and numerous models of war-vessels, of various dates, are also placed here. Reminiscences of the battle of Omdurman (1898) and of the Transvaal War (1900). — The rest of the collection, placed partly in this hall and partly in the BASEMENT, includes weapons and martial equipments from America, Africa, the South Sea Islands, etc.; a *European Armoury*, containing specimens of the armour and weapons of the different European nations; an *Asiatic Armoury*, with Indian guns and armour, etc.; a *Naval Collection*, including models of different kinds of vessels, ships' gear, marine machinery, and the like, including an ingenious little model of a ship, executed by a French prisoner-of-war; relics of Franklin's expedition to the N. pole, and others of the Royal George, sunk at Spithead in 1782; cases containing the swords of Cromwell and General Wolfe; a midshipman's dirk that belonged to Nelson; the pistols of Sir Ralph Abercromby, Bolivar, and Tippoo Sahib; relics of Sir John Moore; personal relics of Drake, Captain Cook, and other famous seamen; numerous other interesting historical relics; quick-firing guns; models of ordnance and specimens of shot and shells; model steam-engines; military models of various kinds: siege-operations with trenches, lines, batteries, approaches, and walls in which a breach has been effected; fortifications, pioneer instruments, etc.; uniforms and equipments of soldiers of different countries; fire-arms and portions of fire-arms at different stages of their manufacture; paintings and photographs of warlike scenes and military equipments and apparatus; trophies from the Crimean War and from the last campaigns in China, Ashantee, etc.

In the garden at the S. end of the building stands a leaden *Statue of James II.*, by Grinling Gibbons, erected behind the Banqueting Hall in 1686 and left undisturbed at the Revolution. It was removed to its present position in 1897.

Whitehall and the neighbourhood now contain various public offices. Near Charing Cross, to the left, is Craig's Court (Pl. R, 26; *IV*), No. 6 in which is the *Royal Almonry*, where the royal alms are distributed at Christmas, Easter, and Whitsuntide.

On Maundy Thursday, *i.e.* the Thursday before Easter, the distribution was formerly made in Whitehall Chapel, but it now takes place in Westminster Abbey. On that day a gift of food, clothing, and money is made to as many poor old men and women as the sovereign has lived years. The 'Maundy Money', which consists of silver penny, two-penny, three-penny, and four-penny pieces, is always fresh from the mint, and, with the exception of the three-penny pieces, is not coined except for this purpose. The name 'Maundy' has been derived from the first words (*mandatum novum*; John XIII, 34) of the Latin anthem usually sung during the ceremony; whence also the baskets in which the doles were placed were called 'maunds'. James II. was the last English sovereign that performed this ceremony in person. This office must not, of course, be confounded with the district in Westminster anciently known as the Almonry, in which Caxton set up his printing-press (comp. p. 272).

Farther on, on the same side of the street, is *Great Scotland Yard*, once the headquarters of the Metropolitan Police (comp. p. 237). Scotland Yard is said to have belonged to the Kings of Scotland (whence its name) from the reign of Edgar to that of Henry II. At a later period Milton, Inigo Jones, Sir Christopher Wren, and other celebrated persons resided here. Opposite, on the right side of Whitehall, is the **Admiralty**, or offices of the governing body of the navy. The building abutting on Whitehall dates from 1722-26, but behind it, in St. James's Park, large and handsome new offices, which when complete will form an extensive quadrangle, have been in course of erection since 1887. The Admiralty Board consists of a First Lord (usually a member of the Cabinet), four Naval Lords, and a Civil Lord, besides a parliamentary and a permanent secretary. To the S. of the Admiralty is the **Horse Guards,** the office of the commander-in-chief of the army, an inconsiderable building with a low clock-tower, erected in 1753 on the site of an old Tilt Yard. It derives its name from its original use as a guard-house for the palace of Whitehall. Two mounted Life Guards are posted here as sentinels every day from 10 a.m. to 4 p.m., and the operation of relieving guard, which takes place hourly, is interesting. At 11 a.m. the troop of 40 Life Guards on duty is relieved by another troop, when a good opportunity is afforded of seeing a number of these fine soldiers together. The infantry sentries on the other side of the Horse Guards, in St. James's Park, are also changed at 11 a.m. A passage, much frequented by pedestrians, leads through the Horse Guards into St. James's Park, but no carriages except those of royalty and of a few privileged persons are permitted to pass.

The vacant space opposite the Horse Guards, between Whitehall Place and Horse Guards Avenue, is to be occupied by the new *War Office* (comp. p. 281), plans for which have been prepared by Mr. William Young.

The **Treasury,** a building 100 yds. in length, situated between the Horse Guards and Downing Street, originally erected during the reign of George I. and provided by Sir Charles Barry with a new façade, is the office of the *Prime Minister (First Lord of the Treasury)* and also contains the *Education Office* and the *Privy Council Office*. The *Office of the Chancellor of the Exchequer* occupies a separate edifice in Downing Street.

To the S., between Downing Street and Charles Street, rise the new **Public Offices**, a large pile of buildings in the Italian style constructed in 1868-73 at a cost of 500,000*l.*, from designs by *Sir G. G. Scott* (d. 1878). They comprise the *Home Office*, the *Foreign Office*, the *Colonial Office*, and the *India Office*. None of these offices are shown to visitors. The effect of the imposing façade towards Parliament Street (the southern prolongation of Whitehall) has been greatly enhanced by the widening of the street to 50 yds., whereby, too, a view of Westminster Abbey from Whitehall is disclosed. The buildings on the W. side of Parliament Street, to the S. of the Home Office, have just been removed (1900), and their site will be occupied by new *Ministerial Offices*, designed by Mr. J. M. Brydon.

The new buildings will be built in line with the other Government Offices, and will ultimately extend back to Delahay Street (comp. Pl. R, 25; *IV*). This widening of the lower part of Parliament Street involved the demolition of *King Street*, a narrow thoroughfare, to the W. of it and the only approach in earlier times from Whitehall to Westminster. At the N. end, removed to make room for the present Government Offices, stood Holbein's great gate (p. 234). Spenser, the poet, spent his last days in King Street, and he was carried hence to Westminster Abbey. Cromwell's mother lived here, often visited by her affectionate son; so did Dr. Sydenham, Lord North, Bishop Goodman, Sir Henry Wotton, and at one time Oliver Cromwell himself. Through this narrow street all the pageants from Whitehall to the Abbey and Westminster Hall passed, whether for burial, coronation, or state-trials. Parliament Street was opened only in 1732, long after Whitehall had ceased to be a royal residence, and was carried through the old privy garden of Whitehall. — No. 17 *Delahay Street* was the home of Judge Jeffreys (d. 1689). The office of the *Society for the Propagation of the Gospel in Foreign Parts* is at No. 19.

The modern edifice on the E. side of Whitehall opposite the Treasury, in the Franco-Scottish Renaissance style, is *Montague House*, the mansion of the Duke of Buccleuch, containing a splendid collection of miniatures and many valuable pictures.

Whitehall Gardens, to the N. of Montague House, occupy the site of the old Privy Garden of Whitehall. The office of the *Board of Trade* is now here. No. 2 was the home of Benjamin Disraeli (Lord Beaconsfield) in 1873-75. No. 4 was the town-house of Sir Robert Peel, whither he was carried to die after falling from his horse in Constitution Hill (June 29th, 1850).

Derby Street, on the E. side of Parliament Street, leads to *New Scotland Yard*, on the Victoria Embankment, the headquarters of the Metropolitan Police since 1891. The turreted building, in the Scottish baronial style, was designed by Norman Shaw, and is impressive by its simplicity of outline and dignity of mass. In the 'Lost Property Office' (entr. from the Embankment) lost articles found and sent to the police headquarters may be reclaimed on payment of 15 per cent of their value.

18. Houses of Parliament and Westminster Hall.
St. Margaret's Church.   Westminster Bridge.

The ***Houses of Parliament**, or **New Palace of Westminster** (Pl. R, 25; *IV*), which, together with Westminster Hall, form a single pile of buildings, have been erected since 1840, from a plan by *Sir*

Charles Barry, which was selected as the best of 97 sent in for competition. The previous edifice was burned down in 1834. The new building is in the richest late-Gothic (Tudor or Perpendicular) style, and covers an area of 8 acres. It contains 11 courts, 100 staircases, and 1100 apartments, and has cost in all about 3,000,000*l*. Although so costly a national structure, some serious defects are observable; the external stone (dolomite) is gradually crumbling, and the building stands on so low a level that the basement rooms are said to be lower than the Thames at high tide. The *Clock Tower (St. Stephen's Tower)*, at the N. end, next to Westminster Bridge, is 318 ft. high; the *Middle Tower* is 300 ft. high; and the S.W. *Victoria Tower*, the largest of the three (75 ft. sq.), through which the Queen enters on the opening and prorogation of Parliament, attains a height of 340 ft. The archway is 65 ft. high. The large clock has four dials, each 23 ft. in diameter, and it takes five hours to wind up the striking parts. A light in the Clock Tower by night, and the Union flag flying from the Victoria Tower by day, indicate that the 'House' is sitting. The great Bell of the Clock Tower, popularly known as 'Big Ben' (named after Sir Benjamin Hall, First Commissioner of Works at the time of its erection) is one of the largest known, weighing no less than 13 tons. It was soon found to have a flaw or crack, and its tone became shrill, but the crack was filed open, so as to prevent vibration, and the tone became quite pure. It is heard in calm weather over the greater part of London. The imposing river front (E.) of the edifice is 940 ft. in length. It is adorned with statues of the English monarchs from William the Conqueror down to Queen Victoria, with armorial bearings, and many other enrichments.

The impression produced by the interior is in its way no less imposing than that of the exterior. The tasteful fitting-up of the different rooms, some of which are adorned down to the minutest details with lavish magnificence, is in admirable keeping with the office and dignity of the building.

The Houses of Parliament are shown on Saturdays from 10 to 4, (no admission, however, after 3.30) by tickets obtained gratis at the entrance. We enter on the W. side by a door adjacent to the Victoria Tower (public entrance also through Westminster Hall; Handbook, 6*d.* or 1*s.*, unnecessary).

Ascending the staircase from the entrance door, we first reach the *Norman Porch*, a small square hall, with Gothic groined vaulting, and borne by a finely clustered central pillar. We next enter (to the right) the QUEEN'S ROBING ROOM, a handsome chamber, 45 ft. in length, the chief feature in which is formed by the fresco paintings by *Mr. Dyce*, representing the virtues of chivalry, the subjects being taken from the Legend of King Arthur. Above the fireplace the three virtues illustrated are Courtesy, Religion, and Generosity; on the N. side are Hospitality and Mercy. The fine

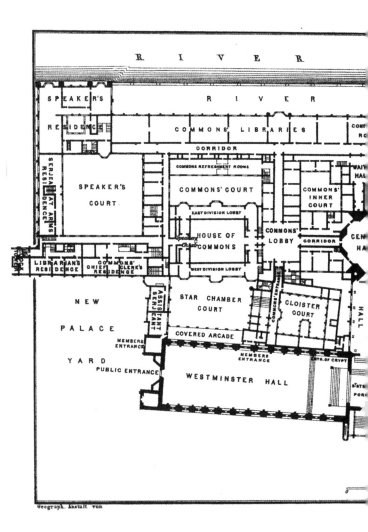

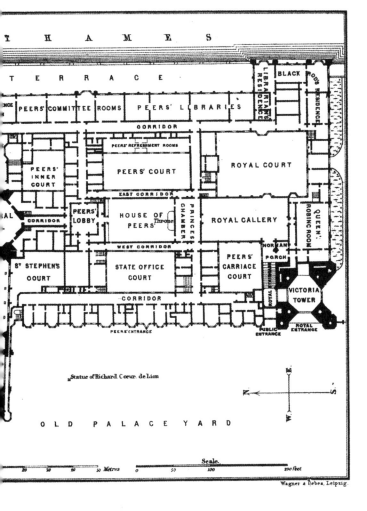

THAMES

TERRACE

PEERS' COMMITTEE ROOMS   PEERS' LIBRARIES

LIBRARIAN'S RESIDENCE   BLACK ROD'S RESIDENCE

CORRIDOR

PEERS' REFRESHMENT ROOMS

PEERS'
INNER
COURT   PEERS' COURT   ROYAL COURT

EAST CORRIDOR

CORRIDOR   PEERS'
LOBBY   HOUSE OF
PEERS   Throne   PRINCESS CHAMBER   ROYAL GALLERY   QUEEN'S ROBING ROOM

WEST CORRIDOR   NORMAN
PORCH

S.T. STEPHEN'S
COURT   STATE OFFICE
COURT   PEERS'
CARRIAGE
COURT   ROYAL

VICTORIA
TOWER

CORRIDOR

PEERS' ENTRANCE   PUBLIC
ENTRANCE   ROYAL
ENTRANCE

Statue of Richard Cœur de Lion

N   E   S   W

OLD   PALACE   YARD

Scale.

20   30   40   50 Metres   0   50   100   200 feet

Wagner & Debes, Leipzig.

dado panelling with carvings by *H. H. Armstead, R. A.*, illustrative of Arthurian legends, the rich ceiling, the fireplace, the doors, the flooring, and the state-chair at the E. end of the room are all worthy of notice. Next comes the ROYAL or VICTORIA GALLERY, 110 ft. long, through which the Queen, issuing from the Queen's Robing Room on the S., proceeds in solemn procession to the House of Peers, for the purpose of opening or proroguing Parliament. On these occasions privileged persons are admitted into this hall by orders obtained at the Lord Chamberlain's Office. The pavement consists of fine mosaic work; the ceiling is panelled and richly gilt. The sides are adorned with two large frescoes in water-glass by *Maclise:* on the left, Death of Nelson at Trafalgar (comp. p. 186), and on the right, Meeting of Blücher and Wellington after Waterloo.

The PRINCE'S CHAMBER, the smaller apartment entered on quitting the Victoria Gallery, is a model of simple magnificence, being decorated with dark wood in the style for which the middle ages are famous. Opposite the door is a group in marble by *Gibson*, representing Queen Victoria enthroned, with allegorical figures of Clemency and Justice. The stained-glass windows on the W. and E. exhibit the rose, thistle, and shamrock, the emblems of England, Scotland, and Ireland. In the panels of the handsome wainscot is a series of portraits of English monarchs and their relatives of the Tudor period (1485-1603).

These are as follows, beginning to the left of the entrance door: 1. Louis XII. of France; 2. Mary, daughter of Henry VII. of England and wife of Louis; 3. Charles Brandon, Duke of Suffolk, Mary's second husband; 4. Marquis of Dorset; 5. Lady Jane Grey; 6. Lord Guildford Dudley, her husband; 7. James IV. of Scotland; 8. Queen Margaret, daughter of Henry VII. of England and wife of James (through this princess the Stuarts derived their title to the English throne); 9. Earl of Angus, second husband of Margaret, and Regent of Scotland; 10. James V.; 11. Mary of Guise, wife of James V., and mother of Mary Stuart; 12. Queen Mary Stuart; 13. Francis II. of France, Mary Stuart's first husband; 14. Lord Darnley, her second husband; 15. Henry VII.; 16. Elizabeth, daughter of Edward IV., and wife of Henry (this marriage put an end to the Wars of the Roses, by uniting the Houses of York and Lancaster); 17. Arthur, Prince of Wales; 18. Catharine of Aragon; 19. Henry VIII.; 20. Anne Boleyn; 21. Jane Seymour; 22. Anne of Cleves; 23. Catharine Howard; 24. Catharine Parr; 25. Edward VI.; 26. Queen Mary of England; 27. Philip of Spain, her husband; 28. Queen Elizabeth.

Over these portraits runs a frieze with oak leaves and acorns and the armorial bearings of the English sovereigns since the Conquest; below, in the sections of the panelling, are 12 reliefs in oak, representing events in English history (Tudor period).

Two doors lead from this room into the *HOUSE OF PEERS, which is sumptuously decorated in the richest Gothic style. The oblong chamber, in which the peers of England sit in council, is 90 ft. in length, 45 ft. broad, and 45 ft. high. The floor is almost entirely occupied with the red leather benches of the 550 members. The twelve fine stained-glass windows contain portraits of all the kings and queens of England since the Conquest. At night the House is lighted by electricity. Eighteen niches between the windows are occupied by statues of the barons who extorted the Magna Charta from King John. The very handsome walls and ceiling are decorated with heraldic and other emblems.

Above, in recesses at the upper and lower ends of the room, are six frescoes, the first attempts on a large scale of modern English art in this department of painting. That on the wall above the throne, in the centre, represents the Baptism of King Ethelbert (about 596), by *Dyce;* to the left of it, Edward III. investing his son, the 'Black Prince', with the Order of the Garter, by *Cope;* on the right, Henry, son of Henry IV., acknowledging the authority of Judge Gascoigne, who had committed the Prince to prison for striking him, by *Redgrave.* — Opposite, at the N. end of the chamber, three symbolical pictures of the Spirits of Religion, Justice, and Chivalry, by *Horsley, W. C. Thomas,* and *Maclise.*

At the S. end of the hall, raised by a few steps, and covered with a richly gilded canopy, is the magnificent throne of the Queen. On the right of it is the lower throne of the Prince of Wales, while on the left is that intended for the sovereign's consort. At the sides are two large gilt candelabra.

The celebrated woolsack of the Lord Chancellor, a kind of cushioned ottoman, stands in front of the throne, almost in the centre of the hall. — At the N. end of the chamber, opposite the throne, is the *Bar,* where official communications from the Commons to the Lords are delivered, and where law-suits on final appeal are pleaded. Above the Bar are the galleries for the reporters and for strangers. Above the throne on either side are seats for foreign ambassadors and other distinguished visitors.

From the House of Lords we pass into the PEERS' LOBBY, another rectangular apartment, richly fitted up, with a door on each side. The brass foliated wings of the southern door are well worthy of examination. The corners contain elegant candelabra of brass. The encaustic tiled pavement, with a fine enamel inlaid with brass in the centre, is of great beauty. Each peer has in this lobby his own hat-peg, etc., provided with his name.

The door on the left (W.) side leads into the PEERS' ROBING ROOM (not usually shown), which is decorated with frescoes by *Herbert.* Two only have been finished (Moses bringing the Tables of the Law from Sinai, and the Judgment of Daniel).

The door on the N. side opens on the PEERS' CORRIDOR, the way to the Central Hall and the House of Commons. This corridor is embellished with the following eight frescoes (beginning on the left): —

1. Burial of Charles I. (beheaded 1649); 2. Expulsion of the Fellows of a college at Oxford for refusing to subscribe to the Covenant; 3. Defence of Basing House by the Cavaliers against the Roundheads; 4. Charles I. erecting his standard at Nottingham; 5. Speaker Lenthall vindicating the rights of the House of Commons against Charles I. on his attempt to arrest the five members; 6. Departure of the London train-bands to the relief of Gloucester; 7. Embarkment of the Pilgrim Fathers for New England; 8. Lady Russell taking leave of her husband before his execution.

The spacious *CENTRAL HALL, in the middle of the building, is octagonal in shape, and richly decorated. It is 60 ft. in diameter and 75 ft. high. The surfaces of the stone-vaulting, between the massive and richly embossed ribs, are inlaid with Venetian mosaics, representing in frequent repetition the heraldic emblems of the English crown, *viz.* the rose, shamrock, thistle, portcullis, and harp. Lofty portals lead from this hall into (N.) the Corridor to the House of Commons; to (W.) St. Stephen's Hall; to (E.) the Waiting Hall (see below); and (S.) the House of Peers (see p. 239). Above the first and last of these doors are St. David and St. George, in glass mosaic, by *Poynter*. Here, too, are statues of Lord John Russell (d. 1878; by Boehm), Lord Iddesleigh (d. 1887; by Boehm), Lord Granville (d. 1891; by Thornycroft), and the Right Hon. W. E. Gladstone (d. 1898; by Pomeroy).

The niches at the sides of the portals bear statues of English sovereigns. At the W. door: on the left, Edward I., his consort Eleanor, and Edward II.; on the right, Isabella, wife of King John, Henry III., and Eleanor, his wife. At the N. door: on the left, Isabella, wife of Edward II., Henry IV., and Edward III.; on the right, Richard II., his consort, Anne of Bohemia, and Philippa, wife of Edward III. At the E. door: on the left, Jane of Navarre, wife of Henry IV., Henry V., and his wife Catharine; on the right, Henry VI., Margaret, his wife, and Edward VI. At the S. door: on the left, Elizabeth, wife of Edward IV., Edward V., and Richard III.; on the right, Anne, wife of Richard III., Henry VII., and his consort Elizabeth. The niches in the windows are filled with similar statues.

Round the handsome mosaic pavement runs the inscription (in the Latin of the Vulgate), 'Except the Lord keep the house, their labour is but lost that build it'.

A door on the E. side of the Central Hall leads to the HALL OF THE POETS, also called the UPPER WAITING HALL (not usually shown). It contains the following frescoes of scenes from English poetry, now in a very dilapidated condition, and mostly covered up: — Griselda's first trial of patience, from Chaucer, by *Cope*; St. George conquering the Dragon, from Spenser, by *Watts*; King Lear disinheriting his daughter Cordelia, from Snakspeare, by *Herbert*; Satan touched by the spear of Ithuriel, from Milton, by *Horsley*; St. Cecilia, from Dryden, by *Tenniel*; Personification of the Thames, from Pope, by *Armitage*; Death of Marmion, from Scott, by *Armitage*; Death of Lara, from Byron, by *W. Dyce*.

Beyond the N. door of the Central Hall, and corresponding with the passage leading to the House of Lords in the opposite direction, is the COMMONS' CORRIDOR, leading to the House of Commons. It is also adorned with 8 frescoes, as follows (beginning on the left): —

1. Alice Lisle concealing fugitive Cavaliers after the battle of Sedgemoor; 2. Last sleep of the Duke of Argyll; 3. The Lords and Commons delivering the crown to William and Mary in the Banqueting Hall; 4. Acquittal of the Seven Bishops in the reign of James II. (comp. p. 244); 5. Monk declaring himself in favour of a free parliament; 6. Landing of Charles II.; 7. The executioner hanging Wishart's book round the neck of Montrose; 8. Jane Lane helping Charles II. to escape.

We next pass through the COMMONS' LOBBY to the —

HOUSE OF COMMONS, 75 ft. in length, 45 ft. wide, and 41 ft. high, very substantially and handsomely fitted up with oak-panelling, in a simpler and more business-like style than the House of Lords. The present ceiling, which hides the original one, was constructed to improve the lighting and ventilation. The members of the House (670 in number, though seats are provided for 476 only) enter either by the public approach, or by a private entrance through a side-door to the E. of Westminster Hall and along an arcade between this hall and the Star Chamber Court. The twelve stained glass windows are adorned with the armorial bearings of parliamentary boroughs. In the evening the House is lighted through the glass panels of the ceiling. The seat of the Speaker or president is at the N. end of the chamber, in a straight line with the woolsack in the House of Lords. The benches to the right of the Speaker are the recognised seats of the Government Party; the ministers occupy the front bench. On the left of the Speaker are the members forming the Opposition, the leaders of which also take their seats on the front bench. In front of the Speaker's table is the Clerks' table, on which the *Mace* lies when the House is in session. The Reporters' Gallery is above the speaker, while above it again, behind an iron grating, is the Ladies' Gallery.

At the S. end of the House, opposite the Speaker, are the galleries for strangers. The upper, or Strangers' Gallery, can be visited by an order from a member of parliament. To the lower, or Speaker's Gallery, admission is granted only on the Speaker's order, obtained by a member. Strangers will add considerably to their intelligent appreciation of the scene before them by obtaining a copy of the Order of the Day from the ushers (small fee). The row of seats in front of the Speaker's Gallery is appropriated to members of the peerage and to distinguished strangers. The galleries at the sides of the House are for the use of members, and are deemed part of the House.

The seats underneath the galleries, on a level with the floor of the House, but outside the bar, are appropriated to members of the diplomatic corps and to distinguished strangers.

Permission to be present at the debates of the Lower House can be obtained only from a member of parliament. The House of Lords, when sitting as a Court of Appeal, is open to the public; on other occasions a peer's order is necessary. On each side of the House of Commons is a '*Division Lobby*', into which the members pass, when a vote is taken, for the purpose of being counted. The '*Ayes*', or those who are favourable to the motion, retire into the W. lobby, to the right of the Speaker; the '*Noes*', or those who vote against the motion, retire into the E. lobby, to the Speaker's left.

Returning to the Central Hall, we pass through the door at its western (right) extremity, leading to ST. STEPHEN'S HALL, which is 75 ft. long, 30 ft. broad, and 55 ft. high. It occupies the site of old St. Stephen's Chapel, founded in 1330, and long used for meetings of the Commons. Along the walls are marble statues of celebrated English statesmen: on the left (S.), Hampden, Selden, Sir Robert Walpole, Lord Chatham, his son Pitt, and the Irish orator Grattan; on the right (N.), Lord Clarendon, Lord Falkland, Lord Somers, Lord Mansfield, Fox, and Burke.

The niches in the corners of the hall are occupied by statues of English sovereigns. By the E. door: on the left, Matilda, Henry II., Eleanor; on the right, Richard Cœur de Lion, Berengaria, and John. By the W. door: on the left, William the Conqueror, Matilda, William II; on the right, Henry I. Beauclerc, Matilda, and Stephen.

A broad flight of steps leads hence through St. Stephen's Porch (62 ft. in height), passing a large stained-glass window, and turning to the right, to *Westminster Hall.*

The present **Westminster Hall** is part of the ancient Palace of Westminster founded by the Anglo-Saxon kings, and occupied by their successors down to Henry VIII. The hall was begun by William Rufus, son of the Conqueror, in 1097, continued and extended by Henry III. and Edward I., and almost totally destroyed by fire in 1291. Edward II. afterwards began to rebuild it; and in 1398 Richard II. caused it to be remodelled and enlarged, supplying it with a new roof. It is one of the largest halls in the world with a wooden ceiling unsupported by columns. Its length is 290 ft., breadth 68 ft., and height 92 ft. The oaken roof, with its hammer-beams, repaired in 1820 with the wood of an old vessel in Portsmouth Harbour, is considered a masterpiece of timber architecture, both in point of beauty and constructive skill.

Westminster Hall, which now forms a vestibule to the Houses of Parliament, is rich in interesting historical associations. In it were held some of the earliest English parliaments, one of which declared Edward II. to have forfeited the crown; and by a curious fatality the first scene of public importance in the new hall, as restored or rebuilt by Richard II., was the deposition of that unfortunate monarch. In this hall the English monarchs down to George IV. gave their coronation-festivals; and here Edward III. entertained the captive kings, David of Scotland and John of France. Here Charles I. was condemned to death; and here, a few years later (1653), Cromwell, wearing the royal purple lined with ermine, and holding a golden sceptre in one hand and the Bible in the other, was saluted as Lord Protector. Within eight years afterwards the Protector's body was rudely dragged from its resting-place in Westminster Abbey and thrust into a pit at Tyburn, while his head was exposed with those of Bradshaw and Ireton on the pinnacles of this same Westminster Hall, where it remained for 25 or 30 years. A high wind at last carried it to the ground. The family of the sentry who picked it up afterwards sold it to one of the Russells, a distant descendant of Cromwell, and it passed finally into the possession of Dr. Wilkinson, one of whose descendants, at Sevenoaks, Kent, claims now to possess it. There is some evidence, however, that the Protector's body, after exhumation, was buried in Red Lion Square, and that another, substituted for it, was deprived of its head and buried at Tyburn.

Many other famous historical characters were condemned to

16*

death in Westminster Hall, including William Wallace, the brave champion of Scotland's liberties; Sir John Oldcastle, better known as Lord Cobham; Sir Thomas More; the Protector Somerset; Sir Thomas Wyatt; Robert Devereux, Earl of Essex; Guy Fawkes; and the Earl of Strafford. Among other notable events transacted at Westminster Hall was the acquittal of the Seven Bishops, who had been committed to the Tower for their opposition to the illegal dispensing power of James II.; the condemnation of the Scottish lords Kilmarnock, Balmerino, and Lovat; the trial of Lord Byron (grand-uncle of the poet) for killing Mr. Chaworth in a duel; the condemnation of Lord Ferrars for murdering his valet; and the acquittal of Warren Hastings, after a trial which lasted seven years.

The last public festival held in Westminster Hall was at the coronation of George IV., when the King's champion in full armour rode into the hall, and, according to ancient custom, threw his gauntlet on the floor, challenging to mortal combat anyone who might dispute the title of the sovereign. The ceremony of swearing in the Lord Mayor took place here for the last time in 1882, and is now performed in the new Law Courts (p. 179). Mr. Gladstone's coffin lay here in state for two days before his interment (May, 1898).

On the E. side of the hall are placed the following marble statues (beginning from the left): Mary, wife of William III., James I., Charles I., Charles II., William III., George IV., William IV. A tablet on the E. wall marks the position of an archway which formed the chief access to the House of Commons from 1547 to 1680. It was through this archway that Charles I. passed to arrest the Five Members on Jan. 4th, 1641-42. A tablet on the steps and another near the middle of the floor mark the spots where Charles I. and Strafford (1641) stood during their trials.

From the first landing of the staircase leading to St. Stephen's Hall a narrow door to the left (E.) leads to ST. STEPHEN'S CRYPT (properly the *Church of St. Mary's Undercroft*), a low vaulted structure supported by columns, measuring 90 ft. in length, 28 ft. in breadth, and 20 ft. in height. It was erected by King Stephen, rebuilt by Edwards II. and III., and, after having long fallen to decay, has recently been thoroughly restored and richly decorated with painting and gilding. *St. Stephen's Cloisters*, on the E. side of Westminster Hall, were built by Henry VIII. and have been lately restored. They are beautifully adorned with carving, groining, and tracery, but are not open to the public. The other multifarious portions of this immense pile of buildings include 18 or 20 official residences of various sizes, libraries, committee rooms, and dining, refreshment, and smoking rooms. The *Terrace*, overlooking the Thames, is much resorted to by members and their friends for afternoon tea. The number of statues, outside and inside, is about five hundred.

Outside Westminster Hall, on the W., stands a fine bronze *Statue of Oliver Cromwell* (1599-1658), by Hamo Thornycroft, erected in 1899. The statue is 10 ft. high, and stands on a pedestal 12 ft. in height.

On the W. side of Westminster Hall, and to the N. of the Abbey, stands **St. Margaret's Church** (Pl. R, 25; *IV*), which, down to 1858, used to be attended by the House of Commons in state on four days in the year, as then prescribed in the Prayer Book. It was erected in the time of Edward I. on the site of an earlier church built by Edward the Confessor in 1064, and was greatly altered and improved under Edward IV. The stained-glass window of the Crucifixion at the E. end was executed at Gouda in Holland, and is said to have been a gift from the town of Dordrecht to Henry VII. Henry VIII. presented it to Waltham Abbey. At the time of the Commonwealth it was concealed, and after various vicissitudes it was at length purchased in 1758 by the church-wardens of St. Margaret's for 400*l.*, and placed in its present position. William Caxton, whose printing-press was set up in 1476-77 in the almonry, formerly standing near the W. front of Westminster Abbey, was buried here in 1491. From the fact of a chapel existing in the old almonry, printers' workshops and also guild-meetings of printers are still called 'chapels'. Sir Walter Raleigh, who was executed in front of the palace of Westminster in 1618, was buried in the chancel. The church, the interior of which was restored in 1878, is open daily, 9-1 and 2-4.30, except Sat. afternoon (entr. by the E. or vestry door, facing Westminster Hall).

The porch at the E. door was erected as a memorial of *Robert Lowe, Viscount Sherbrooke* (d. 1894), and contains a marble bust of him. At the E. end of the S. aisle is a stained-glass window placed here by the printers in 1882 in memory of Caxton, containing his portrait, with the Venerable Bede on his right and Erasmus on his left. On a tablet below the window is a verse by Tennyson, referring to Caxton's motto, '*Fiat lux*'. To the right of the doorway, low down, is a brass memorial of Raleigh, buried here in 1618. The large and handsome window over the W. door was put up by Americans to the memory of Sir Walter Raleigh in 1882; it contains portraits of Raleigh and several of his distinguished contemporaries, and also scenes connected with the life of Raleigh and the colonisation of America. The poetic inscription on the Raleigh window was written by Mr. J. Russell Lowell. There are also windows in the S. wall in memory of Lord and Lady Hatherley, Phillips Brooks, Bishop of Massachusetts (d. 1893), Sir Thomas Erskine May (d. 1886), the great authority on Constitutional Law, etc., and also one erected in 1887 in memory of Queen Victoria's Jubilee, with an inscription by Browning. The window at the W. end of the S. aisle commemorates Lord Frederick Cavendish, assassinated at Dublin in 1882. At the W. end of the N. aisle is a memorial window (erected by Mr. G. W. Childs) to John Milton, whose second wife and infant child are buried here and whose banns are in the parish-register; the inscription is by Whittier. Edmund Waller, Samuel Pepys, and Thomas Campbell were also married in this church. In the N. wall are windows to Mr. Edward Lloyd (1815-90), printer and publisher, with a verse by Sir Edwin Arnold; to Admiral Blake (d. 1657), 'chief founder of England's naval supremacy', who was buried in St. Margaret's churchyard after being exhumed from Westminster Abbey; and to Mr. W. H. Smith (d. 1891), leader of the House of Commons under Lord

Salisbury. Besides Raleigh and Caxton the church shelters the remains of Skelton (d. 1529), the satirist, and James Harrington (d. 1677), author of 'Oceana'. Perhaps the most interesting of the old monuments is that of *Lady Dudley* (d. 1600), with its painted effigy (near the E. end of the S. wall). Near this monument is a brass tablet commemorating Dean Farrar's connection with St. Margaret's.

In Old Palace Yard, to the S., between the Houses of Parliament and Westminster Abbey, rises an *Equestrian Statue of Richard Coeur de Lion*, in bronze, by *Marochetti*. Farther on are the *Victoria Tower Gardens*, abutting on the Thames, and affording a fine view of Westminster Bridge. — Thence to the *Tate Gallery*, see p. 274.

To the N. of St. Margaret's, in Parliament Square, is a bronze *Statue of Lord Beaconsfield* (d. 1881), in the robes of the Garter, by *Raggi*, unveiled in April, 1883. To the right, opposite the entrance into New Palace Yard, stands the bronze *Statue of the Earl of Derby* (d. 1869), in the robes of a peer, 10 ft. high, by *Noble*, erected in 1874. The granite pedestal bears four reliefs in bronze, representing his career as a statesman. A little farther to the right is a bronze statue of *Lord Palmerston* (d. 1865), and on the N. side of the square is that of *Sir Robert Peel* (d. 1850). On the W. side of the square is the bronze *Statue of Canning* (d. 1827), by *Westmacott*, near which, at the corner of Great George Street, is a handsome Gothic fountain, erected in 1863 as a memorial to the distinguished men who brought about the abolition of slavery in the British dominions.

The Surveyors' Institution, 12 Great George Street, contains a *Forestry Museum*, mainly illustrating the diseases of trees, parasite growths, and insect pests. Strangers are admitted on the introduction of a member of the institution. On the opposite side of the street is the *Institute of Civil Engineers* (Pl. R, 25; *IV*), occupying the site of a house in which Lord Byron's body lay in state in 1824. The busts on the exterior represent Telford, Brindley, Watt, Rennie, Stephenson, Brunel, and Smeaton. Great George Street ends at Storey's Gate (p. 329).

*Westminster Bridge (Pl. R, 29; *IV*), erected in 1856-62, by *Page*, at a cost of 250,000*l*., on the site of an earlier stone bridge, is 1160 ft. long and 85 ft. broad (carriage-way 53 ft., side-walks each 15 ft.). It consists of seven iron arches borne by granite buttresses, the central arch having a span of 120 ft., the others of 114 ft. The bridge is one of the handsomest in London, and affords an admirable view of the Houses of Parliament. It was the view from this bridge that suggested Wordsworth's fine sonnet, beginning 'Earth has not anything to show more fair'. Below the bridge, on the left bank, is the beginning of the *Victoria Embankment* (p. 150); above, on the right bank, is the *Albert Embankment*, with the extensive *Hospital of St. Thomas* (p. 380).

19. Westminster Abbey.

Westminster Column. Westminster School. Church House. Westminster Hospital.

On the low ground on the left bank of the Thames, where Westminster Abbey now stands, once overgrown with thorns and surrounded by water, and therefore called *Thorney Isle*, a church is said to have been erected in honour of St. Peter by the Anglo-Saxon king Sebert about 616. With the church was connected a Benedictine religious house *(monasterium,* or *minster)*, which, in reference to its position to the W. of the Cistercian Abbey of St. Mary of the Graces (Eastminster; see p. 164), was called **Westminster Abbey** (Pl. R, 25; *IV*).

The church, after having been destroyed by the Danes, appears to have been re-erected by King Edgar in 985. The regular establishment of the Abbey, however, may be ascribed to Edward the Confessor, who built a church here which seems to have been almost as large as the present one (1049-65). The Abbey was entirely rebuilt in the latter half of the 13th cent. by Henry III. and his son Edward I., who left it substantially in its present condition, though important alterations and additions were made in the two succeeding centuries. The Chapel of Henry VII. was erected at the beginning of the 16th cent., and the towers were added by Wren and Hawkesmore in 1722-40. The façade of the N. transept was restored in 1890 from designs by Sir G. G. Scott and Mr. Pearson; and the view of the exterior was improved in 1895 by the removal of several houses in Old Palace Yard. At the Reformation the Abbey, which had been richly endowed by former kings, shared in the general fate of the religious houses; its property was confiscated, and the church converted into the cathedral of a bishopric, which lasted only from Dec., 1540, to March, 1550. Under Queen Mary the monks returned, but Elizabeth restored the arrangements of Henry VIII., and conveyed the Abbey to a Dean, who presided over a chapter of 12 Canons. — The title Archbishop of Westminster, recently created by the Pope, is not officially recognised in England.

Westminster Abbey †, with its royal burial-vaults and long series of monuments to celebrated men, is not unreasonably regarded by the English as their national Walhalla, or Temple of Fame; and interment within its walls is considered the last and greatest honour which the nation can bestow on the most deserving of her offspring. The honour has often, however, been conferred on persons unworthy of it, and even on children.

'The spaciousness and gloom of this vast edifice produce a profound and mysterious awe. We step cautiously and softly about, as if fearful

---

† The best guide to Westminster Abbey is the *Deanery Guide*, by *M. C.* and *E. T. Bradley*, published by the *Pall Mall Gazette* (illustrated; price 6 d.).

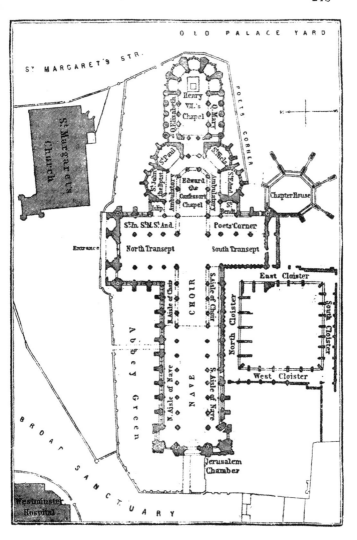

of disturbing the hallowed silence of the tomb; while every footfall whispers along the walls, and chatters among the sepulchres, making us more sensible of the quiet we have interrupted. It seems as if the awful nature of the place presses down upon the soul, and hushes the beholder into noiseless reverence. We feel that we are surrounded by the congregated bones of the great men of past times, who have filled history with their deeds, and the earth with their renown'. — *Washington Irving*.

'When I look upon the tombs of the great, every emotion of envy dies in me: when I read the epitaphs of the beautiful, every inordinate desire goes out: when I meet with the grief of parents upon a tombstone, my heart melts with compassion: when I see the tombs of the parents themselves, I consider the vanity of grieving for those whom we must quickly follow: when I see kings lying by those who deposed them, when I consider rival wits placed side by side, or the holy men who divided the world with their contests and disputes, I reflect with sorrow and astonishment on the little competitions, factions, and debates of mankind'. — *Addison*.

The church is in the form of a Latin cross. The much admired chapel at the E. end is in the Perpendicular style. The other parts of the church, with the exception of the unpleasing and incongruous W. towers by Wren, and a few doubtful Norman remains, are Early English. The impression produced by the interior is very striking, owing to the harmony of the proportions, the richness of the colouring, and the beauty of the Purbeck marble columns and of the triforium. In many respects, however, the effect is sadly marred by restorations and by the egregiously bad taste displayed in several of the monuments. The choir extends beyond the transept into the nave, from which it is separated by an iron screen. In front of the altar is a curious old mosaic pavement with tasteful arabesques, brought from Rome in 1268 by Abbot Ware. The fine wood-work of the choir was executed in 1848. The organ was entirely rebuilt by Mr. Hill in 1884, and stands at the two extremities of the screen between the choir and the nave. It is connected by electric wires with an echo organ in the triforium, above Tennyson's monument (p. 257). The very elaborate and handsome reredos, erected in 1867, is chiefly composed of red and white alabaster. The large figures in the niches represent Moses, St. Peter, St. Paul, and David. The recess above the table contains a fine Venetian glass mosaic, by *Salviati*, representing the Last Supper. In the S. bay of the sanctuary is a portrait of Richard II. on panel, formerly in the Jerusalem Chamber, the oldest contemporary representation of an English sovereign. Behind it is some old tapestry from Westminster School, with the names of Westminster scholars painted on its ends. The Abbey, or, as it is officially termed, the Collegiate Church of St. Peter, is now decorated with upwards of 20 stained-glass windows.

The total length of the church, including the chapel of Henry VII., is 513 ft.; length of the transept from N. to S., 200 ft.; breadth of nave and aisles, 75 ft., of transept, 80 ft.; height of the church, 102 ft., of towers, 225 ft.

The Abbey is usually entered by the door (Solomon's Porch) in the N. transept, near St. Margaret's Church. The nave, aisles, and

transept are open gratis to the public daily (Sun. excepted), except
during the hours of divine service, till 4 p.m. in winter and 6 p.m.
in summer. Daily service at 9.15 (8 on Sun., 9 on Saints' days),
10, and 3 o'clock. In summer there is a special Sunday service
in the nave at 7 p.m. A charge of 6*d*. (except on Mon. and Tues.)
is made for admission to the chapels, which are shown only to
visitors accompanied by a verger. Parties thus conducted start
about every $1/4$ hr. from the S. gate of the ambulatory. Visitors
are cautioned against accepting the useless services of any of the
numerous loiterers outside the church.

The following list of the most interesting monuments, which
do not invariably imply interment in the Abbey, begins with the N.
transept, and continues through the N. aisle, the S. aisle, and the
S. transept (Poets' Corner), after which we enter the chapels.

N. Transept.

On the right, *William Pitt, Lord Chatham*, the statesman
(d. 1778), a large monument by *Bacon*. Above, in a niche, Chatham
is represented in an oratorical attitude, with his right hand outstretched; at his feet are sitting two female figures, Wisdom and
Courage; in the centre, Britannia with a trident; to the right and
left, Earth and Sea. — Opposite —

L. *John Holles, Duke of Newcastle* (d. 1711); large monument
by *Bird*, in a debased style. The sarcophagus bears the semi-recumbent figure of the Duke; to the right is Truth with her mirror,
on the left, Wisdom. — Adjacent —

L. **George Canning*, the statesman (d. 1827); statue by *Chantrey*. — Adjacent, his son —

L. *Charles John, Viscount Canning*, Governor-General of India
(d. 1862), statue by *Foley*.

Close by is their relative, *Viscount Stratford de Redcliffe* (d.
1880), long British ambassador in Constantinople; statue by *Boehm*,
with an epitaph by Tennyson.

L. *William Cavendish, Duke of Newcastle* (d. 1676), and his
wife; a double sarcophagus, with recumbent figures in the costume
of the period. — Adjacent —

L. *Sir John Malcolm*, General (d. 1833), one of the chief pro-
moters of the British power in India; statue by *Chantrey*.

Adjacent, *Lord Beaconsfield* (d. 1881), statue by *Boehm*.

R. *Lord Palmerston*, the statesman (d. 1865); statue by *Jackson*, in the costume of a Knight of the Garter. — Adjoining —

R. *Lord Castlereagh*, the statesman (d. 1822); statue by *Thomas*.
The scroll in his hand bears the (now scarcely legible) inscription,
'Peace of Paris, 1814'. — Next to it —

R. **William, Lord Mansfield*, the statesman and judge (d. 1793),
by *Flaxman*. Above is the Judge on the judicial bench, in his
official robes; on the left is Justice with her scales, on the right,

Wisdom opening the book of the law. Behind the bench is Lord Mansfield's motto: 'uni æquus virtuti', with a youth bearing an extinguished torch. — Opposite —

L. *Sir Peter Warren*, Admiral (d. 1752), by *Roubiliac*. Hercules places the bust of the Admiral on a pedestal, while Navigation looks on with mournful admiration. — Beneath the pavement in front (tablet in the gangway) lies *William Ewart Gladstone* (d. May 19th, 1898). *Mrs. Gladstone* was laid in the same grave in 1900. — Adjacent, by the railing of the ambulatory —

L. *Sir Robert Peel*, the statesman (d. 1850); statue by *Gibson*.

Henry Grattan (d. 1820), *Charles Fox* (p. 253), and the two *Pitts* are all buried in this transept. It was the proximity here of the graves of Fox and the younger Pitt (p. 254) that suggested Scott's well-known lines: —

'Drop upon Fox's grave the tear,
'Twill trickle to his rival's bier'.

W. AISLE OF N. TRANSEPT.

R. *George Gordon, Earl of Aberdeen*, the statesman (d. 1860), Byron's 'travelled Thane, Athenian Aberdeen'; bust by *Noble*.

R. **Elizabeth Warren* (d. 1816), widow of the Bishop of Bangor, by *Westmacott*. The fine monument represents, in half life-size, a poor woman sitting with her child in her arms, in allusion to the benevolence of the deceased. — Adjoining —

R. *Sir George Cornewall Lewis*, statesman (d. 1863); bust by *Weekes*. — Adjacent —

R. *Sir Eyre Coote*, General, Commander-in-Chief of the British forces in India (d. 1783); colossal monument by *Banks*, erected by the East India Company.

R. *Charles Buller* (d. 1848), the statesman; bust by *Weekes*.

R. *Francis Horner*, M. P. (d. 1817); statue by *Chantrey*.

R. *Jonas Hanway* (d. 1786), the philanthropist, by *J. F.* and *J. Moore*. — Opposite —

L. *Sir John Balchen*, Admiral, who in 1744 was lost with his flag-ship and crew of nearly 1000 men in the English Channel; with a relief of the wrecked vessel, by *Scheemakers*.

R. *General Hope*, Governor of Quebec (d. 1789), by *Bacon*; a mourning Indian woman bends over the sarcophagus. — Above —

R. *Warren Hastings*, Governor-General of India (d. 1818); bust by *Bacon*.

R. *Richard Cobden*, the politician and champion of free-trade (d. 1865); bust by *Woolner*. — Above —

Sir Henry Maine, professor of jurisprudence and the 'friend of India' (d. 1888), marble medallion by *Boehm*.

R. *Earl of Halifax*, the statesman (d. 1771); bust by *Bacon*.

At the end of the passage, in three niches in the wall above the door, separated by palm-trees, is the monument of —

Admiral Watson (d. 1757), by *Scheemakers*. The Admiral, in a toga, is sitting in the centre, holding a palm-branch. On the right the town of Calcutta on her knees presents a petition to her conqueror. On the left is an Indian in chains, emblematical of Chandernagore, also conquered by the Admiral.

N. Aisle.

On the left, *Sir Thomas Fowell Buxton* (d. 1845), Member of Parliament, one of the champions of the movement for the abolition of slavery, by *Thrupp*. — Above, *W. E. Forster* (d. 1886), M. P. and educationalist; medallion portrait-head. — Farther on —

L. *Balfe* (d. 1870), the composer, medallion by *Mallempre*.

L. *Hugh Chamberlain*, physician (d. 1728), by *Scheemakers* and *Delvaux*; recumbent figure upon a sarcophagus; on the right and left, two allegorical figures, representing Health and Medicine.

R. Tablets to *Charles Burney* (d. 1814), the historian of music, and *John Blow* (d. 1708), the composer and organist. — Then —

R. *William Croft*, organist of the Abbey (d. 1727), with a bust. On the floor are the tombstones of *Henry Purcell* (d. 1695), organist of the Abbey, and *W. Sterndale Bennett* (d. 1875), the composer. — Above —

R. **George Lindsay Johnstone* (d. 1815); fine monument by *Flaxman*, erected by the sister of the deceased.

L. **Sir Thomas Stamford Raffles*, Governor of Java and founder of the Zoological Society (d. 1826; comp. p. 294), sitting figure, by *Chantrey*.

L. **William Wilberforce* (d. 1833), one of the chief advocates for the emancipation of the slaves; sitting figure, by *Joseph*.

L. *Charles Darwin* (1809–82), the naturalist; bronze medallion by *Boehm*. — *James Prescott Joule* (d. 1889), the physicist; tablet. — *John Couch Adams* (d. 1892), the discoverer of the planet Neptune; medallion by *Bruce Joy*.

L. *Lord John Thynne, D. D.*, Sub-Dean of the Abbey (d. 1881), recumbent figure by *Armstead*.

To the left, at the end of the choir : —

Sir Isaac Newton (d. 1726), by *Rysbrack*. The half-recumbent figure of Newton reposes on a black sarcophagus, beside which are two small Genii unfolding a scroll. Below is a relief in marble, indicating the labours of the deceased. Above is an allegorical figure of Astronomy upon a large globe.

Charles Darwin (p. 252), and *Sir John Herschel* (d. 1871), the astronomer, are buried within a few yards of Newton's tomb (memorial slabs in the floor). — The window above and the following window are respectively memorials of *Robert Stephenson* (d. 1859) and *Joseph Locke* (d. 1860), the engineers.

R. (in the N. aisle) *Richard Mead*, the physician (d. 1754), with bust, by *Scheemakers*. — Above, in the window : —

Spencer Perceval, Chancellor of the Exchequer and First Lord of the Treasury, who was murdered at Westminster Hall in 1812. Recumbent figure upon a sarcophagus, by *Westmacott;* at the head a mourning figure of Strength, and at the foot Truth and Moderation. The relief above represents the murder; the second figure to the left is that of the murderer, Bellingham.

R. *Mrs. Mary Beaufoy* (d. 1705); group by *Grinling Gibbons.*

R. *Thomas Banks* (d. 1805), the sculptor; tablet.

In front of this monument *Ben Jonson* is buried (p. 258), with the words 'O Rare Ben Johnson!' cut in the pavement. The stone with the original inscription is now built into the wall close to the floor beneath Banks' monument. Close by, under a modern brass, lies *John Hunter* (d. 1793), the celebrated surgeon and anatomist, brought here in 1859 from St. Martin's in the Fields. — The window above was erected to the memory of *Isambard Brunel* (d. 1859), the engineer.

R. *Dr. John Woodward* (d. 1728), the 'founder of English geology'; monument by *Scheemakers.* — Above —

R. *Sir Charles Lyell*, the geologist (d. 1875), bust by *Theed* (also slab on the floor). — The next window commemorates *Richard Trevithick* (d. 1833), the engineer.

R. *Charles James Fox* (d. 1806), by *Westmacott*. The famous statesman is supported by the arms of Liberty; at his feet are Peace, with an olive-branch, and a liberated negro slave.

We have now reached the Belfry Tower, called by Dean Stanley the 'Whig Corner'.

R. *Captain Montagu* (d. 1794), by *Flaxman*. Statue on a lofty pedestal, crowned by the Goddess of Victory.

R. *Viscount Howe* (d. 1758); monument by *Scheemakers*, erected by the Province of Massachusetts before its separation from the mother-country.

R. *Sir James Mackintosh*, the historian (d. 1832); bust by *Theed*.

R. *George Tierney*, the orator (d. 1830); bust by *Westmacott*.

R. *Marquis of Lansdowne* (d. 1863); bust by *Boehm*.

R. *Lord Holland*, the statesman (d. 1840); large monument, by *Baily*. Below is represented the entrance to a vault, on the steps to which on the left the Angel of Death, and on the right Literature and Science are posted.

R. *John, Earl Russell* (d. 1878), bust.

R. *Zachary Macaulay* (d. 1838), the father of Lord Macaulay, and a noted advocate of the abolition of slavery; bust by *Weekes*.

R. (above the door), *General Gordon* (d. 1885); bronze bust by *Onslow Ford*.

Having now reached the end of the N. aisle, we turn to the left (S.), where on the N. side of the principal (W.) ENTRANCE, at the end of the nave, we observe the monuments of —

Antony Ashley Cooper, Earl of Shaftesbury (d. 1885), a marble statue by *Boehm*, and —

Jeremiah Horrocks, the astronomer (d. 1641). Above the door is the monument of —

William Pitt, the renowned statesman (d. 1806), by *Westmacott*. At the top stands the statue of Pitt as Chancellor of the Exchequer, in the act of speaking. To the right is History listening to his words; on the left, Anarchy in chains.

R. *James Cornewall*, Captain (d. 1743), by *Taylor*. At the foot of a low pyramid of Sicilian marble is a grotto in white marble, with a relief of the naval battle of Toulon, where Cornewall fell.

S. Aisle.

In the baptistery at the W. end (called by Dean Stanley 'Little Poets' Corner') : —

R. *James Craggs*, Secretary of State (d. 1721); statue by *Guelphi*, with inscription by Pope.

William Wordsworth, the poet (d. 1850); statue by *Thrupp*.

Rev. John Keble (d. 1866); bust by *Woolner*.

The baptistery also contains busts, by *Woolner*, of the *Rev. Fred. D. Maurice* (d. 1872) and the *Rev. Charles Kingsley* (d. 1875), one of *Matthew Arnold* (d. 1888), by *Bruce Joy*, one of *Dr. Thomas Arnold* (d. 1842), by *Gilbert*, and a bronze medallion of *Professor Henry Fawcett* (d. 1884), by *Alfred Gilbert*, with a row of small allegorical figures. The stained-glass windows were placed here by Mr. George W. Childs of Philadelphia in memory of *George Herbert* (d. 1632) and *William Cowper* (d. 1800).

We now continue to follow the S. aisle. Slab on the floor: *Bishop Atterbury* (d. 1732). To the right, above the door leading to the Deanery, is the *Abbot's Pew*, a small oaken gallery, constructed by Abbot Islip in the 16th century.

Below the Abbot's Pew: *William Congreve*, the dramatist (d. 1728), by *Bird*, with a medallion and a sarcophagus of Egyptian marble. The monument was erected by Henrietta, Duchess of Marlborough. — Slab on the floor: *Ann Oldfield* (d. 1730), the actress.

R. *William Buckland*, the geologist (d. 1856), bust by *Weekes*.

R. *Lord Lawrence* (d. 1879), Governor-General of India; bust by *Woolner*. — Above the door to the cloisters (see p. 271) —

George Wade, General (d. 1748), by *Roubiliac*. The Goddess of Fame is preventing Time from destroying the General's trophies, which are attached to a column.

R. *Sir James Outram*, General (d. 1863); bust by *Noble*. Below are Outram and Lord Clyde shaking hands, and between them is General Havelock. At the sides are mourning figures, representing Indian tribes. — Above, occupying the whole recess of the window, —

R. *William Hargrave*, General (d. 1750), by *Roubiliac*. The General is descending from his sarcophagus, while Time, represented allegorically, conquers Death and breaks his arrow.

Adjacent is a tablet recording the burial in the nave of *Sir William Temple* (d. 1699) and his wife, *Dorothy Osborne* (d. 1695).

Sidney, Earl Godolphin (d. 1712), Lord High Treasurer, by *Bird*.

R. *Colonel Townshend*, who fell in Canada in 1759, by *Eckstein*. Two Indian warriors bear the white marble sarcophagus, which is adjoined by a pyramid of coloured Sicilian marble.

R. *John André*, Major, executed in America as a spy in 1780. Sarcophagus with mourning Britannia, by *Van Gelder*. The wreath of autumn leaves above was presented by some Americans. — Opposite, in the nave, by the end of the choir: —

James, Earl Stanhope, ambassador and minister of war (d. 1720), by *Rysbrack*. — Then, returning to the S. aisle: —

L. *Thomas Thynn*, murdered in Pall Mall in 1682 by assassins hired by Count Koningsmarck, whose object was the hand of Thynne's wife, a wealthy heiress, by *Quellin*. The relief on the pedestal is a representation of the murder.

R. *Dr. Isaac Watts*, the famous divine and hymn-writer (d. 1748), with bust by *Banks*.

Below, *Colonel Joseph Lemuel Chester* (d. 1882), a tablet 'in grateful memory of the disinterested labour of an American master of English genealogical learning'.

R. *John Wesley*, founder of the Methodists (d. 1791), and *Charles Wesley* (d. 1788), by *Van Gelder*, relief by *Adams-Acton*.

R. *Charles Burney*, philologist (d. 1818); bust by *Gahagan*.

L. *Thomas Owen*, judge (d. 1598); an interesting old painted monument, with a lifesize recumbent figure leaning on the right arm. — By the adjoining pillar —

L. *Pasquale Paoli*, the well-known Corsican general (d. 1807), formerly buried in old St. Pancras Churchyard, but transferred to Corsica in 1889; bust by *Flaxman*.

R. *Sir Cloudesley Shovel*, Admiral (d. 1707), by *Bird*, recumbent figure under a canopy. — Above —

Sir Godfrey Kneller, the painter (d. 1723), by *Rysbrack*. The monument was designed by Kneller himself, who is the only painter commemorated in the abbey. He was buried in his own garden, at Kneller Hall, Twickenham.

Here is a door leading to the E. walk of the cloisters and to the chapter-house (p. 271).

L. *Sir Thomas Richardson*, judge (d. 1634), old monument by *Le Soeur*.

L. *William Thynne* (d. 1584); a fine old monument in marble and alabaster, with a recumbent effigy.

L. *Dr. Andrew Bell*, the founder of the Madras system of education (d. 1832), with relief representing him examining a class of boys, by *Behnes*.

In the middle of the nave lie, amongst others, *David Livingstone*, the celebrated African traveller (d. 1873), *Archbishop Trench* (d. 1886), *Sir Charles Barry*, the architect (d. 1860), *Robert Stephenson*, the engineer (d. 1859), *Lord Clyde* (d. 1863), *Sir James Outram* (d. 1863; the 'Bayard of India'), *Sir George Pollock* (d. 1872), *Lord Lawrence* (d. 1879), *Sir G. G. Scott*, the architect (d. 1878; with a brass by *Street*), and *G. E. Street* (d. 1881), the architect of the New Law Courts.

We now turn to the right and enter the —

S. Transept and Poets' Corner.

On the right: *George Grote* (d. 1871) and *Bishop Thirlwall* (d. 1875), two historians of Greece who now share one grave. Grote's bust is by *Bacon*.

R. *William Camden*, the antiquary (d. 1623). Above —

David Garrick, the famous actor (d. 1779); large group in relief, by *Webber*. Garrick is stepping out from behind a curtain, which he opens with extended arms. Below are the comic and the tragic Muse. — Below —

Isaac Casaubon, the scholar (d. 1614). On this stone, near the foot, is the monogram I. W., scratched here by Izaak Walton in 1658. — Above —

John Ernest Grabe, the Oriental scholar (d. 1711); sitting figure by *Bird*. — Several uninteresting monuments; then —

Isaac Barrow, the scholar and mathematician (d. 1677).

Joseph Addison, the essayist (d. 1719; p. 265); statue by *Westmacott*. On the base are the Muses in relief.

Lord Macaulay, the historian (d. 1859); bust by *Burnard*.

W. M. Thackeray, the novelist and humorist (d. 1863); bust by *Marochetti*. — Above —

George Frederick Händel, the composer (d. 1759), the last work from the chisel of *Roubiliac*; lifesize statue surrounded by music and instruments; above, among the clouds, a heavenly choir; in the background, an organ. — Below, *Jenny Lind-Goldschmidt*, the singer (d. 1887); medallion portrait-head, by *Birch*.

By the S. wall : —

*John, Duke of Argyll and Greenwich (d. 1743); a large monument by *Roubiliac*. On a black sarcophagus rests the half-recumbent lifesize figure of the Duke, supported by History, who is writing his name on a pyramid; on the pedestal, to the left, Eloquence, to the right, Valour. — *Sir Walter Scott* (d. 1832), replica of the bust by *Chantrey*, placed here in 1897.

A door here leads into the *Chapel of St. Blaise* or *St. Faith*, with its lofty groined roof. The chapel is open for private devotions.

Above the doorway of the chapel: —

Oliver Goldsmith (d. 1774), buried at the Temple (p. 177); medallion by *Nollekens*. — Then —

John Gay, the poet (d. 1732), by *Rysbrack*. A small Genius holds the medallion. The irreverent inscription, by Gay himself, runs: —

> '*Life is a jest; and all things show it:*
> *I thought so once, but now I know it*'.

Nicolas Rowe, the poet (d. 1718), and his only daughter, by *Rysbrack*. Above, the medallion of the daughter. — Then —

James Thomson, the poet of the 'Seasons' (d. 1748); statue by *Spang*. — Adjacent —

*William Shakspeare (d. 1616), designed by *Kent*, and executed by *Scheemakers*. The figure of the Poet, placed on a pedestal resembling an altar, is represented with the right arm leaning on a pile of his works; the left hand holds a roll bearing a well-known passage from 'The Tempest'. On the pedestal are the masks of Queen Elizabeth, Henry V., and Richard III.

Above, *Robert Burns* (d. 1796), bust by *Steell*.

Robert Southey, the poet (d. 1843), bust by *Weekes*.

S. T. Coleridge, the poet (d. 1834), bust by *Hamo Thornycroft*. — Then, opposite Addison's statue, —

Thomas Campbell, the poet (d. 1844), statue by *Marshall*. — The grave of *Charles Dickens* (d. 1870) is between the statues of Addison and Campbell, and is adjoined by the tombs of Händel and Sheridan. Garrick, Francis Beaumont, Sir John Denham, the Rev. Henry Cary (translator of Dante), James MacPherson (of 'Ossian' fame), Dr. Johnson, and Macaulay are also buried in the Poets' Corner.

Passing round the pillar we now enter the —

E. AISLE OF THE POETS' CORNER.

On the right. *Lord Tennyson*, the poet (d. 1892), bust by *T. Woolner* (strangely unlike all the better-known portraits of the poet). — *Granville Sharp* (d. 1813), one of the chief advocates for the abolition of slavery, medallion by *Chantrey*. — Above —

Charles de St. Denis, Seigneur de St. Evremont, author, French Marshal, afterwards in the service of England (d. 1703), bust. — Below —

Matthew Prior, politician and poet (d. 1721), large monument by *Rysbrack*. In a niche is Prior's bust by *Coyzevox* (presented by Louis XIV. of France); below, a black sarcophagus, adjoined by two allegorical figures of (r.) History and (l.) Thalia. At the top are two boys, with a torch and an hour-glass. — Then —

William Mason, the poet (d. 1797); medallion, mourned over by Poetry, by *Bacon*. — Over it —

Thomas Shadwell, the poet (d. 1692), by *Bird*. — Below —

Thomas Gray, the poet (d. 1771); medallion, held by the Muse of poetry, by *Bacon*. — Above —

John Milton (d. 1674; buried in St. Giles's Church, Cripplegate), bust by *Rysbrack* (1737). Below is a lyre, round which is twining a serpent with an apple, in allusion to 'Paradise Lost'. — Below —

Edmund Spenser (d. 1598; buried near Chaucer), 'the prince of poets in his tyme', as the inscription says; a simple, altar-like monument, with ornaments of light-coloured marble above. — Above —

Samuel Butler, author of 'Hudibras' (d. 1680), with bust. — Then:

Ben Jonson (d. 1637), poet laureate to James I., and contemporary of Shakspeare; medallion by *Rysbrack* (1737); on the pedestal the inscription, 'O rare Ben Johnson!' (comp. p. 253). —

Michael Drayton, the poet (d. 1631), with bust.

Barton Booth, the actor (d. 1733), an ancestor of Edwin Booth, with medallion, by *Tyler*.

John Phillips, the poet (d. 1708); portrait in relief.

The tomb of *Geoffrey Chaucer* (d. 1400), the father of English poetry, is on the same side, close by, and consists of an altar-sarcophagus (supposed to be from Grey Friars Church, p. 123) under a canopy let into the wall (date, 1555). The tomb was erected by Nicholas Brigham (d. 1558), who is said to have removed Chaucer's remains from the cloister. — Above it is a fine stained-glass window, erected in 1868, with scenes from Chaucer's poems, and a likeness of the poet.

Abraham Cowley, the poet (d. 1667), with urn, by *Bushnell*.

Robert Browning, the poet (d. 1889), is buried directly in front of Cowley's monument; and side by side with him lies *Lord Tennyson*, poet laureate (d. 1892; comp. p. 257).

H. W. Longfellow, the poet (d. 1882); bust by *Brock*.

John Dryden, the poet (d. 1700); bust by *Scheemakers*.

Archbishop Tait (d. 1883); marble bust by *Armstead* (at the entrance to the choir-ambulatory).

Robert South, the preacher (d. 1716); statue by *Bird*.

Richard Busby (d. 1695; see p. 273); statue by *Bird*.

In front of Dryden's tomb is a blue slab in the floor, believed to commemorate *Robert Hawle*, murdered in the choir in 1378 by the followers of John of Gaunt. The church was closed for four months until the outraged privileges of sanctuary were again confirmed to it. — In the centre of the S. transept is a white slab, covering the remains of 'Old Parr' (d. 1635), who is said to have reached the age of 152 years.

To the left of the entrance to the ambulatory is an old altar decoration of the 13th or 14th cent., below which is the old monument of the Saxon king *Sebert* (d. 616) and his wife *Athelgoda* (d. 615).

We now repair to the *CHAPELS, which follow each other in the following order (starting from the Poets' Corner).

I. CHAPEL OF ST. BENEDICT.

1. *Archbishop Langham* (d. 1376); with recumbent figure.

2. *Lady Frances Hertford* (d. 1598).

3. *Dr. Goodman*, Dean of Westminster (d. 1601).

4. A son of Dr. Spratt.

*5. *Lionel Cranfield, Earl of Middlesex* (d. 1645), Lord High Treasurer in the time of James I., and his wife.

6. *Dr. Bill* (d. 1561), first Dean of Westminster under Elizabeth.

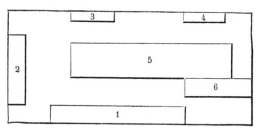

Near this is the tomb of *Ann of Cleves* (d. 1557), fourth wife of Henry VIII.

II. CHAPEL OF ST. EDMUND, King of the East Anglians (d. 870).

*1. *John of Eltham*, second son of Edward II., who died in 1334 in his nineteenth year. Sarcophagus with lifesize alabaster figure.

2. *Earl of Stafford* (d. 1762); slab, by *Chambers*.

3. *Nicholas Monk* (d. 1661), Bishop of Hereford, brother of the famous Duke of Albemarle (p. 263); slab and pyramid, by *Woodman*.

4. *William of Windsor* and *Blanche de la Tour* (d. 1340), children of Edward III., who both died young; small sarcophagus, with recumbent alabaster figures 20 in. in length.

5. *Duchess of Suffolk* (d. 1558), granddaughter of Henry VII. and mother of Lady Jane Grey; recumbent figure.

6. *Francis Holles*, son of the Earl of Clare, who died in 1622, at the age of 18, on his return from a campaign in Flanders, in which he had greatly distinguished himself; sitting figure, by *Stone*.

7. *Lady Jane Seymour* (d. 1560), daughter of the Duke of Somerset.

8. *Lady Katharine Knollys* (d. 1568), chief Lady of the Bed-

chamber to Queen Elizabeth, niece of Anne Boleyn, and grandmother of the Queen's favourite, the Earl of Essex.

9. *Lady Elizabeth Russell* (d. 1601), a handsome sitting figure of alabaster, in an attitude of sleep. The Latin inscription says, 'she sleeps, she is not dead'.

10. *Lord John Russell* (d. 1584), and his son *Francis*; sarcophagus with a recumbent figure, resting on the left arm, in official robes, with the boy at the feet.

11. *Sir Bernard Brocas of Beaurepaire*, Chamberlain to Queen Anne, wife of Richard II., beheaded on Tower Hill in 1399; an interesting old monument in the form of a Gothic chapel, with recumbent figure of a praying knight; at the feet, a lion.

12. *Sir Humphrey Bourchier*, partisan of Edward IV., who fell

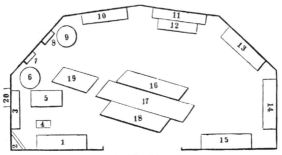

Chapel of St. Edmund.

on Easter Day, 1471, at the battle of Barnet Field. Altar monument, with the figure of a knight, the head resting on a helmet, one foot on a leopard, and the other on an eagle.

13. *Sir Richard Pecksall* (d. 1571), Master of the Buckhounds to Queen Elizabeth; canopy with three niches.

*14. *Edward Talbot, Earl of Shrewsbury* (d. 1617), and his wife; figures lying under a canopy on a slab of black marble with a pedestal of alabaster.

15. *William de Valence, Earl of Pembroke*, who fell at Bayonne in 1296; recumbent wooden figure, overlaid with metal, the feet resting on a lion.

16. *Robert de Waldeby, Archbishop of York* (d. 1397), once an Augustinian monk and the companion of Edward the Black Prince in France, tutor to Richard II.; mediæval monument, with engraved figure.

*17. *Eleanora de Bohun, Duchess of Gloucester*, Abbess of Barking (d. 1399), one of the most interesting monuments in the Abbey, with a fine brass. Her husband was smothered at Calais by order of Richard II., his nephew. She is represented in the dress of a nun of Barking. The inscription is in old French.

18. *Mary, Countess of Stafford* (d. 1693), wife of Lord Stafford, who was beheaded on Tower Hill in 1680.

19. *Dr. Ferne*, Bishop of Chester, Grand Almoner of Charles I. (d. 1661).

Edward Bulwer Lytton, the novelist (d. 1873), and *Lord Herbert* of Cherbury (d. 1678) are buried under slabs in this chapel.

III. CHAPEL OF ST. NICHOLAS, Bishop of Myra.

1. *Lady Cecil*, Lady of the Bedchamber to Queen Elizabeth (d. 1591).

2. *Lady Jane Clifford*, daughter of the Duke of Somerset (d. 1679).

3. *Countess of Beverley*; small tombstone with the inscription, 'Espérance en Dieu' (d. 1812), by *Nollekens*.

4. *Anne, Duchess of Somerset* (d. 1587), widow of the Protector

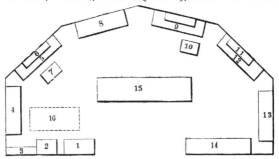

Chapel of St. Nicholas.

(beheaded on Tower Hill in 1552, see p. 162), and sister-in-law of Jane Seymour, third wife of Henry VIII.; recumbent figure.

5. *Westmoreland Family.* — Above —

6. *Baron Carew* (d. 1470) and his wife, mediæval monument, with kneeling figures.

7. *Nicholas Bagenall* (d. 1687), overlain by his nurse when an infant.

*8. *Lady Mildred Burleigh* (d. 1588), wife of Lord Burleigh, the famous minister, and her daughter *Anne*. Lady Burleigh, says the epitaph, was well versed in the Greek sacred writers, and founded a scholarship at St. John's College, Oxford. Recumbent figures.

9. *William Dudley*, Bishop of Durham (d. 1483).

10. *Anna Sophia* (d. 1601), the infant daughter of Count Bellamonte, French ambassador at the court of James I.

11. *Lady Ross* (d. 1591); mediæval monument.

12. *Marchioness of Winchester* (d. 1586).

13. *Duchess of Northumberland* (d. 1776) by *Read*.

14. *Philippa de Bohun, Duchess of York* (d. 1431), wife of Edward Plantagenet, who fell at Agincourt in 1415. Old monument with effigy of the deceased in long drapery.

*15. *Sir George Villiers* (d. 1605) and his wife (d. 1632), the parents of the Duke of Buckingham, favourite of James I.; monument with recumbent figures, in the centre of the chapel, by *Stone*. — The remains of *Katherine of Valois*, wife of Henry V. (d. 1437), lay below this tomb for 350 years (comp. p. 266).

16. *Sir Humphrey Stanley* (d. 1505).

Opposite us, on leaving this chapel, under the tomb of Henry V., is a bronze bust of *Sir Robert Aiton*, the poet (1570-1638), executed by Farelli from a portrait by Van Dyck. Aiton was secretary of two Queens Consort and a friend of Jonson, Drummond, and Hobbes. The earliest known version of 'Auld Lang Syne' was written by him.

IV. A flight of twelve black marble steps now leads into the **CHAPEL OF HENRY VII.**, a superb structure erected in 1502-20 on the site of an old chapel of the Virgin Mary. The roses in the decoration of the fine brass-covered gates are an allusion to the marriage of Henry VII., founder of the Tudor family, with Elizabeth, daughter of Edward IV., which united the Houses of York and Lancaster, and put an end to the Wars of the Roses (comp. p. 178). The chapel consists of nave and aisles, with five small chapels at the E. end. The aisles are entered by doors on the right and left of the main gate. On the left stands the font. The chapel contains about 100 statues and figures. On each side are carved choir-stalls in dark oak, admirably designed and beautifully executed; the quaint carvings on the 'misereres' under the seats are worthy of examination. Each stall is appropriated to a Knight of the Order of the Bath, the lower seats being for the squires. Each seat bears the armorial bearings of its occupant in brass, and above each are a sword and banner.

The chief glory of this chapel, however, is its fan-tracery ceiling with its fantastic pendentives, each surface being covered with rich fret-work, exhibiting the florid Perpendicular style in its utmost luxuriance. The airiness, elegance, and richness of this exquisite work can scarcely be over-praised. The best survey of the chapel is gained either from the entrance-door, or from the small chapel at the opposite extremity, behind the monument of the founder, whose portrait is to be seen in the stained-glass window above.

'On entering, the eye is astonished by the pomp of architecture, and the elaborate beauty of sculptured detail. The very walls are wrought into universal ornament, incrusted with tracery, and scooped into niches, crowded with the statues of saints and martyrs. Stone seems, by the cunning labour of the chisel, to have been robbed of its weight and density, suspended aloft, as if by magic, and the fretted roof achieved with the wonderful minuteness and airy security of a cobweb.' — *Washington Irving.*

We first turn our attention to the S. aisle of the chapel, where we observe the following monuments:

*1. *Lady Margaret Douglas* (d. 1577), daughter of Margaret, Queen

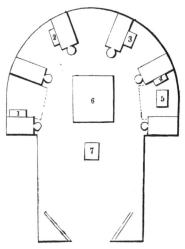

of Scotland, great-granddaughter of Edward IV., granddaughter of Henry VII., niece of Henry VIII., cousin of Edward VI., sister of James V. of Scotland, mother of Henry I. of Scotland (Lord Darnley), and grandmother of James VI. Her seven children kneel round the sarcophagus; the eighth figure is her grandson, King James.

2. *Mary, Queen of Scots*, beheaded in 1587, an inartistic monument by *Cure*, representing a recumbent figure under a canopy, in a praying attitude. The remains of the Queen are buried in a vault below the monument. Adjacent, on the wall, hangs a photographic copy of the warrant issued by James I. in 1612 for the removal of his mother's body from Peterborough Cathedral to Westminster Abbey.

3. *Margaret, Countess of Richmond*, mother of Henry VII. (d. 1509); recumbent metal effigy, by *Torregiano*.

4. *Lady Walpole* (d. 1737), first wife of Sir Robert Walpole, executed by *Valori* after the ancient statue of Pudicitia (so-called) in the Vatican, Rome, and brought from Italy by her son, Horace Walpole.

5. *George Monk* or *Monck, Duke of Albemarle* (d. 1670), the restorer of the Stuarts, by *Scheemakers*. Rostral column, with lifesize figure of the Duke. In Monk's vault, which is in the N. aisle, are also buried *Addison* (d. 1719; p. 256) and *Secretary Craggs* (d. 1721).

In the vault in front of it are buried *Charles II., William III.* and *Queen Mary*, his wife, and *Queen Anne* and her consort, *Prince George of Denmark*. We now enter the nave, which contains the following monuments (beginning from the chapel on the left): —

1. *George Villiers, Duke of Buckingham*, the favourite of James I. and Charles I., murdered in 1628 by the fanatic Felton, and his consort. The monument is of iron. At the feet of the recumbent effigies of the deceased is Fame blowing a trumpet. At the front corners of the sarcophagus are Neptune and Mars, at those at the back two mourning females, all in a sitting posture. At the top, on their knees, are the lifesize children of the deceased.

2. *John Sheffield, Duke of Buckinghamshire* (d. 1721), and his wife, by *Scheemakers*. The figure of the Duke is half-recumbent, and in Roman costume. At his feet is the duchess, weeping. Above is Time with the medallions. Anne of Denmark (d. 1618), consort of James I., is interred in front of this monument. — Within this chapel is preserved an old pulpit of the Reformation period, probably the one in which Cranmer preached the coronation and funeral sermons of Edward VI.

In the E. chapel were interred *Oliver Cromwell* and some of his followers, removed in 1661.

*3. *Duke of Montpensier* (d. 1807), brother of King Louis Philippe, recumbent figure in white marble, by *Westmacott*. — *Dean Stanley* (d. 1881; recumbent statue by *Boehm*), and his wife, *Lady Augusta Stanley* (d. 1876), are buried in this chapel.

4. *Esmé Stuart*, who died in 1661, in his eleventh year; pyramid with an urn containing the heart of the deceased.

5. *Lewis Stuart, Duke of Richmond* (d. 1623), father's cousin and friend of James I., and his wife. Double sarcophagus with recumbent figures. The iron canopy is borne by figures of Faith, Hope, Charity, and Wisdom. Above is a fine figure of Fame.

*6. *Henry VII.* (d. 1509) and his wife *Elizabeth of York* (d. 1502); metal monument, by *Torregiano*. It occupies the centre of the eastern part of the chapel, and is enclosed by a tasteful chantry of brass. On the double sarcophagus are the recumbent figures of the royal pair in their robes. The compartments at the sides of the tomb are embellished with sacred representations. — *James I.* (d. 1625) is buried in the same vault as Henry VII.

George II. and a number of members of the royal family are interred, without monuments, in front of the tomb of Henry VII. Also *Edward VI.* (d. 1553), whose monument by Torregiano was destroyed by the Republicans, and is replaced by a modern Renaissance altar (No. 7 in plan, p. 263). The marble frieze and two of the columns, however, belong to the original. To the left is the tomb of *Elizabeth Claypole* (d. 1658), second daughter of Oliver Cromwell, marked by an inscription in the pavement.

The monuments in the northern aisle of this chapel are not less interesting than those in the southern.

*1. *Queen Elizabeth* (d. 1603), by *Powtrain* and *De Crits*. Here also is commemorated Elizabeth's sister and predecessor *Mary* (d. 1558), who is buried beneath.

2. *Sophia*, daughter of James I., who was born in 1607, and died when three days old. Small recumbent figure in a cradle.

3. *Edward V.* and his brother, the *Duke of York*, the sons of Edward IV., murdered in the Tower when children, by Richard III., in 1483. Some bones, supposed to be those of the unfortunate boys, were found in a chest below a staircase in the Tower (see p. 159), and brought hither. Small sarcophagus in a niche.

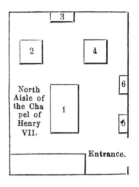

4. *Mary*, daughter of James I., who died in 1607 at the age of two years. Small altar-tomb.

5. *Charles Montagu, Earl of Halifax*, Lord High Treasurer (d. 1715). — The earl was the patron of *Addison* (d. 1719; p. 263), who is commemorated by a slab in front of this monument.

5. *George Saville, Marquis of Halifax*, Lord Keeper of the Privy Seal during several reigns (d. 1695).

After quitting the Chapel of Henry VII. and descending the steps, we see in front of us the *Chantry of Henry V.* (p. 266), with its finely sculptured arch, over which is represented the coronation of that monarch (1413). A slab on the floor marks the vault of the *Earls of Clarendon*, including the distinguished historian (d. 1674).

V. CHAPEL OF ST. PAUL.

1. *Sir Rowland Hill* (1795-1879), the originator of the system of penny postage; bust by *Keyworth*.

2. *Sir Henry Belasyse* (d. 1717), Lieutenant-General and Governor of Galway. Pyramid by *Scheemakers*.

3. *Sir John Puckering* (d. 1596), Keeper of the Great Seal under Queen Elizabeth, and his wife. Recumbent figures under a canopy.

4. *Sir James Fullerton* (d. 1630), First Gentleman of the Bedchamber to Charles I., and his wife. Recumbent marble figures.

5. *Sir Thomas Bromley* (d. 1587), Lord Chancellor under Queen Elizabeth. Recumbent figure; below, his eight children.

6. *Sir Dudley Carleton* (d. 1631), diplomatist under James I.; semi-recumbent figure, by *Stone*.

7. *Countess of Sussex* (d. 1589); at her feet is a porcupine.

8. *Lord Cottington*, statesman in the reign of Charles I. (d. 1652), and his wife. Handsome black marble monument, with the recumbent figure of Lord Cottington in white marble, by *Fanelli*, and, at the top, a bust of Lady Cottington (d. 1633), by *Le Sueur*.

*9. *James Watt* (d. 1819), the improver of the steam-engine; colossal figure in a sitting posture, by *Chantrey*.

*10. *Sir Giles Daubeney* (d. 1507), Lord-Lieutenant of Calais under Henry VII., and his wife. Recumbent effigies in alabaster, painted.

11. *Lewis Robsart* (d. 1431), standard-bearer of Henry V.; an interesting old monument, without an effigy.

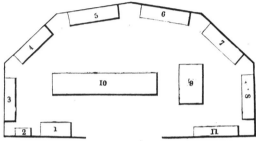

Chapel of S^t. Paul.

This chapel contains an ancient stone coffin found in digging the grave of Sir Rowland Hill.

To the right, on leaving the chapel, is a monument to *William Pulteney, Earl of Bath* (d. 1764), by *Wilton;* and beside it another to *Rear-Admiral Charles Holmes* (d. 1761), also by *Wilton*. Opposite is a screen of wrought iron executed by an English blacksmith in 1293.

*VI. CHAPEL OF ST. EDWARD THE CONFESSOR, forming the end of the choir, to which we ascend by a small flight of narrow steps. (The following chapel, No. VII, is sometimes shown before this.)

1. **Henry III.* (d. 1272), a rich and artistic monument of porphyry and mosaic, with recumbent bronze effigy of the king, by *William Torel* (1290).

2. *Queen Eleanor* (d. 1290), first wife of Edward I., by *Torel*. The inscription is in quaint old French: — 'Ici gist Alianor, jadis Reyne de Engletere, femme al Rey Edeward, Fiz le Rey Henri e fylle al Rey de Espagne e Contasse de Puntiff del alme di li Dieu pur sa pité eyt merci'. Recumbent metal effigy.

3. *Chantry of Henry V.* (d. 1422). On each side a lifesize figure keeps guard by the steps. The recumbent effigy of the king wants the head, which was of solid silver, and was stolen during the reign of Henry VIII. In 1878 the remains of Katherine of Valois (d. 1437), queen of Henry V. (the 'beautiful Kate' of Shakspeare's 'Henry V.') were re-interred in this chantry, whence they had been removed on the building of Henry VII.'s Chapel. On the bar above this monument are placed the saddle, helmet, and shield said to have been used by Henry V. at the battle of Agincourt.

4. *Philippa* (d. 1369), wife of Edward III., and mother of twelve children. She was the daughter of the Count of Hainault and Holland, and was related to no fewer than thirty crowned heads, statuettes of whom were formerly to be seen grouped round the sarcophagus.

5. *Edward III.* (d. 1377), recumbent metal figure on a sarcophagus of grey marble. This monument was once surrounded by statuettes of the king's children and others. The pavement in front of it dates from 1260.

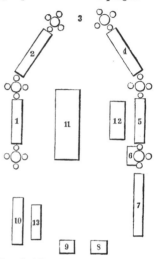

6. *Margaret Woodville* (d. 1472), a daughter of Edward IV., who died in infancy. Monument without an effigy.

7. *Richard II.*, murdered on St. Valentine's Day, 1399, and his queen. The wooden canopy bears an old and curious representation of the Saviour and the Virgin.

8. The old *Coronation Chair*, of oak, made by Edward I., and —

9. The new *Coronation Chair*, made in 1689 for Queen Mary, wife of William III.,

Chapel of St. Edward the Confessor.

on the model of the old one, and last used by Queen Adelaide in 1831. The former contains under the seat the famous *Stone of Scone*, the emblem of the power of the Scottish Princes, and traditionally said to be that once used by the patriarch Jacob as a pillow. It is a piece of sandstone from the W. coast of Scotland, and may very probably be the actual stone pillow on which the dying head of St. Columba rested in the Abbey of Iona. This stone was brought to London by Edward I. in 1297, in token of the complete subjugation of Scotland. Every English monarch since that date has been crowned in this chair. On the coronation day the chairs are covered with gold brocade and taken into the choir of the Abbey, on the other side of the partition in front of which they now stand. Between the chairs are the state sword and shield of Edward III. (d. 1377).

The reliefs on the screen separating Edward's chapel from the choir, executed in the reign of Edward IV., represent the principal events in the life of the Confessor.

10. *Edward I.* (d. 1307), a simple slab without an effigy. The inscription is: — 'Eduardus primus, Scottorum malleus, hic est'

(here lies Edward I., the hammer of the Scots). The body was recently found to be in remarkably good preservation, with a crown of gilded tin on the head, and a copper gilt sceptre in the hand.

*11. *Edward the Confessor* (d. 1066), a large mediæval shrine, the faded splendour of which is still traceable, in spite of the spoliations of relic-hunters. The shrine was erected by order of Henry III. in 1269, and cost, according to an authentic record, 255*l.* 4*s.* 8*d.* A few devout pilgrims still visit this shrine on St. Edward's Day (Oct. 13th).

12. *Thomas of Woodstock, Duke of Gloucester*, murdered at Calais in 1397.

13. *John of Waltham* (d. 1395), Bishop of Salisbury, recumbent metal effigy.

Opposite the Chapel of Edward the Confessor is the entrance to the *Chapel* or *Shrine of St. Erasmus*, a picturesque archway, borne by clustered columns, dating from about 1484. Passing through this chapel, we enter the —

VII. CHAPEL OF ST. JOHN THE BAPTIST.

1. *Sir Thomas Vaughan* (d. 1483), Lord High Treasurer of Edward IV. Old monument, with a brass, which is much defaced.

2. *Colonel Edward Popham* (d. 1651), officer in Cromwell's army, and his wife. Upright figures.

3. *Thomas Carey*, son of the Earl of Monmouth, Gentleman of the Bedchamber to Charles I., who died in 1648, aged 33 years, from grief at the misfortunes of his royal master.

4. *Hugh de Bohun* and his sister *Mary* (d. 1300), grandchildren of Edward I.; tombstone of grey marble.

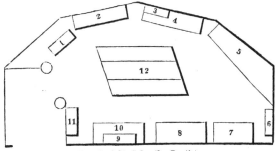

Chapel of St. John the Baptist.

5. *Henry Carey, Baron Hunsdon*, cousin of Queen Elizabeth (d. 1596). Rich canopy without an effigy.

6. *Countess of Mexborough* (d. 1821), small altar-tomb.

7. *William of Colchester*, Abbot of Westminster (d. 1420); a mediæval stone monument with the recumbent figure of the prelate, his head supported by angels, and his feet resting on a lamb.

Above this monument is a slab with a mourning Genius by *Nollekens*, erected to the memory of *Lieut. Col. MacLeod*, who fell at the siege of Badajoz, at the age of 26.

8. *Thomas Ruthall*, Bishop of Durham under Henry VIII., who died in 1524, leaving great wealth. Mediæval recumbent figure.

9. *Thomas Millyng*, Abbot of Westminster (d. 1492); canopy without a figure.

10. *G. Fascet*, Abbot of Westminster (d. 1500).

A slab in front of this tomb, with an inscription by Dean Stanley, marks the resting-place of the third *Earl of Essex* (d. 1646), the only prominent Parliamentarian in the Abbey not disinterred at the Restoration.

11. *Mary Kendall* (d. 1710); kneeling female figure.

12. *Thomas Cecil, Earl of Exeter* (d. 1622), Privy Councillor under James I., and his wife. His wife lies on his right hand; the space on his left was destined for his second wife, who, however, declined to be buried there, as the place of honour on the right had already been assigned to her predecessor.

VIII. The small CHAPEL OF ABBOT ISLIP exhibits the rebus of its founder, 'I slip', in several parts of the carving. The tomb of Abbot Islip (d. 1532), destroyed by the Roundheads, is now represented by a kind of table by the window. The chapel also contains the tomb of *Sir Christopher Hatton* (d. 1619), nephew of the famous Lord Chancellor, and his wife. — A room above this chapel (adm. 3*d.* on Mon. and Tues., on other days 6*d.*) contains the remains of the curious *Wax Effigies* which were once used at the funerals of persons buried in the Abbey. Among them are Queen Elizabeth (restored in 1760), Charles II., William III. and his wife Mary, Queen Anne, General Monk, the Duchess of Buckinghamshire, the Duchess of Richmond (comp. p. 408), William Pitt, Earl of Chatham, and Lord Nelson. The last-mentioned two are not funeral figures.

In the ambulatory, near the chapel of Edward the Confessor, is the ancient monument of the Knight Templar, *Edmund Crouchback* (d. 1296), second son of Henry III., from whom the House of Lancaster derived its claims to the English throne. On the sarcophagus are remains of the figures of the ten knights who accompanied Edmund to the Holy Land. Adjacent is the monument of another Knight Templar, *Aymer de Valence* (d. 1323), Earl of Pembroke and cousin of Edward I., who was assassinated in France. The beautiful effigy of *Aveline, Countess of Lancaster* (d. 1273), first wife of Edmund Crouchback, on an adjoining monument (seen from the choir), merits notice.

To the right is a large marble monument, executed by *Wilton*, to *General Wolfe* (buried in St. Alphage's, Greenwich), who fell in

1759 at the capture of Quebec. He is represented sinking into the arms of a grenadier, while his right hand is pressed on his mortal wound; the soldier is pointing out to the hero the Goddess of Fame hovering overhead. In the background is a mourning Highlander.

Opposite is the monument of *John, Earl Ligonier and Viscount of Inniskilling*, Field-Marshal (d. 1770), by *Moore*.

IX. CHAPELS OF ST. JOHN THE EVANGELIST, ST. MICHAEL, AND ST. ANDREW, three separate chapels, now combined.

1. *Sir John Franklin* (d. 1847), lost in endeavouring to discover the North West Passage, by *Noble*. Inscription by *Tennyson*.

2. *Earl of Mountrath* (d. 1771), and his wife; by *Wilton*. An angel points out to the Countess the empty seat beside her husband.

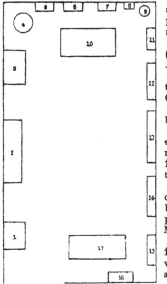

3. *Earl of Kerry* (d. 1818), and his wife; a marble sarcophagus with an earl's coronet, by *Buckham*. Altar-tomb.

4. *Telford*, the engineer (d. 1834); huge statue by *Baily*.

5. *John Kemble* (d. 1823), the actor, in the character of Cato; statue by *Flaxman*.

6. *Dr. Baillie* (d. 1823); bust by *Chantrey*.

7. (above) *Susannah Davidson*, daughter of a rich merchant of Rotterdam (d. 1767), by *Hayward*. Altar tomb with head.

8. *Mrs. Siddons*, the famous actress (d. 1831); statue by *Chantrey*, after Reynolds's picture of her as the Tragic Muse.

9. *Sir James Simpson* (d. 1870), the discoverer of the value of chloroform as an anæsthetic; bust by *Brodie*.

*10. *Lord Norris* (d. 1601), son of Sir Henry Norris who was executed with the ill-fated Anne Boleyn, with his wife, and six sons. The recumbent figures of Lord and Lady Norris are under a catafalque; at the sides are the life-size kneeling figures of the sons. On the S. side of the canopy is a relief of warlike scenes from the life of the deceased nobleman. At the top is a small Goddess of Fame.

11. *Mrs. Kirton* (d. 1603); tablet with inscription, sprinkled with tears represented as flowing from an eye at the top.

12. *Sarah, Duchess of Somerset* (d. 1692). The Duchess is represented leaning on her arm, looking towards the angels, who are appearing to her in the clouds. At the sides are two poor boys bewailing the death of their benefactress.

*13. *J. Gascoigne Nightingale* (d. 1752), and his wife (d. 1731); group by *Roubiliac*. Death, emerging from a tomb, is launching his dart at the dying lady, while her husband tries to ward off the attack.

14. *Lady St. John* (d. 1614), with an effigy.

15. *Admiral Pocock* (d. 1793); sitting figure of Victory with medallion, by *Bacon*.

16. *Sir G. Holles* (d. 1626), nephew of Sir Francis Vere, by *Stone*.

*17. *Sir Francis Vere* (d. 1608), officer in the service of Queen Elizabeth. Four kneeling warriors in armour support a black marble slab, on which lies the armour of the deceased.

This chapel also contains tablets or busts in memory of *Admiral Kempenfelt*, who was drowned with 900 sailors by the sinking of the 'Royal George' in 1782 (commemorated in Cowper's well-known lines); *Sir Humphry Davy* (d. 1829), the natural philosopher; the learned *Dr. Young* (d. 1829), and others.

Beyond this point we dispense with the services of the guide.

A door in the S. Aisle, adjacent to the angle of the Poets' Corner, leads from the abbey to the beautiful Cloisters, dating in their present form from the 13-15th cent., though they include work of as early as the 11th century. The cloisters may also be entered by a passage in the N.E. corner of Dean's Yard (p. 272). They contain the tombs of numerous early ecclesiastics connected with the abbey, and many other graves, including those of *Betterton*, the actor (d. 1710), *Mrs. Bracegirdle*, the actress (d. 1748), *Aphra Behn*, the novelist (d. 1689), *Sir Edmond Godfrey* (murdered 1678), *Dr. Buchan*, author of 'Domestic Medicine' (d. 1805), *Samuel Foote* (d. 1777; no inscription), etc. One slab is inscribed 'Jane Lister, dear childe, 1688'.

From the E. walk of the cloisters we enter the *Chapter House, the 'cradle of all free parliaments', an octagonal room with a central pillar, built in 1250, and from 1282 to 1547 used for the meetings of the House of Commons, which Edward VI., in the latter year, appointed to take place in St. Stephen's Chapel, Westminster Palace. The Chapter House was afterwards used as a receptacle for public records, but these were removed to the New Record Office (p. 174).

In the vestibule, to the left, is a Roman sarcophagus. A stained-glass window, on the right, commemorates *James Russell Lowell*, poet and essayist (d. 1891). — On the wall of the Chapter House are remains of a mural painting of Christ surrounded by the Christian virtues. The old tiled pavement is well executed. The Chapter House, which has recently been ably restored, contains a glass-case with fragments of sculpture, coins, keys, etc., found in the neighbourhood; another case with ancient documents relating to the Abbey, including the Great Charter of Edward the Confessor (1066); and a third with a large illuminated missal and impressions of royal seals. The stained-glass windows were erected in memory of Dean Stanley : the E. window by the Queen, that adjoining on the S. by American admirers, and the rest by public subscription.

Adjoining the Chapter House is the *Chapel of the Pyx* (shown by special order only), which was once the *Treasury of the Kings of England*. The pyx (*i.e.* the box in which the standards of gold and silver are kept) has been removed to the Mint (p. 164).

Opposite the entrance to the Chapter House is a staircase ascending to the *Muniment Room*, or Archives of the Abbey, and to the Triforium, which affords a fine survey of the interior.

In the *Jerusalem Chamber*, to the S.W. of the Abbey (shown on application at the porter's lodge), are frescoes of the Death of Henry IV. and the Coronation of Queen Victoria, some stained glass ascribed to the reign of Henry III., and busts of Henrys IV. and V. It dates from 1376-86, and was the scene of the death of Henry IV.

> *King Henry.* Doth any name particular belong
> Unto the lodging where I first did swoon
> *Warwick.* 'Tis called Jerusalem, my noble Lord. ?
> *King.* Laud be to God! even there my life must end.
> It hath been prophesied to me many years,
> I should not die but in Jerusalem;
> Which vainly I supposed the Holy Land: —
> But bear me to that chamber; there I'll lie
> In that Jerusalem shall Harry die.
> *Shakspeare, King Henry IV., Part II; Act* iv. *Sc. 4.*

It probably derived its name from tapestries or pictures of the history of Jerusalem with which it was hung.

The adjoining *Abbot's Refectory* or *College Hall*, where the Westminster college boys dine, contains some ancient tapestry and stained glass.

For fuller information the curious reader is referred to Dean Stanley's 'Memorials of Westminster Abbey', Sir G. G. Scott's 'Gleanings from Westminster Abbey', and E. T. Bradley's (Mrs. A. Murray Smith) 'Annals of Westminster Abbey'.

To the W. of Westminster Abbey rises the **Westminster Column**, a red granite monument 60 ft. high, designed by *Sir Gilbert Scott*, and erected in 1854-59 to former scholars of Westminster School who fell in the Crimea or the Indian Mutiny. At the base of the column couch four lions. Above are the statues of Edward the Confessor and Henry III. (chief builders of Westminster Abbey), Queen Elizabeth (founder of Westminster School), and Queen Victoria. The column is surmounted by a group of St. George and the Dragon. It is on or near the site of Caxton's house (the 'Red Pale'), in the Almonry.

An archway, passing under the new house to the S. of the column, leads to the *Dean's Yard* and **Westminster School**, or *St. Peter's College* (Pl. R, 25; *IV*), re-founded by Queen Elizabeth in 1560. The school consists of 40 Foundationers, called *Queen's Scholars*, and about 180 *Oppidans* or *Town Boys*. Among the celebrated men educated here were Dryden, Locke, Ben Jonson, Cartwright, Bentham, Barrow, Horne Tooke, Cowley, Rowe, Prior, Giles Fletcher, Churchill,

Cowper, Southey, Hakluyt the geographer, Sir Chris. Wren, Warren Hastings, Gibbon, George Herbert, Vincent Bourne, Dyer, Toplady, Charles Wesley, George Coleman, Dean Aldrich (logician and musician), Elmsley the scholar, Lord Raglan, J. A. Froude, and Earl Russell. Nicholas Udall, author of 'Roister Doister', was appointed Head Master about 1555, and Dr. Richard Busby (p. 258) held the same office here from 1638 to 1695. A comedy of Terence or Plautus is annually performed at Christmas in the dormitory of the Queen's Scholars by the Westminster boys, with a prologue and epilogue alluding to current events. The old dormitory of the Abbey is now used as the great school-room, while the school-library and class-rooms occupy the site of the mediæval Misericorde, of which considerable remains are still traceable. The old tables in the dining-hall are said to be made from the timbers of the Armada. The staircase of Ashburnham House (included in the school-buildings) and the school-gateway are by Inigo Jones.

On the S. side of Dean's Yard is the **Church House** (Pl. R, 25; IV), the ecclesiastical memorial of Queen Victoria's Jubilee. When complete it will occupy the whole area bounded by Dean's Yard, Tufton Street, Little Smith Street, and Great Smith Street; but the only part now ready is the *Great Hall*, at the back, opened in 1896. The architect is *Sir Arthur W. Blomfield*, the material red brick, and the style late - Perpendicular (Tudor). The hall has a fine oaken roof. Besides serving as a kind of ecclesiastical club, the Church House is intended to be the business-centre of the Church of England. Both Houses of Convocation meet here, and it also accommodates many of the Church Societies. Adm. 10–12 and 2–4, Sat. 10–12.

The *Royal Architectural Museum*, No. 18 Tufton Street (adm. daily 10–4, Sat. 10–6, free), to the S. of Dean's Yard (whence a passage leads), contains Gothic, Renaissance, and Classic carvings (mainly casts).

The open space to the N. and W. of the Abbey is the Broad Sanctuary, formerly a sacred place of refuge for criminals and political offenders. Edward V. was born in the Sanctuary in 1470 and his mother and brother again took refuge here in 1483. The poet Skelton (d. 1529) also sought shelter here from Cardinal Wolsey's vengeance.

Westminster Hospital (Pl. R, 25; IV), on the N. side, founded in 1719, was the first of the now numerous hospitals of London supported by voluntary contributions. It contains 205 beds. — To the E. of the hospital is *Westminster Guildhall* or *Sessions House*, recently rebuilt. — To the W. of the hospital is the *Royal Aquarium*, a red brick edifice, 600 ft. in length, with an arched roof of glass and iron. It includes a few fish-tanks, a theatre (p. 68), etc., and music-hall entertainments of all kinds are given here.

From this point Victoria Street (Pl. R, 21, 25; IV), a wide and handsome thoroughfare, opened in 1851 at a cost of 215,000l., leads to the S.W. to Victoria Station (p. 57). Among its buildings are numerous large blocks of flats and chambers, some large hotels, the *Army and Navy Stores* (p. 33), the *American Embassy* (No. 123; p. 75), and the offices of the Canadian High Commissioner and of several Colonial Agents (see pp. 75, 76). At No. 63 is the *Meteorological Office*, where the latest forecast of the weather may be obtained for a fee of 1*s.* (daily 11-8, Sun. 7-8 p.m.).

In Ashley Gardens, just to the S. of Victoria Street, stands the new **Roman Catholic Cathedral of London** (Pl. R, G, 21; *IV*), a simple yet imposing brick and stone building in the early Byzantine style, from the designs of *Mr. J. F. Bentley*, founded in 1895 and to be completed in 1901. It is 360 ft. long, 156 ft. wide, and 117 ft. high (nave), and will cost at least 170,000*l.* The campanile is 293 ft. in height (to the top of the cross).

The plan includes a nave, aisles, transepts, eight side-chapels, a sanctuary (4½ ft. above the nave) flanked by the Chapel of the Blessed Sacrament and the Lady Chapel, and an apsidal choir, raised 13 ft. above the nave. The nave and other parts of the church contain many handsome marble columns. The lower parts of the massive piers and walls are to be encrusted with marble, while the upper parts, the vaulting, and the domes are to be decorated with mosaics illustrating the history of the Roman Catholic church. Below the choir is a crypt. — The remains of Cardinals Wiseman and Manning, at present in Kensal Green Cemetery (p. 375), are to be placed in the vaults below the cathedral.

The Cardinal Archbishop of Westminster resides at *Archbishop's House*, Carlisle Place, close by.

In Caxton Street, to the N., near *St. James's Park Station* (p. 61), is the *Westminster Town Hall*, a Jacobean building of red brick. On the opposite side of the same street, a little farther to the W., is the *Blue Coat School* (Pl. R, 21; *IV*), a small building ascribed to Wren (1709). A little to the S. is the *Grey Coat Hospital* (Pl. R, 25; *IV*), built in the 17th cent. and now used as a school for 400 girls.

20. The National Gallery of British Art.

From the S. side of *Old Palace Yard* (p. 246) Abingdon Street and Millbank Street lead to the S. to *Lambeth Bridge* (Pl. G, 25, 29; *IV*), built in 1862. In Smith Square, a little to the W., rises the large church of *St. John the Evangelist* (Pl. R, 29; *IV*), built in 1721-28, with four heavy corner-towers, erected, it is said, to produce the uniform subsidence of the marshy site. In the E. window is some ancient stained glass brought from Rouen.

From Lambeth Bridge Grosvenor Road skirts the left bank of the Thames to Vauxhall Bridge (p. 279), passing midway the site of *Millbank Penitentiary*, a model prison built and arranged from designs by Jeremy Bentham (d. 1832). The prison was taken down in 1893, and the N. part of the site is now covered by large blocks of workmen's dwellings, erected by the London County Council, while the S. portion, nearest the river, is occupied by the —

*National Gallery of British Art (Pl. G, 25), or **Tate Gallery,**

built and presented to the nation, along with a collection of 65 modern paintings, by *Sir Henry Tate* (d. 1899). The building, opened in 1897 and enlarged in 1899, is in a free classic style. In the centre of the façade is a handsome projecting Corinthian portico, approached by a flight of steps; at each end is a pavilion, with Corinthian pilasters, connected with the central portion by means of a plain ashlar wall, relieved by a niche flanked with pilasters. The pediment over the central portico is surmounted by a colossal Britannia, behind which appears a low dome. The architect was *Mr. Sidney R. J. Smith.*

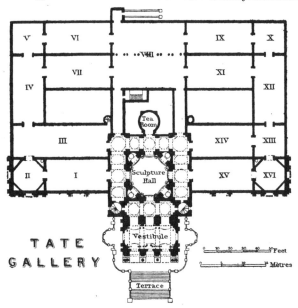

The Tate Gallery affords a fairly adequate view of modern British art. Besides the *Tate Collection* (see above) it contains the works of art purchased under the conditions of the *Chantrey Bequest* (formerly in South Kensington Museum), the *Vernon Collection* and other paintings by artists of the 19th cent., removed hither from the National Gallery, a fine series of paintings by *Mr. G. F. Watts*, presented by him to the nation, and a few paintings given by other donors. There are also a few sculptures. The director is *Mr. Charles Holroyd*. Catalogue 6*d*. Comp. also the 'Handbook to the Tate Gallery', by *Edw. T. Cook.*

The nearest railway stations to the Tate Gallery are Victoria and Westminster (Underground Railway). From the former two lines of omnibuses (Peckham and Elephant and Castle) run past the door (fare 1/2d.).

The Tate Gallery is under the management of the Trustees of the National Gallery and is considered as a branch of that institution. This accounts for the way in which the pictures are numbered. Those brought from Trafalgar Square retain their old numbers, while the other pictures begin with No. 1498, No. 1497 having been the highest number at the National Gallery when the Tate Gallery was opened.

There is a simple *Refreshment Room* in the basement, besides a small *Tea Room* on the groundfloor, at the back of the Central Hall.

On passing through the *Vestibule*, where sticks and umbrellas are given up (no charge), we enter a **Central Hall**, lighted by a dome and enlivened by a fountain. In the recesses are Sculptures: from left to right, *H. Thornycroft*, Teucer; *Lord Leighton*, Sluggard, Athlete struggling with a python; *W. G. John*, Boy at play. — We now turn to the left (W.) and enter —

Room I. In this and the other rooms we begin to the left of the entrance. — 1029. *W. Linton*, Temples of Pæstum; 917. *T. S. Good*, No news; 241. *Sir David Wilkie*, The parish-beadle; 442. *G. Lance*, Red Cap; 423. *D. Maclise*, Malvolio and the Countess ('Twelfth Night'); 1038. *Mulready*, Snow-scene; 921. *Sir D. Wilkie*, 'Blind Man's Buff' (sketch for the painting in Buckingham Palace); 401. *D. Roberts*, St. Paul's, at Antwerp; 1204. *J. Stark*, Landscape; 1225. *Thos. Webster*, Father and mother of the artist; 432. *E. M. Ward*, The South Sea Bubble (1720); 402. *C. R. Leslie*, Sancho Panza and the Duchess (replica of a work now at Petworth); 894. *Sir D. Wilkie*, John Knox preaching; 1428. *R. H. Lancaster*, View at Southampton; 1237. *Constable*, Landscape; 438. *John Linnell*, Wood-cutters; 356. *Etty*, 'Youth on the prow and Pleasure at the helm' (Gray); 4x7. *T. Webster*, A dame's school; 1276. 1244. *Constable*, Landscapes; 1498. *J. P. Knight*, Sacking a church in the time of John Knox; 426. *T. Webster*, The truant; 410. *Sir E. Landseer*, High Life and Low Life; 374. *Richard Bonington*, Column of St. Mark, Venice; 616. *E. M. Ward*, James II. receiving the news of the landing of the Prince of Orange (1688); *Constable*. 1236, 1245. Landscapes, 1235. House in which the artist was born; 1474. *W. J. Müller*, Dredging on the Medway; 403. *C. R. Leslie*, Uncle Toby and Widow Wadman; 430. *Ward*, Dr. Johnson in the anteroom of Lord Chesterfield (1748); 422. *Maclise*, Play Scene in 'Hamlet'; 608. *Sir Edwin Landseer*, Alexander and Diogenes; 353. *Gilbert Newton*, Yorick and the Grisette; 404. *Clarkson Stanfield*, Entrance to the Zuyder Zee; *Wm. Mulready*, 394. Fair-time, 393. The last in; 614. *Etty*, The bather; 1499. *Wm. Hilton*, Nature blowing bubbles for her children; 405. *C. Stanfield*, Battle of Trafalgar (sketch for a larger work); 400 *D. Roberts*, Burgos Cathedral; 406. *Stanfield*, Lake of Como.

Room II contains a number of works by *Sir Edwin Landseer* (1802-73): 1220. A distinguished member of the Royal Humane Society, 607. Highland dogs, 609. The maid and the magpie, 414, 413. (farther on) War and Peace, 411. Highland music, 412. The hunted stag. — *1508. Landseer and Millais*, Equestrian portrait. This work was begun by Landseer for a portrait of Queen Victoria, but left unfinished. Millais added the rider (a portrait of his daughter), the page, the dog, and the background. The picture is also known as 'Nell Gwynne' or 'Diana Vernon'.

Also: 352. *Collins*, Prawn-catchers; 1389. *Willcock*, Landscape; 429. *Creswick*, Pathway to the village-church; 431. *E. M. Ward*, Fall of Clarendon; 1181. *Mulready*, Sea-shore; 439. *Linnell*, Windmill; 231. *Wilkie*, Thomas Daniell, R. A.; 1562. *F. Goodall*, The ploughman and the shepherdess.

Room III. 443. *G. Lance*, Fruit; *F. Goodall*, 451. The tired soldier, 450. Village holiday in the olden time; 615. *W. P. Frith*, 'The Derby Day' (Epsom racecourse in 1856), one of the most 'popular' works in the gallery; 1684 (above), *Jos. Webb*, Mont St. Michel; 620. *Lee*, River-scene, with cattle by *T. S. Cooper*; 898. *Sir Chas. Eastlake*, Lord Byron's Dream; 452. *J. F. Herring*, The frugal meal; 446. *J. C. Horsley*, The pride of the village (from W. Irving's 'Sketch-Book'); 1091. *P. F. Poole*, Vision of Ezekiel;

1142. *Cecil Lawson*, August moon; 1501. *Legros*, Women praying; 416. *Pickersgill.* Robert Vernon; 1502 *H. Macallum*, The crofter's team; no number, *H. Herkomer*, Portrait of Mr. Herbert Spencer (1896); 1677. *A. MacCallum*, Silvery moments (Burnham Beeches); 1205. *F. L. Bridell*, Woods of sweet chestnut above Varenna; 393. *Sir Charles Eastlake*, Haidée, a Greek girl; no number, *D. G. Rossetti*, Portrait of Mrs. William Morris; *A. L. Egg*, 444. Scene from the 'Diable Boiteux', 1335. Beatrix knighting Esmond (from Thackeray); *Wm. Dyce*, 1426. St. John leading the Virgin Mary from the Tomb, 1407. Pegwell Bay; *1394. *Ford Madox Brown*, Christ washing St. Peter's feet (the fair-haired disciple near the middle of the table is a portrait of Holman Hunt, and next him is D. G. Rossetti; the bald disciple is W. M. Rossetti); 563. *Thomas Seddon*, Jerusalem and the Valley of Jehoshaphat; 1500. *R. B. Martineau*, The last day in the old home; 1388. *G. H. Mason*, The cast shoe; *Fred. Walker*, *1391. The harbour of refuge, *1209. The vagrants; 1322. *Wm. Bell Scott*, The eve of the Deluge; 1688. *J. F. Lewis*, Courtyard of the Coptic Patriarch's house in Cairo; 1405. *J. F. Lewis*, Edfou, in Upper Egypt. *Dante Gabriel Rossetti*, *1279. 'Beata Beatrix' (a portrait of the artist's wife, painted in 1863, the year after her death; the date at the top of the frame is that of Beatrice's death, June 9th, 1290); *1210. The Annunciation (the Virgin is a portrait of Christina Rossetti, the poetess, sister of the artist), painted in 1849. 1492. *Geo. Richmond*, Christ and the Woman of Samaria.

Room IV. TATE COLLECTION. 1567. *Mrs. H. M. Stanley*, His first offence; 1518. *Briton Rivière*, A blockade-runner; 1543. *J. W. Waterhouse*, The Lady of Shalott. *Sir John E. Millais* (1829-96), 1510. Mercy (St. Bartholomew's Day, 1572), painted in 1886; 1509. The North-West Passage (1874), with a portrait of Trelawney, the friend of Byron and Shelley; *1507. Vale of rest (1858; note the coffin-shaped cloud); 1508. The knight-errant (1870). 1517. *Briton Rivière*, Companions in misfortune; 1522. *Luke Fildes*, The doctor; 1544. *Stanhope A. Forbes*, The health of the bride; 1524. *Peter Graham*, A rainy day; 1550. *Albert Goodwin*, Sinbad the Sailor; 1542. *J. W. Waterhouse*, St. Eulalia (whose martyred corpse was shrouded by a miraculous fall of snow); 1549. *Albert Moore*, Blossoms; 1504. *John Crome (Old Crome)*, Near Hingham, Norfolk; 1547. *Linnell*, Landscape. *Sir J. Millais*, 1563. St. Stephen (1895); *1564. A disciple (1895); 1506. Ophelia (1852); *1691. Boyhood of Sir Walter Raleigh; 1657. Order of release (1746). 1545. *J. B. Pyne*, Alum Bay; 1526. *J. Faed*, Faults on both sides; 1546. *J. Linnell*, Noonday rest; 1539. *G. H. Boughton*, Weeding the pavement; 1556. *Dendy Sadler*, A good story; 1529. *A. C. Gow*, Musical story by Chopin; 1523. *Alma Tadema*, A silent greeting. — Bust of Sir Henry Tate, by *Brock*; The Singer, statuette by *Onslow Ford*.

Room V. TATE COLLECTION. 1513. *J. C. Hook*, Young dreams; 1653. *Lady Butler*, The remnants of an army; 1533. *Sir E. Landseer*, Uncle Tom and his wife for sale; 1555. *Dendy Sadler*, Thursday; *Orchardson*, 1521. Her mother's voice, 1519. Her first dance, 1520. The first cloud; 1516. *Briton Rivière*, Giants at play; 1548. *Keely Halswelle*, Pangbourne; 1514. *J. C. Hook*, Seaweed raker; *S. E. Waller*, 1552. Sweethearts and wives, 1551. Success; 1541. *Waterhouse*, Consulting the oracle; 1511. *Lord Leighton*, 'And the sea gave up the dead which were in it'; 1540. *B. W. Leader*, Landscape; 1557. *J. R. Reid*, A country cricket-match; 1530. *Gow*, A lost cause; 1554. *John Haynes-Williams*, 'Ars longa, Vita brevis'; *1515. *Briton Rivière*, Miracle of the Gadarene swine; 1559. *S. J. Carter*, Red deer; 1512. *J. C. Hook*, Home with the tide.

Room VI temporarily contains works by foreign artists and watercolours. Among the former (on the N. wall) may be mentioned: 1285. *Horace Vernet*, Portrait of Napoleon I.; 815. *P. J. Clays*, Dutch shipping; 600. *Dyckmans*, Blind beggar; 810. *Charles Poussin*, Pardon-day in Brittany; 1448. *Bonvin*, 1493. *Giov. Costa*, Landscapes; 1686. *H. Fantin-Latour*, Flowers. The water-colours and pastels (other walls) include: 70. *Bonington*, Cheyne Walk; 71. *Copley Fielding*, View in Sussex; 66. *H. Macallum*, Boy of Capri; 77. *Chas. Maundrell*, Château d'O; 56. *H. Dixon*, Lions; 57. *H. S. Hopwood*, Industry; 69. *A. Glendening*, Hay-making; 58. *G. Cockram*, Solitude; 73.

W. Bennett, Richmond Park; 76. *J. P. Gulich*, A violin concerto; 54. *A. W. Hunt*, Windsor Castle; 53. *Rossetti*, Rosa Triplex; 75. *A. MacCallum*, Monarch of the glen; 61. *Leopold Rivers*, Stormy weather.

Room VII. WATTS COLLECTION. This room is devoted to works by *George Frederick Watts*, R. A. (born 1817), mostly of a large size and interesting not only for their fine colouring but in many cases also for their wealth of allegorical or symbolical allusion. To the left, as we enter from Hall VIII: 1635. Death crowning Innocence; 1630. Mammon (dedicated to his worshippers); 1646. The Messenger; 1642. Eve tempted; 1643. 'She shall be called woman'; 1644. Eve repentant; 1633. Dray horses; 1637. The Spirit of Christianity, dedicated to all the churches; *1640. Hope; 1632. 'For he had great possessions'; 1636. Jonah; 1631. The dweller in the innermost; 1638. 'Sic transit gloria mundi'; 1637. The All-pervading; *1641. Love and Life (there are replicas of this painting in the Luxembourg and in the Corcoran Gallery at Washington); 1692. Love triumphant; *1615. Love and Death; 1693. Death and Judgment; 1647. Chaos; 1639. Faith; 1634. The Minotaur; 1561. Portrait of himself (1864). — In the centre, *G. F. Watts*, Clytie, a bronze bust.

Hall VIII. SCULPTURE. To the left: 18. *A. Drury*, Griselda; '19. *E. Onslow Ford*, Folly; 11. *H. Bates*, Pandora; 8. *Brock*, A moment of peril; *28. *Bates*, Hounds in leash; 23. *Pomeroy*, Dionysos: 17. *H. A. Pegram*, Ignis fatuus; 27. *Colton*, The girdle; 1. *John Gibson*, Hylas and the water-nymphs; 10. *H. C. Fehr*, Perseus and Andromeda; 9. *W. Calder Marshall*, Prodigal Son; 21. *R. Stark*, Indian rhinoceros. In the centre of the hall: 20. *Pomeroy*, The nymph of Loch Awe.

Rooms IX-XII are not yet open to the public. We therefore proceed through Room XIV (comp. plan) to —

Room XIII. To the left of the entrance from R. XII: 1590. *T. C. Gotch*, Alleluia; 1604. *Henry Moore*, Catspaws off the land; 1624. *T. M. Rooke*, The story of Ruth (triptych); 1679. *H. J. Draper*, The lament for Icarus; 1603. *H. W. Davis*, Sheep; 1596. *E. A. Waterlow*, Galway gossips; 1592. *M. R. Corbet*, Morning glory; 1698. *J. Young Hunter*, My Lady's garden; 1607. *J. W. North*, The winter-sun; 1622. *Joseph Knight*, A tidal river; 1611. *F. D. Millet*, Between two fires; 1597. *R. W. Macbeth*, The cast shoe; 1648. *David Farquharson*, In a fog.

Room XIV. To the left of the entrance from R. XIII: 1650. *Napier Hemy*, Pilchards; 1605. *La Thangue*, The man with the scythe; 1614. *David Murray*, 'My love has gone a-sailing'; *1615. *J.S.Sargent*, Carnation, Lily, Lily, Rose; 1617. *J. Brett*, Britannia's realm; 1616. *Hon. John Collier*, Last voyage of Henry Hudson; 1618. *H. S. Tuke*, 'All hands to the pump'; 1627. *F. Bramley*, A hopeless dawn; 1603. *Edwin Hayes*, Sunset at sea; 1612. *Geo. Clausen*, The girl at the gate; 1672. *R. Peacock*, Ethel; 1678. *S. Melton Fisher*, In realms of fancy; 1673. *Yeend King*, Milking time; 1595. *Wm. Small*, The last match; 1606. *C. E. Johnson*, Gurth and his swine (from 'Ivanhoe'); 1599. *Vicat Cole*, The Pool of London (p. 147); 1601. *W. Q. Orchardson*, Napoleon on board the 'Bellerophon'; 1602. *H. Herkomer*, Charterhouse Chapel; 1649. *Lucy E. Kemp-Welch*, Colt-hunting in the New Forest; 1613. *H. S. Tuke*, August blue.

Room XV. CHANTREY BEQUEST. To the left of the entrance from R. XVI: 1569. *J. M. Swan*, Prodigal Son; 1570. *Val. Prinsep*, Ayesha; 1571. *J. MacWhirter*, June in the Austrian Tyrol; 1572. *J. W. Waterhouse*, The magic circle; 1573. *P. H. Calderon*, St. Elizabeth of Hungary; 1574. *Lord Leighton*, Bath of Psyche; 1515. *H Herkomer*, Found; 1576. *A. Hacker*, Annunciation; 1577. *Briton Rivière*, Beyond man's footsteps; 1578. *Anna Merritt*, Love locked out; 1579. *Colin Hunter*, Their only harvest; 1580. *W. L. Wyllie*, Toil, glitter, grime, and wealth on a flowing tide; 1581. *W. Hunt*, Dog in the manger; 1582. *J. Pettie*, Vigil; 1583. *Marcus Stone*, 'Il y en a toujours un autre'; 1584. *Sir John Millais*, 'Speak, Speak'; 1585. *G. F. Watts*, Psyche; above, Portrait of Sir Francis Chantrey, by himself; 1586. *Sir E. J. Poynter*, Visit to Æsculapius; 1587. *Frank Dicksee*, Harmony; 1588. *A. C. Gow*, Cromwell at Dunbar; 1589. *A. Parsons*, 'When nature painted all things gay'; 1620. *J. Seymour Lucas*, After Culloden.

Room XVI. CHANTREY BEQUEST. To the left of the entrance from

R. XV: 1625. *J. M. Strudwick*, A golden thread; *1621. *Wm. Logsdail*, St. Martin's in the Fields (p. 186); 1600. *J. R. Reid*, Toil and pleasure; *1626. *Joseph Farquharson*, The cheerless winter-day; 1609. *W. F. Yeames*, Amy Robsart; 1623. *Adrian Stokes*, Upland and sky; 1619. *J. Aumonier*, Sheep-washing in Sussex; 1628. *Ernest Parton*, Waning of the year.

In the corridor on which Rooms XIV and XV open are a relief of Thetis and Achilles, by Thomas Banks, and a *Statue of Sir David Wilkie*, by S. Joseph. — The UPPER FLOOR of the gallery is at present empty.

Immediately in front of the Tate Gallery the Thames is crossed by *Vauxhall Temporary Bridge*, a substantial structure, to serve during the rebuilding of Vauxhall Bridge.

Vauxhall Bridge (Pl. G, 26), originally constructed by Walker in 1816, with nine iron arches, is at present being rebuilt by Sir Alex. Binnie. The span of the new central arch is to be 150 ft. Vauxhall Bridge Road runs hence to the N. to Victoria Station (p. 57; tramway No. 9, p. 54). — A little to the S. of Vauxhall Bridge is *Kennington Oval* (p. 72), a cricket-ground second only to Lord's in public favour and in interest. Just to the W. of the Oval is *Vauxhall Park* (Pl. G, 30), with a terracotta statue of *Professor Henry Fawcett* (d. 1884).

The river is crossed farther up by the *Grosvenor Road Bridge*, used for the various railways converging at Victoria Station, and by Chelsea Suspension Bridge (p. 363).

21. Pall Mall and Piccadilly.

Waterloo Place. York Column. Marlborough House. St. James's Street. Burlington House. Geological Museum. Leicester Square.

Pall Mall (Pl. R, 22, 26; *IV*), the centre of club-life (see p. 102), and a street of modern palaces, derives its name from the old game of *pall mail* (from the Italian *palla*, 'a ball', and *malleo*, a mallet; French *jeu de mail*), introduced into England during the reign of Charles I. In the 16th and 17th centuries Pall Mall was a fashionable suburban promenade, but about the end of the 17th cent. it began to assume the form of a street. Among the many celebrated persons who have resided in this street may be mentioned Marshal Schomberg, the scion of a noble Rhenish family (the Counts of Schönburg), who fell at the Battle of the Boyne (1690). Gainsborough died in 1788 in the house which had once been Schomberg's (house next the War Office). Dodsley, the publisher, carried on business in Pall Mall under the sign of 'Tully's Head', bringing out, among other works, Sterne's 'Tristram Shandy', and the 'Annual Register'. Nell Gwynne lived at No. 79 (rebuilt) from 1671 till her death in 1687 and used to talk over the garden-wall to Charles II., as he walked in St. James's Park. Sir Walter Scott stayed at No. 23, the house of his son-in-law Lockhart, in 1826-27.

The eastern portion of the street, between Cockspur Street and Trafalgar Square, is called *Pall Mall East*. Here, nearly opposite the corner of the HAYMARKET (where Addison once resided), is a bronze statue of *George III.*, by *Wyatt*, erected in 1837. On the N.

side of Pall Mall East are the *Royal Society of Painters in Water Colours* (No. 6) and the *United University Club* (entrance from Suffolk Street). Farther to the W., at the left corner of Haymarket, rises the large *Carlton Hotel* (p. 9), on the site of the Opera House, demolished in 1893. The N. part of the same building, facing Haymarket, is occupied by *Her Majesty's Theatre* (p. 65), opposite which is the *Haymarket Theatre* (p. 65). Then in Pall Mall, at the corner of Waterloo Place, is the *United Service Club*.

To the N. of **Waterloo Place** (Pl. R, 26; *IV*) is *Regent Street* (p. 286), leading to Piccadilly. In the centre of the place is the *CRIMEAN MONUMENT, erected, from a design by *Bell*, to the memory of the 2162 officers and soldiers of the Guards, who fell in the Russian war. On a granite pedestal is a figure of Victory with laurel wreaths; below, in front, three guardsmen; behind, a trophy of guns captured at Sebastopol. On the sides are inscribed the names of Alma, Inkerman, and Sebastopol. — In the S. part of the place or square are five monuments. In the centre is an equestrian statue of *Lord Napier of Magdala* (1810-90), by *Boehm*. To the left is a bronze statue of *Colin Campbell, Lord Clyde*, Field-Marshal (d. 1863), the conqueror of Lucknow, by *Marochetti*. Adjacent is a similar monument (by *Boehm*) to *Lord Lawrence* (d. 1879), ruler of the Punjâb during the Sepoy Mutiny of 1857 and Viceroy of India from 1864 to 1869, erected in 1882 by his fellow-subjects, British and Indian. — To the right, opposite, is the bronze statue of *Sir John Franklin*, by *Noble*, erected by Parliament 'to the great arctic navigator and his brave companions who sacrificed their lives in completing the discovery of the North West Passage A. D. 1847-48'. On the S. of this statue is a bronze figure of Field-Marshal *Sir John Fox Burgoyne* (d. 1871), by *Boehm*.

The broad flight of steps at the S. end of Waterloo Place, known as *Waterloo Steps*, descends to St. James's Park. At the top of the steps rises the **York Column,** a granite column of the Tuscan order, 124 ft. in height, designed by *Wyatt*, and erected in 1833 (no admission). It is surmounted by a bronze statue of the Duke of York (second son of George III.), by *Westmacott*. — To the W. of the column, in Carlton House Terrace (No. 9), is *Prussia House*, the residence of the German ambassador.

Carlton House, the site of which is occupied by Waterloo Place, was built in 1709 for Henry Boyle, Lord Carlton, and was bought in 1732 by the Prince of Wales. It was afterwards the residence of the Prince-Regent (later George IV.), but was pulled down in 1827. Its columns are now said to adorn the façade of the National Gallery (p. 188).

Farther on in Pall Mall (S. side) is a series of palatial club houses, the oldest of which dates from 1829 (see also p. 102). At the corner on the left is the *Athenaeum Club* (with a frieze reproducing that of the Parthenon); then the *Travellers' Club* (with its best façade towards the garden), *Reform Club*, and *Carlton Club* (with polished granite pillars; an imitation of Sansovino's Library of St. Mark at Venice).

John St. leads from this point to the N. to **St. James's Square** (Pl. R, 22, 26; *IV*), which is embellished with an *Equestrian Statue of William III.*, in bronze, by *Bacon*, erected in 1808. The square has been an aristocratic place of residence ever since it was first laid out in the reign of Charles II. At the S.E. corner (No. 31) is *Norfolk House* (Duke of Norfolk), built 1748-52; in an older building, behind, George III. was born in 1733, his parents having been turned out of St. James's Palace by George II. Adjoining, to the N., is *London House* (rebuilt 1820), the official town-residence of the bishops of London since 1771, but seldom occupied (comp. p. 386). Lord Chesterfield (1694-1773) was born in the house originally occupying this site. Next door is the Earl of Derby's mansion. No. 8, on the N. side of the square, was the home and depôt of Josiah Wedgwood the Younger from 1796 till 1830. No. 10 has been the residence of the elder Pitt (1759-62), Lady Blessington (1820-29), Lord Derby (1837-54), and Mr. Gladstone (1890). At No. 13 (now the *Windham Club*) Lord Ellenborough died in 1818. No. 14 (rebuilt 1898) is the *London Library* (p. 281). The *East India United Service Club* (No. 16) replaces the house in which Queen Caroline lived during part of her trial (1820), while Lord Castlereagh, then Foreign Secretary, lived next door (No. 18). No. 21, now a branch of the war-office, is called *Winchester House*, because from 1829 till 1875 it was the London residence of the bishops of Winchester. It was occupied in 1676-78 by Arabella Churchill, mistress of James II. The adjoining house, now incorporated with the Army and Navy Club (see below), was the residence of Mary Davis, the actress, in 1676-87. The S. side of the square is mainly occupied by the N. front of the Junior Carlton Club (see below). — See 'History of St. James's Square', by Arthur Dasent (1895).

Adjoining the Carlton Club, on the S. side of Pall Mall, is the *War Office*, in front of which is a bronze statue of *Lord Herbert of Lea* (d. 1861), once War Secretary, by *Foley*. [The War Office is to be removed to more commodious premises in Whitehall (see p. 236).] Opposite, on the right side of the street, are the *Junior Carlton Club* and the *Army and Navy Club* (known as 'the Rag').

Farther on, at the W. end of Pall Mall, are the *Oxford and Cambridge Club*, the *Guards' Club*, and the *New Oxford and Cambridge Club* on the left, and the *Marlborough Club* on the right. **Marlborough House** (Pl. R, 22; *IV*), on the S. side of Pall Mall, was erected by *Sir Christopher Wren*, in 1710, for the first Duke of Marlborough (d. 1722 at Windsor), and his Duchess Sarah (d. here 1744), and is now the home of the Prince of Wales. The Duke of Marlborough lived in such a magnificent style as entirely to eclipse the court of 'Neighbour George' in St. James's Palace. Prince Leopold of Saxe-Coburg (d. 1865), husband of Princess Charlotte (d. 1817), was tenant of Marlborough House from 1817, when part of the crown-lease on which the property was held terminated, until he accepted the throne of Belgium in 1831. Marlborough House finally reverted to Government in 1835. The house was afterwards occupied by the Queen Dowager Adelaide, subsequently used as a picture-gallery, and has been the residence of the Prince of Wales since 1863. It has been remodelled and considerably enlarged since 1850. The walls of the principal staircases are embellished with mural paintings by La Guerre, representing the battles of the great Duke of Marlborough. The house and grounds occupy about 4³/₄ acres. The chapel on the side next St. James's Palace, built for the Roman Catholic services of Queen Henrietta Maria, wife of Charles I., is now the *German Chapel Royal.*

To the W. of Marlborough House, and separated from it by a narrow carriage-way only, is *St. James's Palace* (p. 327).

In ST. JAMES'S STREET, which here leads N. to Piccadilly, are situated the *Thatched House Club,* the *Conservative Club, Arthur's Club, Brooks's Club, New University Club, White's Club* (the bow window of which has figured in so many novels), *Boodle's Club* (founded about 1760), the *Junior Army and Navy Club,* the *Devonshire Club* (formerly *Crockford's),* notorious for its high play under the Regency), and others. In St. James's Place, to the left, are *Spencer House* (Earl Spencer) and the house (No. 22) occupied by Samuel Rogers, banker and poet, from 1800 till his death in 1855, and the scene of his famous literary breakfasts. To the right, in King Street, is *St. James's Theatre* (p. 65). *Willis's Restaurant,* a little farther along King Street, occupies the site of rooms which were down to 1863, under the name of *Almack's* (from the original proprietor, 1765), famous for the aristocratic and exclusive balls held in them. King Street also contains *Christie and Manson's Auction Rooms,* celebrated for sales of valuable art collections. The chief sales take place on Saturdays, in the Season. — At No. 4 Bennett Street, to the left, Byron wrote 'The Bride of Abydos'.

Piccadilly (Pl. R, 18, 22; *I, IV),* extending from Haymarket to Hyde Park Corner, is nearly 1 M. in length. The eastern portion is one of the chief business-streets of the West End. The western half, which is bordered on the S. by the *Green Park* (p. 330), contains a number of aristocratic and fashionable residences, and the *Naval and Military* (**94;** formerly the house of Lord Palmerston), *Badminton* (100), *Isthmian* (No. 105), *St. James's* (106), *Savile* (107), *Junior Naval and Military* (96), *Junior Athenaeum* (116), and other clubs.

Turning into it to the right, we first notice, on the right, the *Egyptian Hall* (p. 68). On the opposite side are *Old* and *New Bond Streets* (p. 289), leading to Oxford Street. Between Old Bond Street and Sackville Street rises **New Burlington House** (Pl. R, 22; *I),* to the W. of which is the *Burlington Arcade* (p. 31). Old Burlington House, built in 1695-1743 by Richard, Lord Burlington, with the assistance of the architect Campbell, was purchased by Government in 1854 for the sum of 140,000*l.* along with its gardens, on which various new edifices have been built. The incongruous top story and the present façade of the old building are also new. Nearest Piccadilly is a building in the Italian Renaissance style, completed in 1872 from designs by *Banks* and *Barry,* and occupied by several learned societies, to whom the rooms are granted by Government rent-free; in the E. wing are the *Royal, Geological,* and *Chemical Societies,* and in the W. the *Antiquarian* (with a collection of paintings, chiefly old portraits), *Astronomical*, and *Linnaean*.

The **Royal Society**, or Academy of Science, the most important of the learned bodies of Great Britain, was founded in 1660, and received its charter of incorporation from Charles II. three years later. As early as 1645, however, its germ existed in the meeting of a few men of learning, far from the turmoil of the Civil War, to discuss subjects relating to the physical and exact sciences. The first number of its famous *Philosophical Transactions* appeared in 1665. It now comprises about 520 members (including 50 foreign members), each of whom is entitled to append to his name the letters F. R. S. (Fellow of the Royal Society). The *Library* of the society consists of about 50,000 vols. and 5000 MSS. The rooms contain portraits and busts of celebrated Fellows, including Sir Christopher Wren, Sir Isaac Newton, Robert Boyle, Halley, Sir Humphry Davy, Watt, and Sir William Herschel; also a telescope which belonged to Newton, and the MS. of his 'Philosophiæ Naturalis Principia Mathematica'; and the original model of Davy's safety-lamp.

The Copley Medal and two Royal Medals are awarded annually by the society for scientific eminence, and the Davy Medal for chemical investigation. The Rumford and Darwinian Medals are awarded biennially for investigations in light and heat and in biology respectively. Besides the *Transactions* the society also issues its *Proceedings* annually, and a *Catalogue of Scientific Papers* published in all parts of the world.

An arcade leads through the building into the inner court. On the N. side is the exhibition building of the **Royal Academy of Arts** (founded in 1768), in the Renaissance style, erected by *Smirke* in 1868-69. At the top of the façade are 9 statues of celebrated artists: Phidias, Leonardo da Vinci, Flaxman, Raphael, Michael Angelo, Titian, Reynolds, Wren, and Wykeham. The Exhibition of the Royal Academy (transferred in 1869 from Trafalgar Square to Piccadilly), which takes place here every year from May to the beginning of August, attracts immense numbers of visitors (admission 1s., catalogue 1s.). It consists of paintings and sculptures by modern (mainly) British artists, which must have been finished during the previous year and not exhibited elsewhere before. The 'Private View' of the Exhibition, held by invitation of the Academicians before it is thrown open to the public, is always attended by the cream of society and is one of the events of the London Season. The 'Academy Dinner' held about the same time is also a highly important social function. The Academy organises every winter a loan exhibition of works of old masters or of deceased modern artists. The society consists of 40 Royal Academicians, 30 Associates, and 2 Associate Engravers. — A staircase in the corner to the right ascends to the GIBSON and DIPLOMA GALLERIES (open daily, 11-4, free), which contain some valuable works of early art, the diploma pictures presented by Academicians on their election, and the Gibson collection of sculpture. Among the ancient works are:

*Mary with Jesus and St. John, a relief by *Michael Angelo;* *Madonna, Holy Child, St. Anne, and St. John, a celebrated cartoon by *Leonardo da Vinci,* executed in 1503 for the church Dell'Annunziata at Florence; Copy of Leonardo's Last Supper, by his pupil *Marco da Oggionno,* from which Morghen's engraving was taken; Woman at a well, ascribed to *Giorgione* but considered by Frizzoni to be an early work of *Seb. del Piombo;* portrait by *Giorgione.* The diploma works include good specimens by *Reynolds* and *Wilkie.* The *Library,* on the first floor, contains a fine collection of books and prints.

At the back of the Academy, and facing Burlington Gardens, is another Renaissance structure, erected in 1869 from designs by *Pennethorne* and long occupied by *London University.* In 1900 the offices of the University were transferred to the Imperial Institute (p. 345).

The effective façade is decorated with a series of statues. Above the portico are those of Milton, Newton, Harvey, and Bentham, by *Durham;* over the cornice in the centre, Plato, Archimedes, and Justinian, by *Woodington,* and Galen, Cicero, and Aristotle, by *Westmacott;* in the W. wing, Locke, Bacon, and Adam Smith, by *Theed,* and Hume, Hunter, and Sir Humphry Davy, by *Noble;* in the E. wing, Galileo, Laplace, and Goethe, by *Wyon,* and Cuvier, Leibnitz, and Linnæus, by *Macdowell.* A marble statue of Queen Victoria, by *Boehm,* was erected here in 1889.

Close by, at 1 Savile Row, to the N.E., is the *Royal Geographical Society* (sec., Dr. J. Scott Keltie). Richard Brinsley Sheridan died at 17 Savile Row in 1816, and Grote, the historian, died at No. 12 in 1871. — In Albemarle Street, to the W., beyond Bond Street (p. 289), is the *Royal Institution,* founded in 1799 for the promotion and teaching of science, with library, reading-room, laboratories, and weekly lectures from Christmas to Midsummer. The admirably equipped *Davy Faraday Research Laboratory,* at No. 20, presented to the Royal Institution by Mr. Ludwig Mond, was opened in December, 1896. The *Royal Asiatic Society* (No. 22) has a library (open 11-4, on Sat. 11-2). No. 50, the house of Mr. John Murray, the publisher, contains portraits of Scott, Byron, Washington Irving (Wilkie), and other men of letters; also Hogarth's Scene from the 'Beggars' Opera'. No. 13 is the *Albemarle Club* (p. 103), No. 7 the *Royal Thames Yacht Club.*

On the N. side of Piccadilly, a little beyond Burlington House, is the *Albany,* let out in chambers, and numbering 'Monk' Lewis, Canning, Byron (No. 2A), Bulwer Lytton, and Macaulay (No. 1E, second floor) among quondam residents. The last lived here for 15 years and wrote here the first volumes of his 'History of England'. Byron passed the first part of his married life at 139 Piccadilly, where his daughter Ada was born in Dec., 1815.

St. James's Church (Pl. R, 22; *I*), adjoining *Princes' Restaurant* (p. 16) on the S. side of Piccadilly, built by *Wren* in 1682-84, and considered (as to the interior) one of his finest works, contains a marble font by *Grinling Gibbons*, who also executed the handsome foliage over the altar. The stained-glass windows, representing the Passion and other scenes, are modern. The vestry is hung with portraits of former rectors, three of whom (Tenison, Wake, and Secker) became archbishops.

The **Museum of Practical Geology,** erected in 1850, is a little farther to the E. The building contains, besides the geological museum, a lecture-room for 500 hearers, and a library. Entrance by Jermyn Street (Nos. 28-32); admission, see p. 108.

The HALL contains busts of celebrated geologists: on the right, Buckland, Playfair, Greenough, Forbes, William Smith, and Jukes (behind); on the left, Murchison, De la Beche, Hutton, Hall, Sedgwick, and Ramsay; at the pillars near the entrance, Queen Victoria and Prince Albert. At the upper end is a copy of the Farnese Hercules in Portland limestone. Then English, Irish, and Scotch granite; alabaster; Portland limestone from the island of Portland, near Weymouth in Dorsetshire; Derbyshire, Staffordshire, and Irish marbles; auriferous quartz; malachite; a large block of solid copper; lode with galena and pyrites; and numerous varieties of limestone. These are partly in the rough, and partly polished and cut in the shape of large cubes, squares, tablets, or short columns. Two tables inlaid with ancient and modern marbles. Also terracotta statuettes, copies of ancient statues, vases, and pieces of tesselated pavement. The mosaic pavement in the middle of the hall deserves notice. The table-cases contain part of a large mineralogical collection bequeathed by Mr. Henry Ludlam.

On the FIRST FLOOR we first observe a large vase of Siberian aventurine quartz, a gift from the Emperor of Russia; a geological model of London and its vicinity; a gold snuff-box with enamel portrait, given to Sir Roderick Murchison by Alexander II. of Russia; a steel salver, inlaid with gold, presented by the Russian Administration of Mines to Sir Roderick Murchison. On the S. side is a collection of porcelain, glass, enamels, and mosaics from the earliest period down to the present day. Then, in table-cases at the sides of the room, iron, steel, and copper, at different stages of their manufacture. We notice in a standard case on the right side (E. ; No. 14) a penny rolled out into a strip of copper, 10 yds. long. The cases arranged in the form of a horseshoe in the middle of the room contain the collection of non-metallic minerals: here are seen all kinds of crystallisations, particularly of precious stones, from quartz nodules with brilliant crystals in the interior up to the most exquisitely polished jewels. Models of the largest known diamonds, such as the Koh-i-noor and the Regent Diamond, are exhibited in Case A (on the E. side). The metalliferous minerals, or ores, occupy the wall-cases. Other cabinets are filled with agates, some of which are artificially coloured with oxide of iron, and the precious metals, including a model of a huge nugget of pure gold, weighing 2020 oz. (value 8376*l.*).

In the adjoining apartments to the N. are exhibited geological relief plans and models of mines, mining tools, miners' lamps, etc. The two upper galleries, running round the hall, chiefly contain fossils, which are of little interest to the ordinary visitor. At the S. end of the higher gallery is a *Petrographical Room*, with specimens of rocks and rock-structure.

On the N. side of Piccadilly, opposite the Geological Museum, is *St. James's Hall* (p. 69), which has another entrance in the Regent Quadrant (p. 286). We next reach *Piccadilly Circus* (p. 286), and then, on the right, the *Criterion Theatre* (p. 66) and the *Haymarket* (p. 279). At this point Piccadilly proper comes to an end. *Coventry Street*, its eastern prolongation, containing the *Prince of*

Wales Theatre (p. 66), leads on to **Leicester Square** (Pl. R, 27; *I*), a quarter largely inhabited by French residents, and adorned in 1874 with flower-beds and a marble statue of *Shakspeare*, in the centre, bearing the inscription, 'There is no darkness but ignorance'; at the base are four water-spouting dolphins. The corners of the garden are embellished with marble busts of *Reynolds, Hunter, Hogarth,* and *Newton,* all of whom lived in or near the square. After the revocation of the Edict of Nantes (1685) this neighbourhood became a favourite resort of the more aristocratic French Protestant exiles. Leicester House and Savile House, once situated in the square, were occupied by members of the royal family during the first half of last century; and Peter the Great was entertained at Savile House by the Marquis of Carmarthen (1698). Down to the beginning of the present century the open space in the centre was a frequent resort of duellists. — The *Alhambra Theatre* (p. 67), on the E. side, burned down in 1882, was rebuilt in 1883-84. The site of Savile House, on the N. side of the square, is occupied by the *Empire Theatre* (p. 67).

The line of Coventry Street is continued on the other side of the square by Cranbourn Street, in which are *Daly's Theatre* (p. 66) and the *Hippodrome* (p. 67), leading to Charing Cross Road (p. 188). The *Reynolds Galleries*, in Cranbourn Street, occupy a house in which Sir Joshua Reynolds lived for several years.

22. Regent Street. Oxford Street. Holborn.

All Saints' Church. Wallace Collection. University College. St. Pancras' Church. Foundling Hospital.

Regent Street (Pl. R, 23, 26; *I*), one of the finest streets in London, and containing a large number of the best shops, was laid out by *Nash* in 1813, for the purpose of connecting Carlton House (p. 280), the residence of the Prince Regent, with Regent's Park. It is 1 M. in length, and extends from Waterloo Place, Pall Mall (p. 280), across Oxford Street, to Portland Place. To the right (E.), at the corner of Charles Street, stands the *Junior United Service Club*, and on the same side is the *Raleigh Club*. Jermyn Street (with the *Geological Museum*, p. 285) is a little farther on. The street then reaches *Regent Circus, Piccadilly* (see p. 285; known as *Piccadilly Circus*), whence Piccadilly leads to the W., Coventry Street to the E., and the wide Shaftesbury Avenue (p. 188) to the N.E. The triangle in the centre of the Circus is occupied by a *Memorial Fountain to Lord Shaftesbury* (d. 1885), by Alfred Gilbert, A. R. A., unveiled in 1893 and adorned with eight plaques of scenes from the philanthropist's life. Beyond the Circus Regent Street describes a curve to the W., forming the so-called *Quadrant*. On the left is the entrance to *St. James's Hall* (see p. 285). Farther on, to the left, we pass New Burlington Street, Conduit Street, and Maddox Street.

Hanover Street and Prince's Street both lead to the W. to HANOVER SQUARE, which is embellished with a bronze statue of *William Pitt* (d. 1806), by *Chantrey*. On the W. side of the square is the *Oriental Club*; and at the N.W. angle, in Tenterden Street, the *Royal Academy of Music*. In George Street, leading out of the square on the S., is **St. George's Church**, built by *James* (1713-24), with a classic portico, and three stained-glass windows, made in Malines about 1520 and brought to England early in the 19th century. It has long been a favourite resort for fashionable weddings. Lady Mary Wortley Montagu died in George Street in 1762.

The intersection of Regent Street with Oxford Street (see p. 288), which extends for a long distance in both directions, is called *Regent Circus*, *Oxford Street*, or simply *Oxford Circus*. Margaret Street, the second cross-street beyond Oxford Street, leads to the W. (left) to CAVENDISH SQUARE, which contains an equestrian statue in marble of the *Duke of Cumberland* (the victor at Culloden in 1746), by *Chew*, and a bronze statue of *Lord George Bentinck* (d. 1848), by *Campbell*. *Harcourt House*, on the W. side of the square, is the mansion of the Duke of Portland. Lord Byron was born in 1788 at 24 Holles Street, between Cavendish Square and Oxford Street; the house, which has since been rebuilt, is now marked by a bust of the poet. He was baptised in *Old Marylebone Church*, at the top of Marylebone High Street (Pl. R, 20), where Charles Wesley was buried in 1788 and Robert Browning was married in 1846. This was the old church (rebuilt in 1741) which figures in the 'Rake's Marriage' by Hogarth (see p. 231). [The house of Mrs. Browning's father, which she left secretly for her marriage, was No. 50, Wimpole Street, a little to the E. of High Street; it is now marked by a tablet.] In Margaret Street, to the E. (r.) of Regent Street, is **All Saints' Church** (Pl. R, 24; *I*), built by *Butterfield* in 1850-59, in the Early English style, and lavishly decorated in the interior with marble and gilding. The E. wall of the choir is frescoed by Dyce in the style of early Christian art. The spire is 227 ft. high. — At No. 74a Margaret Street is the *Parkes Museum of Hygiene* (open on week-days, 10-6).

The *Polytechnic Young Men's Christian Institute*, between Cavendish Square and Regent Street, has occupied since 1882 the old Polytechnic Institution. The Institute has numerous technical and other classes (11,000 students), reading-rooms, a gymnasium, etc. The good genius of the institution is Mr. Quintin Hogg, who has spent 150,000*l.* upon it. On the opposite side of the street is the County Council's *School of Arts* (p. 98). Farther on, on the right side of Regent Street, are *St. George's Hall* (p. 70) and the handsome *Queen's Hall* (p. 69). The latter has accommodation for 3000 persons; the ceiling is painted by Carpégat.

At the N. end of Regent Street is *Langham Place*, with *All Souls' Church*, erected by Nash. The large building on the other side is the *Langham Hotel* (p. 11). From this point PORTLAND PLACE, one of the widest streets in London (120 ft.), leads to *Park Crescent, Park Square,* and *Regent's Park* (p. 294).

Oxford Street (Pl. R, 19, 23, 27; *I, II*), the principal artery of traffic between the N.W. quarter of London and the City, extends from the Marble Arch (at the N.E. corner of Hyde Park, p. 332) to Holborn, a distance of 1½ M. The E. portion of this imposing street contains a number of the most important shops in London, and presents a scene of immense traffic and activity; while the W. end, with the adjoining streets and squares (particularly Grosvenor Square and Berkeley Square on the S. and Portman Square on the N.), comprises many aristocratic residences. — *Edgware Road,* which begins at the W. end of Oxford Street (see Pl. R, **15**), follows the line of the old Roman road to St. Albans. In Harrow Road, leading to the W. from Edgware Road, is *St. Mary's Churchyard* (Pl. R, 12), now a public park, near the N.W. angle of which is the grave of Mrs. Sarah Siddons (d. 1831), the famous actress. A *Statue of Mrs. Siddons,* by Chavalliaud, was erected in 1897 on Paddington Green, close by. — Portland Street and Orchard Street lead to the N. (left) from Oxford Street to *Portman Square,* No. 15 in which is the residence of the Duke of Fife. The 'Blue Stocking Club' met at Mrs. Montagu's (d. 1800) in the N.W. corner of the square. Anthony Trollope lived in Montagu Square, just to the N. From the N.E. corner of Portman Square Baker Street runs due N. to *Baker Street Station* (Pl. R, 20; p. 58), a little to the W. of which is *Marylebone Station* (Pl. R, 16; p. 56), in Marylebone Road. Blandford Street, diverging from Baker Street to the E., contains the house (No. 2) in which Faraday, the chemist, served his apprenticeship (tablet). Lower Berkeley Street runs to the E. from Portman Square to Manchester Square (see below). Adjacent, at 13 Mandeville Place, is *Trinity College,* an incorporated institution for the study of music and arts.

Duke Street leads to the left (N.) from Oxford street, farther on, to *Manchester Square,* on the N. side of which stands **Hertford House** (Pl. R, 20; *I*), formerly the residence of the fourth marquis of Hertford, and said to be the original of Gaunt House in Thackeray's 'Vanity Fair'. Hertford House was afterwards occupied by Sir Richard Wallace (d. 1890), who added three fine galleries for the reception of the famous Hertford Collection, which he greatly extended. This magnificent collection of paintings, armour, furniture, porcelain, and art-treasures of every kind, now known as the ****Wallace Collection** and valued at 4,000,000*l.,* was bequeathed to the nation by Lady Wallace (d. 1897), and 80,000*l.* were voted by parliament to purchase the house and adapt it as a public gallery. The collection was opened to the public in June, 1900. Adm., see p. 108. Catalogue of the pictures 6*d.,* of the armour 6*d.* The director is *Mr. Claude Phillips.*

The *_Picture Gallery_ (over 750 works) includes an admirable series of Dutch and Flemish paintings, and a few choice canvases of the Italian, Spanish, and British schools; but its special importance is due perhaps to the exceptionally fine collection of French art of the 18th and early 19th cent., which rivals and in some points excels that in the Louvre, while it fills a serious gap in the national collections of Great Britain. — The *_French Furniture_, chiefly of the periods of Louis XIV., XV., and XVI., which is distributed through the rooms containing the paintings, at least equals the corresponding collections in the Louvre and the Garde Meuble of Paris. — The *_Armoury_, though collected more with a view to illustrate the art of the armourer than the art of war, is the finest in England.

Beyond the entrance (where sticks and umbrellas are given up) we enter the Lower Hall. Immediately in front rises the _Great Staircase_, with a handsome balustrade of the period of Louis XIV., and busts of Sir Richard and Lady Wallace and the fourth Marquis of Hertford.

Most of the paintings and much of the finest furniture are on the first floor; visitors are therefore recommended to ascend the staircase at once, and, turning to the right at the top, to traverse RR. XX, XIX, XVIII. and XVII in order to begin with R. XVI, which contains the gems of the picture-gallery, other than those of the French school. — The numbers of the rooms are painted above the doors, on the inside.

First Floor. — Room XVI. Various Schools. To the left: *1. _Cima da Conegliano_, St. Catharine of Alexandria (panel from an altar-piece); 2. _Bianchi_, Allegorical subject; 5. _Copy of Titian_, Rape of Europa (original in Boston, U.S.A.); *9. _Andrea del Sarto_, Virgin and Child, with St. John and two angels; 10. _Luini_, Virgin and Child. — *11. _Titian_, Perseus and Andromeda.

Mr. Claude Phillips, who discovered this painting in a neglected condition in a bathroom in Hertford House, identifies it with a work mentioned by Vasari as painted for Philip II. of Spain about 1562. It afterwards belonged to the Orléans Gallery, and on the dispersal of that collection in London in 1798 disappeared from public view.

21. _Velazquez_, Don Baltasar Carlos; 13. _Murillo_, Virgin and Child; 15. _Alonso Cano_, Vision of St. John the Evangelist (in the master's earlier style); 17, 21. _J. van Ostade_, Village-scenes; 23, 27. _P. de Hooghe_, Dutch interiors; 25. _Berghem_, Coast-scene; 29. _Rembrandt_, The artist's son Titus; 30. _Rubens_, Isabel Brandt, first wife of the artist. _Reynolds_, 31–33. Portraits; 36. 'Love me, love my dog'; *28. Portrait of Nelly O'Brien. 37. _Romney_, Mrs. 'Perdita' Robinson; 39. _Lawrence_, Portrait; *40. _Reynolds_, The Strawberry Girl; 41. _Hoppner_, Portrait; _Gainsborough_, *42. Mrs. 'Perdita' Robinson, 44. Miss Haverfield; *45. _Reynolds_, Mrs. 'Perdita' Robinson; 49. _A. Cuyp_, River-scene; 52, 55. _Rembrandt_, Portraits of himself; *53. _Van Dyck_, Portrait of an Italian nobleman; 57. _Pynacker_, Landscape; 58. _Murillo_, Holy Family; 60. _Hobbema_, Landscape; 61. _C. Drost_, Portrait; *63. _Rubens_, The 'Rainbow' landscape; 65. _Ph. Wouverman_, Horse-fair; 68. _Murillo_, Annunciation; *73. _J. van_

Ostade, Winter-scene; 74. *F. Bol*, Toper; 77. *W. van de Velde*, Sea-fight; *79. *Van Dyck*, Madame Philippe le Roy (comp. No. 94); *Rubens*, 81. Holy Family, *82, *90 (farther on), Burgomaster Jan Pellicorne and his wife; *84. *F. Hals*, The laughing cavalier; *86. *Rembrandt*, The Unmerciful Servant; *88. *Velazquez*, 'La Femme à l'eventail'; 89. *Backer*, Portrait; 92. *Gonzales Coques*, Family group; *94. *Van Dyck*, Philippe le Roy; 99, *Hobbema*, Landscape. — The magnificent cabinets and bronzes in this room should also be noticed.

Room XVII. Schools of the 17th Century. 102. *J. B. Weenix*, Flowers and fruit; 107. *C. de Heem*, Stillife; 108. *N. Poussin*, Dance of the Seasons; 110. *B. van der Helst*, Family group; 111. *Jan Steen*, Supper-scene; 116. *Salv. Rosa*, River-scene, with Apollo and the Sibyl; 119. *Ph. de Champaigne*, Marriage of the Virgin; 121. *Hackaert*, Landscape; 122. *Largillière*, Louis XIV. and his family; *127. *Ph. de Champaigne*, Portrait of Fénelon; 130. *H. Rigaud*, Cardinal Fleury; 132. *Camphuysen*, Landscape; 137. *W. van de Velde*, Sea-piece ('Le Coup de Canon'). — In the centre, *Sèvres Porcelain* of the 18th century. — A flight of steps descends from this room to R. VII (Armoury; see p. 289).

Room XVIII. This room, the two following, and the great staircase, are devoted to the French School of the 18th Century. The sumptuous contemporary *Furniture and bric-à-brac which are placed in these rooms are admirably in harmony with the decorative character of the paintings. Room XVIII contains a charming series of fêtes champêtres, conversations galantes, pastoral and romantic scenes, etc., by *Watteau* (1684-1721), *Lancret* (1690-1743), *Pater* (1696-1736), *Boucher* (1704-1770), and *Fragonard* (1732-1806), the delicacy and grace of which will repay careful inspection. *Greuze* (1725-1805) is represented by a number of characteristic heads and several other works, including *402, Portrait of Mlle. Sophie Arnould, the actress; *Lemoine* (1688-1737) by two works (Nos. 392, 417); and *Nattier* (1685-1766) by the portrait of a French prince (No. 414). — The glass-cases contain *French Snuff Boxes* (18th cent.) and *Sèvres Porcelain* (18th cent.).

Room XIX. contains decorative pieces by *Boucher*. Also: 435. *Boilly*, The dead mouse; 437. *Nattier*, Queen Marie Lesczinska; *439. *Watteau*, The toilet; 442. *Greuze*, The broken mirror.

Room XX. 449. *Mme. Le Brun*, Boy in red; 451. *C. A. Van Loo*, Concert given by the Grand Turk; 456. *Nattier*, Portrait of Mlle. de Clermont; *De Troy* (1679-1752), The hunt-breakfast; *Lépicié*, 464, 466. Domestic scenes; 469. *Marne*, The elixir; 470. *De Troy*, Stag at bay; 477. *Callet*, Louis XV. — We now proceed to —

Room XXIII, *i. e.* the landing at the top of the great staircase. On the walls above the staircase are huge allegorical and mythological compositions by *Boucher* and *Lemoine;* above the doors to the right and left, 483, 488. *Fragonard*, Cupids sporting, Cupids reposing.

Room XXI (entered from R. XX). WATER COLOURS by *Copley Fielding*, *Richard Bonington*, *Decamps*, *Lami*, *Derby*, *H. Vernet*, *Brascassat*, *Raffet*, *Downman*, *Géricault*, etc.

Room XXII. WATER COLOURS by *Decamps*, *Turner*, *Bonington*, *Clarkson Stanfield*, *Roberts*, *Pils*, *Cogniet*, etc. On a screen are sketches in oil by *Rubens*. — The furniture, etc., in these two rooms should also be noticed. — Beyond R. XXII we enter —

Room XII, on the walls of which is an important series of Venetian views by *Canaletto* (No. 498 the best), with a few by *Guardi*. This room also contains several fine cabinets and other sumptuous furniture. In a long wall-cabinet are porcelain and plate; above, several fine bronzes. Two glass-cases in the centre contain Sèvres porcelain (18th cent.), and a third contains repoussé and chased plate (16-18th cent.).

Room XIII. DUTCH SCHOOLS OF THE 17TH CENTURY. To the left: 234. *G. Metsu*, Woman selling fish; *Terburg*, 235. Lady at her toilet, 236. Lady reading a letter; *237. *Netscher*, Lace-maker; 238. *Rembrandt*, Negro archer; 239. *N. Maes*, Housewife at work; *240. *Metsu*, The letter-writer surprized; 241. *K. du Jardin*, Portrait; 243. *E. van der Neer*, Lady in a red dress; 246. *W. van de Velde*, Landing from ships of war; 249. *Wynants*, Landscape; *251. *Metsu*, Sleeping sportsman; 252. *P. Potter*, Cattle in stormy weather; 254. *Eman. de Witte*, Church-interior. — 209. *Jan Steen*, A boor household; 210. *Teniers*, Delivery of St. Peter; 211. *Brouwer*, Boor asleep; 217. *A. van der Neer*, Skating-scene; 219. *P. Potter*, Milkmaid; 224. *Bakhuisen*, Sea-piece; 226. *Wouverman*, Landscape; 227. *Teniers*, Boors carousing; 230. *J. van der Heyden*, Exterior of a church; 233. *Jan Weenix*, Dead birds.

Room XIV. DUTCH SCHOOLS OF THE 17TH CENTURY. To the left: *W. van Mieris*, 176. Lady and cavalier, 178. Boy with a drum; 177. *G. Dou*, Hermit; 180. *Cuyp*, Cattle; 183, 185, 186. *Berghem*, Landscapes; 192. *J. Duck*, Card-party; 198. *J. Both*, Italian coast-scene; 202. *A. van Ostade*, Buying fish. — 143, 145. *W. van de Velde*, Sea-pieces; 147. *J. van Stry*, Cattle; 151. *A. van der Werff*, Venus and Cupid; 152. *P. Neeffs the Elder*, Church-interior; *Jan Steen*, 154. Harpsichord lesson, 158. Tavern-scene; 160. *Wynants*, Landscape; 164. *Hobbema*, Landscape; 166. *E. Boursse* (b. 1630), Woman cooking; *Schalcken*, 168. Girl watering plants, 171. Girl threading a needle.

Room XV. FRENCH AND BRITISH SCHOOLS OF THE 19TH CENTURY. To the left: 317. *Marilhat* (1811-47), Palm-trees; *318. *Decamps*, Eastern women; 320. *Delaroche*, State-barge of Card. Richelieu; *Bonington* (1801-28), 322. Francis I. and Margaret de Navarre, 323. Henri III. and the English ambassador; 324. *Delacroix*, Faust and

Mephistopheles; *Meissonier*, 325. The print-collector, *327. The bravoes. Farther on and on the opposite wall several others by this master, one of which (No. 369. Dutch Burghers) is supposed to be his earliest picture. 344. *Troyon*, Watering cattle; 345. *Decamps*, Punishment of the hooks; *Prud'hon*, 347. Venus and Adonis, 348. Sleep of Venus; *351. *Bonington*, Henri IV. and the Spanish ambassador; *Sir David Wilkie*, 352. Scottish lassies dressing, 357. (farther on), Sportsman refreshing; 360. *Isabey*, Promenade by the sea; 365. *Rosa Bonheur*, A shepherd's dog; 370. *Couture*, The duel; 375. *Bonington*, Piazza di San Marco. — 258. *David Roberts*, Louvain Cathedral; *Decamps*, 259. Arabs reposing, 261. Finding of Moses, 263. A well in the East; 264. *Prud'hon*, Puppies; *Diaz*, 266. Venus and Cupid, 268. Cupid and nymphs; 274. *Géricault*, Cavalry skirmish; 279. *Cogniet*, Rebecca and the Templar; *281. *Corot*, Macbeth and the witches; 282. *Delacroix*, Execution of Marino Faliero; 283. *Rousseau*, Forest of Fontainebleau; 301. *Gérome*, Draught-players; 308. *Gallait*, The Duke of Alva administering an oath; 314. *Delaroche*, Cardinal Mazarin's last illness. — This room also contains two cabinets of Sèvres porcelain (18th cent.). — We now retrace our steps to the Great Staircase and descend to the —

Ground Floor. — ROOM I, to the left at the foot of the staircase, contains portraits of royal personages (564. *Sully*, Queen Victoria; 559. *Lawrence*, George IV.; 560. *Allan Ramsay*, George III.), and is adjoined on the N. by —

ROOM II, handsomely decorated in the 18th cent. style, with sumptuous furniture to match. — To the right is —

ROOM III. This room contains the choice collection of Italian *Majolica*, arranged in glass-cases near the N. end of the room. By the E. wall are cases containing caskets in metal and stamped leather; also, terracotta head of John the Baptist (Ital.; 16th cent.); on the wall farther on, Virgin and Child, in glazed terracotta, by *Andrea della Robbia*. The desk-cases in the centre of the room contain *Enamels*, *Medals*, *Plaquettes*, *Ivory and Boxwood Carvings* (14-17th cent.); *Reliefs and Portraits in Coloured Wax* (16-17th cent.); and small works in *Metal* (12-17th cent.). On the mantelpieces are bronzes, vases, etc. — The paintings hung here belong to the EARLIER ITALIAN AND FLEMISH SCHOOLS: *Bramantino*, *538 (over the N. fire-place), Gian Galeazzo reading Cicero (fresco), 537 (adjacent), Head of a girl (fresco); *531 (over the S. fire-place), *P. Pourbus*, Allegorical love-feast; on the opposite wall, 555. *Bronzino*, Eleanora di Toledo, Grand Duchess of Florence. — On the other side of R. II is —

ROOM XI, with large paintings of dogs and game by *Oudry* (1686-1755) and one by *Desportes* (No. 628). Three cases in this room contain the collection of *Miniatures*, chronologically arranged. Another case contains Italian *Bronzes* (16-17th cent.).

Room X. French and British Schools of the 19th Century.
To the left: *H. Vernet*, 607. Dog of the regiment wounded, 613.
Dead trumpeter; 617. *G. S. Newton*, Portrait; 618. *Achenbach*,
Ebb-tide; 620. *Bellangé*, The despatch; *Robert*, 590-592. Brigand
scenes; 594. *Desportes*, Dogs and dead game; 601. *Saint-Jean*,
Flowers and fruit; 602. *Sant*, Portrait-study.

Room IX. 568. *Schopin*, Divorce of the Empress Josephine;
573. *Schelfhout*, Winter in Holland; 574. *Morland*, The visit; 580.
Gudin, Coast-scene; 586. *Bellangé*, A grenadier.

*Armoury. Room VIII, adjoining R. X on the W., contains the
Oriental Arms and Armour. In a glass-case opposite the entrance is
a collection of *Tobacco Pipes* (chiefly Oriental). On the middle shelf,
at the end next the window, is Sir Walter Raleigh's smoking
apparatus.

Room VII. This and the following rooms accommodate the *European Armoury*, which is arranged rather decoratively than chronologically, The finer and richer specimens are exhibited in glass-cases.
— In R. VII the visitor should notice the series of early swords, from
the 11th cent. onwards (Nos. 12, 13, 18, etc.); the rapiers in *Case 1*
(16-17th cent.); and the arquebus and wheel-lock muskets in
Cases 2-3. *Case 4* contains helmets of the 14-16th century.

Room VI. In the centre: *564. Gothic suit of equestrian armour
(late 15th cent.). *Case 6*. Decorative helmets, swords, and daggers
of the Italian Renaissance. *Case 8*. Flint and wheel-lock pistols.

Room V includes various objects of historical interest. 864.
Russet and gold armour of Sir Thomas Sackville; *1164. Damascened
suit of Alfonso II., Duke of Ferrara (16th cent.); *1198. Equestrian
suit in black and gold, ascribed to the Elector Joseph of Bavaria,
and taken from the arsenal at Munich by Napoleon I. *Cases 10 & 11*.
Decorative defensive armour (16th cent.); No. 1330. Circular shield,
attributed to the Emp. Charles V. *Case 12*. Nos. 1302, 1303. Sword
and gauntlet of Henry, Prince of Wales (d. 1612); 1306. Dagger
presented by the city of Paris to Henri IV. on his marriage with
Marie de Médicis (1599); *1308. Oval shield, embossed and damascened, surmounted by the monogram of Diana of Poitiers.

Room IV, the walls and ceiling of which are lined with coloured
tiles, contains a few busts. A flight of steps at the N. end of the
room ascends to R. XV, while at the S. end it is adjoined by R. III,
whence we may return to the entrance.

To the S. of Oxford Street are *Grosvenor Square* (Pl. R, 19) and
Berkeley Square (with its plane-trees; Pl. R, 22, 23), many of the
houses in which still have bits of fine old iron-work in front of
their doors, with extinguishers for links or torches. Horace Walpole died at 11 Berkeley Square in 1797; Clive killed himself at
No. 45 in 1774. No. 38, now the town-house of Lord Rosebery, was
the house from which the daughter of Mr. Child, the banker,
eloped with the Earl of Westmorland in 1782, and was afterwards

the residence of their daughter Lady Jersey (d. 1867) and her husband. Pope lived at No. 9 Berkeley Street, to the S. of Berkeley Square, and presented the lease of it to Martha Blount. Bulwer Lytton spent his later years at No. 12 Grosvenor Square. At the foot of South Audley Street, which runs to the S. from the S.W. corner of Grosvenor Square, is *Chesterfield House* (Pl. R, 18; *IV*), with a fine marble staircase and the library in which the 'Chesterfield Letters' were written. In the same street is a tasteful *Free Public Library*, opened in 1895. In *Brook Street*, which runs E. from Grosvenor Square to Hanover Square (p. 287), is a house (No. 25) distinguished by a tablet indicating that Händel used to live here.

New Bond Street (Pl. R, 23; *I*), which diverges to the right (S.) from Oxford Street, farther on, is continued by *Old Bond Street* to Piccadilly (p. 282). This thoroughfare contains numerous attractive and fashionable shops, the *Grosvenor Club* (No. 135), and several picture-galleries (comp. p. 70). — *Hanover Square, Cavendish Square, Regent Street*, and *Oxford Circus*, see pp. 286, 287. — In Oxford Street, on the left, farther on, is the *Princess's Theatre* (p. 67), nearly opposite which is the *Pantheon*, which has successively been a concert-room, a theatre, and a bazaar, and is now the extensive wine warehouse of Messrs. Gilbey. Then on the right (No. 58) is the *Soho Bazaar* (p. 31), with an exit at the other end to Soho Square (Pl. R, 27). On the N. side of this square is the new *French Protestant Church*, one of the best examples of terracotta architecture in London; and on the E. side is the new Roman Catholic *Church of St. Patrick*.

The district of Soho contains a large colony of Italian cooks. couriers, waiters, tailors, restaurant-keepers, servants, teachers, etc. — No. 37 Gerrard Street, ¼ M. to the S. of Soho Square, was for several years the home of Edmund Burke (tablet); and Dryden lived at No. 43 (tablet) from 1686 till his death in 1700. Mozart, when a boy of eight years (March, 1763), lodged with his father and sister at 51 Frith Street, leading to the S. from Soho Square. — In the churchyard of *St. Anne's* (Pl. R, 27; *I*), Wardour Street, are a tablet to Theodore, King of Corsica, who died (1756) in poverty near by, and the grave of William Hazlitt (d. 1830).

Oxford Street proper ends at *Tottenham Court Road* (see below), which runs to the N., and *Charing Cross Road* (p. 188), leading to the S. to Charing Cross.

Tottenham Court Road, which runs to the N. to Euston Road, passes the **Whitefield Memorial Church** (Pl. R, 28), a conspicuous red brick edifice, built in 1899, on the site of a chapel originally erected by George Whitefield in 1756. The churchyard, now open to the public as the *Whitefield Gardens*, contains the graves of Bacon, the sculptor (d. 1799), and Whitefield's wife. The line of this street is continued beyond Euston Road, towards the N. (Camden Town, Hampstead) by *Hampstead Road*, No. 263 in which is the house of George Cruikshank, the caricaturist, where he died in 1878 (tablet).

Great Russell Street, running off Tottenham Court Road a little to the N. of Oxford Street, leads to the W. to the British Museum (p. 299).

The eastern prolongation of Oxford Street, extending to Holborn, and called *New Oxford Street*, was laid out in 1849 at a cost of 290,000*l.* through the 'Rookery of St. Giles', one of the most disreputable quarters of London. A little to the S., in High Street, is the church of *St. Giles-in-the-Fields*, the third church on this site, completed in 1734. Chapman, the translator of Homer (tombstone against the exterior S. wall, erected by Inigo Jones), Shirley, the dramatist, and Andrew Marvell are buried here. Close to the S.E. corner of the church is the square tomb of Richard Pendrell (d. 1671), who helped Charles II. to safety after the battle of Worcester, with a quaint epitaph, describing him as 'Unparalleled Pendrell'. On the N. side of New Oxford Street, at the corner of Museum Street, is *Mudie's Library* (p. 20). — *Museum Street* leads to the N. to the *British Museum* (p. 299), in Great Russell Street.

The residential district bounded by New Oxford Street and Holborn on the S., Tottenham Court Road on the W., Euston Road on the N., and Gray's Inn Road on the E., is known as **Bloomsbury**, a corruption of 'Blemundsbury', the manor of the Blemunds or the Blemontes. It has many literary and historical associations. Among its squares are, to the W. of the British Museum, BEDFORD SQUARE; to the E., BLOOMSBURY SQUARE and RUSSELL SQUARE, the one containing a statue of *Charles James Fox* (d. 1806), and the other one of *Francis, Duke of Bedford* (d. 1802), both by *Westmacott*. In Bloomsbury Square stands the *College of Preceptors* (1889), an examining institute which grants diplomas to teachers (F. C. P., L. C. P., A. C. P.).

Gower Street, which leads to the N. from Bedford Square, contains **University College** (Pl. B,28), founded in 1828, chiefly through the exertions of Lord Brougham, for students of every religious denomination. A long flight of steps leads to the dodecastyle Corinthian portico fronting the main edifice, which is 400 ft. in length and surmounted by a handsome dome. It contains numerous lecture rooms, a laboratory, the Slade School of Fine Art, and a museum with original models and drawings by Flaxman (d. 1826), the celebrated sculptor (open to visitors in the summer months, Sat. 10-4). The new laboratories, etc., built next the street in 1892, somewhat mask the view of the main edifice. The subjects studied at the college comprise the exact and natural sciences, the classical and modern languages and literatures, history, law, and medicine. The number of professors is about 40, and that of students about 1100, paying over 20,000*l.* in fees. The building also contains a well-known school for boys (4-500), at which Mr. John Morley, Mr. Joseph Chamberlain, and Lord Leighton were pupils. The whole is maintained without aid from Government. In Gower Street, opposite, and connected with it as a clinical establishment, stands the **University College Hospital**, where about 45,000 patients are annually treated by the medical professors of the college.

Close by, in Gordon Square, is the **Catholic Apostolic Church**, built in 1850-54, one of the largest ecclesiastical edifices in London.

The INTERIOR is a fine example of modern Gothic (Early English), though unfinished towards the W. The *Choir*, with its graceful triforium and diapered spandrels, is very rich. The most beautiful part of the church is, however, the *English Chapel*, to the E. of the chancel, with its polychrome painting, stained-glass windows, and open arcade with fine carving (particularly on the three arches to the S. of the altar).

In Woburn Square (Pl. B, 28), to the S. of Gordon Square, is *Christ Church*, containing a reredos in memory of the poetess *Christina Rossetti* (d. 1894). The paintings are from designs by Sir Edward Burne-Jones.

In Tavistock Place, to the E. of Gordon Square, is the *Passmore Edwards Settlement* (p. 101), the seat of a University Settlement formed largely under the inspiration of Mrs. Humphry Ward's 'Robert Elsmere'.

John Ruskin (1819-1900) was born at No. 54, *Hunter Street*, leading to the N. from Brunswick Square (Pl. B, 32).

At the N. end of Gower Street is the *Gower Street Station* (Metropolitan; p. 60). Thence Euston Road runs to the E. to *Euston Square Station*, terminus of the *London and North Western Railway* (p. 55), the entrance-hall of which contains a colossal statue of George Stephenson, by *Baily*.

St. Pancras' Church (Pl. B, 28), in Euston Square, was built by the Messrs. Inwood in 1819 at a cost of 76,679*l*. It is an imitation of the Erechtheum at Athens; while its tower, 168 ft. in height, is a double reproduction of the so-called Tower of the Winds.

Old St. Pancras' Church (Pl. B, 27), with its historical churchyard, is situated in Old St. Pancras Road, next to the Workhouse. Part of the churchyard, with the adjacent St. Giles burying-ground, has been converted into public gardens. A monument was erected here in 1879 by the Baroness Burdett-Coutts to those whose graves were disturbed in the process. Among the gravestones preserved here are those of William Godwin (1756-1836) and his wife. It is said that Shelley first met his second wife, Mary Godwin, at her mother's grave in this churchyard.

Farther to the E. is the *St. Pancras Station*, terminus of the *Midland Railway* (p. 55), with the terminus hotel, a very handsome building in an ornate Gothic style, by Sir G. G. Scott. Adjacent is the *King's Cross Station*, terminus of the *Great Northern Railway* (p. 56).

To the N. of King's Cross lie the populous but comparatively uninteresting districts of SOMERS TOWN, CAMDEN TOWN, KENTISH TOWN, ISLINGTON, HIGHBURY, and HOLLOWAY. In Great College Street, Camden Town, is situated the *Royal Veterinary College* (Pl. B, 23), with a museum to which visitors are admitted daily (9 to 5 or 6) on presenting their cards. *Charles Dibdin* (d. 1814), the writer of nautical songs, is buried in St. Martin's Burial Ground, Camden Street (now a public recreation-ground), a little to the N.W. of the Veterinary College. He is commemorated by a Scandinavian cross. The *Royal Agricultural Hall* (p. 68) is in Liverpool Road, Islington (Pl. B, 35), and the *Grand Theatre* (p. 67) is close by, in High Street. *Alex. Cruden* (1701-70), of 'Concordance' fame, lived in Camden Passage, off High Street (Pl. B, 35). About ³/₄ M. to the N., in Canonbury Square (Pl. B, 38), is *°Canonbury Tower*, an interesting relic of the country-residence of the Priors of St. Bartholomew. The tower, now used as a free library and reading-room, was probably built by Prior Bolton (p. 128), though restored at a later date, and contains a fine carved oak room. Oliver Goldsmith occupied rooms in the tower in 1762. Charles and Mary Lamb lived at No. 19 Colebrooke Row (Pl. B, 35) in 1823-1827.

Holloway Gaol or *City Prison* (beyond Pl. B, 25), a rather handsome building, is mainly used for short-sentence or unconvicted prisoners (about 350 men and 650 women); *Pentonville Prison* (Pl. B, 30), constructed on the radiating principle, accommodates about 1000 male prisoners and is conducted on a modified silent and separate system. Grimaldi, the famous clown, is buried in St. James's Churchyard, Pentonville Road (Pl. B, 32). The great *Metropolitan Cattle Market* (Pl. B, 25, 26, 29, 30), Copenhagen Fields, repays a visit on Thursdays, when 3-4000 cattle and 12,000 sheep are usually on sale (comp. p. 32). The market, opened in 1855, covers an area of 30 acres. Around the lofty clock-tower in the centre are grouped a post-office, a telegraph-station, banks, an enquiry-office, shops, etc. At the sides are interminable rows of well-arranged stalls for the cattle, of which about 4,000,000 are sold here every year. The 'Pedlars' Market' on Friday afternoons brings together an extraordinary assortment of second-hand goods. — Lord Beaconsfield (Benjamin Disraeli) was born in a house near *Highbury Station* (Pl. B, 33, 34), now occupied as a draper's shop.

The eastern prolongation of New Oxford Street is **High Holborn** (Pl. R, 32, and *II*; so called from the '*Hole Bourne*', or Fleet Brook, which once flowed through the hollow near here), a street which survived the Great Fire, and still contains a considerable number of old houses. Milton once lived here, and it was by this route that condemned criminals used to be conducted to Tyburn. The increasing traffic indicates that we are approaching the City. On the right are several side-streets, leading to *Lincoln's Inn Fields* (with the *Soane Museum*, etc., see pp. 228-232). Red Lion Street on the left, continued by Lamb's Conduit Street, leads to *Guilford Street*, on the N. side of which stands the —

Foundling Hospital (Pl. R, 32), a remarkable establishment founded by Captain Thomas Coram in 1739 for 'deserted children'. Since 1760, however, it has not been used as a foundling hospital, but as a home for illegitimate children, whose mothers are known. (Neither in London nor in any other part of England are there any foundling hospitals in the proper sense of the term, such as the 'Hospice des Enfants Trouvés' in Paris.) The number of the children is about 520, and the yearly income of the Hospital, 19,000l.

In the *Board Room* and the *Secretary's Room* are a number of pictures, chiefly painted about the middle of last century. They include the following: *Hogarth*, °March to Finchley, and Finding of Moses; portraits by *Ramsay, Reynolds*, and *Shackleton*; views of the Foundling Hospital and St. George's Hospital by *Wilson*; view of the Charterhouse by *Gainsborough*. The Picture Gallery contains a good portrait of Coram by *Hogarth*. Most of the pictures were presented to the institution by the artists themselves. (The success with which the exhibition of these pictures was attended is said to have led to the first exhibition of the Royal Academy in 1760.) The hospital also possesses Raphael's cartoon of the Massacre of the Innocents, a bust of Händel and some of his musical MSS., a collection of coins or tokens deposited with the children (1741-60), etc. The *Chapel* is adorned with an altar-piece by *West*, representing Christ blessing little children ; the organ was a gift from *Händel*. Divine service, at which the children are led in singing by trained voices, is performed on Sundays at 11 a.m. and 3.30 p.m. The Hospital is shown to visitors on Mondays from 10 to 4 and on Sundays, after morning-service, when the children in their quaint costumes may be seen at dinner. The attendants are forbidden to accept gratuities, but a contribution to the funds of the institution is expected from the visitor on entering or in the church-offertory.

To the E. of Lincoln's Inn are *Chancery Lane* (p. 174) on the right (after which we are in the City), and *Gray's Inn Road* (p. 176) on the left. Then *Holborn Viaduct, Newgate*, etc., see pp. 124, 125.

23. Regent's Park.

Regent's Park (Pl. B, 15, 16, 19, 20) was laid out during the last years of the reign of George III., and derives its name from the then Prince Regent, afterwards George IV. It occupies the site of an earlier park called *Marylebone Park*. The name Marylebone is said to be a corruption of *Mary on Tyburn (Mary-le-bourne)*, Tyburn being a small brook, coming from Kilburn and flowing into the Thames. It crossed Oxford Street a little to the E. of the Marble Arch and flowed through St. James's Park, leaving its mark upon *Brook Street*, Grosvenor Square, and notably upon 'Tyburn', that melancholy old place of execution situated about the lower corner of Edgware Road. It has also given its name to *Tyburnia*, the quarter of London situated to the N. of Hyde Park.

In the time of Queen Elizabeth Marylebone Park was filled with deer and game. Under the Commonwealth the land was cleared of the woods and used as pasturage. Afterwards trees were again planted, footpaths constructed, and a small artificial lake formed.

The Park, which is one of the largest in London, embraces 472 acres of ground, and extends from York Gate, Marylebone Road, to Primrose Hill. Within its precincts are situated several private residences, among which is St. Dunstan's Villa, with the clock and the automatic figures from the church of St. Dunstan's in Fleet Street (see p. 173). The gardens of the *Zoological Society* (founded by Sir Humphry Davy and Sir Stamford Raffles in 1826) occupy a large space in the N. part of the Park, which also contains the gardens of the *Botanical Society* and the *Toxopholite (Archery) Society*. The Park is surrounded by a broad drive known as the *Outer Circle*. In summer a band plays in the Park on Sun. afternoons in the *Kiosk* (rfmts.) a little to the S. of the Zoological Gardens (Pl. B, 20).

The **Zoological Gardens** are bounded on the N. by the Regent's Canal and intersected by the Outer Circle, which here runs parallel with the canal. They are thus divided into two portions, which, however, communicate with each other by means of a *tunnel* constructed under the drive. The principal entrance is in the Outer Circle (the *Main Entrance* on the Plan); ingress may also be obtained from the Broad Walk, at the S.E. angle of the gardens (see Pl., *South Entrance*), or from Albert Road, Primrose Hill, on the N. side of the canal (*North Entrance*, near No. 43 on the Plan). The Main Entrance is about $^3/_4$ M. from the *Portland Road Station* of the Metropolitan Railway, from which the S. Entrance is a little less remote, while both gates are about $^3/_4$ M. from the *Chalk Farm Station* of the North-Western and North London Railways. The *Baker Street Station* (Metropolitan) is about $^3/_4$ M. from the S. entrance, which

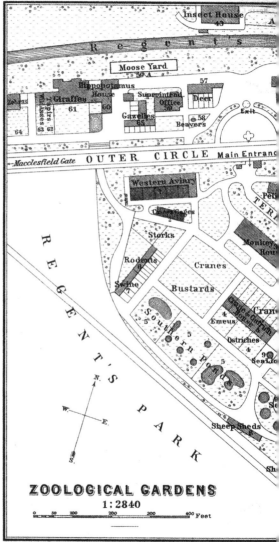

ZOOLOGICAL GARDENS

1:2840

0 50 100   200   300   400 Feet

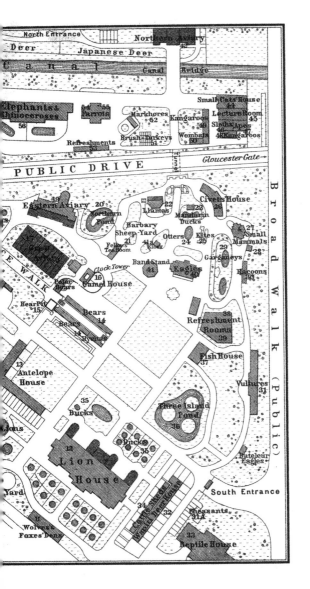

North Entrance · Northern Aviary 42

Deer · Japanese Deer

C a n a l · Canal · Bridge

Elephants & Rhinoceroses 56 · Parrots 54 · Small Cats House 44 · Lecture Room 45 · Sloths, Apes 46 · 47 Kangaroos 48

Markhores 52 · Kangaroos 49 · Wombats 50

Refreshments · Brush-Turkeys 51

PUBLIC DRIVE · Gloucester Gate →

Eastern Aviary 20 · 49 · Civets House

Northern Pond · 21 Llamas · 22 · 23 · Mandarin Ducks 27 · Small Mammals 28

Barbary Sheep-Yard · Otters 24 · Kites 25 · 26 · Garganeys 29

Fellows' Tea-Room · 41a Rhenoc

Clock Tower 16 · Band Stand 41 · Eagles 40 · Racoons 34

Polar Bears · Camel House · Refreshment Rooms 39 · 38

BearPit 15 · Bears 14 · Fish House 37

Bears · Hyaenas · Vultures 31

13 Antelope House · 35 Ducks · Three Island Pond 9 · Bateleur Eagles

Lions · 12 L i o n · Ducks 35 · H o u s e · South Entrance

Yard · 11 Wolves & Foxes' Dens · 34 · 32 · Pheasants 31a · Reptile House 37

B r o a d   W a l k   (P u b l i c)

E · W A L K

is only 300 yds. from Park Street, where 'Waterloo' omnibuses (No. 64 ; p. 46) pass at frequent intervals. The *North Entrance* is $1/2$ M. from *Chalk Farm* and $3/4$ M. from *St. John's Wood Road* (Metropolitan), and is passed by Camden Town and Bayswater omnibuses (No. 86; p. 50). (Carriages are not allowed to drive along the Broad Walk.)

The Zoological Gardens are open daily from 9 a.m. to sunset ; adm. 1*s.*, on Mon. 6*d.*, children half-price except on Mon.; on Sun. only by order obtained from a member. The number of visitors in 1899 was 696,707. The number of animals is about 2750, including 820 mammals and 1470 birds. A military band usually plays here on Saturdays in summer at 4 p.m. Official Catalogue 6*d.* A more attractive guide is 'A Walk through the Zoological Gardens' by *F. G. Aflalo* (illus.; 3*s.* 6*d.* ; London, 1900).

Many of the animals conceal themselves during the day in their holes and dens, under water, or among the shrubbery ; the best time to visit them, accordingly, is at the feeding-hour, when even the lethargic carnivora are to be seen in a state of activity and excitement. The pelicans are fed at 2.30, the otters at 3, the eagles at 3.30 (except Wednesdays), the beasts of prey at 4 (in winter, Nov.-Feb., at 3), the seals and sea-lions at 4.30 (in winter at 3.30), and the diving birds in the fish-house (Pl. 37) at 12 and 5 p.m. Children may enjoy the delight of riding on elephants, camels, and so on for a small fee.

Those who have not time to explore the Gardens thoroughly had better follow the route indicated below, so as to see the most interesting animals in the shortest possible time.

On entering from the Outer Circle (Pl., *Main Entrance*), we turn to the right, and first reach the *Western Aviary* (Pl. 1), which is 170 ft. long, and contains 200 different kinds of birds, chiefly from Australia, the Indian Archipelago, and South America. Then, returning between the *Crows* (Pl. 2) and the *Crane and Bustard Paddocks*, we reach, on the left, the —

Monkey House (Pl. 3), which always attracts a crowd of amused spectators. The unpleasant odour is judiciously disguised by numerous plants and flowers. The bats are also kept here.

We next turn to the S. and enter the *Crane and Ostrich House* (Pl. 4), on one side of which are the storks and cranes, and on the other (by which we return) the ostriches, rheas, emeus, and cassowaries. Quitting this house by the door at which we entered, we turn to the left and then take another turning on the right leading to the *Rodents* (Pl. 6), *Swine* (Pl. 7), and *Southern Ponds* for *Water Fowl* (Pl. 5; about 50 different kinds). We then proceed to the left, along the other side of the Southern Ponds and past the *Sheep Sheds* (Pl. 8), to the *Sea-Lions' Pond* (Pl. 9). To the right is the *Sheep Yard* (10), built in 1885 for the *Burrhel*, or blue wild sheep, from the Himalayas. To the S.E. of this point are the *Wolves'* and

Foxes' Dens (Pl. 11). Opposite, to the N. (see Plan), is the large
Lion House (Pl. 12), which is 230 ft. long and 70 ft. wide and
contains 14 dens for lions, tigers, leopards, pumas, and jaguars.
It also contains a bust of *Sir T. Stamford Raffles* (1781-1826), the
first president of the Zoological Society. To the E. of the Lion House
are the *Cattle Sheds* (Pl. 34), containing, among other specimens, the
yak, the bison, the gayal, and the wild cattle of Great Britain.

We now retrace our steps, and pass along the open-air enclosures
at the back of the Lion House to the *Antelope House* (Pl. 13).
Issuing thence, we proceed straight on, past the *Bear Pit* (Pl. 15),
to inspect the dens containing *Bears* and *Hyenas* (Pl. 14) on each side
(below) of the terrace-walk; we then ascend to the terrace to view the
bear-pit and the *Polar Bears' Den*, from above. A little farther on we
leave the terrace-walk, to the right, and reach the *Pelicans' Enclosure* (Pl. 18). Then, passing the *Great Aviary* (Pl. 17; flamingo,
ibis, night-herons, etc.) on the right, and the *Eastern Aviary*
(Pl. 19) on the left, we reach the *Camels* (Pl. 16), stabled below the
Clock Tower.

We here turn to the left, and pass in front of the *Fellows' Tea
Room* to the *Northern Pond* (Pl. 20), which contains more water-
fowl. To the right is the *Barbary-Sheep Yard* (Pl. 21), beyond which
is the *Llamas' House* (Pl. 22). This should not be approached too
closely on account of the unpleasant expectorating propensities of
its inmates. On the other side of the path descending hence to the
tunnel (p. 294), which we pass in the meantime, is the pond of the
Mandarin Ducks (Pl. 23). Opposite, on the right, are the *Otters* (Pl. 24)
and the *Kites* (Pl. 25); to the N.E., on the left, lies the *Civet House*
(Pl. 26). We now turn to the right and proceed to the south.

We first reach, on the left, the *Small Mammals* (Pl. 27; the
house may be entered), on the right the *Garganey Ducks* (Pl. 29);
then, on the left, the *Flying Squirrels* (Pl. 28) and the *Racoons*
(Pl. 30). Continuing in a straight direction past the back of the refreshment-rooms (see p. 297), the *Vultures* (Pl. 31), and another
small aviary containing *Bateleur Eagles*, we reach the S. Entrance,
which we leave on the left. Near the entrance is the *Wapiti Deer
House* (Pl. 32), behind which are the Cattle Sheds (see above). Opposite the Deer House are aviaries containing *Pheasants* and *Peacocks* (Pl. 31a). We now turn to the left, and after a few paces
reach the *Reptile House* (Pl. 33), in the S.E. angle of the gardens.
This contains an extensive collection of large serpents, lizards, al-
ligators, crocodiles, snapping turtles, frogs, and toads. Just beyond
it is the *Tortoise House*, with fine specimens of giant tortoises. At
this point we turn back and walk straight on, past the front of the
Cattle Sheds, to the *Three Island Pond* (Pl. 36), stocked with water-
fowl, among which are specimens of the black-necked swan. The
path leading first to the left and then to the right, passing (opposite) more *Water Fowl* (Pl. 35), leads to the *Fish House* (Pl. 37), con-

taining fish and small aquatic birds. The *Refreshment Rooms* (Pl. 38, 39) here afford an opportunity for a rest.

From the Refreshment Rooms we proceed towards the N.W. past the *Eagles' Aviaries* (Pl. 40), having on our left the *Band Stand* (Pl. 41) and the *Kiosk* (Pl. 41 A), where tickets for rides on the elephants, etc., are sold, and pass through the tunnel leading into the N. section of the gardens. Here we first go straight on, across the canal-bridge, on the other side of which are the *Northern Aviary* (Pl. 42; for owls and birds of prey), and the *Insectarium (Pl. 43), containing insects, land crustaceans, and an electric eel (fee for electric shock 1s.). Here also are various birds, including two mynahs (a kind of starling), which talk as well as parrots. Between the last two houses is the North Entrance, opposite which are paddocks containing *Japanese* and *Axis Deer*.

We now recross the bridge and turn to the left to the *Small Cats' House* (Pl. 44) and *Lecture Room* (Pl. 45), the latter adorned with water-colour sketches of animals. Close by are the *Kangaroo Sheds* (Pl. 48, 49), the *Sloths' House* (Pl. 46), and the **Apes' House* (Pl. 47), the last usually containing some of the most interesting inmates of the Gardens, in the form of specimens of the anthropoid or manlike apes. We now turn to the right and pass the *Wombats' House* (Pl. 50), the *Brush Turkeys* (Pl. 51), and the *Markhore House* (Pl. 52) on the right, and a *Refreshment Stall* (Pl. 53) on the left. Opposite this stall is the *Parrot House* (Pl. 54, 55), containing about ninety different species of that gaudy and harsh-voiced bird, next to which is the **Elephant and Rhinoceros House* (Pl. 56), containing the African and Asiatic varieties of these animals.

No. 57 is a *Deer Shed;* No. 59 is the *Superintendent's Office.* The *Moose Yard* (No. 59a), below, to the right, on the bank of the canal, contains moose-deer and reindeer from Labrador. Proceeding in a straight direction, we reach the *Hippopotamus (Pl. 60) and the *Giraffe House* (Pl. 61). Beyond are the *Tapirs* (Pl. 62), the *Wild Asses* (Pl. 63), and the *Zebras* (Pl. 64). Returning along the S. side of these houses, we reach, on the left, the *Gazelles* (Pl. 65) and the *Beavers* (Pl. 58). A little way beyond the Beaver House we reach an *Exit*, which takes us into the Outer Circle.

Part of the southern portion of Regent's Park is occupied by the **Botanic Gardens** (Pl. B, 20), which are circular in shape, and are enclosed by the drive called the *Inner Circle*. Large flower-shows take place here on three Wednesdays in May and June, which are largely attended by the fashionable world (tickets of admission sold at the gate and by the principal ticket-agents). Musical promenades are held on each other Wed. from May to August (adm. 2s. 6d.). On Mon. and Sat. visitors are admitted for a fee of 1s., and on Tues., Thurs., and Frid. on presenting an order of admission given by a Fellow of the Botanical Society. Foreigners are admitted on application to the officials. The Museum and the collections of economic, medicinal, and water plants are very interesting. — *Skating Fêtes* are held at the Botanic Gardens in winter (comp. p. 74).

On the E. side of the Park stands *St. Katharine's Royal Collegiate Hospital*, with its chapel. This building was erected in 1825 in substitution of one which formerly stood on the site of the St. Katharine Docks (p. 166). The Hospital was originally founded by Matilda, wife of King Stephen (1148), and was renewed by Queen Eleanor, wife of Edward I. (1273). The patronage is vested in the queens of England and forms part of their dower. The foundation consists of a master and two brothers, in holy orders, and three sisters, who together form the chapter. Schools for boys and girls are within the precincts. The chapel contains a canopied tomb of a duke of Exeter (15th cent.), stalls of the 14th cent., and a fine organ, all brought from the original hospital. A house in the close has been granted by Queen Victoria to the superintendent of the *Queen Victoria Jubilee Nurses*, whose office adjoins the chapel.

To the S. of Regent's Park runs the MARYLEBONE ROAD, containing the imposing premises of *Madame Tussaud's* well-known waxwork exhibition (adm., see p. 68), which are close to the Baker Street station of the Metropolitan railway. The large building opposite Mme. Tussaud's is the *Marylebone Workhouse* (see Pl. R, 20). Adjacent, in York Place, is *Bedford College*, a university college for women, including an art-school and a teachers' training department. Charles Dickens lived at No. 1 Devonshire Terrace (corner of Marylebone Road and High Street) from 1839 to 1851, writing there 'Barnaby Rudge', 'Martin Chuzzlewit', the 'Christmas Carol', 'Dombey and Son', 'David Copperfield', and other works. In Marylebone Road, a little farther to the W., rises the large new *Hôtel Great Central* (p. 10), behind which is the *Marylebone Station*, the terminus of the new London extension of the Great Central Railway (p. 56).

The summit of **Primrose Hill** (Pl. B, 14; 205 ft.), an eminence to the N. of Regent's Park, from which it is separated by the canal and a road, commands a very extensive view. On the E. and S., as far as the eye can reach, nothing is seen but the roofs and spires of the stupendous city of London, while on the N. the green hills of Hampstead and Highgate form the picturesque background of a landscape which contrasts pleasantly with the dingy buildings of the Metropolis. At the S. base of the hill there is an open-air gymnasium; a refreshment-room has also been opened. A 'Shakspeare Oak' was planted on the S. slope of the hill in 1864, on the tercentenary celebration of the great dramatist's birth.

To the N.W. in Finchley Road, near the *Swiss Cottage Station* (Metropolitan; Pl. B, 10), stands *New College*, for the education of Congregational ministers. Among its professors have been some men of considerable note. It contains a good theological library. The building was erected about 40 years ago in the midst of what was then green fields, and is admired for its style and proportions. —

Farther out in the Finchley Road (beyond Pl. B, 5) is *Hackney Congregational College*, erected in 1887 at a cost of about 23,000*l*.

At 44 Abbey Road, about 1/2 M. to the W. of the Swiss Cottage, John Gibson Lockhart (d. 1854), son-in-law and biographer of Sir Walter Scott and editor of the *Quarterly Review*, spent some of his later years.

Lord's Cricket Ground (Pl. B, 12; p. 72), in St. John's Wood Road (Metropolitan station, see p. 60), to the W. of Regent's Park, is thronged with a large and brilliant crowd of spectators on the occasion of the principal cricket-matches, particularly when Cambridge is disputing the palm of victory with Oxford, or, better still, Eton with Harrow; and it then presents a characteristic and imposing spectacle, which the stranger should not fail to see. Admission on ordinary days 6*d.*; during great matches, which are always advertised beforehand, 1*s.* or 2*s.* 6*d.* The ground was purchased by the Marylebone Cricket Club for a large sum, to prevent it from being built upon. The pavilion and stands enable all the spectators to have a good view of the game. There are also several luncheon-bars and a telegraph-office.

In Maida Hill West (Pl. R, 12), a little to the S. of this point, is a handsome *Catholic Apostolic Church*, by Pearson.

24. The British Museum.

The nucleus of the now vast contents of the ****British Museum** (Pl. R, 28; *II*) was the notable *Cottonian Library* (state papers, Biblical and other MSS.), bequeathed to the nation by *Sir John Cotton* in 1700. The injury this library received from a fire at Ashburton House in 1731 showed the necessity of proper provision for the safeguarding of such public collections. This was obtained by the Act of 1753, providing for the purchase of the *Sloane* and *Harleian Collections* and for depositing these, along with the Cottonian Library, in one 'general repository' (*Montagu House*, bought for the purpose). The sum paid to the executors of Sir Hans Sloane was 20,000*l.*, being in his opinion about one-fourth of the value of his books and collections. The Act provided for the raising of 300,000*l.* by a lottery, which, however, produced only 95,000*l.* Of this sum 30,000*l.* was specially invested to form a capital fund, and still appears in the Trustees' annual estimate of expenditure. The Sloane Collection contained only a few specimens of ancient sculpture, and the development of this important branch of the Museum may be dated from 1772, when a parliamentary grant rendered possible the acquisition of the valuable antiquities collected by *Sir William Hamilton*. The presentation by George III. of a collection of Egyptian antiquities in 1801, and the purchase of the Townley Marbles in 1805 and the Elgin Marbles in 1816, made such additions to the original contents that a new wing had to be built for their reception. The Museum continued to increase, and when George IV. presented it in 1823 with the King's Library, collected by George

III., old Montagu House was felt to be quite inadequate for its purpose, and a new building, designed by *Sir Robert Smirke* and completed by his younger brother *Sydney Smirke*, was erected on its site between 1823 and 1855. The new Reading Room (see p. 326) was added in 1857, and since 1879 a new gallery for the Mausoleum marbles and the entire 'White Wing', on the S.E. side (p. 325) have been erected from a bequest by Mr. William White. The contents of the British Museum are at present arranged in eight sections, each under the special superintendence of an Under Librarian or Keeper. These sections are as follows: Printed Books (Maps and Plans), Manuscripts, Oriental Printed Books and Manuscripts, Prints and Drawings, Egyptian and Assyrian Antiquities, British and Mediæval Antiquities and Ethnography, Greek and Roman Antiquities, and Coins and Medals. The Natural History sections are now at S. Kensington (see p. 346). Wherever it is practicable, the names are attached to the different objects. For a thorough study of the collections the excellent official catalogues are indispensable; for a hasty visit the following directions may suffice. Courses of lectures on the various antiquities of the Museum are delivered here by experts from time to time. — The number of visitors to the British Museum in 1899, exclusive of readers and students, was 663,724.

The Museum is open free on every week-day from 10 a.m. till 6 p.m., but after 4 p.m. in Jan., Feb., Nov., and Dec., and after 5 p.m. in March, Sept., and Oct., some only of the galleries remain open, *viz.*: on Mon., Wed., and Frid., the MSS., King's Library, Porcelain and Glass, Prints and Drawings, and the Prehistoric, British, Ethnographical, and Mediæval Collections; and on Tues., Thurs., and Sat. the Greek and Roman, Egyptian, Assyrian, Semitic, Religious, and American Collections. The Museum is open on Sun. afternoon from 2.30 (2 in winter), but is shut on Good Friday and Christmas Day. — Sticks and umbrellas are left in the hall. The excellent general 'Guide to the Exhibition Galleries' (price 2*d*.), as well as various special guides and catalogues may be obtained in the hall, or from the attendants in the various sections. Good photographs of several of the most interesting drawings and sculptures in the Museum may be purchased in the chief librarian's office.

The PRINCIPAL FAÇADE, towards (S.) Great Russell Street, with two projecting wings and a portico in the centre, is 370 ft. in length. In front it has an Ionic colonnade of 44 columns. The pediment above the *Portico*, which is borne by two rows of eight columns, is adorned with sculptures by *Westmacott*: on the right, Progress of the Human Race; on the left, allegorical figures of Mathematics, the Drama, Poetry, Music, and Natural Philosophy.

The ENTRANCE HALL, which in 1877 was enlarged by an extension towards the N., measures 62 ft. in length. The statue of *Shakspeare* on the right, at the entrance to the library, chiselled by Roubiliac, was bequeathed by Garrick, the actor. Beside it is a bust of *Sir A. H. Layard* (d. 1894). On the W. side of the hall is the principal staircase, ascending to the first floor. To the left of it is a bust of the *Duke of Marlborough*, by Rysbrack, to the right, a bust of

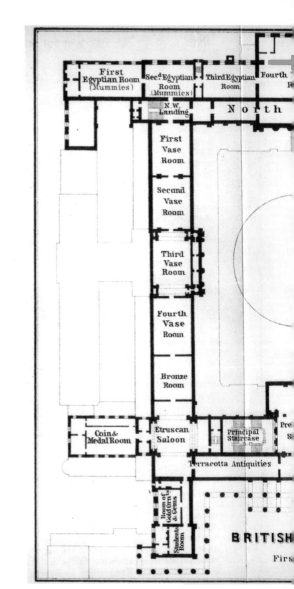

First
Egyptian Room
(Mummies)

Sec.ᵈ Egyptian
Room
(Mummies)

Third Egyptian
Room

Fourth
R

N.W.
Landing

North

First
Vase
Room

Second
Vase
Room

Third
Vase
Room

Fourth
Vase
Room

Bronze
Room

Coin &
Medal Room

Etruscan
Saloon

Principal
Staircase

Pre
S

Terracotta Antiquities

Room of
Gold Orn.ᵗˢ
& Gems

Students
Room

BRITISH

First

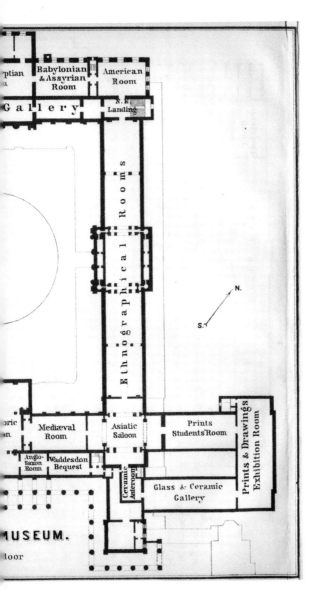

ptian
a

Babylonian & Assyrian Room

American Room

G a l l e r y

N. E.
Landing

E t h n o g r a p h i c a l   R o o m s

N.

S.

oric
an

Mediæval Room

Asiatic Saloon

Prints Students'Room

Prints & Drawings Exhibition Room

Anglo-Saxon Room

Waddesdon Bequest

Ceramic Anteroom

Glass & Ceramic Gallery

M U S E U M.

loor

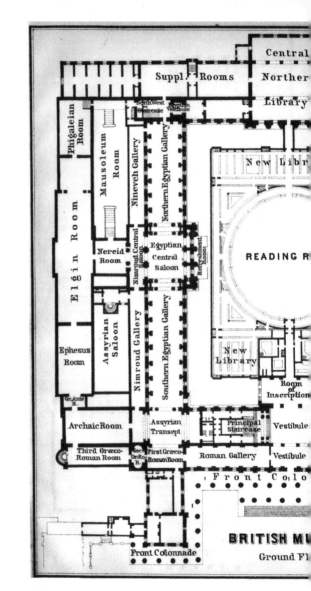

Central
Norther
Library

New Libr

READING R

New
Library

Room
of
Inscription

Suppl. Rooms

NorthWest
Staircase
Egyptian
Vestibule

Phigaleian
Room

Mausoleum
Room

Nineveh Gallery

Northern Egyptian Gallery

Elgin Room

Nereid
Room

Nimroud Central
Saloon

Egyptian
Central
Saloon

Refreshment
Room

Ephesus
Room

Assyrian
Saloon

Nimroud Gallery

Southern Egyptian Gallery

Gr.Ante
R.

Archaic Room

Assyrian
Transept

Principal
Staircase

Vestibule

Third Graeco-
Roman Room

Secd
Gr.Ro.
R.

First Graeco
Roman Room

Roman Gallery

Vestibule

Front Colo

BRITISH MU

Front Colonnade

Ground Fl

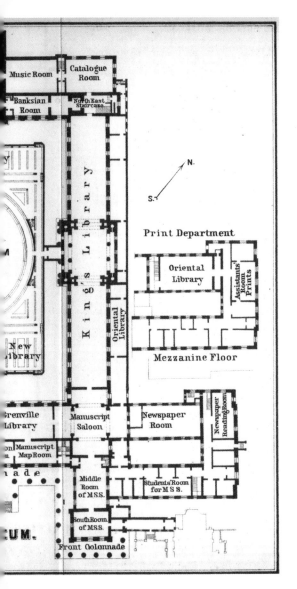

Music Room

Catalogue Room

Banksian Room

North East Staircase

King's Library

Oriental Library

New Library

N.

S.

Print Department

Oriental Library

Assistants' Room Prints

Mezzanine Floor

Grenville Library

Manuscript Saloon

Newspaper Room

Newspaper Reading Room

Manuscript Map Room

Middle Room of MSS.

Students' Room for MSS.

South Room of MSS.

Front Colonnade

:UM.

the *Earl of Chesterfield*. By the door leading into the sculpture-room is a statue of *Mrs. Damer*, the sculptress, from a model by Ceracchi. Various Buddhist sculptures from Amravati in South India, dating from the 4th cent. A.D., are also exhibited on the staircase.

The ROOM OF INSCRIPTIONS, to the N. of the entrance-hall, contains a representative series of Greek and Roman inscriptions, round the walls, and also a few sculptures:

To the left: Marble vases with Bacchic reliefs; Greek portrait-busts, including Sophocles and Antisthenes; 1301. Female statue from Cnidus; 19. Figure in armour, with the head of Hadrian. In the centre of this part of the room: 134a. Cratera from the Villa of Hadrian, round the upper part of which are reliefs of Satyrs making wine; on pedestals round the last, four cinerary urns. — To the right: Greek portrait-busts of Epicurus, Diogenes(?), Hippocrates, Demosthenes, and °Euripides (92°; ?); °Head of an old woman, dating, in spite of its marked realism, from the 5th cent. B.C.; 1383. Bust of Cornelius Lentulus Marcellinus, proprætor of Cyrene. In the centre: 45. Equestrian statue, restored as Caligula. Near the last, 54. Group of two dogs.

From the Hall we first turn to the right into the **Library,** and enter the room which contains the collection of 20,240 vols. bequeathed to the Museum by *Thomas Grenville*.

The glass-cases contain a chronological series of *Illuminated MSS.* from the 10th to the 16th century. CASE I (to the left). Greek MSS. of 10-13th cent.: MSS. illuminated by English artists, 10-11th centuries. — CASE II. MSS. of 12-13th cent.: Psalters; 18. Diurnale; °19. Roll with tinted outline drawings from the life of St. Guthlac of Croyland. — CASES III & IV. MSS. of 14th cent.: copies of the Apocalypse; breviaries; summaries of ancient history in French. — 41. Durandus de Divinis Officiis; 42. Latin poems by Petrarch's tutor; 43. Latin treatise on virtues and vices; 44. Dante's Divine Comedy with miniatures; 45. French MS. with portrait of Richard II. — CASE V. English and French MSS. of 15th cent.: 51. Roman de la Rose; 56. French romances, presented by Talbot, Earl of Shrewsbury, to Margaret of Anjou, consort of Henry VI.; 57. Froissart's Chronicle. — CASE VI. Latin, French, and Italian MSS. of the 15th cent.: 58. Lectionary, with portrait of Siferwas, the illuminator; copies of Hours of the Virgin. — CASE VII. MSS. of 15th and 16th cent.: 69. Plutarch's Lives; 70. Ethics of Aristotle, in Spanish; 88. Splendor Solis, an alchemical work in German; Books of Hours. — In the lower divisions of Cases I, IV, V, and VII are large MSS., chiefly of the 15th century. — CASE VIII, between Cases II and III, contains specimens of *Bindings of MSS.* of the 10-16th centuries.

We next enter the hall containing the **Manuscripts,** the cases in which are filled with numerous interesting autographs and treasures of a kindred nature. Comp. 'Illustrated Guide to the MSS.' (1899; 6d.).

CASE I (on the left, divided into 6 sections) contains autographs of English Sovereigns: Richard II., Henry IV., Henry V., Henry VI., Edward IV., Edward V.; Henry VII., Henry VIII., Catharine of Aragon, Anne Boleyn, Edward VI.; Jane Grey, Queen Mary, Queen Elizabeth, James I., Charles I.; Oliver Cromwell, Charles II., James II., William III., Mary II., Queen Anne; George I., George II., George III., George IV., William IV., and Queen Victoria (pencil signature written in 1823, at the age of four years). The last section contains autographs of foreign sovereigns: Charles V., Henri IV., Louis XIV., Peter the Great, Frederick the Great, and Napoleon I.

CASE II contains historical autographs and papers from 1432 to 1595. Autographs of Perkin Warbeck, Card. Wolsey, Sir Thos. More, Abp. Cranmer, and Bishop Latimer; declaration signed by Cranmer and seven bishops; letter and leaf from the diary of Edward VI.; letter of Lady Jane Grey; description of the execution of Queen Mary Stuart, and sketch of the room at Fotheringay in which her trial was held; autographs of Mary, Queen of Scots, Lord Burghley, James VI., Sir Walter Raleigh, Sir Francis Drake, Sir John Hawkins, Sir Philip Sidney, and others.

CASE III (opposite the last) contains historical autographs and documents of 1595-1689. Autographs of Bacon, Queen Elizabeth, Robert Cecil, Arabella Stuart, Abp. Laud, Hampden, Pym, Cromwell, Prince Rupert, Milton, Charles II., Claverhouse, Duke of Monmouth (begging his life), and William III.; instruction by Charles I. for the impeachment of the Five Members (1642), and a letter by him when a captive at Carisbrooke Castle (1648).

CASE IV (opposite Case I) contains similar documents of 1690-1885, including autographs of the Old Pretender, Marlborough, Robert Walpole, Bolingbroke, the Young Pretender, Clive, Pitt (Earl of Chatham), Warren Hastings, 'Junius', George Washington, the younger Pitt, Burke, Fox, Sheridan, Queen Caroline, Nelson (sketch-plan of the battle of the Nile, 1798, and unfinished letter to Lady Hamilton on the eve of Trafalgar, 1805), Duke of Wellington (list of his cavalry at Waterloo, written just before the battle), Palmerston, Peel, Disraeli, Gladstone, Gen. Gordon (last page of his diary), and Queen Victoria (letter to Miss Gordon).

CASE V, at right angles to Case III, contains a collection of charters, ranging in date from 785 to 1216 and including documents of the Saxon Eadred, Canute the Dane, Richard Cœur-de-Lion, Henry I., etc. In the triangular part of the case is a collotype copy of the articles of Magna Charta (1215), the original of which is preserved in the Museum. — CASE VI, at right angles to Case II, contains charters from 1220 to 1508.

CASES VII and VIII, on either side of the entrance to the Students' Room (to the S.), contain literary and other autographs. Those in Case VII are English and include autograph writings of Jeremy Taylor, Wren, Dryden, Locke, Newton, Swift, Pope, Steele, Addison, Richardson, Chesterfield (letter to his son), Hogarth, Wesley, Goldsmith, Reynolds, Johnson, Boswell, Chatterton, Hume, Gibbon, Garrick, Kemble, Mrs. Siddons, Kean, Flaxman, Wilkie, Turner, Burns (song), Cowper, Coleridge, Wordsworth, Lamb, Byron, Shelley, Keats, Browning, Mrs. Browning, Tennyson, Bulwer Lytton, Dickens (his last letter), Thackeray, Carlyle, and Macaulay. — Among the foreign autographs in Case VIII are those of Erasmus, Luther, Calvin, Michael Angelo, Titian, Ariosto, Galileo, Rubens, Van Dyck, Rembrandt, Montaigne, Molière, Corneille, Racine, Voltaire, Rousseau, Victor Hugo, Leibnitz, Kant, Goethe, Schiller, Heine, Händel, Haydn, Mozart, Beethoven, Mendelssohn, and Wagner.

The corresponding CASES IX and X, at the opposite end of the room, to the left and right of the entrance to the King's Library, exhibit a series of autograph literary works, etc. In Case IX: treatise on the Sacrament by Edward VI.; the prayer-book of Lady Jane Grey; a book of prayers copied out by Queen Elizabeth; original MSS. of James I. and Charles I.; Milton's Family Bible, with notes in his hand; autographs of Ben Jonson, Francis Bacon, Butler (part of 'Hudibras'), Locke, Defoe, Pope, Sterne ('Sentimental Journey'), Dr. Samuel Johnson, and Gibbon. — In Case X: Autographs of Cowper ('John Gilpin'), Gray ('Elegy'), Burns ('Autobiography'), Byron ('Childe Harold'), Scott ('Kenilworth'), Coleridge, Lamb, Southey, Keats, Macaulay, Newman ('Dream of Gerontius'), Tennyson ('Idylls of the King'), Charlotte Bronte, George Eliot ('Adam Bede'), Leonardo da Vinci (note-book), Michael Angelo, Albrecht Dürer (sketch-book), Lope de Vega, and Tasso ('Torismondo').

Against the pilasters are four upright cases (G-K) containing early Biblical manuscripts. In CASE G, adjoining Case X (N.W.), are a volume of the Codex Alexandrinus and the Gospel of St. Luke in Greek (Codex Nitriensis). The former, dating from the 5th cent., ranks with the Codex Sinaiticus at St. Petersburg and the Codex Vaticanus at Rome as one of the three oldest Greek MSS. of the Bible. — CASES H and I contain illuminated copies of the Vulgate (840 and 1097). — In CASE K is a copy of Wycliffe's Bible (14th cent.), with illuminations. Adjoining Case I, on the pilaster, are an autograph of Edmund Spenser; the deed of sale of 'Paradise Lost', with Milton's signature; and an autotype facsimile of a mortgage by Shakspeare.

Cases A-E, in the middle of the room, contain Greek, Latin, and other MSS., arranged to show the progress of the art of writing. A. Greek papyri, brought from Egypt, including portions of Plato, Bacchylides, Homer, and Aristotle (only extant MS. of his 'On the Constitution of Athens'). Other Greek MSS. hang on the pilasters near Cases A and C. — B. Greek MSS.; wax-tablet containing two lines written by a schoolmaster and copied twice by a pupil. — C, D. Latin and other MSS. — E. English MSS.: a unique copy of Beowulf, on vellum (ca. 1000 A.D.); Anglo-Saxon Chronicle to 1066; Piers Plowman (before 1400); poem by Occleve, with a portrait of Chaucer on the margin (early 15th cent.). — Case F, in the centre, contains chronologically arranged MS. sources of English history, shewing how the history was recorded before the invention of printing; 2. Bede's Ecclesiastical History; 3. Anglo-Saxon Chronicle; 4. Wace's Roman de Rou; 12. Matthew Paris, etc.

In frames attached to the wainscot to the left (W.) of the entrance to the King's Library are hung several *Deeds*, including photographs of two copies of Magna Charta preserved in the Museum. — To the left is a series of *Papyri* (four in Coptic, one in Greek), relating to the monastery of St. Phœbammon, near Hermonthis, Egypt. — On the pilaster beside Case H is a counterpart of the deed of conveyance of the land on which Melbourne now stands.

At the entrance to the Newspaper Room (E.) are two glass-cases (L and M) with impressions of the Great Seals of the British sovereigns (left) and of various baronial and ecclesiastical seals (right).

To the S.E. of the Manuscript Saloon is the **MS. Room for Students.** The door to the E. opens on the corridor leading to the **Newspaper Reading Room** and to the staircase ascending to the **Print Department** (see p. 325). — On the N. it is adjoined by the **King's Library,** a collection of 65,000 vols., 20,000 pamphlets, and numerous maps, prints, and drawings, made by George III. and presented to the nation by George IV., and arranged in a hall built for the purpose, which extends along the whole breadth of the building. The collection is remarkable for the beauty and rarity of the works contained in it. Changes in the arrangements are not infrequent, and temporary exhibitions illustrating special periods are held here from time to time.

At the S. end of the hall are four cases containing a selection of Oriental MSS., some of which are of great beauty and value.

Twenty-two cases arranged on each side of the hall contain typographical specimens in illustration of the history of printing, in chronological order.

Cases I and II contain a collection of 'block-books', *i.e.* books printed from carved blocks of wood. Among them are several specimens of the Biblia Pauperum; Defensorium Inviolatæ Virginitatis Beatæ Mariæ Virginis (1470); Temptationes Demonis; Ars moriendi; Mirabilia Romæ; some old German calendars, including that of Regiomontanus printed at Nuremberg in 1474, the earliest known; Planetenbuch, or book of the planets (1470), etc.

Cases III and IV are occupied by the earliest German printed books, including the Mazarin Bible, the first printed Bible, printed by Gutenberg and Fust (Mayence, 1455; a copy of this Bible was sold in 1873 for 3400*l.*); the first psalter, printed on parchment in 1457 by Fust and Schœffer (the first printed book bearing a date); Bible printed by Fust and Schœffer in 1462 (the first printed Bible bearing a date); Decretum Gratiani, printed at Strassburg by Eggesteyn in 1471; Latin Bible, printed at Bamberg in 1461; the first German Bible (printed at Strassburg about 1466).

Case V contains early German and Dutch books: Steinhœwel's German Chronicle (Ulm, 1473); Rynaert die Vos (Gouda, 1479), the first printed edition in any language.

CASE VI contains examples of Italian typography: Cicero, De Oratore, printed at Subiaco by Schweinheim and Pannartz in 1465, the first work printed in Italy; Livy, printed at Rome in 1469 by Schweinheim and Pannartz, on vellum; Petrarch (Fano, 1503); Lactantius (Subiaco, 1465); Cicero, Tusculanæ Questiones (Rome, 1469); the first printed edition of Dante (Foligno, 1472); Virgil, by Aldus (Venice, 1501); Cicero, Epistolæ ad Familiares, on vellum (Venice, 1469).

CASE VII contains Italian and French printing: Valturius de re militari (Verona, 1472); Lascaris, Greek Grammar (Milan, 1476), the first printed Greek work; Æsop (Milan, ca. 1480); Barzizius, Liber epistolarum (Paris, 1470), the first book printed in France; L'Art et Science de Rhétorique, copy belonging to Henry VII. (Paris, 1493).

In CASE VIII are specimens of English printing: Recuyell of the Historyes of Troye, by Le Fevre, printed abroad by Caxton about 1475 (the first book printed in English); the original French of the same work, also printed by Caxton (the first book printed in French); The Game and Playe of the Chesse, printed by Caxton about 1476; The Dictes or Sayengis of the philosophers, printed by Caxton at Westminster in 1477 (the first book printed in England); St. Bonaventura, Speculum Vitæ Christi, printed on vellum by Caxton ca. 1490; Prayer-book, printed by Caxton at Westminster ca. 1491 (unique); the first printed edition of Chaucer's Canterbury Tales, by Caxton, about 1478; 'The Book of St. Albans', a book of the chase, printed at the Abbey of St. Albans in 1486.

CASE IX contains early specimens (in several instances the first) of Spanish, Portuguese, Slavonic, Oriental, American, South African, and Australian printing.

In CASE X are examples of Colophons and early Title-pages.

CASE XI contains specimens of early printed music.

CASE XII exhibits portraits of printers and bibliographers.

CASE XIII contains specimens of fine and sumptuous printing: Horace, first edition, from the Aldine press (Venice, 1501); Virgil, printed by Aldus on vellum (1501); Theuerdank, composed by Melchior Pfinzing on the marriage of the Emperor Maximilian with Mary of Burgundy, and printed at Nuremberg by Schœnsperger in 1517; Petrarch, on vellum, printed by Aldus (Venice, 1501), once the property of Isabella Gonzaga, Marchioness of Mantua; Dante, printed in 1502, also by Aldus at Venice, and the first book which bore the anchor, the distinguishing mark of the Aldine Press; Milton's 'Paradise Lost', printed by Baskerville (Birmingham, 1759); Anacreon, printed in capitals (1791); Horace, printed in microscopic type (Paris, Didot, 1828); Homer's Odyssey, in very small type (London, 1831).

CASE XIV contains works illustrated with wood-cuts and engravings. Ariosto (London, 1591), with engravings; Book of the Passion (Wittenberg, 1521), illustrated by Cranach; first and second editions of Holbein's Dance of Death (Lyons, 1538 and 1539); Breydenbach's Journey to the Holy Land (Mayence, 1486), illustrated with folding views.

In CASE XV are specimens of illuminations and sumptuous printing: Euclid, printed by Ratdolt (Venice, 1482); Martial, Aldus (Venice, 1501); Breviaries, missals, and hours; Aulus Gellius, Noctes Atticæ, on vellum (Florence, 1513).

CASE XVI contains books bearing the autographs of the authors or early owners: Wittenberg Bible of 1541, with Luther's signature; autographs of Calvin, Francis Bacon, Melanchthon, Michael Angelo, Tasso, Voltaire, Ben Jonson, Lord Burghley, Bentley, Newton, Coleridge, Napoleon I., and George Washington; proof-sheets of Scott's 'Woodstock', with notes and corrections by the author.

CASES XVII and XVIII are assigned to typographical and literary curiosities: Broadsides and proclamations; the first edition of the Book of Common Prayer (1549); first collected edition of Shakspeare's works (1623); also of Milton, Bunyan, Defoe, and many others. In CASE XVIII are Luther's 95 Theses against the Indulgence of 1517, beside which is one of the Papal Indulgences sold by Tetzel; below, at S. end of case, Official duplicate of Lincoln's proclamation against slavery.

CASE XIX has specimens of Chinese, Japanese, and Corean printing and engraving; and Cases XX, XXI, and XXII, examples of Japanese block-printing in colours.

At the N. end of the hall a series of six cases are filled with bound books, many of which are very beautiful specimens of the art of book-binding, including some by Grolier. Adjacent are four cases with English engraved book-illustrations (1545-1650).

Two cases near the middle of the hall contain specimens of recent acquisitions by the library (changed from time to time).

Case XXIII contains a facsimile (by Rev. F. T. Havergal) of the Mappa Mundi in Hereford Cathedral (1290-1310; see *Baedeker's Great Britain*).

Cases XXIV-XXVIII contain relief-maps of Palestine, Mt. Blanc, the Western Alps, Mt. Vesuvius, and Mt. Etna. Other maps shown are a woodcut of the Siege of Aden (1513), a facsimile of a map made at Madrid by Juan de la Cosa, the pilot of Columbus, containing the first delineation of the latter's discoveries (ca. 1500), a facsimile of Ribero's 'Carta Universal' (Seville, 1529), and one of Cantino's map (1502), the earliest map showing the line drawn by Pope Alexander VI. to divide the discoveries of the New World between Spain and Portugal.

Two other cases contain specimens from a collection of postage-stamps bequeathed by T. K. Tapling, M. P., in 1891.

In the lower portions of several cases are placed the 5020 vols. (bound in about 1000) of the Chinese Encyclopædia, a reprint of standard Chinese works from 1150 B.C. to 1700 A.D., published in 1726.

Near the middle of the hall stand a large celestial globe by Coronelli (Paris, 1693), the constellations on which are very finely engraved, and a model of the ingenious hanging press employed in the museum-library to economize space.

At the end of the King's Library is a staircase, leading to the collections of oriental art and ethnography (comp. p. 326). In the meantime, however, we retrace our steps to the entrance-hall, and pass out of it, to the left, into the *Sculpture Gallery. Comp. 'Guide to the Greek and Roman Antiquities' (1899; 6d.). The first room we enter is the —

Roman Gallery. On the left side are Roman antiquities found in England. The compartments below the windows contain rough-hewn sarcophagi, while by the intervening pilasters are specimens of old Irish characters (Oghams). Above, on the walls to the right and left, are fragments of Roman mosaic pavements, discovered in England. On the right (N.) side of the room is ranged a collection of Roman portrait busts and statues (the numbering begins at the W. end of the gallery): 2. Julius Cæsar; 77*. Marcus Brutus; 3. The youthful Augustus; 4. Augustus; Drusus the younger; 5. Tiberius; 7. Drusus; 8. Caligula; 47. Iconic female figure; 1155. Claudius; 11. Nero; 15. Trajan; above, Head of Titus; 17, 18. Hadrian; 20. Antinous, favourite of Hadrian; 21. Julia Sabina, Hadrian's consort; 23. Statue of Hadrian in civil costume; *24. Antoninus Pius; Faustina the elder; Antoninus Pius; 26, 1464. Marcus Aurelius; 28. Faustina, his consort; 30. Lucius Verus; 32. Lucilla; 33. Commodus; 34. Crispina, consort of Commodus; 35. Pertinax; 36. Septimius Severus; 1415. Iconic female figure; 37. Caracalla; 38. Julia Mamæa, mother of Alexander Severus; 39, 40. Gordian and Sabinia, his wife. — We next reach the —

First Græco-Roman Room. This and the two following rooms contain sculptures, executed in Italy, but chiefly by Greek artists or from Greek models; also a few Greek originals.

To the left of the entrance: 500. Sadly injured Roman copy of the Diadumenos of Polycleitos, from Vaison, in France. To the right of the entrance, 134. Statue of a hero; 75*. Good copy of the head of the Diadumenos of Polycleitos, from Corinth; 501. Diadumenos by an Attic sculptor, perhaps after a figure by Phidias; 76*. Statue of a youth, after an original by Polycleitos (once the property of Westmacott, the sculptor). To the left: 117. Bust of Homer; 119. Bust of Sophocles at an advanced age; 112. Statue of Artemis; 113. Ideal female head; *1380. Apollo Citharœdus, found in the Temple of Apollo at Cyprus (replica in the Capitol at Rome); 115. Bust of Apollo; 116. Statue of Venus; 111. Head of Juno; *118. Dancing Satyr (from the Palazzo Rondanini at Rome); 109. Satyr playing with the infant Bacchus (from the Palazzo Farnese at Rome). By the W. door, Heads of Athena. Statue of Dionysos, from Posilipo, akin to the so-called Sardanapalus in the Vatican and, like it, a work of the 4th cent. B.C.; 126. Caryatide.

Second Græco-Roman Room. In the recess on the left: *136. The Townley Venus, showing the influence of Praxiteles, found at Ostia; opposite, 250. Discobolus, or the 'quoit-thrower' (ancient copy of the statue by Myron). Round the room are several heads: 139. Bearded head, of the Pergamenian school; 137. Aphrodite; 72*. Apollo; 69*. Youthful Dionysos; *70*. Apollo, found in the Thermæ of Caracalla, an easy and vigorous work; 138. Apollo Pourtalès or Giustiniani, from the same original, but harder and more conventional; *71*. Head of Hermes, an excellent copy, restored by Flaxman, of an original by Lysippus (so-called Jason, at Munich).

Third Græco-Roman Room. On the right (N.) side: 141. Colossal head of Hercules, a roughly executed work, resembling the Farnese Hercules in being after an original by Lysippus; 145. Cupid bending his bow; 147. Relief of a youth holding a horse; 148. Shepherd asleep; *38*. Iconic female bust (the so-called Clytie), perhaps of Antonia (b. 36 B.C.), daughter of Mark Antony (this bust appealed strongly to Emerson); 129. Ideal head of a youth, probably used architectonically; 780. Two youths on horseback; 503. Head of an Amazon, after Polycleitos; 37*. Discobolus; Hellenistic portrait-head; 140. Ideal head of a youth, after an original of the 5th cent. B.C.; Child's head from Paphos (Cyprus); 159. Apotheosis of Homer, relief with the name of the sculptor, Archelaus of Priene (found at Bovillæ, of the time of Tiberius); 43. Youthful barbarian, found in Trajan's Forum; 162. Attendant of Mithras, restored as Paris; 163. Mithras, the Persian Sun God, sacrificing a bull; 164. Term, found near Tivoli; 165. Actæon devoured by his dogs (from Lanuvium); above, Head of Aphrodite (? so-called Sappho); 48*. Bust of Hermes, after an original of the

5th cent. B.C.; 47*. Herma with the head of a medical deity (after a 5th cent. original), admirable in execution and expression; *46*. Relief, Victory sacrificing to Apollo. — West side: 171. Statue of Hermes, good copy of a Praxitelian original; Boy extracting a thorn from his foot, found on the Esquiline Hill, a realistic Hellenistic modification of the archaic bronze in the Capitoline Museum. — South side: 43*. Archaic head of an athlete; 42*. Diana (archaistic statue); Bearded head of Mercury from Tivoli; Head of a bearded god, probably Zeus, after an original of the time of Phidias (the eyes were inserted); Head of Dionysos from Baiæ; 104. Head of Minerva; 172. Torso of Venus ('Richmond Venus'); Small basalt head; Youthful Pan; 177. Herma of the Bearded Pan, with a flute; 183, 184. Satyrs; 185. Venus (from Ostia); 41*. Discus with relief of Apollo and Artemis slaying the children of Niobe; 189. Bacchus and Ampelos (personification of the vine in the form of a girl); 186. Part of a group of two boys quarrelling at play; above, 191. Mænad (from Cumæ); 192. Ideal head of a maiden, of great delicacy of execution (the eyes were inlaid); 196. Girl playing with astragali (knuckle bones); 195. Bacchic relief with two sitting satyrs; 128. Minerva (helmet and drapery restored in bronze); 199. Head of youthful Hercules from Genzano, after a Praxitelian original; 776. Relief representing Apollo, Latona, and Diana, with three worshippers; 202. Head of Venus; 204. Head of Hercules.

The door on the right leads into the Archaic Room; the staircase at the extreme end descends to the —

Græco-Roman Basement Room, which contains Greek and Roman sculptures of various kinds: sarcophagi, cinerary urns, reliefs, vases, fountain-basins, candelabra, table-supports, animals, leaden anchors, etc. On the E. wall is a mosaic from a Roman villa at Halicarnassus, representing Aphrodite rising from the sea, with two Tritons. Adjacent are two sacrificial groups in marble, and a relief of two gladiators struggling with a bull. — The annex contains a series of Etruscan sarcophagi and urns, reproductions of Etruscan tombs at Bomarzo and Vulci, an ancient Roman water-wheel (found in Spain), other sculptures, and miscellaneous objects.

The door on the right in the Third Græco-Roman Room leads into the —

Archaic Room, which chiefly contains archaic remains from Asia Minor and the Peloponnesus. At the W. end of the room are ten sitting figures (Nos. 7-16), of the beginning of the 6th cent. B.C., which, with the adjacent lion (17) and the sphinx (18), once formed part of the Sacred Way leading to the Temple of Apollo near Miletus, known as Branchidæ from the priestly clan which ministered in it. The forms of these figures are very full and show little attempt at modelling. On a lofty pedestal by the W. wall is a cast (192) of a statue of Nike (Victory) by Paionios (from Olympia); at each side (190, 191) a cast of a metope from the temple of

Zeus at Olympia. Opposite the Nike: *94. Reliefs from the '*Harpy Tomb*' at Xanthos (at the sides sacrificial scenes; at the ends winged sirens, bearing away small figures intended to represent departed souls). The forms here are also full but more carefully modelled. On the N. and S. walls are archaic marble friezes (81, 82), from Xanthos in Lycia (with clever representations of fighting cocks), above which are imitations of the pediments of a temple, containing casts (160-183) of the pediment sculptures found in Ægina in 1811 (originals in Munich). On the E. wall are plaster casts of four metopes from Selinus in Sicily, probably dating from about 600 B.C. By this wall also are fragments (24-48) from the older temple of Diana at Ephesus. On the column-base from Ephesus are reliefs and the remains of a dedication by King Crœsus. By the N. wall are objects from the temple of Apollo at Naucratis (100-127). By the N.W. exit are objects from Mycenæ (1-6). Among the other works are: *206. 'Strangford' Apollo (severe and scant in form, probably by an Æginetan sculptor); 205. Another archaic figure of Apollo; 96, 97. Female torsos from Xanthos; 154. Headless female figure from Attica; 2*. Cast of a bronze statue of a charioteer found at Delphi (original of the 1st half of the 5th cent. B.C.).

The **Greek Ante-Room**, a small chamber to the N., contains, on the right, *1300. a sitting figure of Demeter, a dignified original of the 4th cent. B.C. (period of Praxiteles and Scopas), found at Cnidus; on the left, 209. Apollo, copy of an archaic work, from the Choiseul-Gouffier collection. Beside the latter are two archaic heads copied from the same original as the statue. Here also are glass-cases with statuettes, small heads, and sculptured fragments from Cyrene and Priene.

The **Ephesus Room** contains fragments of the celebrated *Temple of Diana* (comp. *Acts*, chap. xix), exhumed by Mr. J. T. Wood at Ephesus in 1869-74. The remains consist chiefly of the drums and bases of columns, and fragments of capitals and cornices. Among them is the lowest drum of a column with lifesize reliefs believed to represent Thanatos and Hermes bringing Alcestis back from Hades (1204-6). On the E. side of the room are sculptures from various sources, including a Scylla from Bargylia in Asia Minor; 31*. Head of Perseus (recognizable by the winged cap), copy of an important work of the 5th cent. B.C.; 32*. Torso of a Triton, in high relief, from Delos; and a horse's head from a chariot-group from Civitá Lavinia. To the right of the exit are a fine head (30*) wrongly named Alexander the Great, a characteristic specimen of Alexandrian art, and a colossal seated and draped figure of Dionysos (432), from the choragic monument of Thrasyllos, erected on the S. slope of the Acropolis in 320 B.C. Opposite is a cast of the Olympian Hermes by Praxiteles. In the middle, to the right, 1106. So-called Base of the Muses (probably an altar), with reliefs of the Muses, a late-Hellenic work. We now reach the —

Elgin Room, containing the famous *Elgin Marbles*, being the remains of the sculptures executed to adorn the Parthenon at Athens, and considered the finest specimens of the plastic art in existence. They were brought from Athens in 1801-3 by Lord Elgin, at that time British ambassador at Constantinople, at a cost of 70,000*l.*, and sold to the British Government in 1816 for half that sum. The Parthenon, the Temple of Pallas Athena on the Acropolis of Athens, was built by Ictinos in B.C. 447-434, in the time of Pericles, the golden age of Athens and of Hellenic art. It was in the Doric order of architecture, and occupied the site of an earlier but unfinished temple of Athena. It was adorned with sculptures under the supervision of Phidias. A statue of Athena, formed of gold and ivory, stood in the interior of the cella. The sculptures preserved here consist of the frieze round the exterior of the cella, 15 metopæ, and the relics of the two pediments, unfortunately in very imperfect preservation. The figures of the deities represented are most nobly conceived, admirably executed, and beautifully draped.

The remains of the E. PEDIMENT, representing the Birth of Athena, who, according to the Greek legend, issued in full armour from the head of Zeus, are arranged on the W. (left) side of the room.

In the left angle of the tympanum we observe two arms and a mutilated human head (303A-C), in front of which are two spirited horses' heads, also considerably damaged. These are considered to represent a group of Helios, the god of the rising sun, ascending in his chariot from the depths of the ocean, his outstretched arms grasping the reins of his steeds. Next comes a youthful male figure (303 D), leaning in a half-recumbent posture on a rock covered with a mantle and a panther's skin, formerly called Theseus, but more probably Cephalus, the beloved of Eos. With his outstretched right arm, he seems to be greeting the ascending orb of day. This figure, the only one on which the head remains, is among the best-preserved in the two pediments. Next to Theseus is a group (303 E, F) of two sitting female figures in long drapery, who turn with an appearance of lively interest towards the central group — perhaps the Attic Hours, Thallo and Auxo (or Demeter and Persephone?). Then comes (303 G) a female figure hurrying towards the left, looking backwards in great excitement towards the central group. The girlish forms make it probable that this represents Hebe; the former identification with Iris, messenger of the gods, seems negatived by the absence of wings.

The central group, which probably represented Athena surrounded by the gods, is entirely wanting. The space occupied by it, indicated here by an opening in the middle of the sculptures (partly filled by a Doric capital from the Parthenon), must have measured 33-40 ft. in length.

Next comes (303 J), on the right, a torso of Victory, which, however, probably belongs to the W. pediment. Then (303 K, L, M) a noble group of two sitting female forms, in the lap of one of which reclines a third female, probably representing the three Fates. Adjacent, in the angle of the tympanum (303 N, O), the torso of Selene (the goddess of the moon), as a charioteer, and by her side the head of one of her coursers. This portion of the frieze is thought to have shown the Moon sinking into the sea at the approach of Day. The horse's head is in good preservation.

The remains of the WEST PEDIMENT are on the opposite side of the room. They are by no means so well preserved as those from the East Pediment, and we can only form an idea of their meaning and connection from a drawing executed by the French painter Carrey in 1674, which contains several groups that are now wanting. The subject of the sculptures is the Strife of Athena and Poseidon for the soil of Athens. By a stroke of his trident Poseidon caused a salt-spring to gush forth from the soil, but his gift was outdone by that of Athena, who produced the olive-tree, and was adjudged the possession of the city. In the left angle we observe (304 A) the torso of a recumbent male figure, perhaps the river-god Cephissus. Next to it is a cast (304 B, C) of a group of two figures (the original is in Athens), supposed to be Cecrops, the first king of Attica, and his daughter; the male figure is in a semi-recumbent posture, propping his left arm on the coils of a serpent; the female kneeling beside him has her right arm round his neck. Next (304 H) the torso of a man, perhaps Hermes. The relics of the central group are exceedingly scanty. Of Athena only the right shoulder with part of the armour and a piece of the ægis are preserved (304 L). [No. 328, the upper part of a female head lying on the base, was found near the Parthenon, but is no longer thought to belong to the Athena.] A much mutilated torso (304 M), consisting of the shoulders alone, is all that remains of the rival aeity, Poseidon. The proportions of these two statues, which, as the central figures, occupied the highest part of the tympanum, are on a much larger scale than those of the others.

Next comes a female torso (304 O), perhaps Amphitrite; then (304 P, Q) the lower part of a sitting female form, wrongly named Leucothea, with a boy by her side; then the cast of a kneeling male figure, perhaps the river god Ilissus. Lastly, at the end of the tympanum (304 W), is the torso of a recumbent female form, supposed to represent the nymph Callirrhoë.

Around the whole of the hall, at a height of about 4½ ft. from the ground, we observe the **Frieze (about 175 yds. long), which ran round the outside of the cella (or inner sanctuary) under the colonnade enclosing the Parthenon. It forms a connected whole, and represents, in low relief, the festive procession which ascended to the Acropolis at the end of the Panathenæa, for the purpose of presenting to the Goddess a peplos, or robe, woven and embroidered by Athenian virgins. The priests with sacrificial bulls and horses, the virgins, the warriors on horseback, on foot, and in chariots, and the thronging worshippers of all kinds are executed with admirable taste and skill. The slabs are arranged as far as possible in their original order, the points of the compass being indicated above them. On the E. side, the side of entrance, was represented an august assembly of the gods, looking towards the advancing procession (see N. part of E. wall). In the group to the left of the centre are Zeus, Hera, Isis or Nike (erect), Iacchos (Dionysos), Demeter with her torch, Ares (?), and Hermes with the petasos (hat); to the right are Athena, Hephæstus, Poseidon, Apollo, Peitho, Aphrodite, and Eros with a sunshade. Between the two groups of deities are priests and priestesses, preparing for the reception of the train. To the right and left of the gods are groups of older and younger men, waiting for the procession. The latter moves along both the N. and S. sides, as if it had been divided into two on the W. side. There are girls with baskets, trays, bowls, and torches, cows and rams for sacrifice led by young men, youths with various sacrificial gifts, players on the lute and lyre, oplites springing from four-horse chariots, and troops of noble Athenian youths on horseback. On the W. side other riders are preparing to join their companions. The whole procession is inexhaustibly rich in effective motives, but the finest and most lifelike figures are the mounted youths. — Most of the pieces of this frieze are but slightly damaged, while some of them are perfectly preserved. A few of the slabs are merely casts of portions of the frieze at Paris and Athens.

Above the frieze on the W. wall of the room are 15 *Metopæ and casts of four others from the Parthenon, being the sculptures which filled the intervals between the triglyphs of the external frieze. They represent the battle of the Centaurs and Lapithæ, and are executed in very high relief.

This room also contains a model of the Acropolis and another representing the Parthenon as it appeared after its bombardment by the Venetian General Morosini in 1687. Adjacent are three casts (300, 301, 4*) of small reproductions of the colossal chryselephantine statue of Athena, by Phidias, which stood within the Parthenon. In an adjacent wall-case are votive reliefs, including one (798) with two tresses of hair dedicated to Poseidon. — On the drum of a column on the E. side of the N. section of the room is a fragment (3)2) of the shield of another small reproduction of the Athena Parthenos (Strangford Collection). The reliefs represent the contests of the Greeks and Amazons; the bald-headed old man is said to be a portrait of Phidias himself. There are some traces of colouring on the reverse side, where, on the shield of the original statue, the contests of the Gods and Giants were represented.

On the E. wall are plaster casts (400-404) from the external frieze of the Temple of Theseus at Athens, representing battle-scenes, partly of the contests of the Greeks with the Centaurs, three metopæ from the same temple with sculptures of the feats of Theseus, and (below the Parthenon frieze) casts (430) of the frieze of the Choragic Monument of Lysicrates.

Among the other sculptures in the Elgin Room are casts (G 1 & 2) of two marble chairs from the theatre of Dionysos at Athens (one on each side of the entrance); 549. Head of Pericles (a Roman copy of an original by Cresilas, a contemporary of Phidias); 504. Head of Hera from Agrigentum (probably a modern forgery); *550. Head of Æsculapius from Melos, an original of the time of Praxiteles. Towards the N. end of the room are some remains from the Erechtheum (5th cent. B.C.), the purest existing type of the Ionic style, including a column from the E. portico, a *Caryatid from the S. portico (407), and fragments of friezes, cornices, ceiling coffers, etc. Here, too, is the capital of a Doric column from the Propylæum (433), the magnificent entrance to the Acropolis. Near by are a cast of a colossal owl; a draped torso of Æsculapius from Epidauros (551); and a *Statue of a youth, probably Eros, from Athens. — We now enter the —

Phigaleian Room, containing the marbles from the Temple of Apollo Epicurios at Phigaleia in Arcadia. Round the walls are arranged twenty-three slabs from the frieze adorning the interior of the cella. Those on the N. and W. walls (520-531) represent the contest of the Centaurs and Lapithæ, the others (532-542), battles between the Greeks and the Amazons. Fragments of the metopes of this temple (510-519) hang on the S. wall.

On the wall, in the S.W. angle, are four reliefs and the cast of a fifth (421-425) from the frieze of the temple of the Wingless Victory (Nike Apteros or Athena Nike) at Athens. These represent the Athenians fighting with Greek and Asiatic foes. Near the centre of the W. wall, above, are casts (426-429) from the balustrade of this temple: to the left, *Victory fastening her sandal.

Fine specimens and casts of *Greek Sepulchral Stelae* are also placed in this room. To the left of the entrance, 702. Stele from Macedon with a family group. Of the four tombstones let into the E. wall the finest are that on which an athlete is represented handing his strigil to his slave (625) and that (to the right) representing an athlete standing alone (626). On the floor below, tablet commemorating the victory of a citharist (775); tablet in memory of those who had fallen in battle (750); and a charming relief of dancing nymphs. On the N. wall, curious relief of a physician and patient (629); stele of Xanthippus, who is represented holding a votive foot (628). Beside the N. and W. walls are sepulchral urns. Among the votive reliefs is one relating to the torch-race in honour of the goddess Bendis (Plato, Repub. Bk. I).

To the left and right of the door between this room and the Elgin Room are two good Greek portrait-busts (8*, 9*).

The door in the N.E. corner of the room leads to the Mausoleum Room (see below); we, however, return to the Elgin Room, and by the door in the centre of the E. side reach the —

Nereid Room, containing the sculptures from the so-called *Nereid Monument* at Xanthos in Lycia (end of 5th cent. B.C.). In the centre is a model of the monument, by Sir C. Fellows, and on the S. wall of the room is a 'restoration' of one of the sides of the monument. Eight Nereids, some much mutilated, stand in this room. On the walls are fragments of four friezes that adorned the building. The broad frieze, supposed to have encircled the base, represents a battle between Greeks and Asiatic warriors, some of whom are mounted; the other narrower friezes bear scenes of war, hunting, banqueting, and sacrifice. On each side of the door on the N. wall is a lion from the monument, and above the doorway is the E. pediment of the same.

We now descend the steps on the left to the **Mausoleum Room,** added in 1882, containing remains from the ******Mausoleum at Halicarnassus**, discovered by Newton in 1857.

This celebrated monument (whence the modern generic term 'mausoleum' is derived) was erected by Artemisia in B.C. 352, in honour of her husband Mausolus (Mausollos), King of Caria, and was reckoned among the Seven Wonders of the World. The architects were Satyros and Pythis. The tomb stood upon a lofty basement, and was surrounded by 36 Ionic columns. Above it was a pyramid rising in steps (24 in number), surmounted by a four-horse chariot, with colossal statues of Mausolus and his wife, sculptured by the above-named Pythis. The monument was in all about 140 ft. in height, and was embellished by a number of statues, lions, and other pieces of sculpture. In the centre of the room are (1000) a *Statue of Mausolus (restored from 77 fragments) and (1001) a female figure (perhaps Artemisia) found under the ruins of the pyramid, grouped along with a wheel (largely restored) and fragments of the colossal horses of the chariot of Mausolus, so as to suggest their position in a chariot. The bronze bit and bridle are original. In the S.W. corner of the room is (980) a column from the colonnade, with fragments of the architrave; opposite are its base and lowest drum. A few fragments of the relief-friezes of the monument are also preserved; these are assigned by Pliny to Scopas, Bryaxis, Leochares, and Timotheus; but Vitruvius names Praxiteles in the place of the last-mentioned. On the E. wall are seventeen slabs (*1006-1031) of a frieze representing the contests of the

Greeks with the Amazons, and above are fragments of another frieze, in bad preservation, representing races and the battle of the Greeks with the Centaurs. Low down on the W. wall, near the S. end of the room, is a slab with a charioteer, ascribed to Scopas. Adjoining this is the *Head of a youth, in a somewhat damaged state but of splendid original workmanship and probably from the chisel of Praxiteles (formerly in the collection of the Earl of Aberdeen). At the N.E. end of the room is a reproduction of the cornice of the Mausoleum. Among other fragments are a female torso; eight lions; *1045. Fragment of an equestrian figure in Persian garb; fragments of columns. The room also contains, in the N.W. corner, a number of marbles from the Temple of Athene Polias at Priene (B.C. 334), a colossal arm, hand, foot, and female head, and a female figure (probably a goddess) in the dress and attitude of a charioteer. On the wall (1165-1176) are reliefs from a balustrade of later date, representing the contest with the Giants (ca. 2nd cent. B.C.). On either side of the steps at the S. end is a Lycian Tomb (950, 951), adorned with sculptures of martial scenes. Opposite the steps at the N. end is a colossal lion from Cnidos. To the right of these steps is an alabaster jar inscribed 'Xerxes the Great King', in four languages.

The admirable little lions on the stair-posts were modelled by *Alfred Stevens* (d. 1875) and originally stood with others on a railing (now removed) in Great Russell Street. Similar lions also occupy the stair-posts in other parts of the Museum.

The **Mausoleum Annex** (shown by special permission), which opens off the Mausoleum room near the N.W. angle, contains less important Græco-Roman sepulchral and votive reliefs, sarcophagi, altars, stelæ, etc.

We now ascend to the raised gallery at the N. end of the room, on which are placed four heads, including *1051, a beautiful female head found at Halicarnassus (4th cent. B.C.). By turning to the right we reach the Assyrian and Egyptian collections, which, next to the Elgin Room, are the most important parts of the British Museum.

The **Assyrian Gallery** comprises three long narrow rooms, called the *Nineveh (Kouyunjik) Gallery*, the *Nimroud Central Saloon*, and the *Nimroud Gallery*; the *Assyrian Transept*, adjoining the last of these three; the *Assyrian Saloon*; and finally a room (p. 319) on the second floor. Its contents are chiefly the yield of the excavations of Sir A. H. Layard in 1845-54 at Kouyunjik, the ancient Nineveh, and at Nimroud, the Biblical Calah, but include the collection made by Mr. George Smith in Mesopotamia, as well as contributions from other sources.

The **Nineveh** or **Kouyunjik Gallery** contains bas-reliefs dating from B.C. 721-625, and belonging to the royal palace of Sennacherib (d. B.C. 681) at Nineveh, afterwards occupied by Sennacherib's grandson, Assurbanipal or Sardanapalus. The older reliefs, dating from the time of Sennacherib, are executed in alabaster, the others in hard, light-grey limestone.

We begin our examination at the S.W. corner. No. 1. Esarhaddon, cast from a bas-relief cut in the rock, at the mouth of the Nahr el-Kelb river, near Beirût; 2. Galley with two banks of oars; 3*. Colossal face; 4-8. Row of fragments (upper part damaged), representing Sennacherib's advance against Babylon; 15-17. Return from battle, with captives and spoil; 18-19. Procession of warriors; 20-29. Siege of a fortified town, perhaps Jerusalem (on slab No. 25 is the city itself, while 27-29 represent the triumph of the victors). *Nos. 36-43. Series of large reliefs, which decorated the walls of a long passage between the palace and the Tigris; on one side, descending the slope, are horses, held by attendants; on the other, ascending, servants with dishes for a feast. The figures, rather under lifesize, are beautifully designed. No. 44. Monumental tablet; 45-50. Triumph of Sardanapalus over the Elamites (in limestone, well preserved). Nos. 51-52. Removal of a winged bull on a sledge by means of wooden rollers and levers; to the right, construction of a lofty embankment. Nos. 53-56. Similar scenes in better preservation; 57-59. Sennacherib besieging a city situated on a river (quaintly represented), and receiving the spoil and prisoners; 60. Figure with the head of a lion, bearing a knife in the right hand, which is held up.

The glass-cases in the middle of the hall contain some of the most interesting of the cuneiform tablets and cylinders from the library enlarged by Sardanapalus at Nineveh, including historical, geographical, philological, official, and legal documents of great value. Some of those in Case A give the Babylonian versions of the Creation and the Flood, the latter closely resembling that of Genesis. Other tablets bear prayers, incantations, omens, etc. The collection of cuneiform tablets in the Museum is the richest in Europe. — We now enter the —

Nimroud Central Saloon, containing the sculptures (dating from B.C. 880-630), discovered by Sir A. H. Layard at Nimroud, on the Tigris, situated about 18 M. below Nineveh. They are from the palace built by Esarhaddon, the successor of Sennacherib, but some of them are of a much earlier date than that monarch, who used the fragments of older buildings. The reliefs on the left are from a Temple of the God of War.

We begin to the left of the entrance from the Nineveh Gallery. 67. Large relief, representing the evacuation of a conquered city; below, the triumphal procession of King Tiglath-Pileser III. in his war-chariot. 68. Colossal head of a winged man-headed bull; opposite, another similar, but smaller head. At the central pillars, two statues of the god Nebo (69, 70). Then, black marble obelisk (98), adorned with five rows of reliefs; the cuneiform inscriptions record events in the history of Shalmaneser II. Opposite, in the middle of the room, 849. Seated statue of Shalmaneser II., in black basalt (about 850 B.C.). At the entrance to the Nimroud Gallery, on the right, a colossal winged *Lion (77); on the left, a colossal winged bull (76), both with human heads. Then bas-reliefs (84), evacuation of a conquered town and other scenes from the campaigns of Tiglath-Pileser. 88. Monolith (figure in relief) of Shalmaneser (B.C. 850); 110. Monolith of Samsi-Rammânu, son of Shalmaneser II. (B.C. 825-812). At the entrance to the Kouyunjik Gallery, a colossal lion (£6) from the side of a doorway (B.C. 880).

Nimroud Gallery. We begin at the S.W. corner. The slabs on the W. side are arranged as they originally stood in the palace of Assur-Nasir-Pal (885-860 B.C.) at Nimroud. Nos. 3-16 are martial and hunting scenes in the life of Assur-Nasir-Pal. To the left and right of the N. door are (17, 18) winged figures with a stag and an ibex. On the E. side of the gallery are colossal bas-reliefs; 19. Foreigners bringing apes as tribute; 20. King Assur-Nasir-Pal in a rich embroidered dress, with sword and sceptre;

°21-26. The king on his throne surrounded by attendants and winged figures with mystic offerings; 28, 29. Winged figure with a thunderbolt, chasing a demon; 36. Lion-hunt; 37-41. Representation of religious service. The slabs with the larger reliefs bear inscriptions running horizontally across their centres. The glass-cases in the middle of the room contain bronze dishes with engraved and chased decorations, admirably executed, other bronze articles of different kinds, etc. Cases E, F contain a collection of °Ivory Carvings, some with Egyptian figures. Between the cases (from S. to N.), 42. Part of a broken obelisk of Assur-Nasir-Pal; 89. Statue of that king on its original pedestal; inscribed limestone altar and coffer (71, 73); monolith of Assur-Nasir-Pal (B.C. 880). — The door in the N.W. corner of this room leads into the anteroom of the —

Assyrian Saloon, which consists of a large glass-roofed hall, used chiefly as a lecture-room, with a gallery or balcony round it. On the walls of both hall and balcony are reliefs from Nimroud and from Nineveh, excavated by Messrs. Rassam and Loftus. These reliefs, belonging to the latest period of Assyrian art, are throughout superior to those in the other rooms, both in design and execution. From the vestibule we turn to the left and enter the gallery.

On the E. wall: 33-53. Assurbanipal (668-626 B.C.) hunting lions. — S. or end wall: 103-117. Hunting-scenes. — W. wall: 118, 119. Assurbanipal offering libations over dead lions; 63. Guards; 64-69. Attendants with dead lions and hunting-gear; 70-72. Laden mules; 73, 74. Attendants with hunting-gear; 13, 15. Soldiers; 19, 20 Soldiers and captives; 21-24. Assault on the city of Lachish; 25, 26. Prisoners and booty from Lachish; 27-32. Sennacherib (705-681 B.C.) before Lachish; 17, 18. Mythological subjects; 862. Tiglath-Pileser III. (745-727 B.C.) receiving the submission of a foe; 863. Siege of a city by Tiglath-Pileser III ; 616. Inscription recording the conquests of Tiglath-Pileser III.; 81. Mythological scene.

The last-mentioned reliefs are in the vestibule, which we have again reached. We now descend the staircase to the basement proper, and turn to the right to enter the hall.

On the E. wall: Cuneiform inscriptions; 96, 98. Servants and warriors; 121. Assurbanipal and his wife banqueting in an arbour; 122. Servants carrying a dead lion; 124. Musicians; 83-87. Assurbanipal's war against the Arabians; 88. War against the Ethiopians. — S. or end wall: Large reliefs of the capture of a city in Susiana and the reception of captives. — At this end of the room is a glass-case containing the bronze bands that adorned the gates of Tell-Balawat, with reliefs recording the victories of Shalmaneser II. — W. wall: 89-94. War against the Babylonians; 12, 14. Musicians; 9-11, 16. Warriors; 1-8. Scenes of war; Bringing home the heads and spoil of conquered enemies; Warriors preparing their repast. — High up on the N. wall is a piece of pavement from the palace of Sardanapalus.

The Nimroud Gallery is adjoined on the S. by the **Assyrian Transept,** which in its western half is a continuation of the Nimroud Gallery (monuments from the time of Assur-Nasir-Pal), while the eastern part contains antiquities from Khorsabad (about B.C. 720), from the excavations of Messrs. Rawlinson and Layard

Near the W. side is the monolith of Assur-Nasir-Pal, with a portrait in relief. In front of it is an altar, which stood at the door of the Temple of the God of War. At the N. and S. sides are two colossal winged °Lions, with human heads and three horns, from the sides of a doorway. To the right of the entrance from the Nimroud Gallery is the upper part of a broken obelisk (62; B.C. 880). On the wall are reliefs and inscriptions from the palace of the Persian kings at Persepolis (B.C. 500) and casts of Pehlevi inscriptions from Hadji Abad (near Persepolis). — In the E. or Khorsabad section, two colossal animals with human heads, adjacent to

which are two colossal human figures. Within the recess thus formed
are fragments of bas-reliefs from the same place, and inscribed tablets
from Kouyunjik. To the right, opposite the window, a relief of a hunt-
ing-scene in black marble, the only slab obtained at Khorsabad by Sir
Henry Layard.

The collection of *Egyptian Antiquities fills three halls on the
groundfloor, and four rooms in the upper story. The antiquities,
which embrace the period from B.C. 3600 to A.D. 350, are arranged in chronological order. The Southern Gallery, which we
enter first, is devoted to antiquities of the latest period.

Southern Egyptian Gallery. Monuments of the period B.C. 1333-350.
Those at the S. end of the gallery are of the Greek and Roman periods.
Section 1: monuments of the period of the Roman dominion. Section 2:
time of the Ptolemies. In the middle is the celebrated 'Stone of Rosetta', a tablet of black basalt with a triple inscription. It was found
by the French near the Rosetta mouth of the Nile in 1798, but passed
into the possession of the English in 1802. One of the inscriptions
is in the hieroglyphic or sacred character, the second in the enchor-
ial, demotic, or popular character, and the third in Greek. It was
these inscriptions which led Young and Champollion to the discovery
of the hieroglyphic language of ancient Egypt. — The remaining part
of the gallery contains monuments from the 30th to the 19th Dynasty
(beginning about B.C. 1330). To the left, sarcophagus of Psammetichus,
an official of the 18th Dyn.(?); to the right, sarcophagus of a priest of
Ptah; to the right, sarcophagus of Hanata, a temple official of the 26th
Dyn., upon it, his statue which was found inside; to the left, sarcophagus
of King Nectanebus I. (about B.C. 378), with reliefs; to the right, sarcophagus of a priest of Memphis; right and left, two obelisks erected by
Nectanebus I. before the temple of Thoth at Memphis. To the left,
mummy-shaped sarcophagus from Thebes (26th Dyn.); to the right, *Sarcophagus of the Queen of Amasis II. (from Thebes); to the left, green
granite sarcophagus of a royal scribe, with reliefs; to the right, part of a
seated colossus of Osorkon II. (22nd Dyn.), beside it, its head. — To the
left, granite column from Bubastis, with palm-capital; to the right, statue
of the Nile; to the left, Apries; between them is a colossal scarabæus in
granite; to the left, granite column from Heracleopolis; right and left,
two sitting figures of the goddess Sekhet or Bast (with the head of a cat).
To the right, sitting figures of a man and a woman, in sandstone; to
the left, King Menephtah II. on his throne. Between the columns at the
entrance to the Central Saloon: on the right, wooden statue of a king of
the 19th Dyn. (883); on the left, wooden statue of Ramses II. (882). — The —

Central Egyptian Saloon chiefly contains antiquities of the time
of Ramses the Great, the Sesostris of the Greeks. In the middle are a
colossal fist from one of the statues in front of the temple of Ptah at Memphis, a cast of the Hyksos sphinx inscribed with the names of Ramses II.,
Menephtah I., Ramses III., and Pasebkhanu, and a granite lion, from
Benha el-Assal; to the left, two colossal heads, the one a cast from a
figure of Ramses at Mitrahineh, the other in granite from the Memnonium
at Thebes. To the right, a statue of the king in black basalt. Between
the columns, at the entrance to the Northern Gallery: on the right, granite
statue of Ramses II., from Thebes; to the left, a wooden figure of King Seti I.

[To the E. of the Central Egyptian Saloon, opposite the entrance
to the Nereid Room (p. 312), is the Refreshment Room. The
authorities would assuredly earn the gratitude of the public if they
improved this, the only neglected department under their care.]

Northern Egyptian Gallery, chiefly containing antiquities of the time
of the 18th Dynasty, under which Egypt enjoyed its greatest prosperity.
On the left and right, statues of King Horus in black granite, and two
lions in red granite (from Nubia). In the centre is a colossal ram's head

from Karnak. To the right and left are sitting figures of King Ameno-phis III., called by the Greeks Memnon (B.C. 1500), in black granite, from Thebes. On the left is a tablet recording the Ethiopian conquests of Ame-nophis III. Opposite is a colossal head of Amenophis III.; De Quincey speaks of this head as uniting 'the expressions of ineffable benignity with infinite duration'. On the left, column with a capital in the form of a lotus bud. To the right and left are two colossal heads, found near the 'Vocal Memnon', at Thebes. In the middle, cast of a sphinx inscribed with the name of Thotmes III. (B.C. 1600). Several repetitions of the statue of the goddess Sekhet, which is distinguished by the cat's head (in accordance with the Egyptian custom of representing deities with the heads of the animals sacred to them). Lower part of a black granite figure of Queen Mautemua seated in a boat. In the middle is the colossal head of King Thothmes III., found at Karnak, adjoining which on the right is one of the arms of the same figure. On the right is a monument, the four sides of which are covered with figures of Thothmes III. and gods. To the right, small sandstone figure of an Egyptian prince.

The shelves beneath the windows of the Egyptian galleries contain stelæ, inscribed tablets, funeral jars, etc. Below are larger slabs (some with the inscriptions picked out in red for the convenience of visitors), wall-paintings, etc. Smaller antiquities and fragments are ranged beside the walls (many under glass). — The —

Northern Egyptian Vestibule contains antiquities of the period em-braced by the first twelve dynasties, and particularly that of the fourth dynasty (about 3000 B.C.), when Egypt enjoyed a very high degree of civilisation. No. 1144 is a cast of the figure known as the Shêkh el-Beled (ca. B.C. 3700). Above the door is a plaster cast of the head of the northern colossal figure of Ramses at Abu-Simbel (Upper Egypt).

Opposite the Northern Vestibule is a staircase leading to the UPPER FLOOR. On the wall of the staircase are Mosaics from Hali-carnassus, Carthage, and Utica. The ante-room at the top of the stairs contains glass-cases with Cyprian sculptures (p. 320). To the left are four rooms filled with smaller Egyptian antiquities.

First Egyptian Room, containing a *Collection of mummies and mummy cases or coffins, from about B.C. 3600 to the Roman period. The *Wall Cases*, beginning to the left of the entrance, contain the coffins. *Cases 1-2*. Coffins and coffin-covers of the 11th Dyn. (B.C. 2500). — *Cases 3-6*. Coffins of the 18th Dyn. (B.C. 1600). — *Case 7*. Coffin of the 20th Dyn. (B.C. 1200). — *Cases 8-14*. Specimens of various dates, down to 800 B.C. Farther on are examples from Der el-Bâhri (see below). — *Cases 27-28*. Coffin covers of 600-450 B.C. — *Cases 29-34*. Coffin of Bak-en-Mut, etc. — *Cases 35-55*. Coffins of B.C. 650 and later dates. The mummy in Case 55 is said to have once been in the possession of Nell Gwynne. — The *Standard Cases A to K*, in the centre, contain mummies and coffins. In *Case A*, next the door, are the coffin of King Mycerinus (4th Dyn.; ca. B.C. 3600) and por-tions of the body found with it. — *Case B*. Coffin of Amamu. — *Case E*. Skeleton and coffin of Khati (B.C. 2600). — *Case F*. Skeleton of Heni, an official of the same date. — *Case H*. Coffins from Thebes. 1000-900 B.C. — *Case N*. Mummy of priestess and two others. — *Case Q*. Coffins and mum-my of Seshepeeshet (B.C. 650). — *Case R*. Coffin of Herua. — On the walls of the room are casts and paintings. In Case 55 are photographs of some of the royal mummies discovered in 1882 at Der el-Bâhri (see *Baedeker's Egypt*).

Second Egyptian Room. The *Standard Cases 8-FF* and the *Wall Cases 56-74* contain the continuation of the collection of mummies and mummy cases. *Case 64*. Coffin of the Roman period. — *Case 66*. Mummy, with portrait and Greek inscription. — *Cases 69-71*. Mummies of children with portraits. — *Case 72*. Part of outer coffin of a certain Cornelius (A.D. 110). — *Cases 73-74*. Interesting Coptic pall, with Christian symbols (ca. A.D. 400); portrait of a Greek girl from Memphis (1st cent. A.D.). The above-mentioned are the oldest known portraits on wood. — *Cases 77-80*. Canopic jars, in which were interred the embalmed intestines of the mummies. — *Cases 81-101*. Ushabti figures in limestone, marble, steatite, wood, etc., which were buried with the mummies to serve the deceased in the lower world. — *Case AA*. Mummy of Cleopatra Candace, from Thebes. — *Case BB*. Coffin of Tphous, daughter of Heraclius Soter. — *Cases CC, DD*. Coffins of Cleopatra and Soter. — On the S. side of the room are frames containing sepulchral tablets.

Third Egyptian Room. WALL CASES. *Cases 48-53*. Mummies of animals. *Cases 54-57*. Pillows or head-rests in wood and clay; chests to hold canopic jars (see p. 317). *Case 58*. Sepulchral boxes in the shape of temples. *Cases 59-80* contain an extensive collection of small figures of Egyptian gods in various materials, and of the animals sacred to them. Above Cases 65-75 are two ends of a shrine from a sacred boat, and figures of Osiris, Chnemu, and Anubis. — *Case 81*. Terracotta cones, bearing the names of kings and high officials (chiefly from Thebes). *Cases 82-85*. Sepulchral boxes and tablets (B.C. 1400-200). *Cases 86-91*. Mummies of animals; above Cases 82-90 are terracotta jars, each containing an ibis-mummy. — TABLE CASES. *Case A*. Writing-apparatus and materials; wax-tablets, ostraca or potsherds used for writing on. *Case B*. Armour and weapons: No. 5495. Bronze cylinder bearing the name of Pepi I. (B. C. 3233), perhaps the most ancient bronze article extant. In the lower part of the case are a rope-ladder, crocodile-skin armour, and flints. — *Case C*. Wig found in a temple at Thebes (about B.C. 1500); reed wig-box; toilet articles. In a small adjoining case are some beautiful specimens of Egyptian metal work (No. 2277a. Bronze statuette of Nectanebo II.; 6. Silver figure of Amen-Ra; 86a. Gold figure of Chonsu). *Stands D, H*. Models of obelisks. *Case E*. Food and fruits found in tombs. *Case F*. Tools and implements. *Case G*. Shoes and sandals. *Case I*. Models of boats used to transport dead bodies across the Nile. *Case K*. Spinning implements and weapons in wood: No. 20,648. Box of flint-headed arrows. Below are specimens of ancient Egyptian and Coptic linen. *Case L*. Sepulchral tablets in wood. — Beneath the windows is a long frame containing a facsimile of the Book of the Dead. Between the second and third windows hangs a specimen of coloured worsted work (400 A.D.). In a long case by the S. wall is a hieroglyphic papyrus of Queen Netchemet (21st Dyn.), with chapters and illustrations from the Book of the Dead.

Fourth Egyptian Room. WALL CASES. *Cases 100-105*. Sepulchral vessels, in alabaster, variegated marble, and stone. *Cases 106-113*. Egyptian earthenware (B. C. 1700-400). *Cases 114-119*. Egyptian porcelain. In the lower part of the cases, glazed tiles from Tell el-Yehûdîyeh. *Cases 120-133*. Earthenware (B.C. 600-300): No. 22,356 (Case 123), neck of a wine-jar, sealed with the seal of Aahmes II. (B.C. 572). *Cases 134-137*. Painted earthenware, etc., of the Greek period. *Case 138*. Bricks, stamped with the names of kings. *Cases 139-143*. Figures of gods, men, and animals; terracotta and porcelain lamps, etc. (Græco-Roman period). Series of sunk reliefs in sandstone from Ptolemaic temples. *Cases 144-150*. Domestic articles. *Cases 151-153*. Chairs and seats of various kinds. *Cases 154-162*. Portrait and votive figures of kings, priests, ladies, etc. *Cases 163-167*. Sepulchral vessels. — TABLE CASES. *Case A*. Musical instruments, spoons, ivory ornaments, glass bottles and vases. *Case B*. Beads in porcelain and glass; modern forgeries of Egyptian antiquities. Adjacent, under glass, head of a porphyry statue of Ramses II. from Thebes (ca. B.C. 1330). *Case C*. Bronzes, toys, draughtsmen, dice, etc. Below, models of a granary, houses, potter's yard, boat-cabin, etc. *Case D*. Scarabs and cylinders, used as amulets, in steatite, stone, carnelian, porcelain, etc. *Case E*. Toilet articles; vessels for holding cosmetics, perfumes, etc. *Case F*. Scarabs in stone and porcelain; rings. — *Case G*. °Throne, with gilded ornaments, from Thebes (Græco-Roman period); ivory and wooden draughtsmen; draught-board; blue porcelain beads. *Case H*. Scarabs in basalt, stone, porcelain, etc.; porcelain 'Utchats', or symbolic eyes of the sun; rings; beads; crowns. *Case I*. Jewellery. *Case K*. Miscellaneous porcelain articles. *Case L*. Domestic furniture. *Case M*. Antiquities of late periods: terracottas of Græco-Roman period; ivory ornaments, leaden weights, etc. Coptic crosses, bells, etc.; moulds, bronze stamps, silver and bronze articles. *Case N.* Gnostic gems, engraved with magic formulæ, gods, demons, animals, etc. — The casts on the N. and S. walls are of sculptures in the rock-temple of Bêt el-Walli in Nubia.

Babylonian and Assyrian Room. To the left of the entrance: 90,850. Boundary-stone (B.C. 1320); 92,888. Black basalt figure (headless) of King Gudea of Babylon (about B.C. 2500). Opposite (right; 91,025) is a cast of this king, with an archaic cuneiform inscription. — The *Wall Cases* on the left side of the room (Nos. 1-22) contain inscribed bricks, boundary-stones, landmarks, gate-sockets, and statues from Babylonia, Assyria, Elam, Van, and Persia (B.C. 4500-500). Those to the right (23-44) contain bronzes, glass vessels, alabaster figures, earthenware coffins, and utensils from Babylonia, Assyria, and Van (B.C. 2500 to 100 A.D.). — *Floor Cases* on the left: A, E. Babylonian inscribed tablets of baked clay (B.C. 2300-2000); C. Babylonian inscribed stones, tablets, and cones (B.C. 4500-2400); G. Clay cylinders with inscriptions (B.C. 625-100); I. Babylonian inscribed tablets with hymns, calendars, etc. — *Floor Cases* on the right: B. Sumerian tablets of the Kings of Ur (ca. B.C. 2400); D. Assyrian cylinders and seal-cylinders (B.C. 2500-350); F. Tablets from Tell el-Amarna (letters and despatches of Kings of Mesopotamia; ca. B.C. 1450); H. Assyrian cylinders (B.C. 705-620) and objects in gold and ivory, necklaces, etc., of the Assyrian, Persian, and Parthian periods; J. Seals, rings, and gems with busts and Pehlevi inscriptions (Sasanian period; 226-632 A.D.).

We have now reached the American Room of the Ethnographical Department (see p. 326). It is adjoined by a Staircase descending to the King's Library (p. 303). The SECOND NORTH GALLERY consists of a series of smaller rooms parallel with those just described. The first three (from this end) are occupied by collections illustrating **Religions of the East and Early Christianity**; the three following and the ante-chamber contain the **Semitic Antiquities.**

Religious Collections. Room I (V). EARLY CHRISTIANITY. Wall Cases 1-13. *Latin Christianity.* Bronze lamps; silver spoons, chalices, and patens; in Cases 7, 8. °Silver Treasure found at Rome in 1793, including large silver bridal-casket; ivory carvings; terracotta lamps. — Cases 14, 15. *Greek Church.* Small enamelled ikons; iron penitential crown. — Cases 16-20. *Abyssinian Church.* Silk altar-cloth; gilt and brass crosses; silver patens, chalices, lamps. — Cases 21-26. *Coptic Church.* °Cedar door-panels; woodcarvings; gravestone from Upper Egypt; limestone fragments with writings in Greek and Coptic. In the lower part of Cases 24-26 are so-called Gnostic articles, of uncertain date. — The Table Cases contain smaller objects, of great interest and beauty.

Room II (IV). EASTERN RELIGIONS. Wall Cases 1-24. *Brahmanism* or *Hindoo Mythology.* — Cases 23, 24. *Nepal.* — Cases 25-29. *Java.* — Case 27. *Ceylon.* — Case 30. *Bali* (Asiatic Archipelago). — On the lower shelves of Cases 30-46. *Jainism.* — Cases 32-34. *Judaism.* — Cases 35-37. *Islamism.* — Cases 38-40. *Shintoism.* In the glass-case in the centre of the room is the model of a Shinto shrine for transferring sacred objects from the temple on festivals. — Cases 41-43. *Taoism.* — Cases 44-46. *Confucianism.* — Cases 47, 48. *Shamanism.* — At the E. end of the room is an upright glass-case containing a model of a sacred car for Vishnu (?), from the Carnatic; two table-cases in the centre contain Indian grants of land inscribed on copper plates; and in an upright case at the W. end is a copy of the Adi Grant'h, or sacred book of the Sikhs, with the paraphernalia of the priest who reads it.

Room III. BUDDHISM. Wall Cases 1-18. *Japan.* — Cases 19-22. *Thibet.* — Cases 22-27. *China.* — Cases 28-45. *Burma and Siam.* — Cases 46-58. *India and Ceylon.* — Cases 59-76. *Ancient India.* Sculptures, partly under Classical influence. — At the E. end of the room, under glass, is a machine used in Japan to exorcise the 108 demons that tempt the human heart to sin; in the centre of the room are a Burmese and two Chinese bells, and table-cases with Indian antiquities; at the W. end of the room are two upright cases with relic boxes found in Buddhist topes. In Table Case D are some praying mills from Thibet.

Semitic Antiquities. This collection embraces inscriptions, carvings, gravestones, and other monuments from Phœnicia, Palestine, Carthage, and Cyprus, arranged chronologically under these headings in two rooms and the ante-room mentioned at p. 317. In Case 29, in the first room, is a cast of the *Moabite Stone* (ca. B. C. 900), which was discovered by the Rev. F. Klein in the land of Moab in 1868. The inscription gives an account of the wars of Mesha, King of Moab, with Omri, Ahab, and Ahaziah, Kings of Israel. Soon after Mr. Klein had obtained an impression of the stone the latter was broken into pieces by the Arabs; most of the fragments have, however, been recovered and are now in the Louvre. The sculptures and inscriptions in the ante-room are mainly from Idalium (B. C. 650-150).

The ante-room at the W. end of the Second North Gallery is at the head of the staircase descending to the Egyptian galleries (p. 316). We here enter the rooms to the left, which contain the *Collection of Vases and other objects of Hellenic art.

First Vase Room. The arrangement of the painted terracotta vases in the cases of this room affords an instructive survey of the development of the art of vase-painting. To the left: Cases 1-4. Prehistoric pottery from Greek islands, with the most primitive forms of geometrical decoration. Cases 6-13. Mycenæan period (from Rhodes, etc.), with spiral, waved, and conventionalised patterns. Cases 14-19. Vases from Rhodes and Athens with geometric patterns (Dipylon style). Cases 20-23. Late-Attic, early-Corinthian, and Bœotian vases; fragments from Caria. Cases 24-27. Black and red vases with stamped and incised decoration from Etruria ('bucchero') and Rhodes. Cases 28-32. Vases from Cyprus. To the right of the entrance: Cases 33, 34. Proto-Corinthian lecythi. Cases 35-37. Rhodian pottery. Cases 38-45. Corinthian pottery. Cases 46, 47, 50, 51. Vases from Naucratis. Cases 48, 49. Terracotta sarcophagus from Cameiros in Rhodes. Cases 52-58. Later Corinthian vases. Case 58. Pottery from Corfu. Cases 59-64. Pottery from Cyprus. — Table Case A contains archaic jewellery and weapons from Rhodes; archaic stone figures, etc. Above, Phœnician and Oriental pottery. Table Cases B and C contain antiquities from tombs at Curium and Enkomi, near Salamis in Cyprus. Table Case D. Antiquities from Amathus in Cyprus. Table Case E. Rhodian and Græco-Egyptian work in porcelain, glass, and ivory. Table Case F. Archaic Rhodian pottery. Pedestal Case 2 contains the Burgon lebes from Athens. Two other large cases here contain an important sarcophagus from Clazomenæ, painted within and without with designs representing the death of Dolon, etc. (ca. 550 B. C.).

Second Vase Room (6th cent. B. C.). The vases in this room, also of the archaic period, are almost entirely of Greek design and fabric, and are in most cases adorned with black figures on a red ground. Cases 10, 11, 22, 23 contain vases with black figures on a white ground. In Cases 48, 49, and Table Case C, is a series of vases signed by the potters or painters. In Case I is a series of Panathenaic prize amphoræ. The finest vases are in the middle of the room. The —

Third Vase Room (5th cent. B. C.) contains the red-figure vases of the best period, adorned with human and animal forms. To the right are several large vases adorned with groups of great beauty. Table Cases A, B, D, and E contain a number of kylikes with the artists' signatures. The lecythi in Table Case K come chiefly from Sicily; beautiful Athenian lecythi are shown in Table Case F.

Fourth Vase Room (4th-3rd cent. B. C.). Cases 1-13 contain vases dating from the close of the best period. In the other cases are vases of the period of the decline of the art (end of 4th and beginning of the 3rd cent. B.C.). In the centre of the room are several large craters and a series of ten Panathenaic amphoræ. In Table Case B are rhyta (drinking-vessels) ending in animals' heads. Table-case E. Fragments of moulded reliefs, etc. — The —

*Bronze Room contains Greek and Roman bronzes. Cabinet 1-9. Candelabra, lamps, tripods, etc. Cabinet 10, 11. Strigils and bathing-implements. Cabinet 12-19. Armour; tools. Cabinets 20-30. Vessels of various kinds; weapons; mirrors. Cabinets 31-43. Rich collection of bronze statuettes (chiefly Roman or Græco-Roman), arranged according to the different groups of gods and heroes: 31, 32. Venus and Cupid; 33-35. Jupiter, Pluto, Hecate, Neptune, Minerva, Mars, Vulcan, Apollo, and Diana; 36-39. Bacchus, Silenus, etc.; 40, 41. Hercules and Mercury; 42, 43. Heroes (Atys, Harpocrates). Cabinets 44-47 contain a selection of larger bronzes: *282. Venus putting on her sandals, from Patras; *1327. Youthful Bacchus; 987. Apollo with the chlamys; 909. Jupiter in a sitting posture, with sceptre and thunderbolt (from Hungary); busts of Lucius Verus and Claudius; 816. Boy playing at morra, from Foggia; 827. Hercules with the apples of the Hesperides, from Phœnicia; Statuette of Pomona. Cabinets 48, 49. Statuettes of Fortune, Victory, the Seasons, etc.; 50-53. Figures of Lares and actors, allegorical lamps, and other objects; 54, 55. Roman chair of state (bisellium) inlaid with silver, figure-head of an ancient galley from Actium, etc.; 56-60. Candelabra and lamps. — On a circular table in the centre of the room is (216) a *Head of a goddess, from Cappadocia. — Case B contains several fine works: *269. Marsyas, a Hellenistic modification of a celebrated work of Myron (copy in the Lateran); 284. Silenus carrying a basket; *848. Philosopher (?), found at Brindisi; *847. Head of a poet, from Constantinople (wrongly known as Homer or Sophocles); *267. Winged head (perhaps of Hypnos, the god of sleep), Perugia; 268. Head of an African, from Cyrene; 248. Bronze disk. Also two tablets with archaic inscriptions. — To the right of the entrance is a small case with *Bronzes from Paramythia in Epirus (4th cent. B.C.): Dione (?); one of the Dioscuri; Venus; Jupiter with his left hand outstretched; Poseidon with his right hand outstretched; Apollo bending his bow. — To the left of the entrance is a small case with select Greek bronzes mostly of the archaic period: 303. Mirror, with an alto-relief of Venus and Adonis at the foot (Locri); 192. Beautiful female figure with diamond eyes; 209. Apollo, perhaps a copy of the Apollo Philesios at Branchidæ (p. 307), a work by Canachos. — Table Case A contains the bronzes of Siris, two shoulder-pieces of Greek armour, from Magna Græcia; mirror-cases, richly ornamented; and other specimens of repoussé work. Above the case are some bronze cups from Galaxidi, the port of Delphi. — The following are exhibited singly in small cases: leg of a colossal figure. apparently a warrior, from Magna Græcia; Apollo, a life-sized figure (828). — The other table-cases contain weapons, knives, figures of animals, bracelets, brooches, fibulæ, armlets, pins, locks, keys, and other small bronze articles. The small pedestal-case 3, to the left of the exit, contains small Gallo-Roman bronzes (the best, 823. Hermes). Pedestal-case 4, to the right, contains some other select Greek bronzes of small size.

We next reach the —

Etruscan Saloon, which contains archaic bronces, works in terracotta, pottery, burial urns, cists, and reliefs. Most of the Etruscan sarcophagi and other heavy objects are now placed in the basement, see p. 307. Many of the finest bronzes are in the large detached Case B, including a '*Lebes' with an engraved frieze representing Hercules driving away the oxen of Cacus; at the back are chariot-races and mock combats; on the lid, Hercules carrying off Auge (or Pluto and Proserpine?); round the rim are four mounted Amazons (from Capua). Female figure in long drapery, from Sessa; *Amphora, the handles composed of men bending backwards, with sirens at their feet, from Vulci; Hercules taming the horses of Diomede, from Palestrina; Ceres sitting in a waggon, from Amelia, in Etruria. Noteworthy bronzes in other cases are a strigil (Case A), with a handle formed of a figure of Aphrodite; *Cist with engraved frieze, representing the sacrifice of captive Trojans at the funeral pile of Patroclus, and a Satyr and Mænad on the lid, from Palestrina (Case C); similar cists in Cases I, D, E, and H. To the left of the entrance is a large terracott sarcophagus from Cære, with lifesize male and female figures, modelled in the round. In a large case on the other side: Sarcophagus-cover, with the half-recumbent figure of a woman holding a mirror. The same case contains several cists, urns, and other figures. Table Case F contains ornamented bronze vase-handles. Case G contains antiquities from Cyprus. In Cases K and L are mirrors with incised designs. Case M. Inscriptions upon lead, etc.; inscribed sling-bolts, plummets, nails, etc. On the top of this case are some Roman steelyards. — On the W. side of the room is the entrance to the Coin and Medal Department. Standing cases near this door contain a very interesting and extensive collection of electrotypes of the finest Greek and Roman gold and silver coins, from 700 B.C. down to the Christian era, arranged chronologically and geographically. — The S. section of the Etruscan saloon, containing Roman terracotta reliefs, etc., may be regarded as an annex of the Terracotta Room (see below). Table Case N contains objects in bone, ivory (tessaræ or theatre-tickets), and jet; Case O, examples of ancient glazed ware. In the S.E. corner, adjoining the entrance to the Gold Ornament Room, is a mummy from the Fayûm, with a portrait on panel (comp. p. 190).

The numbering of the Wall Cases around the room begins in this corner. Nos. 1-18. Terracotta slabs; 19-25. Pottery and bronzes (temporarily here); 26-27. Terracottas from Lanuvium (Città Lavinia); 47-63. Terracotta chests and sarcophagi; 65-70. Pottery (in Case 66, two burial urns in the form of a primitive hut); 71-75. Archaic paintings on terracotta panels, probably from a tomb; 76-80. Archaic Etruscan candelabra; 82-87. Bronzes of the primitive period; 88-97. Early Etruscan bronze weapons (in Case 93 an Etruscan helmet, dedicated by Hiero I. of Syracuse to Zeus at Olympia, a relic from the battle of Cumæ, fought in B.C. 474); 99-102 and 121-125. Etruscan black pottery ('bucchero nero'); 103-107. Bronze bowls; 108-115. Bronze statuettes; 126-135. Antiquities from the Polledrara Tomb, near Vulci (ca. B.C. 610).

The *Room of Gold Ornaments and Gems (open till 6 p.m. daily, April to Aug.; in other months closed earlier thrice a week) lies to the S. of the Etruscan Saloon. The collection of medals, gold ornaments, cameos, and gems preserved here is very complete and extremely valuable, being probably the finest in Europe. It is also most admirably arranged. — In the passage leading to the room are specimens of silversmith's work, mostly of the Roman period, including a fine *Service (ministerium) of 36 pieces, found at Chaourse (France) and probably dating from the 3rd cent. A.D. Here also are collections of seal-rings and of gold ornaments from the Oxus (4th cent. B.C.). On the walls hang some mural paintings, six of which are from the tombs of the Nasones, near Rome.

The centre of the Gem Room itself is occupied by a large case (X), with a fine display of cameos (W. side) and intaglios (E. side). The table-case to the N. contains archaic gold ornaments from the Greek islands. On the top stands the famous °°Portland Vase, which was deposited in the British Museum in 1810. In 1845 it was broken to pieces by a madman named Lloyd, but it was afterwards skilfully reconstructed. The vase, which is about 1 ft. in height, is of dark-blue glass, adorned with beautifully cut reliefs in opaque white glass, and was found in a tomb at Rome in the early part of the 17th century. It came for a time into the possession of Prince Barberini, whence it is also called the 'Barberini Vase', and is now the property of the Duke of Portland. The reliefs probably represent the meeting of Peleus and Thetis, and Thetis consenting to be the wife of Peleus. The bottom, which has been detached, is adorned with a bust of Paris. — The table-cases to the S. contain mediæval goldsmith's work and enamels; personal relics (the 'Juxon medal'; Gibbon's snuff-box and watch; Napoleon's snuff-box, etc.); Anglo-Saxon, Teutonic, and later jewellery (on S. slope). Above is placed an *Enamelled Gold Cup or Hanap, formerly in the possession of Kings of France and England and purchased in 1892 for 8000l. It was probably made about 1350. — The table-cases to the W. contain archaic Greek gems and Etruscan scarabs (outer slope) and later Greek and Roman gems (inner slope). In the three windows are frames with casts of gems made in glass and

by the window-wall are three cases with drinking-vessels of various materials and periods, a Roman silver service, small silver statuettes, long
brooch-pins, ivory boxes with low reliefs, and a very valuable series of
Gold Ornaments from a burial-place in Cyprus, some of which are in
the Mycenæan style. — The cases along the N. wall and part of the
E. wall contain Etruscan, Greek (of the best period and later), and Roman
gold ornaments; and above are frescoes from Rome, Pompeii, and Her-
culaneum. — The other cases by the E. wall contain ancient Barbaric,
British, and Irish gold ornaments. Above are silver ornaments from
Algeria, Norway, and Abyssinia. — In the wall-cases to the S. are gold
ornaments from India and Central America, and an extensive collection
of finger-rings. Above are silver ornaments from England, Bolivia, and
Russia, and gold ornaments from Ashantee. In this room are also gold
ornaments and ivory reliefs from Enkomi in Cyprus.

The next room contains the **Terracotta Antiquities.** (The numbering of the cases begins at the end farthest from the Etruscan
Room.) To the right are the Greek and Græco-Phœnician Terracottas, to the left are the Græco-Roman Terracottas. The finest
figures from Tanagra, Eretria, and Asia Minor are in Cases 16-26
(to the right).

Table Case D contains terracotta bowls; on the top, a large *Askos*, or
vase shaped like a wine-skin. Table Case C contains lamps. Table Case
B. Grotesque figures and masks; terracotta moulds. Table Case A. Terracotta jointed dolls; on the top, a sepulchral urn.

The **Central Saloon,** at the top of the Great Staircase, contains
the **Prehistoric Antiquities.**

The numbering of the cases begins in the inner (N.) part of the saloon,
to the left. The wall-cases and table-cases in this portion contain illustrations of the Stone and Bronze Ages in Great Britain and the Continent,
the exhibits being arranged geographically. Cases 21-30 contain the *Greenwell
Collection of Antiquities from British Barrows*. — The wall-cases in the
outer (S.) part of the room illustrate the Palæolithic Stone Age in Great
Britain and the Continent (Cases 51-60), the stone age in Africa (61-62),
late Celtic antiquities (65-74), the stone and bronze ages in Japan (77-78),
and India (79-93). In the table-cases are flint arrow-heads and bone implements; and articles from Swiss lake-dwellings. — Near the top of the
Great Staircase is an interesting clock, constructed in 1589 by Isaac Hab-
recht, the maker of the famous clock at Strassburg.

This room also contains (temporarily) part of the collection of **Anglo-
Roman Antiquities** (43-410 A.D.), brought from the room now occupied
by the Waddesdon Bequest (p. 324). In the middle of the room are a
colossal bronze bust of Hadrian from the Thames valley, and an interesting bronze helmet. The table-cases contain brooches, trinkets, moulds
for coins, and implements of various kinds. This collection also includes
numerous smaller objects found in graves; vessels of glass, pewter, and
metal; bronze figures, among which are three of Mars, several good statuettes found in the valley of the Thames, a fine figure of an archer, and
a gilt figure of Hercules; silver votive ornaments; sculptures, including
a figure of Luna, the finest piece of Roman sculpture found in Britain.

The room occupied by the **Anglo-Saxon Antiquities** is entered
from the S.E. corner of the Prehistoric Saloon.

In the wall-cases are the antiquities found in England, consisting of
cinerary urns, swords and knives (some inscribed), a runic cross, silver
ornaments, bronze articles, etc. In Cases 23-26 is a collection of foreign
Teutonic antiquities of similar date, the most noticeable of which are
the contents of a Livonian grave. In the centre-cases are ornaments,
weapons, and matrices of seals. Near the exit, under glass, is a casket
carved out of whale's bone.

Beyond the Anglo - Saxon Room is the *Waddesdon Bequest Room, formerly the Anglo-Roman Room (see p. 323). This contains a fine collection of works of art of the cinquecento period, bequeathed to the Museum in 1899 by *Baron Ferdinand Rothschild* and valued at 300,000*l.* The objects include plate, enamels, jewellery, boxwood carvings, bronzes, arms and armour, majolica, and glass. Comp. Catalogue by *C. H. Read* (6*d.*).

Case **A** (to the left of the entrance): *1. Bronze medallions from the handles of a litter, with heads of Bacchantes (Greek; 3rd cent. B.C.); 3, 4. Bronze door-knockers (Ital.; 16th cent.); *5. Iron shield with reliefs, damascened with gold, by *Giorgio Ghisi* of Mantua (1554); 19. Reliquary of champlevé enamel (Limoges; ca. 1285). — Case **B**: 7, 8. Arquebuses, with highly ornamented stocks and barrels (French; 16th cent.); 12. Rapier, with damascened hilt (Ital.; 16th cent.); 24. Enamel portrait of Catherine of Lorraine, by *Limousin* (Limoges; late 16th cent.); other enamels. — Case **C**: 30, 31. Enamel dishes by *Martial Courtois* (Limoges; ca. 1580); 33. Similar dish by *Jean Courtois* (Limoges; ca. 1560); 48. Similar dish by *Susanne Court* (Limoges; late 16th cent.); *216 Miniature busts of a man and woman in walnut wood (German; ca. 1590). — Case **D** (in the opposite corner of the room): Enamels, including (395) an interesting portrait of Diana of Poitiers (Limoges; ca. 1550). — Case **E**: 53. Glass goblet, with enamels (Arab work, mounting French; 14th cent.); 54. Mosque lamp (Arab work; 14th cent): other specimens of glass; 60, 63, 64. Italian majolica. — Case **F**: *87. Silver book-cover (German; ca. 1500); 97. Set of twelve silver tazze, embossed and chased (Ger.; ca. 1580); 104. Standing cup and cover of silver gilt (Ger.; ca. 1600); 103, 108. Similar cups. — Case **G** (central row, opposite door): 100. Standing cup (Venetian?); 101, 102, 105, 107, 109. Standing cups; 112. Ostrich-egg cup (Ger.; 1554); *118. Standing cup, with cameos (French; ca. 1550); 121. Onyx cup, with miner as support (Ger.; ca. 1650). — Case **H**: 149. Pendent jewel of gold, with figures of Charity, Faith, and Fortitude (Ger.; 16th cent.); 151. Jewel, with Cleopatra (16th cent.); 156. Jewel in the form of a hippocamp (Ger.; 16th cent.); *167. So-called 'Lyte Jewel', containing a portrait of James I. (by Hilliard) and given by this king to Thomas Lyte (Engl.; 17th cent.); 171. Hat-jewel of Don John of Austria (Ital.; 16th cent.); 177. Pendant (Ger.; 16th cent.). — Case **J**: 66. Gold cup adorned with pearls (Ger.; ca. 1600); *68. Roman vase of mottled agate, in Renaissance mount; 77. Rock-crystal cup, in gold mount (Ger.; 16th cent.); 79. Rock-crystal vase with cartouche containing name of Emp. Akbar of India; 81. Jade cup (Ger.; 16th cent.); 195-200. Gold rings; 201-208. Knives, forks, and spoons. — Case **K**: 231. Devotional carving attached to a ring (carving probably English; ca. 1340); *232. Miniature altar, carved in boxwood (Flemish; 1511); 233. Miniature tabernacle in boxwood, elaborately carved, once perhaps the property of Emp. Charles V. (Flem.; ca. 1520); 242. Medallion of John of Leyden (1510-36) in boxwood (Ger.; 16th cent.). — Case **L**: 131-146. Standing cups and other plate; 217-221. Caskets in ebony and ivory; 234. Retable of black wood, with pearwood panels (Ger.; 16th cent.). — Case **M** (at the E. end of the room): 16. Damascened cabinet (Milanese; 16th cent.); 61, 62. Vases of Urbino ware (16th cent.); 65. Amphitrite, terracotta figure (Ital.; 16th cent.); 259. Wooden statuette of St. George (Ger.; 15th cent.); 260. Statuette of St. Margaret (Flem.; 16th cent.).

The Mediæval Room, parallel with the preceding and entered from the Prehistoric Saloon, contains the mediæval objects, excepting the glass and pottery.

Mediæval Room. Cases 1-9. Arms and armour; 10-20. Oriental, Venetian, and other metal work; 21-26. Astrolabes and clocks, including a timepiece in the form of a ship, probably made for the Emperor Rudolph II. (1576-1612); 27. Chalices; 28-31. Limoges and other enamels; 32. Old English embroideries; 33-34. Paintings from St. Stephen's Chapel at Westminster

(1356); 35-43. Ivory carvings; below, old English work in alabaster; 44-49. Caskets carved in wood and ivory. On the wall, Franconian wood-carving (16th cent.). Cases 50-52. Brasses and other sepulchral objects. Table Case A contains historical and personal relics: Burns's punch-bowl, the 'Glenlyon brooch', enamelled badges, and Russian cups. Table Case B: Domestic objects, English fruit trenchers (16th cent.), keys, calendars. Table Cases C and D: Matrices of English and Foreign Seals. Table Case E: Enamels, including specimens of English, Italian, German, and Limoges workmanship. Table Case F: Carvings in ivory, rock-crystal, mother-of-pearl, and other materials. Table Case G: Watches and dials. Table Case H: Chamberlains' keys; portraits on pressed horn and tortoise-shell; collection of papal rings. Table Case K: Watches, medallions, and dials. Table Case L: Objects used in games; curious set of chessmen of the 13th cent., from the island of Lewis in the Hebrides, made of walrus tusk.

The **Asiatic Saloon** (arrangement unfinished). Cases 1-9. Japanese and Corean terracottas and porcelain; 11-15. Japanese bronzes; 16-18. Corean pottery; 19-45. Japanese pottery; 46-60. Japanese porcelain; 61. Siamese and Burmese pottery; 62-64. Chinese pottery; 65-99. Chinese porcelain. — Cases 100-113. Chinese jade and metal figures, wearing apparel, figures, and implements; 114-118. Indian and Persian works of art, including a handsome inlaid cabinet. — The detached cases contain Japanese and Chinese porcelain and Japanese antiquities, sword-guards, and ivory carvings (small).

From the Asiatic Saloon we turn to the right into the new rooms of the WHITE BUILDING (see p. 300), which contains the collections of *Glass and Pottery* and also the **Department of Prints and Drawings**. The latter contains an unrivalled collection of original drawings, engravings, and etchings. Hitherto the use of this collection has been practically restricted to students, who obtain tickets on written application to the Principal Librarian (see p. 327), but the spacious new rooms now built for it include a fine Exhibition Gallery (see below), the contents of which are changed every three years. Foreigners and travellers may obtain access to the *Students' Rooms* on giving in their names. Comp. the Handbook to the 'Department', by Louis Fagan (3s. 6d.).

We first enter the —

English Ceramic Ante-Room, containing pottery and porcelain chiefly bought from Mr. Willett or given by Sir A. W. Franks. To the right on entering: Wall-tiles from Malvern (1457-58). Cases 1-8 (left). Early English Pottery (11-15th cent.); 9-20. Glazed Ware of the 16-18th cent.; 21-26. English Pottery, chiefly from Staffordshire; 27-32. Pavement Tiles (13-16th cent.); 33. Fulham Stoneware (17th cent.); 35-46. English Porcelain (that in the last four cases inferior); 47-50. Liverpool Tiles, transfer-printed, by Sadler. The upright case contains a collection of so-called 'Chelsea Toys'.

Glass and Ceramic Gallery, including the valuable Slade Collection of Glass. Cases 1, 2. English Delft, chiefly made at Lambeth in the 17-18th cent.; 3-7. Dutch and German Delft; 8. Italian Pottery; 9-23. Italian Majolica; 24-26. Spanish Pottery; 27-31. Rhodian and Damascus Ware; 32, 33. Persian Pottery; 34, 35. French Pottery; 37-45. Antique Glass, chiefly of the Roman period; 46-54. Venetian Glass; 55-58. German Glass; 59. Chinese Glass; 60-61. Oriental Glass; 62. French Glass; 63. English Glass; 64-66. Wedgwood and other Staffordshire Wares and Bristol Delft. The table-cases contain Wedgwood medallions; antique, German, Dutch, and Flemish glass; English engraved glass; Oriental pottery, etc. Above the cases are 13 busts, modelled in clay by Roubiliac, of Milton, Cromwell, Sir Isaac Newton, Sir Hans Sloane, etc.

The **Print and Drawing Exhibition Gallery** is at present mainly occupied by a fine series of *Drawings and Etchings by Rembrandt*, supplemented by characteristic examples of contemporary etchers. The etchings are grouped in three chronological divisions: 1628-39, 1639-49, and 1650-61. In the first of these Rembrandt depended chiefly on the acid (pure etching); in the second, he used the dry-point method more and more; and in the third he gave up the acid almost wholly for dry-point. — In the centre of the room is (No. 141) a cartoon by *Michael Angelo*, belonging to the Malcolm Collection.

We now return to the Asiatic Saloon and begin our inspection of the extensive and interesting **Ethnographical Collection**, which is arranged topographically and occupies the whole of the EAST GALLERY. The Asiatic Section is first entered; then follow the Oceanic, African, and American Sections, each containing a great variety of objects illustrating the habits, dress, warfare, handicrafts, etc., of the less civilised inhabitants of the different quarters of the globe.

At the top of the N.E. Staircase are Mexican sculptures from Tabasco and sculptures from Honduras. On the staircase-walls are casts of heads from monuments at Thebes.

On the N. side of the spacious entrance-hall, facing the entrance door, is a passage leading to the ***Reading Room**, constructed in 1854-57 at a cost of 150,000*l*; it is open from 9 a.m. to 7 or 8 p.m. (closed on the first four days of March and September, as well as on Good Friday and Christmas Day). This imposing circular hall, covered by a large dome of glass and iron (140 ft. in diameter, or 2 ft. larger than the dome of St. Peter's at Rome, and 106 ft. high), has ample accommodation for 458 readers or writers. Around the superintendent, who occupies a raised seat in the centre of the room, are circular cases containing the *General Catalogue* for the use of the readers (now printed and nearly complete in 800 vols.) and various special catalogues and indexes, one of the most generally useful being *Mr. G. K. Fortescue's* 'Subject Index of Modern Books.' On the top of these cases lie printed forms to be filled up with the name and 'press-mark' (*i. e.* reference, indicated in the catalogue by letters and numerals, to its position in the book cases) of the work required, and the number of the seat chosen by the applicant at one of the tables, which radiate from the centre of the room like the spokes of a wheel. The form when filled up is put into a little basket, placed for this purpose on the counter. One of the attendants will then procure the book required, and send it to the reader's seat. About 20,000 vols. of the books in most frequent request, such as dictionaries, encyclopædias, histories, periodicals, etc., are kept in the reading-room itself, and may be used without any application to the library-officials; while coloured plans, showing the positions of the various categories of these books, are distributed throughout the room. Every reader is provided with a chair, a folding desk, a small hinged shelf for books, pens, and ink, a blotting-pad, and a peg for his hat. The reader will probably find the arrangements of the British Museum Reading Room superior to those of most public libraries, while

the obliging civility of the attendants, and the freedom from
obtrusive supervision and restrictions are most grateful. The
electric light has been introduced into the Reading Room and
Galleries. — In the year 1858, the first after the opening of the
New Reading Room, the number of readers amounted to 190,400,
who consulted in all 877,897 books or an average of 3000 a day.
In 1899 there were 188,554 readers, or 620 per day. A *Description
of the Reading Room* may be had from an attendant (1d.).

Persons desirous of using the Reading Room must send a written
application to the Principal Librarian, specifying their names, rank
or profession, purpose, and address, and enclosing a recommendation
from some well-known householder in London. The applicant must
not be under 21 years of age. The permission, which is granted
usually for six months at a time, is not transferable and is subject
to withdrawal. The Reading Room tickets entitle to the use of the
new *Newspaper Room* (comp. p. 303). Tickets for visitors to the
Reading Room are obtained on the right side of the entrance-hall.
Visitors are not allowed to walk through the Reading Room, but may
view it from the doorway. — Besides the main reading-room there is
a special room for students in the Department of MSS. and another
for students of Oriental books and MSS. — The **Libraries** contain a
collection of books and manuscripts, rivalled in extent by the
National Library of Paris alone. The number of printed volumes
is about 2,000,000, and it increases at the rate of about 50,000
volumes per annum. The books occupy about 40 miles of shelving.

25. St. James's Palace and Park. Buckingham Palace.

The site of **St. James's Palace** (Pl. R, 22; *IV*), an irregular brick
building at the S. end of St. James's Street, was originally occupied
by a hospital for lepers, founded before 1190 and dedicated to St.
James the Less. In 1532 the building came into the possession of
Henry VIII., who erected in its place a royal palace, said to have been
designed by *Holbein*. Here Queen Mary died in 1558. Charles I. slept
here the night before his execution, and walked across St. James's
Park to Whitehall next morning (1649). The palace was considerably
extended by Charles I., and, after Whitehall was burned down in
1691, it became the chief residence of the English kings from
William III. to George IV. In 1809 a serious fire completely
destroyed the eastern wing, so that with the exception of the interesting old brick gateway towards St. James's Street, the Chapel
Royal, and the old Presence Chamber there are few remains of the
ancient palace of the Tudors. The state-rooms are sumptuously
fitted up, and contain a number of portraits and other works of art.
The initials HA above the chimney-piece in the Presence Chamber
are a reminiscence of Henry VIII. and Anne Boleyn. It is difficult
to obtain permission to inspect the interior. The guard is changed

every day at 10.45 a.m., when the fine bands of the Grenadier, Coldstream, or Scots Guards play for ¹/₄ hr. in Friary Court, the open court facing Marlborough House. The Duke of York, son of the Prince of Wales, occupies a portion of the palace to the W. of the gateway, known as *York House*. Though St. James's Palace is no longer the residence of the sovereign, the British court is still officially known as the 'Court of St. James's'. See 'Memorials of St. James's Palace', by Edgar Sheppard.

On the N. side, entered from Colour Court, is the *Chapel Royal*, in which the Queen and some of the highest nobility have seats. Divine service is celebrated on Sundays at 10 a.m., 12 noon, and 5.30 p.m. A limited number of strangers are admitted to the two latter services by tickets obtained from the Lord Chamberlain; for the service at 10 no ticket is required. At the service on Epiphany (Jan. 6th) an offering of gold, myrrh, and frankincense is still made. — The marriage of Queen Victoria with Prince Albert, and those of some of their daughters, were celebrated in the Chapel Royal.

Down to the death of Prince Albert in 1861, the Queen's *Levées* and *Drawing Rooms* were always held in St. James's Palace. Since then, however, the drawing-rooms have taken place at Buckingham Palace, but the levées are still held here. A levée differs from a drawing-room in this respect, that, at the former, gentlemen only are presented to the sovereign, while at the latter it is almost entirely ladies who are introduced. Richly dressed ladies; gentlemen, magnificent in gold-laced uniforms; lackeys in gorgeous liveries, knee-breeches, silk stockings, and powdered hair, and bearing enormous bouquets; well-fed coachmen with carefully curled wigs and three-cornered hats; splendid carriages and horses, which dash along through the densely packed masses of spectators; and a mounted band of the Life Guards, playing in front of the palace: — such, so far as can be seen by the spectators who crowd the adjoining streets, windows, and balconies, are the chief ingredients in the august ceremony of a 'Queen's Drawing Room'. A notice of the drawing-room, with the names of the ladies presented, appears next day in the newspapers.

In the life of a young English lady of the higher ranks her presentation at Court is an epoch of no little importance, for after attending her first drawing-room she is emancipated from the dulness of domesticity and the thraldom of the schoolroom; — she is, in fact, 'out', and now enters on the round of balls, concerts, and other gaieties, which often play so large a part in her life.

On the W. side of St. James's Palace lies *Clarence House*, the residence, since 1874, of the Duke of Edinburgh, who succeeded his uncle as Duke of Saxe-Coburg-Gotha in 1893. — *Marlborough House*, on the E. side of the palace, see p. 281.

St. James's Park (Pl. R, 21, 22, 25, 26; *IV*), which lies to the S. of St. James's Palace, was formerly a marshy meadow, belonging to St. James's Hospital for Lepers. Henry VIII., on the conversion of the hospital into a palace, caused the marsh to be drained, surrounded with a wall, and transformed into a deer-park and riding-path. Charles II. extended the park by 36 acres, and had it laid out in pleasure-grounds by *Le Nôtre*, the celebrated French landscape-gardener. Its walks, etc., were all constructed

primly and neatly in straight lines, and the strip of water received
the appropriate name of 'the canal'. The present form of St. James's
Park was imparted to it in 1827-29, during the reign of George IV.,
by *Nash*, the architect (see below). Its beautiful clumps of trees, its
winding expanse of water, and the charming views it affords of the
stately buildings around it, combine to make it the most attractive
of the London parks. In 1857 the bottom of the lake was levelled
so as to give it a uniform depth of 3-4 ft. The suspension-bridge,
across the centre of it, forms the most direct communication for pedestrians between St. James's Street and Westminster Abbey.

The broad avenue, planted with rows of handsome trees, on the
N. side of the park, is called the *Mall*, from the game of 'paille
maille' once played here (comp. p. 279). At the E. extremity, near
Carlton House Terrace, is the flight of steps mentioned at p. 280,
leading to the *York Column* (p. 280). — *Birdcage Walk*, on the S.
side of the park, is so named from the aviary maintained here as
early as the time of the Stuarts. To the right, just inside Storey's
Gate (see below), is a handsome Renaissance structure by Basil
Slade, accommodating *Her Majesty's Office of Works* and the *Institution of Mechanical Engineers* (1899).

At the E. end of Birdcage Walk is *Storey's Gate*, leading to *Great
George Street* and *Westminster*. In *Petty France*, now *York Street*, to
the S. of Birdcage Walk, Milton once had a house. — A battalion
of the Royal Foot Guards is quartered in *Wellington Barracks*, built
in 1834, on the S. side of Birdcage Walk; the interior of the small
chapel is very tasteful (open Tues., Thurs., & Frid., 11-4). The
India and *Foreign Offices* (p. 237), the *Treasury* (p. 236), the *Horse
Guards* (p. 236), and the *Admiralty* (p. 236) lie on the E. side of
St. James's Park. In an open space called the *Parade*, between the
park and the Admiralty (new buildings, see p. 236), are placed a
Turkish cannon captured by the English at Alexandria, and a large
mortar, used by Marshal Soult at the siege of Cadiz in 1812, and
abandoned there by the French. The carriage of the mortar is in the
form of a dragon, and was made at Woolwich. Annually, on the
Queen's birthday (May 24th) or the day officially celebrated as
such, the pretty military ceremony known as 'trooping the colour'
is performed here by the Guards. An invitation to one of the
above-named public offices should be obtained if possible.

Buckingham Palace (Pl. R, 21; *IV*), the Queen's residence,
rises at the W. end of St. James's Park. The present palace occupies
the site of *Buckingham House*, erected by John Sheffield, Duke of
Buckingham, in 1703, which was purchased by George III. in
1761, and occasionally occupied by him. His successor, George IV.,
caused it to be remodelled by Nash in 1825, but it remained empty
until its occupation in 1837 by Queen Victoria, whose town residence it has since continued to be. The eastern and principal
façade towards St. James's Park, 360 ft. in length, was added by

Blore in 1846; and the large ball-room and other apartments were subsequently constructed. The palace now forms a large quadrangle. The rooms occupied by Her Majesty are on the N. side.

A portico, borne by marble columns, leads out of the large court into the rooms of state. We first enter the *Sculpture Gallery*, which is adorned with busts and statues of members of the royal family and eminent statesmen. Beyond it, with a kind of semicircular apse towards the garden, is the *Library*, where deputations, to whom the Queen grants an audience, wait until they are admitted to the royal presence. The ceiling of the magnificent *Marble Staircase*, to the left of the vestibule, is embellished with frescoes by Townsend, representing Morning, Noon, Evening, and Night.

On the first floor are the following rooms : *Green Drawing Room*, 50 ft. long and 33 ft. high, in the middle of the E. side ; *Throne Room*, 66 ft. in length, sumptuously fitted up with red striped satin and gilding, and having a marble frieze running round the vaulted and richly decorated ceiling, with reliefs representing the Wars of the Roses, executed by Baily from designs by Stothard ; *Grand Saloon* ; *State Ball Room*, on the S. side of the palace, 110 ft. long and 60 ft. broad ; lastly the *Picture Gallery*, 180 ft. in length, containing a choice, though not very extensive, collection of paintings.

Among the most valuable works are the following: — *Rembrandt*: ***'Noli me tangere' (1638), °Ship-builder and his wife (1633; cost 5000*l.*), *Adoration of the Magi (1657), *Burgomaster Pancras and his wife (1645), °Portraits of himself, of a lady (1641), and of an old man. *Rubens*: °Pythagoras (fruit by *Snyders*), *The Falconer, *Landscape, *Assumption (sketch). *Van Dyck*: *Madonna and Child with St. Catharine, Charles I. on horseback, and others. *Titian*, *Summer-storm in the Venetian Alps (ca. 1534). Fine examples of *Frans Hals*, *Cuyp*, *A.* and *I. van Ostade*, *Jan Steen*, *Metsu*, *Hobbema*, *Ruysdael*, *Terburg* (including his masterpiece, **Lady writing a letter), *Paul Potter*, *A. van de Velde*, *Teniers*, *Maes*, *Dou*, and *Claude Lorrain*. — In the dining-room are portraits of English sovereigns by *Gainsborough* and others. In an adjoining room is *Sir Frederick Leighton's* Procession in Florence with the Madonna of Cimabue.

Permission to visit the Picture Gallery may occasionally (very rarely) be obtained (during the Queen's absence only) from the Lord Chamberlain on written application.

The Gardens at the back of the Palace contain a summer-house decorated with eight frescoes from Milton's 'Comus', by Landseer, Stanfield, Maclise, Eastlake, Dyce, Leslie, Uwins, and Ross.

The ROYAL MEWS (so called from the 'mews' or coops in which the royal falcons were once kept), or stables and coach-houses (for 40 equipages), entered from Queen's Row, to the S. of the palace, are shown on application to the Master of the Horse. The magnificent state-carriage, designed by Sir W. Chambers in 1762, and painted by Cipriani (cost 7660*l.*), is kept here.

To the N., between Buckingham Palace and Piccadilly, lies the GREEN PARK, which is 60 acres in extent. Between this and the Queen's private gardens is *Constitution Hill*, leading direct to *Hyde Park Corner* (p. 332). Three attempts on the life of the Queen have been made in this road. The *Green Park Arch*, which was originally erected in 1846 immediately opposite Hyde Park Corner, was removed to its present site at the W. end of Constitution Hill in 1883. The *Equestrian Statue of Wellington*, by *Wyatt*, with which it was disfigured, has been re-erected at Aldershot Camp.

26. Hyde Park. Kensington Gardens. Kensington Palace. Holland House.

The district between Bond Street (p. 290) and *Park Lane* (Pl. R, 18, 19; *IV*), a street about ³/₄ M. in length, connecting the W. end of Piccadilly with Oxford Street, is known as MAYFAIR, and is one of the most fashionable in London. At the S. end of Park Lane (W. corner) is *Gloucester House*, the residence of the Duke of Cambridge; and a little farther to the N. is a handsome *Fountain* by Thornycroft, adorned with figures of Tragedy, Comedy, Poetry, Shakspeare, Chaucer, and Milton, and surmounted by a statue of Fame. Lord Beaconsfield died at 19 Curzon Street, to the N.E., in April, 1881. The well-known *Curzon Street Chapel* was pulled down in 1899 and a mansion for the Duke of Marlborough is now being built on its site.

Park Lane forms the eastern boundary of **Hyde Park** (Pl. R, 14, etc.), which extends thence towards the W. as far as Kensington Gardens, and covers an area of 390 acres (with Kensington Gardens, 630 acres). Before the dissolution of the religious houses the site of the park belonged to the old manor of Hyde, one of the possessions of Westminster Abbey. The ground was laid out as a park and enclosed under Henry VIII. In the reign of Elizabeth stags and deer were still hunted in it, while under Charles II. it was devoted to horse-races. The latter monarch also laid out the 'Ring', a kind of corso, about 350 yds. in length, round an enclosed space, which soon became a most fashionable drive. The fair frequenters of the Ring often appeared in masks, and, under this disguise, used so much freedom, that in 1695 an order was issued denying admission to all whose features were thus concealed.

At a later period the park was neglected, and was frequently the scene of duels, one of the most famous being that between Lord Mohun and the Duke of Hamilton in 1712, when both the principals lost their lives. Under Queen Anne a large portion of the park was taken to enlarge Kensington Gardens; and, finally, Queen Caroline, wife of George II., caused the *Serpentine*, a sheet of artificial water, to be formed. The Serpentine was originally fed by the *Westbourne*, a small stream coming from *Bayswater*, to the N.; but it is now supplied from the Thames.

Hyde Park is one of the most frequented and lively scenes in London. It is surrounded by a handsome and lofty iron railing, and provided with nine carriage-entrances, besides a great number of gates for pedestrians, all of which are shut at midnight. On the S.

side are *Kensington Gate* and *Queen's Gate*, both in Kensington
Gore, near Kensington Palace; *Prince's Gate* and *Albert Gate* in
Knightsbridge; and *Hyde Park Corner* at the W. end of Piccadilly.
On the E. side are *Stanhope Gate* and *Grosvenor Gate*, both in Park
Lane. On the N. side are *Cumberland Gate*, at the W. end of Oxford Street, and *Victoria Gate*, Bayswater. The entrances most used
are Hyde Park Corner at the S.E., and Cumberland Gate at the
N.E. angle. At the latter rises the MARBLE ARCH, a triumphal
arch in the style of the Arch of Constantine, originally erected by
George IV. at the entrance of Buckingham Palace at a cost of
80,000*l.* In 1850, on the completion of the E. façade (p. 330),
it was removed from the palace, and in the following year was re-
erected in its present position. The reliefs on the S. are by *Baily*,
those on the N. by *Westmacott*; the elegant bronze gates well deserve inspection. — The handsome gateway at HYDE PARK CORNER,
with three passages, was built in 1828 from designs by *Burton*.
The reliefs are copies of the Elgin marbles (p. 309). Immediately
to the E. is *Apsley House* (p. 341), the residence of the Duke of
Wellington. The house next it is that of *Baron Rothschild*. Opposite Apsley House is a bronze *Equestrian Statue of Wellington*, by
Boehm. At the corners of the red granite pedestal are figures of a
grenadier, a Highlander, a Welsh fusilier, and an Inniskillen dra-
goon, all also by Boehm.

To the N. of Hyde Park Corner, within the park, rises another
monument to the 'Iron Duke', consisting of the colossal figure known
as the *Statue of Achilles*, which, as the inscription informs us, was
erected in 1822, with money subscribed by English ladies, in
honour of 'Arthur, Duke of Wellington, and his brave companions
in arms'. The statue, by *Westmacott*, is cast from the metal of
12 French cannon, captured in France and Spain, and at Waterloo,
and is a copy of one of the Dioscuri on the Monte Cavallo at Rome.
Opposite, in Hamilton Gardens, is a statue of *Lord Byron*, erected
in 1879. No carts or waggons are allowed to enter Hyde Park, and
cabs are admitted only to one roadway across the park near Kensington Gardens. The finest portion of the park, irrespectively of the
magnificent groups of trees and expanses of grass for which English parks stand pre-eminent, is that near the Serpentine, where,
in spring and summer, during the 'Season', the fashionable world
rides, drives, or walks. The favourite hour for carriages is 5-7
p. m., and the fashionable drive is the broad, southern avenue,
which leads from Hyde Park Corner to the W., past the Albert
Gate. Equestrians, on the other hand, appear, chiefly in the
morning, but also in the afternoon, in *Rotten Row*, a track
exclusively reserved for riders, running parallel to the drive on
the N., and extending along the S. side of the Serpentine from
Hyde Park Corner to Kensington Gate, a distance of about $1^1/_2$ M.
The scene in this part of Hyde Park, on fine afternoons, is most

interesting and imposing. In the Drive are seen unbroken files of
elegant equipages and high-bred horses in handsome trappings,
moving continually to and fro, presided over by sleek coachmen and
powdered lackeys, and occupied by some of the most beautiful and exquisitely dressed women in the world. In the Row are
numerous riders, who parade their spirited and glossy steeds before
the admiring crowd sitting or walking at the sides. It has lately
become 'the thing' to walk by the Row on Sundays, and on a fine
day the 'Church Parade', between morning-service and luncheon
(*i.e.* about 1-2 p.m.), is one of the best displays of dress and
fashion in London. Cycling in Hyde Park has also become a fashionable amusement, but all the roads (except that from Victoria
Gate to Alexandra Gate) are closed to cyclists between 3 and 7 p.m.
— The drive on the N. side of the Serpentine is called the *Ladies'
Mile*. The Coaching and Four-in-hand Clubs meet here during the
season, as many as thirty or forty drags sometimes assembling. The
flower-beds adjoining Park Lane and to the W. of Hyde Park Corner
are exceedingly brilliant and the show of rhododendrons in June is
deservedly famous. There is a *Band Stand* near the N.E. angle of
the Serpentine.

A refreshing contrast to the fashionable show is afforded by a
scene of a very unsophisticated character, which takes place in summer on the Serpentine before 8 a.m. and after 8 p.m. At these
times, when a flag is hoisted, a crowd of men and boys, most of
them in very homely attire, are to be seen undressing and plunging
into the water, where their lusty shouts and hearty laughter
testify to their enjoyment. After the lapse of about an hour the
flag is lowered, as an indication that the bathing time is over, and
in quarter of an hour every trace of the lively scene has disappeared.
— Pleasure-boats may be hired on the Serpentine (1*s.*-1*s.* 6*d.* per
hr.); boat-houses on the N. side.

In winter the Serpentine, when frozen over, is much frequented by skaters. To provide against accidents, the *Royal Humane
Society*, mentioned at p. 187, has a 'receiving-house' here, where
attendants and life-saving apparatus are kept in readiness for any
emergency. The bottom of the Serpentine was cleaned and levelled
in 1870; the depth in the centre varies from $5^{1}/_{2}$ to 14 ft. E. of
the bridge and from $4^{1}/_{2}$ to 5 ft. W. of the bridge. It was in the
Serpentine that Harriet Westbrook, first wife of the poet Shelley,
drowned herself in 1816. At the point where the Serpentine enters
Kensington Gardens it is crossed by a five-arched bridge, constructed
by *Sir John Rennie* in 1826. The view from this bridge has 'an
extraordinary nobleness' (Henry James). Near the S. end of the
bridge is a small *Restaurant* (tea, ices, light refreshments).

On the W. side of the park is a powder-magazine. Reviews,
both of regular troops and volunteers, sometimes take place in
Hyde Park. The Park is also a favourite rendezvous of organised

crowds, holding 'demonstrations' in favour or disfavour of some political idea or measure. The Reform Riot of 1866, when quarter of a mile of the park-railings was torn up and 250 policemen were seriously injured, is perhaps the most historic of such gatherings. The gravel expanse adjoining the Marble Arch is also the favourite haunt of Sunday lecturers of all kinds. Near the Victoria Gate (Pl. R, 11) is a curious little *Cemetery for Dogs*, containing about eighty graves.

To the W. of Hyde Park, and separated from it by a sunk-fence, lie **Kensington Gardens** (Pl. R, 10, etc.), with their pleasant walks and expanses of turf (carriages not admitted). They owe their present appearance mainly to Queen Caroline, wife of George II., who planted the noble avenues of stately trees, designed the *Broad Walk* on the W. side, 50 ft. in width, which leads from Bayswater to Kensington Gore, and formed the *Basin* or *Round Pond*. Many of the majestic old trees have, unfortunately, had to be cut down. Near the Serpentine are the flower-gardens; at the N. extremity is a sitting figure of Dr. Jenner (d. 1823), by *Marshall*. The *Albert Memorial* (p. 343) rises on the S. side of the gardens. The handsome wrought-iron gates opposite the Memorial were those of the S. Transept of the Exhibition Buildings of 1851, which stood a little to the E., on the ground between Prince's Gate and the Serpentine, and was afterwards removed and re-erected as the Crystal Palace at Sydenham (see p. 396). In the Broad Walk, with its back to Kensington Palace, is a highly idealized *Statue of Queen Victoria*, in white marble, by the Princess Louise, erected in 1893.

*Kensington Palace (Pl. R, 6), on the W. side of Kensington Gardens, incorporates part of Nottingham House, which was purchased from the second Earl of Nottingham by King William III. in 1689. The present unassuming brick edifice was erected (or altered) partly by *Sir Christopher Wren* for William and Mary in 1689-91 (S. front and N.W. wing), and partly by *William Kent* for George I. in 1721 (N.E. wing). This palace was the scene of the death of William III. and his consort, Mary, of Queen Anne and her husband, Prince George of Denmark, and of George II. (1760), after which it ceased to be the sovereign's residence. Queen Victoria was born (May 24th, 1819) and brought up here, and here she received the news of the death of William IV. and her own accession. Princess May, Duchess of York, also was born here. Various suites of apartments are occupied by aristocratic pensioners of the crown; the S.W. wing has since 1873 been occupied by the Princess Louise and her husband the Marquis of Lorne (now Duke of Argyll). — The STATE ROOMS, on the second floor, have recently undergone an extensive and much needed restoration, and were thrown open to the public in 1899.

They contain a number of paintings (chiefly portraits), of more

historical than artistic interest, and a few pieces of furniture; the
panelling, cornices, and other embellishments, especially in Wren's
portion of the palace, deserve inspection. — Admission, see p. 108.
The entrance is at the N.W. angle of the palace, and is approached
from the Broad Walk (p. 334) by a path passing in front of the
Orangery (p. 336). Illustrated Guide, by *Ernest Law*, 1s.

From the entrance the *Queen's Staircase*, or *Denmark Staircase*, with
good oak wainscoting, ascends to QUEEN MARY'S GALLERY, a handsome
oak-panelled apartment, 88 ft. in length. The first chimney-piece, on the
right, was designed by Wren. Among the portraits here are those of
Queen Mary, George I., William III. as Prince of Orange, Peter the Great,
and William III., all by *Kneller*. — In the QUEEN'S CLOSET are old paintings of London and a fine Tudor chimney-piece, bearing the initial of
Queen Elizabeth, brought hither from Westminster Palace. — QUEEN ANNE'S
PRIVATE DINING ROOM. Over the fireplace: 40. Installation of Knights of
the Garter by Queen Anne; 43. *Jan Wyck*, Duke of Marlborough. — QUEEN
MARY'S PRIVY CHAMBER. On the carved oak cornice appear the united
initials of William and Mary. Paintings: to the right, 50. *Th. Hudson*,
Matthew Prior; *Kneller*, 57. Robert Boyle, 58. John Locke, 59. Sir Isaac
Newton; over the fireplace; 52. *B. Luti*, James Stuart, the Old Pretender.
— The next room, QUEEN CAROLINE'S DRAWING ROOM, is the first of the
suite designed by Kent. The ceiling-painting, Minerva attended by History
and the Arts, is also by Kent. Paintings (several with most elaborate
and handsome frames): to the right, 60. *Drouais*, Mme. de Pompadour.;
61. *Unknown Artist*, Mlle. de Clermont; 62. *Callet*, Louis XVI.; 63. *Rigaud*,
Louis XV.; 68. *Graff* (?), Queen of Prussia; 70. *Ch. Le Brun*, Louis XIV.
on horseback; 71. *A. Pesne*, Frederick the Great. — The CUPOLA ROOM,
or CUBE ROOM, 37 ft. square and 34 1/2 ft. high, the most gorgeous room in
the palace, is elaborately decorated with white marble, painting, and gilding. The slightly domed ceiling is painted in imitation of a cassetted
dome; at the apex is a star of the Order of the Garter. In six white
marble niches in the walls are gilded statues of Minerva, Apollo, Ceres,
Venus, Bacchus, and Mercury. Above the elaborate chimney-piece is a
marble relief, by *Rysbrack*, of a Roman marriage. In the centre of the
room is an ancient musical clock. Queen Victoria was baptized in this
room on June 24th, 1819. — The KING'S DRAWING ROOM has a ceiling-
painting (by Kent) of Jupiter and Semele, best seen from the window
opposite the door. Paintings: above the door, 80. *Benj. West*, Death of
General Wolfe (duplicate of the original in Grosvenor House). Then a
large number of royal portraits by the same artist. Over the fire-place,
89. *Beechey*, George III. reviewing the 10th Dragoons, the Prince of Wales
on the right and the Duke of York on the left. The *View from the
windows of this room over Kensington Gardens is very beautiful; not a
roof or sign of the city is to be seen. — KING'S PRIVY CHAMBER, to the
left of the drawing-room: Portraits of the time of George III. To the
right: *Hoppner*, 90. Fifth Duke of Bedford, 91. Earl of Moira; 92. *Phillips*,
Lord Hutchinson; 96. *Opie*, Mary Granville, Mrs. Delaney; 95. *Joseph*, Spencer Perceval; 99. *Gainsborough*, Bishop Hurd; 94. *Hickel*, R. B. Sheridan;
101. *Robineau*, Abel, the musician; 102. *Angelica Kauffmann*, Duchess of
Brunswick, sister of George III. In the centre of this room is the chair
used by Queen Victoria at her coronation. — On the other side of the
King's Drawing Room is the NURSERY, used by the Queen when a little
girl. Her doll's-house and other toys are placed here. In this and the
following rooms is a collection of prints and engravings, illustrative of
Queen Victoria's life and reign. Princess May was born here (May 26th, 1867).
— The adjoining ANTE-ROOM is hung with engraved portraits of the
Queen's prime ministers. — QUEEN VICTORIA'S BEDROOM. Here Her Majesty
was sleeping when roused early in the morning of June 30th, 1837, to
meet the Lord Chamberlain and the Archbishop of Canterbury, who brought
news of her accession. She passed through the anteroom, whence a staircase descends to the Drawing Room below (see below). — Beyond this

room opens the KING's GALLERY, on the S. façade of the palace, a fine room 96 ft. in length, built by Wren. Over the chimney-piece is a *Wind-Dial*, with a pointer formerly connected with a vane on the roof. The centre of the dial is occupied by a map of N.W. Europe. Above is a carved wooden pediment, with a fresco-painting of the Madonna and Child. The ceiling is painted with allegorical subjects by *Kent*. The naval paintings and portraits of admirals were brought hither from Hampton Court. — At the end of the Gallery we reach the KING's GRAND STAIRCASE, designed by Wren, and decorated later by Kent. On the walls are depicted various persons of George I.'s court, standing behind a balustrade. The ceiling is painted with heads of musicians, etc. — The PRESENCE CHAMBER has an elaborate carving ascribed to *Grinling Gibbons* over the chimney-piece. The pictures hung here are copies of paintings of various ceremonial occurrences in the Queen's reign. The key-plans beside them indicate the various personages. — We now re-enter Queen Caroline's Drawing Room (p. 335), whence we may retrace our steps to the entrance.

Visitors may usually, on application to one of the attendants, have an opportunity of inspecting the apartments on the first floor of Kent's building, which include the Room in which Queen Victoria was born (May 24th, 1818), the Drawing Room in which she received the intimation of her accession to the throne (p. 335), and the Hall in which she held her first council.

On the way out towards Kensington Gardens, we visit the *Orangery*, a masterpiece of garden-architecture, built by Wren for Queen Anne in 1704. The elegant building, 170 ft. in length and 32 ft. in width, with a gracefully proportioned pavilion at each end, stands upon a stone platform. The interior, panelled and enriched with Corinthian pilasters with rich capitals, and other carvings, is at present empty.

The space to the W. of Kensington Palace is now occupied by rows of fashionable residences. Thackeray died in 1863 at No. 2 *Palace Green*, the second house to the left in Kensington Palace Gardens (Pl. R, 6) as we enter from Kensington High Street. Among his previous London residences were 88 St. James's Street, 13 (now 16) Young Street, Kensington (where 'Vanity Fair', 'Pendennis', and 'Esmond' were written), and 36 Onslow Square (re-numbered). *Holly Lodge*, the home of Lord Macaulay, where he died in 1859, is in Campden Hill, a lane leading off Campden Hill Road, a little farther to the W. The next house is *Argyll Lodge*, long the London residence of the Duke of Argyll. Sir Isaac Newton died in 1727 at Campden Hill (Pl. R, 2), in what was afterwards named *Bullingham House* and recently formed part of *Kensington College*.

Farther to the W., on a hill lying between Uxbridge Road, on the N., and Kensington Road on the S., stands **Holland House** (Pl. R, 1), built in the Tudor style by *John Thorpe*, for Sir Walter Cope, in 1607. The building soon passed into the hands of Henry Rich, Earl of Holland (in Lincolnshire), son-in-law of Sir Walter Cope, and afterwards, on the execution of Lord Holland for treason, came into the possession of Fairfax and Lambert, the Parliamentary generals. In 1665, however, it was restored to Lady Holland. In 1762 it was sold by Lord Kensington, cousin of the last representative of the Hollands, who had inherited the estates, to Henry Fox, afterwards Baron Holland, and father of the celebrated Charles James Fox. Holland House now belongs to Lord Ilchester, a descendant of a brother of Henry Fox.

Since the time of Charles I. Holland House has frequently

been associated with eminent personages. Fairfax, Cromwell, and Ireton held their deliberations in its chambers; William Penn, who was in great favour with Charles II., was daily assailed here by a host of petitioners; and William III. and his consort Mary lived in the house for a short period. Joseph Addison, who had married the widow of Edward, third Earl of Holland and Warwick, occupied the house from 1716 until his death there in 1719. During the first half of the 19th century. Holland House was the rallying point of Whig political and literary notabilities of all kinds, such as Moore, Rogers, and Macaulay, who enjoyed here the hospitality of the distinguished third Baron Holland. The house contains a good collection of historical relics and paintings, including several portraits by *G. F. Watts.* Compare Princess Lichtenstein's 'Holland House'.

No. 2, Holland Park Road, to the S. of Holland House, is **Leighton House** (Pl. R, 1), formerly the residence of *Lord Leighton, P. R. A.* (d. 1896). The house, which was presented to the nation by the sisters of Lord Leighton, contains an exquisite *°Arab Hall,* approached by a 'twilight passage' and sumptuously decorated with priceless Persian and Saracenic tiles, Moorish carvings, etc. The other rooms are hung with a large collection of drawings, sketches, and studies by Lord Leighton, and photographs and other reproductions of his works. In the large studio is an important oil-painting by Leighton (212. Clytemnæstra in Argos awaiting the return of Agamemnon), and on a screen at the top of the staircase is an admirable half-length figure of a man (No. 131). Admission daily, 2-5.30; free on Tues. & Sat., on other days by ticket (1s.) obtained at No. 1 Laura Place, close to the house.

Along the N. side of Hyde Park and Kensington Gardens runs UxBRIDGE ROAD, leading to Bayswater and Notting Hill. The rows of houses on this road, overlooking the park, contain some of the largest and most fashionable residences in London. Near the Marble Arch (Pl. R, 15) is the *Cemetery of St. George's,* Hanover Square (now a public playground; open 10-4, on Sun. and holidays 2-4), containing the grave of Laurence Sterne (d. 1768; near the middle of the wall on the W. side). Sterne's body, however, is believed to have been exhumed two days after burial and sold to the professor of anatomy at Cambridge. Mrs. Radcliffe, writer of the 'Mysteries of Udolpho', is said to be buried below the chapel. The old mortuary chapel has been replaced since 1893 by the tasteful *Chapel of the Ascension,* designed by H. P. Horne, and elaborately decorated in the interior with paintings of Scriptural scenes and figures by Frederic Shields. The paintings are executed in oil upon canvas, which is then fixed upon slabs of Belgian slate rivetted to the walls, leaving an air-chamber behind. The chapel was founded by Mrs. Russell Gurney (d. 1897), and is to be open all day for private prayer and meditation.

27. Private Mansions around Hyde Park and St. James's.

Grosvenor House. Stafford House. Bridgewater House. Lansdowne House. Apsley House. Dorchester House. Lady Brassey Museum. Devonshire House.

The English aristocracy, many of the members of which are enormously wealthy, resides in the country during the greater part of the year; but it is usual for the principal families to have a mansion in London, which they occupy during the season, or at other times when required. Most of these mansions are in the vicinity of Hyde Park, and many of them are worth visiting, not only on account of the sumptuous manner in which they are fitted up, but also for the sake of the treasures of art which they contain.

Permission to visit these private residences, for which application must be made to the owners, is often difficult to procure, and can in some cases be had only by special introduction. Some of them are occasionally thrown open for a few Sunday afternoons in connection with the National Sunday League. During winter it is customary to pack away the works of art in order to protect them against the prejudicial influence of the atmosphere.

Grosvenor House (Pl. R, 18; *I*), Upper Grosvenor Street, is the property of the *Duke of Westminster*, and is sometimes shown to visitors in summer, on written application to the Duke's secretary. The pictures are arranged in the private rooms on the groundfloor.

ROOM I (*Dining Room*). No. 1. *Guido Reni*, John the Baptist; 2. *Murillo*, Landscape with Jacob and Laban; 3. *L. Carracci*, Holy Family; 4. *Hogarth*, Distressed poet; 5. *Teniers*, Interior; 6, 13, 16, 15, 25. *Claude Lorrain*, Landscapes; 11. *Rubens*, Landscape; 12. *Cuyp*, Sheep (early work); 23. *Van Dyck*, Portrait of himself; 8. *Van Huysum*, Fruit and flowers; *21. *Claude*, Sermon on the Mount; *Rembrandt*, 14. Portrait of a man with a hawk, *19, *20. Portraits of Nicolas Burghem and his wife (dated 1647); 22. *Adriaen van de Velde*, Hut with cattle and figures (1658); 17. *Wouverman*, Horse-fair; 24. *Cuyp*, Landscape; *18. *Rembrandt*, Portrait of a lady with a fan; *27. *Berchem*, Large landscape with peasants dancing (1656); 28. *Rembrandt*, Portrait of himself; 29. *Claude*, Landscape; 30. *Rubens*, Conversion of St. Paul (sketch); 31. *Sustermans*, Portrait.

ROOM II (*Saloon*). To the left: **33. *Rembrandt*, The Salutation.
'A delicate and elevated expression is here united with beautiful effects of light. This little gem is distinguished for its marvellous blending of warm and cold tints'. — *Vosmaer*.

Above, 32. *Cuyp*, River-scene; *34. *G. Dou*, Mother nursing her child; **35. *Paul Potter*, Landscape with cattle (1647); 38. *N. Poussin*, Children playing; 37. *Velazquez*, Portrait of himself; **39. *Hobbema*, Wooded landscape, with figures by *Lingelbach*; 43. *Andrea del Sarto*, Portrait; 45. *Paolo Veronese*, Annunciation; *46. *Murillo*, John the Baptist; 49. *Rubens*, Dismissal of Hagar; 52. *Canaletto*, Canal Grande in Venice; 59. *Parmigiano*, Study for the altar-piece in the National Gallery (No. 33; p. 202)!; 57. *Dughet (Gaspar Poussin)*, Tivoli; 60. *N. Poussin*, Holy Family and angels; 62. *Giulio Romano*, St. Luke painting the Virgin; 64. *Domenichino*, St. Agnes; *65. *Murillo*, Infant Christ asleep; 68. *Garofalo* (?), Holy Family.

ROOM III (*Drawing Room*). No. 80. *Van Dyck*, Virgin and Child with St. Catharine; *79. *Reynolds*, Portrait of Mrs. Siddons as the Tragic Muse (1784); 77. *Andrea del Sarto*, Holy Family; 72. *Teniers*, Château of the painter with a portrait of himself; *Gainsborough*, *70. The 'Blue Boy', a full-length portrait of Master Buthall, 74. Coast-scene.

ROOM IV (*Gallery*). No. *83. *Rembrandt* (or *A. Brouwer*?), Landscape with figures; 85. *Turner*, Conway Castle; 88. *Raphael* (?), Holy Family; *89. *Velazquez*, Don Balthazar Carlos, Prince of Asturias (sketch); 90. *Titian*, Landscape; *93. *Rubens*, Portrait of himself and his first wife, Elisabeth Brandt, as Pausias and Glycera (the flowers by *Jan Brueghel*); 91. *Titian* (?), Woman taken in adultery; 95. *School of Bellini*, Circumcision; 96. *Titian*, Tribute Money (replica); 99. *Giovanni Bellini* (? more probably an early imitator of *Lorenzo Lotto*), Virgin and Child, with saints; 101. *P. de Koninck*, Landscape.

ROOM V (*Rubens Room*). To the left: *102. Israelites gathering manna, *103. Abraham and Melchizedek, *104. The four Evangelists, three of a series of nine pictures painted by *Rubens* in Spain in the year 1629.

vi. Corridor: 105. *Rubens*, David and Abigail; Landscapes by *Turner*, *Bonington*, *Jules Breton*, *Cotman*, *Gude*, *Calcott*, and *Crome*; sixteen pictures of Oriental subjects by *Goodall*.

vii. Ante-Drawing-Room. No. 126. *Fra Bartolommeo* (?), Holy Family; 131. *Domenichino*, Landscape; 122. *Millais*, Duchess of Westminster; 127. *Gainsborough*, The cottage-door; 130. *J. and A. Both*, Landscape.

The *Vestibule* contains a °Terracotta Bust by *Alessandro Vittoria*.

Stafford House, or **Sutherland House** (Pl. R, 22; *IV*), in St. James's Park, between St. James's Palace and the Green Park, the residence of the *Duke of Sutherland*, is perhaps the finest private mansion in London, and contains a good collection of paintings, which is shown to the public on certain fixed days in spring and summer. Application for admission should be made to the Duke's secretary.

The magnificent Entrance Hall is adorned with well-executed copies of large works by *Paolo Veronese*.

Visitors then pass through the Banqueting Hall and enter the fine Picture Gallery, on the ceiling of which is a painting by *Guercino*. Our enumeration begins to the right: 73. *Zurbaran*, Madonna with the Holy Child and John the Baptist (1653); 68. *Annibale Carracci*, Flight into Egypt; °62. *Murillo*, Return of the Prodigal Son; 61. Ascribed to *Raphael*, Christ bearing the Cross (a Florentine picture of little value); 59. *Parmigiano*, Betrothal of St. Catharine; 58, 54. *Zurbaran*, 88. Cyril and Martin; 57. *Dujardin*, David with the head of Goliath; °53. *Murillo*, Abraham entertaining the three angels; 51. After *Dürer*, Death of the Virgin; 48. *Paul Delaroche*, Lord Strafford, on his way to the scaffold, receiving the blessing of Archbishop Laud (1838). — 47. Ascribed to *Correggio*, Mules and mule-drivers.

This work is described as having been painted by Correggio in his youth, and is said to have served as a tavern-sign on the Via Flaminia near Rome. In reality it is an unimportant work of a much later period.

Farther on: 42. *Tintoretto*, Venetian senator; 36. *Rubens*, Coronation of Maria de' Medici, design in grisaille upon wood for the painting in the Louvre; 33. *Honthorst*, Christ before Caiaphas; 30. *Murillo*, Portrait; °27. *Van Dyck*, Portrait of the Earl of Arundel; 25. *L. Carracci*, Holy Family; 23. *Parmigiano*, Portrait; 22. *Guercino*, Pope Gregory and Ignatius Loyola; °19. *Moroni*, Portrait; 18. Ascribed to *Titian*, Mars, Venus, and Cupid; 15. *Zurbaran*, St. Andrew; 5. *A. Cano*, The Ancient of Days.

A small room, opening off the gallery, contains cabinet-pieces by *Watteau*, *Le Nain*, and *Rottenhammer*.

The pictures in the private apartments, which are not exhibited, include examples of *Velazquez*, *Murillo*, *Veronese*, *Tintoretto*, *Correggio*, *Bordone*, *Pordenone*, *Rubens*, *Van Dyck*, several *Dutch Masters*, *Reynolds*, *Hogarth*, *Lely*, *Landseer*, and others.

Bridgewater House (Pl. R, 22; *IV*), in Cleveland Row, by the Green Park, to the S. of Piccadilly, is the mansion of the *Earl of Ellesmere*, and possesses one of the finest picture-galleries in London. The most important works are hung in the private rooms. Admission to the large picture-hall is granted for Wednesdays and Saturdays, on application supported by some person of influence.

On the walls of the Staircase: *A. Carracci*, Copy of Correggio's 'Il Giorno' at Parma; *N. Poussin*, The Seven Sacraments, a celebrated series of paintings; *Veit*, Mary at the Sepulchre; *Pannini*, Piazza di San Pietro at Rome.

Gallery. To the right of the entrance: °*Guido Reni*, Assumption of the Virgin, a large altar-piece, nobly conceived and carefully finished. To the left: 156. *G. Coques*, Portrait; 225. *Stoop*, Boy with grey horse; 142. *Brekelenkamp*, Saying grace; 31. Ascribed to *Sebastian del Piombo*, Entombment; 125. *Bassano*, Last Judgment; °263. *P. van Slingeland*, The kitchen (1685); 243. *N. Berchem*, River-scene; 217. *Metsu*, Fish-woman; *126. *A. van Ostade*, Man with wine-glass (1677); 137. *Ary de Voys*, Young man in a library; 209. *N. Berchem*, Landscape; *17. *Titian*, Diana and her nymphs interrupted at the bath by the approach of Actæon (painted in 1559); 196. *Rembrandt*, Portrait; 247. *J. van Ruysdael*, Bank of a river; *166. *A. van Ostade*, Skittle-players (1676); 258. *W. van de Velde*, Rough sea (1656); 212. *N. Berchem*, Landscape; *196. *Ruysdael*, Bridge; *65. *Paris Bordone*, Portrait of a man (high up); *281. *J. Wynants*, Landscape, with figures by *A. van de Velde* (1669). — **19. *Titian*, 'The Venus of the shell.'

'Venus Anadyomene rising — new-born but full-grown — from the sea, and wringing her hair ... Titian never gave more perfect rounding with so little shadow'. — *Crowe and Cavalcaselle*. (This work, painted some time after 1520, has unfortunately suffered from attempts at restoration.)

135. *Van der Heyde*, Drawbridge; 222. *A. Brouwer*, Peasants at the fireside; 171. *Van Huysum*, Flowers (1723-24); 177. *A. van Ostade*, Portrait; 242. *Metsu*, Lady caressing her lap-dog. — *18. *Titian*, Diana and Callisto. 'Titian was too much of a philosopher and naturalist to wander into haze or supernatural halo in a scene altogether of earth'. — *C. & C.*

284. *A. van der Neer*, Moonlight-scene; 233. *Netscher*, Lady washing her hands; 154. *A. von Ostade*, Backgammon players; 130. *Teniers*, The alchemist; *141. *W. van de Velde*, Naval piece (an early work).

On the opposite wall: *153. *Jan Steen*, The school-room, a large canvas; 190. *Wynants*, Landscape; 182. *Isaac van Ostade*, Village-street; *168. *Rembrandt*, Mother with sons praying; *280. *Paul Potter*, Cows; 111. *Netscher*, A fashionable lady; *183. *Isaac van Ostade*, Village-street; *191. *J. Steen*, The fishmonger; 267. *Cuyp*, Ruin; *90. *Lorenzo Lotto*, Madonna with saints, an early work (hung high); 109. *Salomon Koning*, The philosopher's study; 214. *W. Mieris*, The violinist; 243. *G. Dou*, The violinist (1637); 165. *Wynants*, Landscape; *129. *A. Brouwer*, Landscape, surrounded with a border of fruit and flowers by *D. Seghers*; *194. *Metsu*, The stirrup-cup (an early work); 257. *Ruysdael*, Landscape; *201. *Pynacker*, Alpine scene with waterfall; *195. *Hondecoeter*, The raven detected, illustrating the well-known fable; 257. *Hobbema*, Landscape; *174. *Rubens*, Free copy with altered arrangement of Raphael's frescoes in the Villa Farnesina at Rome, the landscapes by some other painter.

The following masterpieces on the groundfloor are not shown to visitors. In LADY ELLESMERE'S SITTING ROOM: **Raphael*, Madonna and Child, the 'Bridgewater Madonna' (copy in the National Gallery); *35. *Raphael*, Holy Family ('La Vierge au palmier'); **29. *Titian*, Holy Family (an early work, ascribed to *Palma Vecchio*); *14. *Luini*, Head of a girl (assigned to *Leonardo da Vinci*); **77. *Titian*, The three periods of life (copies in the Villa Borghese and Palazzo Doria at Rome). The DRAWING ROOM and LORD ELLESMERE'S SITTING ROOM contain a number of admirable works of the Dutch school, including the fine *Girl at work, by *N. Maes*.

Lansdowne House (Pl. R, 22; *I*), Berkeley Square, the property of the *Marquis of Lansdowne*, contains a valuable picture-gallery and a collection of Roman sculptures. The ancient sculptures form probably the most extensive private collection out of Rome. Most of them were discovered at Hadrian's Villa by Gavin Hamilton. It was while living here, as librarian to Lord Shelburne, that Priestley discovered oxygen.

SCULPTURES (catalogue provided). In the Dining Room: Woman asleep, by *Canova*, his last work; 31. Bacchus; 35. Mercury. — Ball Room: So-called Antinous of the Belvedere; 63. Marcus Aurelius as Mars; 61. Youthful Hercules; 89. Discobolus of Myron, wrongly restored as Diomede with the palladium; 87. Juno enthroned; 85. So-called Jason untying his sandals; 83. Wounded Amazon. Numerous reliefs, funereal columns, etc. Child soliciting alms, by *Rauch*.

PICTURES (catalogue provided). No. 65. *Tidemand* and *Gude*, Norwegian landscape; 75. *Gonzales Coques*, Portraits of an architect and his wife;

76. *Sir Thomas Lawrence*, Portrait of Lord Lansdowne; *54. *Reynolds*, Lady Ilchester; 7. *Master of Treviso* (assigned to *Giorgione*), Concert; 61, 146. *Both*, Landscapes; *48. *Van Dyck*, Henrietta Maria, wife of Charles I.; 38. *Luini*, St. Barbara; *15. *B. van der Helst*, Portrait of a lady (1648); 51. *Guercino*, The Prodigal Son; *13. *Murillo*, The Conception; *9. *Cuyp*, Portrait of a boy; 88. *C. Dolci*, Madonna and Child; *137. *Sebastian del Piombo*, Portrait of Federigo da Bozzolo; 36. *Gainsborough*, William, first Marquis of Lansdowne (1737-1805).

Apsley House (Pl. R, 18; *IV*), Hyde Park Corner, the residence of the *Duke of Wellington*, was built in 1785 for Earl Bathurst, Lord High Chancellor of England, and in 1820 purchased by Government and presented to the Duke of Wellington, as part of the nation's reward for his distinguished services. A few years later the mansion was enlarged, and the external brick facing replaced by stone. The site is one of the best in London, and the interior is very expensively fitted up. It contains a picture-gallery, numerous portraits and statues, and a great many gifts from royal donors. Admission only through personal introduction to the Duke.

Among the finest works of art in Apsley House are the following, most of which are in the picture-gallery (on the first floor). *Velazquez*, *Water-seller of Seville, Two Boys, *Quevedo, poet and satirist, Portrait of Pope Innocent X. (repetition of the painting in the Doria Gallery at Rome); *°*Correggio*, Christ in Gethsemane (copy in the National Gallery); *Parmigiano*, Betrothal of St. Catharine; *Marcello Venusti*, Annunciation; fine examples of *De Hooghe*, *Breughel*, and *Teniers*; *Watteau*, Court-festival; *Claude*, Palaces at sunset; *Rubens*, Holy Family; *Spagnoletto*, Allegorical picture; *Wouverman*, *Starting for the chase, *Returning from the chase; *Murillo*, St. Catharine; several large and well-executed copies of *Raphael* (Bearing of the Cross, etc.); *P. *Potter*, Deer in a wood; *A. *Cuyp*, Cavalier with grey horse; *A. van Ostade*, Peasants gaming; *Jan Steen*, *Family scene, *The smokers, Peasants at a wedding-feast; *Van der Heyde*, Canal in a town; *N. Maes*, The milk-seller, The listener; *Lucas van Leyden*, Supper; *J. Victor*, Horses feeding; portraits of Napoleon, by *David* and others; *Allan*, Battle of Waterloo; *Wilkie*, Chelsea Pensioners reading the news of Waterloo; *Burnet*, Greenwich Pensioners celebrating the anniversary of Trafalgar.

On the staircase is *Canova's* colossal Statue of Napoleon I.

Dorchester House (Pl. R, 18; *IV*), the residence of *Capt. Holford*, a handsome edifice in Park Lane, contains a good collection of pictures, shown in spring and summer to visitors provided with an introduction. Among the finest works of art are —

Velazquez, *Portrait of the Duke Olivarez, and, opposite, *Portrait of Philip IV., both lifesize, early works in excellent condition; *Paul Potter*, Goats at pasture (dated 1647; *A. van Ostade*, Interior (1661); *Cornelis de Vos*, Portrait of a lady; *Ruysdael*, Landscape with view of Haarlem; *Lorenzo Lotto*, Portrait; *Gaud. Ferrari*, Mary, Joseph, and a cardinal; *Titian* (?), Portrait; *Andrea del Sarto*, Holy Family; *Cuyp*, View of Dordrecht; *Tintoretto*, Portrait; *Luini* (?), Flora; *Fra Angelico* (? or *Pesellino*), Six saints; *Bronzino*, Leonora, consort of Cosimo I.; *Tintoretto* (ascribed to *Bassano*), Conversation-piece of three figures; *Rembrandt*, Portrait of Martin Looten (dated 1632); *Hobbema*, Margin of a forest (1663); *Paolo Veronese* (school-piece), Portrait of the Queen of Cyprus; *Titian*, Holy Family with John the Baptist; *Dosso*, Portrait of the Duke of Ferrara; *Van Dyck*, Portrait of the Marchesa Balbi.

The **Lady Brassey Museum**, at 24 Park Lane, contains a valuable and interesting ethnological collection, antiquities, coral, stuffed birds, jewellery, and curiosities of various kinds, collected by the late Lady Brassey during her voyages in the 'Sunbeam' yacht to almost every part of the world. Admission is sometimes granted on application to Lord Brassey.

The museum-building is fitted up and decorated in the Indian style, with carvings, etc., partly by Hindoo artists and partly executed in London. The lower room was originally the 'Durbar Hall' of the Colonial and Indian Exhibition in London. At the entrance and on the staircase are Oriental arms and armour, embroideries, stuffed birds, etc. A collection of boats and models near the top of the staircase includes a child's toy-boat picked up by the 'Sunbeam' in mid-ocean. — The glass-cases in the museum are numbered from left to right. 1. Personal souvenirs of Lady Brassey, and reminiscences of voyages. 2-4. Ethnological collection from Borneo, Burmah, and the Straits of Malacca. 5. Oriental Arms. 6. Specimens from Australian and other mines. 7. Indian jewellery and works in brass and silver. 8. Pottery and porcelain, including specimens from Fiji, and a sun-baked tea-set from the Shetland Islands. 9. Ethnological collection (excluding the South Seas). 10. Jewellery and ornaments from the Balkan Peninsula, Cyprus, China, South America, etc. Above, Burmese silver bowls; Indian pottery. 11-18. Interesting ethnological collection, mainly from New Guinea and the South Sea Islands. The cases are lined with native cloth, made from the bark of the paper mulberry tree. The birds are from New Guinea. 19-22 Corals. 23-26. Antiquities from Cyprus, Egypt, and South America; some of great rarity. 27. Miscellaneous collection of artistic objects from various sources. 28-29. Japanese objects. 30. Savage ornaments, mainly from the South Seas. 31. Ornaments and jewellery from India. 32. Savage ornaments, from the Sandwich Islands, South Sea Islands, South Africa, etc. Beside the windows are cases of birds of Paradise, flying-fish, etc. In the wall-cases are cloaks made of sea-birds' skins and feathers, from the Aleutian Islands; *Feather-cloak from the South Sea. Doorway from a Buddhist monastery in Tibet; above, specimens of pottery from the Solomon Islands. Articles used by the savage tribes of North Queensland. — The library contains 80 or 90 volumes of photographs taken in all parts of the world.

Devonshire House (Pl. R, 22; *IV*), Piccadilly, between Berkeley Street and Stratton Street, the London residence of the *Duke of Devonshire*, contains fine portraits by *Jordaens, Reynolds, Tintoretto, Dobson, Lely*, and *Kneller*. In the library is a fine collection of gems.

The **Earl of Northbrook's Collection**, at 4 Hamilton Place, Piccadilly, formed out of the famed *Baring Gallery*, is especially notable for its admirable examples of the Quattrocentists, and also contains *Holbein's* fine portrait of Hans Herbster of Strassburg (1516), and important works by Jan van Eyck, Cranach, Mazzolini, Garofalo, Seb. del Piombo, Murillo, Zurbaran, Velazquez, Rembrandt, Bol, Dou, Steen, Ruysdael, Cuyp, Rubens, etc.

Surrey House, 7 Hyde Park Place, just to the W. of the Marble Arch, the residence of *Lord Battersea*, is finely decorated and contains many interesting treasures of art.

The rich collection of early Italian pictures of *Mr. L. Mond*, 20 Avenue Road, N.W., may be seen by appointment on written application. It contains a large altar-piece by Raphael, and works by Fra Bartolommeo, Mantegna, Botticelli, Giovanni and Gentile Bellini, Garofalo, Titian, Ghirlandajo, Cima da Conegliano, Dosso Dossi, Sodoma, and others.

28. Albert Memorial. Albert Hall. Imperial Institute. Natural History Museum.

Along the S. edge of Hyde Park, beginning at Hyde Park Corner (p. 332), runs KNIGHTSBRIDGE (Pl. R, 13, 17), a wide and handsome thoroughfare, passing *Prince's Club* (p. 103; left) and the large *Knightsbridge Cavalry Barracks* (right). Opposite the end of Sloane Street is an *Equestrian Statue of Field-Marshal Lord Strathnairn*, by Onslow Ford, erected in 1895. The statue is in bronze, cast from guns taken in the Indian Mutiny.

Knightsbridge is continued by KENSINGTON GORE (Pl. R, 9), in which, to the right, between Queen's Gate and Prince's Gate, in the S. part of Kensington Gardens, near the site of the Exhibition of 1851, rises the *Albert Memorial (Pl. R, 9), a magnificent monument to Albert, the late Prince Consort (d. 1861), erected by the English nation at a cost of 120,000*l.*, half of which was defrayed by voluntary contributions. On a spacious platform, to which granite steps ascend on each side, rises a podium or stylobate, adorned with reliefs in marble, representing artists of every period (178 figures). On the S. side are Poets and Musicians, and on the E. side Painters, by *Armstead ;* on the N. side Architects, and on the W. Sculptors, by *Philip.* Four projecting pedestals at the angles support marble groups, representing Agriculture, Manufacture, Commerce, and Engineering. In the centre of the basement sits the colossal bronze-gilt figure of Prince Albert, wearing the robes of the Garter, 15 ft. high, by *Foley*, under a Gothic canopy, borne by four clustered granite columns. The canopy terminates at the top in a Gothic spire, rising in three stages, and surmounted by a cross. The whole monument, designed by *Sir G. G. Scott* (d. 1878), is 175 ft. in height, and is gorgeously embellished with a profusion of bronze and marble statues, gilding, coloured stones, and mosaics. At the corners of the steps leading up to the basement are pedestals bearing allegorical marble figures of the quarters of the globe: Europe by *Macdowell*, Asia by *Foley*, Africa by *Theed*, America by *Bell*. The canopy bears, in blue mosaic letters on a gold ground, the inscription: 'Queen Victoria and Her People to the memory of Albert, Prince Consort, as a tribute of their gratitude for a life devoted to the public good.'

On the opposite side of Kensington Gore stands the *Royal Albert Hall *of Arts and Sciences* (Pl. R, 9), a vast amphitheatre in the Italian Renaissance style, destined for concerts, scientific and art assemblies, and other similar uses. The building, which was constructed in 1867-71 from designs by *Fowke* and *Scott*, is oval in form (measuring 270 ft. by 240 ft., and 810 ft. in circumference), and can accommodate 8000 people comfortably. The cost of its erection amounted to 200,000*l.*, of which 100,000*l.* were contributed by the public, 50,000*l.* came from the Exhibition of 1851, and about 40,000*l.* were defrayed by the sale of the boxes. The exterior is tastefully ornamented in coloured brick and terracotta. The terracotta frieze, which runs round the whole building above the gallery, was executed by *Minton & Co.*; and depicts the different nations of the globe. The *Arena* is 100 ft. long by 70 broad, and has space for 1000 persons. The *Amphitheatre*, which adjoins it, contains 10 rows of seats, and holds 1360 persons. Above it are three rows of boxes, those in the lowest row being constructed for 8 persons each, those in the centre or 'grand tier' for 10, and those in the upper tier for 5 persons. Still higher is the *Balcony* with 8 rows of seats (1800 persons), and lastly, above the balcony, is the *Picture Gallery*, adorned with scagliola columns, containing accommodation for an audience of 2000, and affording a good survey of the interior. It communicates by a number of doors with the *Outer Gallery*, which encircles the whole of the Hall, and commands a fine view of the Albert Memorial. The ascent to the gallery is facilitated by two 'lifts', one on each side of the building. The *Organ*, built by Willis, is one of the largest in the world; it has nearly 9000 pipes, and its bellows are worked by two steam-engines. (The organ is occasionally played about 4 p.m., when notice is given in the daily papers; small fee.) Below the dome is suspended a huge *velarium* of calico ($^3/_4$ ton in weight) for lessening the reverberation and moderating the light.

The Albert Hall stands nearly on the former site of **Gore House**, which has given its name to Kensington Gore (p. 343). Although less famous than Holland House, it possessed fully as much political and social influence at the beginning of this century. It was long the residence of William Wilberforce, around whom gathered the leaders of the anti-slavery and other philanthropic enterprises. It was afterwards the abode of the celebrated Lady Blessington, who held in it a kind of literary court, which was attended by the most eminent men of letters, art, and science in England. Louis Napoleon, Brougham, Lyndhurst, Thackeray, Dickens, Moore, Landor, Rogers, Campbell, Bulwer, Landseer, Benjamin Disraeli, and Count D'Orsay were among her frequent visitors (see 'The Most Gorgeous Lady Blessington', by J. Fitzgerald Molloy). During the exhibition of 1851 Gore House was used as a restaurant, where M. Soyer displayed his culinary skill; and it was soon afterwards purchased with its grounds by the Commissioners of the Exhibition for 60,000*l*.

On the W. side of the Albert Hall is the *Alexandra House*, a home for female students, projected by the Princess of Wales and erected in 1886 at the cost of Sir Francis Cook. A little to the E. of the Albert Hall is *Lowther Lodge*, a very satisfactory example of Norman Shaw's modern antique style.

On the S. side of the Albert Hall is a statue of Prince Albert, overlooking the old site of the gardens of the Royal Horticultural Society (p. 387), which are now occupied by various public buildings and intersected from E. to W. by Prince Consort Road and Imperial Institute Road.

In Prince Consort Road is the **Royal College of Music** (Pl. R, 10), incorporated by royal charter in 1883 for the advancement of the science and art of music in the British Empire. The present building was opened in May, 1894, by the Prince of Wales, the president of the institution.   Dr. Hubert Parry is the director of the college, which provides a thorough musical education in the style of the Continental Conservatoires. Upwards of fifty scholarships and exhibitions are open to the competition of students. The teaching staff consists of 11 professors and 30 teachers; and in the first year of its existence the college was attended by 150 pupils, including several from the Colonies and the United States.

The College of Music contains the DONALDSON MUSEUM OF MUSICAL INSTRUMENTS (open free, daily, except Sat., 10-5), comprizing over 200 ancient and historical instruments (16-18th cent.) and musical MSS. Among the most interesting exhibits are a guitar once in the possession of David Rizzio; a guitar made for Henri IV. of France in 1592; spinets and harpsichords of the early 16th cent., one believed to be the earliest keyboard stringed instrument in existence; lutes; pair of presentation mandolins made for the Venetian ambassador to Madrid (1778); guitar belonging to Louis XV. when Dauphin; collections of bagpipes, vielles or hurdy-gurdies, and viole de gamba and viole d'amor (17th cent.); zither originally in the possession of Titian; Italian gradual or service-book of the 15th cent.; MSS. of Mozart, Spohr, J. J. Rousseau, etc.

The entrance-hall of the College contains statues of the Prince and Princess of Wales and a bust of Mr. Samson Fox, to whose munificence the building is due. These are all by the late Prince Victor of Hohenlohe. In the Council Room is a bust of the Duke of Clarence (d. 1892), by Weber.

The *Imperial Institute of the United Kingdom, the Colonies, and India, built in 1887-93, as the national memorial of Queen Victoria's Jubilee, is a huge Renaissance edifice by *Mr. T. E. Colcutt*, with a frontage 600 ft. in length, surmounted by a large central tower (280 ft. high; fine peal of bells), with smaller towers at the corners. In addition to the main building there are a Great Hall, to the N., 100 ft. long and 60 ft. wide, a smaller hall to the E., and Exhibition Galleries covering two acres of ground. In 1899, for financial reasons, the buildings were transferred to Government, the 'Institute' retaining the main W. wing, rent-free, for its offices and as a kind of club-house.

The main objects of the Institute, which was established by funds subscribed by the people of the British Empire and is partly supported by the annual payments of the 'Fellows', are to collect and disseminate by means of collections, exhibitions, lectures, etc., a knowledge of agricultural, commercial, and industrial conditions and progress throughout the Empire; to farther systematic colonization; and generally to promote the unity and the commercial and industrial prosperity of the Empire.

Visitors are admitted to the EXHIBITION GALLERIES (adm. by the side-entrance at the E. end of the façade; see p. 103), which contain a series of collections illustrating the products, manufactures, flora, and fauna of the different British colonies, India, etc. There are also a free *Commercial Reading Room* (trade journals of all kinds) and a *Refreshment Bar.*

Since 1900 the E. main wing and the central block have been occupied by **London University,** founded in 1836, which was formerly established in a building in Burlington Gardens (p. 284). London University (not to be confounded with University College in Gower Street) is not a teaching establishment but an examining board, granting degrees in arts, science, medicine, music, and law, to candidates belonging to either sex wherever educated. Its diplomas are much valued on account of the high standard of the examinations.

Opposite the Imperial Institute a new building for the Royal College of Science (see below) and Museum of Science is under construction. On each side of the Imperial Institute and behind the new College of Science are the *Exhibition Galleries* (p. 363), belonging to South Kensington Museum. In Exhibition Road, to the E. of the Imperial Institute, is the *Central Technical College*, belonging to the *City and Guilds of London Institute* (pp. 98, 137). Adjacent, to the S., a new building is being erected for the *Royal School of Art Needlework*, with collections of ancient and modern furniture, needlework, etc. (for sale). The school is at present accommodated in a temporary building, to the N. of the Technical College; open to visitors from 10 to 5 or 6 (Sat. 10-2).

On the opposite side of Exhibition Road is the *Royal College of Science*, for the training of teachers and others, a building completed in 1872-73, chiefly of terracotta, with fine sgraffito decorations. A little farther to the S. is the present main entrance to the *South Kensington Museum* (p. 351). — Exhibition Road debouches to the S. in *Cromwell Road*, a street of palatial residences, about 1 M. in length, deriving its name from the fact that Henry, son of the Protector, resided in a house that once stood here. Immediately to the right, in a large and handsome building facing Cromwell Road, is the —

*Natural History Museum, containing the natural history collections of the British Museum. The building was erected in the Romanesque style in 1873-80, from a design by Mr. Waterhouse, and consists of a central structure, with wings flanked by towers 192 ft. high. The extreme length of the front is 675 ft. The whole of the external façades and the interior wall-surfaces is covered with terracotta bands and dressings, producing a very pleasing effect. Admission, see p. 108; the Museum is closed on Good Friday and Christmas Day. Really interested visitors should buy the excellent general guide (3*d.*), while there are also illustrated guides (4*d.*-6*d.*) for the different sections. In 1899 the Natural History Collections were visited by 422.290 persons.

We first enter the GREAT HALL, 170 ft. long. 97 ft. wide, and 72 ft. high, at the entrance to which is a bronze statue of Richard Owen (1804-92), by *Brock*, while to the right is a marble statue of Thomas H. Huxley (1825-95), by *Onslow Ford*. The glass-cases in the centre of the hall contain groups illustrating albinism, melanism, the variation of species under the influence of domestication (pigeons, canaries, Japanese cock with tail-feathers 9 ft. long, etc.), the variation of sex and season, the adaptation of colouring to surrounding conditions, protective resemblances and mimicry, and the crossing of what outwardly appear to be quite distinct species. The alcoves round the hall are devoted to the Introductory or Elementary Morphological Collection (still incomplete), 'designed to teach the most

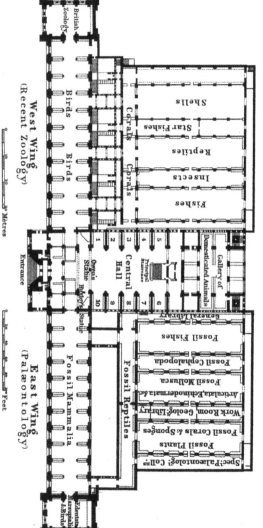

NATURAL HISTORY MUSEUM

Ground Floor

West Wing (Recent Zoology)

British Zoology

Birds

Birds

Corals

Corals

Shells

Star Fishes

Reptiles

Insects

Fishes

Central Hall

Organ Statue

Principal Staircase

Owen's Statue

Entrance

Gallery of Domesticated Animals

General Library

Fossil Fishes

Fossil Cephalopoda

Fossil Mollusca

Articulata, Echinodermata &c.

Work Room   Geolog¹ Library

Fossil Corals & Sponges

Fossil Plants

Spec¹ Palæontolog¹ Collⁿˢ

Fossil Reptiles

Fossil Mammalia

East Wing (Palæontology)

Tasmanian Marsupials & Birds

Métres

Feet

1 2 3 4 5 6 7 8 9 10

important points in the structure of the principal types of animal and plant life, and the terms used in describing them'. The bays to the left (W.) are devoted to the vertebrate animals, including man, while those to the right (E.) illustrate the insects, mollusks, and plants. In the middle of Bay VIII (r.) is a section of the *Sequoia gigantea*, or 'Big Tree' of California, measuring about 16 ft. in diameter and showing 1335 rings of annual growth. — In Bay VI (r.) are exhibited the most recent acquisitions of the museum.

On the groundfloor, behind the great staircase, is a gallery now being fitted up with a collection of *Animals under Domestication*. — Two cabinets on the N. side of this room contain Butterflies and Moths (*Lepidoptera*).

The *Geological and Palæontological Collection occupies the ground-floor of the E. wing (to the right of the entrance). The S.E. GALLERY, 280 ft. long and 50 ft. wide, contains fossil remains of animals of the class Mammalia. Pier Cases 1 and 2, to the right, contain remains of prehistoric man and of animals associated with him, chiefly found in caves in Great Britain and on the Continent. In a wall-case to the right of the window is a series of reproductions of bone implements, with rude carving and representations of animals. Table Case 1 also contains skulls and other remains of the prehistoric cave-dwellers, as well as weapons of reindeer-antler, flint implements, etc. In Pier Case 2 is a fossilised human skeleton, found in the limestone rock on the coast of Guadeloupe, West Indies. Pier Cases 3-5 contain the remains of extinct carnivorous animals, including the skull of the great sabre-toothed tiger (Case 3) and a fine collection of bones of the great cave-bears (Cases 4 & 5). The following cases on this side are devoted to the Ungulata or hoofed animals, such as the rhinoceros, palæotherium, horse, hippopotamus, pig, and the great family of ruminants. Among the most prominent objects are the skull and lower jaw of the Rhinoceros leptorhinus from the Thames Valley (Case 6), the sivatherium, a gigantic Indian antelope (Case 14), and the heads and horns of the extinct British wild ox (Case 18). To this class belong the skeletons of the gigantic Irish elk (*Cervus* or *Megaceros hibernicus*) in the central passage (stands K, L, M).

Most of the cases on the left side of the gallery are occupied by the very complete collection of the molar teeth and other remains of the Proboscidea, or elephants, including the mastodon, mammoth, and twelve other species. In Pier Case 31 is a fragment of the woolly skin of the Siberian mammoth. Closely allied to this species was the Ilford mammoth, found in the valley of the Thames, the skull and tusks of which are exhibited in the middle of the gallery (Case E). On a stand close by is the skeleton of Steller's sea-cow (*Rhytina*), an extinct species, found in the peat deposits of Behring's Island, Kamschatka. On Stand A, at the beginning of the gallery, is a perfect skeleton of the mastodon, found in Missouri, to one side of which are the skulls of a dinotherium (lower jaw a plaster reproduction), from Eppelsheim in Hesse-Darmstadt, and of a mastodon from Buenos Ayres.

At the end of the gallery we enter the *Pavilion*, which contains the fossil Birds, Marsupialia, and Edentata. Among the first (in Pier Cases 23, 24) are remains of the dinornis, or moa, an extinct wingless bird of New Zealand. Table Case 13 contains two specimens of the Archæopteryx, the oldest fossil bird as yet discovered, in which the tail is an elongation of the back-bone. Other cases contain remains of the gigantic extinct kangaroo of Australia (six times larger than its living representative), and of some of the diminutive mammals of the earliest geological period. In Case O, near the centre of the room, is the plaster skeleton of a megatherium from Buenos Ayres, a huge extinct animal, the bony framework of which is almost identical with that of the existing sloth. In the adjoining Case OO is a skeleton of Mylodon robustus, a somewhat similar animal from Buenos Ayres. In Case Q is a cast of a gigantic extinct armadillo (*Glyptodon asper*) from Buenos Ayres, beside which the skeleton of a living species is placed for comparison. The huge eggs of the Æpyornis of Madagascar should be noticed (in Case RR).

The corridor leading to the N. from the E. end of the gallery leads to —
GALLERY D, which is devoted to the fossil Reptiles. In Wall Cases,
and Table Cases 1 & 2 are remains of the Pterodactyles or flying lizards.
To the left (S.) is a large collection of Ichthyosauria, or fish-like reptiles,
while the cases to the right contain remains of the Dinosauria, the largest
of all land-animals. In the middle of the room are a reproduction of a
gigantic Iguanodon (Belgium) and the interesting skeleton of a Pariasaurus
from South Africa (W. end of the gallery).

The various galleries extending to the N. of the reptile gallery, each
about 140 ft. long, contain the fossil Fishes, Corals and Protozoa, Plants,
and Invertebrate Animals.

The connecting corridor at the W. end of the gallery contains the
Chelonia, including a cast of a huge Indian tortoise.

We now return to the entrance-hall and enter the S.W. GALLERY,
to the left, in which is the *Ornithological Collection. The glass-cases
round the sides of the gallery contain the general collection of birds in
systematic arrangement, while those in the middle contain admirably
mounted groups illustrating the nesting habits of British birds (continued
in the Reptile Gallery). The Pavilion at the end of the gallery contains
the eagles, with reproductions of their eyries; also a clever reproduction
of a cliff at the Bass Rock, with gannets (Solan geese), guillemots, and
kittiwakes.

This pavilion also contains a highly interesting *Collection of British
Zoology, including specimens of mammals, birds, and fresh-water fishes, that
are, or recently have been, found in the British Isles. The cabinets by the
W. window contain an almost complete series of the eggs of British birds.

The parallel gallery to the N. contains the Collection of Corals, while
the galleries at right angles to this are devoted to the Fishes, Insects,
Reptiles, and Shells. In the Insect Gallery is a series of models illustrating the life-histories of insects injurious to agriculture. A staircase,
descending from the westernmost of the passages connecting the Bird and
Coral Galleries, leads to the Cetacean Collection, which includes the
skeleton of a common rorqual or fin-whale (*Balaenoptera musculus*), 69 ft.
long, and that of a sperm-whale (*Physeter macrocephalus*), 50 ft. long.

We now again return to the Great Hall and ascend the large flight
of steps at the end of it to the first floor. On the first landing-place is a
statue of *Charles Darwin* (d. 1882), by Boehm. On the first floor, above
the Domesticated Animals Collection, is the *Refreshment Room* (entr. to the
right and left at the head of the staircase). The E. gallery (right) of the Great
Hall contains the *Gould Collection of Humming Birds*; the W. gallery accommodates part of the Mammalian collection. At the end of the former,
above the geological department, is the *Mineralogical Collection, which
contains a most extensive array of minerals, meteorites, etc. A notice at
the door gives instruction as to the best order in which to study the
specimens here. To the right of the entrance is a case containing different
varieties of marble and granite; the contents of the cases to the left
illustrate the characters of minerals and rocks. In Case 1g is the 'Colenso
Diamond' (130 carats), presented by Mr. Ruskin. Among the most remarkable objects in the other cases are a unique crystalline mass of Rubellite
from Ava (Case 33a), a magnificent crystal of light red silver ore from
Chili (Case 8), and the unrivalled groups of topazes and agates (Cases
25 & 16). In Case 13h is a piece of jasper, the veining in which bears a
singular resemblance to a well-known portrait of Geoffrey Chaucer. Case 42
illustrates enclosures in crystals. Among the larger objects in the room
at the E. end is the Melbourne meteorite, the heaviest known ($3^{1}/_{2}$ tons).

The gallery in the W. wing of the first floor, above the Bird Gallery,
contains the Mammalian Collection. To the left are the larger carnivora,
seals, etc.; to the right the kangaroos, hippopotami, camels, and deer.
In the middle of the gallery are the giraffes, elephants, and rhinoceroses;
in the pavilion at the end, buffaloes, cattle, and sheep.

The *Botanical Collection is exhibited on the second floor of the
E. wing. The part of this collection shown to the public is arranged so
as to illustrate the various groups of the vegetable kingdom and the

natural system of the classification of plants. The different orders are represented by dried specimens of the plants themselves, coloured drawings, fruits, and prepared sections of wood. The dicotyledonous plants are shown in the cases on the N. (left) side of the gallery, while in returning along the S. side we pass in turn the monocotyledonous plants, the gymnosperms, and the cryptogams. The series ends with Sowerby's models of the larger British fungi. Near the door is a chalk-like mass of earth containing twelve billion diatoms. Larger specimens are placed in the centre of the gallery, above which hangs a bamboo from Burma, 81 ft. long. At the E. end of the gallery are a palm from Brazil with a swollen stem (*Acrocomia sclerocarpa*) and a grass-tree from Australia (*Kingia australis*). A series of glazed frames contains a collection of British plants. — Among the most interesting herbaria in the students' department are those of Sir Hans Sloane, founder of the British Museum (see p. 299; about 1750), John Ray, Sowerby (English plants), and Sir Joseph Banks (1820), the last including the collection of Ceylon plants made by Hermann and described by Linnæus. The botanical drawings by *Francis* and *Ferdinand Bauer* form the finest collection of the kind in the world, remarkable both for scientific accuracy and artistic beauty.

The second floor of the W. wing is devoted to the **Osteological Collection**, with a very extensive collection of skulls. This room also contains the interesting collection of skeletons and stuffed specimens of monkeys, amongst which the anthropoid apes should be noticed. — At the top of the staircase (second floor) is a sitting figure of *Sir Joseph Banks* (d. 1820), the botanist, by *Chantrey*.

29. South Kensington Museum.

The Museum is about 4 min. walk to the N.E. of the *South Kensington Station* of the Metropolitan Railway (p. 61). *Omnibus Routes* Nos. 10, 15, 21, 27, 70, 92, etc. (pp. 36, etc.) pass along Brompton Road, near the main entrance; and Nos. 1, 6, 13, 79, 88, etc., pass the N. end of Exhibition Road, about 5 min. from the N.W. entrance.

The ****South Kensington Museum** (Pl. R, 9), now officially styled the **Victoria and Albert Museum**, is situated in Brompton, 1 M. to the S.W. of Hyde Park Corner. It consists of two parts. The MAIN BUILDING, at the corner of Exhibition Road and Cromwell Road, has its principal entrance in Exhibition Road, to the S. of the College of Science. The so-called EXHIBITION GALLERIES (p. 363), to the W. of Exhibition Road, are entered from Imperial Institute Road. The Main Building is open gratis on Mondays, Tuesdays, and Saturdays from 10 a.m. to 10 p.m.; on Wednesdays, Thursdays, and Fridays, 10 a.m. to 4, 5, or 6 p.m. according to the season, charge 6d. The Exhibition Galleries are open at the same hours but always gratis. The whole museum (except the libraries) is open free on Sunday, from 2 p.m. till 4, 5, 6, or 7 p.m. Tickets, including admission to the libraries, etc., 6d. per week, 1s. 6d. per month, 3s. per quarter, 10s. per year. In the middle of the main building are *Refreshment Rooms (p. 347; closed on Sun.), to the right and left of which are lavatories for ladies and gentlemen. — The Museum was visited in 1899 by 955,445 persons. The director of the Science Museum is *Major-General E. R.*

Festing; the director of the Art Museum is *Mr. C. Purdon Clarke,*
C. I. E.

The Museum was originally opened in 1857, in a temporary
structure, now used as the Bethnal Green Museum (p. 170). The
erection of permanent buildings was begun immediately afterwards
and various portions were opened as they were completed, but for
many years the building was left unfinished, destitute of a façade,
and quite unworthy of its priceless contents. In 1899, however,
Queen Victoria laid the foundation of new buildings, designed by
Mr. Aston Webb, which will present a handsome façade, 700 ft. in
length, towards Cromwell Road and will double the area of the
main building. The new official name of the Museum was adopted
at the same time by command of Her Majesty.

The Museum is one of the subdivisions of the Department of
Science and Art of the Committee of Council on Education, which
is under the control of the Lord President of the Council for the
time being, assisted by a Vice-President. The object of the Department is the promotion of science and art by means of the systematic training of competent teachers, the foundation of schools of
science and art, public examinations and distribution of prizes,
the purchase and exhibition of objects of science and art, and
the establishment of science and art libraries. It is carried on at
an annual expense of about 600,000*l.*, defrayed by the national
exchequer. Several other institutions in England, Scotland, and
Ireland are administered by the Department. Among its professors,
directors, and examiners are numbered many of the chief English
savants; and the tangible results of its teaching and influence are
seen in the progress of taste and knowledge in the fine arts and
natural science throughout the kingdom.

South Kensington Museum is largely indebted for its rapid progress to the generosity of private individuals in lending the most
costly treasures of art for public exhibition *(Loan Collections);*
but Government has also liberally expended considerable sums in
the acquisition of valuable objects. The art-collection, both in
value and extent, is one of the finest in the world. All the articles
in the museum are provided with a notice of their origin, the names
of the artist and (if on loan) owner, and (when acquired by purchase) a statement of their cost. The following is necessarily but a
limited list of the chief objects of interest permanently belonging
to the institution; and of the numerous plaster casts only such are
mentioned as are not usually met with in other collections. Even a
superficial glance at all the different departments of the museum
occupies a whole day; but it is far more satisfactory, as well as
less fatiguing, to pay repeated visits. Owing partly to the piecemeal
way in which the buildings have been erected, partly to their scattered disposition, partly to the fact that many sections of them are
not open to the public, and finally to the unmanageable size of the

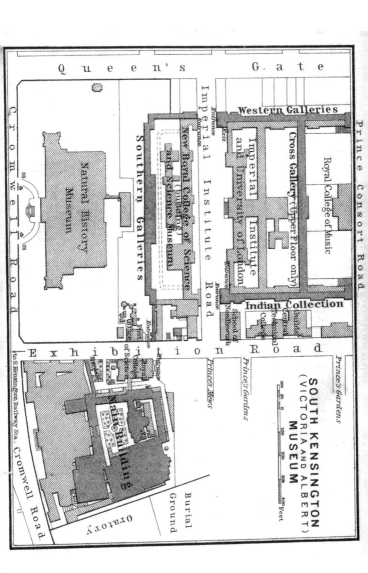

SOUTH KENSINGTON
(VICTORIA AND ALBERT)
MUSEUM

Queen's Gate

Western Galleries

Imperial Institute Road

Entrance

Exit

Entrance

New Royal College of Science (Building) and Science Museum

Southern Galleries

Natural History Museum

Cromwell Road

Imperial and University of London Institute

Cross Gallery (Upper Floor only)

Royal College of Music

Prince Consort Road

Indian Collection

School of Art Needlework

Central Technical College

Goldsmiths College

Exhibition Road

Entrance

Office of Sc...

Prince's Gardens

Prince's Mews

Prince's Gardens

0   50   100   200   300   400 Feet

Main Building

to South Kensington Railway Sta.

Cromwell Road

Oratory

Burial Ground

Main Building (Ground Floor)

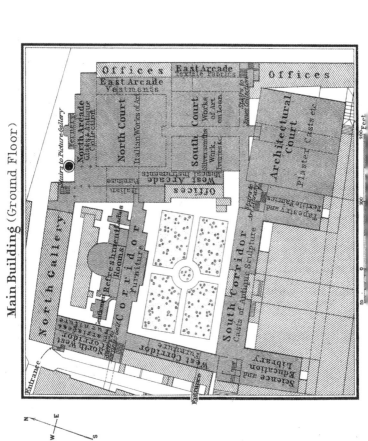

N · E · S · W

Entrance

North Gallery

Stairs to Picture Gallery

North West Corridor Furniture

Refreshment Rooms

Corridor Furniture

West Corridor Furniture

Entrance

Science and Education Library

South Corridor
Casts of Antique Sculpture

Tapestry and Textile Fabrics

Architectural Court
Plaster Casts etc.

West Arcade Musical Instruments

Italian Furniture

Offices

Vermin

North Arcade Glass & Antique Collection

North Court
Italian Works of Art

South Court
Silver, smith's Work, Enamels &c.

Works of Art on Loan

Staircase to

Offices

East Arcade
Vestments

East Arcade
Textile Fabrics

Offices

200 Feet 100 0 50

collections, it can hardly be claimed that the arrangements of the South Kensington Museum are specially perspicuous. As, moreover, the show-cases bear no letters or numbers, it is often difficult to indicate with precision the locale of any particular object. It is hoped, however, that the following description, with the aid of the plans, will neutralize this difficulty as far as possible. The arrangement is especially liable to be altered during the present building operations. Guide-books, catalogues, and photographs are sold at stalls close to the various entrances.

The Museum of Ornamental or Applied Art, a collection of modern and mediæval works of art (about 50,000 in number) and plaster casts or electrotype reproductions of celebrated ancient and modern works, partly belonging to the Museum and partly on loan, is installed in the Main Building, with the exception of the Oriental Collections, which are in the East and Cross Galleries (pp. 365-367). — The Main Building also contains the British Fine Arts Collections, or Picture Gallery, on the upper floor (p. 358); the National Art Library (keeper, *Mr. G. H Palmer*), consisting of upwards of 80,000 vols. and a collection of 240,000 drawings, engravings, and photographs, at the top of the staircase in the S.W. corner of the South Court (p. 355); the Science and Education Library, containing upwards of 66,000 volumes, at the E. end of the S. Corridor (see below); and the Royal College of Art, in which drawing, painting, and modelling are taught, on the top floor. — The Science Museum, incorporating the old *Patent Office Museum*, occupies the S. and W. Exhibition Galleries (pp. 363-365). — The Royal College of Science occupies a separate building (see p. 346).

A. Main Building.

The Main Building comprizes three large *Courts* roofed with glass, surrounded by arcades, three *Corridors* to the W. enclosing an open court, and *Galleries* on the upper floor.

Entering by the present Principal Entrance in Exhibition Road, we first reach the **South Corridor**, containing the admirable *Collection of Casts from the Antique*, which are displayed to great advantage (special catalogue 6d.). They include reproductions of several works of interest rarely met with in collections of this kind.

At the W. end of this corridor is the *Science Library* (see above) and at the E. end is the staircase to the spacious *Art Library*. The staircase walls are hung with pictures, including a work painted by *Millais* at the age of sixteen.

From the S.E. corner of the S. Corridor we enter the hall devoted to *Tapestry and Textile Fabrics*, which is divided into three sections. Among its finest contents are three pieces of Flemish tapestry, dating from 1507, with scenes from the Visions of Petrarch's 'Trionfi' (on the W. wall); one of a set of hangings representing the

Seven Deadly Sins, remarkable for the preservation of the colouring; an exquisite example of Flemish tapestry in silk and gold
and silver thread, representing the Adoration of the Infant Saviour.
This room also contains some Italian cassoni (p. 357) and other furniture. — The door on the E. side of this hall leads to the —

Architectural Court. This is divided into two portions by an
arcade (17 ft. broad) running down the centre, each half measuring
135 ft. by 60 ft., and is devoted to full-size plaster and other reproductions, chiefly of large architectural works, along with a few
original objects. At the S. end of the WESTERN SECTION of the
court is a fine *Rood Loft, of alabaster and marble, from the Cathedral of Bois-le-Duc, North Brabant (1625). Immediately in front is
a cast of the Monument of Sir Francis Vere in Westminster Abbey
(p. 271), behind which is the competition sketch model for the
Wellington Monument in St. Paul's by *Alfred Stevens*. Adjacent
are original models of various figures and groups forming part of the
design. The composition is pleasing, though in a decorative rather
than in a monumental style. In the middle of the room is a copy,
in two parts, of Trajan's Column, the original of which was erected
at Rome in A. D. 114. The reliefs represent Trajan's war with
the Dacians, and include 2500 human figures, besides animals,
chariots, etc. Between the two parts of this column is a cast of
the main W. portal of the Cathedral of St. Sauveur, at Aix in Provence. — To the left from the above-mentioned rood-loft: Copy
of the Chapter House Door in Rochester Cathedral (see *Baedeker's
Great Britain*). Cast of a portion of Rosslyn Chapel, near Edinburgh, with the column known as the 'Prentice's Pillar' (1446).
In front is a case with models of the 'New Model' army of Oliver
Cromwell, from the carved oak originals in Cromwell House, Highgate (p. 374). Cast of the angle of the Cloisters of San Juan de
los Reyes at Toledo (15th cent.), an admirable example of Spanish
Gothic. Cast of the Tabernacle in the church of St. Leonard at
Léau, in Belgium, executed by Cornelis de Vriendt in 1552, and
one of the finest works of the Flemish Renaissance. Cast of a brass
Font (1446), with a curious iron crane for lifting the cover, from the
church of Notre Dame at Hal. Cast of a Fountain by Pieter de Witte
(Pietro Candido; ca. 1548-1628), at the Old Palace in Munich.
Spanish Altar Painting of the 15th cent., representing the history
of St. George. By the wall are casts of early Norwegian Church
Doors, Danish Pew-Ends (15th cent.), and portions of a Danish Carriage (15th cent.) and of a Danish Altar (12th cent.). Adjacent are
reproductions of the Celtic Crosses of Gosforth and Irton (Cumberland) and Ruthwell (Dumfriesshire; 7th cent.?). — To the right:
Carved oak *Front of Sir Paul Pindar's House, formerly in Bishopsgate Without (1600). Cast of the Schreyer Monument, outside the
St. Sebaldus Church at Nuremberg, one of Adam Krafft's masterpieces, executed in 1492 (Deposition, Entombment, Resurrection).

Cast of a Choir Stall, from the Abbey of St. Denis. Then copies of works by Jean Goujon (1515-72): Œil-de-Bœuf from the Louvre; Relief of Victory from the Château d'Ecouen; and six Nymphs from the Fontaine des Innocents at Paris. Cast of a Pillar from Amiens Cathedral, with figures of Christ and King David; and the lower portion of a carved wooden Doorway in Beauvais Cathedral (16th cent.). Cast of Choir Stalls, in carved oak, from the Cathedral of Ulm, by Jörg Syrlin (about 1468). — By the end-wall: *Cast of the Puerta della Gloria of Santiago de Compostella, Spain, by Maestro Mateo, an imposing work in the Romanesque style (end of the 12th cent.). In front is a plaster cast of the Bronze Lion of Brunswick, the original of which is said to have been brought from Constantinople in 1166 by Henry the Lion. — To the left, casts of a portion of the Rood Loft in Limoges Cathedral, erected in 1533. — This section of the court also contains casts of works by Jean Cousin, Germain Pilon, Barye, Adrian de Vries, etc.

The CENTRAL PASSAGE between the two sections of this court contains electrotype reproductions of gold and silver plate from the collections at Windsor and the Tower of London. On one wall is a cast of the celebrated Pala d'Oro of Aix-la-Chapelle (10th cent.).

EASTERN SECTION of the Court. On the S. wall is the cast of a Chimney-piece from the Palais de Justice at Bruges, by Lancelot Blondeel, a fine specimen of Flemish work of the 16th century. Above is a cast of Thorvaldsen's frieze representing the Triumphal Entry of Alexander the Great into Babylon. In front, to the left (W.) are a metal reproduction of the Shrine of St. Simeon at Zara, in Dalmatia (1380), and a cast of the choir-screen of the church of St. Michael, Hildesheim, a Romanesque work of the end of the 11th century. — Behind the last, Cast of the shrine of St. Sebaldus, Nuremberg, the masterpiece of Peter Vischer (1519). — On the other side of the Hildesheim screen are painted and gilded terracotta spandrels (S. French; 14th cent.). — From the ceiling hangs a reproduction of a Corona, or Chandelier, from the Cathedral of Hildesheim (11th cent.). — On the wall to the right (E.) of the Bruges chimney-piece are copies of part of the Coloured Terracotta Frieze in the Ceppo Hospital at Pistoja, by Giov. della Robbia. Farther on, by the same wall, cast of the Marsuppini Monument by Desiderio da Settignano in Sta. Croce, Florence (late 15th cent.), and the original Monument of Marquis Malaspina from Verona (1536). — Almost in front of this monument is a cast of the Pulpit by Benedetto da Maiano in Santa Croce, Florence (15th cent.). — Opposite is a copy of the Font in the Baptistery at Siena. — In the middle of the room are casts of two celebrated Pulpits in Pisa, by Nicola (1260) and Giovanni Pisano (1302-11). — Farther on, to the right, cast of the Shrine of St. Peter Martyr in the church of Sant' Eustorgio at Milan, by Balduccio of Pisa. — To the left, by the W. wall, is a copy of a Seven-branched Candlestick in Milan Cathedral

(13th cent.). — On the E. wall, near the N. end of the room, is a reproduction of Donatello's Singing Gallery, formerly in the Duomo of Florence and now in the Museo Nazionale of that city. — At the N. end is a series of casts of the masterpieces of Michael Angelo, backed by a cast of the great doorway of San Petronio, Bologna. This section also contains casts of works by Donatello, etc.

We now descend the steps at the end of the Central Passage into the —

South Court, which is also divided into an eastern and a western half by an arcade (above it, the Prince Consort Gallery, p. 362). — On the upper part of the walls of these two departments, in sunken panels, are portraits (some in mosaic) of 35 famous artists, each inscribed with the name.

In the northern lunette of the E. section of the court is a fine *Fresco by *Lord Leighton*, representing the 'Arts of War' or the application of human skill to martial purposes (best seen from the gallery upstairs). The corresponding *Fresco in the S. lunette, by the same artist, illustrates the 'Arts of Peace'.

The Court contains an extremely valuable **Collection of small objects of art in metal, ivory, amber, agate, jade, and porcelain, many of which are lent to the Museum by private owners. The W. half of the court is devoted to European objects, while the E. half contains works of art from China and Japan (but comp. p. 367).

The WESTERN SECTION contains Ivory Carvings, Gold and Silver Work, and Loan Collections. At the S. end is a very representative collection of ivory carvings, affording a complete and highly instructive survey of the development of this mediæval art. In the 3rd case in the first row running from S. to N. are some works of world-wide celebrity, such as the leaf of the diptych of a *Bacchante of the 4th cent. (probably the finest early ivory carving extant), the leaf of a Byzantine Diptych formerly in the Cathedral of Liège, and the Diptych of Rufinus Gennadius Probus Orestes, Consul of the East, A.D. 530. The *Veroli Casket, of the 11th cent. (?), is in the same case. In other cases are triptychs, figures, etc., of French workmanship of the 14th century. Then, tankards, caskets, combs, etc., of a later date. The best works of other collections are here represented by admirable casts in fictile ivory (scientific catalogue by *Westwood*). — Other cases contain a valuable collection of silversmith's work (notably a silver-gilt *Salt Cellar with hall-mark for 1586-87 and a *Cup and Cover with hall-mark for 1611), ecclesiastical vessels, jewellery, personal ornaments, clocks and watches, carvings in amber, engraved crystal, bishops' croziers, etc. Among the single objects of greatest importance are a *Cup in repoussé work, attributed to Jamnitzer, but probably by an imitator; a *Mirror made for the royal family of Savoy; an Astronomical Globe made at Augsburg for the Emp. Rudolf II. in 1584; a *Byzantine crystal ewer of the 9th or 10th cent.; the 'Gloucester Candlestick' (early 12th cent.); and a chess-table in damascened work (Milan). At the N. end are a collection of arms and armour, four cases of bronzes and brass repoussé work, and a case of pewter-work, including specimens of François Briot (16th cent.).

The CENTRAL PASSAGE contains an admirable collection of finger-rings, arranged according to countries and destined uses (wedding, mourning, motto, charm, iconographic, etc.); cameos, gems, precious stones; snuff-boxes, bracelets, earrings, necklaces of various nations; and a collection of military and naval medals and other decorations. In one case is a large and varied collection of precious stones bequeathed by the *Rev. Chauncy Hare Townshend.* This passage also contains collections of gold and silver plate and jewellery lent by *Mr. J. Dunn-Gardner,* and of arms and armour lent by *Mr. D. M. Currie.* In one case are some admirable reproductions of Etruscan jewellery by Castellani of Rome.

The WEST ARCADE of this court is subdivided into three rooms, each fitted up with old oak panelling, brought in one instance from Sizergh Castle in Westmorland (16th cent.) and in another from 'Bromley Palace' (1606; destroyed 1894), at Bromley-by-Bow. The rooms contain English furniture of the 17th and 18th centuries.

The EAST SECTION of the South Court is at present mainly occupied by the fine collection of Chinese and Japanese porcelain, majolica, and Damascus, Rhodian, and Persian ware, lent by *Mr George Salting.* At the N. end are three table-cases containing illuminated books, portraits in wax, and carved boxwood medallions, and a fourth with knives, forks, and a fine Italian sword.

EAST ARCADE. Textile fabrics, embroideries, and furniture. At the S. end is a *Parisian Boudoir of the time of Louis XVI., originally belonging to the Marquise de Serilly, Maid of Honour to Marie Antoinette (bought for 2100*l.*). The paintings are by Lagrenée and Rousseau de la Rottière, the chimney-piece by Clodion, the metal work by Gouthière.

In the SOUTH ARCADE is the Museum Collection of Lace.

From the S.W. corner of this court we may enter the South Corridor, with the antique casts (see p. 351).

Leaving the S. Court, we next enter the **North Court**, devoted to Italian art, comprising numerous original sculptures of the Italian Renaissance. — Over the S. doorway is placed a marble *Cantoria or singing gallery from the church of Santa Maria Novella at Florence, by *Baccio d'Agnolo* (about 1500).

EAST SECTION. The following are the most noteworthy objects in this part of the court. Statues of *Cupid and Jason, by pupils of *Michael Angelo.* — *Christ in the sepulchre (bought for 1000*l.*), Delivering the Keys to St. Peter, two bas-reliefs by *Donatello.* — Lifesize figure of the Virgin, with worshippers, formerly the tympanum of a doorway at Santa Maria della Misericordia, Venice, attributed to *Bartolommeo Buon* (15th cent.). — Tabernacle, ascribed to

Desiderio da Settignano, a pupil of Donatello. — Relief in marble, with portrait of a man, by *Matteo Civitale*. — Altar or shrine of a female saint, from Padua, by a pupil of *Donatello*. — An ancient Roman Column. — *Large Chimney-piece ascribed to *Desiderio da Settignano*. — *Fragments from the Tomb of Gaston de Foix, by *Agostino Busti* (dated 1523). — Chimney-piece from the palace of the Rusconi family at Como. — Tabernacle from the church of San Giacomo at Fiesole, by *Andrea Ferrucci* (ca. 1490). — *Bronze busts of Popes Alexander VIII. and Innocent X., attributed to *Bernini*. — Bronze bust of Henry VII. (1457-1509), ascribed to *Torregiano* (1470-1522). — In the cases are Italian bronzes of the 14-17th centuries. In the 1st case are the famous *Martelli Bronze, a mirror-cover by *Donatello*, and four beautiful bronze Candlesticks from Florence (late 15th cent.). On a screen is a bronze bas-relief of the Entombment ascribed to *Donatello*. — Among the admirable busts of the early Renaissance in this part of the court are : *Giov. di San Miniato , by *Antonio Rossellino*, signed and dated 1456, with strongly marked characteristics; Portrait of a man, a vigorous work of the school of Rossellino; *Marble bust of a Roman emperor, crowned with laurel, a masterpiece of the Lombard school (15th cent.), of extraordinarily careful execution. — Against the E. wall is a cast of a Singing Gallery by *Luca della Robbia* (1432-38), originally in the Cathedral of Florence.

The E. ARCADE contains a collection of European tapestry and textile fabrics, including the superb *Sion Cope, from the convent of Sion at Isleworth (p. 414), English embroidery of the 13th century. One large case is occupied by a Venetian bed and furniture of the 18th century.

At the N. end of the court are the tribune and the high-altar of the conventual church of Santa Chiara at Florence, the latter by *Leonardo del Tasso* (ca. 1520). — Near this chapel are models of certain of the best examples of architectural ornament in Italy: portion of the Borgia Apartment in the Vatican; portion of the Villa Madama on Monte Mario, Rome; the great 'bancone' in the Sala del Cambio, Perugia; the Chapel of St. Peter Martyr in Sant' Eustorgio, Milan; the Chapel of St. Catherine in San Maurizio, Milan; part of the tribune of the Riccardi Chapel at Florence; and part of a room in the Palazzo Macchiavelli, Florence.

WEST SECTION. Collection of glazed terracotta works, some attributed to *Luca* and *Andrea della Robbia* of Florence (15-16th cent.). Those in white or uncoloured enamel are the oldest, while the coloured pieces date from the first decade of the 16th century. Among the most interesting specimens are twelve *Medallions representing the months, ascribed to *Luca della Robbia*; large medallion executed by *Luca della Robbia* for the Loggia de' Pazzi, with the arms of King René of Anjou in the centre; Adoration of the Magi, with a portrait of Perugino (looking over the shoulder of the king in the green robe and turban); Virgin and Child, by *Andrea della Robbia.* — Collection of Florentine terracotta busts, including one of a *Lady, attributed to *Donatello.* Terracotta group of the Virgin and Child, by *Jacopo della Quercia.* Terracotta statuette of the Virgin, ascribed to *Antonio Rossellino.* Terracotta bas-reliefs, being studies for three of the reliefs on the pulpit of Benedetto da Maiano at Santa Croce, Florence (p. 353). — *Sketch in stucco for one of the panels of the singing boys on the singing gallery executed by *Luca della Robbia* for Florence Cathedral (p. 356). — Case containing small models in wax and terracotta by Italian sculptors of the 16th cent., including twelve ascribed to Michael Angelo. — Terracotta model ascribed to Raphael. — Sketch for the statue of Jonah in the Chigi Chapel in Santa Maria del Popolo at Rome. — Extensive collection of Italian *Majolica,* including a famous plateau with a portrait of Pietro Perugino. — This court, which represents the Italian section of the Museum, also contains examples of Italian art in carved furniture, tarsia work, etc.

Part of the WEST ARCADE (see also p. 355) is occupied by a valuable collection of *Musical Instruments:* Harpsichord which belonged to Händel; German finger-organ, said to have once belonged to Martin Luther; Spinet of pear-tree wood, carved and adorned with ebony, ivory, lapis lazuli, and marble, by *Annibale de' Rossi* of Milan (1577); spinet, stated to have been the property of Elizabeth of Bohemia; Harpsichord inscribed 'Hieronymus Bononiensis faciebat, Romæ MDXXI'.

The NORTH ARCADE contains Italian and other glass vessels, antique pottery, mummy-cases, Spanish woodwork, mural decorations from Puteoli, etc.

The **Fernery,** which forms a pleasant object at the windows of this arcade, was fitted up to enable the art-students to draw from plants at all seasons.

To the W. of the North Court are three ROOMS, the first of which contains a collection of Hispano-Moresque ware, including a lustred *Vase from Malaga (ca. 1500) and other specimens of great beauty and rarity. The other two rooms are mainly devoted to *Italian Woodwork* and *Furniture,* including several fine marriage-coffers ('cassoni') and gilt mirror-frames (16th cent.).

From the last (southernmost) of these rooms a CORRIDOR leads to the *Refreshment Rooms (p. 349). This passage contains a number of modern marble statues and original models. Among these may be mentioned the Cupid and Pan of *Holme Cardwell,* and the Savonarola and other busts by *Bastianini* (1830-68), celebrated for his admirable imitations of the style of the 15th century. The windows contain interesting specimens of stained glass, partly from German churches. At the end of the corridor is a staircase leading to the Keramic Gallery (p. 363). We turn to the left into the —

West Corridor, which contains part of the *Museum Collection* *of Furniture*, including specimens of French, Spanish, Flemish, German, English, and Dutch workmanship. The walls are covered with wood-carvings, tapestries, and paintings.

The **North-West Corridor**, to the N. of the W. Corridor, contains another part of the collection of furniture and also some old state carriages and sedan chairs. At its N.W. corner is an exit into Exhibition Road (see p. 363).

At the N.W. angle of the N. court is a broad flight of steps leading to the upper floor, which contains the —

*British Fine Arts Collections a valuable and representative gallery of English paintings. It includes the collections given or bequeathed by *Messrs. Sheepshanks, Parsons, Forster, W. Smith,* and others, and a **Historical Collection of British Water-colour Drawings,* of great interest to the student and lover of art. It also contains the famous *Cartoons of Raphael,* formerly in Hampton Court. At the top of the stairs by which we have just ascended are some original cartoons of the frescoes in the Houses of Parliament (p. 240), and an original model of a group of the Graces, by *Baily.* — In addition to the paintings the following rooms contain a fine collection of electrotype reproductions of gold and silver plate, etc., of various countries, exhibited in glass-cases. Comp. Plan, p. 360.

Room I contains a collection of *Water-colour Drawings bequeathed by Sir Prescott Gardiner Hewett and a number of recently acquired water-colour drawings of the English school, including examples of *Rossetti, Madox Brown, Millais, Holman Hunt, Sir John Gilbert, Sam Bough, Sir Ed. Burne-Jones, Tenniel, Sir J. Linton, Birket Foster, Cuthbert Rigby, Albert Moore,* etc. On the end-wall are some interesting drawings on wood by *G. F. Watts, G. Cruikshank, Burne-Jones, Leighton, Fred. Walker, Madox Brown,* etc.

Room II is hung with works by *R. Caldecott, R. Doyle, W. H. Hunt, D. Roberts, W. C. Stanfield, G. Cattermole, J. Holland, J. Nash, F. W. Topham, E. Duncan, J. F. Lewis, W. L. Leitch, F. Tayler, L. Haghe, T. M. Richardson, S. Cooper, F. Walker, Sir John Linnell,* etc. On screens are specimens of *Copley Fielding, J. F. Lewis, A. Penley, David Cox,* etc.

Room III. Water-colours and drawings by *Gilpin, Barnet, Gainsborough, Benj. West, Cipriani, P.* and *T. Sandby, Pocock, Loutherbourg, Rooker, Hearne, Girtin, Cleveley, Wheatley, W. Alexander, J. T. Serres,* etc.

Room IV. On the walls are water colours by *Richards, Bewick, Young, W. Payne, A. Wilson, Pyne, Josh. Wallis, H. W. Williams, Gandy, De Wint, Müller, Wm. Blake, S. Howitt, Crome, Glover, Barker, Reinagle, T. Rowlandson,* etc. On screens are works by *W. Havell, H. Edridge,* and *De Wint;* also oil-paintings by *Karl Heffner* and *Vicat Cole.* On the S. wall are pastel heads, by *John Russell.*

Room V contains works by *Richard Bonington, Stothard, J. Cristall, Turner, Varley, G. F. Robson,* etc.

The following three rooms are at present in the builder's hands, and their former contents (as given below) are temporarily distributed among the other rooms of the suite.

Room VI. FORSTER COLLECTION. On the walls: Illustrations of Douglas Jerrold's 'Men of Character', by *W. M. Thackeray;* paintings and drawings by *Stanfield, Turner, Cattermole, Stothard,* and *Cipriani.* *Frans Hals, Man with a jug; °Gainsborough, His daughters; Reynolds, Portrait; Perugini, John Forster (donor of the collection); Boxall, Walter Savage Landor; Frith, Charles Dickens; °Maclise, Macready as 'Werner'; Maclise, Scene from Jonson's 'Every Man in his Humour', with portrait of Forster; Watts, Thomas Carlyle; Wynfield, Death of Cromwell. On the screen: Drawings by *Maclise*, *Leech*, *Thackeray*, *Landseer*, and *Count d'Orsay*. The glass cases in the middle of the room contain autographs of Queen Elizabeth Charles I., Cromwell, Addison, Pope, Johnson, Byron, Keats, etc.; the MSS. of several of Dickens's novels, including the unfinished 'Edwin Drood', with the last words he wrote; Dickens's desk; three sketch-books of Da Vinci, which the master used to carry at his belt; chair, desk, and Malacca cane of Oliver Goldsmith. Small model of a curious Chinese Temple, with a grotto. — The door to the right leads to the *Keramic Gallery* (p. 363).

Room VII. DYCE COLLECTION. Pictures. To the left: Ascribed to *Janssens*, Dr. Donne; *Halls*, Edmund Kean as Richard III.; *West*, Saul and the Witch of Endor; *Worlidge*, Garrick as Tancred; *Unknown Artist*, Kemble as Coriolanus; *Loutherbourg*, Garrick as Don John; *Richardson the Elder*, Portrait of Pope; *Unknown Artist*, Mrs. Siddons. To the right: *G. Romney*, Serena; *Unknown Painter*, John Milton; *Reynolds*, Portrait. The room also contains books (fine editions of the classics), drawings, and miniatures. — The books, MSS., and drawings of the *Dyce and Forster Bequests* may be consulted in the reading-room of the Art Library, where catalogues are provided.

Room VIII. DYCE COLLECTION. Books, Engravings, and Drawings.

We 'now return to Room III and thence enter the NORTH GALLERY, or —

****Raphael Room**, containing the marvellous cartoons executed by the great painter for Pope Leo X., in 1515 and 1516, as copies for tapestry to be executed at Arras in Flanders. Two sets of tapestry were made from the drawings, one of which, in a very dilapidated condition, is preserved in the Vatican; the other, after passing through the hands of many royal and private personages, is now in the Old Museum at Berlin. The cartoons were originally ten in number, but three, representing the Stoning of St. Stephen, the Conversion of St. Paul, and St. Paul in prison at Philippi, have been lost (represented here by copies). The cartoons rank among Raphael's very finest works, particularly in point of conception and design.

The cartoons here are as follows, beginning to the right on entering: — *Christ's Charge to Peter. — Death of Ananias. — Peter and John healing the Lame Man. — Paul and Barnabas at Lystra. Then, on the opposite wall: — *Elymas the Sorcerer struck with blindness. — Paul preaching at Athens. — *The Miraculous Draught of Fishes.

The room also contains copies of the tapestries worked from the three missing cartoons (see above) and some old Italian furniture.

At the E. end of the hall we turn to the right, and reach the three rooms occupied by the SHEEPSHANKS COLLECTION.

Room A. To the left are a number of works by *C. R. Leslie*: *114. Florizel and Perdita. *109. Scene from the 'Taming of the Shrew', 115. Autolycus, etc. Also: *171. *Redgrave*, Ophelia; 121. *Sir T. Lawrence*, Queen Caroline, wife of George IV.; 59. *Cope*, Il Penseroso; 172. *Redgrave*, Bolton Abbey; 166. *Newton*, Portia and Bassanio; 210. *Turner*, East Cowes Castle, Isle of Wight; 58. *Cope*, L'Allegro; 226. *Wilkie*, The refusal ('Duncan Gray'); 11. *Callcott*, Dort (a sunny meadow); 213. *Uwins*, Italian mother teaching her child the tarantella; 207. *Turner*, Line-fishing off Hastings; *Constable*, Landscape study (on loan); 74. *Frith*, Honeywood introducing the bailiffs to Miss Richmond as his friends; 212. *Uwins*, Suspicion. — *Turner*, 208. Venice, 209. St. Michael's Mount, Cornwall; 10. *Callcott*, Slender and Anne Page; 223. *Webster*, Contrary winds; *Constable*, Landscape study (on loan); 1403. *Morland*, Horses in a stable; *Collins*, 31. Seaford, coast of Sussex;

579. *Angelica Kauffmann*, Lady Hamilton; 1405. *Geo. Cruikshank*, Cinderella 113. *Leslie*, Uncle Toby and Widow Wadman (comp. p. 276); 211. *Turner*, Vessel in distress off Yarmouth; 110. *Leslie*, Characters in the 'Merry Wives of Windsor'; and several landscapes by *Richard Wilson*. — The cases in the centre of the room contain a collection of fine enamels and miniatures.

Room B. To the left: 61. *Creswick*, Scene on the Tummel, Perthshire; 37. *Morland*, The reckoning; 895. *Lance*, Fruit; 126. *J. H. Wilson*, Coast-

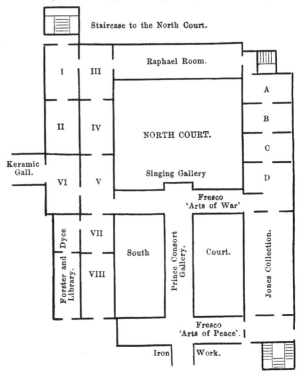

Staircase to the North Court.

I   III

Raphael Room.

II   IV

NORTH COURT.

A

B

C

Keramic Gall.

VI   V

Singing Gallery

D

Fresco 'Arts of War'

Forster and Dyce Library.

VII

South

Prince Consort Gallery.

Court.

Jones Collection.

VIII

Fresco 'Arts of Peace'.

Iron   Work.

scene; *Gainsborough*, 136. Daughters of George III.; 91. Queen Charlotte; 83. *J. C. Horsley*, Rival performers; *Linnell*, 1407. Driving cattle, 134. Milk-ing-time; *165. *P. Nasmyth*, Sir Philip Sidney's Oak, Penshurst. — *Mulready*, 152. Portrait of Mr. Sheepshanks, 141. First love, 143. Open your mouth and shut your eyes!, 146. The sonnet, 148. The butt, 139. The fight in-terrupted, 142. Interior with portrait of Mr. Sheepshanks, 138. Seven ages of man, 145. Choosing the wedding-gown. — *222. *Webster*, Village-choir; *103. *C. Landseer*, Temptation of Andrew Marvell; 232. *Creswick*, The Land's End, Cornwall; 15. *Callcott*, Sunny morning; 197. *Stothard*,

Shakspeare's principal characters; 219. *Webster*, Sickness and health. — 62. *Creswick*, A summer's afternoon; 1828. *Hering*, Arona, on Lago Maggiore; 167. *Redgrave*, Cinderella; 374. *Loutherbourg*, Landscape; 233 *Danby*, Mountain-scene in Wales; *189. *Stanfield*, Market-boat on the Scheldt; 225. *Wilkie*, The broken jar; 188. *Stanfield*, Near Cologne; 1360. *Sir T. Lawrence*, Lady Carrington. — The frame in the centre contains drawings and sketches by *Mulready*.

Room C. To the left: Landscapes by *Dawson* (No. 177), *Barret* (No. 4), and *Glover* (No. 165); 16. *J. R. Reid*, The Thames at evening; 15. *T. Graham*, Wayfarers; *261. *De Wint*, Woody landscape; 242. *Howard*, Peasants of Subiaco; 1827. *Lee* and *Cooper*, Wooded glen, with cattle; 258. *De Wint*, Corn-field; 155. *MacCallum*, Sherwood Forest; 249. *Monamy*, Old East India Wharf at London Bridge; 220. *Ward*, Bulls fighting. — *190. *Stanfield*, Sands near Boulogne; 236. *Crome*, On the skirts of the forest; *88. *E. Landseer*, The drover's departure, a scene in the Grampians; 176. *Roberts*, Gate at Cairo; 501. *Dawson*, Shipping; 9. *Callcott*, Brisk gale. Then a number of works by *Sir E. Landseer*: 92. The 'Twa Dogs'; *93. The old shepherd's chief mourner ('one of the most perfect poems or pictures', says Mr. Ruskin, 'which modern times have seen'); *87. Highland breakfast; 91. 'There's no place like home', etc. — 232. *J. Crome*, Household Heath; 354. *H. Andrews*, Garden scene; 234. *Chalon*, Hastings, with fishing-boats making for shore in a breeze; 164. *Mulready Junior*, Interior; 64. *Crome*, Woody landscape. — The radiating frames contain drawings by *Mulready*, *Eugène L. Lami* (d. 1890), *Ditchfield*, *Leech*, etc.

Room D. This room is devoted chiefly to a collection of paintings and studies by *John Constable*, *R. A.*, given by Mr. Sheepshanks and Miss Isabel Constable. To the left: *34. Dedham Mill, Essex; *33. Salisbury Cathedral; *35. Hampstead Heath; 1632. Water-mill at Gillingham; 1631. Cottage in the corn-field. To the right: *38. Water-meadows near Salisbury; *37. Boat-building near Flatford Mill; 1630. Near Hampstead Church; *36. Hampstead Heath. On five screens and on the walls are sketches by the same artist. — Between the exits into the next gallery is an oil painting of an old English homestead by *R. Redgrave*, *R. A.* On one of the screens are sketches by the same artist.

In the adjacent long GALLERIES is the superb **Collection of French marquetry and other furniture, porcelain, miniatures, bronzes, paintings, and sculptures of the 18th cent., bequeathed to the Museum by *Mr. John Jones* (d. 1882), officially valued at 250,000*l*. Special handbook, with numerous illustrations, 1*s*.

The LEFT GALLERY contains furniture, nearly all of the best period of French art in this department. Among the most interesting pieces are an Escritoire à toilette, in light-coloured wood, which is said to have belonged to Marie Antoinette, and was probably executed by *David Röntgen*; two escritoires by the same; a writing-table and a small round table with Sèvres plaque, both belonging to Marie Antoinette (the two valued at upwards of 5000*l*.); cabinet of black boule (purchased by Mr. Jones for 3500*l*.); a marquetry cabinet inlaid with Sèvres plaques, etc. In one of the central cases is one of the fifty copies of the Portland Vase (p. 322) made by Wedgwood.

RIGHT GALLERY. Collection of Sèvres, Oriental, Dresden, and Chelsea porcelain. Among these may be mentioned the 'gros bleu' Sèvres vases, the green porphyry vases, the 'Rose du Barry' service, etc. — Collection of jewellery and miniatures, including *Portraits of Louis XIV. by *Petitot*. — The fine collection of snuff-boxes includes

many with miniatures by Isabey, Petitot, Blaremberghe, and others.
— Sculptures, among which are busts of Marie Antoinette and the
Princess de Lamballe, in the style of *Houdon*. — At the N. end
of this gallery is a magnificent *Armoire, with inlaid work by
André Boule or *Buhl*, the court cabinet-maker of Louis XIV. —
The pictures on the walls include examples of *Gainsborough, Land-
seer, Linnell, Mulready*, and other English artists. The foreign works
are mostly school-copies, but there is a genuine, signed work by
Crivelli (Madonna), on the right wall at the end of the left gallery.

The lunettes in the galleries contain decorative paintings to
illustrate the different branches of Art Studies. At the S. end of the
Gallery is a staircase leading down to the E. section of the S.
Court (p. 355).

We now return to Room D., and turn (to the left) into the
Gallery which separates the N. from the S. Court, passing Leighton's great fresco described at p. 354. The W. portion of the Gallery contains a few unimportant oil-paintings and three cases with
specimens of *Bookbinding*. The balcony on our right, from which
we look down into the N. court midway in this gallery, is the singing gallery, mentioned at p. 355. Opposite it is the ***Prince Consort Gallery,** which contains a rich selection of small mediæval
works of art, arranged in glass-cases, on the left, and German,
French, Papal, and Italian medals in frames, on the right.

The first glass-case, higher than the others, holds ancient enamelled
works, the most important of which are a *Shrine in the form of
a church with a dome (Rhenish Byzantine of 12th cent., bought for
2142*l.*), a *Triptych of champlevé enamel (German, 13th cent.),
and an *Altar-cross of Rhenish Byzantine work with enamel medallions (12th cent.). The following cases contain examples of ancient and modern enamels, especially some fine *Limoges Enamels*
of the 15th, 16th, and 17th centuries. The most valuable objects
are the oval *Portrait of the Cardinal de Lorraine (bought for 2000*l.*),
the large *Casket, enamelled on plates of silver, with a band of
dancing figures, ascribed to *Jean Limousin* (16th cent.), and a small
*Cup and cover, decorated with translucent enamel, known as 'email
de plique à jour', all in Case 3; and a gold *Missal Case, with translucent enamels, said to have belonged to Queen Henrietta Maria
(Italian, ca. 1580), in Case 10. In the last case are English enamels (made at Bilston and Battersea). To the right, at the end of
the gallery, are three cases containing specimens of *French Lock-
smiths' Work* and two others with *Caskets and Coffers* of various
dates and origins.

The Gallery of the *Architectural Court*, reached by a few steps at the
S. end of the Prince Consort Gallery, contains the collection of Ornamental Ironwork, of Italian, French, German, and English origin: balconies, window-gratings, lamps, etc. — Five iron screens designed by
Jean Tijou, though long attributed to Huntington Shaw of Nottingham,
for Hampton Court Palace (about 1693; see p. 411).

The *Keramic Gallery, entered from Room VI of the picture galleries (p. 359), contains an admirable collection of earthenware, porcelain, and stoneware. We first reach the collection of English pottery of the 17th and 18th cent.; Wedgwood ware; Chelsea, Worcester, and Derby porcelain; enamelled earthenware. The following cases contain the *Collection of English Pottery* given to the Museum by Lady Charlotte Schreiber, including fine examples of most of the older wares. This is succeeded by a collection of German and Flemish stoneware, including several large German stoves. Adjoining are specimens of French earthenware of the 16th cent., including 6 pieces of the famous Henri-Deux ware (in a small case by itself), probably made at St. Porchaire; choice collection of Palissy ware; Sèvres porcelain; Delft; Dresden china; Italian porcelain, including 4 pieces of the rare *Florentine porcelain of the 16th cent., probably the earliest porcelain made in Europe; some Hispano-Moresco (Spanish) ware. The windows on the right, in grisaille, designed by *W. B. Scott*, represent scenes connected with the history of pottery.

At the W. end of the Keramic Gallery is a highly decorated staircase, on which is a memorial tablet with portrait of *Sir Henry Cole, K. C. B.* (d. 1882), the first Director of the Museum. The staircase descends to the S. end of the N. W. Corridor (p. 358), at the N.W. corner of which is a door opening on Exhibition Road, on the opposite side of which are the Exhibition Galleries.

B. Exhibition Galleries.

These galleries, which contain the Science Museum and the Oriental Art Collections, extend behind the new buildings of the College of Science in Imperial Institute Road and on each side (E. and W.) of the Imperial Institute (comp. p. 346). They owe their name to the fact that they were originally erected in connection with the International Exhibitions held in the Horticultural Society's Gardens (p. 344) in 1871-74. — Admission, see p. 349.

In Exhibition Road, immediately opposite the N.W. exit from the Main Building, is the entrance to the S. GALLERY, which contains the *Machinery and Inventions Division*. Some of the machinery is shown in motion or may be set in motion by the visitor. We first reach the *Models of Mining Machinery*. Farther on are *Metallurgical Models, Textile Models and Machinery* (including a historical collection of sewing and knitting machines, in a wall-case to the left), and *Printing and Writing Machines* (with a hand-press said to have been used by Benjamin Franklin). The wall-case to the left, at the foot of the staircase, contains a historical series of type-writing machines. — The adjacent bay, to the right, contains *Agricultural Models*, with the original Bell Reaping Machine (1826). The next section contains *Machine Tools for Metal Working, Woodworking Machines*, the original model of *Nasmyth's Steam Hammer* (2nd case from the door), models of *Gun Mountings*, *Rifles*, etc. In the wall cases to the left are models of *Agricultural Implements*, *Cooking* and *Washing Machines*, and *Lighting Appliances*.

The collection of *Steam Engines*, arranged as far as possible in historical sequence and showing the most primitive types contrasted with the most recent, begins at the end of this section. To the right are working models of the Newcomen engine as it was in 1720, and of the 'Old Bess' engine of 1877, which replaced the engine to which James Watt applied for the first time his separate condenser (patented 1769). — We now enter the Central Hall, which contains the most interesting specimens.

To the right is Watt's first Sun and Planet Engine, erected at Soho near Birmingham, in 1788. — The visitor should also notice the admirable models of beam-engines by James Watt, worked by compressed air; a model of an atmospheric engine worked by steam ('shewing the state of the development of the steam engine in 1730, in which form it remained until 1760, when J. Watt commenced his improvements'). In the centre of the hall are, on the left, the *'Agenoria'*, a locomotive built in 1829 by Foster and Rastrick, and *'Puffing Billy'*, the first locomotive engine ever constructed, in use at the Wylam Collieries from 1813 to 1862. On the right, *Stephenson's first locomotive, the *Rocket*, constructed to compete in the trial of locomotives on the Liverpool and Manchester Railway in 1820, where it gained the prize of 500l.; and the *Sans Pareil*, by Hackworth of Darlington, another competitor at the above-mentioned trial. A glass case in front of the Rocket contains a number of personal relics of Stephenson. These early engines may be compared with the fine models of modern locomotives in the annexe behind. To the left, as we quit the central hall, is Heslop's Winding and Pumping Engine, patented 1790 and erected for raising coals about 1795.

The following room contains a historical series of *Gas Engines*. At the end are three fine models of modern fire-engines. In the wall-cases to the left are *Gas* and *Water Meters* and a series of *Speed Indicators*. — To the left, at the beginning of the next room we may note a model of the *Westinghouse Brake* and the original *Brougham*, built for Lord Brougham in 1838. To the right are a historical series of rails for railways, models of railway carriages and tramways, etc. Farther on, beyond the cranes and apparatus for lifting heavy weights, we reach the *Marine Machinery*. Among the most noteworthy objects here are the *Engine of Bell's 'Comet'*, the first commercially successful steamship, which plied on the Clyde in 1812, and the model of the engines and paddle-wheels of the 'Great Eastern' (1857). At the end are the engines and a model of Maxim's *Flying Machine* (1894).

The visitor is recommended to retrace his steps to the E. staircase and to ascend to the upper floor of the gallery. Here are a collection of *Telegraphic Instruments*, a large collection of *Educational Models for teaching Mechanics*, and a collection of models illustrating the construction of *Bridges and Roofs*. Farther on we reach the most interesting collection of *Ship Models*, in three rooms devoted respectively to *War Ships* from 1670 to the present day; *Ocean Liners* (including nine models of the Cunard steamers from 1840 to 1894); British and foreign *Boats*, *Docks*, etc. The models of lifeboats and lighthouses should be noticed. — Descending to the groundfloor by the W. staircase, we turn to the left and enter the *Museum of Economic Fisch Culture*, at the end of which is exit into Imperial Institute Road (p. 346).

We now cross Imperial Institute Road in order to reach the W. GALLERY, containing the *Collections of Scientific Apparatus used in Education and Research*, comprising much that is of great value and interest to students. In the vestibule may be seen the standard weights and measures of Great Britain; the clock of Glastonbury Abbey, constructed by one of the monks in 1325, and showing the phases of the moon; Dover striking clock of 1348; clock with stone weights, from Aymestrey Church, Herefordshire. — In the Lower Gallery are the *Clocks and Chronometers*, and the *Astronomical*, the *Physiographical*, the *Meteorological*, and the *Geological Divisions*.

We then ascend the S. staircase, on the walls of which are specimens, drawings, etc., of *Injurious Insects* and the damage they cause. At the top of the staircase is the *Mathematical Division*, in which is Babbage's calculating machine. Next follows the *Physical Division*, among the most interesting objects in which are the electrical machines, the apparatus used by Joule in his discovery of the mechanical equivalent of heat, copies of the original air-pump and hemispheres of Otto von Guericke, and the historical series of photographic apparatus. Beyond this are the *Chemical Division* and the *Metallurgical Division*, comprising a collection of metallic elements bequeathed by Prince Lucien Bonaparte. [To the E. or right diverges the Cross Gallery, described at p. 367.] — The *Biological Division*, at the end of the gallery, includes a copy of the first compound microscope (ca. 1590), various recording instruments, models illustrating the structures of flowers, models of organs of the human body, and models of invertebrate animals.

The E. GALLERY, entered from Imperial Institute Road to the right (E.) of the Imperial Institute, is devoted to the *Indian Section of South Kensington Museum. This collection was formerly known as the *India Museum*, and was kept until 1880 in the India Office (p. 237).

The **Entrance Hall** contains original and reproduced examples of Hindoo architecture, including the stone front of a house from Bulandshahr; the façade of a shop in Cawnpore; the large façades of two dwelling-houses from Ahmedabad, in teak wood, carved and painted (17th cent.); and various carved windows, doorways, balconies, etc. In the centre of the hall are a brass model of the Palace of the Winds, Jeypore, a wooden model of the Kutb Minar, near Delhi, a model of the city of Lahore, and a copy of a tomb in Mooltan tile-work.

We next pass the Staircase, ascending to the right to the upper floor, and enter the **Lower Gallery**. — ROOM I. On the walls, Indian carpets. Plaster casts of architectural details and sculptures. Carved stone-work. Portions of stone columns from a temple at Ajmir, destroyed in 1200. Marble throne. Model of the 'Golden Temple' at Amritzar. — ROOM II. Cases with figure-models of Indian divinities, handicraftsmen, agriculturalists, etc., and (above the wall-cases) models of ships and boats. On the walls, Persian carpets and cotton carpets from the Deccan. — Room III. Embroidery, brucades, state carpets, and canopies; peasant dresses from the Punjâb, turbans, caftans. — Room IV. Embroidered shawls from Delhi; garments decorated with beetles' wings; fine muslins from Dacca. On the walls, embroidered coverlets and printed chintzes. — Room V. Saddles and trappings. Printed and painted fabrics.

We now reach the N. staircase, at the foot of which are cases with costumes, including a royal dress from Lucknow. On the walls of the staircase are Indian sketches bv *George Landseer* (d. 1878). At the head of the staircase we enter the **Upper Gallery**, in which are placed the collections of furniture, carvings, lacquer-work, arms, pottery, jewellery, and bronzes.

Room VI. The first cases on the left contain Buddhist and Hindoo sacred figures, and brass and marble idols and vessels used in the worship of Buddha. Among these is a figure of *Buddha as Siddhartha before his conversion taking part in a grand procession; also two Siamese figures of Buddha (19th cent.), of gilt metal decorated with glass spangles. The other cases contain Indian works in metal, arranged according to countries. The most interesting are the brass vessels with reliefs from Thibet; the Bidri work from Purneah (in the N.W. Provinces); *Objects in dark metal, damascened with silver, from the Deccan; bells from Burmah and Tanjore. Among the most valuable pieces are the large *Ewer, with enamels of Indian scenery, in Bidri work (on a separate stand); Samovar, of tinned copper, from Cashmere (18th cent.); °Bowl and stand, in pierced silver, from Ahmedabad. Reproductions of the 'Perak Regalia.' On the walls are native paintings on talc and sketches of Indian craftsmen, by *J. L. Kipling*.

Room VII. Jewellery and articles in jade, crystal, gold, and silver. Bracelets and necklaces; °'Ankus', or elephant goad, of gold, richly ornamented with a spiral board of diamonds, and set with rubies (from Jeypore); necklace of tiger-claws; carvings in jade. Seven cases with the Treasure from the King of Burmah's Palace at Mandalay, captured in 1885-86. *Silver filigree work. °Golden relics from Rangoon, discovered in levelling a Buddhist temple, consisting of three 'Charifas' or relic shrines, a tassel, a leaf-scroll, a bowl with cover, a small cup, a helmet, and a jewelled belt (dated the year 846, *i.e.* 1484-85 A.D.). Buddhist Reliquary in gold (said to date from B. C. 50), with interesting figures, resembling later Christian works. °Ancient silver patera (4th cent. A.D.), found at Badakshan, with representations resembling those of classical antiques (worship of Bacchus?). Indian crystal vessels; right, niellos; left, Kuftgari and enamel work. Here also are the golden throne of the Maharajah Runjeet Singh, and a model illustrating the way in which Hindoo women wear jewellery. — By the walls: Ornaments of various kinds.

Room VIII. By the walls: Arms and Armour, arranged according to provinces; the swords in the cases to the left are particularly interesting. *Howdah, with embroidered covering. *Palanquin, of ivory, with representations of battles and beautiful ornamentation. Guns from Afghanistan. Bronze gun from Burmah, in the form of a dragon. On the wall to the right is the banner of Ayoub Khan, captured at the battle of Candahar in 1880. — [Off this section, to the right, opens the Cross Gallery (see next page).]

Room IX. Pottery and Tiles, arranged by provinces. The most important are the manufactures of the N.W. Provinces (left), Sinde (right), and Madras (left). On the walls, copies of the paintings in the Ajanta caves. In the centre of the room, a collection of Patna glass and a large earthenware bowl used for storing grain.

Room X. Wood and Ivory Carvings, Mosaics, Lacquer Work, Musical Instruments, Carvings in Marble and Stone. — 4th Case to the left: Models of tombs and vessels in soapstone. — 5th Case on the right: Wind Instruments. — 4th, 6th, and 8th Cases to the right: Stringed Instruments. In the 8th case also are conches and two 'nyastarangas'. — In the 7th case are Instruments of percussion. — In the centre: Tiger devouring an Eng-

lish officer, a barbaric mechanical toy that belonged to Tippoo Sahib. —
To the left: Drums and other musical instruments. — In the centre:
Bedstead from Theebaw's Palace, Mandalay; swinging bedstead of painted
wood, from Sinde. Steering Chair of carved teak wood from Burmah. —
Wooden articles, lacquered, the ornamentation of which is more striking
than the forms. — Wood and Ivory Mosaics, of great delicacy of execution. — Carvings in ivory and sandal-wood. — Furniture made of ivory
and various kinds of wood. — On the walls is a fine collection of 274
water-colour drawings of Indian scenery, costumes, customs, etc., by *Wm.
Carpenter*. On the left wall are hung fine old Persian carpets.

*Cross Gallery (see p. 366). This gallery, consisting of a series
of rooms with a total length of 900 ft., connects the upper floor of
the India Museum with the upper floor of the W. Exhibition Gallery (comp. p. 365). It contains the SARACENIC, TURKISH, PERSIAN,
CHINESE, and JAPANESE ART COLLECTIONS, all of which will richly
repay inspection.

Room XI. 'Meshrebiyeh', or lattice window, from Cairo. *'Mimbar', or
pulpit, from a mosque at Cairo, of carved wood inlaid with ivory and ebony,
and still bearing traces of painting (1480). Casts of Saracenic ornamentation. — Room XII. Turkish textile fabrics and embroideries (18th cent.).
Coloured casts of cornices in Cairo; painted panelling from Damascus. —
Room XIII. Saracenic wood and metal work. Fine Mosque lamps of
bronze and glass. Turkish and Damascus tiles. — Room XIV. Persian
carpets, including (left wall) the splendid 'Holy Carpet' from the Mosque
of Ardebil (1540). — Room XV. Persian textile fabrics; embroideries; carpets. — Room XVI. Persian arms and armour; woodwork, bookbindings,
illuminations. Cast of the 'Archer Frieze' from the palace of Darius at
Susa (500 B.C.), now in the Louvre. — Room XVII. Persian tiles. Fine
collection of Persian pottery and glass. — Room XVIII. Blue and white
Chinese porcelain; models of Chinese buildings, sent by the Emperor of
China to Josephine, wife of Napoleon, but captured by the British. On
the walls are fans; embroideries; screen of porcelain plaques. — Room XIX.
Chinese enamels, bronzes, and coloured porcelain. — Room XX. Lacquer
work. Chinese enamels on copper, including a staff with a Runic inscription (1st case on the left). Carvings in wood, ivory, soapstone, etc.
Japanese arms and armour. Japanese lacquered screens. — Room XXI.
Old Chinese lacquered screens; model of Japanese pagoda; Japanese sedan-
chair; Japanese cabinet adorned with coloured straw; Chinese lantern of
carved wood; Japanese domestic shrine; lacquered chest, formerly the
property of Napoleon I. — Room XXII. Carvings in wood and ivory;
lacquer. Historical collection of *Japanese pottery formed by the Japanese
government. — Room XXIII. *Japanese Collection of bronzes, lacquer-
work, textile fabrics, and enamels. To the left of the entrance, large bronze
incense-burner. Bronze equestrian statue of Kato Kiyomasa. *Eagle in
hammered iron, with extended wings, admirably executed by a Japanese
metal-worker of the 16th cent., named Miyôchin Munêharu (purchased for
1000*l.*). Opposite is an elaborate modern incense-burner, with peacocks
and other birds. At the top of the steps at the end of the room is a
colossal bronze figure of a *Bodhisattva, or sacred being destined to become a Buddha.

The lofty building to the E. of South Kensington Museum is
the Roman Catholic **Church of the Oratory** (see p. 78), the finest
modern example in London of the style of the Italian Renaissance.
The façade was completed in 1897. The interior is remarkable
for its lofty marble pilasters and the domed ceiling of concrete
vaulting. In the Lady Chapel are a superb altar and reredos, inlaid
with precious stones, brought from Brescia. The chapels are embel-

lished with mosaics and carvings, and it is intended to cover the walls with mosaics. The choir-stalls are beautifully carved in Italian walnut, the floor is of rich marquetry, and the altar-rail is formed of *giallo antico* marble. The two seven-branched candlesticks of gilt bronze are accurate copies of the Jewish one on the Arch of Titus. — In front of the W. wing, known as the 'Little Oratory', is a *Statue of Cardinal Newman* (1801-90), by Chavalliaud, unveiled in 1896.

30. Belgravia. Chelsea.

Chelsea Hospital. Royal Military Asylum. Carlyle's House.

The southern portion of the West End, commonly known as **Belgravia,** and bounded by Hyde Park, the Green Park, Sloane Street, and Pimlico, consists of a number of handsome streets and squares (*Belgrave Square, Eaton Square, Grosvenor Place*, etc.), all of which have sprung up within the last few decades. It derives its general name from Belgrave Square, the centre of West End pride and fashion. Like *Tyburnia*, to the N., and *Mayfair*, to the E., of Hyde Park, it is one of the most fashionable quarters of the town. At Pimlico on the S.E. stands *Victoria Station*, the extensive West End terminus of the South Eastern and Chatham Railway, and of the London and Brighton Railway (p. 57), whence Victoria Street (p. 273), opened up not many years ago through a wilderness of purlieus, leads N.E. to Westminster; Vauxhall Bridge Road S.E. to Vauxhall Bridge; Buckingham Palace Road and Commercial Road S.W. to Chelsea Bridge and Battersea Park (p. 383).

In Buckingham Palace Road, opposite Victoria Station, is the *National School of Cookery* (Pl. G 2, *IV;* on view 2-4), an institution for teaching the economical preparation of articles of food suitable to smaller households, and for training teachers for branch cookery-schools, of which there are now several in London and other towns.

St. Peter's (Pl. R, 17; *IV*), Eaton Square, is a favourite church for fashionable marriages.

Chelsea, now a suburb of London, lies on the N. bank of the Thames, to the W. of *Chelsea* or *Victoria Suspension Bridge* (Pl. G, 18), which was built in 1858 and leads to the E. end of Battersea Park (p. 383). For many ages before it was swallowed up, Chelsea was a country village, like Kensington, with many distinguished residents. It appears in Domesday Book as *Chelched, i.e.* 'chalk hythe', or wharf; but the name has also been derived from *chesl* (Ger. *Kiesel*), meaning gravel, and *eye*, an island.

Skirting the Thames between the suspension-bridge and *Battersea Bridge* (Pl. G, 10, 11; opened in 1891), is the *Chelsea Embankment* (opened in 1873), which passes the *Albert Suspension Bridge* (central span, 450 ft.) and ends, beyond Battersea Bridge, near the site of *Cremorne Gardens*, so named from an early owner, Lord Cremorne, and formerly a very popular place of recreation, but closed in 1877 and now covered with buildings.

The E. end of Chelsea Embankment skirts the grounds of **Chelsea Hospital** (Pl. G, 18, 14), an institution for old and invalid soldiers, begun in the reign of Charles II. by *Wren*, on the site of a theological college (the name 'college' being sometimes still applied to the building), but not completed till the time of William and Mary. The hospital, consisting of a central structure flanked by two wings, and facing the river, accommodates 540 pensioners. In addition to these about 80,000 out-pensioners obtain relief, varying from $1\frac{1}{2}d.$ to 5s. a day, out of the invested funds of the establishment, which is also partly supported by a grant from Parliament. The annual expenses are about 28,000*l.*

The centre of the quadrangle in front of the hospital is occupied by a bronze statue of Charles II., by *Grinling Gibbons*. The hospital (small fee to pensioner who acts as cicerone) contains a chapel with numerous flags, 13 French eagles, and an altar-piece representing the Ascension of Christ; the ceiling above the latter is by *Seb. Ricci*. In the dining-hall is an equestrian portrait of Charles II., by *Verrio*. Visitors may attend the services in the chapel on Sun., at 11 a.m. and 6.30 p.m. The gardens are open to the public.

To the N. of the hospital lies the **Royal Military Asylum** or **Duke of York's Military School** (Pl. G, 13, 17), founded in 1801 by the Duke of York, an institution in which about 550 sons of soldiers are annually maintained and educated. The building has a Doric portico. The school may be visited daily, from 10 to 4; Friday is perhaps the best day. — In Chelsea Bridge Road, near the hospital, are the largest and finest of all the *Barracks* (Pl. G, 17, 18) for the Foot Guards, with accommodation for 1000 men.

To the S.E., on part of the ornamental grounds of Chelsea Hospital, there stood in the reigns of George II. and George III. a place of amusement named the *Ranelagh*, which was famous beyond any other place in London as the centre of the wildest and showiest gaiety. Banquets, masquerades, fêtes, etc., were celebrated here in the most extravagant style. Kings and ambassadors, statesmen and literati, court beauties, ladies of fashion, and the *demi-monde* met and mingled at the Ranelagh as they now meet nowhere in the Metropolis. Its principal building, the 'Rotunda', 185 ft. in diameter, not unlike in external appearance to the present Albert Hall, was erected in 1740, by William Jones. Horace Walpole describes it as 'a vast amphitheatre, finely gilt, painted, and illuminated, into which everybody that loves eating, drinking, staring, or crowding is admitted for twelve pence'. This haunt of pleasure-seekers was closed in 1805, and every trace of it has long been obliterated.

To the S.W. of the hospital, adjoining the Embankment, lies the Chelsea *Botanic Garden*, presented by *Sir Hans Sloane* to the Society of Apothecaries, on condition that 50 new varieties of plants grown in it should be annually furnished to the Royal Society, until the number so presented amounted to 2000. It was famed for its fine cedars, of which but one survives. In the middle is a statue of Sloane, by Rysbrack. The garden is now under the care of the Trustees of the London Parochial Charities.

To the W. of this point the Embankment passes *Cheyne Walk*

(Pl. G, 10, 14), a row of red-brick Queen Anne or Georgian houses, with wrought-iron gates. Maclise (d. 1870), the painter, lived at No. 4, which afterwards became the home of George Eliot (Mrs. Cross), who died here in 1880. Count D'Orsay lived at No. 10. No. 16, known as the *Queen's House* and associated with Queen Catherine of Braganza, was the home of Dante G. Rossetti (d. 1882); and a bust of the painter and poet, by Ford Madox Brown, has been placed in the Embankment Gardens in front of it. No. 18 was *Don Saltero's*, a coffee-house and museum opened in 1695 by a barber named Salter and often mentioned by Swift, Steele, and other contemporary writers. The houses between this and Oakley Street occupy the site of Henry VIII.'s *Manor House*, where Katherine Parr lived with her second husband, Thomas Seymour, and the Princess, afterwards Queen, Elizabeth. Sir Hans Sloane also lived at the historic manor house and made the collection which formed the beginning of the British Museum (see p. 299). His name is commemorated in Sloane Street, Sloane Square, etc.

A little farther to the W., opposite Cheyne Row (Pl. G, 14), which runs to the N. from Cheyne Walk, is a *Statue of Thomas Carlyle* (d. 1881), by Boehm. At No. 24 (formerly No. 5) Cheyne Row is ***Carlyle's House**, the unpretending residence of Thomas Carlyle, the 'Sage of Chelsea', from 1834 till his death in 1881. It is now fitted up as a memorial museum (open from 10 till sunset; adm. 1s., Sat. 6d., parties of ten 6d. each).

The *Dining Room* and *Back Dining Room*, on the groundfloor, contain a few pieces of furniture that belonged to Carlyle, a bookcase full of his books, and a case containing fragments of his writing and other relics. — In the *Drawing Room*, on the first floor, are other pieces of furniture and a case containing mementoes of Carlyle's intercourse with celebrated persons such as Goethe, Bismarck, and the Emp. Frederick of Germany, the Prussian Order of Merit given to Carlyle, notes from Carlyle to his wife, Disraeli's offer of a baronetcy and Carlyle's reply, etc. On the walls are several portraits of Mrs. Carlyle, and adjacent is her *Bedroom*. — On the second floor are *Carlyle's Bedroom* and the *Spare Room*, in which Emerson slept. — At the top of the house is the famous *Study*, double-walled for the exclusion of sound. Here 'Frederick the Great' was written. It contains many interesting personal relics. — Comp. 'The Carlyles' Chelsea Home', by *Reginald Blunt* (illus.; 1895).

Leigh Hunt lived at No. 10 Upper Cheyne Row. — The manufacture of Chelsea china was carried on in a pottery in Lawrence Street, the first parallel street to the W. of Cheyne Row.

Hard by, at the corner of Cheyne Walk and Church Street, stands ***Chelsea Old Church** (*St. Luke's*; Pl. G, 10), one of the most interesting churches in London. It was originally built in the reign of Edward II. (1307-27), but in its present form dates mainly from about 1660, though some older work remains in the chancel and its side-chapels. Among the numerous monuments it contains are those of Lord Bray and his son (1539); several of the Lawrence family, the 'Hillyars' of H. Kingsley's interesting novel 'The Hillyars and the Burtons' (see recent edition, with a note on Chelsea Old Church by Clement Shorter); the sumptuous monument of

Lord and Lady Dacre (1594-95); the Duchess of Northumberland (d. 1555; mother-in-law of Lady Jane Grey and grandmother of Sir Philip Sidney); Sir Arthur Gorges (1625), the friend of Spenser; Sir Robert Stanley (d. 1632); and Lady Jane Cheyne (d. 1669), a large monument by Bernini, the only work now remaining that he did for England. Sir Thomas More built the chapel on the S. side of the chancel, and erected a monument to himself, which is now in the chancel. In all probability his remains are in this church, except his head, which is at Canterbury (see *Baedeker's Great Britain*). In the churchyard is the monument of Sir Hans Sloane (d. 1753; see p. 370). In the church or churchyard are also buried, though their monuments have disappeared, Shadwell, poet laureate (d. 1692), Henry Sampson Woodfall, printer of the celebrated Letters of Junius (d. 1805), and John Cavalier, the Huguenot leader (d. 1740). In the church are the 'Vinegar Bible', Foxe's Book of Martyrs (2 vols.), and two other books, chained to a desk. The keys of the church may be had from the *Rev. R. H. Davies*, 106 Oakley Street.

This old church ceased to be the parish-church of Chelsea in 1824. The new church, also dedicated to St. Luke, is a large building of 1820-24, in Sydney Street (Pl. G, 13). — In Church Street is the old *Rectory*, for several years the home of Charles, George, and Henry Kingsley, whose father was Rector of Chelsea.

Joseph Turner, the landscape-painter, died in 1851 in lodgings at the extreme W. end of Cheyne Walk (No. 119).

The *Public Library*, in Manresa Road (Pl. G, 10), contains a collection of Keats relics, presented by Sir Charles Dilke, a valuable series of Chelsea prints and sketches, busts of Carlyle and Leigh Hunt, a statuette of Sir Thomas More, and other exhibits of local interest.

The past associations of Chelsea are full of interest and have barely been touched upon above. Sir Thomas More resided in Chelsea, in a house afterwards named *Beaufort House*, the site of which is marked by Beaufort Street (Pl. G, 10). Here he was often visited by Henry VIII., Holbein, and (probably) Erasmus. The old *Moravian Burial Ground*, with the grave of *Count Zinzendorf* (d. 1760), occupies part of the site of More's garden. The adjoining Danvers Street marks the site of *Danvers House*, the home of the witty and hospitable Lady Danvers, the friend of Dr. Donne and Francis Bacon. Hard by is *Lindsey House*, now divided into five, once occupied by Brunel and Bramah. Bishop Atterbury, Dean Swift, and Dr. Arbuthnot all resided in Church Street. Sir Richard Steele resided not far off. Mrs. Somerville lived at Chelsea Hospital, where her husband was physician. *Walpole House* occupied the site of the W. wing of the Hospital, and Ward 7 of the infirmary was its dining-room (1723-46). Sir Robert Walpole was visited here by Swift, Gay, and Pope. The beautiful Duchess of Mazarin ended her life in a small house in Chelsea, where she was often visited by St. Evremond. Lord Burleigh, Gay, Newton, Smollett, Miss Mitford, Letitia Landon ('L. E. L.'), George Meredith, Swinburne, and Shelley were also among the famous residents of Chelsea. Prince Rupert is said to have invented his 'drops' here. Addison occasionally resided at *Sandford Manor House*, Sandy End (Pl. G, 7). Among the other famous old houses of Chelsea were *Shrewsbury House*, where dwelt 'Bess', Countess of Shrewsbury, who built Chatsworth, Hardwick Hall, and Oldcotes (see *Baedeker's Great Britain*), and *Winchester House*, long the palace of the Bishops of Winchester.

A little to the W. was Little Chelsea, now West Brompton, where the famous Earl of Shaftesbury of the 'Characteristics' resided in Shaftesbury House. This mansion, where Locke, who had been Lord Shaftesbury's tutor, was a guest, and where Addison wrote parts of the 'Spectator', has been converted into a workhouse.

See 'Handbook to Chelsea', by *Reginald Blunt* (illus.; 1900), and 'Old Chelsea', by *B. E. Martin* (illus. by Joseph Pennell).

31. Hampstead. Highgate. Kensal Green Cemetery.

The visitor should go to *Hampstead* by omnibus (p. 50), tramway (Nos. 5, 6, p. 54), or train (North London Railway, p. 56), and walk thence to *Highgate*.

Highgate also may be reached direct by omnibus (p. 50), tramway (Nos. 2, 3, 4, 6; p. 54), or train (Great Northern Railway, p. 56).

The two hills of Hampstead and Highgate, occupied by the N.W. suburbs of London, are well worth visiting for the extensive views they command of the Metropolis and the surrounding country.

The village of **Hampstead** ('home-stead') has been long since reached by the ever-advancing suburbs of London, from which it can now scarcely be distinguished. It is an ancient place, known as early as the time of the Romans; and various Roman antiquities have been found in the neighbourhood, particularly at the mineral wells. These wells (in Well Walk, to the E. of the High Street) were discovered or re-discovered about 1620, and for a time made Hampstead a fashionable spa; the old well-house is now used as a church. Well Walk also contains the house in which John Keats and his brother lodged in 1817-18, and at the bottom of John Street, near Hampstead Heath Station, is *Lawn Bank* (then called Wentworth Place; memorial tablet), where Keats lived with his friend Charles Brown in 1818-20. Part of 'Endymion' was written in the first of these, and much of Keats's finest work, including parts of 'Hyperion' and the 'Eve of St. Agnes', was done at Lawn Bank. Leigh Hunt long lived in a cottage in the Vale of Health, a cluster of houses in the centre of the S. part of the heath; the site is now occupied by the Vale of Health Hotel. The parish-church of *St. John* dates from 1744, and with its square tower forms a conspicuous object in the view from many parts of London. It contains a bust of Keats, by *Miss Anne Whitney* of Boston (U.S.A.), placed here in 1894 by a few American admirers of the poet. In the churchyard are buried *Sir James Mackintosh* (d. 1832), *Joanna Bailie* (d. 1851; memorial tablet in the church), her sister *Agnes* (d. 1861, aged 100 years), *George Du Maurier* (d. 1896), and *Constable*, the painter (d. 1837), who has left many painted memorials of his love for Hampstead (see, *e.g.*, his pictures of Hampstead in the Tate Gallery, p. 276, and at S. Kensington, p. 361). The well-known Kit-Cat Club, which numbered Addison, Steele, and Pope among its members, held its first meetings in a tavern at Hampstead.

***Hampstead Heath** (430 ft. above the sea-level) is one of the most open and picturesque spots in the immediate neighbourhood of London, and is a favourite and justly valued resort of holiday-makers and all who appreciate pure and invigorating air. The heath is about 240 acres in extent. Its wild and irregular beauty, and picturesque alternations of hill and hollow, make it a refreshing contrast to the trim elegance of the Parks. The heath was once a notorious haunt of highwaymen. In 1870 it was purchased by the Metropolitan Board of Works for the unrestricted use of the public. *Parliament Hill* (265 acres), to the S.E. of the heath proper, has also been acquired for the public. A supposed tumulus, known as 'Queen Boadicea's Grave', was investigated here in 1895 with disappointing results. Near the ponds at the S.E. corner of the heath the Fleet Brook (p. 172) takes its rise. The garden of the *Bull and Bush Inn*, on the N. margin of the heath, contains a holly planted by Hogarth, the painter; and *'Jack Straw's Castle'*, on the highest part of the heath, near the flag-staff, is another interesting old inn. Lord Chatham (1708-78) died at *Wildwoods*, near the Bull and Bush, in a room with an oriel window on the upper floor (N.E. angle of the house). On public holidays Hampstead Heath is generally visited by 25-50,000 Londoners and presents a characteristic scene of popular enjoyment.

The *View from the highest part of the heath is extensive and interesting. On the S. lies London, with the dome of St. Paul's and the towers of Westminster rising conspicuously from the dark masses of houses; while beyond may be discerned the green hills of Surrey and the glittering roof of the Crystal Palace at Sydenham. The varied prospect to the W. includes the Welsh Harp (p. 417), Harrow-on-the-Hill (p. 420; distinguishable by the lofty spire on an isolated eminence), and, in clear weather, Windsor Castle itself. To the N. lies a fertile and well-peopled tract, studded with numerous villages and houses and extending to Highwood Hill, Totteridge, and Barnet. To the E., in immediate proximity, we see the sister hill of Highgate, and in clear weather we may descry the reach of the Thames at Gravesend.

We leave Hampstead Heath at the N. end, near 'Jack Straw's Castle', and follow *Heath* or *Spaniards' Road*, leading to the N.E. to Highgate. We soon reach, on the left, the *'Spaniards' Inn'*, the gathering-point of the 'No Popery' rioters of 1780, and described by Dickens in 'Barnaby Rudge'. The stretch of road between 'Jack Straw's Castle' and this point is perhaps the most open and elevated near London, affording fine views to the N.W. and S.E. To the left, just beyond the inn, is the course of the *Hampstead Golf Club*. The road then leads between *Caen Wood*, with its fine old oaks, on the right, and *Bishop's Wood*, on the left. Caen Wood, or Ken Wood House, was the seat of the celebrated judge, Lord Mansfield, who died here in 1793. Bishop's Wood once formed part of the park of the Bishops of London. We now follow *Hampstead Lane*, passing the grounds of *Caen Wood Towers* on the right, and reach *Highgate*. To the right diverges The Grove, in the third house

in which, to the right, Coleridge died in 1834. A little farther on
we reach Highgate High Street, whence a cable-tramway (p. 54)
plies down Highgate Hill.

There is also a pleasant path from Hampstead to Highgate leading
past the Ponds and over *Parliament Hill* (p. 373) to Highgate Road. Turning
here to the left, we pass the tramway-terminus (No. 4c, p. 54) at the end
of Swain's Lane, and ascend West Hill, skirting the spacious grounds of
Holly Lodge, the residence of Baroness Burdett Coutts, to the Highgate High
Street (see above). — Swain's Lane. diverging to the right, leads to Highgate
Cemetery (see below) and to the S.W. entrance of Waterlow Park (see below).

Highgate, which is situated on a hill about 30 ft. lower than
Hampstead Heath, is one of the healthiest and most favourite sites
for villas in the outskirts of London. The view which it commands
is similar in character to that from Hampstead, but not so fine. The
new church, built in the Gothic style in 1833, is a handsome edifice,
and, from its situation, very conspicuous. The Highgate or North
London *Cemetery, lying on the slope of the hill just below the
church, is very picturesque and tastefully laid out. The catacombs
are in the Egyptian style, with cypresses, and the terraces afford a fine
view. *Michael Faraday*, the great chemist (d. 1867; by the E. wall),
Lord Lyndhurst (d. 1863), and *George Eliot* (d. 1880; near the
Swain's Lane entrance to the lower part of the cemetery) are buried
here. *Samuel Taylor Coleridge* (d. 1834) is interred in a vault below
the adjacent Grammar School, which, founded in 1565, was lately
rebuilt in the French Gothic style. To the E. of the upper part of
Highgate Cemetery is *Waterlow Park*, 29 acres in extent, formerly
the grounds of Fairseat House, the residence of Sir Sidney Waterlow, and presented to the public by that gentleman in 1891. The
main entrance of Waterlow Park is at the top of Highgate Hill. In
this park is the quaint old *Lauderdale House*, once occupied by Nell
Gwynne, restored in 1893 and now used as refreshment rooms.

On the opposite side of Highgate Hill, facing Lauderdale House,
is *Cromwell House*, said to have been built for Cromwell's son-in-
law, General Ireton, and now a Convalescent Hospital for Children.
It is a plain red-brick mansion, with a fine oak staircase, on the newel
of which are small carved figures representing officers of Cromwell's
army, etc. A little lower down is *St. Joseph's Retreat*, the chief seat
of the Passionist Fathers in England, with a handsome new church
opened in 1891. The *Whittington Almshouses* at the foot of the
hill were established by the famous Lord Mayor of that name, and
are popularly supposed to occupy the very spot where he heard the
bells inviting him to return. Close by is the stone on which he is
said to have rested, now forming part of a lamp-post; it is needless
to say that its identity is more than doubtful.

The *Highgate Archway Tavern*, at the foot of Highgate Hill, is
an important omnibus and tramway terminus (comp. pp. 50, 54).
Archway Road leads thence to the N. to (1/3 M.) the site of *Highgate
Archway*, now replaced by a viaduct-bridge, by means of which

Hornsey Lane is carried across the road. *Highgate Station* lies ½ M. farther on, near the entrance to the *Highgate Gravel Pit Wood*, 70 acres in extent and about 1 M. to the N., opened as a public park in 1886.

Highgate used to be notorious for a kind of mock pilgrimage made to it for the purpose of 'swearing on the horns.' By the terms of his oath the pilgrim was bound never to kiss the maid when he could kiss the mistress, never to drink small beer when he could get strong, etc.. 'unless he liked it best'. Some old rams' heads are still preserved at the inns. Byron alludes to this custom in 'Childe Harold', Canto I.

About 2 M. off, on the elevated ground to the E. of *Muswell Hill* and N. of *Hornsey*, is the *Alexandra Palace* (p. 69), an establishment resembling the Crystal Palace. The palace is near the *Alexandra Palace* and the *Woodgreen Stations* of the G. N. R. and the *Palace Gates Station* on the G. E. R.

Kensal Green Cemetery forms an exception to most of the cemeteries of London, which are uninteresting, owing to the former English custom of burying eminent men in churches. It lies on the N.W. side of London and is most easily reached by omnibus from Edgware Road. We may also travel by the Metropolitan Railway to Notting Hill or Westbourne Park Station (p. 61), each of which is about ¾ M. to the S. of the cemetery; or by the North London Railway to Kensal Rise Station (p. 57), ½ M. to the N.

Kensal Green Cemetery, laid out in 1832, covers an area of about 70 acres, and contains about forty thousand graves. It is divided into a consecrated portion for members of the Church of England, and an unconsecrated portion for dissenters. Most of the tombstones are plain upright slabs, but in the upper part of the cemetery, particularly on the principal path leading to the chapel, there are several monuments handsomely executed in granite and marble, some of which possess considerable artistic value. Four of the most conspicuous monuments are those of Ducrow, the circus-rider, Robins, the auctioneer, Morrison, the pill-maker, and St. John Long, the quack. Among the eminent people interred here are: — Brunel, the engineer; Sydney Smith, the author; Mulready, the painter; Sir Charles Eastlake, the painter and historian of art; Tom Hood, the poet; Leigh Hunt, the essayist; Sir John Ross, the arctic navigator; Thackeray, the novelist; John Leech, the well-known illustrator of 'Punch'; Gibson, the sculptor; Mme. Tietjens, the great singer; Charles Kemble and Charles Mathews, the actors; Anthony Trollope, the novelist; John Owen, the social reformer. Adjoining the grave of the last is the Reformers' Memorial. — Cardinals Wiseman and Manning are interred in the Roman Catholic Cemetery, adjacent to Kensal Green (comp., however, p. 274).

Highgate Cemetery (p. 374) to the N., and *Norwood Cemetery* to the S. of London, are worth visiting for the sake of the excellent *Views they afford. The Greeks have a special enclosure in Norwood Cemetery. Abney Park Cemetery (p. 144) is much used as a burying-ground by Nonconformists. The chief Jews' Burial Ground is in Mile End Road, adjoining the People's Palace (Pl. R, 60). — See 'London Burial Grounds: Notes on their History from the Earliest Times to the Present Day', by Mrs. Basil Holmes (London, 1896).

III. THE SURREY SIDE.

32. St. Saviour's Church.

Guy's Hospital. Barclay and Perkins' Brewery. Southwark Park.

The 'Surrey Side' of the Metropolis, with a population of over 750,000 souls, has in some respects a character of its own. It is a scene of great business life and bustle from Lambeth to Bermondsey, but its sights, institutions, and public buildings are few. *Southwark*, or that part of it immediately opposite the City, from London Bridge to Charing Cross, is known as 'the Borough', a name which it rightly enjoys over the heads of such newly created boroughs as Greenwich or the Tower Hamlets, seeing it has returned two members to Parliament for more than 500 years. We note a few of its objects of interest.

Mention must be made, in the first place, of *St. Saviour's Church (Pl. R 38, III; open 11-4), one of the oldest churches in London, situated opposite the London Bridge Station, immediately to the W. of the S. end of London Bridge. The original Norman nave, of which fragments still remain, was built in 1106 by Gifford, Bishop of Winchester, as the church of the then established Priory of St. Mary Overy. Peter de Rupibus, another Bishop of Winchester, built the choir and Lady Chapel in 1207, and altered the character of the nave, which had been damaged by fire, from Norman to Early English. The building was converted into a parish-church by Henry VIII. in 1540. The interesting choir, transept, and Lady Chapel of Peter de Rupibus still survive; the choir and Lady Chapel were restored, with but partial success, in 1822 and 1832-34. The nave was taken down in 1838, and replaced by an incongruous new structure, which was in turn removed to make way for a fine new nave, in the 13th cent. style, built in 1890-96 by *Blomfield*. Above the cross is a quadrangular tower, flanked by pinnacles. After extensive restorations St. Saviour's was opened as a collegiate church in Feb., 1897, and may one day become the cathedral for South London. — The entrance is on the E. side of the S. transept.

Interior. Though the interior at present produces a first impression of newness, and even of rawness, a tribute must be paid to the unusual congruity with which the dignified modern nave has been adapted to the earlier work. — The large window in the S. TRANSEPT was restored and filled with stained glass (Tree of Jesse) at the expense of Sir Fred. Wigan. On the wall opposite the door is a monument to *William Emerson* (1483-1575), 'who lived and died an honest man', and is believed to have belonged to the same stock as Ralph Waldo Emerson. The window above commemorates *Elizabeth Newcomen* (d. 1675), a benefactor of the parish. On the pillar immediately to the N. of the door in this transept are carved

the arms and hat of *Cardinal Beaufort* (son of John of Gaunt), a benefactor of the church. — The windows in the NAVE commemorate illustrious
men connected with the church or with Southwark. In the S. wall, from
E. to W., are memorial windows to *William Shakspeare* (see below), *Philip
Massinger* (d. 1639), *John Fletcher* (d. 1625), *Francis Beaumont* (d. 1616), and
Edward Alleyn (p. 401), once churchwarden of the parish. The next two
windows contain figures of *SS. Paulinus* and *Swithin*. The large W. window
(by H. Holiday), representing the Creation, was presented by Mr. Withers
in 1893. The fine old Norman doorway and the recess at the W. end of
the N. wall are relics of the original nave. The windows in the N. wall
are destined for memorials to *Dr. Johnson, Cruden, Sacheverell, Bunyan,
Baxter*, and *Chaucer*. Near the E. end of this wall is the monument of
the poet *John Gower* (1325-1402), the friend of Chaucer. It consists of a
sarcophagus with a recumbent marble figure of the poet (repainted in
1832), whose head rests upon his three principal works, the *Speculum
meditantis, Vox clamantis*, and *Confessio amantis*, while his feet are supported by a lion. — The N. TRANSEPT has a memorial window to the
Prince Consort (by Kempe; unveiled in 1898), bearing figures of Gregory
the Great, King Ethelbert, Archbp. Stephen Langton, and William of
Wykeham. The aumbry, the stone coffin (12th cent.) below it, the carved
oaken bosses from the former roof, and the fine muniment chest should
be noticed. On the N. wall is the effigy and tomb of *Lockyer* (d. 1672),
a famous quack ('his pills embalm him safe'). — The chandelier hanging
below the tower was presented in 1680. — The *Altar Screen* in the
CHOIR was erected by Fox, Bishop of Winchester, in the early years
of the 16th century. In the N. choir-aisle are the painted tomb, with
effigies, of *John Trehearne*, gentleman-porter to James I., and the recumbent wooden figure of a *Crusader* (13th cent.). Opposite the latter is
the canopied tomb of *Alderman Humble*, on which some beautiful verses
are inscribed. — The beautiful °LADY CHAPEL, now used as the parish
church, is flanked with aisles and contains the monument of *Lancelot
Andrewes*, Bishop of Winchester (d. 1625). The trials of the reputed heretics
under Queen Mary in 1555 took place in this chapel. The martyrs are
commemorated by stained-glass windows. In the N.E. bay, above the
bench of the old Consistorial Court, is a window in honour of St. Thomas
à Becket, Charles I., and Archbp. Laud. In the S. choir-aisle are a
memorial window to *Geo. Gwilt* (d. 1856), the architect, and a slab in
memory of *Abraham Newland* (1730-1807), long chief-cashier of the Bank
of England. On the pavement at the W. end of the aisle are some Roman
tesseræ, and on the pillar to the N. is a brass (1652), with a quaint inscription.

Among those who are buried in St. Saviour's but have no monuments
are *Sir Edward Dyer* (d. 1607), the poet, *Massinger* and *Fletcher*, the dramatists, *Edmund Shakspeare* (d. 1607, aged 27), a player, brother of the
poet, and *Lawrence Fletcher*, who was a lessee, along with Shakspeare and
Burbage, of the Globe and Blackfriars Theatres. — *John Harvard*, founder
of Harvard College. Cambridge, Mass., was baptized at St. Saviour's on
29th Nov., 1607; his parents kept the 'Old Queen's Head' in Southwark.
James I. of Scotland and Joanna Beaufort were married in this church
in 1425.

On the river, near St. Saviour's, once stood *Winchester House*,
the residence of the bishops of Winchester, whose diocese included
South London until 1877, when the latter was transferred to the
diocese of Rochester.

The Borough High Street runs to the S. from London Bridge.
Thomas Street, diverging to the left (E.) near the N. end of Borough
High Street, leads to **Guy's Hospital** (Pl. G, 42), founded in 1721
by Guy, the bookseller, who had amassed an immense fortune by
speculation in South Sea stock. The institution contains 500 beds,

and relieves 5000 in-patients and 70,000 out-patients annually. It includes a residential college for 50 students and a dental school. The yearly income of the hospital is about 31,000*l*. The court contains a brazen, and the chapel a marble statue of thef ounder (d. 1724), the latter by *Bacon*. Sir Astley Cooper, the celebrated surgeon, to whom a monument has been erected in St. Paul's (see p. 118), is buried here. John Keats was a student at Guy's, and the Rev. F. D. Maurice was chaplain here from 1836 to 1846.

Southwark Street, which diverges to the right (W.) from Borough High Street a little farther on, leads to the *Borough Market* (p. 32). Redcross Street, which intersects Southwark Street, leads on the left to *Redcross Hall*, with paintings commemorating deeds of heroism in humble life, and on the right to Park Street, in which is situated **Messrs. Barclay, Perkins, and Co.'s Brewery** (Pl. R, 38; *III*), partly on the former site of the *Globe Theatre*. This is one of the most extensive establishments of the kind in London, and is well worthy of a visit, on account both of its great size and its admirable arrangements. It was founded more than 200 years ago.

The brewery covers an area of about 12 acres, forming a miniature town of houses, sheds, lofts, stables, streets, and courts. At the entrance stand the Offices, where visitors, who readily obtain an order to inspect the establishment on application by letter, enter their names in a book. The guide who is assigned to the visitor on entering expects a fee of a shilling or so. In most of the rooms there is a somewhat oppressive and heady odour, particularly in the cooling-room, where the carbonic acid gas lies about a foot deep over the fresh brew. Visitors are recommended to exercise caution in accepting the guide's invitation to breathe this gas.

In spite of the vast dimensions of the boilers, vats (one of which has a capacity of 112,000 gallons, or more than twice that of the Great Tun of Heidelberg), fermenting 'squares', and other apparatus, none but the initiated will have any idea of the enormous quantity of liquor brewed here in the course of a year, amounting to nearly 20 million gallons. About 200,000 quarters of malt are annually consumed, and the yearly duty paid to government by the firm amounts to the immense sum of 180,000*l*. The head brewer is said to receive a salary of 1000*l*. per annum. One of the early owners of the brewery was Dr. Johnson's friend Thrale, after whose death it was sold to Messrs. Barclay and Perkins. Dr. Johnson's words on the occasion of the sale, which he attended as an executor, though often quoted, are worthy of repetition: 'We are not here to sell a parcel of boilers and vats, but the potentiality of growing rich beyond the dreams of avarice.' Most of the water used in brewing is supplied by an artesian well, sunk on the premises. — The stables contain about 150 strong dray-horses, used for carting the beer in London, and many of them bred in Yorkshire.

The brewing-trade in London has become a great power within the last twenty or thirty years, and is felt to have a serious bearing upon the results of parliamentary and municipal elections. It is no longer a merely manufacturing trade, but promotes the consumption of its own goods by the purchase or lease of public-houses, where its agents are installed to conduct the sale. These agents are nominal tenants and are possessed of votes, and their number and influence are so great, that the power of returning the candidate who favours the 'trade' is often in their hands. All the great brewers are now understood to be extensive proprietors of such 'tied houses.'

The central station of the *Metropolitan Fire Brigade* (comp. p. 97), is in Southwark Bridge Road, farther to the W.

Among other interesting associations connected with this locality the following may be noticed. The name of *Park Street* reminds us of the extensive Park of the Bishops of Winchester, which occupied the river side from Winchester House to Holland House. In the fields to the S. of this park were the circuses for bull and bear baiting, so popular in the time of the Stuarts. Edward Alleyn was for many years the 'Keeper of the King's wild beasts' here, and amassed thereby the fortune which enabled him to found Dulwich College (see p. 401). A dingy passage in Bankside still shows the name 'Bear Garden' (Pl. R, 38). — Richard Baxter often preached in a church in Park Street, and in Zoar Street there was a chapel in which John Bunyan is said to have ministered. — *Mint Street* recalls the mint existing here under Henry VIII. — In High Street there stood down to 1875 the old *Talbot* or *Tabard Inn*, the starting-point of Chaucer's 'Canterbury Pilgrims'. — The *George* (rebuilt after a fire in 1676) is an interesting specimen of an old-time inn, with galleries round its inner court. — The *White Hart*, a similar structure in the Borough High Street, mentioned by Shakspeare in 'Henry VI'. (Part II, iv. 8) and by Dickens in the 'Pickwick Papers' (as the meeting-place of Mr. Pickwick and Sam Weller), was pulled down in 1889. — The *Marshalsea Gaol*, the name of which is familiar from 'Little Dorrit', stood near *St. George's Church*, at the corner of Great Dover Street and Borough High Street. In the graveyard of this church lies the arithmetician Edward Cocker (d. 1675), whose memory is embalmed in the phrase 'according to Cocker'.

Southwark Park (Pl. R, 49, G, 49, 53), in Rotherhithe (p. 95), much farther to the E., laid out by the Metropolitan Board of Works at a cost of more than 100,000*l.*, covers an area of sixty-three acres, and is in the immediate neighbourhood of the extensive *Surrey Docks* (p. 167).

The Borough High Street is continued on the S. by Newington Causeway to the *Elephant and Castle* (Pl. G, 33; p. 35), a well-known inn and omnibus-centre (electric railway, see p. 62). In Newington Butts, a little to the W., stood the *Tabernacle* of the late popular preacher Mr. Spurgeon (d. 1891), built in the classic style and accommodating 6000 persons (comp. p. 77). It was burnt almost to the ground in April, 1898, but has been rebuilt on the old lines, though on a somewhat smaller scale. — Walworth Road, leading to the S. from the Elephant and Castle, is continued by Camberwell Road, ending at *Camberwell Green* (Pl. G, 39). Church Street leads hence towards the E. and is continued by Peckham Road, near the beginning of which, on the right, is *Camberwell Grammar School*. Farther on (No. 63) is the *Camberwell School* of *Arts and Crafts*, opened in 1898, with technical and trade classes intended to encourage the industrial application of decorative design. Connected with the school is the **South London Fine Art**

Gallery (Pl. G, 43), founded in 1868, as the Working Men's College for South London. It includes a picture-gallery of works either permanent (including a fine cartoon by F. Madox Brown) or on loan, a free library, a small museum, and a lecture-hall (open daily, 3-5, 7-9.30).

33. Lambeth Palace. Bethlehem Hospital, Battersea Park.

St. Thomas's Hospital. St. George's Cathedral. Battersea Polytechnic.

On the right bank of the Thames, from Westminster Bridge to Vauxhall Bridge, a distance of about ⁴/₅ of a mile, stretches the ALBERT EMBANKMENT (Pl. G, 29, R, 29; *IV*), completed in 1869. It has a roadway 60 ft. in breadth, and cost more than 1,000,000*l*. On it, opposite the Houses of Parliament, stands **St. Thomas's Hospital** (Pl. R, 29; *IV*), a spacious edifice built by *Currey* in 1868-71, at a cost of 500,000*l*. It consists of seven four-storied buildings in red brick, united by arcades, and is in all 590 yds. long. The number of in-patients annually treated in the 572 beds of the hospital is over 5000, of out-patients about 80,000. Its annual revenue is 40,000*l*. Professional visitors will be much interested in the admirable internal arrangements (admission on Tuesdays at 10 a.m.). The hospital was formerly in a building in High Street, Southwark, which was sold to the South Eastern Railway Company in 1862 for 296,000*l*. — In Paris Street, to the E. of the hospital, is the entrance to *Archbishop's Park*, a portion (ca. 10 acres) of the grounds of Lambeth Palace opened to the public in 1900.

Lambeth Palace (Pl. R, 29; *IV*), above the hospital, has been for over 600 years the London residence of the Archbishops of Canterbury. It can be visited only by the special permission of the archbishop (apply to the chaplain). The entrance is by the S. gateway, a massive brick structure, flanked by two towers, which was erected by Cardinal Morton in the end of the 15th century. The part of the palace actually occupied by the archbishop dates from 1829-34; visitors are shown over the older portions usually in the following order (small fee to guide). The '*Lollards' Tower*' (properly the *Water Tower*), so called because the Lollards, or followers of Wycliffe, were supposed to have been imprisoned and tortured here, is an old, massive, square keep, erected by Archbishop Chicheley in 1434. A small room in the upper part of the tower, 13¹/₂ ft. long, 12 ft. wide, and 8 ft. high, called the 'prison' and forming part of a staircase-turret more than 200 years older than the time of Chicheley, still contains several inscriptions by prisoners, and eight large rings fastened in the wall, to which the heretics were chained. The Earl of Essex, Queen Elizabeth's favourite (1601), Lovelace, the poet (1648), and Sir Thomas Armstrong (1659), were also confined here. The name of Lollards' Tower, applied to what is really a group of three buildings distinct in character and architecture, dates only from the beginning of the 18th century. The real Lollards' Tower was the S.W. tower of old St. Paul's Cathedral (see p. 111), as mentioned in Stow's Survey of London (1598). — The *Chapel*, 72 ft. long and 26 ft. broad, which opens off the lower part of the water-tower, was built in 1245 by Archbishop Boniface in the Early English style, and is the oldest part of the building. The screen and windows were placed here by Archbishop Laud; the latter were destroyed in the Civil War and replaced by Archbishop Tait, his family, and friends. The musicians' gallery and the lancet-windows at the W. end are due to Juxon. The roof is modern and is copied from the vaulting of the crypt. Parker (d. 1575) is the only archbishop buried here. The chapel was the scene of Wycliffe's second trial (1378) and of the consecration of the first American bishops (1787). The *Guard Chamber*, 60 ft. long, and 25 ft. broad, contains portraits of the archbishops since 1533, including Archbishop Laud, by *Van Dyck;* Herring, by *Hogarth;* Secker, by *Sir Joshua Reynolds;* Sutton, by *Sir Thomas Lawrence;* Howley, by *Shee;* Tait, by *Sant;* Benson, by *Herkomer;* and a portrait of Archbishop War-ham, after *Holbein* (1504), a copy of the original in the Louvre (or perhaps, according to Woltmann, the original itself). The dining-room contains portraits of Luther and his wife. — The *Great Hall*, 92 ft. long and 40 ft. broad, was built by Archbishop Juxon in 1663 on the site of the old hall, and has a roof in the style of that of Westminster Hall, with Italian instead of Gothic details. The early-Renaissance doorway, bearing Juxon's arms, should be noticed. The hall now contains the *Library*, established by Archbishop Ban-croft in 1610, and consisting of 30,000 vols. and 2000 MSS., some of which, including the Registers of the official acts of the arch-bishops from 1274 to 1744 in 41 vols., are very valuable. The glass-cases contain some interesting MSS. and relics. The library is accessible daily, except Saturdays, between 10 a.m. and 4 p.m. (in summer, 5 p.m; Tues., 10-1; closed from Sept. 1st to Oct. 15th). — See 'Lambeth Palace and its Associations', by *Rev. J. Cave-Browne* (2nd ed., 1883), and 'Art Treasures of the Lambeth Library', by the librarian, *S. W. Kershaw, F. S. A.* (1873).

The parish-church of *St. Mary*, immediately to the S. of the palace, was rebuilt in 1851 but retains its old Perpendicular tower. It contains the graves of six archbishops (Bancroft, Tenison, Hutton, Secker, Cornwallis, and Moore). The 'Pedlar's Window' commem-orates a pedlar who is said to have bequeathed an acre of land (the 'Pedlar's Acre') to the parish.

The church is situated close to the E. end of *Lambeth Suspension Bridge* (built in 1862), whence Lambeth Road runs to the E., passing **Bethlehem Hospital** (Pl. R, 33; popularly corrupted into *Bedlam*), the oldest charitable institution for the insane in the world.

The hospital was founded in Bishopsgate Street by Sheriff Simon Fitz-Mary in 1247, as a priory for the Order of St. Mary of Bethlehem. The priory was seized by the Crown in 1375, and there is evidence that insane persons were confined in it as early as 1403. In 1547 Henry VIII. granted a charter to the City of London for the management of the institution, and it has remained ever since one of the 'royal' hospitals. The building in Bishopsgate Street was taken down in 1675, and a new hospital built in Moorfields, to replace which the present building in St. George's Fields, Lambeth, on the site of the notorious 'Dog & Duck Tavern', was begun in 1812. The cost of construction of the hospital, which has a frontage 900 ft. long, was 122,000l.; the architect was *Lewis*, but the dome was added by *Smirke*.

The hospital is now used as a charitable institution for persons of unsound mind of the educated classes whose means are insufficient to provide for their proper treatment elsewhere, and admits mainly acute and curable cases. Since the opening of the State Criminal Asylum at Broadmoor criminal patients are no longer confined here. Between 1820 and 1899 the number of patients was 17,972, of whom more than half were dismissed cured. The establishment can accommodate 300 patients, and is fitted up with every modern convenience, including hot air and water pipes, and various appliances for the amusement of the hapless inmates, including a fine recreation-hall. There is also a convalescent-establishment at Witley, in Surrey. Professional men, who are admitted on application to the Resident Physician, will find a visit to the hospital exceedingly interesting.

St. Luke's Hospital (Pl. B, 40), Old Street, City Road, accommodates 200 patients. There are also extensive asylums for the insane of the pauper class at *Claybury* (near Woodford, p. 415) and *Cane Hill* (near Coulsdon, S. E. R.), as well as older institutions at *Hanwell* (p. 422), 7 1/2 M. to the W. of London (G. W. R.), and *Colney Hatch*, 6 1/2 M. to the N. of London (G. N. R.).

Beyond the hospital, at the corner of Lambeth Road and St. George's Road, stands **St. George's Cathedral** (Pl. R, 33), a large Roman Catholic church, begun by *Pugin* in the Gothic style in 1840, and completed, with the exception of the tower, in 1848. It was not, however, consecrated till 1894, when it was finally freed from debt. — A little to the N. W., in Westminster Bridge Road, is *Christ Church*, an elegant Nonconformist chapel, erected for the congregation of the late celebrated *Rowland Hill*, of Surrey Chapel. The beautiful tower and spire were built with American contributions as a memorial of President Lincoln. The pulpit, brought from Surrey Chapel, bears an appropriate inscription.

Farther on in Lambeth Road rises the large *School for the Indigent Blind*, to which visitors are admitted on Thurs. from 3 to 5 p.m.; on other days an order from the chaplain or a member of committee is required.

Lambeth Road ends at *St. George's Circus* (Pl. R, 33), whence Westminster Bridge Road runs to the W. to Westminster Bridge (p. 246); Waterloo Road to the N.W. to Waterloo Station (p. 58) and Waterloo Bridge (p. 183); Blackfriars Road, passing the *Surrey Theatre* (p. 67), to the N. to Blackfriars Bridge (p. 152); Borough

Road to the E.; and London Road to the S. to the Elephant and Castle (p. 379) and Spurgeon's Tabernacle (p. 379). In the centre of the circus rises an *Obelisk*, erected in 1771 in honour of Lord Mayor Crosby, who obtained the release of a printer imprisoned for publishing the parliamentary debates.

At the *Lambeth Free Library*, in Brixton Road (Pl. G, 31, 32), considerably to the S. of this point, a medallion was erected in 1900 to the poet *William Blake* (1757-1828), who spent most of his life on the Surrey side of the Thames.

From this point we return (by tramway if desired) to the Thames at Lambeth Palace, and skirt the river towards the S. by the Albert Embankment (p. 380), passing the handsome buildings of *Doulton's Pottery Works* (Pl. G, 29), which have obtained a high artistic reputation and are well worth a visit. At the end of the Embankment Vauxhall Bridge (p. 279) lies to our right, and Harleyford Road, leading to *Kennington Oval* (p. 72), to our left. Wandsworth Road, straight in front, leads to the neighbourhood of *Clapham Common*, a fine public park of 220 acres.

Clapham Parish Church (Holy Trinity), on the Common, was built in 1776 and is about to be restored. It is interesting from its connection with the 'Clapham Sect', a coterie of rich evangelical philanthropists at the end of the 18th cent., among whom were Lord Teignmouth, Zachary Macaulay (father of Lord Macaulay), William Wilberforce, Henry Thornton, and James Stephen.

We diverge to the right, however, from Wandsworth Road by Nine Elms Lane (Pl. G, 26), which is continued farther on by Battersea Park Road, leading to **Battersea** ('Peter's ey', or island), a suburban district on the S. bank of the Thames, opposite Chelsea (p. 368), with about 150,000 inhabitants. Battersea is noted chiefly for its park and contains numerous important manufactories. The making of Battersea enamel (see p. 362) has long been discontinued.

In Battersea Park Road, close to the Battersea Park Road Station (Pl. G, 23), is the *Home for Lost Dogs and Cats* (open to visitors 10-6, in winter 10-4; small donation expected). In 1899 about 20,000 dogs and 550 cats were received here, most of which came to a painless death in the lethal chamber. Cats may be boarded at the Home for 1s. 6d. per week.

A little farther on in Battersea Park Road is the **Battersea Polytechnic Institute** (comp. p. 98), a handsome building by *Mountford*, erected in 1892. It includes workshops for various trades, laboratories, art, music, and photographic rooms, several lecture and class rooms, gymnasia for men and women, and club and social rooms. Recitals are given on a fine organ presented by the late Sir Henry Tate (p. 274).

Battersea Park (Pl. G, 14, 15, 18, 19), at the S.W. end of London, on the right bank of the Thames, opposite Chelsea Hospital, was laid out in 1852-58 at a cost of 312,890l., and is about 200 acres in extent. It is most conveniently reached by taking a steamboat to Battersea Park Pier. At the lower end of the park is the elegant *Chelsea Suspension Bridge* or *Victoria Bridge*, leading to Pimlico, and $^1/_2$ M. distant from Victoria Station (p. 57; omnibus). From the upper end of the park the *Albert Suspension Bridge* crosses to the Chelsea Embankment. Near the S.E. angle of the park are *Battersea Park Station* of the West London Extension and the *Battersea Park Road Station* of the Metropolitan Extension (see p. 57). The principal attraction of the extensive pleasure grounds, which are provided with an artificial sheet of water, groups of trees, etc., is the *Sub-tropical Garden*, 4 acres in extent, containing most beautiful and carefully cultivated flower-beds and tropical plants, which are in perfection in August and September. The park contains large open spaces for cricket, football, lawn tennis, and bowls, and is also one of the favourite resorts of cyclists (cycles for hire near the N.E. gate). It contains two or three unpretending refreshment-rooms.

The parish-church of *St. Mary*, adjoining Battersea Square Pier (Pl. G, 11), rebuilt in 1776, contains some memorials and stained glass from the earlier edifice, including the monument of Henry St. John, Viscount Bolingbroke (1678-1751), and his second wife (a niece of Mme. de Maintenon). The monument, in the N. gallery, is adorned with their medallions by Roubiliac and bears epitaphs written by Bolingbroke himself. The E. window contains ancient stained glass, relating to the St. John family. William Blake, the poet and artist, was married at St. Mary's in 1782; and Turner used to sketch from the vestry windows. — *Dives' Flour Mills*, to the E. of the church, occupy the site of Bolingbroke's manor-house, of which the W. wing still remains, containing the cedar-wainscotted room, overlooking the Thames, in which Pope wrote the 'Essay on Man'.

EXCURSIONS FROM LONDON.

34. The Thames from London Bridge to Hampton Court.

STEAMBOATS from *London Bridge* to *Hampton Court*, see p. 63. Sometimes the boats are unable to proceed farther than *Kew*. By embarking at *Chelsea* or *Battersea Park* the traveller may shorten the trip by about 1 hour. STEAM LAUNCHES also ply from *Richmond* to *Staines*, etc. The scenery, after London is fairly left behind, is of a very soft and pleasing character, consisting of luxuriant woods, smiling meadows, and picturesque villas and villages. The course of the river is very tortuous. — The words right and left in the following description are used with reference to going upstream.

ROWING AND SAILING BOATS may be hired at Richmond, Kingston, Hampton Wick, and several other places on the river, the charges varying according to the season, the size of the boat, etc. (previous understanding advisable). ELECTRIC and other MOTOR LAUNCHES may also be hired. The prettiest part of the river near London for short boating-excursions is the stretch between Richmond and Hampton Court. A trifling fee, which may be ascertained from the official table posted at each lock (*3d.-1s.* for rowing-boats), has to be paid for passing the locks. Rowing boats going upstream generally keep near the bank to escape the current. Boats pass each other to the right, but a boat overtaking another one keeps to the left.

For the river above Hampton Court, see *Baedeker's Great Britain*.

The prominent objects on both banks of the Thames between London Bridge and Battersea Bridge have already been pointed out in various parts of the Handbook, so that nothing more is required here than a list of them in the order in which they occur, with references to the pages where they are described: — *South Eastern Railway Bridge, Southwark Bridge* (p. 155), *St. Paul's Cathedral* (right; p. 111), *South Eastern and Chatham Railway Bridge* (p. 152), *Blackfriars Bridge* (p. 152), *Victoria Embankment* (right; p. 150), the *City of London School* (right; p. 152), the *Temple* (right; p. 176), with the *Law Courts* (p. 179) appearing above it, *Somerset House* (right; p. 182), *Waterloo Bridge* (p. 183), *Savoy* and *Cecil Hotels* (right; p. 7), *Cleopatra's Needle* (right; p. 151), *Charing Cross Railway Bridge, Montague House* (right; p. 237), *New Scotland Yard* (right; p. 237), *Westminster Bridge* (p. 246), *Houses of Parliament* (right; p. 237), *Westminster Abbey* (right; p. 247), *Albert Embankment* (left; p. 380), *St. Thomas's Hospital* (left; p. 380), *Lambeth Palace* (left; p. 380), *Lambeth Bridge* (p. 381), *Tate Gallery* (right; p. 274), *Vauxhall Temporary Bridge* (p. 277), *South Eastern and Chatham Railway Bridge* (*Grosvenor Road Bridge*, p. 277), *Chelsea Suspension Bridge* (p. 368), *Battersea Park* (left; p. 383), *Chelsea Hospital* (right; p. 369), *Albert Bridge* (p. 368), *Battersea Bridge* (p. 368).

A little way above Battersea is another *Railway Bridge*, beyond which we reach *Wandsworth Bridge* and —

L. **Wandsworth** (railway-station, see p. 422), an outlying suburb of London, containing a large number of factories and breweries. *Wandsworth Prison* accommodates about 1000 male prisoners. The old *Huguenot Burial Ground* here is interesting. The scenery now begins to become more rural in character, and the dusky hues of the great city give place to the green tints of meadow and woodland. About 1 M. above Wandsworth the river is spanned by *Putney Bridge*, erected in 1886, connecting Fulham, on the right, with Putney, on the left.

R. **Fulham**, principally noted for containing a country-residence of the Bishops of London, who have been lords of the manor from very early times. The Episcopal Palace, which stands above the bridge, dates in part from the 16th century. Its grounds contain some fine old trees, and are enclosed by a moat about 1 M. in circumference. In the library are portraits of *Sandys*, Archbishop of York, *Laud*, *Ridley* the martyr, and other ecclesiastics, chiefly Bishops of London. The first bishop who is known with certainty to have resided here was Robert Seal, in 1241. A handsome, but somewhat incongruous, chapel was added to the palace in 1867. *Fulham Church*, rebuilt in 1881, has a tower of the 14th cent., and contains the tombs of numerous Bishops of London. Theodore Hook (d. 1841) and Vincent Bourne (d. 1747) are buried in the churchyard. In a house at the N. end of Fulham, on the road to Hammersmith, Richardson wrote 'Clarissa Harlowe'. In Fulham (Parson's Green station, p. 61), are the pleasant premises of the *Hurlingham Club*, with grounds for pigeon-shooting, polo, lawn-tennis, etc.

L. **Putney** (railway-station, p. 422) is well known to Londoners as the starting-point for the annual boat-race between Oxford and Cambridge universities (p. 74), which takes place on the river between this village and Mortlake (p. 387).

Thomas Cromwell, Wolsey's secretary, and afterwards Earl of Essex, was the son of a Putney blacksmith; and Edward Gibbon, the historian, was born here in 1737. In 1806 William Pitt died at Bowling Green House, on the S. side of the town, near Putney Heath, where, eight years before, he had engaged in a duel with George Tierney. Lord Castlereagh and George Canning also fought a duel on the heath in 1809. The tower of Putney Church is about 400 years old.

*Beautiful walk from Putney over Putney Heath, through the village of Roehampton (1½ M. to the S.) and Richmond Park, to (4 M.) Richmond.

The fine old house, called *Barn Elms*, which we now soon observe on the left, was granted by Queen Elizabeth to Sir Francis Walsingham, who entertained his sovereign lady here on various occasions. It was afterwards occupied by Jacob Tonson, the publisher, who built a room here for the famous portraits of the Kit-Cat Club, painted for him by Sir Godfrey Kneller. The *Ranelagh Club* here has grounds for polo, golf, lawn tennis, etc.

On the opposite bank, a little farther on, formerly stood *Brandenburgh House*, built in the time of Charles I.; it was once inhabited by Fairfax, the Parliamentary general, by Queen Caroline, consort of George IV., who died here in 1821, and by various other notabilities.

R. **Hammersmith** (railway-station), now a town of considerable size, but of little interest to strangers. The *Church of St. Paul*, consecrated in 1631, containing some interesting monuments, a ceiling painted by Cipriani, and an altar-piece carved by Grinling Gibbons, was pulled down in 1882 to make room for a new and larger edifice. The town contains numerous Roman Catholic inhabitants and institutions. Some of the houses in the Mall date from the time of Queen Anne. Hammersmith is connected by a suspension-bridge with the cluster of villas called *Castelnau.* — *St. Paul's School*, founded in 1512, was transferred to Hammersmith from behind St. Paul's Cathedral in 1884. Among its eminent alumni are Camden, Milton, the first Duke of Marlborough, Pepys, Jeffreys, Major André, and Jowett. A little to the N., near Addison Road Station, is the huge building of *Olympia* (p. 69). In Blythe Road, just behind Olympia, is the large new *Post Office Savings Bank,* the foundation stone of which was laid by the Prince of Wales in 1899.

R. **Chiswick** (railway-station, p. 422) contains the gardens of the *Royal Horticultural Society* (p. 344), which, however, are soon to be removed. Opposite Chiswick lies *Chiswick Eyot.*

In *Chiswick House,* the property of the Duke of Devonshire, Charles James Fox died in 1806, and George Canning in 1827. It was built by the Earl of Burlington, the builder of Burlington House, Piccadilly (p. 282), in imitation of the Villa Capra at Vicenza, one of Palladio's best works. The wings, by Wyatt, were added afterwards. — The churchyard contains the grave of Hogarth, the painter (d. 1764), who died in a dwelling near the church, now called Hogarth House.

L. *Barnes* (railway-station, p. 422), a village with a church partly of the 12th cent., freely restored, and possessing a modern, ivy-clad tower. At the next bend lies —

L. **Mortlake** (rail. stat., p. 424), with a church occupying the site of an edifice of the 14th cent.; the tower dates from 1543. In the interior is a tablet to *Sir Philip Francis* (d. 1818), now usually identified with *Junius.* Mortlake is the terminus of the University Boat Race course (comp. p. 386).

The two famous astrologers, Dee and Partridge, resided at Mortlake, where Queen Elizabeth is said to have consulted the first-named. Sir Richard (d. 1891) and Lady Burton are buried here, under a tent of white marble. — *Pleasant walk through (S.) East Sheen to Richmond Park.

L. *Kew* (p. 412) has a railway-station on the opposite bank, with which a temporary bridge connects it. (The old stone bridge was removed in 1899, and a new one is being erected.) Picturesque walk to Richmond. It was on an 'eyot' between Richmond and Kew that Prince William (William IV.) used to meet Perdita Robinson.

R. *Brentford* (p. 414), near which is *Sion House* (p. 414).

R. **Isleworth** (rail. stat.), a favourite residence of London merchants, with numerous villas and market-gardens. The woods and lawns on the banks of the river in this neighbourhood are particularly charming. The course of the stream is from S. to N. A new lock, the first on the river, was opened here in 1894; beyond it we pass under a railway-bridge, and then a stone bridge, the latter at —

L. *Richmond* (see p. 411); boats may be hired here (p. 385).

L. *Petersham* (Dysart Arms), with a red brick church, in a quaint classical style, dating from 1505 but enlarged since. Capt. Vancouver (d. 1798) is buried in the cemetery. Close to the church is *Ham House* (Earl of Dysart), also of red brick, facing the river, the meeting-place of the Cabal during its tenancy by the Duke of Lauderdale.

A little farther from the river stands *Sudbrook House*, built by the Duke of Argyll (d. 1743), and now a hydropathic establishment. It is immortalised by Scott in the 'Heart of Midlothian', as the scene of the interview between Jeanie Deans and the Duke.

On the opposite bank of the Thames is —

R. **Twickenham** (*Railway; King's Head; Albany; White Swan,* by the river), with a great number of interesting historical villas and mansions. The name most intimately associated with the place is that of Pope, whose villa, however, has been replaced by another (occupied by Mr. Labouchere), while his grotto is also altered. The poet was buried in the old parish-church, and its present modern successor still contains his monument, erected by Bishop Warburton in 1761. The monument erected by Pope to his parents 'et sibi' is now concealed by the organ. On the exterior of the E. wall of the N. aisle is a tablet placed by Pope in memory of his nurse who served him for 38 years. Kitty Clive (d. 1785), the actress, is also buried in the churchyard. Below Twickenham stands *Orleans House*, a building of red brick, once the residence of Louis Philippe and other members of the Orleans family. *York House*, said to owe its name to James II., was until 1900 the residence of the present Duc d'Orléans. Farther up the river, about $1/_2$ M. above Twickenham, is *Strawberry Hill*, Horace Walpole's famous villa; it was long the residence of the late Countess Waldegrave, who collected here a great many of the objects of art which adorned it in Walpole's time. Among other celebrities connected with Twickenham is Henry Fielding, the novelist. *Eel Pie Island* (inn), opposite Twickenham, is a favourite resort of picnic parties.

R. *Teddington* (p. 411), with the second lock on the Thames and a foot-bridge.

L. **Kingston** (*Griffin; Sun; Wheatsheaf;* rail. stat., p. 424), an old Saxon town, where some of the early kings of England were crowned. In the market-place, surrounded by an ornamental iron railing, is the *Stone* which is said to have been used as the king's seat during the coronation-ceremony. The names of those believed to have been crowned here are carved on the stone. The *Town Hall*, with an old leaden statue of Queen Anne over the doorway, dates from 1840; the Renaissance *County Hall* from 1893. The former contains a stained-glass window put up in 1899 to commemorate the septcentenary of the borough's charter. The *Church of All Saints* is a fine cruciform structure, dating in part from the 14th century. Kingston is united with *Hampton Wick* on the other bank by a stone bridge, constructed in 1827. It is surrounded by numerous villas and country-residences, and is a favourite resort of Londoners in summer.

Rowing and sailing boats may be hired either at Kingston or Hampton Wick. — Pleasant walks to *Ham Common*, and through *Bushy Park* to (2 M.) *Hampton Court*. — The Guildford coach (p. 55) passes through Kingston.

Steaming past *Surbiton*, the southern suburb of Kingston, and *Thames Ditton* (p. 406), on the left, we now arrive at the bridge crossing the river at —

Hampton Court, see p. 406. (The village of *Hampton* lies on the right, about 1 M. farther up.)

35. The Thames from London Bridge to Gravesend.

STEAMBOATS from *London Bridge* to *Gravesend*, see p. 63. To Gravesend by railway, see R. 45.

The scenery of the Thames below London contrasts very unfavourably with the smiling beauties of the same river higher up; yet the trip down to Gravesend has attractions of its own, and may be recommended as affording a good survey of the vast commercial traffic of London. — The words right and left in the following description are used with reference to going downstream.

Leaving *Fresh Wharf* or *Old Swan Pier* at London Bridge, the steamboat steers through the part of the Thames known as the *Pool* (p. 147). The principal objects seen on the banks are the *Monument* (left; p. 148), *St. Olave's Church* (right), *Billingsgate* (left; p. 149), *Custom House* (left; p. 149), and *Tower* (left; p. 155). We then pass under the *Tower Bridge* (p. 165) and, beyond *St. Katharine's Docks* and *London Docks* (both right), proceed between *Wapping* (p. 167), on the left, and *Rotherhithe* (p. 167), on the right, which are connected by the *Thames Tunnel* (p. 167). The steamer calls at *Cherry Gardens Pier* in Wapping and at *Thames Tunnel Pier* in Rotherhithe. — On the left bank lies the district of *Shadwell* (p. 167). To the right are the *Surrey Commercial Docks* (p. 167), and opposite them is *Limehouse Dock*. At *Limehouse Pier*, in Limehouse Reach, the Pool ends. For the next three miles we skirt the *Isle of Dogs* (p. 168), on the left, on which are the *West India Docks* and *Millwall Docks*. Opposite *Millwall Pier* lies *Deptford*, with the Royal Victualling Yard and the foreign cattle-market (p. 168).

R. **Greenwich Pier**, whence there is a ferry to *North Greenwich* (p. 168). *Greenwich*, see p. 391. — Immediately beyond the pier rises Greenwich Hospital (p. 392), on a river-terrace 860 ft. long, and behind it are *Greenwich Park* and *Observatory* (p. 394).

We now steer to the N., down Blackwall Reach, with *Greenwich Marshes* on the right. On the left, farther on, lie *Blackwall* and the *East India Docks*, beyond which we pass over *Blackwall Tunnel* (p. 168), just before reaching *Blackwall Pier*. — At the mouth of *Bow Creek* (left), by which the Lea enters the Thames, is *Trinity Wharf*, belonging to the Trinity House (p. 163). On the left are the *Royal Victoria Docks* (p. 168), continued on the E. by the *Albert Docks* (p. 168), with the workmen's quarters of *Canning Town* and *Silvertown*. Off *Charlton Pier* (right) lies the 'Warspite' training-ship of the Royal Marine Society.

R. **Woolwich Pier**, *Woolwich*, see p. 394. — Near the pier there is a steam *Ferry* (p. 394) to *North Woolwich* (p. 168).

The banks of the Thames below Woolwich are very flat and marshy, recalling the appearance of a Dutch landscape. Shortly after leaving Woolwich we enter a part of the river called *Barking Reach*, with *Plumstead Marshes* on the right. To the left are the huge gas-works at *Beckton*. Farther on, at Barking Creek on the N., and Crossness on the S. bank, are situated the outlets of London's new and gigantic system of drainage (p. 97). The pumping house at Crossness is a building of some architectural merit, with an Italian tower (visitors admitted on application at the office). Passing through *Halfway Reach* and *Erith Reach*, with *Belvedere House* (p. 432) and *Erith Marshes* on our right, we next arrive at —

R. **Erith** (Prince of Wales), a village pleasantly situated at the base of a wooded hill, with a picturesque, ivy-clad, old church. It is a favourite starting-point for yacht-races. — On the opposite bank of the river, 2 M. lower down, lies —

L. *Purfleet* (Royal Hotel, fish-dinners), the seat of large Government powder-magazines, capable of containing 60,000 barrels of powder. The training-ship *Cornwall* is moored in the Thames at Purfleet. Opposite is the mouth of the small river Darent. In *Long Reach*, between Purfleet and Greenhithe, is the Admiralty 'measured mile.' — The Essex bank here forms a sharp promontory, immediately opposite which, in a corresponding indentation, lies —

R. *Greenhithe* (Pier; White Hart), a pretty little place, with a number of villas. The training-ships '*Arethusa*' and '*Chichester*' and the higher class school-ship '*Worcester*' lie in the river here. Greenhithe is also a yachting-station. A little way inland is *Stone Church*, supposed to have been built by the architect of Westminster Abbey, and restored by Street (p. 179); it contains some fine stone-carving and old brasses. Just beyond Greenhithe the eye is attracted by the conspicuous white mansion of *Ingress Abbey*, at one time occupied by the father of Sir Henry Havelock. Two miles below Greenhithe, on the opposite bank, is —

L. **West Thurrock** (Old Ship), with the Norman church of St. Clement (12th cent.) and some remains of an old monastery.

L. *Grays Thurrock* (King's Arms), near which are some curious caves. The training-ships '*Shaftesbury*' and '*Exmouth*' are moored here. — Next, 3 M. lower down, —

R. *Northfleet*, with chalk-pits, cement-factories, and a fine old church containing some monuments and a carved oak rood-screen of the 14th century. Northfleet also possesses a college for indigent ladies and gentlemen, and a working-men's club, the latter a large red and white brick building. An electric tramway runs from Northfleet station (S. E. R.) to the top of Northfleet Hill (1*d.*), where it connects with another tramway to Rosherville and Gravesend (through-fare 2*d.*).

The steamer next passes *Rosherville* (p. 433), with a pier (right), and finally reaches —

R. **Gravesend**, p. 433. Thence by rail to *London* or *Rochester*, see R. 45.

On the Essex bank, opposite Gravesend, we observe the low bastions of *Tilbury Fort*, originally constructed by Henry III. to defend the mouth of the Thames, and since extended and strengthened. It was here that Queen Elizabeth assembled and reviewed her troops in anticipation of the attack of the Armada (588), appearing in helmet and corslet, and using the bold and well-known words: 'I know I have the body of a weak, feeble woman, but I have the heart and stomach of a king. and of a king of England too!' The large docks at *Tilbury* (Tilbury Grand Hotel), opened in 1886, comprise 588 acres, of which 73 are water. They have frequent railway-communication with Fenchurch Street (p. 58).

36. Greenwich Hospital and Park.

Greenwich may be reached by *Steamboat*, see R. 35 (pleasant in fine weather); by *Tramway*, see Nos. 13, 14, 15, p. 54; or by *Railway* in 25-35 min. from *Charing Cross Station* (p. 57; trains every 20 min.; fares 11*d.*, 7*d.*, 6*d.*), *Cannon Street* (fares 9*d.*, 6*d.*, 4½*d.*), *London Bridge*, *Victoria* (fares 10*d.*, 9*d.*, 6*d.*), or *Holborn Viaduct*. — This excursion may also be combined with a visit to *Blackwall* and the *Docks*, starting from *Fenchurch Street Station* (see R. 9).

Greenwich. — Hotels: Ship Tavern, King William St., near the pier (fish dinner from about 7*s.*). Connected with the Ship Tavern is a restaurant, called the Ship Stores, which is cheaper; lunch from 1*s.* 6*d.*

Greenwich, with 78,167 inhab. (1891), is situated in Kent, on the S. bank of the Thames, 4½ M. below London Bridge. — At the close of the parliamentary session the Cabinet Ministers and other members of the Government used to meet annually to partake of a banquet at Greenwich, known as the *Whitebait Dinner*, from the whitebait, a small fish not much more than an inch in length, for which Greenwich is famous, and which is considered a great delicacy. It is eaten with cayenne pepper, lemon juice, and brown bread and butter. The Whitebait Dinner was resumed, after a hiatus of 15 years, in 1895. Greenwich Fair was discontinued in 1856.

In Church Street, a little to the S. of the station, is the parish-church of *St. Alphage* or *St. Alfege* (rebuilt in the Italian style in 1718), which contains the tombs of General Wolfe (d. at Quebec 1759) and of Thomas Tallis (1529-85), 'father of English church-music'. The stained-glass window above the gallery, at the N.W. end of the nave, commemorates the baptism of Henry VIII. (comp. p. 392) in the old parish-church; and the window opposite was placed in memory of Wolfe in 1896. — From Nelson Street, which diverges to the right from Church Street, King William Street leads to the N. to Greenwich Park (p. 394) and to the S. to the entrance of —

*Greenwich Hospital and Royal Naval College (Pl. G, 70), occupying the site of an old royal palace, built in 1433 by Humphrey, Duke of Gloucester, and called by him Placentia or Plaisance. In it Henry VIII. and his daughters, Mary and Elizabeth, were born, and here Edward VI. died. During the Commonwealth the palace was removed. In 1667 Charles II. began to rebuild it, but he only completed the wing which is named after him. Twenty years later, after the accession of William III., the building was resumed, and in 1694 the palace was converted into a hospital for aged and disabled sailors. The number of inmates accommodated in the hospital reached its highest point (2710) in 1814, but afterwards decreased considerably. In 1865 the number was 1400, and of these nearly 1000 took advantage of a resolution of the Admiralty, which gave the pensioners the option of remaining in the hospital or of receiving an out-door pension, and chose the latter alternative. There are now no pensioners left. The revenue of the hospital amounts to about 160,000l. per annum, being derived mainly from landed property; and upwards of 9000 seamen and marines derive benefit from it in one form or another. The funds also support Greenwich Hospital School (p. 393). The hospital is now used as a *Royal Naval College*, for the instruction of naval officers; but many of the suites of rooms are at present unoccupied. The expenses of the college and the maintenance of the building are defrayed by votes of Parliament.

The building consists of four blocks or sections. On the side next the river are the W. or KING CHARLES BUILDING, with the library, and the E. or QUEEN ANNE BUILDING, which now contains a naval museum. These are both in the Corinthian style. Behind are the S.W. or KING WILLIAM BUILDING, and the S.E. or QUEEN MARY BUILDING, each furnished with a dome in Wren's style. The *River Terrace*, 860 ft. long, is embellished with two granite obelisks, one in commemoration of the marine officers and men who fell in the New Zealand rebellion of 1863-64; and the other (of red granite) in honour of *Lieutenant Bellot*, a French naval officer, who lost his life in a search for Franklin. The quadrangle in the centre contains a marble statue of *George II.*, in Roman costume, by Rysbrack; an Elizabethan gun found in the Medway and supposed to have belonged to a ship sunk by the Dutch in 1667; and a gun which was on board the 'Victory' at Trafalgar (1805). In the upper quadrangle is a colossal bust of *Nelson*, by Chantrey. — On the S.W. side is the *Seamen's Hospital*, for sailors of all nationalities, transferred hither in 1865 from the *Dreadnought*, an old man-of-war formerly stationed in the Thames.

The Painted Hall (p. 393) is open to the public daily from 10 to 4, 5, or 6 (on Sun. after 2 p.m.), and the Chapel and Royal Museum are open daily, except Sun. and Frid., at the same hours.

The chief feature of the King William section is the PAINTED
HALL, 106 ft. long, 50 ft. broad, and 50 ft. high, containing the
Naval Gallery of pictures and portraits which commemorate the naval
victories and heroes of Great Britain. The paintings on the wall and
ceiling were executed by *Sir James Thornhill* in 1707-27. The
Descriptive Catalogue (price 3*d*.) supplies brief biographical and
historical data.

The VESTIBULE contains, amongst other pictures, Portraits of Columbus and Andrea Doria (from Italian originals), Vasco da Gama (from
a Portuguese original), Duquesne by *Steuben*, and the Earl of Sandwich
by *Gainsborough*; statues of Admirals St. Vincent, Howe, Nelson, and
Duncan; a memorial tablet to Sir John Franklin and his companions,
executed by *Westmacott* (on the left); and a painting of the turret-ship
'Devastation' at a naval review in honour of the Shah of Persia (1873),
by *E. W. Cooke* (to the right). — The HALL. The four corners are filled
with marble statues: to the left of the entrance, Adm. de Saumarez, by
Steele; to the right, Capt. Sir William Peel, by *Theed*; to the left of
the exit, Viscount Exmouth, by *Macdowell*; to the right, Adm. Sir Sidney
Smith, by *Kirk*. The numbering of the pictures begins in the corner to
the right. Among the most interesting are the following: 10. Hawkins,
Drake, and Cavendish, a group after *Mytens*; *Loutherbourg*, 11. Destruction
of the Spanish Armada in 1588, 29. Lord Howe's victory at Ushant; 28.
Briggs, George III. presenting a sword to Lord Howe in commemoration
of the victory at Ushant in 1794; 24. Lord St. Vincent; 30. Admiral Hood;
35. *Drummond*, Battle of Camperdown (1797); 42. *Reynolds*, Lord Bridport;
48. *Chambers* (after *Benjamin West*), Battle of La Hogue, 1692; 46. *Kneller*,
George, Duke of Cumberland; 53. *Dance*, Captain Cook; 54. *Zoffany*, Death
of Captain Cook in 1779; 57. *Lely*, James II.; 55. Sir James Clark ROSS;
63. Adm. Kempenfeldt; 75. Sir Charles Napier; 87. *Devis*, Death of Nelson
in 1805; 83. Nelson; 88. *Turner*, Battle of Trafalgar; 89. Collingwood;
93. *Arnold*, Battle of the Nile; 101. *Jones*, Battle of St. Vincent; 90. Capt.
G. Duff; 112. *Allen*, Nelson boarding the San Nicholas, 1797; *Lely*, 104.
Monk, Duke of Albemarle, 109. Sir W. Penn. — In the UPPER HALL are
busts of (left) Rivers, Goodenough, Tschitchagoff (a Russian admiral), Sir
Joseph Banks, Blake, William IV., Adam, Nelson, Vernon, and Liardet.
The upper hall also contains glass-cases with relics of Nelson, including
the coat and waistcoat he wore at Trafalgar, when he received his death-
wound; the coat he wore at the battle of the Nile; his watch; his pigtail,
cut off after death; an autograph letter; a Turkish gun and sabre presented
to him after the battle of the Nile; the silken hangings of his hammock,
etc. — The NELSON ROOM (to the left of the upper hall) contains pictures
by West and others in honour of the heroic Admiral, a series of portraits
of his contemporaries, portraits of General Barrington by *Reynolds* and
Admiral Hope (d. 1881) by *Hodges*, etc.

In the S.E. or Queen Mary edifice is the CHAPEL, which contains
an altar-piece by *West*, representing St. Paul shaking the viper off his
hand after his shipwreck, and monuments of Adm. Sir R. Keats,
by *Chantrey*, and Adm. Sir Thomas Hardy, by *Behnes*.

The ROYAL NAVAL MUSEUM, in the E. or Queen Anne wing (admission free), contains models of ships, rigging, and various apparatus; relics of the Franklin expedition; mementoes of Nelson;
a model of the Battle of Trafalgar; a number of paintings and
drawings, etc.

At the *Royal Naval School*, lying between the hospital and
Greenwich Park, 1000 sons of British seamen and marines are
educated.

To the S. of Greenwich is *Greenwich Park (Pl. G, 71), 174 acres in extent, laid out during the reign of Charles II. by the celebrated *Le Nôtre*. The park, with its fine old chestnuts and hawthorns (in blossom in May) and herds of tame deer, is a favourite resort of Londoners of the middle classes on Sundays and holidays, particularly on Good Friday, Easter Monday, and Whit-Monday. A hill in the centre, 180 ft. in height, is crowned by the famous Greenwich *Royal Observatory* ('astronomical' visitors sometimes admitted on application to the Director, Mr. W. H. M. Christie), founded in 1675, from the meridian of which English astronomers make their calculations. The new building was completed in 1899. About 350 yds. to the E. is the *Magnetic Pavilion*, placed here to avoid the disturbance of the instruments that would be caused by the iron in the main building. The correct time for the whole of England is settled here every day at 1 p.m.; a large coloured ball descends many feet, and the time is telegraphed hence to the most important towns throughout the country. The fine astronomical apparatus in the observatory includes a 28-inch refracting telescope and a 26-inch photographic telescope. A large number of chronometers are tested here annually. A standard clock (with the hours numbered from 1 to 24) and various standard measures of length are fixed just outside the entrance, *pro bono publico*. The terrace in front of the observatory and the other elevated portions of the park command an extensive and varied view over the river, bristling with the masts of vessels all the way to London, over the Hainault and Epping Forests, backed by the hills of Hampstead, and over the plain extending to the N. of the Thames and intersected by docks and canals.

On the S. and S.E. Greenwich Park is bounded by *Blackheath*, a common, now 267 acres in extent, across which runs the Roman road to Dover. Here Wat Tyler in 1381 and Jack Cade in 1450 assembled the rebellious 'men of Kent', grown impatient under hard deprivations, for the purpose of attacking the Metropolis, and here belated travellers were not unfrequently robbed in former times. *Blackheath Golf Club*, founded in 1608, is the oldest existing golf club in the world, and the heath is still frequented by golfers, though better 'links' have been laid out within the last few years elsewhere near London (comp. p. 72). — To the S. of Blackheath, beyond the *Blackheath Station* of the S. E. R., lies *Lee*, in the churchyard of which is the grave of Edmund Halley (d. 1742), the astronomer.

37. Woolwich.

Woolwich may be reached by *Steamboat*, see R. 35; or by *Railway* in 25-45 min. from *Charing Cross* (trains every 20 min.; fares 1s. 6d., 1s., 9d.), *Cannon Street*, or *London Bridge*. There are four railway-stations at Woolwich: *Woolwich Dockyard* (to the W.), *Woolwich Arsenal* (near the Arsenal), *Woolwich Town*, and *North Woolwich*. — North Woolwich (p. 168), whence there is a free ferry to Woolwich, may be reached by rail from

Liverpool Street or *Fenchurch Street*. — A tramway (No. 18; p. 54) connects Woolwich with Greenwich.

Woolwich (King's Arms, near the Dockyard Station; Royal Mortar, near the Arsenal Gates) is situated on the Thames, 9 M. below London Bridge. Pop. (1891) 40,848.

The ROYAL ARSENAL, one of the most imposing establishments in existence for the manufacture of materials of war, is shown on Tuesdays and Thursdays between 10 and 11.30, and 2 and 4.30, by tickets, obtained at the War Office, Pall Mall. Foreigners must receive special permission by application through their ambassador. The chief departments are the *Gun Factory*, established in 1716 by a German named Schalch (the new Woolwich guns are not cast, but formed of forged steel and wire); the *Laboratory* for making cartridges and projectiles; the *Gun-carriage and Waggon Department*; and the *Stores Department*. The arsenal covers an area of 593 acres, and affords employment to over 15,000 men. The magazines, which extend along the Thames for a mile to the E. of the pier, contain enormous stores of war-materials. — The *Dockyard*, established by Henry VIII. in 1532, was closed in 1869, but is still used for military stores. It lies to the W. of the pier.

To the S. of the Dockyard Station, and higher up the slope, lie the *Red Barracks*, eight buildings connected by a corridor, and now partly occupied by the *Royal Artillery College* for training artillery officers for appointments in the arsenal. Still higher up, at the N. end of Woolwich Common, are the *Royal Artillery Barracks*, 1200 ft. in length, with accommodation for 4000 men and 1000 horses. In front of the building are placed several pieces of ordnance, including a cannon $16^1/_2$ ft. long, cast in 1677 for the Emperor Aurungzebe, and 'looted' at Bhurtpore in 1827; and a *Statue of Victory*, by John Bell, in memory of the artillery officers and men who fell in the Crimea. — To the E. are the *Royal Artillery Institution*, the *Military Train Barracks*, and *St. George's*, the garrison-church.

Woolwich Common, which extends hence to the S.W. for about 1 M., is used for the manœuvres of the garrison. On its N.W. side stands the *Royal Military Repository*, where soldiers are instructed in mounting and dismounting guns, pontooning, etc. Within its limits is the *Rotunda* (113 ft. in diameter), built by Nash in 1814, containing a military museum, with models of fortifications and designs and specimens of artillery (open to the public daily from 10 to 12.45 and 2 to 5).

The *Royal Military Academy*, established in 1719, and transferred in 1806 to the present building on the S.E. side of Woolwich Common, trains cadets for the Engineers or Artillery.

On the opposite (W.) side of the Common is a *Hut Camp* for two field-batteries; and at the S. end is the huge military *Herbert Hospital*, built in 1865. The extensive *Telegraphic Works* of Sie-

mens Brothers, where submarine cables are made, are worth visiting (card of admission necessary, procured at the London office, 12 Queen Anne's Gate, by visitors provided with an introduction).

About 1½ M. to the S. of Woolwich Common rises *Shooters' Hill*, a conspicuous eminence, commanding an extensive and charming view of the richly-wooded plains of Kent.

On Shooters' Hill, not far from the Herbert Hospital (p. 395), is *Severndroog Castle*, a triangular tower erected in 1784 by his widow to the memory of Sir William James (1721-83), who distinguished himself by the capture of Severndroog (1775) and other exploits in the Indian Seas.

38. The Crystal Palace at Sydenham.

Trains for the Crystal Palace leave *London Bridge Station* (p. 58), *Ludgate Hill Station* (p. 58), *Holborn Viaduct Station* (p. 58), and *Victoria Station* (p. 57) nearly every ¼ hr. Fares from Victoria, 1s. 3d., 1s., and 7d.; return-tickets 2s., 1s. 6d., 1s.; return-tickets including admission to the Palace (on the 1s. days) 2s. 6d., 2s., and 1s. 6d. Frequent trains also run from *Addison Road, Kensington* (fares 1s. 9d., 1s. 4d., 9d.), on the North London Railway (p. 57). Through-tickets, with or without admission to the Palace, are issued at all stations on the North London and the Metropolitan lines, and a glance at the Railway Plan of London in the Appendix will enable the visitor to choose his route.

The *Crystal Palace* is situated at Sydenham, 8 M. to the S.E. of Charing Cross. Admission 1s.; annual season-ticket 21s.; special annual ticket for employees and students 10s. 6d. On special occasions, duly advertised in the newspapers beforehand, the prices are raised. Children under 12 years of age pay half-price. The Palace is opened at 10 a.m., and closed at 7.30 p.m. in winter (except on nights when the interior of the Palace is illuminated) and at 10 p.m. in summer, when illuminated garden fêtes are a great feature (comp. p. 400).

A hasty visit to the Palace and gardens, including the journey there and back, occupies at least half-a-day. Meals may be taken at the Palace, where there are good restaurants with various charges. Refreshments may be obtained at any of the counters distributed throughout the building, and there are also public and private dining-rooms in three or four different parts of the Palace.

The Palace also contains a library and reading-room (adjoining the transept in the N.E. section, admission 2d.), a large smoking-lounge, letter-boxes, lavatories, railway time-tables, shoeblacks, a hair-cutting room, and other conveniences. If fatigued, the visitor may hire a wheel-chair and attendant at the rate of 1s. 6d. per hr. within the Palace or 2s. in the grounds.

The Crystal Palace at Sydenham, designed by *Sir Joseph Paxton*, consists entirely of glass and iron. It was constructed mainly with the materials of the first great Industrial Exhibition of 1851, and was opened in 1854. It is composed of a spacious central hall or nave, 1608 ft. long, with lateral sections, two aisles, and two transepts. (A third transept at the N. end, which formed a palm-house of imposing dimensions, was burned down in 1866.) The central transept is 390 ft. long, 120 ft. broad, and 175 ft. high. The S. transept is 312 ft. long, 72 ft. broad, and 110 ft. high. The two water-towers at the ends are 282 ft. in height. The cost of the whole undertaking, including the magnificent garden and grounds, and much additional land outside, amounted to a million and a half sterling.

ENTRANCES. (1.) The *Low Level Station* of the Brighton and South Coast Railway, and of the South London Line (London Bridge, Crystal Palace, Clapham Junction, Victoria Station), is on the S.E. side of the Palace, and connected with it by a glass gallery. — (2.) From the *High Level Station* of the South Eastern and Chatham Railway (Victoria Terminus or Holborn Viaduct Station), on the W. side of the Palace, we pass through the subway to the right, and ascend the staircase, where we observe the notice 'To the Palace only', leading direct to the W. portion of the Palace. If we leave the subway on the right, and ascend the stairs past the booking office, we reach a broad road at the top, on the other side of which is the principal entrance in the central transept. — Those who approach from Dulwich (p. 401) alight at Sydenham Hill Station, $1/2$ M. from the Palace.

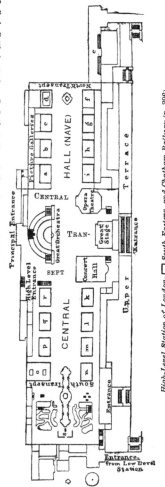

The Crystal Palace is of such vast extent, that in our limited space we can only indicate the order in which the chief objects of interest are most conveniently visited (comp. Plan). A fuller description will be found in the official *Guide* (price 1s.; smaller guide-books 2d., programme for the day 2d.).

Approaching from the Low Level Station (p. 397) through the glass arcade, 720 ft. in length, we first enter the *S. Transept*, whence, opposite the great partition (Pl. s), we obtain a good general survey of the Palace (better still from the clock-gallery above the partition). The effect produced by the contrast between the green foliage of the plants, distributed along the whole of the nave, and the white forms of the statuary to which they form a background, is most pleasing. Behind the statues are the richly-coloured façades of the courts, and high above is the light and airy glass vaulting of the roof. The whole presents, at a single *coup d'oeil*, a magnificent and unique view of the art and culture of nations which are widely separated from each other in time and space.

In order to obtain a general idea of the arrangements of the Palace we walk to the opposite end of the nave, and then visit the various courts, beginning with the Egyptian Court on the N.W. side of the central transept.

In the SOUTH TRANSEPT we first observe, in recesses in the partition mentioned above, a series of plaster casts of the statues of English monarchs in the Houses of Parliament (see p. 241). The equestrian statue of Queen Victoria in the middle of the transept is by Marochetti. A little beyond it is a water-basin containing the *Crystal Fountain* (by Osler), which once adorned the original Crystal Palace of 1851 in Hyde Park, and is now embellished with aquatic plants and ferns. The casts from modern sculptures are arranged for the most part in the S. nave and transept, and those from the antique in the N. half of the building. On the left (W.) of the CENTRAL TRANSEPT is the great *Händel Orchestra*, which can accommodate 4000 persons, and has a diameter (216 ft.) twice as great as the dome of St. Paul's. In the middle is the powerful organ, with 4384 pipes, built by Gray & Davison at a cost of 6000*l.* and worked by hydraulic machinery (a performance usually given in the afternoon). Opposite, at the garden end of the transept, is the *Great Stage*. The *Concert Hall*, on the S. side of the stage, in which good concerts are given from time to time, can accommodate an audience of 4000. The *Opera House*, on the N., opposite the Concert Hall, accommodates 2000 persons, and is used for plays and pantomimes as well as for operas.

On each side of the nave is a range of so-called *Courts, containing copies of the architecture and sculpture of the most highly civilised nations, from the earliest period to the present day, arranged in chronological order. The collection of casts, especially those in the Greek and Roman courts, ranks among the best in the

country; and the careful reproductions of the most famous architectural bits of the different epochs merit more than passing inspection. All the exhibits are distinctly labelled.

On the W. side of the nave are the EGYPTIAN COURT (Pl. a),
with imitations of ancient Egyptian architecture; the GREEK COURT
(Pl. b), with portions of Greek buildings and casts of Greek sculpture; the ROMAN COURT (Pl. c), with casts and restored models of
Roman buildings; and the ALHAMBRA COURT (Pl. d), a copy of part
of the Alhambra, the Moorish palace at Granada.

The north end of the Palace, which, like the other, boasts of a
handsome *Fountain with a basin of aquatic plants, is now occupied
by the TROPICAL DEPARTMENT, containing specimens of tropical
vegetation, and aviaries of foreign birds. This is used as a smoking
lounge. — From this part of the building a staircase descends to
the right by the buffet to the *Aquarium* (trout fed at 4 p.m.), *Monkey
House*, and gardens.

We now proceed to the E. side of the nave, where we first enter
the BYZANTINE AND ROMANESQUE COURT (Pl. f), with specimens of
architecture and sculpture of various dates from the 6th to the 13th
century. The three MEDIÆVAL COURTS (Pl. g; 12-16th cent.) illustrate *German, English*, and *French Gothic*. Then follow the RENAIS-
SANCE COURT (Pl. h), with the ELIZABETHAN VESTIBULE; and the
ITALIAN COURT (Pl. i), now occupied by the *Crystal Palace Club*.

Behind the courts on this side are the *Library* and *Reading
Room* (adm. 2d.) and the *Skating Rink* (adm., incl. roller skates,
1s.-1s. 6d.).

On the S. side of the Central Transept, which we now traverse,
most of the courts are now used for special purposes. We first observe, next to the Concert Hall, the FRENCH COURT (Pl. k), now
used as an afternoon tea room; then a COURT (Pl. l) used for private
dining-rooms; next, the FABRICS COURT (Pl. m), with its billiard
tables; and then the MUSIC COURT (Pl. n). Behind these four courts
is the *Grill Room*, adjoined by the *New Dining Room*.

We have now again reached the South Transept. Among the
shrubberies around the water-basin mentioned at p. 398 are groups
of figures representing the different races of mankind, stuffed
animals, and other objects. On the W. side is the POMPEIAN COURT
(Pl. o), which is intended to represent a Roman house of the reign
of Titus, having been carefully copied, both in form and pictorial
decoration, from a building excavated at Pompeii. — Adjoining is
a cabinet with views of Pompeii (admission 3d.).

The CHINESE COURT (Pl. p) contains Chinese art and manufactures, including a collection of Oriental china.

The MANUFACTURING COURT (Pl. q) shows interesting processes
of manufacture, including a steam loom for ornamental weaving.

The ENTERTAINMENT COURT (Pl. r) is now used for exhibitions
of various kinds.

Ascending now to the WEST GALLERY, by a staircase near the Central Transept (W. side), we find to our right (N.) the PORTRAIT GALLERY, consisting of a series of busts of eminent men of all nations, and to our left (S.) the collection of OIL AND WATER-COLOUR PAINTINGS, which includes some fine modern works. Passing under the clock by the S. Gallery, we reach the EAST GALLERY, the S. half of which contains the *Wurtemberg Collection of Stuffed Animals* (about 1500 in number), while the N. half is devoted to a *Technological Museum* and various miscellaneous collections (Tasmanian; Modern Egyptian; Palestine Exploration; Lifeboat Society, etc.). — Other portions of the galleries are filled with stalls for the sale of trinkets, toys, millinery, confectionery, and knick-knacks of all sorts. The Palace also possesses a gymnasium, a cinematograph (seats 6d), a palace of illusions (adm. 6d.), and many other attractions of which it is needless to give an exhaustive list.

The highest *Terrace*, the balustrade of which is embellished with 26 marble statues representing the chief countries and most important cities in the world, affords a magnificent view of the park and of the rich scenery of the county of Kent. The prospect is still more extensive from the platform of the N. TOWER, which rises to a height of 282 ft. above the level of the lowest basins, and is ascended by a winding staircase and by a lift; it extends into six counties, and embraces the whole course of the Thames (adm. 3d., children 1d.).

The chief exit from the Crystal Palace into the *Gardens is in the S. basement, below the Central Transept; they may also be entered from the covered arcade leading to the Palace from the Low Level Station (p. 397), or by any one of the small side-doors in different parts of the building. The Gardens, covering an area of 200 acres, and laid out in terraces in the Italian and English styles, are tastefully embellished with flower-beds, shrubberies, fountains, cascades, and statuary. The numerous seats offer grateful repose after the fatigue of a walk through the Palace. At the head of the broad walk is a monument to Sir Joseph Paxton, surmounted by a colossal bust by *Woodington*. The two great fountain basins have recently been converted into SPORT ARENAS, each about 8½ acres in extent. During the season football, cricket, lawn tennis, lacrosse, and other games are played here (comp. pp. 72-74). Various other fountains, however, still remain and play on firework nights (see below) and other special occasions. A great display of fireworks (by Messrs. C. T. Brock & Co.) takes place every Thursday and Saturday evening in summer, often attracting 10-20,000 visitors. — The *GEOLOGICAL DEPARTMENT in the S.E. portion of the park, by the Boating Lake, is extremely interesting and should not be overlooked. It contains full-size models of antediluvian animals, — the Megalosaurus, Ichthyosaurus, Pterodactyl, Palæotherium, Megatherium, and the Irish Elk (found in the Isle of Man)

— together with the contemporaneous geological formations. — The N.E. part of the park is laid out as a CRICKET GROUND, and on summer afternoons the game attracts numerous spectators. This is the headquarters of the London County Cricket Club, of which Dr. W. G. Grace is captain. The grounds of the *London Polo Club* (public matches) and the *Football Grounds and Cycle Track* are on opposite sides of the Grand Central Walk. At the N. end of the terrace are a swimming-bath, dancing platform, monkey-house, and aviaries; and the gardens also contain open-air gymnasia, a 'switch-back' railway, a maze, a curling pond, swings, etc. Near the Rosery is a *Panorama of the Siege of Paris* (adm. 6d.).

In the London Road, Forest Hill, about 1¼ M. from the Crystal Palace and the same distance from the Dulwich Gallery (see below), is the *Horniman Free Museum*, a large collection formed by Mr. F. J. Horniman, M. P., originally opened in 1890 and rebuilt in 1900 (Curator, Mr. R. Quick). The park (15 acres) is also open to the public. The collections include china and porcelain, ethnographical curiosities, historical relics, carved furniture, enamels, arms and armour, fans, musical instruments, Greek, Roman, and Egyptian antiquities, Oriental objects, etc. The natural history department includes an interesting collection of insects and a brilliant array of moths and butterflies. The Museum is about 3 min. walk from *Lordship Lane*, on the South Eastern and Chatham Railway, and 5 min. walk from *Forest Hill*, on the London, Brighton, & South Coast Railway.

39. Dulwich.

Dulwich, 5 M. to the S. of St. Paul's and 2 M. to the N. of the Crystal Palace, is most conveniently reached from Victoria Station (p. 57; S. E. & C. Railway) in 20 min., or from St. Paul's Station (p. 58) in 25-30 min. (fares 9d., 7d., 5d.; return-tickets 1s., 10d., 8d.). This excursion may be conveniently combined with the preceding, the morning being spent at Dulwich. Lunch at Dulwich or at the Crystal Palace.

On leaving the station at Dulwich we turn to the right. After proceeding for about 100 paces we observe in front of us the new building of **Dulwich College**, a handsome red brick structure in the Renaissance style, built in 1870 at a cost of 100.000l.

The *College of God's Gift* at Dulwich was founded in 1619, by Edward Alleyn, the actor, a friend of Shakspeare, and included an almshouse. The school was reorganized in 1857 and 1882 and now comprises this *New College*, providing an upper grade education for 600 boys, and a *Lower Grade School*, about 1 M. to the N., under separate management, where only nominal fees are charged.

Gallery Road, a broad road diverging to the left (N.) before the New College, leads in 5 min. to the old college-buildings and ***Dulwich Picture Gallery**, the entrance to which is indicated by a notice on a lamp-post. Apart from some unimportant paintings bequeathed to the College by Alleyn and by William Cartwright

(d. 1688), the present valuable collection was formed by *Noel Desenfans* (d. 1807), a picture-dealer in London, and left by him to *Sir P. F. Bourgeois*, the painter (d. 1811), who in turn bequeathed it to God's Gift College, along with 17,500*l.* for its maintenance and the erection of a suitable gallery to contain it. Admission, see p. 108.

This collection possesses a few excellent Spanish works by *Murillo* (1618-82) and one by his master *Velasquez* (1599-1660), and also some good examples of the French school (particularly *N. Poussin*, 1594-1665, and *Watteau*, 1684-1721); while, among Italian schools, later masters only (such as the Academic school of the Carracci at Bologna) are represented. The small pictures catalogued as by Raphael have been, unfortunately, freely retouched. The glory of the gallery, however, consists in its admirable collection of Dutch paintings, several masters being excellently illustrated both in number and quality. For instance, no other collection in the world possesses so many paintings (fifteen) by *Albert Cuyp* (1605-72), the great Dutch landscape and animal painter. The chief power of Cuyp, who has been named the Dutch Claude, lies in his brilliant and picturesque treatment of atmosphere and light. Similar in style are the works of the brothers *Jan* and *Andrew Both*, also well represented in this gallery, who resided in Italy and imitated Claude. Andrew supplied the figures to the landscapes of his brother Jan (Utrecht, 1610-56). The ten examples of *Philip Wouverman* (Haarlem, 1620-68), the most eminent Dutch painter of battles and hunting-scenes, include specimens of his early manner (Nos. 193 and 77), as well as others exhibiting the brilliant effects of his later period. Among the fine examples of numerous other masters, two genuine works by *Rembrandt* (1607-69) are conspicuous (Nos. 99 and 163). About twenty pictures here were formerly assigned to *Rubens* (1577-1640), but traces of an inferior hand are visible in most of them. Among the works of Flemish masters the large canvasses of Rubens' rival *Van Dyck* (1599-1641), and those of *Teniers the Elder* (Antwerp, 1582-1649) and *Teniers the Younger* (1610-94), call for special notice. The specimens of the last-named, one of the most prominent of all genre painters, will in particular well repay examination. — Catalogue (1892; 1*s.*), with biographies of the painters, by *J. P. Richter* and *J. Sparkes*. The numbers given below in brackets are those of earlier catalogues and are still shewn on the pictures, along with the new numbers in red.

ROOM I. On the left: 2 (334). *Bolognese School*, St. Cecilia; 3, 5 (8, 10). *W. Romeyn* (Utrecht, pupil of Berchem; d. 1662), Landscapes with figures; 4 (9). *Cuyp*, Landscape with cattle; *8, 10, 12, 15 (30, 199, 41, 205). *Jan* and *Andrew Both*, Landscapes with figures and cattle; 16 (178). *Unknown Master of Haarlem*, Landscape with figures; 23, 26 (16, 15). *Bartolommeo Breenberg* (of Utrecht, settled in Rome; d. after 1663), Small landscapes; 25 (14). *Corn. van Poelenburg* (Utrecht; d. 1667), Dancing nymph; *31, *33 (155, 61). *Teniers the Younger*, Landscapes with figures; °34, *36 (64, 63). *Wouverman*, Landscapes; 35 (52). *Teniers the Elder*, Cottage and figures.

*39 (104). *Corn. Dusart* (Haarlem, d. 1704), Old building, with figures.
A remarkably careful and choice picture by this scholar of Adriaen van Ostade, who approaches nearest to his master in the glow of his colouring'. — *Waagen.*

45 (107). *Adriaen van Ostade* (Haarlem; d. 1685), Interior of a cottage with figures; 46 (365). *Antonio Belucci* (d. 1726), St. Sebastian with Faith and Charity; °47 (147). *Jan Weenix* (Amsterdam, 1640-1719; son and pupil of Jan Baptist Weenix), Landscape with accessories, dated 1664; 49 (84). *Teniers the Younger*, Road near a cottage; 50 (85). *Brekelenkam*, Old woman eating porridge; 51 (72). *Adriaen van de Velde* (Amsterdam; d. 1672), Landscape with cattle; 52, 54 (86, 50). *Teniers the Younger*, Cottage with figures, Guard-room; *56 (106). *Gerard Dou*, Lady playing on a keyed instrument; 62 (329). *Spanish School*, Christ bearing the cross; *Cuyp*,

63 (5). Cows and sheep, an early work, °65 (114). White horse in a riding-school. — Room VII, to the left of R. I, contains the *Cartwright Collection of Portraits*.

Room II. On the left: 331 (362). *Gainsborough*, Son of Thomas Linley; 67 (93). *Wouwerman*, View near Scheveningen, early work; 65 (113). *Willem van de Velde the Younger* (Amsterdam; d. 1707), Calm; 71 (156). *Cuyp*, Two horses; °77, 78, *79 (125, 173, 126). *Philip Wouwerman*, Landscapes with figures; 81 (124). *Van Dyck*, Charity; *82 (229). *Karel du Jardin* (Amsterdam, pupil of Berchem, painted at Rome; d. 1678), Smith shoeing an ox; 86 (130). *Adam Pynacker* (of Pynacker, near Delft, settled in Italy; d. 1673), Landscape with sportsmen; *87 (131). *Meindert Hobbema* (Amsterdam; d. 1709), Landscape with a water-mill; 90 (135). *Van Dyck*, Virgin and Infant Saviour (repetitions at Dresden and elsewhere); 92 (137). *Wouwerman*, Farrier and an old convent (engraved under the title 'Le Colombier du Maréchal'); 95 (139). *Teniers the Younger*, Château with the family of the proprietor; 96 (141). *Cuyp*, Landscape with figures; °97 (144). *Wouwerman*, Halt of travellers; °99 (189). *Rembrandt*, Portrait, early work, dated 1632; 102 (143). *Sir Joshua Reynolds* (d. 1792), Mother and sick child.

°103 (166). *W. van de Velde*, Brisk gale off the Texel.
'A warm evening-light, happily blended with the delicate silver tone of the master, and of the most exquisite finish in all the parts, makes this one of his most charming pictures.' — W.

105 (154). *Ruysdael*, Waterfall, painted in an unusually broad manner; *108 (54). *Adriaen Brouwer* (Haarlem, pupil of F. Hals, d. 1640), Interior of an ale-house, a genuine specimen of a scarce master; 112 (116). *Teniers the Younger*, Winter-scene; 114, *117 (12, 11). *Jan Wynants* (Haarlem, d. 1682), Landscapes; *115 (190). *A. van Ostade*, Boors making merry, 'of astonishing depth, clearness, and warmth of colour'; 120 (140). *Jan van Huysum* (Amsterdam, d. 1749), Flowers; 122 (160). *Nic. Berchem* (Haarlem, d. 1683), Wood-scene; *124, **128 (163, 169). *Cuyp*, Landscapes with cattle and figures; 127 (168). School of *Rubens*, Samson and Delilah; 131 (182). *Rubens*, Helen Fourment, the artist's second wife; 133 (176). *Unknown Master*, Landscape with cattle; 137 (159). *Salvator Rosa* (Naples and Rome; d. 1673), Landscape; 140 (358). *Gainsborough*, Portrait of Thomas Linley.

Room III. On the left: 144 (243). *Cuyp*, Landscape near Dort, with cattle; °146 (60). *Teniers the Younger*, Sow and pigs; 147 (191). *Adriaen van der Werff* (court-painter to the Elector Palatine; d. 1722), Judgment of Paris.

152 (194). *Velazquez*, Portrait of the Prince of Asturias, son of Philip IV.. a copy of the original at Madrid.

°155 (196). *Jan van der Heyde* (Amsterdam, d. 1712), Landscape, figures by *A. van de Velde*; *156 (210). *Antoine Watteau* (Paris, d. 1721), Le bal champêtre; 157, 166 (200, 209). *Berchem*, Landscapes; *163 (206). *Rembrandt*, A girl at a window; *167 (197). *A. Watteau*, La fête champêtre; °168 (241). *Ruysdael*, Landscape with mills; 171 (215). *Wilson*, Tivoli; 172 (183). *Northcote*, Sir P. F. Bourgeois (p. 402); 173 (218). After *Van Dyck*, Portrait; 178 (359). *Sir Thos. Lawrence* (d. 1830), Portrait of Wm. Linley, the author; 181 (145). *Cuyp*, Winter-scene; 182 (228). *Wouwerman*, Peasants in the fields; 291 (53). *H. P. Briggs*, Charles Kemble; 183 (150). *Pynacker*, Landscape with figures; 191 (238). *G. Schalcken*, Ceres at the old woman's cottage, from Ovid; °192 (239). *Cuyp*, Landscape near Dort, with cattle; 194 (242). *Van Dyck*, Lady Venetia Digby, taken after death; 188 (363). School of *Le Brun*, Molière; 197 (186). *W. van de Velde*, Calm.

Room IV. On the left: °199 (248). *Murillo*, Spanish flower-girl; 202 (252). *Charles Le Brun* (pupil of N. Poussin; d. 1690), Massacre of the Innocents; *205 (244). *Claude*, Landscape, with Jacob and Laban ('one of the most genuine Claudes I know', writes Mr. Ruskin); *208 (36). *Both*, Landscape; *210 (278). *Ruysdael*, Landscape, with figures by *A. van de Velde*; 213 (269). *Gaspar Poussin* (pupil of N. Poussin; d. 1675), Destruction of Niobe and her children; *215 (275). *Claude Lorrain* (d. 1682), Italian seaport; 216 (271). *Salvator Rosa*, Soldiers gaming ('very spirited, and in a deep glowing tone'); 220 (270). *Claude*, Embarkation of St. Paula at Ostia.

°222 (283). *Murillo*, Two Spanish peasant boys and a negro boy.
'Very natural and animated, defined in the forms, and painted in a golden warm tone'. — W.

°224 (286). *Murillo*, Two Spanish peasant boys. *N. Poussin*, 227 (291). Adoration of the Magi; 229 (295). Inspiration of Anacreon. 230 (335). *Annibale Carracci* (Bologna; d. 1609), Virgin, Infant Christ, and St. John. *N. Poussin*, 234 (300). Education of Jupiter; 236 (305). Triumph of David; 238 (315). Rinaldo and Armida, from Tasso; 240 (310). Flight into Egypt. °241, °243 (307, 306). *Raphael*, SS. Francis of Assisi and Anthony of Padua (retouched); 242 (337). *Carlo Dolci* (Bologna; d. 1686), St. Catharine of Siena; 244 (319). *Le Brun*, Horatius Cocles defending the bridge; °245 (83). *Cuyp*, Landscape with figures (bright and calm sunlight); 249 (309). *Velazquez*, Portrait of Philip IV. of Spain.

ROOM V. On the left: 251 (327). *Andrea del Sarto* (d. 1530), Holy Family (repetition of a picture in the Pitti Palace at Florence, and ascribed by Mr. Crowe to Salviati); 256 (287). *Umbrian School*, Virgin and Child; 260 (226). *Italian School*, Venus gathering apples in the Garden of the Hesperides; 262 (331). *Guido Reni* (d. 1642), St. John in the wilderness; 263 (336). *N. Poussin*, Assumption of the Virgin; 264 (240), *Van Dyck* (ascribed to *Rubens*), The Graces; 267 (343). After *Cristofano Allori* (d. 1621), Judith with the head of Holofernes; 268 (339). *After G. Reni*, St. Sebastian; °270 (333). *Paolo Veronese* (d. 1583). Cardinal blessing a donor; 271 (277). *German School*, Salvator Mundi; 281 (347). *Murillo*, La Madonna del Rosario; 283 (249). *Domenichino*, Adoration of the Shepherds; 285 (351). *Rubens*, Venus, Mars, and Cupid, a late work; 290 (355). School of *Rubens*, Rubens's mother(?).

ROOM VI. On the left: 297 (55). *Loutherbourg*, Landscape; 299 (46). *Teniers the Elder*, Landscape with shepherd and sheep; 300, 306 (110, 111). *J. Vernet*, Landscapes; 302 (361). *Gainsborough*, Samuel Linley; 314 (35). *Teniers the Elder*, Landscape, with the repentant Peter.

316 (366). *Gainsborough*, Mrs. Moodey and her two children; 318 (340). *Sir Joshua Reynolds*, Mrs. Siddons as the Tragic Muse, painted in 1789. — °320 (1). *Gainsborough*, Portraits of Mrs. Sheridan and Mrs. Tickell, the daughters of Thomas Linley.

Mrs. Tickell sits on a bank, while Mrs. Sheridan stands half behind her. Waagen characterises this work as one of the best specimens of the master, and Mrs. Jameson says: 'The head of Mrs. Sheridan is exquisite, and, without having all the beauty which Sir Joshua gave her in the famous St. Cecilia, there is even more mind'.

°322 (102). *Daniel Seghers* (Antwerp; d. 1661), Flowers encircling a bas-relief.

'A very admirable picture of this master, so justly celebrated in his own times, and whose red roses still flourish in their original beauty, while those of the later painters, De Heem, Huysum, and Rachel Ruysch, have more or less changed. The vase is probably by Erasmus Quellinus'. — Waagen.

323 (34). *Teniers the Elder*, Landscape, with the Magdalen; 66 (111). *Gainsborough*, P. T. Loutherbourg, R. A.; 339 (89). *Loutherbourg*, Landscape; 340 (112). *Adriaen van der Neer* (Amsterdam; d. 1691), Moonlight-scene.

The adjacent building, at one time the school, is now used as almshouses. In the chapel is the tomb of Alleyn, the founder. — A few min. walk to the N. of the Picture Gallery is the village of *Dulwich* (Greyhound Inn; Crown), beyond which ($^3/_4$ M. from the Gallery) is the station of *North Dulwich*. — College Road leads to the S. from the village to ($1^3/_4$ M.) the Crystal Palace (p. 396), passing *Dulwich Park* (72 acres), on the right, presented to the public in 1890 by the governors of the college, ($^1/_2$ M.) Dulwich College (p. 401), and (1 M.) *Sydenham Hill Station* (p. 397), beside which is *St. Stephen's Church*, containing a fresco by Sir E. J. Poynter, P. R. A.

A little to the W. of Dulwich, near *Herne Hill Station*, is *Brockwell Park* (78 acres), opened to the public by the London County Council in 1892. John Ruskin spent his youth (1823-40) at Herne Hill in a house still occupied by his cousins, Mr. and Mrs. Arthur Severn.

40. Hampton Court. Richmond. Kew.

These places are frequently visited on a Sunday, as the Palace of Hampton Court, with its fine picture-gallery, is one of the few resorts of the kind in or about London which is not closed on that day.

One of the best ways to make this excursion is to go to Hampton Court by railway; to walk or drive through Bushy Park to the Teddington station; to take the train thence to Richmond; and the tramway thence to Kew. The return to London may be made by railway (see below), on the top of an omnibus, or by steamboat (1½-2 hrs.; fare to London Bridge 1s. to 1s. 10d.; comp. pp. 63, 64). One of the coaches mentioned at p. 55 runs to Hampton Court. Omnibuses, chars-a-bancs, and brakes ply frequently on Sun. afternoon from Charing Cross, Piccadilly, etc., to Kew (6d.-1s.), Richmond (1s.-1s. 6d.), and Hampton Court (1s. 6d.-2s. 6d.).

Another pleasant round, involving more walking, is as follows: by train to Richmond; drive viâ Strawberry Hill to Teddington; walk through Bushy Park to Hampton Court (ca. ½ hr.) and through Richmond Park to Richmond (ca. 2 hrs.); then back to London by train. The least agreeable part of the walk to Richmond may be saved by taking the omnibus to Kingston.

RAILWAY. We may travel by the *South Western Railway* from *Waterloo Station* to *Hampton Court;* or by the *North London Railway* from *Broad Street*, City (comp. p. 57), to *Kew* and *Richmond*, and *Teddington* (p. 411); or by the *Metropolitan District Railway* from the *Mansion House, Charing Cross, Victoria, Westminster,* or *Kensington* to *Richmond*, and thence to *Teddington*.

The SOUTH WESTERN RAILWAY (from Waterloo Station to Hampton Court ¾ hr.; fares 2s., 1s. 6d., 1s. 2½d.) runs for a considerable distance on a viaduct above the streets of London. To the right are the picturesque brick buildings of *Doulton's Pottery* (p. 383). *Vauxhall*, the first station, is still within the town; but we emerge from its precincts near (4½ M.) *Clapham Junction*, the second station. The first glimpse of the pretty scenery traversed by the line is obtained after passing through the long cutting beyond Clapham. To the left is the *Victoria Institution* for children of soldiers and sailors. — 7½ M. *Wimbledon* lies a little to the S. of *Wimbledon Common*, once the scene of the great volunteer rifle-shooting competition now held at Bisley. *Wimbledon House* was once occupied by Calonne, the French minister, and by the Duc d'Enghien, shot at Vincennes in 1804. About ¾ M. from the station is a well-preserved fortified camp of cruciform shape, probably of Saxon origin.

Beyond Wimbledon a line diverges to the left to *Epsom*, near which are *Epsom Downs*, where the great races, the 'Derby' and the 'Oaks', take place annually in May or June (see p. 71). Before reaching (10 M.) *Coombe & Malden*, we pass, on a height to the right, *Coombe House*, formerly the property of Lord Liverpool, who in 1815, when Prime Minister, entertained the Emperor of Russia, the King of Prussia, and the Prince Regent here. Just beyond (12 M.) *Surbiton*, to the left, lie the extensive nurseries of *Barr & Sons*, where the show of daffodils in April and May is worth making a special journey to see. There are millions of bulbs, representing 600 varieties. About 2 M. from Surbiton the branch-line to Hampton Court diverges to the right from the main line, passing *Thames Ditton* (Swan), pleasantly situated in a grassy neighbourhood.

On arriving at (15 M.) **Hampton Court** (*Thames*, Pl. a, near the station, with boats and steam and electric launches for hire, R. & A. from 3s., D. from 2s. 6d.; *Castle*, also near the station, with verandah overlooking the river, D. from 2s. 6d.; *Mitre*, Pl. b, beyond the bridge, R. & A. from 4s. 6d., D. from 2s. 6d.; *King's Arms*, *Greyhound*, Pl. c, first-class inns, at the entrance to Bushy Park; *Park Cottage; Queen's Arms*, D. from 1s. 6d.), we turn to the right, cross the bridge over the Thames, which commands a charming view of the river, and follow the broad road to the Palace on the right. Admission to the Palace, see p. 108. The Gardens are open daily (from 12 on Sun.) until dusk. Hampton Court is annually visited by about a quarter of a million persons; the highest record is 370,000 in 1862. Comp. Plan.

The Palace, the largest royal palace in Great Britain, was originally founded in 1515 by *Cardinal Wolsey*, the favourite of Henry VIII., and was afterwards presented by him to the King. It was built of red brick with battlemented walls, and lay on the site of a property mentioned in Domesday Book. It was subsequently occupied by Cromwell, the Stuarts, William III., and the first two monarchs of the house of Hanover. In 1604 the Hampton Court Conference between the Puritans and the Episcopalians met here under James I. as moderator. Under Queen Anne the Palace was the scene of the event celebrated in Pope's 'Rape of the Lock'. The present state apartments were built by Sir Christopher Wren to the order of William III., who died in 1702 in consequence of a fall from his horse in the park here. Since the time of George II. Hampton Court has ceased to be a royal residence, and over 800 of its 1000 rooms are now occupied in suites by aristocratic pensioners of the Crown.

Approaching from the W., we pass through the *Trophy Gates* into the *Barrack Yard*, so named from the low barracks on the left, built by Charles II. and enlarged by William III. In front of us rises the *Great Gate House*, recently restored, through which we gain the turfed *Green* or *Base Court*, the first and largest of the three principal courts comprised in the palace. On the towers of the archways between the different courts are terracotta medallions of Roman emperors (the best being that of Nero), obtained by Wolsey from the sculptor, *Joannes Maiano*. The fine oriel windows on the outside and inside of the gate-house are Wolsey's originals.

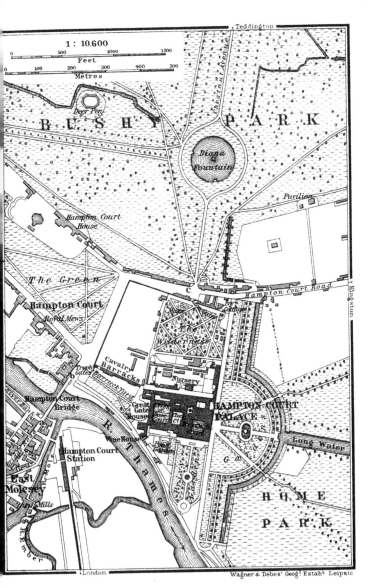

1 : 10.600

500   1000   1500

Feet

0   100   200   300   400   500

Métres

Deer Pen

B U S H Y   P A R K

Chestnut Avenue

Diana Fountain

Pavilion

Hampton Court House

Kingston

The Green

Hampton Court Road

Hampton Court

Royal Mews

The Wilderness

Maze

Ivy Cottage

Cavalry Barracks

Nursery

Trophy Gates

Barrack Yard

River Mole

Hampton Court Bridge

Great Gate House

Tennis Court

HAMPTON COURT PALACE

Wine House

R. Thames

Long Water

Hampton Court Station

Dutch Garden

Garden

East Molesey

Flour Mills

R. Ember

H O M E

P A R K

Beneath both are the arms of Henry VIII. To the left in *Anne Bo-leyn's Gateway*, which leads to the next court (see below), is the staircase ascending to the *Great Hall*, 106 ft. in length, 40 ft. in breadth, and 60 ft. in height, begun by Henry VIII. immediately after the death of Wolsey, and completed in 1536. It contains good stained-glass windows (mostly modern) and fine tapestry representing scenes from the life of Abraham, supposed to be from the designs of *B. van Orley*. The high-pitched timber *Roof is a noble specimen of the Perpendicular Gothic style. The room at the end is identified as *Henry VIII.'s Great Watching Chamber*. This and the adjoining *Horn Room*, from which a staircase descends to the kitchens, also contain tapestries.

We return to Anne Boleyn's Gateway and enter the *Clock Court*, above the entrance to which are seen the armorial bearings of Wolsey, with his motto 'Dominus mihi adjutor'. The court is named from the curious *Astronomical Clock*, originally constructed for Henry VIII., and recently repaired and set going again. From the S. side of this court we pass through an Ionic colonnade, erected by Wren, to the *King's Grand Staircase*, adorned with allegorical paintings by *Verrio*, which ascends to the State Rooms. Bags and parcels are left at the foot of it. The names of the rooms are written above the doors, on the inside; we always begin with the pictures on the left. Visitors are required to pass from room to room in one direction only. The gallery is rich in Italian pictures, especially of the Venetian school, but the names attached to them are often erroneous. The following list pays no regard to the names on the pictures themselves. Comp. *E. Law's* 'History of the Palace in Tudor Times' (1885) and 'Historical Catalogue of the Pictures at Hampton Court' (1881). The 'Illustrated Guide' (1899; 1s.) is an abridgment of the latter.

Room I (*The King's Guard Chamber*). The upper parts of the walls are tastefully decorated with trophies and large star-shaped groups of pistols, guns, lances, and other modern weapons. The best of the pictures are: 9. *Canaletto*, Colosseum and Arch of Constantine at Rome; 20. *Zucchero*, Queen Elizabeth's porter; several military scenes by *Rugendas*.

Room II (*The King's First Presence Chamber*) contains the canopy of the throne of King William III. The wood-carving above the chimney-piece and doors in this and several of the following rooms is by *Grinling Gibbons;* the candelabrum dates from the reign of Queen Anne. The upper row of portraits are the so-called 'Hampton Court Beauties', or ladies of the court of William and Mary, painted by *Sir Godfrey Kneller*, after the model of the 'Windsor Beauties' of Charles II.'s Court, by *Sir Peter Lely*, formerly in Windsor Castle, and now in Room VI of this gallery. The following pictures may also be remarked: 29. *Kneller*, William III. landing at Torbay, a large allegorical work; 35, 36. *Denner*, Portraits; 39, 52. *Schiavone*, Frieze-like landscapes with figures; 707. *Janssen*, Villiers, Duke of Buckingham; 58. *Unknown Master*, Portraits of Villiers, Duke of Buckingham, and his family; 60. *Unknown Painter*, Man's head; °64. Good Dutch copy, in the style of *Mabuse*, of a sketch by *Leonardo da Vinci*, Infant Christ and St. John; 66. *De Bray*, History of Mark Antony and Cleopatra, the figures being portraits of the artist's family.

Room III (*The Second Presence Chamber*). On the left: 69. *Tintoretto*, Esther before Ahasuerus; °80. *Dosso Dossi*, Portrait of a man, well preserved; 72. *Leandro Bassano*, Sculptor; 79. *After Titian*, Holy Family; *73. *Bonifazio Veronese*, Diana and Actæon in a fanciful landscape, one of the artist's masterpieces; 78. *Jacopo Bassano*, Dominican; *85. *Van Dyck*, Equestrian portrait of Charles I.; *90. *Velazquez*, Consort of Philip IV. of Spain; *91. *Tintoretto*, Knight of Malta; 98 (above the mantel-piece), *Van Somer*, Christian IV. of Denmark; 104. *Pordenone*, His own family (dated 1524).

ROOM IV (*The Audience Chamber*). On the left: 117. *Giov. Bellini* (? or of his school; forged signature), Portrait of himself; 113. *Titian* (?), Ignatius Loyola; *114. *Lorenzo Lotto*, Portrait; *115. *Palma Vecchio*, Holy Family; 130. *Unknown Artist*, Portrait; 224. *Girol. da Treviso*, Marriage of the Virgin; 125. *Giorgione* (?), Portrait; 128. *Honthorst*, Elizabeth, Queen of Bohemia, wife of Frederick V. of the Palatinate (above the mantel-piece); 138. *Savoldo*. Warrior; 581. *Mazzolino of Ferrara*, Turkish warrior; 710. *Dutch Master*, Portrait (*not* of Raphael); *144. Wrongly ascribed to *Lor. Lotto*, Family-concert; 235. *Bordone* (? more probably Palma Vecchio), Lucretia, injured by repainting; *148. *Lotto*, Portrait of Andrea Ordini, a sculptor; *149. *Titian*, Portrait.

ROOM V (*The King's Drawing Room*). On the left: 153. *J. Bassano*, Boaz and Ruth; 175. *Schiavone*, Judgment of Midas; 182. *Master of Treviso*, Lawyer; *183. *Dosso*, St. William taking off his armour.

ROOM VI (*King William the Third's Bedroom*) contains the bed of Queen Charlotte. The clock in the corner to the left of the bed goes for a year without re-winding; though in good repair it is no longer wound up. On the walls are the 'Beauties' of the Court of Charles II., chiefly painted by *Lely* (comp. Room II), including 190. Duchess of York (above the mantel-piece); 195. Duchess of Richmond, who was the original of the 'Britannia' on the reverse of the British copper coins; 196. Marie d'Este (?, misnamed Nell Gwynne); all three by *Lely*. The ceiling, by *Verrio*, is emblematic of Sleep.

ROOM VII (*The King's Dressing Room*). Ceiling-paintings by *Verrio*, representing Mars, Venus, and Cupid. *589. *Dürer*, Portrait; *595. *Mabuse*, Children of Christian II. of Denmark; *608. *Holbein*, The artist's parents; *590. *School of Van Eyck*, Head of a young man; *Holbein*, 751. Landscape, *610. Reskemeer (the hand beautifully painted); 563. *Holbein* (?), Henry VIII. as a youth; 601. *Remée* (Antwerp; d. 1678), Henry VII. and his queen Elizabeth, Henry VIII. and his queen Jane Seymour, copy of a fresco by *Holbein* in Whitehall, which was burned with that palace; *561. *Janet*, Queen Eleanor of France; *603. *Holbein*, Frobenius, the famous printer.

ROOM VIII (*The King's Writing Closet*). Beginning at the window: *353. *Gainsborough*, Colonel St. Leger; 680. *Rottenhammer*, Judgment of Paris; *Van Dyck*, 638. Dying saint, 47. Mrs. Margaret Lemon, the artist's mistress; *Artemisia Gentileschi*, 227. Sibyl, 226. Her own portrait; 267. *Dutch Master*, Sophonisba; 734. *P. Brill*, Landscape. The mirror above the chimney-piece here is placed at such an angle as to reflect the whole suite of rooms.

ROOM IX (*Queen Mary's Closet*). On the left: 634. *Hendrik Pot*, Play-scene (the actor here is supposed to be Charles I); 657. *Verdussen*, Windsor Castle; 676. *School of Frans Hals*, Portrait; 731. *J. B. Weenix*, Dead game.

ROOM X (*The Queen's Gallery*) is a hall, 69 ft. long and 26 ft. broad, with tapestry representing scenes from the life of Alexander the Great, after *Le Brun*.

ROOM XI (*The Queen's Bedroom*) contains Queen Anne's bed, and has a ceiling painted by *Thornhill*, representing Aurora rising from the sea. To the left: *307. *Francesco Francia*, Baptism of Christ; 251. *Giulio Romano*, Holy Family; 278. *L. Giordano*, Offerings of the Magi; *97. *Dosso Dossi*, Holy Family; *276. *Correggio*, Holy Family, with St. Jerome on the left, a small and admirable work of the painter's early period; 259. *Holbein* (?), Countess of Lennox, mother of Lord Darnley.

ROOM XII (*The Queen's Drawing Room*), with ceiling painted by *Verrio*, representing Queen Anne as the Goddess of Justice. The allegorical paintings on the walls, with portraits of Queen Anne and her husband, Prince George of Denmark, also by Verrio, were restored to view in 1899, after having been concealed by canvas and wall-paper for over 160 years. The windows command a fine *View of the gardens and canal (³/₄ M. long).

ROOM XIII (*The Queen's Audience Chamber*). On the left: *Holbein*, °340. Henry VIII. and his family; 342. Meeting of Henry VIII. and Francis I. of France, at the Field of the Cloth of Gold. 666. Ascribed to *Holbein*, Face at a window, misnamed Will Somers, court-jester of Henry VIII.

ROOM XIV (*The Public Dining Room*). On the left: *W. van de Velde*, 754, 745. Sea-pieces (sketches); 560. *Zucchero*, Mary, Queen of Scots; 365. *Walker*, Portrait of himself; 366. *Gainsborough*, Jewish Rabbi; 361. *Knapton*, Family of Frederick, Prince of Wales (the boy with the plan on his knee is George III.); 363. *Sir T. Lawrence*, Friedrich von Gentz; above the fire-place, 663. *Van Dyck*, Cupid and Psyche; 376. *Dobson*, Portrait of himself and his wife. We proceed in a straight direction; the door to the left leads to the Queen's Chapel, etc. (see below).

ROOM XV (*The Prince of Wales's Presence Chamber*). On the left: *Rembrandt*, 381. Rabbi; 382. Dutch lady. °385. *Mabuse*, Adam and Eve; 380. *N. Poussin*, Nymphs and Satvrs; 394. *Zucchero*, Calumny. an allegory; 576. *Van Orley*, Death of Adonis; 578. *Schoreel*, Virgin and Child. 88. Andrew and Michael; *L. Cranach*, 600 St. Christopher and other saints, 588. Judgment of Paris; 654. *After Rubens*, Venus and Adonis; 579. *Hemmessen*, St. Jerome; 871. *Zucchero*, Adoration of the Shepherds; 404. *Heemskerck*, Quakers' meeting.

ROOM XVI (*The Prince of Wales's Drawing Room*). On the left: 407. *Van Belchamp*, Louis XIII. of France; 748. *Brueghel the Elder*, Slaughter of the Innocents, thoroughly Dutch in conception; 629, 637. *Gonzales Coques*, Portraits; 411. *Pourbus*, Maria de' Medici; °334. *Palamedes*. Embarking from Scheveningen; *746. *Wynants*, Landscape; 662. *Molenaer*, Dutch merry-making; 418. *Pourbus*, Henri IV. of France.

ROOM XVII (*The Prince of Wales's Bedroom*) contains tapestry representing the Battle of Solebay (1672), and a few portraits.

We now return to Room XIV (*Public Dining Room*), and pass through the door on the right, indicated by notices pointing the 'Way Out'.

QUEEN's PRIVATE CHAPEL. On the left: °463. *Hondecoeter*, Birds; 464. *Snyders*, Still-life; *De Heem*, °467, 469. Still-life pieces. — The BATHING CLOSET adjoining the chapel contains the queen's marble bath. The PRIVATE DINING ROOM contains three bright red beds (William III.'s to the left; Queen Mary's to the right; George II.'s in the middle). Adjoining it is a CLOSET with 12 saints by *Feti* (506).

QUEEN's PRIVATE CHAMBER. In the centre: °106. *Unknown Flemish* or *German Master*, Triptych with the Crucifixion in the centre, the Bearing of the Cross to the left, the Resurrection to the right. and the Ecce Homo on the exterior, of admirable colouring. The KING's PRIVATE DRESSING ROOM contains some poor copies of various well-known works. We then pass through GEORGE II.'s PRIVATE ROOM, with fruit and flower pieces, and a dark corner-room into the long —

SOUTH GALLERY, where Raphael's famous cartoons, now at South Kensington (p. 359), were preserved until 1865. Among the few pictures here are: 571. *Hannemann*, William III. as a boy; 704. *Snyders*, Boarhunt; *Benj. West*, Death of Epaminondas.

We now pass through the small, dark KING's LOBBY, and enter the last long gallery, called the —

°°MANTEGNA GALLERY, which contains the gem of the whole collection, the Triumphal Procession of Cæsar, by *Mantegna* (No. 797), extending the whole length of the wall, and protected by glass. The series of pictures, painted in distemper upon linen, is in parts sadly defaced, and has also been retouched. Mantegna began the work, which was intended for stage-scenery, in 1485, and finished it in 1490-92. The series was purchased by Charles I. along with the rest of the Duke of Mantua's collection in 1628, and was valued by the Parliament after the king's death at 1000*l.* It was rescued by Cromwell, along with Raphael's cartoons. The lighting of the room prevents these paintings being seen to advantage.

Section I. Beginning of the procession with trumpeters, standard bearers, and warriors; on the flag-poles paintings of the victories of Cæsar. — II. Statues of Jupiter and Juno in chariots, bust of Cybele, warlike instruments. — III. Trophies of war; weapons, urns, tripods, etc. — IV. Precious vessels and ornaments; oxen led by pages; train of musicians. — V. Elephants bearing fruit, flowers, and candelabra. — VI. Urns, armour, etc., borne in triumph. — VII. Procession of the captives; men, women, and children, and mocking figures among the populace. — VIII. Dancing musicians, standard-bearers with garlands; among them a soldier of the German Legion, bearing a standard with the she-wolf of Rome. — IX. *Julius Caesar*, with sceptre and palm-branch, in a triumphal car; behind him Victoria; on his standard the legend, 'Veni, vidi, vici'.

'With a stern realism, which was his virtue, Mantegna multiplied illustrations of the classic age in a severe and chastened style, balancing his composition with the known economy of the Greek relief, conserving the dignity of sculptural movement and gait, and the grave marks of the classic statuaries, modifying them though but slightly with the newer accent of Donatello. ... His contour is tenuous and fine and remarkable for a graceful and easy flow; his clear lights, shaded with grey, are blended with extraordinary delicacy, his colours are bright and variegated, yet thin, spare, and of gauzy substance.' — *Crowe and Cavalcaselle*.

The Mantegna Gallery also contains a few other paintings, including an alleged portrait of Jane Shore, mistress of Edward IV. (No. 793; immediately to the right of the door by which we enter) and a portrait of the dwarf Sir Jeffery Hudson, immortalized in Scott's 'Peveril of the Peak' (No. 798; by *Mytens;* over the fire-place).

To the left, at the end of this gallery, are three small rooms the most interesting of which is CARDINAL WOLSEY'S CLOSET, with a fine ceiling, panelled walls, and a frieze of paintings on panel from the History of the Passion.

We now pass the top of the QUEEN'S STAIRCASE, embellished with ceiling-paintings by *Vick,* and a large picture by *Honthorst,* representing Charles I. and his wife as Apollo and Diana, and reach two other rooms, which contain the remainder of the pictures.

ROOM I *(The Queen's Guard Chamber).* On the left: 811. *Ciro Ferri,* Triumph of Bacchus; *Fialetti,* 526. Four doges of Venice, 507. Venetian senators; 850. *Romanelli,* after *Guido Reni,* Triumph of Venus, with Bacchus and Ariadne. The wrought-iron railings, long ascribed to Huntington Shaw (p. 362) but more probably by Jean Tijou, are two of twelve formerly in the gardens. Here also are two pieces of timber from Nelson's flagship, the *Victory.* — We now pass through a small *Ante-Room* into —

ROOM II *(The Queen's Presence Chamber).* W. *van de Velde,* *879. British ship engaged with three Spanish vessels; 880. Close of the same action; on each side of the fire-place, 888. *L. Giordano,* Myth of Cupid and Psyche, in twelve small pictures (painted upon copper); 369. *Michael Wright,* John Lacy, comedian, in three characters. This room contains also a number of sea-pieces.

We now return and descend the Queen's Staircase, at the foot of which we turn to the left and enter the *Fountain Court,* surrounded by cloisters, built by *Wren.* On the S. wall are twelve circular paintings of the Labours of Hercules, by Laguerre, now almost obliterated. Farther on we enter the gardens, in front of the E. façade of the Palace.

The *Garden* is laid out in the French style, and embellished with tasteful flower-beds and shady avenues. Immediately opposite the centre of the façade is the *Long Canal,* $3/4$ M. long and 150 ft. wide, constructed by Charles II. On each side of the canal is the House Park. — In the Pond Garden, to the W. of the Privy Garden, on the S. side of the Palace, is exhibited a vine of the Black Hamburgh variety, planted in 1768 by Lancelot ('Capability') Brown, the stem of which is 38 in. in circumference, and the branches of which spread over an area of 2200 sq. ft. The yield of this gigantic vine amounts annually to 1200 or 1300 bunches of grapes, weighing about 3/4 lb. each. — The old *Tennis Court*, opening from the garden to the N. of the Palace, is still used.

The *Maze* (adm. 1d.), or labyrinth, in the so-called *Wilderness* to the N. of the Palace, may be successfully penetrated by keeping invariably to the left, *except the first time* we have an option, when we keep to the extreme *right*; in coming out, we keep to the *right*, till we reach the same place, when we turn to the *left*. — Near the Maze are the *Lion Gates*, by which we quit Hampton Court. The piers, with the carved stone lions, were erected by Queen Anne; the iron gates are ascribed to Tijou (p. 410).

Outside the gates are the hotels mentioned at p. 406. Omnibuses from Hampton Court to *Richmond* (6d.) and to *Kingston* pass this point; and on Sun. waggonettes ply hence through Bushy Park to *Teddington* (2d.). Carriage from Hampton Court to Teddington 2s. 6d., to Richmond 6s. Comp. also p. 406.

Immediately opposite the Lion Gates is one of the entrances to **Bushy Park**, a royal domain of about 1000 acres. There are three other gates: viz. one near Teddington, one at Hampton Wick (p. 388), and one at Hampton village. Its white-thorn trees in blossom are very beautiful, but its chief glory is in the end of spring or in early summer, when the horse-chestnuts are in full bloom, affording a sight quite unequalled in England ('Chestnut Sunday', usually announced in the London papers). These majestic old trees, planted by William III. and interspersed with limes, form a triple avenue, of more than a mile in length, from Hampton Court to Teddington. Near the Hampton Court end of the avenue is a curious basin with carp and gold-fish and the 'Diana Fountain', dating from 1699. The deer in the park are so tame that they scarcely exert themselves to get out of the way of visitors. They even thrust their heads in at the open windows of the houses that look on the park, insisting on being fed. The residence of the ranger is a sombre red brick house, screened off by railings, near one margin of the park.

We turn to the left on quitting Bushy Park. The road almost immediately forks, when we keep to the right, and then take the third turning on the right, passing the garden of the *Clarence Hotel* and leading to (1¼ M.) *Teddington Station*. The train from Teddington to Richmond passes *Strawberry Hill* (p. 388), *Twickenham* (p. 388), and *St. Margaret's*. From Richmond to London by rail, see p. 405. — The walk from Teddington to (3 M.) Richmond is very picturesque (fine cedars).

Richmond. — Hotels. °STAR AND GARTER, near the Park Gate, on Richmond Hill, L. from 2s. 6d., D. 6s. 6d., with restaurant; °TALBOT, in

High St., near the bridge, R., A., & B. from 6s. 6d., D. from 3s. 6d., pens. from 10s. 6d.; MANSION RESIDENTIAL HOTEL, below the upper end of the terrace; CASTLE, GREYHOUND, in the town. — Numerous *Restaurants*, *Confectioners*, and *Tea Gardens*. 'Maids of Honour', a kind of sweet cheese-cake, are a specialty of Richmond.

Approaches. Richmond may be reached direct from London by the *South Western Railway* (N. Entrance, p. 59), the *North London Railway* from Broad St. (p. 56), or the *Metropolitan District Railway* every half-hour, or, in summer, by the *Steamboat*. Comp. also p. 405.

Richmond is a small town on the right bank of the Thames, charmingly situated on the slope of a hill (pop. in 1891, 22,684). The original name of the place was *Sheen* ('beautiful'), which still survives in the neighbouring *East Sheen*. Edward I. possessed a palace here, which was rebuilt in 1499 by Henry VII., the founder of the Tudor dynasty, who named it Richmond, after his own title. Henry VIII. and his daughter Elizabeth often held their courts in this palace, and the latter died here in 1603. In 1648 the palace was demolished by order of Parliament, and all that now remains of it is a stone gateway in Richmond Green.

From the station George Street leads to the W. to the main street. To the right lies *Richmond Green*, with numerous houses in the Queen Anne style and the *Theatre Royal*, a conspicuous terracotta erection, opened in 1900. We, however, turn to the left and ascend the main street, passing the *Town Hall* (1893), beside which is the small *Richmond Theatre*, opened in 1890, to the charming *Terrace Gardens*, which command a beautiful and famous *View. Above the terrace is *Doughty House*, the residence of Sir Francis Cooke, containing a collection of paintings by old masters and a number of antiquities (accessible on personal introduction). Farther up, at the top of Richmond Hill, is the *Park Gate*, an entrance to **Richmond Park**, 2255 acres in area and 8 M. in circumference. The park is a favourite summer-resort, both of Londoners and strangers, and is frequented in fine weather by crowds of pedestrians, horsemen, cyclists, and carriages. Large herds of deer here also add to the charms of the park. *Pembroke Lodge* in this park was the seat of Lord John Russell (d. 1878), and *White Lodge*, long a royal residence, was the scene of the interview between Jeanie Deans and Queen Caroline in Scott's 'Heart of Midlothian'. — The small church of Richmond contains the tombs of James Thomson (d. 1748), the poet of the 'Seasons', and Edmund Kean, the famous actor (d. 1833). — On the N. side of the town is the *Old Deer Park*, with a golf-course, cricket-ground, etc. In this park stands the *Kew Observatory*, eminent for its important work in meteorology, magnetism, electricity, and the verification of scientific instruments. Footpath to Kew, see p. 414.

From Richmond we may take the tramway (2d.; from near the Station) to **Kew** (*Star and Garter*, near the bridge; *Kew Gardens Hotel*, close to Kew Gardens Station, R. & A. 3s., B. 2s.), skirting the E. side of the Old Deer Park and the Botanic Gardens. The *Church of St. Anne*, on *Kew Green*, dates from 1714; it contains memorial windows to the Duchess of Teck, the Duchess of Cambridge, and other royalties. Gainsborough (d. 1788), the artist, is buried in the churchyard. Close by are *Cambridge Cottage*, the residence of the aged Duchess of Cambridge (d. 1889), and *Kew Cottage*. — Kew, which is reached from London direct by any of the routes to Richmond (see p. 405), has two railway-stations, *Kew Bridge Station* on the left, and *Kew Gardens Station* on the right bank of the Thames. Leaving the first of these, we cross the Thames to Kew Green, and thence proceed to the right to the principal entrance of the Gardens. From Kew Gardens station a short road leads direct to the Victoria Gate, which is visible from the station. Cycles may be left at the cycle-shelter, just outside the principal entrance (charge, 2d. each machine). The beautiful *Botanic Gardens at Kew are open gratis daily from 10 a.m. in summer and from 12 in winter (on Sundays always from 1 p.m.) till sunset; the hothouses are open daily from 1 p.m. Visitors may not bring eatables into the Gardens, or pluck even the wild flowers. Smoking is strictly prohibited in the houses. The present Director of the gardens is Sir W. T. Thiselton-Dyer, whose predecessors were the distinguished botanists Sir Joseph D. Hooker and Sir William J. Hooker. Plan of the Gardens (useful) 2d.

The BOTANIC GARDENS proper lie to the left (S.) of the broad walk leading from the principal entrance. Taking the first side-walk to the left, we reach a range of hothouses, containing the interesting ferns and cacti. A little farther on are the houses with the orchids and pitcher-plants and the tank for the *Victoria Regia, which flowers in July or August. To the E. is a Rock Garden, and a little to the S. is a pond enlivened by pelicans and numerous kinds of foreign waterfowl. On the E. side of the pond is one of the three *Museums* in the gardens, and on the W. side are the *Palm House* (362 ft. long, 100 ft. broad, and 66 ft. high), where the temperature is kept at 80° Fahr., and the *Water Lily House*. We may now cross the lawns to the N. to visit *Kew Palace* (10-6 daily, except Frid.) before going on to the Arboretum (see below). The quaint red brick palace, a favourite residence of George III. and Queen Charlotte (who died here in 1818), was thrown open to the public in 1898. It is at present practically empty. The Gardens contain a number of small ornamental *Temples*.

To the S. and W. of the Botanic Gardens proper lies the AR-BORETUM, covering an area of 178 acres, which extends to the Thames, and is intersected in every direction by shady walks and avenues. In the N. part is a small *American Garden*, with magnolias and fine azaleas (best about the end of May), and near the Thames (on the W.) is the *Hollow Walk*, famous for its show of rhododendrons in May and June. Near the middle of the Arboretum is a picturesque artificial *Lake* (water-fowl), skirted on the N.W. by a broad grassy avenue known as the 'Sion Vista'. Adjoining the S.W. end of the Arboretum are the private grounds surrounding the *Queen's Cottage*, which have been open to the public since 1898. The **Winter Garden*, or *Temperate House*, built in 1865 at a cost of 35,000*l.* in the S. part of the Arboretum, is designed for keeping plants of the temperate zone during winter. The central portion is 212 ft. long, 137 ft. wide, and 60 ft. high; with the wings the total length is 582 ft. A short distance to the E. of this stands the elegant *North Gallery*, the gift of Miss North (d. 1891), opened in 1882. It contains, in geographical sequence, a most interesting collection of paintings of tropical flowers, etc., executed by Miss North in their native localities (catalogue 3*d.*). The neighbouring *Flag-Staff* is a single Douglas pine, 160 ft. in height. Near the Winter Garden is a *Refreshment Pavilion* (tea, ices, etc.). At the S. extremity of the Arboretum is the *Pagoda*, rising in ten stories to a height of 165 ft. (no admission), not far from which is the *Lion Gate*, opening on the Richmond Road.

A footpath on the right bank of the Thames leads from Kew to Richmond, skirting the W. side of Kew Gardens and of the Old Deer Park (p. 412).

On the left bank of the Thames lies *Brentford* (p. 387), the official county-town of Middlesex (ferry a short distance to the S. of Kew Palace). The name of Brentford often occurs in English literature; thus the 'two Kings of Brentford on one throne' are mentioned by Cowper and in the 'Rehearsal'. Adjacent is *Sion House*, a place of great historic interest, which was a nunnery in the 15th cent., and is now a seat of the Duke of Northumberland.

41. Epping Forest. Waltham Abbey. Rye House.

Great Eastern Railway to (11½ M.) *Loughton*, in ³/₄ hr. (fares 2s. 1d., 1s. 5d., 1s.). From Loughton, which may also be reached from *Chalk Farm* and other stations of the *North London Railway* (viâ *Dalston Junction*), we go on foot, through *Epping Forest*, to (5 M.) *Waltham Abbey*. From Waltham Abbey to (6 M.) *Rye House* by railway. — Railway direct from London (Liverpool St.) to (13 M.) *Waltham Cross* in ³/₄ hr. (fares 2s., 1s. 6d., 1s. 1d.) and (19 M.) *Rye House* in 1 hr. (fares 3s. 8d., 2s. 10d., 1s. 8d.). See p. 416.

We may start either from *Fenchurch Street Station* (p. 58) or from *Liverpool Street Station* (p. 56). The first stations after Liverpool Street are *Bishopsgate*, *Bethnal Green* (p. 169), *Globe Road*, *Coborn Road*, and *Stratford*, where the train joins the North London line. Then *Leyton* (with the ground of the Essex County Cricket Club and a Technical Institute) and *Leytonstone*. At (8 M.) *Snaresbrook* is an *Infant Orphan Asylum*, with accommodation for 300 children (to the left of the line). To the E. lies *Wanstead Park* (184 acres), in which is a heronry, and farther to the S. are *Wan-*

stead Flats, another public park. 8¾ M. *George Lane; 9¾* M. *Woodford*, 3 M. from Chingford (see below). About 1½ M. to the E. of (**11 M.**) *Buckhurst Hill* lies *Chigwell*, where the 'King's Head' is the original of the 'Maypole' in 'Barnaby Rudge'. Then (**12 M.**) **Loughton** *(Railway Hotel)*, within a few hundred paces of the Forest. About ¾ M. from the station is the *Oriolet Vegetarian Hospital & Convalescent Home.*

Beyond Loughton the railway goes on viâ *Chigwell Lane, Theydon Bois*, (17 M.) **Epping** *(Thatched House; Cock)*, with 230ʋ inhab., *North Weald*, and *Blake Hall* to the terminus at (**22 M.**) *Chipping Ongar*, an ancient place (9ʋ0 inhab.), with the remains of a castle. *Greenstead*, 1 M. to the W. of Ongar, has a remarkable wooden church, the walls of the nave being formed of upright tree-trunks said to date from Anglo-Saxon times.

Another route to Epping Forest is by the Great Eastern Railway from Liverpool Street, viâ *Wood Street*, the station for *Walthamstow*, to (9 M.) *Chingford* (fares 1*s.* 5*d.*, 1*s.* 1*d.*, 10*d.*), which may also be reached from the *North London Railway* viâ *Dalston Junction* and *Hackney* or viâ *Gospel Oak*. — Chingford (*Royal Forest Hotel, R. & A. from 4*s.*, table d'hôte 5*s.*), which lies 2 M. to the W. of Buckhurst Hill, about 4½ M. to the S.E. of Waltham Abbey, and 2½ M. to the S. of High Beach (see below), is perhaps the best starting-point from which to visit the most attractive parts of the Forest. Open conveyances of various kinds run from Chingford station and from the Royal Forest Hotel to High Beach (6*d.* each), Waltham Abbey, Chigwell, Epping, and other points of interest; the best conveyance is the four-horse coach starting at the hotel. The quaint old house adjoining the hotel, known as 'Queen Elizabeth's Hunting Lodge' and supposed to have been a stand for watching the chase, contains a small museum intended to illustrate the history, natural history, and archæology of Epping Forest and Hainault Forest (see below) Adjacent is a drinking fountain. The *Connaught Grounds* contain several lawn-tennis courts (1-2*s.* per hr.), and there is also a good golf-course. On an eminence to the W. of Chingford is an obelisk, due N. from Greenwich Observatory, and sometimes used in verifying astronomical calculations.

Epping Forest, along with the adjoining *Hainault Forest*, at one time extended almost to the gates of London. In 1793 there still remained 12,000 acres unenclosed, but these have been since reduced to about 5600 acres. The whole of the unenclosed part of the Forest was purchased by the Corporation of London, and was opened by Queen Victoria in May, 1882, as a free and inalienable public park and place of recreation. The forest contains fallow deer and a few roe deer; its bird-life is very varied (herons, kingfishers, jays, owls, and many small songsters); and it is frequented by many rare kinds of butterflies. Perhaps the finest point in the Forest is *High Beach, an elevated tract covered with magnificent beech-trees, about 1½ M. from Loughton. Tennyson was living here when he wrote 'The Talking Oak' and 'Locksley Hall'. There is an inn here, called the 'King's Oak', which is much resorted to by picnic parties. About 2½ M. farther on, on the northern verge of the Forest and 2 M. to the W. of Epping (see above), stands *Copped* (or *Copt*) *Hall*, a country mansion in the midst of an extensive park. Near *Buckhurst Hill* (see above) is the *Roebuck Inn*, and there is also a small inn (the *Robin Hood*) at the point where the road from Loughton joins that to High Beach.

On the highroad between Loughton (or Chingford) and Epping lies *Ambresbury Bank*, an old British camp, 12 acres in extent, and nearer Loughton is another similar earthwork. Tradition reports that it was here that Boadicea, Queen of the Iceni, was defeated by Suetonius, on which occasion 80,000 Britons are said to have perished. — A good map of Epping Forest, price 2*d*., may be obtained of H. Sell, 10 Bolt Court, Fleet Street. Good handbooks to the Forest are those of *E. N. Buxton* (Stanford; 1*s*. 6*d*.) and *Percy Lindley* (6*d*.).

*Waltham Abbey lies on the river Lea, about 2 M. from the W. margin of the forest, and 6 M. to the W. of Copped Hall. The abbey was founded by the Saxon king Harold, and after his death in 1066 became his burial-place. The nave of the old abbey has been restored, and now serves as the parish-church. The round arches are specimens of very early Norman architecture, and may even have been built before the Conquest. Adjoining the S. aisle is a fine Lady Chapel, in the Decorated style. The tower is modern.

The direct railway from Liverpool Street to Rye House runs viâ *Bishopsgate, Bethnal Green, Cambridge Heath, London Fields* (near the public park of that name), *Hackney Downs*, and *Clapton*, beyond which it crosses the *Lea*.

The river *Lea*, near which the line now runs, is still, as in the days of its old admirer Izaak Walton, famous for its fishing; and the various stations on this line are much frequented by London anglers. Nearly the whole of the river is divided into 'swims', which are either private property, or confined to subscribers. Visitors, however, can obtain a day's fishing by payment of a small fee (at the inns). The free portions of the river do not afford such good sport.

From (7³/₄ M.) *Angel Road* a branch-line diverges to Edmonton and Enfield (see below). — 10 M. *Ponder's End;* 12 M. *Enfield Lock.* — 13 M. Waltham Cross *(Four Swans).* The station lies ³/₄ M. to the W. of the abbey (see above) and ¹/₄ M. to the E. of *Waltham Cross*, one of the crosses which Edward I. erected on the different spots where the body of his queen Eleanor rested on its way from Nottinghamshire to London. The cross has been well restored. Another of these monuments, that at Charing Cross, has been already mentioned (see p. 185). Near one of the entrances to *Theobalds Park*, near Waltham Cross, stands the re-erected *Temple Bar* (comp. p. 179).

At (14 M.) *Cheshunt*, famous for its rose-gardens, is a large Nonconformist *Theological College*. Richard Cromwell died at Cheshunt in 1712.

Cheshunt may also be reached by another line from Liverpool St., viâ (9 M.) Edmonton (*Bell*, rebuilt since Cowper's time). Charles Lamb (1775-1834) died at Bay Cottage, Church St., Edmonton, whither he removed in 1833, and is buried in the churchyard, along with his sister Mary (d. 1847). John Keats (1795-1821) served his apprenticeship with a surgeon in Church St. (1810-16) and there wrote his 'Juvenile Poems'. In the church is the Butterworth Memorial to Lamb and Cowper, and in the Free Library are medallion portraits of Lamb and Keats. — A short branch-line runs from Edmonton to Enfield, with the Royal Small Arms Factory (open to visitors on Mon. & Thurs.). The church contains several interesting monuments. The *Palace* (now a school) still retains some work of the Tudor period. Lamb (see above) lived from 1827 to 1833 at Enfield; Keats and Captain Marryat (1792-1821) were educated here; and Isaac Disraeli (1766-1848) was a native of the town.

Beyond (17 M.) *Broxbourne* (Crown, with fine rose-garden) our line diverges to the left from the main line to Cambridge.

19 M. **Rye House,** a favourite summer-resort for schools, clubs, societies, and workshop picnics, was built in the reign of Henry VI.; it belonged, with the manor, to Henry VIII., and afterwards passed into private hands. It is now a hotel (R., B., & A. from 4s., pens. 7s. 6d.). There are still some remains of the old building, particularly the embattled *Gate House.* The grounds are large and beautiful, affording abundant open-air amusements, and the attractions include the 'Great Bed of Ware', which measures 12 ft. both in length and in breadth. This bed formerly stood at Ware (see below) and is alluded to by Shakspeare (*Twelfth Night*, iii, 2).

Rye House gave its name in 1683 to the famous 'Rye House Plot', which had for its object the assassination of Charles II. and the Duke of York, as they travelled that way. The supposed conspiracy, which was headed by Rumbold, then owner of the manor, is said to have failed on account of the premature arrival of the King and his brother. It led to the execution of Rumbold, Algernon Sidney, Lord William Russell, etc. Whether a conspiracy, however, existed at all, is doubtful.

From Rye House the railway goes on viâ (20¼ M.) *St. Margaret's* (branch to Widford and Buntingford) and (22¼ M.) *Ware*, to (24¼ M.) *Hertford* (Salisbury Arms, Dimsdale Hotel), with a castle of the 10th cent., and one of the 17th cent., now used as a school. To the W. of Hertford is *Panshanger*, the seat of Earl Cowper, with a fine collection of paintings. See *Baedeker's Great Britain*.

42. St. Albans.

Midland Railway, from St. Pancras, 20 M., in ½-1 hr. (fares 2s. 8d., 1s. 7½d., no second class); *North Western Railway*, from Euston Square, 24 M., in ¾-1¼ hr. (fares 2s. 8d., 2s., 1s. 7½d.); or *Great Northern Railway*, from King's Cross, 23½ M., in ¾-1 hr. (fares 2s. 8d., 1s. 7½d.). Our chief description applies to the first-mentioned route, for which through-tickets may be obtained at any of the Metropolitan Railway stations. — During the summer-months a four-horse *Coach* runs to St. Albans daily, starting at 11 a.m. from the Hôtel Victoria, and, for the return-journey, from the Peahen, St. Albans, at 4 p.m. (2½ hrs.; fare 10s., return 15s.). The drive, passing the Welsh Harp, Hendon, Edgware, Bushey, and Watford, is picturesque and pleasant.

The first stations on the Midland Railway are *Camden Road*, *Kentish Town*, *Haverstock Hill*, *Finchley Road*, and *West End*, where we leave London fairly behind us and enter the open country. Hampstead here lies on the right and Willesden on the left, while the spire of Harrow church, also on the left, may be seen in the distance. 5 M. *Child's Hill*. — 6½ M. *Welsh Harp*, with an artificial lake, formed as a reservoir for the Regent Canal. It attracts large numbers of anglers (fishing-tickets at the inn, 'Old Welsh Harp'; 1s. and 2s. 6d. per day). It is also a favourite resort of skaters in winter. — 7 M. *Hendon*, with a picturesque ivy-grown church. — 9 M. *Mill Hill*, with a Roman Catholic Missionary College and a noted *Public School* for boys, founded in 1807 by Nonconformists. *Sir Stamford Raffles* died here in 1826; and *William Wilberforce* lived here, and built the Gothic *Church of St. Paul* (1836).

About 1 M. to the W. lies *Edgware*, and a little more remote is *Whitchurch*, also called *Little Stanmore*. While Händel was choir-master to the Duke of Chandos at Canons, a magnificent seat in this neighbourhood, now demolished, he acted as organist in the church of Whitchurch (1718-21). The church still contains the organ on which he played, and also some fine wood-carving, and the monument of the Duke of Chandos (d. 1774) and his two wives. A blacksmith's shop in Edgware is said to be the place where Händel conceived the idea of his 'Harmonious Blacksmith'. — There is a good golf-course at *Stanmore*, near Edgware.

12 M. *Elstree*, a picturesque village in Hertfordshire, which we here enter. Good fishing may be obtained in the Elstree reservoir. — 15 M. *Radlett*. — 20 M. **St. Albans**, see below.

If the *London and North Western Railway* route be chosen, the traveller is recommended to visit, either in going or returning, *Harrow on the Hill* (p. 420; station 1 M. from the town).

The traveller who is equal to a walk of 10 M., and is fond of natural scenery, may make the excursion to St. Albans very pleasantly as follows. By railway from King's Cross (*Great Northern Railway*) to (9 M.) *Barnet;* thence on foot, viâ (1 M.) *Chipping Barnet* and (5 M.) *Elstree* (see above), to (10 M.) *Watford*, a station on the London and North Western Railway; and from Watford by rail to (7 M.) *St. Albans*. If the traveller means to return by the Great Northern Railway, he should take a return-ticket to Barnet. — Near *Hatfield*, the first station on this line in returning from St. Albans, is *Hatfield House*, the seat of the Marquis of Salisbury, a fine mansion built in the 17th cent. on the site of an earlier palace, in which Queen Elizabeth was detained in a state of semi-captivity before her accession to the throne (comp. *Baedeker's Great Britain*).

St. Albans (*Peahen, George*, both near the Abbey, unpretending) lies a short distance to the E. of the site of *Verulamium*, the most important town in the S. of England during the Roman period, of which the fosse and fragments of the walls remain. Its name is derived from St. Alban, a Roman soldier, the proto-martyr of Christianity in our island, who was executed here in A.D. 304. Holmhurst Hill, near the town, is supposed to have been the scene of his death. The Roman town fell into ruins after the departure of the Romans, and the new town of St. Albans began to spring up after 795, when Offa II., King of Mercia, founded here, in memory of St. Alban, the magnificent abbey, of which the fine church and a large square gateway are now the only remains. Pop. (1891) 12,895.

The ***Abbey Church** is in the form of a cross, with a tower at the point of intersection, and is one of the finest and largest churches in England. It was raised to the dignity of a cathedral in 1877, when the new episcopal see of St. Albans was created. It measures 550 ft. in length (being the second longest church in England, coming after Winchester), by 175 ft. in breadth across the transepts; the fine Norman *Tower* is 145 ft. high. The earliest parts of the existing building, in which Roman tiles from Verulamium were freely made use of, date from the 11th cent. (ca. 1080); the *Choir* was built in the 13th cent. and the *Lady Chapel* in the 14th century. An extensive restoration of the building, including a new E.E. *W. Front*, with a large Dec. window, and large new windows in the N. and S. transepts, has been completed at an expense of 130,000*l*., by Lord Grimthorpe, who acted as his own architect without conspicuous success. St. Albans, 320 ft. above the sea, lies higher than any other English cathedral. See Froude's 'Annals of an English Abbey'.

The fine **Interior** (adm. to nave free; to E. parts of the church 6*d.*, tickets from the verger) has recently been restored with great care. The NAVE, the longest Gothic nave in the world, shows a curious intermixture of the Norman, E. E., and Dec. styles; and the change of the pitch of the vaulting in the S. aisle has a singular effect. The *Stained Glass Windows* in the N. aisle date from the 15th century. The painted ceiling of the CHOIR dates from the end of Edward III.'s reign (1327-77), that of the CHANCEL from the time of Henry VI. (1422-61). Some traces of old fresco painting have also been discovered in the N. TRANSEPT. The *Screen* behind the altar in the PRESBYTERY is of very fine mediæval workmanship, and has lately been restored and fitted with statues. To the N. is the curious old *Watch Gallery*. Many of the chantries, or mortuary chapels of the abbots, and other monuments deserve attention. The splendid brass of *Abbot de la Mare* is best seen from the aisle to the S. of the presbytery. In the *Saint's Chapel* are the tomb of Duke Humphrey of Gloucester (d. 1447), brother of Henry V., and the shrine of St. Alban. In the N. aisle of the presbytery are parts of the *Shrine of St. Amphibalus*. The *Lady Chapel* has been restored with great richness and provided with a marble floor.

The *Gate*, the only remnant of the conventual buildings of the abbey, stands to the W. of the church. It is a good specimen of the Perp. style. It was formerly used as a gaol, and is now a school.

About ³/₄ M. to the W. of the abbey stands the ancient *Church of St. Michael*, which is interesting as containing the tomb of the great Sir Francis Bacon, Baron Verulam and Viscount St. Albans, who lived at Gorhambury House here. The monument ('sic sedebat') is by *Rysbrack*. To reach the church we turn to the left (W.) on leaving the cathedral and descend to the bridge over the *Ver*. The keys are kept at No. 13 St. Michael's Cottages. The present *Gorhambury House*, the seat of the Earl of Verulam, 1¹/₂ M. to the W. of St. Michael's, is situated in the midst of a beautiful park, and contains a good collection of portraits.

St. Albans was the scene of two of the numerous battles fought during the Wars of the Roses. The scene of the first, which ushered in the contest, and took place in 1455, is now called the *Key Field*; the other was fought in 1461 at *Barnard's Heath*, to the N. of the town, just beyond St. Peter's Church.

43. Harrow. Rickmansworth. Chenies. Chesham.

27 M. METROPOLITAN RAILWAY from *Baker Street Station* to *Chesham* in 1-1¹/₂ hr. (fares 3*s.* 10*d.*, 2*s.* 10*d.*, 1*s.* 11*d.*). This line is an extension of the St. John's Wood branch of the Metropolitan Railway. For some distance it runs side by side with the *Great Central Railway* (p. 56).

Baker Street Station (Pl. R, 20), see p. 58. — Passing the suburban stations of *St. John's Wood Road* (for Lord's Cricketground, p. 299), *Marlborough Road*, *Swiss Cottage*, *Finchley Road*, *West Hampstead*, *Kilburn-Brondesbury*, and *Willesden Green*, the train quits London and enters a pleasant open country. To the N. of (6 M.) *Kingsbury-Neasden*, with the works of the Metropolitan Railway Co., lies the *Brent* or *Welsh Harp Reservoir* (p. 417). At

(8 M.) *Wembley Park* is a popular recreation-ground (see p. 69), disfigured with an apparently futile attempt to erect a tower higher than the Eiffel Tower at Paris. On the other (N.E.) side of the railway is the course of Wembley Golf Club.

10 M. Harrow-on-the-Hill *(King's Head; Roxborough; Railway)*, a town of 13,000 inhab., famous for its large public school, founded in 1571 by John Lyon, a yeoman of the parish, and scarcely second to Eton. It has numbered Lord Byron, Sir Robert Peel, Sheridan, Spencer Perceval, Palmerston, Card. Manning, and numerous other eminent men among its pupils. The oldest portion of the school is the red brick building dating from 1608-15, now known as the 'Fourth Form Room'; its panels are covered with the names of the boys, including those of Byron, Peel, and Palmerston. The chapel (1857), library (1863), and speech-room (1877) are all modern. The number of scholars is now about 630. Harrow church has a lofty spire which is a conspicuous object in the landscape for many miles round. The churchyard commands a most extensive *View. A flat tombstone, on which Byron used to lie, when a boy, is still pointed out. Harrow may also be reached by the London & North-Western Railway (see p. 418) or by the Great Central Railway. — A branch-line runs from Harrow (N. W. R. station) to (2 M.) *Stanmore* (p. 418).

12¹/₂ M. *Pinner* (Queen's Head, a quaint 'Queen Anne' building), a prettily situated little town. A little to the W. lie *Ruislip Park* and *Reservoir*. — About 3 M. to the S.W. of (14¹/₂ M.) *Northwood*, with numerous suburban villas and an excellent golf-course, is *Harefield*, the scene of Milton's 'Arcades'.

18 M. **Rickmansworth** *(Victoria; Swan)*, a small paper-making town (7000 inhab.) on the *Chess*, near its confluence with the Colne, is a good centre for excursions. Large quantities of water-cress are grown here for the London market. To the S.E., on the other side of the Colne, lies *Moor Park* (Lord Ebury), with its fine timber.

Walkers are advised to quit the railway here and to proceed to (9¹/₂ M.) Chesham on foot, through the *Valley of the Chess. We turn to the right on leaving the station, pass under the railway-bridge, ascend a few steps immediately to the left, cross the railway by a foot-bridge, and enter *Rickmansworth Park*, with its fine old trees. The walk across the park brings us in 25 min. to a road, which we cross obliquely (to the left) to a meadow-path leading to (¹/₄ hr.) the highroad to Chenies, at a point near the village of *Chorley Wood* (¹/₂ M. from the station, p. 421). About 1³/₄ M. farther on we turn to the right (sign-post) for (¹/₂ M.) the picturesque and neatly-built village of Chenies (*Bedford Inn*). The *Mortuary Chapel* attached to the church here contains the tombs of the Russells from 1556 to the present day, affording an almost unique instance in England of a family burial-place of this kind (admission only by order obtained on application to the Duke of Bedford at Woburn Abbey; key kept by Mr. White, whose house adjoins the above-mentioned signpost). The finest monument is that of *Anne, Countess of Bedford (d. 1558), the builder of the chapel. Lord William Russell (beheaded in 1683; p. 417), Lord John Russell (d. 1878), and Lord Ampthill (d. 1884) are buried here. Adjoining the church is a fragment of the fine old manor-house.

Matthew Arnold and J. A. Froude frequently visited Chenies for the sake of the
angling in the Chess. — To reach Chesham we follow the lane between the
church and the manor-house, and then turn to the left along a path through
beech-wood on the slope of the valley of the Chess. View of the Elizabethan
mansion of *Latimers* (Lord Chesham), on the other side of the stream.
After about ¼ hr. we pass through two gates. 20 min. Lane, leading to
the left to Chalfont Road station (see below). In 10 min. more we descend to
the right to the road and follow it to the left to (2 M.) *Chesham* (see below).

Perhaps no walk in England of equal length combines more literary
interest and rural charm than that from Rickmansworth to Slough described
below (ca. 18 M.). Turning to the left as above and passing under the
railway, we follow the road to (2 M.) *Maple's Cross*. A field-path to the
right brings us in 10 min. to another winding road, which we follow (to
the right) to (about 2 M.) the lodge-gates of *Newlands Park*. We here pass
through a gate on the left and continue by an avenue of trees to (8 min.)
a gate and road. We cross the stile and follow a field-path (several stiles)
descending to (½ M.) *Chalfont St. Giles* (see below) in the valley. — From
Chalfont St. Giles we follow the road to the S., passing, after 1¾ M., the
solitary old Quaker meeting-house of *Jordans* (to the right), in the little
graveyard attached to which lie Elwood (Milton's secretary), William Penn
(d. 1718), his wife, and five of his children. About ½ M. farther on we
turn to the right and follow the road (or through *Wilton Park*) to (1½ M.)
Beaconsfield (p. 422). Thence, as at p. 422, to (3 M.) *Burnham Beeches*,
(4 M.) *Stoke Poges*, and (2 M.) *Slough* or *Burnham Beeches Station*.

20 M. *Chorley Wood* and (22 M.) *Chalfont Road* are each about
1½ M. from *Chenies* (p. 420). They are also nearly equidistant
(3-3½ M.) from the charming little village of *Chalfont St. Giles*.
The cottage, at the S.E. end of this village, in which Milton finished
'Paradise Lost' and began 'Paradise Regained' (1665-68), has been
left unchanged since the poet's time and contains a few relics
(adm. 6*d*., a party 3*d*. each).

From Chalfont Road a branch-line runs to (5 M.) **Chesham**
(Crown; George), a quaint old town with 8000 inhab., mainly employed in the manufacture of furniture and other articles in beech
wood, cricket-bats, tennis-rackets, wooden spades, French hoops,
etc. Ducks and water-cress are also largely produced. Fine view
from the *Park*.

Beyond Chalfont Road the railway is continued viâ Amersham and
Great Missenden to *Wendover* and *Aylesbury* and thence to *Verney Junction*
(see *Baedeker's Handbook to Great Britain*).

44. Windsor. Eton.

Windsor is reached by the *Great Western Railway*, from Paddington Station (21 M., in 35-75 min.; fares 3*s*. 6*d*., 2*s*. 3*d*., 1*s*.
9*d*.; return-tickets, available for 7 days, 5*s*. 6*d*., 4*s*., available
from Frid. to Tues., 4*s*. 6*d*., 3*s*. 6*d*.); or by the *South Western
Railway*, from Waterloo Station, N. side (25½ M., in 1¼ hr.;
same fares).

GREAT WESTERN RAILWAY. The first station is *Royal Oak*,
where, by a clever piece of engineering, the rails for local trains
are carried under those for through trains, by a descent and then
an ascent. The second station, called *Westbourne Park*, is the junc-

tion of a line to Hammersmith (p. 386). Farther on *Kensal Green Cemetery* (p. 375) lies on the right. The next stations are *Acton*, *Ealing*, *Castle Hill*, and *Hanwell*, at which last, on the left, is the extensive *Middlesex County Lunatic Asylum*, with a fine park and accommodation for 1000 inmates. At (9 M.) *Southall* a branchline diverges on the left to *Brentford*. 11 M. *Hayes*. From (13¹/₂ M.) *West Drayton* branch-lines run to *Uxbridge*, a busy little town, prettily situated on the *Colne*, 3 M. to the N., and to *Staines* (p. 424). — 16¹/₂ M. *Langley*, or *Langley Marish*, has an old church, the S. porch of which contains an interesting parish library, established here by Sir John Kederminster in the reign of James I. The walls of the library are carved and painted in late-Jacobean style, and the doors of the cupboards are adorned with views of Eton and Windsor as they were in the early 17th century. Tradition says that Milton (whose father's estate was at Horton, 2 M. distant) was in the habit of studying here, and his chair is still shown. Key at the almshouses near the churchyard gate. — At (18¹/₂ M.) **Slough** *(Crown; Royal)* the branch to Windsor diverges to the left from the main line, and passengers who are not in a through Windsor carriage change. Omnibus to Windsor, see p. 424.

Sir William Herschel (d. 1822) and *Sir John Herschel* (d. 1871), the celebrated astronomers, made many of their important discoveries in their observatory at Slough.

A pleasant ramble, through picturesque scenery, may be made from Slough to (2 M.) *Stoke Poges* and (4 M.) *Burnham Beeches*. [*Burnham Beeches Station*, 1¹/₂ M. beyond Slough, is slightly nearer the Beeches, but there is no public conveyance thence.] The churchyard at Stoke Poges is the scene of Gray's famous 'Elegy', and now contains his grave. He lies in his mother's tomb, close to the S. wall (tablet) of the church. The touching epitaph on the tomb, written by Gray himself, describes Mrs. Gray as the mother of several children, 'only one of whom had the misfortune to survive her'. A monument to the poet's memory has been erected in the adjacent *Stoke Park*, a fine property which once belonged to the descendants of William Penn. Sir Edward Coke entertained Queen Elizabeth at Stoke Park in 1601. — *°Burnham Beeches*, to the N.W. (omn. from Slough in summer, fare 1s. 6d.), the finest in England, have been secured as a public resort by the Corporation of London, and walks and drives have been cut through them. Their autumnal colouring is very lovely (see 'Burnham Beeches', by F. G. Heath; 1s.). — About 3 M. to the N. of Burnham Beeches lies *Beaconsfield* (Saracen's Head), with a house (named *Gregories*) once occupied by *Edmund Waller* (d. 1687) and *Edmund Burke* (d. 1797), of whom the one lies buried in the churchyard, and the other in the church (memorial tablet, erected in 1898). It furnished the title of *Benjamin Disraeli, Earl of Beaconsfield* (d. 1881), who lived at *Hughenden*, 8 M. to the W., and is buried in a vault near the village-church.

Before reaching Windsor the train crosses the Thames, passing Eton College (p. 429) on the right. The station is on the S.W. side of the town, in George Street, about ¹/₄ M. from the Castle.

South Western Railway. Route to *Clapham Junction*, see p. 405; the branch-line to Richmond and Windsor diverges here to the right from the main South Western line, and approaches the Thames at *Wandsworth* station (p. 385). We next pass *Putney* (p. 386), *Barnes* (p. 387; branch-line to *Chiswick*, p. 387, and *Kew*

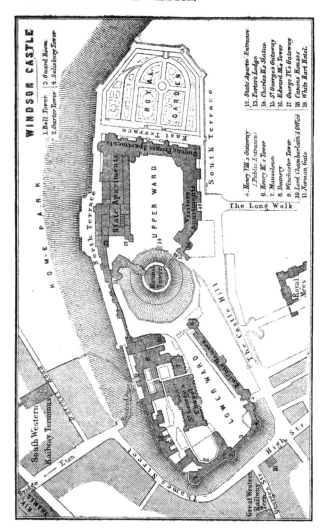

Bridge, p. 413), *Mortlake* (p. 387), and *Richmond* (p. 411). The line skirts Richmond Park, crosses the Thames by a bridge of three arches, and reaches *Twickenham* (p. 388; on the left a branch-line to *Teddington*, p. 388, *Hampton Wick*, p. 388, and *Kingston*, p. 388). Next stations, *Feltham*, with a large reformatory for youthful criminals, *Ashford*, and *Staines*, a picturesque old town, deriving its name from the 'stones' which once marked the limits of the jurisdiction of London in this direction.

A branch of the South Western Railway runs hence to the left to *Virginia Water* (p. 431), *Ascot* (p. 431), and *Reading*. Near *Egham*, the first station beyond Staines on this line, is the plain of *Runnimede*, where King John signed the Magna Charta in 1215 (see p. 85). Above the town rises *Cooper's Hill* (view), celebrated in Denham's well-known poem; on it stands the *Royal Indian Engineering College*. Beyond Egham is *Mt. Lee*, on the top of which is the enormous **Holloway College for Women**, erected and endowed by Mr. Holloway (of the 'Pills') at a cost of 1,000,000*l*. The buildings, which are very handsome and elaborate, form a quadrangle 550 ft. long by 376 ft. wide and have accommodation for 300 students. Orders to view the college and picture-gallery on Wednesday afternoons may be obtained by writing to the secretary.

Our train runs in a N.W. direction. Stations *Wraysbury* and *Datchet* (Manor House; Stag). On the left rise the large towers of Windsor Castle, round the park of which the train describes a wide circuit. Before reaching Windsor we cross the Thames, on the N. bank of which lies Eton College (p. 429). The station lies in Datchet Road, on the N.E. side of the town, 1/4 M. from the 'Hundred Steps' (p. 426), and 1/2 M. from the main entrance to the Castle.

Windsor. — Hotels. WHITE HART, R. & A. 4*s*.-7*s*. 6*d*., B. 1*s*. 6*d*.-3*s*., D. 4-6*s*.; CASTLE; ROYAL ADELAIDE, facing the Long Walk; BRIDGE HOUSE, R. from 2*s*. 6*d*., well spoken of, CHRISTOPHER, these two at Eton. — Restaurants. At the hotels; also *Layton*, 1 Thames St.; *Ivey*, 18 Thames St.

Cab to any part of Windsor 1*s*. 6*d*., to Eton 2*s*. *Carriage* to Virginia Water and back 13*s*., with two horses 21*s*., to Burnham Beeches and Stoke 15*s*. and 22*s*., to Burnham Beeches and Dropmore 16*s*. and 26*s*.

Omnibus several times daily to *Eton* (1*d*.) and *Slough* (3*d*.); to *Maidenhead*, twice daily (9*d*.). Excursion Brakes in the season to *Virginia Water* (return-fare 2*s*.), *Burnham Beeches* (2*s*.), *Stoke Poges* (2*s*.), etc. — Brakes to *Ascot* in the race-week (p. 71), return-fare 5*s*., on cup-day 7*s*.

Windsor, a town in Berkshire, with 19,000 inhab., is prettily situated on the right bank of the *Thames*, opposite *Eton* (p. 429) and *Datchet*, with both of which it is connected by bridges. The *Town Hall*, completed by Sir Christopher Wren, contains some good royal portraits, an ancient mayor's chair in carved oak, and a marble bust of Charles Knight (1791-1873), a native of Windsor. On the outside are statues of Queen Anne and Prince George of Denmark. The *Parish Church*, High Street, has some quaint monuments, carved railings by Grinling Gibbons, and mosaics by Salviati. The *Garrison Church (Holy Trinity)* contains numerous military memorials. There are also several interesting old houses in the town, but the absorbing attraction is —

**Windsor Castle, which towers above the town on the W. side.

Windsor (Anglo-Saxon *Windlesofra*, in Domesday Book *Windesores*), an estate presented by Edward the Confessor to the monks of Westminster

Abbey, was purchased by William the Conqueror for the purpose of erecting a castle on the isolated hill in it centre. The building was extended by Henry I. and Henry II.; and Edward III., who was born at Windsor, caused the old castle to be taken down, and a new one to be erected on its site, by *William of Wykeham*, the art-loving Bishop of Winchester. Under succeeding monarchs Windsor Castle was frequently extended; and finally George IV. began a series of extensive restorations under the superintendence of *Sir Jeffrey Wyattville*. The restoration, completed in the reign of Queen Victoria at a total cost of 900,000*l.*, left the Castle one of the most magnificent royal residences in the world.

The Castle consists of two courts, called the *Upper* and *Lower Wards*, surrounded by buildings; between the two rises the *Round Tower* (p. 427). The wards and the northern terrace are always open to the public; admission to the eastern terrace is granted on Saturdays and Sundays only, from 2 to 6 p.m., in the absence of the Queen. (The Guards' band usually plays here on Sundays.) The *State Apartments* and the *Albert Chapel* are shown (in the absence of the Queen) on Mondays, Tuesdays, Thursdays, Fridays, and Saturdays, from 1st April to 31st Oct., 11-4; from 1st Nov. to 31st March, 11-3. The *Round Tower* is open at the same hours, but in summer only. *St. George's Chapel* is open daily, except Wednesday, from 12.30 to 4; divine service is celebrated on Sundays at 11 a.m. and 5 p.m.; on week-days, at 10.30 a.m. and 3 p.m. (5 p.m. in winter). The *worst day* for a visit to Windsor is, therefore, Wednesday. Tickets of admission for the State Apartments are obtained in the Lord Chamberlain's Stores (Pl. 10) at the castle. The Private Apartments of the Queen are shown only by a special order from the Lord Chamberlain, which it is difficult to obtain. Visitors are particularly requested not to offer gratuities to the attendants.

From High Street we ascend the *Castle Hill*, at the foot of which is the Jubilee *Statue of Queen Victoria*, by Boehm, and, passing through *Henry VIII.'s Gateway* (Pl. 5), first enter the Lower Ward. On the S. side of this ward, between the *Salisbury Tower* and *Henry III.'s Tower*, are the residences of the Military Knights of Windsor; and on the N. side are the Horseshoe Cloisters, St. George's Chapel (p. 426), and the Albert Chapel (p. 426). The *Horseshoe Cloisters*, originally built by Edward IV. in the shape of a fetter-lock, one of that king's badges, were thoroughly restored by Sir G. G. Scott. At their N.W. angle is the entrance to the *Bell Tower* (Pl. 1; apply to the keeper), built by Henry III., the oldest part of the castle as it now stands. This tower contains a peal of eight bells and is also known as the *Curfew Tower* and as *Julius Caesar's Tower*. Anne Boleyn is said to have passed her last night here, and the dungeons contain the names and dates of interesting prisoners. On the E. side of the cloisters are the principal (W.) entrance to St. George's Chapel and a cross indicating the site of the burial-vaults. To the N. are the Chapter Library and the residences of the Canons. A passage, skirting the N. side of St. George's Chapel, leads hence to the *Dean's Cloisters*, whence a covered passage leads to the S., between St. George's Chapel and the Albert Chapel, to the Lower Ward, and another to the N., through the *Canons' Cloister*, to the *Hundred Steps* (open till sunset), which descend to Thames Street.

On the N.W. side of the lower ward stands *St. George's Chapel, or chapel of the Knights of the Order of the Garter, begun in 1474, in the late-Gothic style, by Edward IV. on the site of a chapel of Henry I., and completed by Henry VIII. We enter by the S. door.

The *Interior possesses a handsome, fan-shaped, vaulted roof. In the *Braye Chapel*, to the right of the entrance, is a cenotaph of the Prince Imperial, with a recumbent figure in white marble, erected by the Queen. At the W. end of the S. aisle is *Beaufort Chapel*, adjoining which is the tomb of the Queen's father, the Duke of Kent, consisting of an alabaster sarcophagus with the recumbent marble effigy of the Duke, designed by *Sir G. G. Scott* (d. 1878), and executed by *Boehm*. The large W. window contains old stained glass, with portraits of Knights of the Garter. At the end of the N. aisle is a marble statue of Leopold I. of Belgium (d. 1879), by *Boehm*. In the angle a brass tablet commemorates a son of King Theodore of Abyssinia, who died in England in 1879 and is buried here. In the adjoining *Urswick Chapel* is the monument of Princess Charlotte, designed by *Wyatt*. Near the middle of the N. wall is a mural tablet to George V. of Hanover, by *Count Gleichen*. The *Rutland Chapel*, opposite the Braye Chapel, contains a monument of 1513. — The richly-adorned *Choir contains the stalls of the Knights of the Garter, with their coats-of-arms and banners. At the E. end, above the altar, is a fine stained-glass window to the memory of Prince Albert, erected from designs by *Sir G. G. Scott*. The reredos below the window, sculptured in alabaster marble, is very fine. The subjects are the Ascension, Christ appearing to his Disciples, and Christ meeting Mary in the Garden. To the left of the altar, below the *Queen's Closet*, is some fine wrought iron-work, formerly on Edward IV.'s tomb and said to have been executed by the Antwerp painter *Quinten Matsys*. The vault in the middle of the choir contains the remains of Henry VIII., his wife Jane Seymour, and Charles I. In the N. choir-aisle are a monument to Dean Wellesley (d. 1882), by *Boehm*; the *Hastings Chantry*, a statue of Earl Harcourt (d. 1830); and the plain tomb of Edward IV. At the E. end of this aisle is the entrance to the *Chapter Room*, in which is preserved the state-sword of Edward III. At the E. end of the S. choir-aisle is a fine statue of the German Emperor Frederick III., by *Boehm*, beside which is the *Lincoln Chapel*. In the S. choir-aisle also are the plain marble tombstone of Henry VI.; the *Oxenbridge Chantry* (1522); and a handsome monument erected by Queen Victoria to her aunt, the Duchess of Gloucester (d. 1857). — A subterranean passage leads from the altar to the royal *Tomb House* under the Albert Chapel, situated on the E. side of St. George's Chapel, in which repose George III., George IV., William IV., and other royal personages. (Divine service, etc., see p. 425.)

The *Albert Chapel (Pl. 7), adjoining St. George's Chapel on the E., was originally erected by Henry VII. on the site of the ancient chapel of St. Edward as a mausoleum for himself; but, on his ultimate preference of Westminster, it was transferred for a similar use to Cardinal Wolsey. On the fall of that prelate it reverted to the Crown, and was subsequently fitted up by James II. as a Roman Catholic chapel. An indignant mob, however, broke the windows and otherwise defaced it, and 'Wolsey's Chapel', as it was called, was doomed to a century of dilapidation and neglect, after which George III. constructed the royal tomb-house beneath it. Queen

Victoria undertook the restoration of the chapel in honour of her deceased husband, Prince Albert, and has made it a truly royal and sumptuous memorial.

The interior, beautified with coloured marble, mosaics, sculpture, stained glass, precious stones, and gilding, in extraordinary profusion and richness, must certainly be numbered among the finest works of its kind in the world, though, it must be owned, rather out of harmony with the Gothic architecture of the building. The ceiling, which resembles in form that of St. George's Chapel, is composed of Venetian enamel mosaics, representing in the nave angels bearing devices relating to the Prince Consort, in the chancel angels with shields symbolical of the Passion. The false window at the W. end is of similar workmanship, and bears representations of illustrious personages connected with St. George's Chapel. At the sides of the W. entrance are two marble figures — the Angels of Life and Death. The walls are decorated with a series of pictures of scriptural subjects inlaid with coloured marbles, by *Triqueti*, in which 28 different kinds of marble have been introduced. Above each scene is a white marble medallion of a member of the royal family, by *Miss Susan Durant*, while between them are bas-reliefs, emblematical of the virtues. Round the edges of the pictures are smaller reliefs in white and red marble, and other ornamentation. Below the marble pictures is a dark-green marble bench; and the floor, which is very handsome, is also of coloured marbles. Most of the modern stained glass windows exhibit ancestors of the Prince Consort; those in the chancel are filled with Scriptural subjects. The reliefs of the reredos, which was designed by *Sir G. G. Scott*, and is inlaid with coloured marble, malachite, porphyry, lapis lazuli, and alabaster, have for their subject the Resurrection. At the E. end of the nave stands the °*Cenotaph* of the Prince, by Triqueti, consisting of a handsome sarcophagus, enriched with reliefs, bearing the recumbent figure of Prince Albert in white marble. Near the W. door is a sarcophagus with a recumbent figure, in white marble, of the Duke of Albany (d. 1884), in the dress of the Seaforth Highlanders. Between these is the sarcophagus of metal and Oriental onyx of the Duke of Clarence (d. 1892), elder son of the Prince of Wales, with a recumbent bronze figure, in the uniform of the 10th Hussars. — The restoration was superintended by *Sir G. G. Scott*. The mosaics are by *Salviati*. The chapel is 68 ft. long, 28 ft. wide, and 60 ft. high.

The **Round Tower**, or *Keep*, used as a prison down to 1660, rises on the E. side of the Lower Ward, on an eminence 42 ft. high, surrounded on three sides by a deep moat. The scarps are embellished by beds of flowers. The battlements, 80 ft. above the ground (entrance from the Upper Ward, near the Norman Gate, Pl. 11), command a charming **View, embracing, in clear weather, parts of no fewer than twelve counties. The bell, weighing 17 cwt., was brought from Sebastopol. The tower is not perfectly symmetrical, measuring 102 ft. by 95 ft.; admission gratis, 11-4. (The custodian points out the principal places in the environs.)

On the N. side of the tower is the vaulted *Norman Gateway* (Pl. 11), flanked by pinnacled towers, and leading to the Upper Ward. Opposite, by the *Porter's Lodge* (Pl. 13), is the entrance to the State Apartments (Pl. 12), which lie on the N. side of the large *Quadrangle*. On the E. are the *Queen's Private Apartments*. *George IV.'s Gateway* (Pl. 17), in the middle of the S. side, at the end of the Long Walk (p. 431), is the principal entrance to the palace, and is used by royal carriages only. At the foot of the

Round Tower, on its E. side, is a bronze statue of Charles II. (Pl. 14), by *Strado*, with reliefs on the pedestal by *Grinling Gibbons*.

The **State Apartments** are usually shown in the following order, though the route is sometimes changed. They are handsomely decorated and contain many good pictures; but the barriers, which leave a narrow passage only for the public, and the hurried manner in which the rooms are shown, render it difficult for visitors to see them satisfactorily. The vestibule contains a good portrait of Sir Jeffrey Wyattville, the architect (see p. 425), by Lawrence.

The OLD BALL ROOM, or VAN DYCK ROOM, is exclusively devoted to portraits by that master. The best are those of Henry, Count de Berg; *Charles I. and his family; Mary, Duchess of Richmond; Henrietta Maria, wife of Charles I. (four portraits); Lady Venetia Digby; George, second Duke of Buckingham, and his brother Lord Francis Villiers; *Children of Charles I.; Head of Charles I. from three different points of view, painted as an aid in the execution of a bust; Lucy, Countess of Carlisle; Charles II. when a boy; Portrait of the master himself; *The three eldest children of Charles I.; Charles I. on horseback. — There are also in this room two small bronzes of the Laocoon and Prometheus Bound, and some valuable cabinets.

The ZUCCARELLI ROOM contains several large landscapes by *Zuccarelli*, and portraits of George I., George II., George III., Frederick Prince of Wales (father of George III.), and the Duke of Gloucester. Between two cabinets containing fine specimens of old china is a bust of the German Emperor William II.

The STATE ANTE-ROOM, originally the 'King's Public Dining Room', contains carvings by *Grinling Gibbons*, an allegorical ceiling-painting, by *Verrio* (Banquet of the Gods), some good Gobelins tapestry, and a portrait of George III. after *Reynolds* (on glass, above the chimney-piece).

The GRAND STAIRCASE, with *Chantrey's* statue of George IV. Beside the statue are two sedan-chairs, used by George III. and Queen Charlotte. At the top of the staircase are cannon from Seringapatam and Borneo.

The GRAND VESTIBULE, 46 ft. long, 28 ft. broad, and 46 ft. high, is decorated with armour and banners, and contains Her Majesty's Jubilee presents of 1887; and a statue of Queen Victoria, by *Boehm*.

The RUBENS ROOM contains ten pictures by *Rubens*, including portraits of himself and his wife Helena Fourment. In the ANTE THRONE ROOM are five historical paintings by *West*, being scenes from the reign of Edward III.

The WATERLOO CHAMBER, or GRAND DINING ROOM, 98 ft. long by 47 ft. broad, in the Elizabethan style, is hung with portraits of Wellington, Blücher, Castlereagh, Metternich, Pius VII., Emp. Alexander, Canning, W. von Humboldt, and others associated with the events of 1813-15, painted by *Lawrence, Beechey, Pickersgill, Wilkie*, etc. The carvings are by *Grinling Gibbons*. This room is often fitted up and used as a theatre.

The THRONE ROOM, formerly used for investitures of the order of the Garter, is decorated in garter-blue. It contains a painting of the Establishment of the Order of the Garter, by *West*; portraits of George III., George IV., William IV., Victoria, and Prince Albert, all in the robes of the Garter; and busts of Napoleon III., Victor Emmanuel II., and Prince Albert. The ivory throne was presented by the Maharajah of Travancore.

The GRAND RECEPTION ROOM, originally meant for a ball-room, is magnificently decorated in the rococo style, and is hung with tapestry representing the story of Jason and Medea. At the N. end is a vase of malachite, the gift of the Emperor Nicholas of Russia.

ST. GEORGE'S HALL, 200 ft. long and 34 ft. wide, has a ceiling adorned with the armorial bearings of the Knights of the Garter since 1350. The banners are those of the twenty-six original knights. On the walls are portraits of the English kings from James I. to George IV., by *Van Dyck*, *Lely*, *Kneller*, *Gainsborough*. etc. At the E. end is the carved oak throne, a copy of the coronation-chair in Westminster Abbey. The grand organ has two keyboards, one playing in the Private Chapel.

The GUARD CHAMBER contains suits of old armour and trophies of arms and armour; four bronze cannon captured in India; in a pedestal-case, under glass, a silver shield inlaid with gold, presented by Francis I. of France to Henry VIII., and said to have been executed by *Benvenuto Cellini* from the design of *Andrea Mantegna;* a colossal bust of Nelson by *Chantrey*, on a pedestal formed of a piece of the foremast of the 'Victory', on board which Nelson was shot, with a hole made by a ball at that battle; chair made of oak from the roof of Alloway Kirk, near Ayr; chair made from an elm-tree from Waterloo; busts of Marlborough, after *Rysbrack*, and Wellington, by *Chantrey*. Over the busts hang two small silken bannerets, with the arms of the heroes, which are annually replaced on June 18th and August 13th, the anniversaries respectively of the battles of Waterloo (1815) and Blenheim (1704), by the dukes of Wellington and Marlborough as a condition of the tenure of the estates voted them by Parliament.

The PRESENCE CHAMBER has a ceiling painted by *Verrio*, representing Catharine of Braganza, consort of Charles II., attended by Virtues. The walls are hung with tapestry depicting the story of Esther and Mordecai. The carvings are by Grinling Gibbons.

The AUDIENCE CHAMBER. The ceiling is decorated with paintings by *Verrio* (Catharine of Braganza as Britannia). The walls are hung with tapestry, continuing the story of Esther and Mordecai, with portraits of Prince Frederick Henry and William II. of Orange, by *Honthorst*, and an old portrait of Mary, Queen of Scots, by *Janet*. This room also contains a magnificent ormolu cabinet by Gouthière.

The *Council Chamber*, *King's Closet*, and *Queen's Closet* are also sometimes shown. They are hung with valuable works by Italian, French, and Netherlandish old masters.

Those who are fortunate enough to gain admittance to the **Private Apartments** will enjoy one of the greatest artistic treats that England has to offer. The rooms are most sumptuously fitted up, and contain a magnificent collection of Chelsea, Oriental, Dresden, and Sèvres china, mediæval and Oriental cabinets, gold and silver plate, pictures, etc. In the *Library* are a valuable collection of drawings and miniatures by *Holbein, Leonardo da Vinci, Raphael*. and *Michael Angelo;* numerous bibliographical and other treasures, including an unpublished MS. by *Dickens*, a Bible once belonging to *Luther*, with his portrait on the cover, and a copy of Shakspeare's works belonging to *Charles I.*, with that king's autograph; Queen Charlotte's reading-desk, etc.

The *N. Terrace*, 625 yds. in length, is always open to the public, and commands a charming view; the **E. Terrace* is open on Sat. and Sun. only, 2-6 (see p. 425). From the latter, which affords a good view of the imposing E. façade of the castle, broad flights of steps descend into the *Flower Garden* (shown on application to Mr. Thomas, Royal Gardens, Frogmore), which is tastefully laid out, and embellished with marble and bronze statues and a fountain.

The *Royal Stables*, or *Mews*, on the S. side of the castle, built at a cost of 70,000*l.*, are open daily from 1 to 3 p.m. Tickets of admission are obtained at the entrance from the Clerk of the Mews.

On the left bank of the Thames, 10 min. to the N. of Windsor Bridge, is **Eton College**, one of the most famous of English schools, founded in 1440 by Henry VI. The number of pupils on the foundation, or *Collegers*, who live at the college, and wear black gowns, is about 70; the main portion of the establishment consists of the *Oppidans*, numbering about 950, who live at the residences of the masters, or in the authorised 'Dames' houses', in the town, but under the jurisdiction of the college. The Eton boys, in their short jackets, broad collars, and tall hats, represent a large section of the youthful wealth and aristocracy of England. The governing-body comprises a provost and ten fellows, the head-master, and lower master, besides whom there are about 50 assistant masters. — Those who desire to see the schools should apply to *Mr. Gaffrey*, at the School Office; the chapel is shown on application to *Mr. Mitchell*, 116 High Street, Eton.

The main school-buildings, the oldest part of which dates from 1523, enclose two large courts, united by the archway of the clock tower. The centre of the *Outer Quadrangle*, or larger court to the W., is occupied by a bronze statue of Henry VI. On its W. side is the *Upper School*, extending along the whole side of the quadrangle, above the arcade, which was built by Sir Christopher Wren. The main room contains marble busts of English monarchs and of distinguished Etonians, including Chatham, Fox, Canning, Peel, and Wellington. The oak panelling on the walls and even the master's desk are covered with the names of former pupils carved by the authorities at the boys' expense. A few older 'autographs' (*e. g.* C. J. Fox, Shelley) are also to be seen. On the N. side of the Quadrangle is the *Lower School*, subdivided by modern wooden partitions, but retaining the old wooden pillars. — The *Chapel* on the S. side, the only part of the college that is not of brick, is a handsome Gothic building somewhat resembling the contemporary King's College Chapel at Cambridge. It dates from 1476 but has been much altered. It is decorated internally with modern wood-carving, stained-glass windows, and mosaics. In the ante-chapel is a marble statue of Henry VI., by *Bacon* (1786). On the outside of the W. wall is a statue of Bishop Waynflete, first headmaster of the school (unveiled 1893). The *Inner Quadrangle* is bounded by cloisters. On the S. side are the dining-hall (restored 1858) of the collegers, and the library, containing a rich collection of classical and Oriental MSS. In Keate's Lane, to the S.W. of the main buildings, are the *Science Schools*, the *Racquet Court*, and the new *Queen's Schools* (1888-90), including a museum and a chapel for the Lower School. The *Playing Fields*, entered from the inner quadrangle, should be visited. Comp. *Maxwell Lyte's* 'History of Eton College' (1889). See also the amusing little book entitled 'A Day of My Life at Eton'.

To the N. and E. of Windsor lies the **Home Park,** or smaller park, surrounded on three sides by the Thames, and about 4 M. in circumference. A carriage-road leads through it to the village of *Datchet* (p. 424), situated on the left bank of the Thames, 1 M. to the E. of Windsor. *Herne's Oak*, celebrated in Shakspeare's

'Merry Wives of Windsor', formerly stood by Queen Elizabeth's Walk (in a private part of the park); in 1863, however, the old tre e was destroyed by lightning, and a young oak planted in its place by the Queen. Opposite Datchet is the small royal cottage *Adelaide Lodge*, near which are the *Royal Kennels*, with the Queen's fancy dogs. Farther to the S. is *Frogmore House*, once the seat of the Queen's mother, the Duchess of Kent (d. 1861). Its grounds contain the Duchess's tomb and the magnificent mausoleum erected by the Queen to her husband, Prince Albert (d. 1861). In the latter are also monuments to Princess Alice (d. 1878) and Prince Leopold (d. 1884). The *Royal Dairy* and *Shaw Farm* can be seen by tickets obtained from *Mr. W. Tait*, Shaw Farm, Old Windsor.

The **Great Park**, 1800 acres in extent, lies to the S. of Windsor, and is stocked with several thousand fallow deer. The *Long Walk*, a fine avenue of elms planted in 1680, leads from *George IV.'s Gateway* (p. 427), in a straight line of nearly 3 M., to *Snow Hill*, which is crowned by a statue of George III., by *Westmacott*. From the end of this avenue a road leads to the left to Virginia Water, passing *Cumberland Lodge*, the residence of Prince and Princess Christian, and *Smith's Lawn*, an open space with an equestrian statue of Prince Albert, by Boehm, presented to the Queen as a jubilee-gift by the women of England. *Virginia Water* (Wheatsheaf Hotel; carriage from Windsor and back 10-13s; omnibus, see p. 424; coach from London, see p. 55), an artificial lake about 2 M. long, was formed in 1746 by the Duke of Cumberland, the victor at Culloden, in order to drain the surrounding moorland. The views from various points around the lake are very pleasing. The *Virginia Water* station of the S.W. Railway (p. 424) is about $1^{1}/_{2}$ M. from the lake. — *Queen Anne's Ride*, running almost parallel with the Long Walk, leads to the right to *Ascot* (p. 424), the scene of the *Ascot Races* in June, on the occasion of which some members of the Royal Family usually drive up the course in state (comp. p. 71).

On the W. Windsor is adjoined by *Clewer*, with several religious and charitable institutions under the care of the 'Clewer Sisters'.

45. Gravesend. Chatham. Rochester.

NORTH KENT RAILWAY from Charing Cross, Cannon Street, and London Bridge, to *Gravesend* (24 M., in 1-1$^{1}/_{3}$ hr.; fares 3s. 6d., 2s. 8d., 2s.); thence to *Strood*, *Rochester*, and *Chatham* in 10-20 min. more (fares 5s. 4d., 3s. 4d., 2s. 8d.); or to Strood by rail, and thence across the Medway to Rochester and Chatham. The return-journey may be made by the SOUTH EASTERN AND CHATHAM RAILWAY, which runs *viâ* Bromley and Beckenham to Victoria, Holborn Viaduct, Ludgate Hill, and King's Cross (in 1 hr. 5 min. to 1$^{3}/_{4}$ hr.; fares 5s. 4d., 3s. 4d., 2s. 8d.).

During the summer-months *Gravesend* may also be reached by a Thames STEAMBOAT from London Bridge, see R. 35.

A pleasant way of making this excursion is as follows: by river to Gravesend, and thence on foot by *Cobham Hall* (p. 433) to (7 M.) *Rochester* and *Chatham*, the return-journey being effected by the South Eastern and Chatham Railway. A whole day will thus be occupied.

On quitting London Bridge station the train first traverses the busy manufacturing districts of *Bermondsey* ('Bermond's isle') and *Rotherhithe*; in the churchyard of the latter is buried Prince Lee Boo (d. 1784), son of the king of the Pellew Islands, who in 1783 treated the shipwrecked crew of the Antelope with great kindness. The train then stops at *Spa Road* and (3 M.) *New Cross*. To the W. of the latter lies the district of *Hatcham*, with *Telegraph Hill* (Pl. G, 56), opened as a public park in 1895. — 5 M. *St. John's*; 6 M. *Lewisham Junction*. We next pass through a tunnel, about 1 M. in length, and arrive at (7 M.) *Blackheath* (p. 394). Then (9 M.) *Charlton*, close to the station of which is the old manor-house of the same name, ascribed to Inigo Jones. [Another service reaches Charlton viâ *Spa Road, Deptford, Greenwich*, and *Westcombe Park*.] Beyond two tunnels we reach (10 M.) *Woolwich Dockyard* and (10³/₄ M.) *Woolwich Arsenal*. — 11¹/₄ M. *Plumstead*, with Plumstead Marshes on the left. — 13 M. *Abbey Wood*, a small village of recent origin, with pleasant surroundings, and some scanty remains of *Lesnes Abbey*, an Augustine foundation of the 12th century. *Bostall Heath* and *Bostall Woods*, ¹/₂ M. to the S., now form a public park (132 acres), under the London County Council. — Close to (14 M.) *Belvedere* lies Belvedere House, now the Royal Alfred Institution for Merchant Seamen. — (15¹/₂ M.) *Erith*, see p. 390. The train crosses the river Cray, and reaches —

17 M. **Dartford** *(Bull; Victoria)*, a busy town of 12,000 inhab., with a large paper-mill, a machine and engine factory, a gunpowder factory, and the City of London Lunatic Asylum. The first paper mill in England was erected here at the end of the 16th century. Foolscap paper takes its name from the crest (a fool's cap) of the founder, whose tomb is in the church. Dartford was the abode of the rebel Wat Tyler (p. 128).

Another route from London to Dartford passes the interesting little town of (9 M.) Eltham *(Greyhound; Chequers)*, prettily situated among trees, with the villas of numerous London merchants. About ¹/₄ M. to the N. of the station lie the remains of *Eltham Palace*, a favourite royal residence from Henry III. (1216-72) to Henry VIII. (1509-47). Queen Elizabeth often lived here in her childhood. The palace is popularly known as *King John's Barn*, perhaps because the king has been confounded with John of Eltham, son of Edward II., who was born here. Part of the old moat surrounding the palace is still filled with water, and we cross it by a picturesque old bridge. Almost the only relic of the building is the fine *Banqueting Hall* (key kept in the adjacent lodge), somewhat resembling Crosby Hall in London in general style and dating like it from the reign of Edward IV. (1461-83). The hall was long used as a barn, and some of its windows are still bricked up. The *Roof is of chestnut. Adjoining the hall on the left is the *Court House*, a picturesque gabled building, formerly the buttery of the Palace.

There were originally three Parks attached to Eltham Palace, one of which, the *Middle Park*, has attained some celebrity in modern days as the home of the Blenkiron stud of race-horses, which produced the Derby winners, Gladiateur and Blair Athole. The *Great Park* has been built over. — The *Church* of Eltham was rebuilt in 1874; in the churchyard are buried *Bishop Horne* (d. 1792), the commentator on the Psalms, and

Doggett, the comedian, founder of 'Doggett's Coat and Badge' (p. 74). *Van Dyck* was assigned summer-quarters at Eltham during his stay in England (1632-41), probably in the palace.

A visit to Eltham may be conveniently combined with one to Greenwich (p. 391), which is reached by a pleasant walk of ¼ M. across Blackneath (p. 391) and Greenwich Park; or to Woolwich (also ¼ M.), reached viâ Shooters' Hill (p. 396). Another pleasant walk may be taken to (3 M.) *Chiselhurst*.

Beyond Dartford we cross the Darent, pass (20 M.) *Greenhithe* (p. 390) and *Northfleet* (p. 390), and reach (24 M.) *Gravesend*.

Gravesend *(Clarendon Royal Hotel; Old Falcon; New Falcon; Rosherville)*, a town with 24,000 inhab., lying on the S. bank of the Thames, at the head of its estuary, has greatly increased in size in recent years, and is much resorted to by pleasure-seekers from London. Vessels on their way up the Thames here take pilots and custom-house officers on board, and outward bound vessels also usually touch here. The newer parts of the town are well built, but the streets in the lower quarter are narrow and crooked. Gravesend possesses two good piers, the *Town Pier* and the *Royal Terrace Pier*, from the former of which a steam-ferry plies to Tilbury, on the opposite bank of the Thames. On the W. side, towards Northfleet, are *Rosherville Gardens* (see p. 69), a favourite resort, where music, dancing, archery, and other amusements find numerous votaries. The parish-church *(St. George's)* was built in 1731, on the site of an earlier church which had been burned down in 1520. The register contains the entry of the burial of Pocahontas (d. 1616), the Indian princess who married Thomas Wrolfe or Rolfe. *Windmill Hill*, at the back of the town, now almost covered with the buildings of the increasing suburbs, commands a fine view of the Thames, Shooters' Hill (p. 396), London, with the hills of Highgate and Hampstead beyond, and (to the S.) over the county of Kent, with Cobham Hall (see below) and Springhead as conspicuous points.

Pleasant excursion to *Cobham Hall, the seat of the Earl of Darnley, in the midst of a magnificent park (fine rhododendrons, in bloom in June), 7 M. in circumference, lying about 4 M. to the S. of Gravesend. (Tickets of admission to the house, which is open to visitors on Fridays from 11 to 4 only, may be obtained at Caddel's Library, King Street, Gravesend, and High Street, Rochester, price 1s.; the proceeds are devoted to charitable purposes.) The central portion of this handsome mansion was built by *Inigo Jones* (d. 1653); the wings date from the 16th century. The interior was restored during the present century. The fine collection of pictures includes a *Portrait of Ariosto and *Europa and the Bull by *Titian*, *Tomyris with the head of Cyrus by *Rubens*, and examples of *Van Dyck*, *Lely*, *Kneller*, and other masters. — The *Parish Church* of Cobham contains some fine old brasses.

The railway from Gravesend to (7 M.) Strood passes only one station, called *Higham*, 3½ M. from which is *Cowling Castle*, built in the time of Richard II., and now a picturesque ruin. Beyond Higham the train penetrates a tunnel, 1¼ M. in length, and enters the station of *Strood*, a suburb of Rochester, on the opposite bank

of the river Medway. A few of the North Kent trains go no farther
in this direction, but most of them cross the Medway, and proceed
to Rochester and Chatham, which practically form one town, surrounded by fortifications defending the entrance to the river.

7½ M. **Rochester** *(Crown; Victoria & Bull; King's Head)*, to
the N. of Chatham, a very ancient city, with a pop. of 26,309,
a fine Norman *Castle*, and an interesting *Cathedral*, is described at
length in *Baedeker's Great Britain*.

8 M. **Chatham** *(Sun; Mitre)*, with 37,711 inhab., on the E. bank
of the Medway, below Rochester, is one of the chief naval arsenals
and military stations in Great Britain. See *Baedeker's Great Britain*.

ALPHABETICAL LIST

OF

EMINENT PERSONS MENTIONED IN THE HANDBOOK

The following is a list of distinguished persons mentioned in the Handbook in connection with their birth, death, residence, burial-place, and the like. It does not profess to give the names of architects and other artists where mentioned in connection with their works, nor does it enumerate the subjects of the portraits in the National Portrait Gallery and elsewhere.

INDEX.

A Street Map of London, 1843

One of the earliest detailed street maps of London published over a century and a half ago so that passengers in Hansom cabs could check that they were being taken by the shortest route. Faithfully reproducing the original hand colouring, it shows street names, prominent buildings, docks, factories, canals and the earliest railways in minute detail.

Beyond the limits of the developed area, which in 1843 extended no further than Hyde Park in the west and Stepney in the east, can be seen the orchards and market gardens of Chelsea and Southwark, the marshes of the Isle of Dogs and the outlying villages of Earls Court, Kentish Town and Bow. A history describes London in 1843.

Bacon's Up to date map of London, 1902

The reign of no other monarch saw such massive change as that which took place when Queen Victoria was on the throne. This street map of London originally published at the end of her long life provides a perfect contrast with the map of London 1843. Many villages lying beyond the built up area at the beginning of her reign have now been swallowed by the expanding conurbation. There is massive development and activity on the lower reaches of the Thames where there is much evidence of the new docks servicing the needs of both the Empire and the mother country. Many of the underground railway lines we know today have already been built. But there was much more to be completed during the coming century and places such as Willesden and Herne Hill were still surrounded by countryside in 1902.

A 20 page illustrated booklet describes Public Buildings, Museums, Palaces, Picture Galleries, Bridges, Hospitals, Markets, Parks, Churches & Places of Amusement in and around London.

Old House Books, Moretonhampstead, Devon, TQ13 8PA. UK
www.OldHouseBooks.co.uk   01647 440707

Other Victorian and Edwardian facsimile reprints from
Old House Books

Dickens's Dictionary of London, 1888

Over 700 entries printed facsimile from the original edition describing buildings from the fashionable gentlemen's clubs in St. James' to the appalling slums of the East End. The remarks on the principal buildings, the churches and the great railway stations, the banks, theatres and sporting facilities are informative and well observed, the comments of someone who obviously knew London like the back of his hand.

Equally revealing and very entertaining are the wealth of tips on social behaviour. There is essential advice on everything from the hiring of servants to the benefits of cycling and how to avoid the attention of carriage thieves.

Dickens's Dictionary of The Thames, 1887

This 320 page companion to *Dickens's Dictionary of London* describes the entire length of the Thames valley from its source at Cricklade to the estuary shores of Essex and Kent and the distant Nore lightship with the exception of London.

Detailed entries describe the carefree era of regattas and riverside picnics on the upper reaches of the Thames while London's tideway and great docks were busy with barges, steamers and sailing ships servicing the world's greatest empire and the needs of the mother country.

Published as the country celebrated Queen Victoria's Golden Jubilee, the book vividly brings to life a time when steamboats with 1000 passengers plied regularly between Westminster and Southend and an annual season railway ticket between Windsor and Paddington was a mere £18.

Old House Books, Moretonhampstead, Devon, TQ13 8PA. UK
www.OldHouseBooks.co.uk   01647 440707

The Oarsman's and Angler's Map of the Thames, 1893

Explore Britain's best loved waterway with the map that must surely have been used by the *Three Men in a Boat*. Very detailed, one inch to the mile and over 8 feet in length, it shows all 164 miles from the source to London Bridge. Riverside towns and villages are marked with historical information, details of riverside inns, the locks and even instructions on how to operate them.

For fishermen, the best pools where trout, pike, perch and others were to be found. There are also details of toll charges and angling laws and a booklet describing life on the river over a century ago when the Thames was the nation's favourite place for recreation and sport.

The British Empire world map, 1905

As the twentieth century dawned the British Empire enjoyed its heyday. It spanned 11½ million square miles with 400 million inhabitants. This detailed colour reproduction of a contemporary world map shows details of global trade, including: the furs of fox, bear, seal and otter brought from the shores of Canada's Lake Athabasca by canoes in summer and dog sleds in winter; cochineal; teak and bamboo from Siam; cinnamon and pearls from Ceylon; tortoise shells and birds of paradise from New Guinea as well as minerals and foodstuffs from all over the world.

Coaling stations, telegraph cables, railways and caravan routes are all marked. A ten-page gazetteer describes over 200 British countries and possessions as well as 33 (including Normandy and the USA) which had been lost to the crown.

Old House Books, Moretonhampstead, Devon, TQ13 8PA. UK

www.OldHouseBooks.co.uk   01647 440707

Index
to
Street Plans of
London

1 General Plan of London in three sections.

a) The Northern section in brown
Page 1 Finchley Road and Kilburn Park, Page 2 Belsize Park and Regent's Park, Page 3 Camden Town, Page 4 Highbury and Islington, Page 5 Shacklewell and Bethnal Green, Page 6 Hackney Wick and Oldford, Page 7 Stratford and West Ham.

b) Central section in red
Page 1 Bayswater and Kensington, Page 2 Marylebone and Hyde Park, Page 3 Bloomsbury and Westminster, Page 4 The City and Southwark, Page 5 London Docks and Bermondsey, Page 6 Limehouse and West India Docks, Page 7 East India Docks.

c) The Southern section in grey
Page 1 West Brompton and Fulham, Page 2 Chelsea and Battersea, Page 3 South Lambeth and Stockwell, Page 4 Walworth and Camberwell, Page 5 Rotherhithe and Peckham, Page 6 Isle of Dogs and Deptford, Page 7 Greenwich.

2 Four Special Plans of the most important quarters of London.

I The West End from Baker Street to Soho. II Holborn, Fleet Street, Strand. III The City from St. Paul's to The Tower. IV West End, Hyde Park and Belgravia The Thames.

3 Railway Map of London and its suburbs.

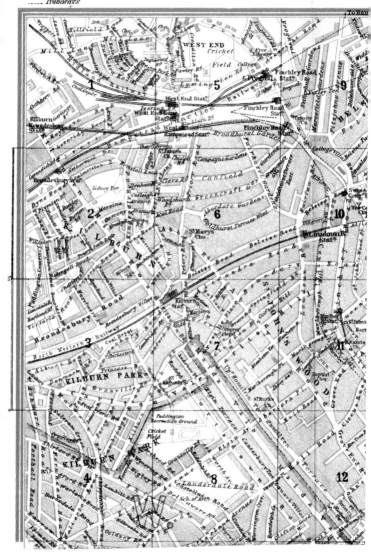

P A D D I N G T O N
B A Y S W A T E R
N O T T I N G H I L L
K E N S I N G T O N
K E N S I N G T O N G A R D E N S
H O L L A N D P A R K
Paddington Workhouse
Lock Hospital
Westbourne Park Station
Royal Oak Station
Westbourne Grove
Round Pond
Kensington Palace
Holland House
Leighton Ho.
Kensington Union Ho.
Natural History Museum
Royal Albert Hall
Albert Memorial
Cromwell Road
Kensington High Str. Station
Bayswater Road
Harrow Road
Gloucester Terrace
Westbourne Terrace
Sussex
1
2
3
4
5
6
7
8
9
10
11
12

28
32
4
27
31
3
26
30
2
25
29
21
British Museum
Bedford Squ.
Russell Square
Holborn
St. Lincoln's Inn Fields
Courts of Justices
The Temple
Temple Pier
Somerset House
Waterloo Bridge
Soho Squ.
Princess Thea.
Charing Cross Station
Charing Cross Pier
County Council Off.
Admiralty
War Office
Parade
Treasury
Government Offices
St. James's Pal.
Marlbro Ho.
Birdcage Walk
Wellington Barracks
Westminster Abbey
Houses of Parliament
St. Thomas Hosp.
Lambeth Palace
Waterloo Sta.
Christ Ch.
Bethlehem Lunatic
Commercial Rd.
Victoria
Romney Str.

Charterhouse
Farringdon Str. Stat.
Aldersgate Str. Stat.
Moorgate Str. Stat.
Finsbury Circus
Liverpool Street Station
Broad St. Stat.
Bishopsgate Stat.
Gt. Eastern Goods Sta.
St. Bartholomew Hospital
Snow Hill
Holborn Viaduct Stat.
G.P.O.
Guild Hall
Ludgate Hill
St. Paul's Cathedral
Cheapside
Bank of England
Royal Exchange
Cornhill
Leadenhall Str.
Fenchurch Str.
Aldgate Station
Mansion Ho. Stat.
Cannon Str.
Upper Thames S.
Blackfriars Stat.
Blackfriars Br.
Blackfriars Stat. (Goods)
Southwark Bridge
London Bridge
London Bridge Station
Guy's Hospital
Lower Thames Str.
Custom Ho.
The Tower
Tower Bridge
Trinity Sq.
Barclay & Perkins's Brewery
Union Str.
Borough
Borough Rd.
Bermondsey Market
Industrial Dwellings
Surrey Theatre
Recreation Gd.
T H A M E S
H O R S E L Y D O W N
B E R M O N D S E Y
33
34
35
36
37
38
39
40
41
42
43
44

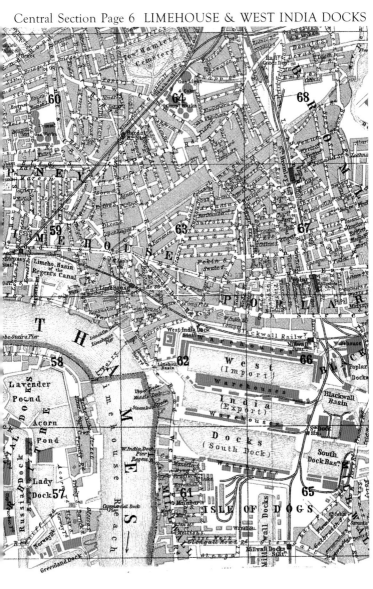

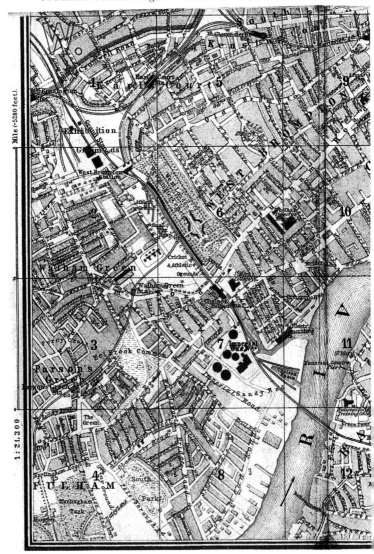

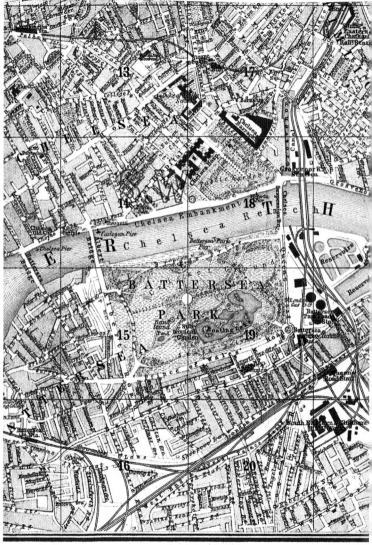

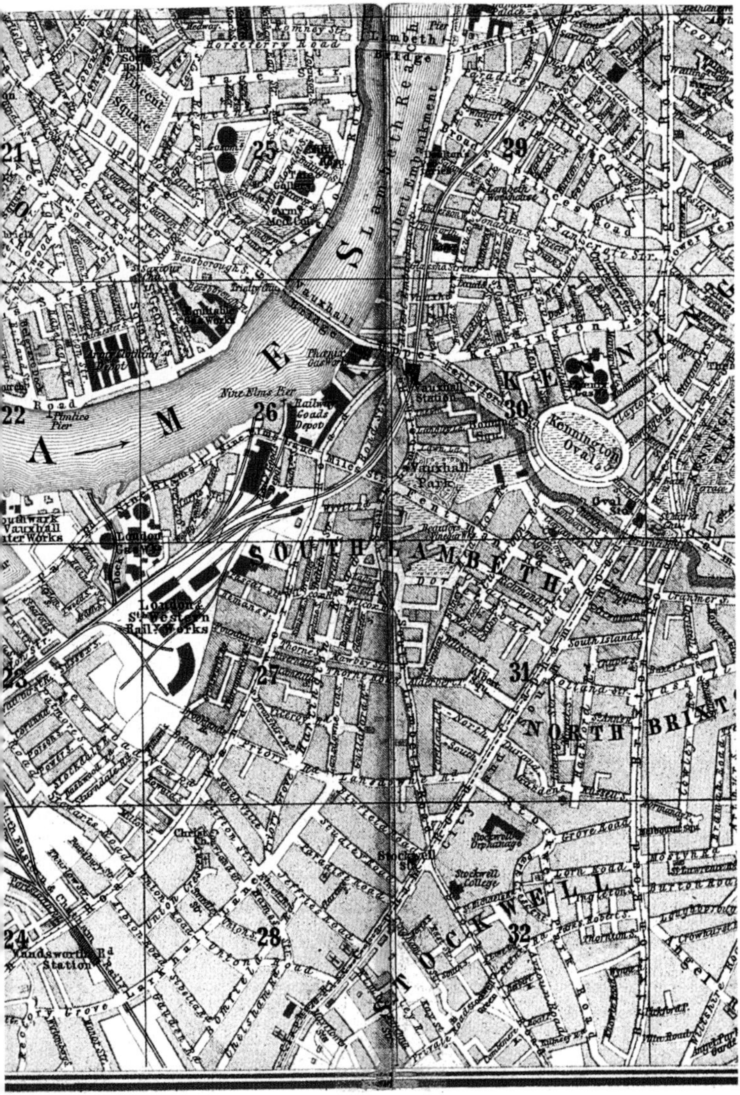

Horseferry Road
Romney Str.
Lambeth Bridge
Vincent Square
Page Str.
Vauxhall Bridge Road
Bessborough S.
Vauxhall Bridge
Army Clothing Depot
Equitable Gas Works
Phœnix Gas Wks
Nine Elms Pier
Pimlico Pier
Railway Goods Depot
Vauxhall Station
Albert Embankment
Broad S.
Lambeth Workhouse
Princes Road
Sancroft Str.
Kennington Lane
Kennington Oval
Oval Sta.
Vauxhall Park
Miles Str.
Nine Elms
Southwark & Vauxhall Water Works
London Gas Wks
London & Sth. Western Railway Works
SOUTH LAMBETH
NORTH BRIXTON
Holland Str.
South Island Pl.
Lansdowne Rd.
Stockwell Orphanage
Stockwell College
Stockwell Sta.
Grove Road
Lorn Road
STOCKWELL
Wandsworth Rd Station
Larkhall Lane
Union Road
Priory Grove
Jeffreys Road
Chelsham Rd.
Angel Road
Brixton Road
21
22
23
24
25
26
27
28
29
30
31
32
T H A M E S
K E N N I N G T O N

33
34
35
36
37
38
39
40
41
42
43
44
WALWORTH
CAMBERWELL
Kent Road
Deacon Street
Kennington Lane
Westmoreland Road
Boyson Road
Grand Surrey
Addington Square
County Court
Camberwell New Rd. Station
Metropole Theatre
Vestry Hall
Denmark Hill Station
DENMARK HILL
Grove Park
Ruskin Park
Loughborough Pk. Station
South Coast

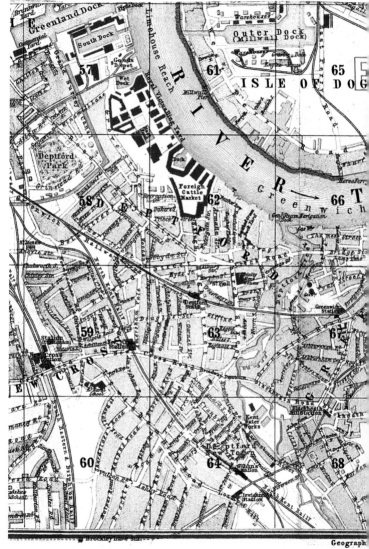

Geograph

1:21.300

Mile (-5280 feet.)

e Anstalt von Wagner & Debes, Leipzig.

Geograph. Anstalt von Wagner & Debes, Leipzig.

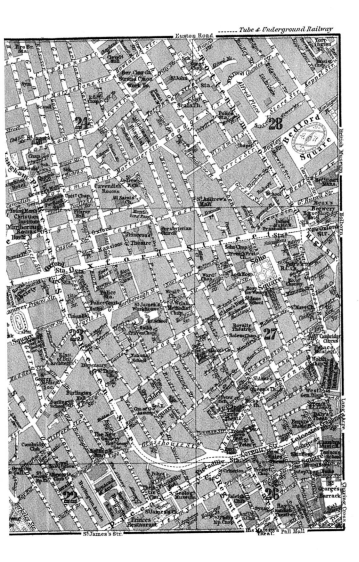

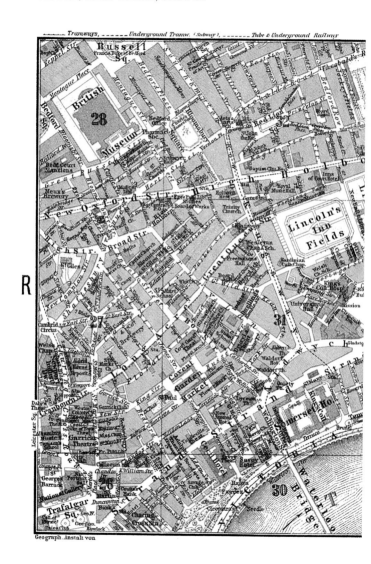

Geograph. Anstalt von

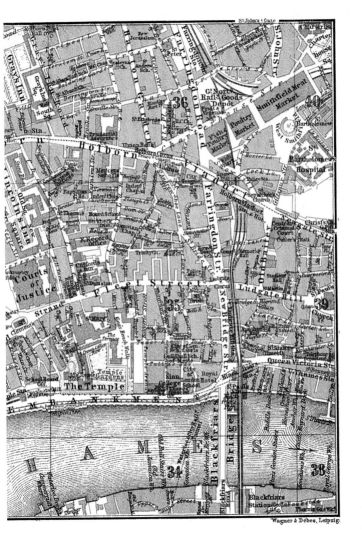

St. John's Gate

Wagner & Debes, Leipzig.

Geograph. Anstalt von

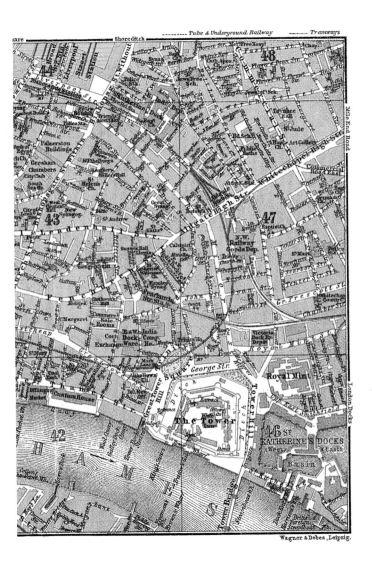

44

48

43

47

46 ST KATHERINE'S DOCKS

42

The Tower

Royal Mint

Mile End Road

London Docks

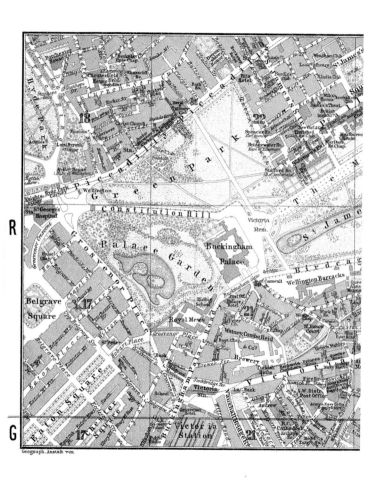

Geograph. Anstalt von

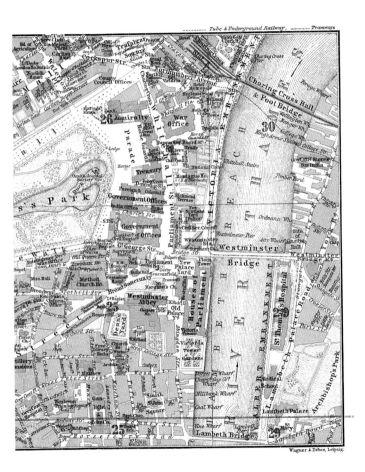

RAILWAY MAP OF LONDON AND ITS SUBURBS

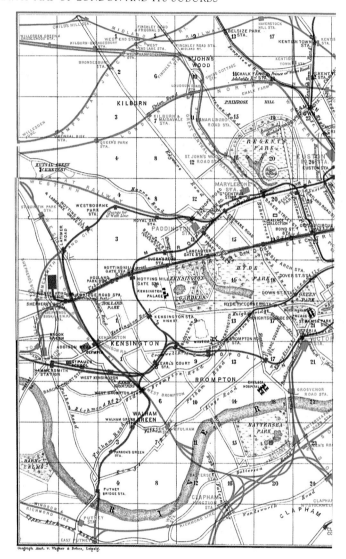

Geograph. Anst. v. Wagner & Debes, Leipzig.

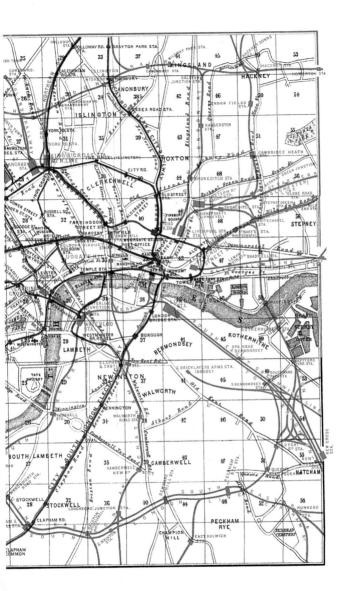

The first edition of this book was
published in 1900 by
Karl Baedeker, Leipzig.
This facsimile edition published in 2002 by
Old House Books,
The Old Police Station, Pound Street,
Moretonhampstead, Newton Abbot,
Devon, TQ13 8PA.
Tel: 01647 440707, Fax: 01647 440202
info@OldHouseBooks.co.uk,
www.OldHouseBooks.co.uk.
Printed and bound in China
ISBN 1 873590 26 1

For details of other facsimile Victorian and
Edwardian maps and guidebooks published by
Old House Books see pages 452 - 454 before the
colour street plan section of this book. Further
information is available by requesting a
catalogue from Old House Books, The Old Police
Station, Moretonhampstead, Newton Abbot,
Devon UK. TQ13 8PA or from
www.OldHouseBooks.co.uk, Tel: 01647 440707,
or Email info@OldHouseBooks.co.uk.